D0966979

The Reader's Digest

Legal Question & Answer Book

The Reader's Digest

Legal Question & Answer Book

The Reader's Digest Association, Inc.
Pleasantville, New York • Montreal

The Reader's Digest

Legal Question & Answer Book

Editor: Sharon Fass Yates
Art Editor: Henrietta Stern
Associate Editor: Robert V. Huber
Assistant Editor: Thomas A. Ranieri

Contributors:
Editors: Sherwood Harris, Edmund H. Harvey, Jr., Rita Christopher
Research Editor: Enid Klass
Copy Editor: Patricia M. Godfrey
Indexer: Sydney Wolfe Cohen
Editorial Assistant: Rena G. Dubow
Artist: Christopher Calle

HYATT LEGAL SERVICES

The questions and answers in this book are based on research provided by the attorneys of Hyatt Legal Services and the firm's Publishing Project staff. The editors of Reader's Digest gratefully acknowledge the assistance of Hyatt Legal Services in the preparation of this book.

READER'S DIGEST GENERAL BOOKS

Editor in Chief: John A. Pope, Jr.
Managing Editor: Jane Polley
Art Director: David Trooper
Group Editors: Norman B. Mack, Joel Musler (Art), Susan J. Wernert
Chief of Research: Monica Borrowman
Copy Chief: Edward W. Atkinson
Picture Editor: Robert J. Woodward
Rights and Permissions: Dorothy M. Harris
Head Librarian: Jo Manning

Library of Congress Cataloging in Publication Data

The Reader's Digest legal question & answer book.
p. cm.
Includes index.
ISBN 0-89577-291-4
1. Law—United States—Miscellanea. 2. Law—United States—Popular works. I. Reader's Digest Association. II. Title: Reader's Digest legal question and answer book. III. Title: Legal question & answer book. IV. Title: Legal question and answer book.
KF387.R424 1988
349.73—dc19 87-25963
[347.3] CIP

Printed in the United States of America
Third Printing, April 1991

Contents

About This Book 11

Chapter 1
You and Your Lawyer 13

What Is a Lawyer? 14
When Do You Need a Lawyer? 17
Finding the Right Lawyer 21
Legal Expenses 26
Working With Your Lawyer 31
Legal Ethics 38

Chapter 2
Marriage and Family 43

Getting Married 44
Prenuptial Agreements 49
Unmarried Couples 52
Common-law Marriages 54
Family Responsibilities 55
Adoption and Surrogate Parenting 64
Unwed Parents 71
Children's Rights 75
Rights of Adopted Children 80
Children in Trouble 81
Going to School 85
Guardians for Children 90
Family Problems 92
Changing Your Name 96
Rights of Grandparents 98
Taking Care of the Elderly 100
Guardians and Conservators 104
Nursing Homes 107

Chapter 3
Divorce and Child Custody 113

Thinking About Divorce 114
Separation 119
Annulment 123
Types of Divorce 124
The Divorce Process 127

Division of Property 133
Support for Spouse (Alimony) 138
Child Custody 140
Visitation 146
Child Support 148

Chapter 4 Your Home 153

Renting a Home 154
Landlord Difficulties 159
Buying Your Home 163
Buyer Beware 172
Building a New Home 174
Financing a New Home 176
Home Improvements and Repairs 180
You and Your Neighbors 185
Homeowners' Problems 187
Ways You May Lose Your Home 193
Selling Your Home 195

Chapter 5 Your Personal Property 201

Owning Personal Property 202
Pets as Property 203
Entrusting Property to Others 207
Borrowing and Lending 214
Gift Giving 216
Lost and Found 217
Selling Personal Property 218
Patents, Copyrights, Trademarks 221

Chapter 6 Your Car 225

Buying a Car 226
Renting or Leasing a Car 230
Selling a Car 232
Car Warranties 234
Car Repairs 236
Licenses and Registrations 240
Tickets and Violations 242
Drinking and Driving 247

At the Scene of an Accident 252
Liability for Automobile Accidents 254

Chapter 7 **Your Money** 263

Financial Institutions 264
Establishing Credit 273
Credit Cards and Charges 278
Personal Loans 282
Payment Problems 290
Your Investments 295
Income Taxes 299
Personal Bankruptcy 303

Chapter 8 **Insurance** 307

The Basics of Insurance 308
Life Insurance 313
Beneficiaries 316
Health and Disability Insurance 320
Insuring Your Home 326
Insuring Personal Property 329
Liability for Personal Injury 333
Insuring Your Car 335
Car Insurance Rates 341
Hit-and-run and Uninsured Drivers 342
Adjusters and Settlements 344

Chapter 9 **Consumer Rights** 347

Deceptive Advertising 348
Sales Tactics 351
Buying by Mail 356
Door-to-door Sales 358
Telephone and TV Sales 360
Prizes, Gifts, and Rebates 362
Consumer Contracts 364
Warranties and Service Contracts 367
Defective and Unsafe Merchandise 372
Your Rights at a Restaurant 375
Travel Troubles 377
When You Have a Complaint 379

Chapter 10 — Your Job — 383

Applying for a Job 384
On the Job 390
Pay and Benefits 395
Workers' Compensation 401
Unions and Strikes 404
Job Discrimination 408
Sexual Harassment 411
Hazardous Work Conditions 412
If You Lose Your Job 414
Unemployment Compensation 420

Chapter 11 — Your Own Business — 423

Starting a Business 424
Forming a Partnership 430
Incorporating 433
Buying a Franchise 438
Running a Business 441
Selling or Ending a Business 448

Chapter 12 — Your Individual Rights — 451

Our Rights as Citizens 452
U.S. Citizenship 455
Your Right to Vote 458
Freedom of Religion 459
Freedom of Speech 460
Freedom of the Press 462
Your Right to Have Firearms 464
Equality Under the Law 465
Your Right to Privacy 468
Dealing With the Police 472

Chapter 13 — Accidents — 475

Accidents Inside Your Home 476
Accidents Outside Your Home 478
Accidents on Public Transportation 483
Accidents in Public Places 485
Boating Accidents 491

Chapter 14 *Your Medical Rights* 493

Your Rights With Doctors 494
Your Rights in the Hospital 496
Consent for Medical Treatment 500
Malpractice 503
Your Medical Records 507
Paying the Bills 509
Living Wills 510
Organ Donations 513

Chapter 15 *Pensions, IRA's, Social Security* 515

Pension Plans 516
IRA's and Keogh Plans 523
Qualifying for Social Security 526
Collecting Social Security 529
Social Security for Dependents 532
Medicare 535
Medicaid 543
Disability and SSI Benefits 545

Chapter 16 *Wills and Estates* 547

Your Estate 548
Making a Will 552
Naming Your Heirs 556
Establishing Trusts 562
The Role of the Trustee 566
Changing or Revoking a Will 567
Contesting a Will 570
Dying Without a Will 573
Settling an Estate 574
Funerals and Burials 581

Chapter 17 *Victims and Crimes* 589

If You Are a Victim 590
What Is a Crime? 597
Rights of the Accused 603
Posting Bail 609
Juvenile Offenders 611
Witnessing a Crime 618

Chapter 18 *Going to Court* 621

The Judicial System 622
Pretrial Procedures 627
Courtroom Protocol 633
Trial Procedures 635
Small Claims Court 640
Selecting Jurors 643
Serving on a Jury 646
Serving on a Grand Jury 649
Being a Witness 651

Glossary 656

Index 677

About This Book

THE READER'S DIGEST LEGAL QUESTION & ANSWER BOOK takes a practical approach to the law. It tells you what you need to know to deal with hundreds of situations that arise in everyday life. We hope you will consult it again and again about everything from getting married to writing a will. You can use it today, tomorrow, and for the rest of your life to protect your family, your possessions—and your peace of mind.

In clear question-and-answer form, this book dramatizes commonplace legal problems that could involve you, your family, your job, your money, your rights, and your safety. You will see the law in action and learn how to solve and prevent problems. The answers are short and to the point. They do not confound you with technical theory, unintelligible Latin phrases, or legal gobbledygook. They tell you, simply, how to deal with the problem.

More than 2,000 questions are answered in these pages. To make sure that we included the most commonly asked questions, Reader's Digest joined forces with Hyatt Legal Services, the largest personal services law firm in the nation. That firm, which serves more than a million clients across the country, submitted the questions most frequently asked in every area of the law and then provided solid, informative answers. Reader's Digest added questions that would be of particular interest to our readers and asked the experts at Hyatt Legal Services to answer them. Then all the answers were put into plain language, free of any trace of legalese.

You don't have to have a subject in mind to use THE READER'S DIGEST LEGAL QUESTION & ANSWER BOOK. You can pick it up at any time and enjoy leafing through its pages, stopping when something catches your eye. Some questions will seem as though they were put there just for you; others will arouse your curiosity. You'll read on to see how the people portrayed in the questions solved their problems. You'll learn what you are entitled to and what actions you can take in circumstances that may confront you. Reading this book may also help you steer clear of legal entanglements.

When you have a specific problem, turn to the Contents and consult the chapter and section titles. The book is arranged by subject for easy reference. If you want information about traffic tickets, for example, look in Chapter 6, *Your Car,* under the section "Tickets and Violations." If you want an even more specific reference, check the Index, which uses ordinary words such as *traffic, parking,* and *speeding.* The cross-references that appear at the beginning of some sections will lead you to related information elsewhere in the book.

Special box features supplement the material covered in the questions and answers, and give sound advice on legal and practical nonlegal matters. Some offer step-by-step instructions, such as how to take your case to small claims court. Others have checklists of important questions to ask or points to consider—for example, "Questions to Ask When Choosing a Lawyer" and "How to Hire a Contractor." The Glossary at the back of the book provides concise, easy-to-understand definitions of more than 400 key legal terms.

Of course, not even 2,000 questions will cover every situation—although if you don't find a question describing your exact predicament, you will probably be able to find one that is similar enough to be helpful. Nor can any one book discuss all the different state and local laws. Laws vary from state to state and city to city, and they can change rapidly as a result of court decisions and new legislation. To give you the most helpful information, the answers to the questions are based on general rules of law and on what the laws say in the majority of states. In many answers, specific states are used as examples. But even if your state is mentioned, you should always check to find out what the law currently says where you live.

Sometimes this means consulting a lawyer. At other times you can find out about the law in your locality by contacting (1) your city, county, or state bar association; (2) the government agency that oversees the area of law you are interested in—for example, the motor vehicle bureau or the state insurance department; (3) your state attorney general's office or the office of another government official, such as the mayor, the county clerk, or a state legislator; (4) a public service group, such as the League of Women Voters; or (5) a consumer advocate group, such as the Center for Auto Safety. But regardless of how much research you do on your own, you should always consider consulting an attorney before starting any legal action.

The information, guidelines, and advice offered in THE READER'S DIGEST LEGAL QUESTION & ANSWER BOOK can protect you against lawsuits, alert you to fraud, help you to avoid falling into legal traps, and inform you about available remedies. By consulting this book before you talk to a lawyer, you can save both time and money. You may even discover you don't need a lawyer to solve your problem. If it turns out that you do need legal counsel, this book will help you prepare the right questions to ask in order to get the best advice possible.

—The Editors

CHAPTER
1

You and Your Lawyer

What Is a Lawyer?

Do the terms* lawyer, attorney, *and* counselor *mean exactly the same thing?

Yes. The terms are interchangeable. They all refer to someone trained in the law who is licensed to practice law in one or more states and is in the business of giving legal advice.

Tony has noticed that his lawyer writes* Esq. *after his name. What does this abbreviation stand for?

Esq. is the abbreviation for *esquire*, or *squire*. In England a squire was a country gentleman who informally settled disputes among the people living on his land. In the United States *esquire* is a title commonly used by lawyers, but it does not refer to any legal certification or specialty.

What is a justice of the peace?

A justice of the peace is a state judicial officer who presides over certain types of minor cases, such as those involving trespassing or disturbing the peace. To many people, the justice of the peace is best known for performing marriages, but not all justices of the peace have the legal authority to do so. A justice of the peace may be either elected by majority vote or appointed by the governor. In some states, the functions of justices of the peace are fulfilled by judges in small claims courts or by magistrates (public officials with limited judicial authority).

Does a judge have to be a lawyer?

Generally, yes. The qualifications for becoming a judge are set by state and federal law. Although standards for education and experience vary from state to state, most states require judges to have been licensed lawyers. Some states allow certain judicial positions to be held by people who are not lawyers. These positions are generally in traffic court or small claims court.

Why do lawyers and judges use such complicated language?

Although legal language is often difficult for the layman to understand, it is more precise than everyday language, and enables lawyers and judges to interpret the law as carefully as possible. If you don't understand the language your lawyer uses, ask him to translate it into plain English.

Bill Barrister, a lawyer, has an ad in the Yellow Pages that says he handles consumer cases. Does this mean he is a specialist?

Not necessarily. Some states, such as Arkansas and California, permit lawyers to qualify as specialists in certain fields of law. To become specialists, lawyers must take additional hours of classroom instruction and pass a special examination. Most states, however, prohibit lawyers from advertising themselves as specialists in a particular area. In other words, Bill Barrister can advertise only that he handles consumer cases, not that he is an expert in consumer law. You should investigate Mr. Barrister's qualifications further if you are looking for an experienced consumer lawyer.

Family Lawyer or Specialist?

No matter how experienced your family lawyer may be, there are certain legal problems that he may not be qualified to handle. A general practitioner may be adequate for reviewing a contract or drawing up a will, for example, but if you're contesting a divorce or have been charged with a crime, you'll be better off with a lawyer who commonly handles such cases. If your legal problem calls for a specialist, ask your family lawyer to recommend one. If he's unable to provide you with any names, consult a legal directory (such as the *Martindale-Hubbell Law Directory*), which lists lawyers and firms for all branches of law, including the following common specialties:

- Admiralty Law
- Bankruptcy Law
- Business Law
- Civil Litigation
- Civil Rights Law
- Conservatorship and Guardianship Law
- Constitutional Law
- Consumer Law
- Contract Law
- Corporation and Partnership Law
- Criminal Law
- Divorce, Adoption, and Family Law
- Environmental Law
- Health Care and Hospital Law
- Immigration and Naturalization Law
- Insurance Law
- Juvenile Law
- Labor Law
- Military Law
- Patent, Trademark, and Copyright Law
- Pension and Profit-Sharing Law
- Personal Injury and Property Damage
- Real Estate Law
- Social Security Law
- Tax Law
- Transportation Law
- Veterans' Law
- Wills, Trusts, and Estate Planning
- Workers' Compensation Law

What Is a Lawyer?

Walter needs a lawyer to handle a minor legal matter, but the only lawyer he knows specializes in corporate law. Should Walter look for another lawyer?

No. Just because this lawyer concentrates on corporate cases does not mean that he will automatically refuse a more routine case. Many lawyers who specialize in one or more areas of law began as general practitioners and are qualified to handle basic legal matters as well as complex ones.

When should I consult a tax lawyer instead of an accountant?

Whenever you could be subject to monetary penalties or to charges of fraud or other criminal wrongdoing. If you are simply seeking advice about preparing tax returns, planning your estate, or getting the best tax advantages, either a lawyer or an accountant should be able to help you.

My supervisor's daughter is going to school to become a paralegal. Does this mean she'll be a lawyer when she graduates?

No. A paralegal is a person who has some legal skills, but who is not a lawyer. A paralegal usually does legal research or other work to assist a lawyer in preparing a case or handling a legal matter.

Stuart discovered that one of his checks had been stolen and cashed. To make a claim, Stuart had to fill out a bank form that required the seal and signature of a notary public. What is that?

A notary public is a person who verifies that signatures on a document are genuine. He also administers oaths to people taking public office and to witnesses at legal proceedings. A notary does not confirm the truth of the statements made in the documents or in testimony; he only certifies that the person presenting them has sworn to their truth. State law determines who is eligible to become a notary public, but generally a person must be of good character, have passed a test on the rules and duties of a notary, and have taken an oath of office.

My father told me that he knows a lawyer who accepts* pro bono *cases. What is that?

Free legal work for charity or for the public. *Pro bono* is a shortened version of the Latin phrase *pro bono publico*, meaning "for the public good." A lawyer who provides *pro bono* service does legal work for the public good without charging a fee. For example, in addition to taking clients who pay him, a lawyer might take a client who cannot afford his services, or he might do free legal work for a community project he believes in, such as one involving the rights of the homeless.

A man in my town confessed to assaulting and robbing a number of elderly women. How can a lawyer agree to defend such a person and still sleep at night?

At the heart of our legal system is the belief that every person charged with a crime is presumed innocent until proven guilty and has the right to be defended by a lawyer. When a lawyer represents a person charged with a crime, it doesn't mean that he condones the crime, but that he believes the accused person is entitled to a fair trial.

When Do You Need a Lawyer?

How do I decide whether or not I need a lawyer?

Begin by analyzing your problem. If a dry cleaner has ruined your dress, for example, you may be able to resolve the matter yourself by asking the cleaner for a reimbursement. On the other hand, a more complicated problem, such as suing someone, will probably require the services of a lawyer. If you're not sure if your situation calls for a lawyer, it might be worth a small consultation fee to find out. In some cases, a lawyer may even be able to show you how to resolve the problem yourself.

Cory wants to buy a new sports car. Should he have his lawyer review the sales agreement and loan papers before he signs them?

Although a car is a major purchase, Cory does not need to consult a lawyer if he understands the terms and conditions of the sales contract. Even if Cory isn't clear about certain provisions, a bank officer should be able to answer any questions he may have.

Sam and Ruth want to sell their house. Their neighbor George has read a book on real estate and has sold several houses. Can he represent them at the closing even though he is not a lawyer?

Possibly. Laws vary from state to state, but in most cases the person selling a house does not have to be represented by a lawyer at a real estate closing. However, since the sale of their house may be the largest financial transaction Sam and Ruth will ever make, they would be wise to find a lawyer who knows local real estate law to represent them.

While George may be familiar with the sale process, he may not be well versed enough in the law to solve any legal problems that may arise. In fact, George's ignorance of the fine points of real estate law could lead to unnecessary expenses for Sam and Ruth, and could even invalidate the sale of their house. If George were to go beyond simply representing Sam and Ruth at the closing and offer them legal advice, he could be charged with practicing law without a license, which is a criminal offense.

Situations Requiring Legal Advice

No matter how lucky or careful you may be, chances are that sooner or later you will find yourself with a legal problem. Deciding whether or not the situation requires a lawyer, however, may not be easy. Many problems fall somewhere between a minor dispute that can be settled in small claims court and a criminal charge that calls for a skillful trial lawyer. If you are in doubt, consult a lawyer, especially if the problem is complex or the consequences far-reaching. Generally, you will need a lawyer if:

- You are about to sign a contract you don't understand or agree with.
- You are served with a summons or other legal document.
- You and your fiancée are considering a prenuptial agreement.
- You want to adopt a child.
- Your child gets into trouble with the law.
- You or your spouse is seeking a separation, divorce, or annulment.
- Your ex-spouse wants to modify or terminate child support or maintenance payments, or alter your custody arrangements.
- You buy or sell your home or any other real estate.
- You are starting your own business or buying a franchise.
- You are threatened with eviction or foreclosure.
- Your personal property is in danger of being repossessed by creditors.
- You have been notified that a creditor plans to garnishee your wages.
- You suffer property damage because of someone's negligence.
- You are injured in an accident.
- You are asked to make an out-of-court settlement.
- You want to draw up a power of attorney.
- You are writing, changing, or contesting a will.
- You want to create a guardianship or conservatorship for a loved one.
- You are charged with any crime, even a misdemeanor.

Martha received a traffic ticket for driving over the speed limit. It's her third speeding ticket this year. Should she hire a lawyer?

Yes. Although traffic violations can usually be handled without the assistance of a lawyer, a driver who has received several tickets during a short period of time stands a greater chance of being jailed or having driving privileges suspended. If Martha doesn't want to lose her driver's license, she should contact a lawyer. The lawyer may be able to help Martha keep her license or reduce the penalty for the third ticket.

My girlfriend was riding a bicycle when a car raced around the corner and hit her. The driver just kept on going. My girlfriend and some neighbors got a good look at the driver and the car. Can a lawyer help us find the driver and sue him for damages?

Yes. A lawyer can help find the driver, either by investigating on his own or with the assistance of a private detective. But before you see a lawyer, you should go to the police, who have more expertise in dealing with such matters. If they locate the hit-and-run driver who injured your girlfriend, and she wishes to file criminal charges against him, that's the time when she should consult a lawyer.

Peter is scheduled to appear in small claims court next month. Should he ask a lawyer to accompany him?

No. Procedures in small claims courts are simplified to enable people to represent themselves. Although most states do not prohibit a lawyer from being present, the cost of the lawyer may turn out to be greater than the amount in dispute.

Is it a good idea to have a family lawyer, even if I don't need one right now?

Yes. Many legal problems arise when you least expect them. By taking the time now to select a family lawyer, you will have someone you trust ready to help you when a crisis occurs.

Can I act as my own lawyer?

Yes, but it is not always advisable. Generally, only an expert in the field—that is, a lawyer—is knowledgeable enough to handle legal issues. If you act as your own lawyer in a trial and you are unclear about the laws relating to your case or even about correct courtroom procedure, you might jeopardize your chance of success. You may also be too emotionally involved in your case to remain objective—even lawyers hire other lawyers when they are personally involved in a legal matter.

My cousin Randall is a lawyer in a neighboring state. Can he write my will or file some legal papers in court for me?

Usually a lawyer must pass an examination that tests his knowledge of a particular state's laws and be issued a license before he may practice law in that state. Sometimes a lawyer is permitted to practice in another state on a one-time basis. At other times, he may be permitted to work under the guidance of a local lawyer who is familiar with the state's laws. Your cousin may be able to help you with your will or file court papers for you in one of these ways. If your cousin is unfamiliar with the laws of your state, however, you should seek the services of a local lawyer.

I will be out of the country during a period when a lot of personal business matters will need to be handled. Do I have to hire a lawyer, or can I authorize my brother-in-law to act in my name?

You can appoint anyone you feel confident will best represent you, but regardless of whether the person is your relative or a lawyer, you must give him your power of attorney. The person you designate to act on your behalf is referred to as your attorney-in-fact. A power of attorney is a document giving someone else the legal authority to act for you in situations involving your property, finances, or personal needs. For example, a power of attorney can authorize the person you name to grant consent in an emergency for medical treatment for your child or to conduct business for you if you are out of town or are too ill to do so. A durable power of attorney authorizes the person you name to continue to act on your behalf even if you become mentally incompetent—for example, from Alzheimer's disease. In that case, the person would not have to be appointed your legal guardian in order to continue to act for you.

Oliver wants to set up a power of attorney. Will he need a lawyer?

No. But if Oliver is unfamiliar with the legal requirements of such a document and makes a mistake in drawing it up, the document could be declared invalid. If Oliver wants to give someone the power to sell his real estate, it is particularly important for him to consult a lawyer, since the agreement may have to be filed in the local real estate public records office to make the sale of the property legal.

Should I have my power of attorney notarized?

Yes. This will prevent someone from using a forged or fraudulent power of attorney, and, for example, selling your property. A notary will be able to confirm the authenticity of your signature because he watched you sign the document or because he can identify your signature.

If I consult a lawyer, will he give me advice even if I don't hire him to handle my legal matters?

Yes, but only to a limited extent. When you first contact a lawyer, he will try to determine what kind of legal problem you have, and how you can go about solving it. In most circumstances, the lawyer will provide general legal advice at this initial meeting, but he may also offer some specific recommendations as to what you should do next. Sometimes a lawyer is unable to give legal advice without first making a preliminary investigation or doing some additional research. If you do not want the lawyer to go that far, be sure to say so; otherwise, you will have to pay him for his time and effort.

Finding the Right Lawyer

Is an older lawyer better than a younger one?

Not necessarily. Age should not be the deciding factor in selecting a lawyer. The most important things are that you should be confident the lawyer can handle your legal problem and that you should feel comfortable with him. Although an older lawyer has more experience, this does not automatically make him more competent. The younger lawyer may have special training in the area of law relating to your problem, while the older lawyer may have handled only a few such cases because he has a general practice. On the other hand, a young lawyer who charges a lower hourly rate will not necessarily be less expensive than an older lawyer. A younger lawyer may take longer to research or prepare a case than a more experienced one.

I consulted a prominent lawyer with an impressive reputation, but he turned out to be rude and intimidating. Should I let my personal feelings stop me from hiring him?

Perhaps. Hiring a lawyer is a very personal matter—not only because you will probably be discussing confidential matters with him, but also because your relationship with the lawyer could affect the outcome of your case. If you conceal important information, for example, because you don't feel you can confide in your lawyer, you risk losing your case if this information is discovered by your opponent's lawyer and used against you. If you have several qualified lawyers to choose from, you should hire the one who not only is competent, but with whom you feel compatible as well.

Arthur has been our family lawyer for years, but when I asked him to help me sue a large corporation he refused, saying the case was too complex for him. Doesn't he have to take my case?

No. If Arthur did not believe he could adequately represent you, he was obligated to reject the case. Professional ethics require a lawyer to turn down a legal case if he knows he is not competent to handle it. A lawyer may take a case in an unfamiliar area of the law, however, if he has time to research the law involved—or obtain the assistance of another lawyer familiar with this type of lawsuit—without delaying the case or causing his client additional expense.

Since Lucy didn't know any lawyers who could help her, her friend Irene suggested that she use a lawyer referral service. What kind of service is this?

Lawyer referral is a service offered by each state's bar association for people who don't know any lawyers and don't have access to a lawyers' directory, which is available in law school libraries, county courthouses, and many public libraries. If Lucy uses such a service, she should bear in mind that because most lawyer referral services rotate the names they recommend, she may be assigned a lawyer on the basis of chance rather than expertise or price. Lucy should follow up any referral by checking the lawyer's reputation with people who have used his services. She might even ask the lawyer to give her the names of clients she could call for references.

My neighbor's insurance company is suing me for the cost of repairing the damage I accidentally caused to his property. Would I be better off hiring a lawyer at a big law firm or one who works on his own?

There are advantages and disadvantages to both. In terms of cost, an individual lawyer may be less expensive because he has a lower overhead, but sometimes a large law firm can be cheaper because its expenses

Finding a Lawyer

If you have a legal problem but you don't know any lawyers, begin by asking friends and relatives if they can suggest someone. But even when a lawyer comes highly recommended, you should still do some comparison shopping for cost and expertise as well as for compatibility. To find the names of more lawyers, consult the following:

- ☑ Your accountant, insurance salesperson, banker, or other professional whose judgment you respect.
- ☑ Your employer's lawyer or law firm.
- ☑ Law directories, such as the *Martindale-Hubbell Law Directory*, available at most libraries.
- ☑ Court clerks, court reporters, and clerks to judges.
- ☑ Government offices and agencies (listed in a special section of your telephone directory) that deal with the subject of your legal problem.
- ☑ The alumni offices of law schools.
- ☑ Your local, county, or state bar association.
- ☑ A national bar association, such as The Association of Trial Lawyers of America.
- ☑ Advertisements in newspapers and magazines, and on radio and television.
- ☑ The Yellow Pages.

are divided among more clients. As far as service is concerned, an individual lawyer may be able to give your case more personal attention, depending on his case load at the time; but a firm may have additional resources, such as research assistants, an extensive law library, and a staff with diverse expertise.

Bernie lives on a farm 120 miles from the nearest city. To be compensated for an injury he received while driving his tractor, he must sue the tractor's manufacturer and a local dealer. Should he use a lawyer from his community or one from the big city?

Bernie should not automatically assume that a lawyer from his own community will not be as good as one from the big city. What really matters is whether a particular lawyer is competent to handle Bernie's case. If Bernie is considering a local lawyer, he should first find out whether that lawyer has any business connections with the manufacturer of the equipment or the local dealer that could possibly pose a conflict of interest. If no conflict exists, Bernie may well prefer a local lawyer who is more experienced in handling farm-related cases and more familiar with the local courts.

Finding the Right Lawyer

I'm confused about whether I should go to a law firm or a legal clinic. What is the difference?

If the type of legal problem you have is a fairly common one, such as an uncomplicated divorce, a routine real estate transaction (for example, a closing), bankruptcy, or accident case, a legal clinic would be able to give you the help you need. These clinics are usually located in shopping centers and storefront locations, and are staffed by lawyers who are familiar with everyday legal problems. Many of these clinics charge standard fees for their services, such as for drawing up a simple will. You can find out what the fee would be over the telephone.

If your problem is a complex or unusual one, however, a law firm might be a better choice. Law firms are usually staffed with lawyers who specialize in different areas of the law, and they often have assistants and extensive private law libraries to help them with their research. The fees charged by these firms are generally higher than those of the legal clinics, since law firms generally have higher expenses and pay their lawyers higher salaries.

My company has just announced that it will be offering a prepaid legal plan as a new fringe benefit for all full-time employees. How do such plans work?

Typically, legal plans provide a variety of legal services for which your employer has paid in advance, or for which a payroll deduction is made from your salary. Under some plans, you and your family can use these services without any additional payment.

Make sure, however, that you understand any special limitations that are included in your company's plan. For example, some legal plans provide coverage for a divorce only when both husband and wife can agree on the terms, but do not cover divorces where the partners cannot agree on how to divide their property or who will get custody of the children, and must therefore go to court to resolve such matters. A detailed description of your plan's benefits should be available from your employer or union.

Darlene needs to hire a lawyer to help defend her in court, but she can't afford one. How can she find someone who will handle her case for free?

Many organizations, both public and private, provide legal services for individuals who are unable to afford their own lawyers. In criminal cases, the defendant is entitled to have a court-appointed lawyer, or public defender, if he is unable to afford his own. This appointment is handled by the court during the arraignment stage of the criminal proceedings. Once a public defender is assigned to a case, he represents his client no differently from the way a lawyer who is hired privately does.

In some civil cases, such as those involving abusive family members, legal aid societies, the Legal Services Corporation, and other organizations offer free legal services to the needy. Darlene should contact her local legal association, or bar association, to find out which services are available in her community. In some areas, the bar association will have a list of lawyers willing to donate their services in certain cases.

Questions to Ask When Choosing a Lawyer

Even if a lawyer comes highly recommended, you should base your decision to hire him on your own opinion rather than someone else's. Since many of the qualities that distinguish a good lawyer from a bad one are intangible and difficult to define, you'll need to ask some specific questions. Listen to the lawyer's answers carefully, but also pay attention to his manner. It is just as important to have a lawyer who is patient, affable, and willing to explain things you don't understand as it is to have one who's skillful and knowledgeable. Here are some key questions you should be sure to ask:

- ☑ Will you charge me for an initial consultation?
- ☑ How long has your firm been in business?
- ☑ Are your clients primarily individuals or companies?
- ☑ What materials should I bring to our first meeting?
- ☑ Can you start working on my case immediately?
- ☑ What are the strengths and weaknesses of my case?
- ☑ What kind of strategy do you propose to follow?
- ☑ About how long will it take to complete the case?
- ☑ How much of the work required will you do yourself, and how much will you delegate to another lawyer or a paralegal?
- ☑ How will you keep me informed about the progress of my case?
- ☑ Will you give me copies of all relevant documents and correspondence?
- ☑ What is your fee for my kind of case? Which services are included in that fee, and which are not?
- ☑ Will you provide a written estimate of all costs before you begin work on my case?
- ☑ Will you send me an itemized bill?
- ☑ Will you work on a contingent-fee basis? If so, will you compute the fee before or after expenses are paid?
- ☑ Do you anticipate any additional costs? If you do, will they have to be paid in advance or as they are incurred?

Legal Expenses

How does a lawyer decide how much to charge?

Attorneys set their fees on the basis of their experience, the nature of the case, the amount of time they expect it will require, and their office expenses. For example, if you need a prenuptial agreement to make sure the children of your first marriage are protected financially, your lawyer may be able to quote you a flat fee based on how much time similar prenuptial agreements have taken. However, if you and your fiancée have difficulty agreeing on certain terms, your lawyer may prefer to charge you an hourly rate, since he may not be able to estimate how much of his time the document will require.

Are lawyers' fees negotiable?

Experienced lawyers generally know their fees and rarely will settle for a lower rate, but some lawyers are willing to negotiate. Your lawyer may be willing to give you an extended period of time to pay the fee. If a lawyer changes his fee too readily, however, make sure he will still provide all the legal services for your case, and not try to raise the fee back to his original quotation by claiming additional services are needed.

Which is better—an hourly fee or a flat fee?

It depends on how long or complex a case will be, which is difficult to predict. Most flat-fee arrangements cover standard services, such as drawing up a will; if your case turns out to be more complicated, you will either have to accept an increase in the standard fee or convert to an hourly rate. Don't be misled by an extremely low flat fee; watch out for unreasonable additional charges, such as an extra payment to have your lawyer appear in court on your behalf in a criminal matter.

What kinds of legal services are generally covered by a flat-fee arrangement?

Prenuptial agreements, marital separation agreements, routine divorces, annulments, simple wills, bankruptcies, incorporating businesses, setting up partnerships, and minor criminal matters, such as traffic violations, are all areas generally covered by flat-fee arrangements. Though a lawyer may agree to handle these types of cases for a flat fee, there may be additional costs if a particular case becomes unusually complicated or involves a long court battle. You should always get a fee agreement, in writing, which describes the specific services that will be provided.

How to Save on Legal Costs

Once you've decided to hire a particular lawyer, have him put the details of your agreement in writing, including his fee, his estimate of any additional costs and expenses, and a statement that he will not exceed a specific dollar amount without first getting your permission. Be sure to ask your lawyer what you can do to help save him time, and therefore save you money. Here are some suggestions:

- ☑ Organize and write down the facts of your situation and any questions you have before talking to your lawyer.
- ☑ Bring all relevant papers and information (such as names and addresses of people involved in the matter) to your lawyer's office. Have it organized so you can find what you need quickly.
- ☑ Do not deluge the lawyer with information; this will take up more time and cost you more money.
- ☑ Be as truthful and accurate as possible, even if the facts are unpleasant. Omissions that come to light later may result in extra costs.
- ☑ Listen attentively to what your lawyer tells you. Be sure you understand what he wants you to do.
- ☑ Be punctual for your appointments and court appearances.
- ☑ Telephone your lawyer only if you have something definite to ask or tell him about.
- ☑ Offer to obtain necessary documents, such as police or medical reports, to save him the work of doing so himself.
- ☑ Offer to help locate witnesses.
- ☑ If the case involves property damage, get a professional estimate of the dollar amount of the damage.
- ☑ Don't change your mind about what you want your lawyer to do, or ask him to do anything extra unless you are prepared to pay for it .

A lawyer told Justin that he could give him only an estimate of his fees. Should Justin get the estimate in writing?

Yes. But Justin should keep in mind that a written estimate would not include costs that could arise from unforeseeable legal complications.

My lawyer won't take my case without a retainer. Why?

A retainer is, in effect, the act that authorizes a lawyer to begin work on a case. If your lawyer were to begin work before you actually hired him, his actions would not be considered legally binding. A lawyer generally asks for a retainer so that he will have a fund available from which he can draw his salary and any miscellaneous out-of-pocket expenses. This fund is put into a trust account and can be used only to pay for expenses related to your case. If you change lawyers, or if the fees and expenses do not exceed the advanced amount, the remaining balance will be refunded to you.

My lawyer says that I have to pay the costs for filing my lawsuit. Since he's charging me so much already, why can't he at least pay for this as part of his overhead?

The fee you pay your lawyer is for his knowledge and experience, the time he spends working for you, and any office expenses associated with your case. Legal ethics forbid lawyers to pay for court filing costs, copies of official documents, court reporters (who take testimony from witnesses who can't attend the trial), and expert witnesses, such as doctors and engineers. If lawyers were permitted to pay for court costs, the person bringing the claim would not have to risk losing any of his own money or property, and this might result in a great deal of unnecessary litigation.

My lawyer charges me the same hourly rate for work done by his assistant as he does for his own work. Is this legal?

Since your lawyer is ultimately responsible for all of the work done on your case, he will be reviewing his assistant's work as your case progresses, and so he may feel justified in charging the same rate for his assistant's time as he does for his own. Still, some large law firms do charge different rates for different lawyers, depending on the experience and position of the person who has been assigned to do the work. Before your lawyer begins working on your case, check your agreement to see if its terms are clearly spelled out.

Lynn's lawyer has had to make several lengthy long-distance calls while working on her case. Does Lynn have to pay for them?

Yes. Incidental expenses, such as the cost of telephone, photocopying, and express mail, are usually added to a lawyer's final bill. Lynn will probably have to pay for any long-distance calls related to her case.

Am I entitled to an itemized bill from my lawyer?

If your lawyer is billing you by the hour, you have the right to an itemized bill that details how that time was spent. However, if your lawyer is charging a flat fee, he usually will not give you an itemized breakdown of the time spent on your case.

My lawyer says that he will work on a contingent-fee basis. What does this mean?

This means that the lawyer's fee will be a percentage of the money you win. If you do not win any money, your lawyer earns no fee. Traditionally, contingent-fee arrangements are common in accident and debt collection cases. But you will still be required to pay any court costs and expenses arising out of your lawsuit. Though your lawyer may advance the money to pay for these expenses, you are expected to reimburse him, regardless of the outcome of your case.

Terence was arrested for drunk driving. Can his lawyer agree to be paid only if Terence is not convicted?

No. Contingent fees are strictly forbidden in criminal cases throughout the United States. Courts have ruled that such arrangements could corrupt justice if the defense lawyer were paid only if his client were acquitted. Terence must pay his lawyer whether he wins or loses his case.

Can I pay my lawyer with a percentage of the money I hope to get from my divorce case?

No. Contingent fees are not permitted in divorce cases.

Is there a maximum percentage of the money a person wins in a lawsuit that a lawyer can receive as a contingent fee?

Contingent fees can range from as low as 20 percent to as high as 50 percent or more. Some states limit the percentage a lawyer may receive in certain cases, such as those involving medical malpractice. A lawyer must inform his client of such a limit before he takes a case; if he exceeds the limit he violates state law.

I gave a lawyer $2,000 as a retainer to take my case, but now I don't want to go through with the lawsuit. Can I get my money back? If so, how long does the lawyer have to return it?

If you decide to discontinue your lawsuit you are not entitled to a full refund, but you may be able to get any unused portion of your money back. You can determine how much money, if any, was not used by checking your lawyer's bills. Since lawyers generally prepare such statements as part of their regular 30-day billing cycle, you might expect to receive any refund within 30 days of the date you told your lawyer to stop working on your case. However, if your lawyer has already invested $2,000 worth of time and services in your case, you will not be entitled to a refund. If, on the other hand, he has spent no time at all on it, you may be able to get the full amount back.

Diane agreed to pay her lawyer a flat fee, but he had to withdraw before completing the case. Does she owe him the entire fee?

No. Diane should pay her lawyer only for the work he actually completed. If Diane's agreement with her lawyer does not specify a way to determine how much of the fee has been earned, the lawyer is entitled to the reasonable value of his services. This value will be based on the time and labor he invested, the difficulty of the questions involved, the extent to which Diane's case prevented him from accepting other cases, customary local fees for services, and the amount in dispute between Diane and her opponent. If, after taking all of these factors into consideration, Diane is entitled to a refund, her lawyer must pay it promptly.

Marjorie was injured when an elevator she was in crashed to the basement. She paid her lawyer a $500 advance to sue the building, but now that her case is coming to court, the lawyer wants another $500 or he'll quit. Marjorie doesn't have the money. What can she do?

First, Marjorie should try to resolve the fee dispute with her lawyer on an informal basis. Most fee agreements in accident cases are put in writing and provide that any payments beyond an initial advance depend on how much, if anything, the client wins. If Marjorie's lawyer still insists on the $500, she should fire him in writing and instruct him to ask for an adjournment of her trial when he notifies the court that he is no longer her lawyer. Then she should find a new lawyer.

Marjorie should also report her fee dispute with her original lawyer to the local bar association or the state supreme court, where she can file a formal grievance. If her chances of winning her lawsuit have been damaged by the lawyer's behavior, she may consider filing a malpractice suit against him. Marjorie should also try to get a refund for any portion of the $500 advance that the lawyer did not earn.

Can I get the other side to pay for my lawyer's fees?

Whether or not the other side will pay your lawyer's fees and expenses depends on the nature of your case. In a divorce case, for example, if a husband has earned all the family income and his wife has always remained at home, the husband may be ordered to pay for his wife's lawyer. In other cases, such as those involving accidents, the losing side in a lawsuit may be required to reimburse the other for certain types of costs and lawyer's fees. But whatever the nature of the case, there is no way to make the other side pay unless it is ordered to do so by the court. Furthermore, neither you nor your lawyer can guarantee that the court will order your opponent to pay.

Are fee splitting and referral fees among lawyers legal?

While fee splitting is usually legal, referral fees are generally legal only when the lawyer who receives the referral fee keeps some control over the case. As the law has become more complex and as more lawyers have chosen to specialize, it has become increasingly common for lawyers to consult other lawyers and to divide their fees accordingly. This happens most often in complicated cases when a lawyer needs the assistance of a lawyer with expertise in another area. In such a case, the lawyer must obtain his client's approval for the arrangement and explain the division of fees in detail.

Working With Your Lawyer

How can I tell if my lawyer is handling my case properly?

At the very least, your lawyer should keep you up-to-date on the status of your case, give you copies of correspondence and court documents, and let you know about court dates and deadlines. Most lawyers will provide this information routinely. If you feel your lawyer has not kept you thoroughly informed, or if you're not satisfied with the progress of your case, you should discuss the matter with him. But remember, the legal process is often slow, with long periods when nothing seems to happen. To a large extent, these delays are beyond the control of your lawyer, who may well feel as frustrated about the situation as you do.

If Dolores questions the wisdom of her lawyer's advice while her case is under way, should she get a second opinion?

Generally speaking, lawyers avoid giving second opinions. Attorneys do not like to second-guess the judgment of other lawyers, because they may be unaware of a particular development or issue relating to the case in progress. Therefore, if Dolores seeks another lawyer's advice, it's probably best that she not mention that she is looking for a second opinion.

Working With Your Lawyer

What is an opinion letter?

An opinion letter is a written statement by your lawyer in which he sets forth his opinion of your case or of a question you have asked him. If you are considering a product liability lawsuit, for example, your attorney may provide you with an opinion letter that summarizes the facts of your case, describes the outcome of cases similar to yours, explains which laws apply to your case, and assesses your chances of winning.

What should I do if I'm dissatisfied with the way my lawyer is handling my case?

Dissatisfaction frequently stems from a lack of communication between a lawyer and his client. For example, you may not understand the reasons for your lawyer's actions, or you may feel that your lawyer has failed to keep you properly informed of the progress of your case. The best way to clear up any confusion is to discuss your concerns with your lawyer as early as possible.

If you remain dissatisfied, you should contact your local lawyers' association, known as the bar association. These associations often have a committee that will try to resolve a problem to your satisfaction. If you suspect that your lawyer has seriously mishandled your case, you can file a formal grievance against him with your state's supreme court or sue him for malpractice.

Can my lawyer give me a timetable so that I'll have some idea when my case will come to court?

Your lawyer may be able to provide a rough timetable if he's had experience with similar cases, but since no two cases are exactly alike, your case may not follow a predictable schedule. The date when your case goes to trial is determined by many factors that are beyond your lawyer's control, such as the caseload of the court. In addition, if your opponent is not as eager as you are to see the case resolved, his lawyer may use delaying tactics to slow up the legal process.

Will my lawyer automatically provide me with copies of all the correspondence and documents relating to my case, or should I ask him to do so?

Usually, a lawyer will provide you with copies of all relevant documents and letters. However, there may be some minor correspondence, such as requests for insurance or police reports, that he will not forward to you. If you want to receive copies of all documents, including those of minor importance, you should specifically ask your lawyer to forward them to you. Most lawyers will be happy to furnish this material, although they may bill you for duplicating costs.

Lenore was injured when she slipped on the wet floor of a supermarket. One month ago she hired a lawyer to handle her case, but all he has done so far is send a letter to the store. Why hasn't he filed a lawsuit yet?

Generally, a lawsuit is only necessary in an accident case when both sides can't agree on a satisfactory settlement. It's also possible that Lenore's lawyer needs more time to investigate the accident or prepare his case. Lawsuits do not have to be filed immediately after an accident, but there is usually a deadline set by state law after which Lenore can no longer sue. If Lenore is worried about missing this deadline or is concerned about the way her lawyer is handling her case, she should discuss these matters candidly with him.

Herb's son Gary got into a fight at school and was suspended. Herb called his lawyer in a rage, claiming that the school's principal was just picking on the boy. Herb wants his lawyer to start a lawsuit against the principal "just to shake him up." The lawyer said he couldn't do this. Why not?

It is against the law to waste a court's time with lawsuits that have no legal basis. If Herb were to sue the principal solely for the purpose of harassing him, the principal could turn around and file a countersuit for malicious prosecution—the offense that is committed when a lawsuit is filed without legal justification.

Hal quit his job to start a partnership with his best friend, Danny. Three months into their venture, Hal discovered that Danny was stealing money from the business. Hal has decided to sue Danny, but Hal's lawyer wants to settle the case out of court. Who gets to decide the course of the case?

Hal. It's his lawsuit, and all decisions regarding its settlement are ultimately his. Hal's lawyer should point out to him, however, that refusing to settle will involve additional time and expense. The lawyer should also discuss what the chances are of winning the amount Hal wants. If Hal's lawyer feels that the settlement is fair, Hal should at least consider taking his lawyer's advice.

Working With Your Lawyer

The person who is suing me suggested that we submit our dispute to arbitration. If I agree, do I give up my right to a court trial?

Only if the arbitration agreement says so. Even if the agreement contains such a clause, however, you can appeal an arbitrator's decision if he (1) exceeded his authority, (2) failed to render a final and definite award, or (3) was guilty of corruption, fraud, or misconduct.

Will my lawyer report me to the authorities if I tell him I was involved in a crime that nobody else knows about?

No. Everything you tell your lawyer is considered confidential information. Without your permission, a lawyer may not disclose what you tell him to anyone. Even if you admit that you committed a crime, your lawyer cannot inform the police.

Ivy was arrested on a drug charge, and her parents have hired a lawyer to defend her. Aren't Ivy's parents entitled to know the details of her case, since they are paying for her lawyer?

No. A lawyer cannot reveal confidential information about his client, even to the person who is paying his fee, without the client's consent.

What an Arbitrator Can Do for You

If you need to settle a dispute, but want to avoid a long, expensive trial, one of the alternatives you should consider is arbitration. Arbitration is a process by which an impartial person or panel listens to both sides and makes what it considers to be a fair ruling. To use arbitration, both sides must agree to do so. The process can be used to settle any difference of opinion, including disagreements about alimony, contracts, or wills. In some states, disputes involving claims of less than a certain dollar amount are automatically sent to arbitration.

The arbitrator can be anyone whom both sides approve of, such as a teacher, lawyer, accountant, or business executive. However, if your disagreement involves a technical subject, such as home construction, you will probably need an arbitrator who has expertise in that area. If you don't know anyone suitable, contact the American Arbitration Association, a nonprofit organization located in New York City that maintains a roster of experts in various fields.

After having a few beers at lunch, Drew returned to work and cut his hand while using a power saw. Should he tell his lawyer that he had been drinking?

Yes. A client should always reveal the complete details of his case to his lawyer. If Drew's lawyer is to prepare and present Drew's case properly, he must be completely informed of all the circumstances surrounding the accident. By admitting that he had a few beers, Drew will allow his lawyer to prepare for testimony from witnesses who may have seen Drew drinking at lunch.

Art has been charged with driving while intoxicated. He confided to his lawyer that, while he wasn't drunk, he may have been "a little tipsy" at the time. Will this admission affect how his lawyer handles the case—especially if Art wants to plead not guilty?

Yes. Art's lawyer will use this information to prepare a strategy to defend Art. For example, it may be better if Art does not take the witness stand in his own defense. If Art were to testify, the prosecuting attorney might raise the issue of Art's "tipsiness" even though Art was not legally intoxicated and turn Art's admission against him. Knowing about Art's physical condition may also lead his lawyer to seek a plea-bargain agreement with the prosecutor. Art would then agree to plead guilty to a less serious offense in order to avoid the severe penalties associated with being convicted of driving while intoxicated.

The cost of arbitration includes (1) expenses incurred by the arbitrator, which are split between both sides, and (2) the administrative fee charged by the American Arbitration Association, which is paid by whichever side initiates the process. An arbitrator must be fair and neutral, and must disclose any information that could disqualify him, such as having a personal interest in the outcome of the case. Although he cannot be sued for failing to exercise skill or care, he may be held liable if he agrees to favor either side before the case has been presented.

Once both sides consent to arbitration, they should confirm in writing the subject of their dispute and the time and place of the proceeding. The hearing itself may have some of the features associated with a court proceeding—such as opening statements, witnesses, and exhibits. However, the hearing will be closed to the public and usually will last no longer than several hours. The decision of the arbitrator is legally binding, and may be appealed only if the arbitrator (1) exceeded his authority, (2) failed to make a final and definite award, or (3) was guilty of misconduct, fraud, or corruption.

Working With Your Lawyer

My lawyer wants to meet with me before my trial to review his questions and my answers to them. Is this legal?

Yes. In fact, most lawyers meet with their clients before a trial for this very purpose. If you have never before testified, your lawyer will prepare you for the experience by helping you organize the facts you are likely to tell the court. If your case involves a robbery, for example, your lawyer will try to refresh your memory of the details of the event. Your lawyer will also want to prepare you for any difficult questions the other side's lawyer may ask during cross-examination. Finally, your lawyer may want to describe the physical layout of the courtroom and explain how the trial will be conducted. The more relaxed you are, the more reliable your testimony will seem to the judge and jury.

Clara wants to take the stand in her own defense at her trial, but her lawyer thinks this is a bad idea. Can Clara insist on testifying even if her lawyer objects?

Yes, but she may have to fire her lawyer and hire another one who is willing to let her testify. If Clara's lawyer feels she would not make a good witness, she ought to consider his opinion carefully. If she testifies, anything Clara says can be used to help convict her. Moreover, Clara has the right not to testify, and if she refuses to take the stand, the prosecutor cannot force her to do so. For all these reasons, her lawyer is probably acting in her best interest by urging her not to take the stand.

My lawyer didn't cross-examine all of the other side's witnesses. Was this irresponsible of him?

Not necessarily. Cross-examination helps your case only if your lawyer can show an outstanding weakness in a witness's story. If your lawyer feels he cannot do this, he may prefer to move on without cross-examination. Your lawyer may also decline to cross-examine a witness in order to suggest that what the witness has to say is not very important.

On several occasions, Arlene's lawyer has gotten so carried away with his courtroom histrionics that the judge has charged him with contempt of court. Does this mean he'll be dismissed from Arlene's case?

No. Arlene's lawyer is not required to withdraw from the case just because the judge has charged him with contempt of court. However, if the judge imposes a fine for contempt of court, Arlene's lawyer could be suspended from all cases, including Arlene's, until he pays it.

Mason would like to fire his lawyer, but his case is well under way. What should he do?

If the case has already come to court, Mason must ask the judge for permission to fire his lawyer. If the judge decides that Mason's case might be harmed by such an action, he may deny Mason's request. If the judge does permit Mason to dismiss his lawyer, Mason should make sure that his lawyer requests an official postponement so that the case is not dismissed before a new lawyer has had time to familiarize himself with the issues involved.

If I fire my lawyer, do I still have to pay his fee?

It depends on how your lawyer has been charging you for his services. If he has been charging on an hourly basis, you must pay him for any time he has spent on your case. If you paid a flat fee, your lawyer may be allowed to keep a portion of that fee to cover the work he has completed. If your lawyer was hired on a contingent-fee basis, you may not owe him anything if you have not yet won any money in a settlement. However, you are not allowed to dismiss your lawyer before a settlement is reached just to avoid paying him his share.

Louise dismissed her lawyer because she wasn't pleased with his performance. Can she ask him to return all the documents relating to her case?

Yes. When you dismiss your lawyer, you are entitled to have any documents, reports, and other materials that you provided returned to you. These materials are your property, and your lawyer may not keep them after he has been fired.

Theodore's lawyer is retiring. What will happen to all of Theodore's personal documents?

Since all of the personal documents contained in Theodore's file are his property, he can arrange for their safekeeping however he chooses. If Theodore's lawyer does not automatically return all of his client's documents before he retires, Theodore should ask him to do so. If another lawyer is taking over Theodore's lawyer's practice and Theodore decides not to use him, Theodore should pick up his file from the office.

Legal Ethics

Do lawyers have a code of ethics that they must follow?

Yes. Lawyers have a written code of ethics—known as the Rules of Professional Conduct, or Code of Professional Responsibility—that guides their professional behavior. While each state has its own code of legal ethics, most state codes are based on those developed by the largest lawyers' group in the country, the American Bar Association. The Code of Professional Responsibility and the Model Rules of Professional Conduct define the standards of conduct that lawyers must follow. If a lawyer violates any of these standards, he can be disciplined or even barred from practicing law.

If I report a lawyer to the bar association for unethical conduct or malpractice, will I have to testify and be cross-examined?

Yes. When the malpractice case comes up for a hearing, you will be required to testify about your lawyer's misconduct, and if he wants to cross-examine you, he can do so at that time.

What are some examples of legal malpractice?

A lawyer commits malpractice if he damages his client's case by failing to exercise a proper degree of skill, knowledge, or diligence; if he doesn't prepare adequately for the case or neglects it completely; if he delays working on the case for so long that the case is dismissed; if he takes money that isn't his or deliberately misleads his client about how much money he could win from a lawsuit; or if he reveals confidential information. It is also malpractice for a lawyer to accept a case that he knows, or should know, he is not competent to handle.

My lawyer suggested that I name him as executor of my will, since I have no close relatives. Would this be all right?

Yes. Many people choose their lawyer as the executor or alternate executor of their will. As long as you feel that your lawyer is experienced and trustworthy, there is no reason for not selecting him for this function.

William's lawyer has assigned his associate to take over the case. Is it ethical for a lawyer to do this?

A lawyer should always obtain his client's consent when turning over part or all of a case to another lawyer. It is common practice to have associates assist with cases, such as doing research and handling routine court appearances. But a lawyer should explain what aspects of the case will be handled by the associate and assure his client that he will closely supervise and check the associate's work. If a client is not comfortable with this arrangement, he should discuss it with his lawyer.

My husband and I listed our house for sale with a real estate broker. Afterward, we received a letter from a lawyer we don't know, who offered to help us close the deal. Should we hire him?

Perhaps. Rules about how lawyers find business have changed quite a bit over the last few years. At one time it was considered improper conduct for a lawyer to send a letter asking for business, but since many states have relaxed their rules, this may be an acceptable practice in your area. Check with your local lawyers' association, called the bar association, or with the disciplinary committee of your state's supreme court. If it is not proper in your area for a lawyer to ask for your business in this manner, you might be better served by finding another lawyer, who abides by the rules of his profession.

When my son was hospitalized because of a bus accident, a lawyer we didn't know started to pester us about suing. We don't want to get involved in legal matters. What can we do?

Report the lawyer's conduct to the disciplinary committee of your state's supreme court and your local lawyers' association, called the bar association. This lawyer is guilty of ambulance chasing, which is forbidden by every state. A lawyer who engages in such behavior could be suspended or even barred from practicing law.

When Stella mentioned to an attorney that she needed a lawyer to handle her divorce, he told her that the family court judge was one of his best buddies, and that if she hired him, she wouldn't have any trouble cleaning out her husband. Has Stella found the perfect lawyer?

Probably not. Stella should look for a lawyer who stresses the quality of his work rather than his connections. Even if the lawyer were to try to use his friendship to influence her case, the judge is bound by oath not to let personal relationships interfere with his decisions. In fact, the judge's close friendship with the lawyer might backfire. If the judge rules in Stella's favor, her husband's lawyer might claim that the judge's decision was in fact influenced by his friendship with her lawyer, and might succeed in having the case tried again before a different judge.

Legal Ethics

Connie's neighbor Neil recently built a fence that crosses a part of her property, so Connie filed a lawsuit against him. Neil's lawyer turns out to be the same one who handled Connie's child custody case 10 years ago. Should Neil find another lawyer?

Nothing in the legal code of ethics specifically prohibits Neil's lawyer from defending him in this lawsuit just because he handled Connie's child custody case, especially since that case was 10 years earlier. But if there is any connection between Neil's lawsuit and Connie's child custody case, then the lawyer should reject the case and Neil should find another lawyer.

Angelo was injured in a two-car accident. He would like his friend Larry to take the case. But Larry is representing the other driver on a reckless driving charge resulting from the same accident. Can Larry handle Angelo's case?

No. A lawyer must serve the best interests of his client. By accepting Angelo's case, Larry would be placing himself in a conflict of interest between Angelo and the other driver. If the other driver gives Larry confidential information about the accident that is damaging to Angelo's case, Larry might have to use this information against Angelo. If Larry represents both drivers, he would be subject to disciplinary action for violating the code of ethics that governs the conduct of lawyers.

Troy and Perry were arrested and charged with destroying property. At their first meeting with a lawyer, Troy swore that everything was Perry's fault; Perry claimed to be innocent and pointed an accusing finger at Troy. Can the same lawyer defend both of them?

No. When a lawyer agrees to represent a client, he commits himself to giving that client the best defense possible. In this case, the lawyer is caught in a clear conflict of interest. He can't represent both, since in defending Troy he must argue that Perry is guilty, and in defending Perry, he would have to argue that Troy committed the crime. Troy and Perry should ask to be represented by different lawyers.

My lawyer can't represent me because of a conflict of interest. Can another lawyer in his firm take the case?

No. If your lawyer can't take your case or has to withdraw from it because of a conflict of interest, no other lawyer affiliated with the firm can represent you in this particular matter. To do so would be to violate the rules of professional ethics of the legal profession. You will have to find a lawyer from a different firm.

Several days after Jerry met with his lawyer, he discovered that the lawyer's secretary was gossiping around town about confidential matters she had learned while transcribing her boss's notes. What can Jerry do?

All members of a lawyer's staff, including secretaries, are bound by the same confidentiality that a lawyer promises his client. If someone breaches this confidentiality, the lawyer must assume full responsibility. Jerry should file a complaint with the state bar's disciplinary committee.

Priscilla asked her lawyer to testify as a witness at her trial, but he told her that he couldn't honor her request. Why not?

A lawyer is ethically bound to keep everything a client has told him confidential. If he were called as a witness, he could be forced to disclose information that Priscilla might not want him to reveal. If the lawyer's testimony is crucial to her case, Priscilla should allow him to withdraw and hire another lawyer to represent her. Then the new lawyer could call the former lawyer to testify as a private citizen at the trial.

I just read a book by a famous lawyer in which he explains how he won a criminal trial. Isn't it a violation of the lawyer-client relationship to publish facts about the case?

Not if he has the client's consent, and any agreement regarding publication rights was made after the case was over. A lawyer is ethically required to avoid situations that would influence how he represents his client. Acquiring publication rights while the case is in progress could tempt the lawyer to place his own interests ahead of those of his client.

Hugh filed a lawsuit against a pharmaceutical company. The company offered a $22,000 settlement, but Hugh's lawyer rejected the claim without telling Hugh, then lost the case. When Hugh found out about the offer, he was furious with his lawyer for not giving him a chance to accept it. Can Hugh sue his lawyer?

Yes. A lawyer must inform his client of all options and give the client an opportunity to make the final decision. Hugh's lawyer should have notified him of any offer of settlement, since the decision to accept or reject the offer was Hugh's. In addition to suing his lawyer for malpractice, Hugh could report him to the ethics committee of his local lawyers' association, called the bar association, or he could report him to the disciplinary committee of the state supreme court.

Lorna lost her case in court and told her lawyer to file an appeal. He didn't file the appeal within the time limit required. What action can Lorna take?

She can file a complaint with the state disciplinary committee for lawyers. Since her lawyer agreed to file her appeal but failed to do so, he violated the Rules, or Code, of Professional Responsibility. Lorna may also sue her lawyer for any losses she suffered as a result of his inaction.

My lawyer met with me for just a few minutes after I was mistakenly arrested for shoplifting. He hardly asked me any questions. Just before my trial began, he told me that if I pleaded guilty, I would get a suspended sentence. I took his advice, and now I'm facing a jail sentence. What can I do?

You should consult with a new lawyer immediately for a review of your situation. If your new lawyer can prove that the first one did not give you appropriate advice before your trial, he might be able to get the court to reconsider your case, or even reverse its decision.

CHAPTER
2

Marriage and Family

Getting Married

What are the legal requirements for getting married?

Each state has its own rules and regulations for obtaining a marriage license and having a ceremony. In general, the requirements concern the age of consent and the mental and physical capacity of each person.

To get a license, the bride and groom must have reached the age of consent, which ranges from 15 to 21, with 18 the most common. If their parents agree to the marriage, the minimum age is lower. Each state makes exceptions to its age of consent—for example, if the bride is pregnant, or if it's a second marriage.

For the marriage to be valid, the couple must have the mental capacity to understand the rights, duties, and obligations created by the marital relationship. They must also be aware of any physical problems that might prevent them from consummating the marriage.

Most states require blood tests and a waiting period—either between the blood test and the day the license is issued or between the license and day of the ceremony. Other formalities that may be necessary are having witnesses attend the ceremony and filing a record of the marriage with the county or state. The clerk of the court in your nearest town or county court can provide information on all these details.

My 16-year-old daughter wants to get married. Can I stop her?

Only in a state that requires parental consent for a 16-year-old to marry. If your daughter lives in a state where women must be 18 to obtain a marriage license, for example, you can prevent her from marrying by withholding your consent. If your daughter lies about her age and marries without obtaining your approval, you can petition the court to have the marriage annulled.

Why is a waiting period required before marriage?

The waiting period dates back to the old practice of announcing banns, or public notices, which gave those opposed to the marriage time to object. Today the waiting period offers the prospective bride and groom a few days' pause to reflect on their decision. Most states have a waiting period before the license is issued; a few require one between the issuance of the license and the ceremony. The waiting period ranges in length from one to five days; the usual period is three days.

Helen and Frank want to get married right away, but their state requires a three-day waiting period between the issuance of the

license and the ceremony. Is there some way for them to have this delay eliminated?

Yes. Most states will waive the waiting period for an emergency or other extraordinary circumstances, such as a terminal illness, active military duty, pregnancy, or the birth of a child out of wedlock. A judge or other official designated for this purpose signs an authorization permitting the ceremony to take place before the end of the waiting period.

If a couple does not have a valid reason for the waiting period to be waived and they wish to marry immediately, they can do so—but they risk having a penalty imposed on them or on the individual who performs the ceremony for failing to observe all the requirements of state law. However, failing to observe such a formality will not make the marriage void or invalid.

What is the reason for requiring a blood test?

The purpose of a blood test is to detect venereal disease. The test may also reveal other health problems, such as tuberculosis or drug addiction. If a communicable venereal disease is found, a marriage license will not be issued. Some states, such as Kansas, Maryland, and South Carolina, do not require a blood test before a marriage license can be issued.

Greg and Nancy obtained their marriage license two weeks before their wedding day, but then Nancy was injured in an accident and was hospitalized for two months. Is the license still valid?

Each state sets its own deadline for the validity of a marriage license. In states that have adopted the Uniform Marriage and Divorce Act, a marriage license is valid for 180 days. In other states the license is good only for periods ranging from 30 to 60 days. Usually, the time limit is shown on the license. Greg and Nancy may have to get a new license, depending on the state where they're getting married.

Wally told Janet two days before their wedding that he had changed his mind about marrying her. Can Janet get Wally to pay for the cost of canceling the wedding?

It depends on where Janet lives. In the past the person left standing at the altar could sue for breach of promise to marry and, if successful, be awarded damages for wedding expenses, lost wages if that person had stopped working, mental anguish, loss of reputation, and loss of a higher social status. Additional money was awarded when the promise to marry had been made with no intention of carrying it out. However, many states no longer recognize the right to sue for breach of promise to marry. Others have placed limits on the kinds of damages awarded or the circumstances under which a lawsuit can be filed. In Maryland, for example, the bride-to-be can sue for breach of promise to marry only if she is pregnant.

My son began an ardent courtship of a girl who was engaged to a soldier stationed overseas. Eventually she broke her engagement. Does the soldier have any legal recourse against my son?

No. Courts are reluctant to interfere when a third person causes a breach of promise to marry. This reluctance is, in part, an effort to protect parents who step in and advise their children about the wisdom of marrying a particular person.

Our son gave his great-grandmother's diamond ring to Andrea for their engagement. Can Andrea keep the ring if they break up?

Not in most cases. Engagement gifts are given with the expectation that the marriage will take place. If the wedding falls through and Andrea insists on keeping the ring, your son can go to court to enforce his

The Marriage Contract

When a man and a woman wed, they are generally full of ideas of love and happiness and a lifetime of caring. They rarely realize that they are also making a legal contract, which will bind them with rights and responsibilities that are defined, regulated, and enforced by the state. A husband and wife are not free to devise the rules by which a marriage may be conducted; they must comply with the laws of their state, and these laws are not negotiable.

As soon as a man and a woman are pronounced husband and wife, they acquire certain rights under the law: the right to be free from parental control, the right to sexual relations and marital privacy, the right to share in each other's property, the right to have society regard their children as legitimate, and the right of one spouse to inherit from the other. In return a husband and wife are given certain responsibilities by state law: above all, they must support each other and their children and make sure that the children are properly educated.

Traditionally, the law expected a husband to support his wife, paying for her food, clothing, home, and furniture; the wife upheld her part of the ownership right. The court could order Andrea either to return the ring or to pay your son an amount equal to the ring's value. Because this ring is an heirloom, the court would probably make Andrea give it back. An exception might occur if the court found that your son broke the engagement without good reason, or did something—such as run off with another woman—that caused the engagement to be broken.

Jim gave Betty a sapphire ring a month before they became engaged. If they never marry, is Betty entitled to keep the ring?

Yes. This was a gift, like a birthday or Christmas present. Jim did not give it to her in exchange for her promise to marry him.

Are some kinds of marriages illegal?

Yes. Every state has restrictions on who can marry whom. No lawful marriage can exist between persons of the same sex or if one of the prospective spouses is already married to someone else. Relatives who are prohibited from marrying each other are brother and sister, parent and child, grandparent and grandchild, aunt and nephew, and uncle and niece. States differ on whether first cousins can marry. Any blood relationship more distant than this is generally acceptable.

Many states also restrict marriages between people who are related by

contract by keeping the home clean, preparing the food, and caring for the children. In recent years the law has given married couples greater freedom in dividing their responsibilities, especially in regard to earning wages and supporting family members. Today both spouses in a marriage may work and share family expenses, or a wife may be the sole support of the family while the husband stays home and minds the children. Moreover, the law expects that a wife will help support her husband and family when necessary, and she may be held equally liable with her husband to pay family expenses.

Generally, the law will not interfere with an ongoing marriage. For example, a judge will not order a working man to give his wife an allowance as long as the family is being provided with the bare essentials of life. Nor will a judge meddle in arguments over the family budget. But when a marriage is dissolving, the law will intervene to help settle disputes, preserve the property rights of those involved, and make sure that the children's best interests are protected. Although other contracts can be terminated by mutual consent, a marriage contract is considered to be so special that it can be ended only by the death of a spouse or by an act of the state—the issuance of a divorce decree.

marriage; unions between stepparents and stepchildren are the most frequently prohibited. Other states have completely eliminated restrictions for people related by marriage.

Brian and Jody are first cousins. They were married in one state and then moved to a state where it is illegal for first cousins to marry. Are they still legally married?

Yes. The general rule is that the validity of a marriage is determined by the laws of the state in which it was performed. There is an exception, however. If Brian and Jody married in one state in order to avoid the prohibition of first-cousin marriages in another state, their marriage would not be recognized.

Jason was adopted by Karen and Mike. Three years later they had a girl, Tammy. When Jason and Tammy grew up, they wanted to marry each other. Is this possible?

Some states would not let them marry, because they are brother and sister as far as the law is concerned. Others would permit the marriage, because Jason and Tammy are not blood relatives. The main concern of laws prohibiting intrafamily marriages is to prevent undesirable genetic traits in children born to couples who are too closely related. Since Jason is adopted, this concern is removed.

I just discovered that my husband's divorce from his first wife was never made final by the court. Are we legally married? Are our children legitimate?

You are not legally married. Until his divorce is final, your husband remains married to his first wife. He could be found guilty of bigamy and punished according to the laws of your state. Although your marriage is invalid, your children are considered legitimate.

Who may perform a marriage ceremony?

People authorized by the state to perform marriage ceremonies include clergymen, judges, and justices of the peace. If an unauthorized person performs a marriage ceremony, he is breaking the law and may be subject to a penalty. An unsuspecting couple would still be considered married and would face no penalty for having an unlawful ceremony.

Can a ship's captain perform a legal marriage ceremony?

The validity of marriages performed on ships is determined by the location of the vessel at the time of the ceremony. If the ceremony takes place in territorial waters, the laws of the state or nation claiming those waters determine the ceremony's validity. Unless the laws of those states or nations specifically prohibit captains from performing marriage ceremonies, couples would be lawfully married. If the wedding takes place while the ship is in international waters, the governing law is generally that of the place where the shipowner lives. Some courts have ruled, however, that the controlling laws are those of the state or country in which the couple resides.

Frank and Myrna met at a vacation resort in the Bahamas. They were so happy they decided to get married there before returning home. Is their marriage valid?

If Frank and Myrna complied with all the requirements for getting married in the Bahamas, they would be legally married when they returned to the United States. However, Frank and Myrna should check their state laws. They may require that for the foreign marriage to be valid, the couple must be legally qualified to marry in their home state. For example, if Frank and Myrna were first cousins and they lived in a state that does not allow first-cousin marriages, then that state would not recognize their Bahamian marriage.

I have heard that a marriage must be consummated for it to be recognized as legally valid. Is this true?

No. Once the ceremony is over, a couple is considered to be legally married. The idea that you are not legally married until you have had sexual relations is mistaken.

Prenuptial Agreements

Both Scott and Mary went through painful property disputes while ending their previous marriages. Neither wants to go through the same ordeal if their new marriage does not work out. What is the best thing for them to do?

Many states permit contracts to be drawn up before or after marriage to establish property rights between husband and wife. If Scott and Mary live in one of these states, they should have a contract drawn up stating what each person owned before the marriage, what each person will own if the marriage ends, and what to do with property acquired during the marriage. Everything should be in writing to avoid future misunderstandings. Scott and Mary should have their own attorneys advise them on the terms and language to include in the contract. They should sign the agreement and have it witnessed and notarized. Some states require that the agreement be recorded in the county where it is made.

George wants Anne to sign a prenuptial agreement containing a provision that Anne will not contest a divorce. Is such an agreement enforceable?

Probably not. Our society values the family as a source of strength and stability. The courts are therefore interested in preserving the institution of marriage. By including a provision that prevents Anne from contesting a divorce, George has tried to make it easier for himself to divorce her. Contracts that facilitate divorce are not viewed as promoting or supporting the institution of marriage.

Jeff is in love with Susan, but he is afraid that Susan wants to marry him only for his money. So he had her sign a prenuptial contract in which she agreed to make no claims against his estate upon his death. Is this binding?

Yes. One purpose of a prenuptial agreement is to define property rights in the event of death. If Jeff wants to make sure his property is inherited by his relatives and not his wife, a copy of the prenuptial agreement should be presented after his death to the court that handles estates. The agreement would be enforceable even though the law in most states gives the wife a right to a share of her husband's estate when he dies.

David and Emily signed an agreement prior to their marriage five years ago, outlining how their property would be divided in the event of death or divorce. Can they cancel the agreement?

Yes, if they both agree. The termination of the prenuptial agreement should be in writing, dated, signed, witnessed, and notarized. A written termination agreement is solid evidence that the original agreement has been canceled. The original and all copies of the prenuptial agreement should be destroyed. If a missing copy of the original prenuptial agreement should turn up later and be presented to a court, a written termination agreement would prove that David and Emily had definitely ended their original agreement. They should also find out if their state has any further legal requirements for terminating a prenuptial agreement.

Before we married, Calvin and I agreed that if we ever divorced, neither of us would make a claim to property the other brought into the marriage. But we never put this in writing. Is our oral agreement enforceable if we divorce?

Probably not. Most states that enforce prenuptial agreements require them to be in writing. In addition, the agreement must be signed,

What to Include in a Prenuptial Agreement

Signing a prenuptial agreement—a marital contract spelling out who gets what if the marriage breaks up—may seem cold and unromantic, but with America's divorce rate at about 50 percent, more and more couples are finding these agreements a sensible precaution. If a marriage does end in divorce, a properly drawn prenuptial agreement will eliminate bitter settlement battles and minimize court costs and lawyers' fees. When drafting a prenuptial agreement, you should avoid such trivialities as who's going to put out the cat or wash the dishes; inconsequential matters like these cannot be enforced by a court. If you think some of your considerations may be inappropriate or invalid, be sure to discuss them with your lawyer. The following are the basics you should consider including:

- ☑ A statement of who will contribute what to family expenses.
- ☑ An agreement on the means of supporting any children or a spouse of a former marriage or other dependent relatives.
- ☑ A declaration that each of you is being honest about all individually owned property and its value at the time of your marriage.
- ☑ An agreement on how premarital property, owned singly or jointly, will be divided if there's a divorce.
- ☑ An agreement on how property that each contributes during the marriage will be divided in the event of a divorce.
- ☑ An agreement on what happens to the property acquired jointly during the marriage.
- ☑ An agreement on how any business partnership between husband and wife will be dissolved.
- ☑ A statement declaring whether the wife intends to use her maiden or married name.
- ☑ A statement that the agreement was not drawn up with the intention of ending the marriage by separation or divorce. (Courts will not accept agreements that tend to promote separation or divorce.)
- ☑ Instructions on how the agreement can be altered or terminated.

witnessed, and in some cases, recorded. Even if you live in a state that does not require a written agreement, it is best to put everything in writing. Not only will this serve as evidence that a binding agreement was made, but it will also remind both you and Calvin of the promises you made to each other.

My spouse's parents forced us to sign a prenuptial agreement. Will this agreement hold up in court?

No. One of the requirements for a valid prenuptial agreement is that no pressure be used to get either person to sign. A court will not enforce a contract that was not freely entered into by those who signed it. Other factors the court would consider in determining the contract's validity: Were both of you fully aware of each other's property and its value? Was the property divided fairly under the terms of the contract? Did the agreement encourage divorce or separation?

Before they were married, Arthur and Lillian agreed to raise their children in a particular religion. But after the children were born, Arthur changed his mind. Can Lillian get a judge to rule in her favor about the children's religious upbringing?

Probably not. A judge would be hesitant to rule in this case; courts do not usually interfere with the upbringing of children in an ongoing marriage unless the children are being neglected or harmed in some way.

Unmarried Couples

My girlfriend and I are planning to move in together next month. Some friends of ours have a "living together agreement." Should we also have one?

It would be wise for the two of you to sit down and discuss how property should be divided if one of you moves out. Topics to discuss include property owned before moving in, property acquired while living together, real estate or leases, pets, income, and joint bank accounts. Once you have come to an agreement, you should put it in writing and have it signed just as you would any other contract. Although such a contract is not mandatory, it would make it easier to prove that an agreement was reached and to have its terms enforced by a court if the time ever came when you had a serious property dispute.

Jim and Bonnie have lived together for several years. During this time they have bought a house, furniture, and appliances. What rights does each one have if they split up and cannot agree on how to divide the property?

If Jim and Bonnie made no agreement before they began living together, it will be more difficult for a court to divide the property. Generally, each of them is entitled to keep any property he or she owned before they began their joint living arrangement. The biggest problem lies in distributing property that they acquired while living together. If Jim and Bonnie live in one of the eight states that have community property laws for married couples (Arizona, California, Idaho, Louisiana, Nevada, New Mexico, Texas, and Washington), there is a good chance a court would divide the property between them, 50-50.

In other states a court would divide the property as fairly as possible, using the theory of equitable distribution. If Jim's name is on the title to the house but Bonnie contributed an equal amount toward its purchase, the court may give each a one-half interest in the property. Appliances and furniture may also be divided equally unless one person contributed more than the other. The court may then divide this property in proportion to what each contributed, taking into account money paid for the item's purchase or nonfinancial contributions, such as child care.

My boyfriend left me with six months to go on our apartment lease, and the rent is too high for me to pay by myself. How can I get money from him to help out?

If both of you signed the lease, you alone can be held responsible for the balance due. One recourse is to go to small claims court to compel your boyfriend to pay his share of the rent. Since small claims courts have a maximum amount that you can seek, check with court personnel to make sure your case qualifies.

If this route is unsuccessful, and your lease permits it, you can try to find someone else to complete the terms of your lease. You could then be relieved of any liability for the balance of the rent. A landlord cannot refuse to accept a new tenant without good reason. If you moved into your boyfriend's apartment and did not add your name to the lease, you are an illegal tenant, and the landlord can evict you—even if you kept up the rent payments in full.

Beatrice and Andrew had lived together for 14 years when Andrew died. Does Beatrice have any claim on Andrew's estate?

If Andrew did not include Beatrice in his will, she may not be able to claim a penny of his estate. Although the laws of each state automatically give the surviving spouse of a marriage a part of the estate when there is no will, they do not protect unmarried couples.

Nevertheless, Beatrice may be able to claim a share of the estate on principles of fairness, or equity. As society becomes more willing to accept living-together arrangements, the courts have become more willing to divide property on an equitable basis. If Andrew and Beatrice were equally responsible for entering and sustaining their relationship, the court might consider it unfair for her contribution to the relationship to go to someone else. A judge might well rule that if Beatrice is denied a share of Andrew's property, his heirs would unjustly benefit.

Common-law Marriages

Are common-law marriages accepted in every state?

Fourteen states and the District of Columbia recognize common-law marriages. These states are Alabama, Colorado, Georgia, Idaho, Iowa, Kansas, Montana, Ohio, Oklahoma, Pennsylvania, Rhode Island, South Carolina, Texas, and Utah.

Teresa and Ben consider themselves married although they never had a formal wedding ceremony. What requirements must they meet in order to qualify legally as husband and wife?

Teresa and Ben must meet four basic requirements: First, they must live in one of the 14 states, or the District of Columbia, that recognizes common-law marriages.

Second, is the capacity to marry. Each must understand the rights and duties that result from the decision to marry. Both must meet the age requirements of their state for a marriage ceremony; however, some states have lower age requirements for common law marriages.

Third, they must agree to be husband and wife, and they must agree on a specific date for the relationship to start. Teresa and Ben cannot, for example, move in together on July 1, decide to be married on December 1, and then claim they were husband and wife since July 1.

Fourth, they must present themselves to the public as husband and wife. Joint checking and savings accounts, joint tax returns, and similar papers indicating the other person as spouse, or using the same last name on driver's licenses all provide evidence to the public that Teresa and Ben consider themselves husband and wife.

Some states add a fifth requirement: for the common-law marriage to be valid the couple must live together once they decide to become husband and wife. But no state sets a time limit for this qualifying cohabitation. The belief that couples must live together seven years to be legally married is a mistaken one.

How is a common-law marriage different from living together?

Common-law husbands and wives have the same rights and obligations as spouses who were married in a formal ceremony. They have a duty to support each other financially and a joint responsibility for the upbringing of their children. One spouse may inherit the other's property when a death occurs. In contrast, couples who live together do not enter into their relationship with the agreement to be husband and wife. They often keep their own names, introduce themselves as individuals rather than as a married couple, and keep separate property. People who live together have no claim to a deceased partner's estate, nor are any marital rights or duties required of them.

John and Susan lived together as husband and wife for three years in a common-law state before moving to a state that does not recognize common-law marriages. Are they still married?

Since John and Susan had a valid common-law marriage in their old state, their new state is likely to recognize them as husband and wife. However, some states have strict requirements for validating a common-law marriage, regardless of where the marriage takes place. Marriages that fail to meet these standards may not be recognized as valid by a court.

Elizabeth and James had lived together as husband and wife for several years when James left and moved in with Janice. He now claims Janice is his wife. Which one is his real wife?

Elizabeth continues to be James's wife. Although a common-law marriage is established without any government action, its termination requires divorce proceedings. There is no common-law divorce. Until James obtains a divorce decree, Janice has no legal claim as James's wife.

Family Responsibilities

Do both husband and wife have an obligation to provide support for the family?

In the past the husband carried the full burden of providing financial support. But with the increasing number of families in which both husbands and wives work at jobs outside the home, this is no longer considered a strictly male responsibility.

If both spouses work, who is legally responsible for paying the household bills?

Generally, both the husband and wife are responsible. The practice of imposing financial responsibility on the husband, and letting the wife escape liability, is no longer the rule. The new trend is to hold working spouses jointly responsible for family debts and individually responsible for personal debts. Some states have enacted family expense statutes that hold spouses equally liable for family expenses. Other states continue to make the husband liable for household bills but allow creditors to ask the wife for payment if the husband's assets are insufficient.

We have been married for two years, but my husband refuses to pay me a dime for support. I've had to use an inheritance from my mother for my expenses. My husband says that he is entitled to half the inheritance and that I should get a job. Do I have to work, or does he have to pay my bills?

The law does not require that both spouses work. As long as you are receiving adequate financial support, the courts will not interfere with who provides it or how it is provided.

Your husband does have a legal obligation to provide you with such basic necessities as food, clothing, a place to live, and medical care. If your husband does not provide these things or give you the money to buy them, you have every right to charge them to him. If your husband won't pay the bill, the creditors may take you to court, where a judge may issue an order requiring him to pay.

If a wife has an income that can adequately support her, a court might rule that any debts she incurs are her own. A court might expect you to pay for your necessities out of your inheritance. However, your husband does not have a right to any of this money; the inheritance is yours to dispose of as you please.

Charlie was disabled because of an accident. His wife, Mabel, has never worked. Must Mabel go out and get a job now that Charlie can't earn a living?

Yes. States do not want families to become dependent on public support when one spouse has the ability to work. Since Charlie is unable to support himself or his family, Mabel must take over that responsibility. If Charlie is disabled to the point that he requires Mabel's constant attention, or if there are other family circumstances that prohibit her from working outside the home, the state would be more willing to consider providing some form of assistance to them.

If I am a homemaker, financially dependent on my husband, and he is close with the money, do I have any legal recourse?

Generally the breadwinner is allowed to determine the standard of living for the family. If your husband is providing you with the basic necessities, a court would not step in and order him to give you additional money. However, if you are not receiving the necessities of life and must seek welfare assistance, a court may require your husband to provide you with more money to help meet your needs.

Carrie bought some clothing on a layaway plan, expecting that her husband would pay for it. Is he required to do so?

No. A husband is not automatically required to cover all of his wife's obligations. If Carrie's husband is adequately providing her with clothing or giving her a sufficient allowance to buy it, he is not liable for completing her layaway purchases.

My husband bought a $2,400 stereo system for his den. He made a $200 down payment and signed a contract to make monthly payments over the next two years. If he stops paying, could I be required to take over the payments?

No. If what your husband bought was a family necessity, you might be required to pay for it. But since a stereo is not a necessity, you cannot be held responsible. Generally, one spouse is not responsible for contracts made by the other. If the debt is in your husband's name, he is responsible for paying it. Under the married women's acts, a creditor cannot force you to settle your husband's debts for items that are not family necessities.

My wife used my credit card to buy a brand-new $2,500 fur coat. Am I obligated to pay for it?

Your duty to pay will be based in part on your past history with that particular credit card. If you have routinely given the card to your wife to use, you would be liable. By allowing her to use the card, you have given her your permission to make charges on that credit card in your name.

If your name alone was on the credit card application, but you requested a duplicate card for her use, you are still liable for the coat. However, if both names were on the application, you are both equally responsible for all charges, regardless of who made them.

Am I liable for the monthly mortgage payments if my husband purchases a home in his own name?

No. Since the title of the house is in his name and you did not sign any papers relating to the purchase, you have no legal interest in the property. The bank, or other holder of the mortgage, cannot force you to make payments on the property.

Is a husband responsible for debts incurred by his wife before they were married?

Not necessarily. Some states will not impose any liability on the husband unless a contract outlined his responsibility for his wife's debts. Other states impose a limited liability on the husband. For example, if no agreement was made about the debts prior to the marriage, a husband's maximum liability is limited to the value of any property his wife transferred to him when they married. If she conveyed to him property worth $15,000 and her premarital debts totaled $21,000, he could be held responsible for only $15,000. The remaining $6,000 is her debt.

If I run a newspaper notice stating that I am not responsible for my spouse's debts, will this protect me in any way?

A newspaper notice may not be an acceptable way to notify creditors of your limited liability. Actual notice should be sent to the merchants who have given you and your spouse credit in the past. However, some states require that you take out an advertisement in a local paper warning merchants who have never extended credit to you that you are no longer responsible for your spouse's debts.

Can I be held responsible for my husband's unpaid taxes?

If this is an income tax matter, it will depend on the type of income tax return that was filed. If you and your husband filed a joint return, you are equally liable for any tax. If your husband refuses to contribute to the unpaid taxes, the Internal Revenue Service can legally require you to pay the entire amount.

Payment of real estate and personal property taxes depends on your legal interest in the property. You do not automatically have a duty to pay taxes that are assessed on your spouse's property. The primary duty falls on the person who holds legal title to the property. If the property is held jointly, you would have to pay the taxes.

Even if the property is not in your name, you may want to pay the taxes to avoid losing the property. For example, if title to the family car is in your husband's name, you may want to pay the taxes to prevent its being sold to meet tax obligations. There is nothing to prevent one person from paying another's taxes.

Noreen earns $20,000 a year as a data processor and puts all her earnings into a savings account. Her husband wants to invest the money in a get-rich-quick scheme. He claims that as her husband he has just as much right to her earnings as she does. Is Noreen's husband correct?

Only if they live in Arizona, California, Idaho, Louisiana, Nevada, New Mexico, Texas, Washington, or Wisconsin. Under community property laws in those nine states, any property or income earned or acquired during a marriage is considered joint property. In other states Noreen's husband would have no claim on his wife's salary and would have to rely on her choosing to share her earnings with him.

Bonnie's grandmother gave her a valuable collection of old coins. Does Bonnie's husband have any claim to this property?

No. Gifts and inheritances acquired while someone is married remain the individual property of that spouse even in community property states.

When Ellen died, she left her niece, Joyce, a $5,000 bracelet. Eight months later Joyce married Christopher. Does he automatically obtain a half interest in the bracelet as a result of their marriage?

No. Christopher has no valid claim to this bracelet, since Joyce inherited it before their marriage. Property rights in a marriage are determined in one of two ways, depending on the state in which the couple is living. In most states anything acquired by a spouse's own efforts, both before and during the marriage, remains the property of that spouse. But in nine states (Arizona, California, Idaho, Louisiana, Nevada, New Mexico, Texas, Washington, and Wisconsin) anything earned or acquired by an individual during a marriage becomes community property, with each spouse owning a one-half interest in it. However, even in these nine states the property owned by a spouse before getting married remains that person's own property.

How much of a joint bank account can a spouse withdraw? Does a large withdrawal require both signatures?

The general rule is that each person named on the joint bank account can withdraw funds without the other person's consent. Nothing prevents one spouse from making a total withdrawal, leaving a zero balance. Some states make exceptions to this rule. In New York, for example, each person has the right to only half the money in a joint account.

Catherine's stepfather refuses to pay any of her bills. Does he have the right to do this?

At one time Catherine's stepfather would have had every right to refuse to support her, even while she is still a minor. The law recognized only the obligation of the natural mother and father to support their children,

The Changing Role of Stepparents

In the past the law did not require stepparents to support their stepchildren; child support was viewed solely as the responsibility of the natural parents. Nowadays many states expect stepparents to help pay the cost of raising their stepchildren.

In at least 10 states—Delaware, Illinois, New Hampshire, New Jersey, Oregon, South Carolina, South Dakota, Utah, Vermont, and Washington—statutes make stepparents responsible for supporting their stepchildren merely as a result of their status as stepparents. A few other states limit a stepparent's financial role to specific situations. For example, statutes in Alaska and New York impose a financial duty only if the stepchild would otherwise be on welfare. Even in states without such support laws, stepparents are being required by the courts to help support their new family, especially if they promised to support or contributed money in the past or if they are the child's only means of support.

Many stepparents have legally adopted the children of their spouse, which gives them the same rights and obligations as natural parents. This means they have an equal say in the children's upbringing and can give consent in a medical emergency. And the children can inherit from them if there isn't a valid will.

regardless of their marital status. The decision to have a child was viewed as a contract, with the natural parents agreeing to provide for the child as a term of the contract. Since the stepparent was not a part of that contract, the law imposed no obligation on the stepparent for support.

Today some states have passed laws that require stepparents to help support their children. In other states stepparent support may be limited to situations where the minor child is receiving public assistance, or where the natural parents are unable to support the child.

Even without specific statutes, courts are more frequently imposing a duty to support stepchildren in certain situations. If Catherine's stepfather had promised to support her, and Catherine's mother relied on this promise and quit her job, the court would require him to pay for Catherine's necessities. If he is Catherine's only means of support, and his past actions and statements made her rely on him as her provider, he must continue in that role until she becomes an adult.

With six children in the family, Anita is having a difficult time making ends meet. Her oldest daughter has taken a job after school. Is Anita entitled to the money her daughter makes?

Yes. The law gives Anita a right to claim any money earned by her minor children in exchange for her duty to support them.

Claire and David are engaged. Claire has a daughter from a previous marriage and wants to make certain the child is protected financially. What is Claire's best course of action?

David and Claire should work out a prenuptial agreement that will provide the financial protection Claire wants for her daughter. Provisions can be included requiring David to support Claire's daughter financially or to give up his share of Claire's estate if she dies first.

Laurie and Andrew have put away a modest amount of money for their retirement. Recently their son was involved in a serious car accident that will keep him hospitalized for a long time. Are they obligated to pay their son's medical expenses?

They could be required to pay for continuing medical services if their son was injured before he reached the legal age of adulthood—18 in most states, still 21 in some. Some states require parents—and even other relatives—to assist indigent family members, but the support is limited to an amount that will not burden the family. The government encourages family members to help each other stay out of poverty, but only to the extent that they don't become impoverished themselves.

Family Responsibilities

Against his parents' wishes, Victor moved in with some friends after graduating from high school. Are his parents still obligated to support him?

No. A parent's duty to provide necessities ends when a child becomes emancipated by reaching adult age, getting married, entering military service, or leaving home and becoming self-supporting. In this case, Victor would be considered emancipated and responsible for his own debts. However, if Victor's parents' conduct forced him to leave home before he reached adulthood—18 in most states but still 21 in some—they could be required to support him until he becomes an adult or is able to support himself, whichever is earlier.

Can a child sue his parents for not providing a good education?

No. A child's right to sue his parents has traditionally not been recognized. The courts want to preserve family unity and the right of parents to provide for their children in the ways they deem best. On the other hand, education is considered a necessity, and parents have a duty to provide it for their children. If parents prevented their child from going to school without just cause, a state would enforce local attendance laws. And in some divorce cases, parents have been required by the court to pay their child's college tuition.

Is it true that parents can lose custody of their children if they are too poor to support them?

Although courts are reluctant to take children away from their parents, state agencies will intervene to protect the children if the parents neglect or abuse them, or are unwilling or unable to support them. However, courts require that clear and convincing evidence be presented about the abuse, neglect, or lack of support before parental rights will be terminated and custody given to someone else.

What rights do natural parents have when their child is taken from them and placed in a foster home?

Unlike adoption, a child's placement in a foster home does not mean that the rights of the natural parents have ended. The state is considered to have physical custody of a child in a foster home, but the parents continue to be responsible for the child's support. Parents may or may not be allowed to visit the child, depending on the reasons for the child's

Becoming a Foster Parent

To qualify as a foster parent, you must be at least 18 or 21 years old (depending on state law), pass a medical examination, and be fully self-supporting. You can be single or married, divorced, widowed, or separated—as long as you are of sound character and reputation. You need not own a home, but your dwelling place should have airy, well-lighted bedrooms that will not be used for any purpose but sleeping, and you must meet strict standards for the health and comfort of the children. By law, the children's natural parents are allowed to visit if it is considered to be in the children's best interests.

As a prospective foster parent you must undergo a series of searching interviews with people from a state-approved child-assistance agency. These talks will give the agency some idea of your character, interests, and personal outlook, and thus help them to match you with the right children.

If all goes well, you will be given approval to board up to six children under the age of 18—the number of children varies from state to state. This approval must be renewed yearly. The states hope that in addition to providing day-to-day care you will also bring the youngsters into the life of your community—with after-school programs, religious observances, and other activities that will teach them to get along well with others. Your reimbursement will be a monthly fee for the children's household expenses, plus possible further stipends for medical and dental care and other special needs. The fees are not intended to pay you for your services, but merely to cover each child's bed, board, and other expenses. In short, nobody gets rich from being a foster parent. It is a labor of love.

removal from their home. Foster care is a temporary measure that occurs voluntarily or involuntarily as the result of a court order. Usually, the parent is unable or unwilling to provide adequate care. This could be the result of an extended illness, abuse or neglect of the child, or a decision to put the child up for adoption.

Is it legal for my husband to sign my name without first getting permission from me?

No. The marital relationship does not automatically create a right to sign the other spouse's name on checks, promissory notes, or contracts. But if you know that your spouse frequently signs your name to such things as checks on your bank account and you have done nothing to stop it, you have ratified these acts and will probably be liable for your spouse's forgery. If you benefit financially from a loan obtained by your husband's forging your signature, you may also be responsible for repaying it. If a creditor cannot prove that a spouse participated in obtaining the loan or received any benefits from it, liability will not be imposed.

Does a spouse have a right to sexual relations?

Yes. A right to sexual relations is established when a marriage takes place. A spouse cannot deny sex to the other spouse without good cause—illness, for example. If one spouse continually refuses, the only remedy is divorce or annulment. Forcing a spouse to have sexual relations could result in charges of rape or assault and battery.

Is it true that a wife must move to a new city with her husband?

Traditionally, the husband, as the head of the household, had the right to determine where the family would live. The wife had a duty to follow him; her failure to do so was legal desertion and grounds for a divorce. Today, there is no legal requirement that a couple live together, although a refusal to move may still be used as a ground for divorce.

Adoption and Surrogate Parenting

Alice and Mark want to adopt a child. Will they need a lawyer even if they are working through an adoption agency?

Yes, because the agency will have an attorney seeing to its interests throughout the adoption process. While Alice and Mark and the agency all share a common goal—a happy, successful adoption—it is always possible that some unexpected conflict of interest will arise. In that event, the agency's attorney will act exclusively on behalf of his client. So Mark and Alice should retain an attorney to act on their behalf and advise them about how to protect their interests.

Recently Ruth and Edward adopted a baby privately—that is, they and their lawyer dealt with the expectant mother directly instead of going through an agency. They had their lawyer pay all of the expectant mother's medical expenses plus a $5,000 bonus as well. Was this adoption legal?

No. Although private adoptions are legal in many states, adoptions that involve a bonus or other form of profit for the natural mother are against the law. Private adoptions are arranged directly between the natural and the adoptive parents without going through an adoption agency. In a private adoption the same legalities are followed as in an agency adoption. All necessary consents are obtained, changes are made in the birth certificate, and there is a probationary period before the court issues a final decree. Any money given to the natural mother can only be to pay medical and hospital expenses.

The $5,000 bonus that Ruth and Edward paid makes their adoption illegal. Not only would a court refuse to recognize the adoption, but also the attorney who worked it out could face criminal charges. Many states have laws that restrict the attorney's role in an adoption to advising clients and appearing in court for the adoption proceedings. The purpose of these restrictions is to ensure that only those persons licensed by the state can act as placement agents.

Can an unmarried couple adopt a child?

Yes, although state laws and the policies of adoption agencies generally make it more difficult for an unmarried couple to adopt. Courts and placement agencies have always given distinct preference to married couples. Adoption agencies are usually stricter in this regard than state laws. Nevertheless, opportunities for unmarried couples to adopt have been increasing, for two reasons: one is the growing need to find homes for older, less easily placeable children; the other is society's growing acceptance of unmarried couples who live together.

Can a single person adopt a child?

Yes. Most states allow single persons to adopt children, although some courts still take the view that a child's well-being is best served if he is adopted by a married couple. Nonetheless, if a prospective single parent shows that he can provide the child with a stable home environment, financial security, and a supportive family, the courts are likely to approve the adoption.

Joan and Fred have been reading ads that say many foreign children are waiting to be adopted by American couples. What special problems and procedures do overseas adoptions involve?

Adopting a child from abroad is complicated and frequently expensive because there is a great deal of paperwork to process, not only in the United States but in the child's country, and a trip to that country is often required. However, the entire adoption process may take no longer than similar proceedings in this country. The process is complex because you must meet three sets of adoption requirements: those of your home state, those of the United States, and those of the foreign country. These requirements may include the following: adoption of the child before he is brought to the United States; the presence of at least one adoptive parent at the adoption proceedings; and obtaining both exit and entry visas for the child. The process also requires the adoptive parents to produce numerous supporting documents, such as birth and marriage certificates and statements of their financial worth.

Is it a crime to adopt a baby by buying one on the black market?

Yes. It is illegal to buy or sell a child for profit. Violation of adoption laws can lead to criminal charges and stiff penalties.

Larry and Edith adopted a child from Mexico. Does this automatically make the child an American citizen?

No. As soon as the adoption becomes final, Larry and Edith should file a

Adopting a Child Through an Agency

If you want to adopt a child through an agency, don't be deterred by the long conferences with caseworkers, the blizzard of paperwork, and a seemingly endless wait between application and final adoption. The process helps to protect the adopted child's well-being.

The first step in adopting a child is finding the right agency. Every state has both public and private adoption agencies. Contact your local department of social services for information about public agencies. You can find private agencies by looking in the telephone directory, asking families who have adopted, or checking with church and adoptive-parent groups. Write or call the agencies you find, and ask about the availability of children, age and medical requirements for prospective parents, restrictions about religion or family size, residence requirements, fees, income requirements, and post-placement services or support groups.

Once you have selected an agency, you will be asked to fill out an application. You may also have to produce numerous documents, including your marriage certificate, birth certificate, financial records, photographs, verification of your employment, and divorce decrees, if any.

When your application is approved, a home study period of several weeks or months will begin. During this time caseworkers will visit your petition with the U.S. Immigration and Naturalization Service to have the child become a naturalized American citizen. There is no waiting period.

If my wife and I adopt a child and things don't work out, can we return the child to the adoption agency?

Yes, under certain circumstances. At the time of adoption, the court awards temporary custody of the child for a trial period usually lasting from 6 to 18 months. During this period representatives of the adoption agency conduct home studies to evaluate how the adoption is working out. Meanwhile, the adoptive parents themselves are constantly assessing the situation. If the trial period proves a disappointment, the final adoption papers are not issued. The child is then returned to the agency, which tries to arrange for a new adoption.

When Polly and Don got divorced, Polly won custody of their children. Don then left town and has not been heard from in five years. Can Bill, Polly's present husband, adopt the children without Don's consent?

Yes, but only under special conditions. First, every reasonable effort must

home to get a clear picture of your lifestyle. The questions will be penetrating, and your answers should be frank. Caseworkers also investigate the background and special needs of the child to be adopted to help make a successful match. If you decide to adopt the child the agency offers, you will generally sign a placement agreement stating your willingness to accept financial responsibility for the child and your intent to adopt. The agency continues to be the child's legal guardian until the adoption is final.

To begin formal adoption you must file a petition with the court. A hearing will then be held in the judge's chambers or in a closed court. In some states the court may issue a temporary decree of adoption at this point. In any case, a probationary period of 6 to 18 months (depending on state law) will follow. During that time your caseworker will continue to visit your home to see how you and the child are adjusting to each other and to help smooth the transition. After the probation, a second court hearing will be held and a final decree issued. In some states there is only one hearing, and it is preceded by the probationary period.

When the judge issues a final decree of adoption, an amended birth certificate is generally prepared, showing you as the child's parent. Adoption records are then placed in the court's files, and in many states, they are sealed and can be opened only by a court order.

be made to find Don and let him know about Bill's adoption petition so that he can, if he wishes, appear at the adoption hearing and argue against the termination of his parental rights. Some courts would approve the adoption if Don could not be found to give his consent, or if he were located but did not respond to the notice of the hearing. Other courts would give importance to Don's failure to communicate with his children for five years in determining whether or not his consent was required.

Beth and David, who are in their late forties, want to adopt her deceased brother's two young orphaned children. The couple, married for 20 years, have two children of their own, ages 18 and 16. Are Beth and David too old?

There is a good chance that the adoption will go through. While courts do take age into account, the likelihood here is that Beth and David will live long enough to care for the children until they reach maturity. Beth and David's situation is further strengthened by the fact that they are relatives of the children, have been married for many years, and have successfully raised their own children.

Harold's wife, Eleanor, has children by her previous marriage. Harold wants to adopt them. Is her consent to this enough?

No, there are several additional requirements. Harold's petition must be approved by a court that will consider many factors in addition to Eleanor's wishes. These factors include the children's feelings toward Harold and the couple's ability to provide a sound, stable family environment. Eleanor's consent will, of course, count strongly in favor of Harold's adoption petition. In addition, Eleanor's first husband must consent to the proposed adoption if he is still living.

How do you put a child up for adoption?

Adoptions are arranged in two main ways: through a licensed adoption agency or through private placement. Both methods are closely monitored by the courts. Usually, the mother makes preliminary arrangements with a recognized agency while she is pregnant. When the child is born, the mother signs a consent form saying she is freely and willingly agreeing to end her parental rights by giving the baby to the agency for placement with another family.

In the second, less frequent method—private placement—a doctor or attorney, rather than a licensed adoption agency, acts as an intermediary between the natural and adopting parents. Some states limit or prohibit adoptions arranged through anyone not licensed by the state.

In both methods of adoption, any agreement reached must be approved by the court. Relevant details—such as any payments made to the natural mother and proof of voluntary consent—must be disclosed before a judge will approve the adoption.

Paul and Gail had known each other for only a few months when Gail became pregnant. Gail wants to put the baby up for adoption, but Paul wants to keep it. What are Paul's rights?

Paul faces an uphill fight, but he has a fair chance of winning custody. The key point in his favor is that as one of the natural parents, he has legal rights superior to those of a prospective adoptive parent. The procedure would be for the court to notify Paul of Gail's adoption petition. Paul could then object—showing, for example, that he can provide the baby with a good home and adequate financial support.

The courts usually respond favorably to a well-grounded request by the father to keep the child. However, some courts might declare Paul unfit to keep the baby because he did not marry Gail when he learned that she was pregnant.

Sally had a baby out of wedlock and gave the child up for adoption. Now, two years later, Sally is married to the baby's father. Can the couple get their baby back?

Probably not. The big obstacle is the couple's two-year delay. Once an adoption is finalized, the court is very reluctant to return a child to his natural parents. The courts usually assume that the child has developed a strong emotional bond with the adoptive parents, and that pulling him out of this setting might be traumatic.

The fact that Sally has since married the natural father adds little weight to her request. Unless there is evidence that fraud or threat was used to get Sally's consent to give her baby up for adoption, her request will in all likelihood be denied.

If an unwed mother marries a man who is not the father of her child, is it necessary for him to go through adoption proceedings to have full rights as a father?

Yes. Until there is an adoption, there is no legal relationship between the child and the husband. Adoption is the procedure used to create the same legal status and rights that are automatically given to natural children. For instance, until a stepchild is adopted, he can inherit from his mother's husband only if he is specifically mentioned in the will. In some states adoption is the only way that a stepparent can be held financially responsible for a stepchild.

If my son wants to put my grandson up for adoption, is there any way I can stop him?

No. The fact that you are the child's grandparent gives you no more legal rights in the matter than any stranger would have. So your son can terminate his parental rights if he wishes to. What you can do, however, is petition the court to allow you to adopt your grandson. If you can show that you have played a significant role in your grandson's life, and that there is a strong emotional bond between you, the court will be more likely to treat your petition favorably. Your age will no doubt count against you, but you may be able to get around this objection by showing that you can offer the child a fine home atmosphere.

Another approach would be to ask the court for the right to visit your grandson after his adoption takes place. All the states now have laws guaranteeing grandparents the right to ask the court for visitation rights. You should check your local statutes, however, since many of them do not cover cases involving voluntary termination of parental rights.

Mike and Ellen arranged for a surrogate to have a child for them with Mike as the father. In the last month of her pregnancy, the surrogate announced that she planned to keep the baby. Can Mike and Ellen force her to give the child to them?

Mike and Ellen may have to go to court to try to obtain custody of the child. Most states have not revised their laws to clarify the surrogate mother situation; thus it remains for the courts to interpret each case individually. Mike would have to satisfy the court that he is the child's father. Once that was done, Mike could sue for custody.

Steve and Dorothy have arranged for a surrogate mother to bear Steve's child for them. If the baby is born mentally or physically handicapped, must they accept and raise the child?

There is no clear-cut answer to this question. Essentially, everything depends on the agreement or contract Steve and Dorothy made with the surrogate mother. What does the contract say about genetic and birth defects? Does it require the mother to take medical tests to detect certain physical abnormalities in the unborn child? Does the contract guarantee the surrogate mother's right to continue the pregnancy despite the adopting parents' contrary wishes?

In some states surrogate births are illegal and come under laws that make adoption for profit a crime. If Steve and Dorothy live in a state with these laws, they would not have to take the baby born by the surrogate even if they had signed a contract that stated they must take the child.

Is it legal for a couple to pay a fee to a surrogate mother to bear a child for them?

In most states, a couple may pay a surrogate mother's medical and living expenses. In these states it is illegal for the surrogate mother to make a profit. However, courts in Kentucky and New York have upheld fee payments for surrogate mothers.

Unwed Parents

I had a child out of wedlock when I was 16. I am now 22 and about to marry the child's natural father. What can I do to get my child declared legitimate?

Even if you do nothing, your child will, in most states, be considered legitimate the moment you and the natural father marry. Once you are married, you should write to your state's bureau of vital statistics, applying for a new birth certificate for your child, and listing your husband as the natural father. The certificate should be issued to you routinely, since your husband acknowledges the child as his own.

My husband and I got divorced while I was pregnant. Is my son considered legitimate?

Yes. Your child is presumed to be legitimate, since he was conceived while you were married. In fact, wherever possible, the law presumes that children are legitimate. Some state laws set a time limit for establishing legitimacy in situations involving annulment, separation, or divorce.

If I am pregnant and I marry a man who is not the natural father of the child, whose name goes on the birth certificate as the child's father?

If both you and your husband agree to it, your husband's name will appear on the birth certificate, and the law will presume that he is the child's father. Each state has laws providing that when the natural mother marries a man who is not the baby's natural father, this man can have his name put on the child's birth certificate.

I was born out of wedlock, but my father later acknowledged me. Can I have my birth certificate changed?

Yes. For a small fee, your state's bureau of vital statistics will change the name of a parent or a child on the certificate. Write to your state's bureau of vital statistics and tell them what corrections you want. The bureau will send you the appropriate forms and instructions for completing them.

A woman I know has filed a paternity suit against me. Can she force me to submit to a blood test?

Probably. Most states have laws that call for blood tests in paternity cases. The courts feel that any concern about this intrusion on your right to privacy is outweighed by the state's concern for the child's welfare, and by its wish to reduce the number of children receiving public assistance.

The court can order that you be given either of two blood tests. One is the ABO test, named after the major blood types, which may prove conclusively that you are not the parent but cannot establish that you are the parent. The other is the HLA (human leukocyte antigen) test, which cannot flatly prove parentage but can indicate the percentage of likelihood that a child is the offspring of the mother and the alleged father.

Jim's wife, Penny, is pregnant, and he is convinced that the child is not his. What can Jim do about the situation?

If Jim does nothing and the child is born, the law will presume that Jim is the natural father. He can, however, go to court to prove he is not the father. Such proof might include evidence that he and Penny could not have had sexual relations during the time when she became pregnant. Or Jim might produce blood tests that indicate he could not be the father. If Jim could not prove his case, he would have to provide support until the child reached the age of adulthood.

If a woman has a child by artificial insemination, will the child be considered legitimate?

A child's legitimacy depends solely on whether the mother is married or single. The fact of artificial insemination has no bearing on the matter. Many state laws make a married woman's husband the legal father even if he did not contribute genetically to the child. These states believe that legitimizing children is one way of ensuring that they get adequate care and support. However, these laws apply only to children born to couples. If an unmarried mother wants her child to be considered legitimate, she must persuade the father to initiate legitimacy proceedings, or otherwise to acknowledge his child. This holds true regardless of the method used to conceive the child.

Is it a crime for a father not to support his illegitimate child?

Yes. The law says that if a man has admitted being the father, or if a paternity suit has established that he is, he must support his child —whether or not the child is illegitimate. Many states impose criminal penalties for failure to support a child, especially if this failure makes the child eligible for public assistance.

Linda had a child by her boyfriend, Philip. They are not married, and Philip denies that the child is his. Can Linda force him to contribute to the cost of raising the child?

Yes. Linda's first step would be to go to court and bring a paternity suit against Philip to prove that he is the natural father. If Linda is successful in proving paternity, she can then petition the court for an order compelling Philip to pay child support.

John left me after we had lived together out of wedlock for a year. Six months later I had his baby. Now I want to bring a paternity action against him because I need financial help. What information must be presented to the court?

You will have to prove, first, that John is the father—unless, of course, he freely acknowledges that he is. Usually, you will have to file a formal complaint giving the date or dates on which you and John had sexual intercourse, the date you believe you became pregnant, and your child's date of birth. The complaint will also contain information on John's current employment and financial status, and on your expenses as a result of the pregnancy.

John will be notified of your complaint and given a chance to contest your paternity charge in court. Here the burden will be on him to establish that he could not be the child's father. He can do this by presenting the results of blood tests and other evidence showing that the child has not inherited his blood type.

Unwed Parents

My teenage daughter has had a child out of wedlock. Are we, the grandparents, responsible for the child's support?

Not in most cases. In most states your only legal responsibility is to your daughter, whom you must support till she reaches adulthood (18 years of age in most states, 21 in others), or until she becomes emancipated by getting married or by moving out of your home and living on her own. However, at least one state—Wisconsin—includes support of a grandchild as part of the obligation of parents to support their children who have not yet reached adulthood.

Jenny had a daughter out of wedlock seven years ago. Is it too late for Jenny to sue the father for aid in supporting the child?

Jenny's chances of winning a child-support case depend on which state she and her daughter live in. In some states the court will rule that Jenny has waited too long to sue the child's alleged father. But even so, Jenny's daughter may still be able to sue him for nonsupport—if the time limit for starting such a suit has not expired. Some states have strict time limits within which a child may start such a lawsuit.

On the other hand, many courts recognize the importance of having two adults supporting a child. This duty to support is seen by these courts as a continuing obligation, and they impose no time limit for filing a support complaint. Other courts recognize the time limits stated in the statutes but use the dates only to limit retroactive child support. In these states the father would probably not have to make support payments for both the future and all of the past seven years.

My son, who is 21, got his 18-year-old girlfriend pregnant. He does not want to marry her but is willing to help with the child's upbringing. Can we draw up a contract establishing how much support he has to pay?

Yes, but in most states the contract will need the approval of a court if it is to be binding. Laws in some states—among them Illinois, Wisconsin, and New York—specify what can be included in such an agreement.

Susan, who is now married to Brad, had a son by Joseph when she was still single. Joseph insists on visiting his son, often without notice. Can Susan keep Joseph from seeing his son?

Susan has only a moderate chance of legally denying Joseph the right to visit. If the case comes to court, and Joseph proves that he is the natural father, the court will determine how much child support Joseph must pay. Unless there is evidence that visits from Joseph will not be in the child's best interest, the court will then set up a reasonable visiting schedule.

However, Susan can prevent such an arrangement by showing that Joseph's visits would have a bad effect on the child. If she can also show that Joseph has not made any effort to support his son, the court may issue an order forbidding Joseph to visit Susan and her family.

Does an illegitimate child have the right to inherit money from his natural father's estate?

Yes, in some cases. Traditionally, an illegitimate child had no right to inherit from his natural father unless he was named in the father's will. But today illegitimate children are beginning to gain some inheritance rights. Many states allow an illegitimate child to inherit from his mother and also from his natural father if the child can prove paternity, or if the father has acknowledged paternity or was ever declared to be the father in a court of law.

Children's Rights

Do children have the same legal rights as adults?

No. Children are denied the right to vote and, with some exceptions, to enter into valid contracts. State laws define when they can marry, drive a car, purchase alcoholic beverages, write a will, select a guardian, or consent to adoption. Parents and other responsible persons have also been given the right to decide where children shall live, when they can quit school, and how their earnings should be spent. Some of these rights are granted fully when the child reaches maturity, 18 years of age in most states, 21 years in others. Other rights take effect when young people become emancipated by leaving home and living on their own.

However, children do have some rights similar to those enjoyed by adults—among them due process for juvenile court proceedings; a right to privacy in matters involving birth control and abortion; and a right to the full protection of the law in matters of school discipline.

We are encouraging our children to earn their own spending money. At what age can we let them work outside the home?

Federal and state child labor laws strictly limit the age at which children can begin working and the types of jobs they can have. No child under the age of 16 is permitted to work—unless he gets a special work permit from the state or is helping with certain family enterprises and jobs normally performed around the house, such as lawn mowing, babysitting, and snow shoveling. Such jobs are not allowed, however, if they are done during the hours when school is in session.

Children between 16 and 18 may work at gasoline stations, restaurants, retail stores, and jobs that are part of a career employment program administered by a school. They are prohibited from jobs that are considered hazardous or detrimental to their health, such as working in a fireworks factory or a chemical plant.

Karen and Chuck have a 10-year-old son who works after school and on weekends in the small health food store the couple own and run. Isn't this against the law?

No, in this instance the youngster's activity is legal. Although there are federal laws prohibiting child labor, an exception is made when the minor is the employer's child. The law allows a minor to be employed by his parents even when he is under 16 years of age.

However, even when employed by a parent, the child cannot engage in mining or manufacturing, or work in any field that the U.S. secretary of labor has found to be detrimental to a child's well-being. Since Karen and Chuck run a small store that seems to pose no danger to their son's health, no laws are being broken.

My son is 14 years old and wants to get a job. State law prohibits him from working until he is 16. Can we get special permission for him to work?

Yes. Your son can get a work permit that will allow him to hold certain types of jobs before he reaches 16. Such permits, however, impose definite restrictions. Your son may not work more than 40 hours a week. The permit will be denied if the job involves safety hazards (for example, working around machinery or chemicals) or environmental hazards (excessive heat, poor ventilation, or high dust concentrations).

For information about work permits and their restrictions, get in touch with your state's department of labor. Be prepared to give a description of the job, the proposed hours of work, and the name and phone number of the prospective employer.

When our son Alex, who is 15, applied for a job, the manager told him he would be expected to work four hours on each

weeknight and eight hours on weekends. Isn't there a limit on the number of hours schoolchildren are allowed to work?

Yes. The number of hours schoolchildren can work is limited by the Fair Labor Standards Act. Under this law, 14- and 15-year-olds can work after school in a limited number of occupations. During the school year, someone Alex's age can work only between 7 A.M. and 7 P.M., not including the hours in which he attends school; he can work 3 hours a day for a total of no more than 18 hours a week. So the schedule of hours proposed to Alex went far over the limit. However, from June 1 through Labor Day—roughly, summer vacation time—Alex can work from 7 A.M. to 9 P.M., for up to 8 hours a day, or 40 hours a week.

In addition to these federally prescribed hours, your state has its own laws regulating child employment—laws that often limit a youngster's hours and types of work even more sharply than the federal laws. You should check with your state department of labor or local employment office about restrictions imposed by state law.

What happens to money that a child inherits?

Money inherited by a child is usually placed in trust for the benefit of that child until he reaches adulthood or some later, specified age. This procedure is followed because a child is not considered capable of managing large sums of money. Unless the court appoints someone else, a parent acts as guardian of the inheritance and is legally responsible for handling it properly.

Edna inherited $5,000 from her grandmother, and the court appointed Edna's father to handle the money until Edna reached 21. Edna is now 21 and finds that her father has spent the money for his own purposes. Can Edna sue her father for these funds?

Yes. As the court-appointed trustee, her father had a legal duty to (1) act in Edna's best interest, (2) use care and skill in managing her money, and (3) not use her funds for his personal enrichment. By spending Edna's money for his own purposes, her father violated his duties as trustee. He is personally liable and accountable to Edna. She may go to court and sue him for the missing money.

My 15-year-old daughter does a lot of babysitting. Can she be sued if a child is injured while in her care?

Yes. A babysitter—even a child—has a duty to take reasonable precautions to ensure the safety of others. Your daughter's youth will not relieve her of liability if a child in her care is injured because of her negligence. She is responsible for her actions and can be sued if she contributes in any way to a child's injury.

Can a babysitter give consent to emergency surgery or medical treatment for an injured child if the parents cannot be reached?

No. A babysitter has no authority to give consent to any sort of medical treatment. Unless an emergency exists, medical personnel will delay treatment and try to reach the parents, who ordinarily are the only ones who can give such consent. When a parent cannot be reached in an emergency, it is up to the doctor or hospital staff to decide whether a minor shall be given treatment.

My three-year-old son, Bobby, was injured while playing outside at a day-care center. I've noticed before that the center has poorly maintained playground equipment. Who should be notified about this problem?

You should first try to find out what state agency is responsible for licensing and regulating day-care centers. Then contact this agency and report your concern about the safety of the playground equipment. The name of this agency varies from state to state, but there is almost always a department of social services that will be able to help you or direct you to the right place.

There may be additional state or local agencies charged with enforcing health, sanitation, fire, and building codes. The state licensing agency for day-care centers can also tell you what local agencies to call if you learn of problems in these other areas.

Andrew's parents were killed in a two-car crash in which the driver of the other car was intoxicated. Can Andrew sue the other driver, and if so, what sort of damages might be awarded?

Yes. Andrew can sue under his state's wrongful-death statute. Considerations that will have some bearing on Andrew's possible award are the loss of his parents' wages; the loss to Andrew of their advice, guidance, and companionship; compensation for his parents' own pain and suffering; and the loss of his parents' services at home. Andrew may also be awarded punitive damages. That is, the reckless driver may be required to pay an amount in addition to Andrew's actual losses as a punishment for his wrongdoing.

Choosing a Day-care Center

If you work days and cannot have a person come in and care for your child at home, you'll need to find a day-care center that will give him all the loving care he needs. In checking out possible day-care centers, you should remember that they have legal obligations to the youngsters who attend them. Some of the obligations are spelled out in specific laws. Others derive from more general laws, such as those calling for safe and sanitary facilities in places of public assembly. The following checklist is adapted from a booklet published by the U.S. Department of Health and Human Services:

- ☑ Does the center have a valid license to operate?
- ☑ Is there reliable transportation to and from the center? Are the drivers bonded and properly licensed? Are the vehicles in good condition? Do they have seat belts?
- ☑ Does the center have an efficient safety system for fires and other emergencies? Are fire drills held regularly?
- ☑ Is there enough heat, light, and ventilation?
- ☑ Are there safety caps on the electrical outlets?
- ☑ Are there toddlerproof screens or bars on upper-floor windows, and protective gates on stairs?
- ☑ Are the radiators covered or the heaters protected?
- ☑ Are incandescent lights at least three feet from the ground?
- ☑ Is the equipment safe and in good repair?
- ☑ Is there a well-stocked medicine chest and a "sick bay" area?
- ☑ Are medicines, cleansers, matches, sharp instruments, and other dangerous items stored out of the children's reach?
- ☑ Are there enough clean bathrooms?
- ☑ Are there cribs, cots, and other napping facilities?
- ☑ Are there indoor and outdoor play areas that allow each child a generous amount of personal space?
- ☑ Are employees thoroughly screened before being hired? How much does the director know about their credentials and prior experience in working with children?
- ☑ Do the employees take yearly physical exams?
- ☑ Are the employees warm and friendly? Are there enough employees to give sufficient attention to all the children?
- ☑ Do the employees respect your cultural values and religious beliefs?
- ☑ Is the center equipped to keep food from spoiling?
- ☑ Do the employees encourage healthful habits, such as always washing hands before meals?
- ☑ Are the toys and activities appropriate to the age of your child?
- ☑ Are the children given opportunities to learn about their own culture and the culture of others through art, music, and games?
- ☑ Are the premises secure against intruders?
- ☑ Are parents free to visit unannounced, without appointments?

Rights of Adopted Children

What rights does a child have regarding his own adoption?

Children today have considerable say about what happens in their own adoptions. State adoption laws now require that children above a certain age consent to the adoption. In the few states that have enacted the Uniform Adoption Act, the minimum age of consent is 10. Other states set the minimum age at 12 or 14. Children also have the right to decide whether they want to keep their original surname or change it to the adopting parents' last name.

In some situations the child's consent is not required for adoption. For instance, the child's consent might be waived if a stepparent has petitioned to adopt a child, and the child is unaware that the stepparent is not the natural parent.

Do adopted children have the same legal rights as the natural children in the family?

Yes. Adopting parents must agree at the time of the adoption that the child will have all the legal rights possessed by a natural-born child. This agreement is necessary because adoption terminates all the legal obligations that the natural parents have toward their children. The courts want to ensure that an adopted child will not be left without legal rights when he becomes a member of his new family.

Patrick's adoptive father died without making a will. Can Patrick claim part of the estate?

Yes. An adopted child has the same legal right to inherit from his adoptive parents as a natural child does from his parents. However, the laws of inheriting when there is no will vary from state to state, regardless of whether or not an heir is adopted. So Patrick should find out exactly what his state's inheritance laws say.

Christine was adopted when she was two years old. She is now 35 and has learned that her natural mother has died. Does Christine have a right to share in her mother's estate?

Whether Christine has a right to inherit from her natural mother depends on the laws in the state where her mother lived. Some states allow adopted children to inherit from their natural parents; others deny such inheritance rights. If a law is unclear, courts generally rule in favor of allowing an adopted child to inherit.

Children in Trouble

Juvenile misdemeanors and crimes are covered in "Juvenile Offenders" in Chapter 17, *Victims and Crimes.*

My six-year-old accidentally broke a vase in a department store. Must I pay for it?

You do not have to pay, since it was broken accidentally. In most states the parent-child relationship does not automatically create liability for the child's actions. But if you knew your child frequently had "accidents" of this kind, and you did nothing to prevent them, you could be held liable for the resulting damage.

MARRIAGE AND FAMILY

My son hit a home run through someone's $900 front window. Is it true I don't have to pay?

Yes. Your son is responsible for his own actions. The only times a parent is liable for a child's actions are (1) when the parent knew the child was doing something wrong and didn't try to prevent it, (2) when the child was acting on the parent's behalf, or (3) when the parent contributed to the damage by giving the child something dangerous to play with. The homeowner with the broken window is not without recourse, though. He can file a claim with his insurance company. If the cost to repair the damage is more than his deductible, he would be reimbursed.

Am I liable if my child has an accident while driving my car?

Yes, you may be liable. Some states—including Arkansas, California, Florida, and Utah—have statutes that require parents to sign their child's driver's license application and to assume responsibility for accidents resulting from the child's negligence or willful misconduct.

Even if your state does not have this type of law, you might be liable if (1) you allowed your child to drive, knowing he was reckless, incompetent, or too inexperienced to handle the situation, or (2) he was running an errand for you or otherwise acting on your behalf.

Mike's 14-year-old son borrowed a motorcycle from a senior at his high school. He lost control of the bike, hit the maintenance building at school, and set it on fire. Is Mike responsible for the $15,000 damage to the building?

No, not in this case. Parents are not responsible for the negligent acts of their children except in three situations: if they are aware of their child's tendency to act irresponsibly, if the child is acting on the parent's behalf at the time of the accident, or if the parent contributed to the child's negligence in some way. None of these three cases apply to Mike's son.

My son's driver's license has been revoked, and I have prohibited him from driving our car. If he goes ahead and drives it anyway, what is my liability?

If you have expressly forbidden him to drive your car, you are not liable. It would be to your benefit to establish that you not only refused to allow your son to drive but also tried to make sure he did not get another set of keys. If you live in a state that requires your signature on your son's driver's license application, the expiration or revocation of that license relieves you of any further responsibility.

Harvey lives next door with his 14-year-old son, Maurice. My son received some bad cuts and bruises when Maurice beat him up recently. How can I make Harvey pay for what happened?

Ordinarily you could not make Harvey pay for the injuries Maurice inflicted on your son, because the law does not hold parents liable for their children's actions.

But check the laws in your state. About half the states have enacted parental responsibility laws that make parents liable for the payment of damages resulting from the intentional acts—as opposed to accidents—committed by their minor children—up to a fixed dollar amount. This varies from $250 in Vermont to $15,000 in Texas.

Connie and David allow their 17-year-old son to drink beer at home. Are they breaking the law? What if they also let his friends drink beer in their home?

Every state has laws prohibiting the sale, gift, or furnishing of alcohol to minors. In the past, these laws were not applied when children received alcohol in their own home with the consent of their parents, because of the special relationship that exists between parents and their children.

With the growing concern about alcohol abuse in our society, however, some states have moved to curb the practice of children drinking with their parents' approval. In Colorado, for example, it is a crime for a parent to serve or furnish alcohol to his or her minor child. Other states have prosecuted parents who supplied alcoholic beverages to their children under child abuse statutes.

As to the son's friends, Connie and David could face prosecution if they served them alcohol before they reached the legal drinking age.

If the Police Ask Questions About Your Child

Suppose an officer of the law arrives at your front door and tells you that the police are investigating a recent crime—an outbreak of, say, vandalism in the neighborhood—and he wants to question you about your child. How should you respond? Here are some guidelines:

- Ask for details of the crime and find out precisely how your child is supposed to be involved.
- Provide only general information about your child, such as name, age, and a physical description.
- Don't volunteer information that could be damaging to your child—anything you say might be used against your child in court.
- If you want to talk to your child before answering any questions, request a later meeting with the police.
- Remember that both you and your child have the right to refuse to answer questions even if you have nothing to hide.
- If the police take your child into custody, you have the right to know where he will be taken and held. The police may not place your child in a jail cell with adults; he must be held in an area for juveniles only.
- He must be brought before a judge as soon as possible. The judge will decide if it is necessary for him to remain in detention.

My son used false identification to buy some liquor the other night. Can he be arrested for this?

Yes. Not only could your son face criminal charges, but the person who let him use the false identification could be charged as well. Your son's use of false identification is a misdemeanor punishable by a jail sentence, a fine, or both. If the identification that he presented when he bought the liquor was a false or altered driver's license, he could also have his driving privileges suspended.

Ralph and Betty's 15-year-old son is completely out of control. He doesn't go to school, stays out all night, drinks, and steals money from his parents. What will the authorities do if Ralph and Betty can't stop this behavior?

Most states have laws that allow authorities—or the parents themselves—to initiate court action against minors who are out of control. In Illinois, for example, anyone under the age of 18 who is uncontrollable or dangerous can be put in the custody of juvenile authorities through court proceedings. If it is in the best interest of Ralph and Betty's son, and of the public in general, the court can place him under detention until it is no longer necessary to restrain him, or until he reaches the age of adulthood.

MARRIAGE AND FAMILY

Children in Trouble

My 19-year-old son is a troublemaker. Am I within my rights in making him leave the house and support himself?

Yes. The law does not impose a legal obligation on parents to support children who have reached the age of adulthood unless a child is physically or mentally disabled. Many states have reduced the age of adulthood from 21 to 18 years.

If you live in a state where it is 18, you no longer have a duty to support your child. You are within your rights in getting your 19-year-old son to leave home and support himself. If the age of adulthood is 21, your son has a right to your support until he reaches that age.

To what degree are parents held responsible if their children are caught using or selling illegal drugs?

Parents are not responsible if their children are caught using or selling illegal drugs. The special relationship of parent to child does not make a parent liable for a child's criminal act. Some states hold parents liable when their children intentionally cause property damage, but these laws do not apply to criminal cases.

What to Do If Your Child Is Missing

You are far from helpless if your child is missing: a nationwide computer network of police departments, several social service agencies, and even the FBI stand ready to assist you in locating your youngster. The steps you should take are as follows:

1. Make a quick check of your home and neighborhood, looking into such places as abandoned refrigerators and little-used crawl spaces.
2. Ask your neighbors and the child's closest friends if they have seen him; many children are found surprisingly close to home.
3. Assemble background information the police may ask for: photographs, names of the child's teachers, favorite hangouts, and a full physical description, including height, weight, color of hair and eyes, birth date, and other identifying characteristics.
4. Notify the police. Ask them to forward data about your child to the FBI's National Crime Information Center computer. This information will then be available to law enforcement officials throughout the nation. If your child shows up far from home, he can be readily identified.
5. Mount a campaign of your own. Distribute posters and leaflets with the child's picture and description, date of disappearance, reward offered, if any, and where you can be reached.

Should I call the police if my child has run away?

Yes. Many police departments have computer networks that are linked to state and federal systems designed to help locate missing children. The police can also supply you with names and telephone numbers of local and national social service organizations that can help you.

Going to School

Whose responsibility is it to see that children attend school?

Parents of school-age children, as well as foster parents and guardians, are required to see that their children attend school regularly.

Can parents be held criminally responsible if their child doesn't attend school?

Yes. A parent or guardian who fails to send a child to school commits a misdemeanor, and a court may impose a fine or even a prison sentence in unusually blatant cases.

6. Publish this information in local newspapers, shopper's guides, and any other publications that will accept it. Post it on shopping center bulletin boards and any other places you can think of.

7. Call 1-800-555-1212 for the name and number of one of the national hotlines for missing children.

8. Check with local hospitals, medical centers, and morgues. The police will probably have done this already, but hearing from you directly may encourage these facilities to check more thoroughly.

9. If your child is a teenager, call the nearest armed forces recruiting office to find out if he has tried to sign up.

10. Check with the nearest Social Security office for possible leads on where he might be working.

11. Ask the Passport Office of the U.S. Department of State in Washington, D.C., whether the youngster has applied for a passport. If so, the application may give an address where he can be located.

12. If the child has a credit card, ask the issuing company if it has a record of any current purchases, which might supply clues to the place where the child may be staying.

Don't give up hope—thousands of runaway, kidnapped, and missing children have been located by parents who have doggedly run down leads furnished by sources such as these.

Going to School

Howard's parents are not pleased with his progress in their public elementary school. Is it legal for them to take Howard out of school and teach him at home?

It may be, if Howard's parents can provide him with an education that is equivalent to what he's receiving in school. Usually, this means (1) one of the parents must be competent to teach the subjects Howard studies in school, or (2) they must provide him with a qualified teacher. In addition, the amount of time Howard spends in home study each day must roughly equal the time he would have spent in school. The school district might also require Howard to use approved textbooks and other materials.

I've just discovered that my child has been sneaking out of school. What will happen to him if he continues to be absent?

A child who refuses to attend school as required by law is classified as a truant, and the law provides a variety of disciplinary tools. These range from reducing the child's grades to sending him to a special school or even charging him as a juvenile delinquent.

Pete, our neighbors' 15-year-old son, was picked up for truancy. Does he have to go to court for such a minor incident?

If Pete was truant just this once, the school authorities would expect his parents to deal with the problem themselves. But if he becomes a chronic truant and his parents are unable to remedy the situation, Pete will have to go to court.

Greg's son, Matthew, was expelled from school for arguing with a teacher. Isn't the school required to readmit him?

If Matthew's only offense was arguing with a teacher, he will probably be allowed to return to school soon. Students who disobey reasonable rules may be punished, but the punishment must also be reasonable. Only those students who are so disruptive that they prevent the school from performing its function may be expelled permanently.

Can a girl be suspended from school because she is pregnant?

No. A student cannot be excluded from a public school simply because she is pregnant. A pregnant student's presence in school is not considered disruptive enough to warrant suspension. School boards may require pregnant students to be separated from other students, however, as long as their education is equal to that given in regular classes.

John does not want his daughter to participate in the sex education classes in her junior high school. Does he have a right to keep her from going to the classes?

At one time courts gave their consent when parents insisted that their children be excused from sex education classes. Recently courts have been stricter about this issue and have been requiring students to attend a class even when they or their parents object to its contents. But many school authorities recognize that the issue of sex education is a sensitive one, and have established guidelines for excusing students who object. John should contact his local school board to learn its policy regarding sex education classes.

When our family transferred to a new city, we were surprised to learn that our children started their school day with a moment of silence for prayer. Isn't this against the law?

Yes. The courts have consistently held that time set aside for prayer in the public schools violates the First Amendment of the U.S. Constitution. No law or regulation can require a student to participate in a religious activity such as prayer, even silent prayer.

Can we take our children out of public school during the week to attend religious instruction classes at a church school? Could we have someone from the church come to the public school to conduct religious classes?

You can take your children out of school to attend religious instruction classes, but a church teacher cannot come to a public school to conduct religious instruction. The U.S. Constitution requires strict separation of church and state. Your children's religious instruction cannot be held in public classrooms. No expenses can be incurred or administrative time allotted by a public school for religious instruction.

Our school requires children to be vaccinated against certain diseases. Must we comply?

In most instances students must be vaccinated to prevent the spread of communicable diseases. Some states permit exceptions for members of certain religious groups that oppose vaccinations. If you are not a member of one of these religions, you may be subject to criminal penalties for failing to have your child vaccinated.

The high school principal has decided that boys who wear earrings may not attend school. Is this enforceable?

Schools are entitled to make reasonable regulations concerning the dress and appearance of students. In the past 20 years, a number of courts have wrestled with what constitutes reasonable regulations. It is impossible to state a hard-and-fast rule, since much depends on the facts of each case as well as current social attitudes and the standards of the community.

Correcting Your Child's Public School Records

Inaccurate public school records may prejudice teachers and school officials against your child as he moves up through the grades and may reduce his chances of getting into the college of his choice. Under the Family Educational Rights and Privacy Act (FERPA) you can lawfully inspect your child's public school records and request the correction of inaccurate entries. Once the child is 18 years old or attends a post-secondary school, he too has the right to see these records. Corrections should be limited to matters other than grades: a grade will not be changed unless it was incorrectly recorded.

If you suspect that your child's school record is inaccurate, write the principal and ask to see the file. If you get no reply after 45 days, or if the school refuses to let you see the file, write to the Family Educational Rights and Privacy Act Office, Department of Education, Washington, D.C. The FERPA office will see to it that the school complies.

After examining the file, discuss your concerns with the principal and present a written request detailing the changes you want and your reasons for making them. If the school refuses to make the changes, contact the principal or the superintendent of the school district and request a hearing. If they refuse to give you a hearing, write to FERPA, and they will make sure that the school grants you one.

At the hearing you will be given an opportunity to present evidence of why the statements in your child's record should be changed. You may have a lawyer represent you, if you wish. Afterward, the hearing officer will inform the school officials of his decision, and they will decide whether or not to change the records—they have the right to disregard the hearing officer's decision. If you are not satisfied, you may exercise your right to insert your side of the case in your child's record.

Some students have attacked this type of rule by arguing that their dress constitutes "symbolic speech." They claim that the First Amendment prohibits regulations that infringe on their right to express themselves by the way they dress as well as by what they say. But this argument has met with mixed success.

Kevin plays on the high school football team. He broke a leg during a scrimmage. Isn't the school liable for his medical bills?

Not unless the school or its employees were responsible in some way for Kevin's injury. For example, if Kevin's accident occurred because the football field was improperly maintained, or if the school didn't provide adequate protective equipment, the school would probably be held liable. The school cannot be responsible for Kevin's absolute safety. Most courts would say that since football is known to be dangerous, Kevin had assumed the risk of injury when he played.

Eddy's fourth-grade teacher slapped his face for talking in class. Can his parents have the teacher reprimanded for her actions?

It depends on state law and school district policy. Some states have an outright ban on corporal punishment; others permit only the principal to administer it; some require the parents to be notified first. No state permits excessive or unreasonable punishment.

Eddy's parents should call this incident to the attention of the principal and the school board. If the slapping was unreasonable or unauthorized, the teacher may be subject to reprimand or dismissal.

Margo is a third-grade public school teacher. She has noticed that one of her students has come to school several times with bruises on his arms and neck. Should she report this to someone?

Yes. Child abuse laws require certain individuals to report suspected cases of abuse. Professionals such as doctors, nurses, teachers, and other school personnel are generally included among those who must report. In some states Margo would report her observations directly to the appropriate agency; in others she would tell her principal of her suspicions, and he would turn in the report.

Does a college assume my parental rights and responsibilities when my child lives on campus?

Although it was once agreed that colleges stood *in loco parentis* ("in the place of a parent") in matters of discipline, very few colleges today attempt to regulate their students' behavior the way they used to. Except at some private and religious schools, students are generally held responsible for their actions.

Guardians for Children

Under what circumstances does a child need a guardian?

A child needs a guardian if his parents are dead, or unfit or unable to protect, discipline, feed, or take care of him. The fact that parents have financial difficulties is not enough to create a need for the appointment of a guardian. If there is severe financial need, state or local agencies will help the family obtain food stamps or other forms of assistance before considering the appointment of a guardian.

What factors are considered when a judge is deciding whom to appoint as guardian?

The judge will consider age, health, financial condition, moral character, and emotional stability in choosing a guardian. The judge will also try to appoint a guardian who holds the same religious beliefs as the child. The child's own preferences will be taken into account if he is mature enough to understand what is going on.

Can a child ever choose who will be his guardian?

If a child is in his early teens, he may choose his own guardian, subject to the court's approval. If the court rejects the child's nomination, he has a right to make another selection. If the child does not meet the age requirements for selecting his own guardian, the court will consider the child's wishes when making its decision.

What are the duties of a guardian?

A guardian must provide for the support, education, and religious training of his ward, just as a parent would. Guardians are legally obligated to protect the financial assets of their wards. Courts will generally allow a guardian to use income—but not the principal— from a ward's property, or estate, to pay for the child's needs and educational expenses.

As a guardian, do I have to spend any of my own money to provide proper care for my ward?

Yes, in some situations. If there are insufficient assets in the estate to pay for your ward's care, and government benefits and programs do not provide enough to meet these needs, you may have to use your own money to provide support for your ward. If you fail to provide adequate support, the court may award custody to someone else.

The court wants to appoint someone as guardian for Barbara's son. What effect will that have on her rights as a mother?

The decision to appoint a guardian for Barbara's son is a serious matter involving a court ruling that she is unfit or unable to care for him. Thus her son will be expected to live with the guardian, and the guardian will take on full responsibility for the boy's upbringing and education. However, if the court decides it is in the child's best interest, it may grant Barbara the right to visit her son.

If I agree to be a guardian, am I paid for my time?

A guardian may be paid for his services. The amount may be a percentage of the money earned each year by the ward's estate, or the court may establish payments based on the amount of work done by the guardian during that year.

As guardian for my nephew, I invested some of his funds in stock whose value took a huge drop. Will I have to replace the money that was lost through this bad investment?

You might well have to replace the money. As your nephew's guardian you are expected to protect his estate from losses. In addition, many states have statutes specifying the qualifications a stock must have before a guardian can invest in it. If you invest in stock that does not meet these requirements, you could be charged with mismanagement of your nephew's estate.

If my ward gets married, does that end my guardianship?

It depends on the laws in your state. As a general rule, the marriage would end your authority and control over your ward's personal life. But it might not affect your responsibility for your ward's estate. You might still remain responsible for your ward's financial affairs.

What are a woman's legal rights to have an abortion?

The U.S. Supreme Court has ruled that statutes prohibiting abortion unconstitutionally infringe a pregnant woman's rights. During the first three months of a pregnancy, a woman has an unlimited constitutional right to have an abortion. During the second three months, a state may establish certain medical criteria to determine whether or not a woman may have an abortion. A state may take steps to protect an unborn child during the last three months of pregnancy.

The laws regulating abortion after the first three months vary according to how the states have interpreted the Supreme Court rulings. A woman contemplating an abortion after the first three months of pregnancy should seek legal advice about any laws her state may have enacted regarding the later stages of pregnancy.

Does a married woman have to get her husband's permission to have an abortion?

A married woman does not need to obtain her husband's permission for an abortion. The U.S. Supreme Court has stated that, although it is important that the decision to terminate a pregnancy be a joint one by the husband and wife, it is equally clear that if they disagree, the woman must prevail, since it is she who physically bears the child, and it is she who is more directly affected by the pregnancy.

Kermit's girlfriend is pregnant and wants to have an abortion. He doesn't want to marry her, but he does want her to go ahead and have his baby. Can he prevent her from having the abortion?

No. A husband cannot prevent his wife from having an abortion, nor can a man who is not married to the pregnant woman prevent her from ending the pregnancy with an abortion.

Roy's 16-year-old daughter plans to have an abortion. Is there anything Roy can do to stop her?

U.S. Supreme Court guidelines allow state and local governments to require the consent of either the parents or the court if a minor seeks an abortion. Roy's daughter would have to go to court if her father refused to give his consent. If the court determined that she was mature enough to make the decision after consulting with her doctor, or if the abortion was ruled to be in her best interest, Roy would not be able to prevent it.

If a test shows that a fetus is brain-damaged, does the father have the right to force his wife to have an abortion?

No. Since a married woman does not need her husband's permission for an abortion, the opposite is also true—she does not need her husband's permission to have the baby.

My husband physically abuses me. What legal steps can I take to protect myself?

You should call the police and report the abuse. In most states you will have to file a formal complaint before the police will conduct an investigation. If necessary, they will arrest your husband as the first step in criminal proceedings against him. In several states—such as Connecticut, Delaware, Minnesota, Oregon, and Utah—the police can arrest an abusive husband without a signed complaint by the wife.

To protect yourself in the future, you can, in most states, request a court to issue an order restraining your husband from further violence. If he ignores this order, you can bring criminal charges against him.

If it is impossible for you to remain in the home with your husband, you should find a family shelter where you and your children can reside temporarily. An attempt should be made to have your husband receive counseling to help him come to grips with his problems. If you do not believe your husband will stop abusing you, you should consider a legal separation or a divorce.

My husband attacked me, and I injured him while trying to defend myself. Would this be considered self-defense under the law?

Yes, it is self-defense as long as your actions do not continue to the point of retaliation or vengeance. You can take whatever steps are necessary to resist force and avoid harm to yourself. Using a weapon is considered self-defense if you are smaller and weaker than your husband. However, if you pursue and injure him with a weapon after he has retreated, this would not be considered self-defense, and you could be prosecuted.

Anne and Phil have been married for 10 years. Recently Phil has been drinking heavily and physically abusing Anne. Phil says that there is nothing she can do about it, because a wife cannot testify against her husband. Is this true?

No. Husbands and wives may testify against each other in marital disputes. A wife may always testify against her husband when she has accused him of physical abuse.

Family Problems

Mary called the police and reported that she had been raped by her husband, Bill. When the police arrived, Bill just laughed and claimed he was only exercising his "rights as a husband." Can the police arrest Bill?

In the past Bill would have been correct. Legislatures and courts did not define rape to include an act by one spouse against the other. But this is an area in which the law has changed substantially in recent years. Today a number of states—including Florida, Kansas, Nebraska, New Jersey, and Vermont—would allow Bill to be prosecuted for raping Mary. In other states a husband would not likely be prosecuted for raping his wife unless the couple were legally separated, in the process of divorce, or simply not living together.

Sandra left her husband and is afraid that he will hurt her if he finds her. Does she have any way of getting legal protection?

Yes. If Sandra's husband has hurt her in the past, she should ask her local prosecuting attorney's office to petition the court for an order of protection. Once the court issues an order of protection, she should carry it with her at all times. If her husband threatens her, she can call the police, show them the order, and have her husband arrested. In some states Sandra may first have to file for a legal separation or a divorce to be eligible for an order of protection.

I have just discovered that my husband has been sexually abusing our daughter. How can I protect her?

Your first concern is your daughter's physical and mental health. She should be examined by a doctor to assess the extent of injury and abuse. By law, medical personnel are required to report this abuse to the proper authorities in your community.

You could also make the report to your local child protection agency yourself and have them initiate an investigation. A court order could be obtained requiring your husband to move out of your home and not attempt to see your daughter until counseling has been completed.

I believe in spanking my children, but my husband is taking matters too far. Last month my daughter Jill needed six stitches after a "spanking." What can I do?

If you are not able to persuade your husband to seek counseling to help him with his problems, you should file a complaint with the local or state agency dealing with child abuse. After the agency verifies the abuse, they will press charges against your husband and obtain a court order to prevent it from happening again. In extreme situations, the agency may have your husband removed from the home.

Some states—including Colorado, Florida, and Nevada—have child abuse laws that impose penalties on parents who knowingly allow their children to be in situations where abuse can occur. If you do not take steps to protect your child or persuade your husband to seek counseling, you too could face criminal charges.

If we take our child to the doctor for treatment of some serious cuts and bruises, is he required to report this to the authorities if he suspects child abuse?

Yes. A physician is required by law to report to the appropriate agency whenever he has reasonable cause to believe a child has been abused or

Reporting Child Abuse

If you suspect or are aware of a case of child abuse, you should report the matter immediately to your state's child protection agency (many states have toll-free child abuse hotlines). Under the law, your name must be kept confidential; so you need not worry that the abuser will learn your identity. Nurses, doctors, teachers, and other professionals who deal with children are legally required to report child abuse cases that come to their attention. If you are the parent of a child who is being abused at home and you do nothing to stop the abuse, you may be committing a crime. Some states—including Colorado, Florida, and Nevada—impose penalties on a parent who allows a child to remain in a situation where he is abused by another member of the household. If you do not take steps to stop your spouse from abusing your child, for example, you as well as your spouse could face criminal charges.

The first step in a child abuse investigation is a visit to the child's home by a social worker. If the report of the child's situation proves accurate, the social worker will make recommendations—such as moving the child to a safer environment. The state then draws up a plan to improve the family situation. This plan may include counseling, day-care services, financial assistance, or other forms of court-directed help for the parents. The court may also place the child temporarily in a foster home. If the family cannot iron out its problems despite all efforts to help, the parents' right to bring up the child may be terminated, and the child put up for adoption.

neglected. A physician who fails to report suspected abuse may be subject to criminal penalties. If your doctor concludes that the cuts and bruises are only the normal bangs and scrapes of growing up, he will not report anything.

What should I do if I suspect that my neighbor down the street is abusing his child?

Report your suspicions immediately to the child and family service agency that monitors child abuse. After a report is made, the agency will investigate and determine whether the allegation is well-founded. Your name will be kept confidential.

Jack and his wife have been taking care of his 70-year-old mother in their home. I've heard arguments over there, and it sounds as if someone is being hit. I'm afraid Jack's mother is being abused. Would I get in trouble if I called the police? Are they the right people to call?

The police will be able to provide immediate assistance to the family. Many communities also have hotlines for reporting child, spouse, or adult abuse. You do not have to give your name, and you will not get into trouble if you report an instance of abuse.

Changing Your Name

Must a woman change her surname when she gets married?

No. There is no law that requires a woman to take her husband's name. In all states except Iowa and Hawaii, the wife can simply continue to use her maiden name or start using a hyphenated name (Donna Woods-Johnson, for example). Iowa requires a woman to sign the marriage license with the name she intends to use. Hawaii asks the bride to decide at the time of the wedding which name she will use.

If a woman initially takes her husband's surname and then decides to change back to her maiden name or use a hyphenated one, there are two ways to do it. She can request a court hearing to grant permission to do so, or she can have her name changed on her driver's license, voter's registration, bank accounts, credit cards, employment records, and other pieces of identification. But if she lives in Alabama, Hawaii, Louisiana, Maine, or Oklahoma, a court hearing is mandatory.

Jane wants to change her name to Melody Anne. Can she make this change without going to court?

Yes, Jane can lawfully change her name without going to court, except in Alabama, Hawaii, Louisiana, Maine, and Oklahoma. In these five states a person must go to court to obtain a name change.

In states other than these, all she needs to do is start using the new name. If she intends to use the new name consistently, she should notify her employer, bank, post office, credit card companies, and other businesses that she deals with. She should also change her name on her driver's license, voter's registration, passport, and other official papers. The only restriction is that the name change cannot be done for fraudulent purposes such as avoiding creditors and bill collectors or obtaining a passport illegally.

In addition to the states listed above, which have mandatory court proceedings for a name change, many other states will give Jane the option of going through a court procedure to change her name. If she chooses to use the court procedure, she should find out what the requirements are in her state.

Is there a waiting period for a name change? How long does the entire process take?

If you change your name by merely assuming a new name, there is no waiting period. Additional time may be required if you decide to go through a court procedure. Some states require that you reside in the state for a certain period of time before filing the petition. A state may also require that your petition be published in newspapers for a number of consecutive weeks. If all these conditions have to be fulfilled, a legal name change could take several months.

Our 16-year-old son wants to change his name. Does he need our approval before this can be done?

States have different requirements for changing a child's name, but all require parental approval of some kind. In some states both parents must join in the petition to change their child's name. In others only one parent is needed to petition for a name change.

When my husband and I got married, I chose to retain my maiden name for business reasons. What last name should our children have—my husband's or mine?

You and your husband can choose which name your children will use.

Changing your Name

Traditionally, the father had the right to have his children bear his last name. However, as women began working outside the home and became substantial financial contributors to the household, the courts began to give them more rights and privileges. You now have as much right as your husband to select your children's surname. If both of you agree that your name will be used, the courts will not interfere.

Joe and Anne are planning to marry. Each of them has two children from a previous marriage. How can Anne change her children's last name to that of their new stepfather?

The children can have Joe's last name if he legally adopts them or if the children have their names changed by a court. If Anne's ex-husband is still alive, she may have to get his consent. Some states allow one parent to file a petition for a name change provided the other parent is notified and given an opportunity to contest the change.

My son lives with his mother and stepfather and uses his stepfather's last name. Which is considered his legal name—my last name or that of his stepfather?

Your son retains your last name unless a court grants a petition to change it to his stepfather's last name. Courts generally recognize your interest in having your son bear your last name; and unless you have failed to support, visit, or take an interest in your son, the court would probably deny the petition.

Rights of Grandparents

For additional information on visitation rights in divorce cases, see "Visitation" in Chapter 3, *Divorce and Child Custody*.

My son died three years ago. My daughter-in-law is remarrying, and her new husband wants to adopt my two grandchildren. If the adoption is approved, I'm afraid I'll never get to see them. What can I do?

The courts in recent years have increasingly recognized the visitation rights of grandparents, and some states permit visitation when one parent has died, even if the child is later adopted by a stepparent. If your state recognizes grandparent visitation rights in adoption cases, you can petition the court to enforce your rights.

Sheila's daughter and son-in-law were found to be unfit parents by the court, and the judge took custody away from them. Will Sheila be able to see her grandchildren?

Yes, but Sheila may have to go to court. Every state now has laws about grandparent visitation rights, but the laws differ over whether or not the rights are triggered by death, divorce, or the unfitness of the parents. Even if the law does not specifically cover Sheila's situation, she may still be granted visitation rights if it is in the children's best interest.

If the grandchildren are eventually adopted by another couple, Sheila may find that her visitation rights end.

Can grandparents adopt a grandchild if the parents are not able to support the child adequately?

Grandparents may petition the court for adoption, and if it is in the grandchild's best interest, the adoption will be granted. Although some courts express concern over the wide age difference, this does not mean adoption will be denied. If the grandparents are in good health and the child has lived with them, or if there is a close relationship, the court is more likely to rule in the grandparents' favor.

The fact that the parents are financially unable to provide for the child does not automatically justify a termination of their parental rights. The court must establish that they are unfit or have seriously neglected the child before considering an adoption.

Do grandparents have the same authority as parents when the grandchildren are in their care?

No. Grandparents have no more authority over their grandchildren than any other nonparent who takes care of the children. For example, grandparents do not have the authority to consent to emergency medical treatment for their grandchild. However, a parent can give the grandparents a medical power of attorney, which will authorize them to consent to medical treatment in emergencies. This is a simple, inexpensive method of avoiding unnecessary delays at the hospital.

Ben's 19-year-old granddaughter, Amy, borrowed a large sum of money from him and hasn't made any effort to repay it. Are Amy's parents responsible for repaying the debt?

In most states 19-year-old Amy would be considered an adult and would be held responsible for her own debts. Ben would have to go to court to force Amy to repay the loan. If he feels uncomfortable doing this and does not need the money immediately, he could deduct the amount of the loan from any inheritance his granddaughter would receive in his will. Amy's parents would not be liable for the debt, regardless of Amy's age.

Taking Care of the Elderly

My father is 80 years old and still drives his own car. I worry about the possibility of an accident. I don't want to limit his independence, but I do want to ensure his safety. What can I do?

In most states drivers over the age of 65 are required to take eye and driving tests annually to make sure they are still able to drive safely. You might want to make sure your father has been tested recently. Unless your father failed the eye or driving test or has had traffic accidents or tickets, it will not be possible to have his driver's license restricted or revoked. You should also check your father's automobile insurance to make sure he is adequately covered.

Am I responsible for my elderly parents' medical bills?

Generally, no. However, you could be liable for payment if you signed a contract with a hospital, doctor, or other health care provider guaranteeing that the bills would be paid. In addition, some states, including Indiana and South Dakota, have laws requiring close relatives to reimburse the state for the support provided to a welfare recipient. The state will usually seek reimbursement for the welfare support from the closest relatives first—usually the children—but the reimbursement will be limited to an amount that will not burden the relatives.

My mother-in-law lives with us. Do I have to support her?

Children are usually not required to support parents. But sometimes a duty to support exists because of a contract you may have signed with a parent or because of state laws.

For example, if your mother-in-law agreed to give you real estate or personal property in exchange for taking care of her, you would have a legally enforceable duty to support her. Some states require relatives to support a poor person who might otherwise become a state expense. Your obligation in such a situation would be limited to providing necessities—food, housing, clothing, medical care—and by your ability to provide them.

My 63-year-old mother has a heart condition, and the doctor has advised her not to work. My father died without leaving a pension, life insurance, or any means of financial support for her. My husband and I can't afford to support her. What can we do?

Your mother may be eligible for several benefits under both federal and state programs. If your father was entitled to receive Social Security retirement benefits, your mother should receive some of this money. If your mother herself has worked over the years, she may qualify for Social Security disability insurance benefits. If not, she still may be entitled to Supplemental Security Income benefits. She may also be eligible for food stamps and some state-sponsored welfare programs.

In almost every community there are a variety of local programs that provide assistance to older citizens. These programs are coordinated by your local office of aging or department of social services.

I want my younger brother to handle my bills and other financial matters when I am no longer able to do so. Is there any way I can set this up now?

You could use a durable power of attorney. This document outlines the duties your brother will have and specifies that they will become effective when you are no longer able to manage your affairs. A regular power of attorney comes to an end when you become incompetent, but a durable power of attorney remains in effect during the period of incompetence.

Another option under a durable power of attorney is to give your brother responsibility now for the things you want him to handle and have this responsibility continue after you become incompetent.

Three months ago I gave Scott a power of attorney to handle my business affairs. I don't like the way he is running things. How do I cancel this power of attorney?

Scott should be informed in writing that his authority is canceled as of a specific date, and you must carry out any other provisions in the original power of attorney relating to cancellation. Anyone Scott dealt with on your behalf should get a copy of the cancellation notice as well.

Most states require that certain powers of attorney be recorded. For example, if Scott's authority included the right to sell or transfer land, he might have had to record it with the registrar of deeds. If you did record Scott's power of attorney, be sure you also record its termination.

Bob gave Gina power of attorney five years ago. At a court hearing last week, the judge declared Bob incompetent and appointed

Jay as his guardian. Does Gina continue with her duties under the power of attorney now that Jay has become Bob's guardian?

If Bob gave Gina a general power of attorney, it would end when he was declared incompetent. But if Bob established a durable power of attorney, Gina's authority would continue despite Bob's incompetence. However, she would now be accountable to Jay just as she had been to Bob. If Jay decides that Gina's powers should be changed or revoked, he has the authority to do so.

I want to give my cousin Jane a power of attorney to handle my financial matters. How specific do I need to be when writing down all her duties?

You should be very specific when you create the power of attorney. If you make Jane's authority too general, you risk having her conduct business you didn't intend her to handle or having the power of attorney challenged because it is too vague or too broad.

Corrine knows she needs help with her finances, but she does not want to give anyone total authority to take over all her financial matters. She is mainly interested in making sure her monthly checks are deposited and rent payments are made. Is there some way for Corrine to do this?

Since Corrine does not want to give someone broad power over all her finances, she would not want to create a power of attorney, conservatorship, or guardianship. She may be able to set up a direct deposit arrangement with her bank, whereby her Social Security and other checks are mailed to the bank and are deposited directly to her account. She could then establish a direct withdrawal arrangement whereby funds are automatically withdrawn to pay the rent and other bills that she specifies, before they become overdue.

Sarah got a power of attorney so that she could handle her mother's financial affairs. Sarah is the sole heir to her mother's estate. Can Sarah use the power of attorney to transfer her mother's bank account to her name after her mother dies?

No. Sarah's power of attorney expires when her mother dies. A power of attorney may not be used as a substitute for the powers of an executor in the administration of an estate.

My uncle Ralph is in his seventies and suffers from serious health problems, but his mind has always seemed clear. Now we are not so sure. Last week he announced to the family that he was going to adopt his 22-year-old nurse. Will a court let him do this? Can we stop him?

The court will permit Ralph to adopt any person, regardless of age, if he follows the procedure of his state's adoption law.

In order to stop him, you would have to file a petition challenging Uncle Ralph's competence to handle his personal and financial affairs. A judge would then decide if Uncle Ralph needed a guardian to handle his affairs. If a guardian were appointed, Uncle Ralph would not be able to begin adoption proceedings.

My 84-year-old grandfather has been having some problems recently. He refuses to take his medicine, he won't eat properly, and he insists that the mailman has planted a listening device in his mailbox. I'm very worried about him, but I live 700 miles away. What can I do?

Each state has an agency that can investigate and if necessary, petition the court to provide a guardian when one is needed. Your grandfather may only need someone to look after him and provide companionship. If you prefer to avoid legal proceedings, contact the local office on aging in your grandfather's hometown. It will tell you what services are available and advise you about how to help your grandfather.

An employee of the welfare department came to my door wanting to discuss a report that I am not eating properly or keeping my house clean. Do I have the right to refuse to answer his questions and to make him leave?

Yes. Any information you give may be used against you in a court or administrative hearing. Get the name of the agency and of the person who came to see you, and of his supervisor. Then contact the agency to find out what's going on and to obtain copies of any papers relating to the investigation about you.

An old woman lives outside of town in an old wooden shack, with six dogs and eight cats. She goes through garbage cans to find food. I think she should be taken to a home for proper care. Is there anything I can do?

This woman's behavior may seem unusual to you, but every person has the right to determine his lifestyle. She could be completely competent and happy with her way of life. However, if you believe this woman is harming herself or receiving inadequate nutrition, contact a local social service agency that provides services for the elderly. There may be local programs that can provide proper nutrition and health care without intruding on her way of life.

Guardians and Conservators

My aunt wants me to be her guardian. I am not sure I want to do this. What would my obligations be?

Your duties and obligations would depend on whether the court appointed you guardian of your aunt's person or conservator of your aunt's estate. As guardian of your aunt's person, you would be responsible for providing her food, housing, health care, and any other necessities. As your aunt's conservator, you would be responsible for administering and managing her financial affairs. In some circumstances, you would be appointed to carry out the duties of both guardian and conservator.

Evelyn has received notice of a guardianship hearing. If the court appoints a guardian, will Evelyn still be able to sign checks, vote, and make other decisions about her life?

It depends on the type of guardianship ordered by the court. Any powers not given to the guardian will be retained by Evelyn. If there is a court order appointing a conservator, the conservator will be responsible for all the financial decisions, but Evelyn will still be entitled to vote and make other personal decisions.

If the court orders a guardianship over Evelyn's person, the guardian will have the power to make all of Evelyn's personal decisions, including where she will live. Evelyn's ability to vote will depend on her mental capacity and any state laws that apply to voters who are under guardianship or who are mentally incapacitated.

Will Kathleen need an attorney if she is asking the court to have her daughter appointed as her guardian?

Yes. Even if Kathleen has complete trust in her daughter she should nevertheless have an attorney at the hearing who is on her side. The appointment of a guardian means that Kathleen will lose many of her

When Conservators Can Help

If a person has difficulty dealing with bills, bank statements, and other routine financial matters, the appointment of a conservator can help considerably. A conservator is a guardian whose authority is limited to taking care of an individual's financial affairs.

Conservators are often appointed for people who are unable to keep track of their financial obligations, or for those who are ill, or who squander their assets because they are compulsive gamblers, alcoholics, or drug addicts. A person who needs a conservator can ask the court to appoint one, or a close relative can make the request.

Conservatorship is a much less drastic step than appointing a guardian who takes full charge of a person's life. The person being helped has the right to consult with his conservator, who is generally required to take the conservatee's wishes into account when making any decision about his affairs. The conservatee also avoids the stigma of being declared incompetent by a court, which must be done before a guardian can be appointed.

Conservators are usually a person's next of kin, although the court may appoint a more distant relative, a lawyer, or a bank official if this is in the individual's best interests. The conservator may have to post a bond—pay a lump sum of money to the court to be used if he fails to carry out his duties. The court will supervise the conservator and will demand regular accountings to make sure he continues to act in the conservatee's best interests. Conservatorships can be permanent or temporary—for example, if a conservator is appointed for a person who is seriously ill for a long time, the conservatorship can be ended when the person recovers and is once again able to assume full responsibility for his affairs.

rights. In order to protect her interests, she needs a legal representative as an advocate on her behalf. If Kathleen cannot afford an attorney, the court can appoint one.

When Eddie goes to court about an involuntary guardianship, can he have the court appoint an attorney to represent him?

All states allow Eddie to be represented by an attorney at his own expense, but not all states require that one be appointed to represent him in an involuntary guardianship situation. Some states will appoint a guardian *ad litem* ("for the suit") instead of an attorney. The function of the guardian *ad litem* in the court proceedings is to determine what is in Eddie's best interest. An attorney, on the other hand, would follow his client's instructions and would actively present Eddie's side of the case.

Guardians and Conservators

I think my grandmother needs a guardian. If I initiate a court proceeding to have myself appointed as her guardian, will I have to pay all the costs out of my own pocket?

Yes. However, since you are initiating the guardianship action on your grandmother's behalf, you can reimburse yourself from your ward's property upon your appointment.

My sister and mother live in the same town. I live in another state. Won't my sister have to be the guardian, since she lives closer?

Not necessarily. The court has the authority to select the person who will best serve your mother's interest. Unless the state where your mother lives bars nonresidents from serving as guardians, you could be appointed if the court thought you would do a better job than your sister. If you are appointed, you may have to choose someone within the state to accept legal documents.

I just received notice that my children have filed a petition seeking a guardianship over me. I don't think I need anyone to handle my affairs for me. What can I do to stop this?

You have the right to appear at the court hearing and to contest the guardianship petition proceedings. You are not required to have an attorney, but you have the right to be represented by one. In some states, writing a letter is sufficient to inform the court that you wish to contest the guardianship proceedings.

Harold, 80, and Ethel, 81, met and fell in love while living in a nursing home. Can Harold marry Ethel without first obtaining his guardian's consent?

It depends on state laws. Some states require a guardian's consent before a marriage license can be issued; others do not. Some state guardianship laws do not give the guardian the power to prohibit a ward's marriage.

My cousin was appointed by the court to be our grandmother's conservator. I have never trusted my cousin. How can I be sure she is properly handling our grandmother's financial affairs?

The court will require your cousin to file regular accountings of your grandmother's financial affairs. These accountings are a matter of public record and are available for your inspection. The court may also require your cousin to post bond to ensure that she is handling your grandmother's financial affairs properly.

Richard has had a guardian for six years, but now he is sure he is capable of taking care of himself. Can the guardianship be ended?

Yes. Depending on state procedures, Richard can either write a letter to the judge who appointed his guardian or file a formal petition with the court to initiate proceedings to terminate the guardianship.

Nursing Homes

Can an elderly parent be forced to go to a nursing home?

No. No individual can be restrained or placed in a residential facility against his will without a court order. To do so would violate rights guaranteed by the U.S. Constitution. It takes a court order to give one adult custody of another or control over another adult's residence. Unless a court determines that an elderly person is mentally or physically incompetent and that residential care is in his best interest, the person's own consent is essential to place him in a nursing home.

My father was just admitted to a nursing home. He could not sign the admission agreement because of poor health. The facility had me sign as the "responsible party." Does that mean I may have to pay all his bills?

When an adult member of the immediate family signs admission papers to a nursing home, he usually becomes obligated to pay the bills if the relative doesn't have sufficient assets to cover them.

Since you have already assumed some responsibility for your father and he is in poor health, you should consider becoming his legal guardian. This would make you his legal representative, acting with the authority of the court, and you would be allowed to use your father's assets to pay his bills. A legal guardianship would also place you in a stronger position to help protect your father's rights if a problem arises in the nursing home.

My wife and I are getting older, and we are thinking about moving into a continuing care facility. Will it be simple enough for us

to handle, or should we have a lawyer review the papers before we sign anything?

Moving into a continuing care facility could be the last decision about where to live that you and your wife make. Because it is such an important decision, it would be wise to have an attorney help you throughout the entire admission process. The financial operations of a continuing care community are extremely complicated; and unless you have an attorney on your side, you could end up paying a great deal of money and not get what you're hoping for.

Your attorney should review the contract before you sign it to make sure it complies with all the legal requirements of your state and that it clearly outlines your rights if the facility goes bankrupt or fails to deliver on any of its obligations. A number of states have laws that specifically

Choosing a Nursing Home

Information on nursing homes is available from your local or state agency on aging and your state department of health. You may be able to get further leads from your doctor or pastor and by writing to the National Citizens Coalition for Nursing Home Reform, Washington, D.C.

Once you have assembled a list of possibilities, visit the homes that seem most likely to meet your needs. Question the personnel thoroughly and inspect the premises carefully. Here are some specifics:

- ☑ Do the home and its administrator have a state license?
- ☑ Is the home in a safe neighborhood? Is it easy for visitors to get to? Are there parks, libraries, and other senior centers nearby?
- ☑ Are the rooms and halls clean and well-lighted? Are there no more than four beds to a room? Is there a window in each bedroom?
- ☑ Are there curtains and a nurse's call bell for each bed?
- ☑ Are fire doors kept closed, with exits clearly marked? Do the hallways and bathrooms have hand rails and grab bars, wheelchair ramps, and skidproof floors?
- ☑ Is the food appetizing, and nutritious? Are special diets available? Can relatives visit the dining room without an appointment?
- ☑ What is the ratio of staff to residents?
- ☑ Are a doctor and registered nurse on call around the clock? Is there adequate dental care provided?
- ☑ Do the residents seem satisfied? Are they allowed to have their own clothing and personal possessions? Do they have access to religious services? Is there a residents' council? (If so, be sure to talk with a council officer.)
- ☑ Are advance payments refunded if the resident decides to leave?

govern continuing care contracts; among them are Arizona, California, Colorado, Florida, Illinois, Indiana, Michigan, Minnesota, and Texas.

My family has been visiting different nursing homes before selecting one for our mother. One facility wants a contribution to assure her of a place. Is this legal?

No. If a nursing home administrator requests or receives money to guarantee admission to the facility, he may be guilty of bribery. If your mother receives Medicaid, any demand for a donation, gift, or money as a condition of admission is a felony under federal law. Your state may have additional criminal laws covering this type of situation.

I do volunteer work at a local nursing home. Lately it seems dirty, and some of the residents are not taken care of properly. Is it my duty to report this?

As a volunteer, you are probably not included among those who must report suspected abuse. State laws generally specify only licensed professionals as those bound to report abuse, neglect, or exploitation.

If you do want to report your concerns, you should contact the state agency that licenses nursing homes—usually the department of health. The long-term-care or nursing home ombudsman or other official who investigates nursing home complaints would also be interested. The ombudsman can be contacted by calling the state office of aging.

Audrey and Scott have lived in a continuing care retirement community for three years. They are unhappy with the facility. Can they terminate their contract? Can they get a refund?

Their contract should clearly describe what must be done to terminate the agreement and how refunds are calculated. In a typical continuing care contract, residents pay a substantial admission fee plus a monthly charge. The amount of Audrey and Scott's refund will depend on how long they have lived at the facility. Continuing care contracts usually allow the facility to keep 1 to 2 percent of the admission fee for each month of residency. Since Audrey and Scott lived at the facility for three years, they stand to lose anywhere from 36 to 72 percent of the admission fee plus other charges that may be specified in their contract. They would not get refunds of the monthly fees they paid over the past three years.

My 76-year-old mother signed over all her property to a nursing home in exchange for lifetime care. She is very sick, and we don't

think she is being properly taken care of. Can we force the home to return her property so that we can move her to a better facility?

You should review the contract for provisions about returning a patient's property. Some contracts include a probationary period clause, which allows either your mother or the facility to terminate the agreement within a specified time. If your mother's contract has such a clause, and if she has not been at the facility very long, you can use this clause to have her property returned. You will of course have to pay a reasonable sum to cover expenses incurred while she was at the nursing home.

A number of states have enacted laws that regulate lifetime care contracts. If the facility did not comply with this law, you could sue to have the original contract declared invalid.

Rights of Nursing Home Patients

All states have laws and regulations designed to protect nursing home patients and guarantee them a large degree of personal security and control over their lives. Depending on the state, if you are a nursing home patient, you may have these rights:

- To be informed of all available services and their cost.
- To be kept advised of your medical condition, have a voice in your treatment, and have access to your records.
- To have your personal records kept confidential.
- To keep and use personal possessions, as space permits.
- To have privacy during visits by your spouse.
- To be free to communicate privately with others.
- To manage your financial affairs or be given a regular accounting by the nursing home.
- To receive mail unopened.
- To refuse to do any work at the facility, such as vacuuming halls.
- To be free from physical and mental abuse.
- To take part in social and religious activities.
- To receive advance notice of any discharge or transfer to another facility and have some say in it.

If these rights are violated or if you have other complaints about a nursing home, write or call your local or state long-term-care or nursing home ombudsman. The ombudsman is an official who specializes in helping to correct injustices. The ombudsman's office is usually listed in the telephone book under the state government's office of aging. If you write or call the ombudsman, your name will be kept confidential.

When we go to the nursing home to visit our uncle, his roommate always takes over the conversation. We have asked about being allowed to meet in a private room, but with no result. Isn't my uncle entitled to some private time with his family?

Yes. Under the law, every nursing home patient has a right to talk privately with anyone without someone else being present all the time. You or your uncle should ask the administrator or director of nursing to reserve a room for family meetings. Most facilities have a family conference room for this purpose.

When Margaret went to visit her aunt at the nursing home, she found that her aunt had been transferred to another room. This is the fourth transfer in six months, and her aunt is very upset about all these moves. Is there something that can be done to keep Margaret's aunt in the same room?

Doctors and lawyers recognize that frequent room reassignments can disorient nursing home patients and cause psychological stress. Frequent moves also increase the potential for physical injuries from such things as falls in an unfamiliar room. Margaret should alert the administrator to these room changes and request that adequate notice be given so that her aunt can prepare for them.

It is also possible that the facility is violating state or federal laws regarding patients' rights. For example, under the Medicaid Patients' Bill of Rights, a transfer can be made only for medical reasons, or if it is in the best interest of the patient or the other residents. State laws may be even more restrictive about excessive moving of nursing home patients.

Nathan lived in a private nursing home but was sent to a nearby hospital for a medical emergency. He has now recovered enough to return, but the nursing home refuses to allow him back. Isn't it required to readmit him?

Several states, including Connecticut and Michigan, have laws that require nursing home facilities to reserve beds for patients who are temporarily hospitalized for emergency treatment or are receiving therapy under a doctor's orders. There have been cases where Medicaid patients have been transferred to make room for more profitable private patients. This kind of discrimination against nursing home patients is illegal in all states.

When Frances moved into her nursing home last year, she took a favorite chair, a TV set, and other personal items. Some of her

possessions are missing, and she believes they have been stolen. Does she have any recourse against the nursing home?

Yes. Frances can take the nursing home to court for violating regulations that guarantee a resident's right to keep and use personal possessions and to have a secure, private place in which to keep them.

Alvin is a difficult resident and sometimes slaps aides when they try to help him. Yesterday, a nurse's aide lost her temper and hit Alvin back. Can she be held responsible for her action?

Under no circumstances is a nursing home employee allowed to hit a patient. The facts of the matter should be investigated, and the nurse's aide disciplined or fired. If Alvin or his family or guardian wishes to take the matter to court, they have a good case for suing the aide for battery, since she intentionally struck him.

My mother is in a nursing home, but I want to take care of her at our house. How do I get her released?

If your mother is competent to request the release, she should first check with her physician and then write a note informing the facility that she wants to leave. You should reread the admission agreement for any special conditions or requirements concerning release—some facilities for example, want two weeks' notice. If your mother has a guardian, that person would have to make the request, and a court may also have to approve the move.

CHAPTER
3

Divorce and Child Custody

Thinking About Divorce

My husband and I have grown apart, and we have begun talking about a divorce. But neither of us wants to hurt the other with a lot of accusations. Does one of us have to pin the blame on the other, or can we just get a divorce because we both want one?

No accusations are needed if you both agree that the marriage is beyond reconciliation. If one spouse wants to continue the marriage, however, the one who wants the divorce may have to prove the other guilty of some wrongdoing that is grounds for divorce, such as abandonment or cruelty.

Must a couple live apart before being granted a divorce?

Not necessarily. However, more than 20 states, including Arkansas, Hawaii, and North Carolina, permit couples to obtain a no-fault divorce if they have lived apart under a separation agreement for a specified time.

If my wife and I live apart from each other for seven years, will we be considered divorced?

No. Living apart does not make you divorced, no matter how long you do so. Divorce requires a judgment from a court legally terminating the marriage. Without a court decree, there is no divorce.

Carole and Ted remained married for their children's sake. Now the children are grown-up, and Ted and Carole want a divorce. Carole is not self-supporting. What steps should she take?

There are many things that Carole should do to protect her interests. The first is to make an appointment with an attorney. The earlier she does so, the better prepared she will be when she and Ted actually separate.

Before meeting with her attorney, Carole should draw up a list of all the family assets and debts, including any business interests she and Ted may have. If she is not familiar with these matters, she risks not getting a fair property settlement. She should also know the location of deeds, insurance policies, titles to property, and other important documents.

If Carole has been financially dependent on Ted, she will probably need support. To prepare herself for this, she should draw up a budget, estimating all of her monthly living expenses—including those expenses, such as car insurance and Christmas presents, that don't come up every month. It is important that the budget be accurate because the amount of her support will depend upon her needs.

Carole should try to set aside some money before the separation, to be used while the divorce is pending. She should establish credit in her own name and—since there is no guarantee of support or it may not meet her needs—she should also consider getting a job.

What should I discuss with my lawyer the first time I see him about a divorce?

You can get the most out of an initial consultation by being prepared to give your attorney as much information as possible. You should expect to discuss the reasons why you want a divorce. You should also decide on

What to Take to Your Lawyer

The more information you can give your lawyer at your first meeting about a possible divorce, the better he will be able to help you. Since decisions will have to be made about money, property, and custody, the better prepared you are to discuss these matters, the less time, expense, and unnecessary complications there will be. The following checklist will help you compile the facts your lawyer will need:

- ☑ A copy of your marriage certificate.
- ☑ Children's and spouses' names and dates of birth.
- ☑ Copies of any written agreements between you and your spouse that deal with finances, such as a prenuptial agreement.
- ☑ Copies of the deed to your home and to any other real estate you or your spouse may own.
- ☑ A list of valuable personal property, such as cars, jewelry, appliances, cameras, and electronic equipment.
- ☑ A list of bank accounts, stocks, bonds, or other investments that you and your spouse have, and whether they are held singly or jointly.
- ☑ A list of debts, including mortgages, personal loans, credit cards, and charge accounts.
- ☑ A list of monthly expenses and copies of paid bills for one month.
- ☑ Stubs from recent paychecks for each working spouse.
- ☑ Copies of federal and state income tax returns for you and your spouse for the past three years.
- ☑ If you own a business, copies of the tax returns for the business for the past three years.
- ☑ Copies of medical insurance and life insurance policies for both you and your spouse.
- ☑ Copies of pension plans and Social Security earnings statements.
- ☑ If either you or your spouse has been married before, a copy of the divorce papers.
- ☑ The name of your spouse's attorney.

what outcome you are seeking. If you want custody of the children, support, or any specific property, you should let your attorney know. The more information you give your attorney, the better advice you will get—and the more accurate the estimate of legal fees will be.

Martha's marriage is falling apart. Does it make a difference if she moves out first?

Yes. If Martha moves out, her husband may be able to claim in a divorce proceeding that she abandoned him. If Martha and her husband have children and Martha does not take them with her, the court may see this behavior as evidence of her unfitness to have custody of them. Martha's move may also affect how much support she may receive, and requests to have her husband pay her attorney's fees may be denied. These problems can be avoided if both Martha and her husband agree that the marriage is not working and sign a separation agreement.

Do my wife and I have to go through marriage counseling before we can get a divorce?

Some states—such as Nebraska and New Hampshire—require a couple to make all reasonable efforts at reconciliation, including counseling, before a divorce can be granted. In other states the court may order counseling before granting a divorce if one spouse requests it.

Does a husband have to pay his wife's living expenses until a final divorce decree is issued?

The court may order temporary alimony if the wife is not able to support herself while the divorce is pending. However, no spouse has an absolute right to temporary alimony, and it may be denied if the dependent spouse left the household without good reason or committed adultery or some other type of marital misconduct. The amount of temporary alimony will be based on the wife's need, the husband's ability to pay, and the wife's cost of living in a style similar to that she enjoyed during the marriage.

Henry came home one day to find that his wife had left him, taking almost all their possessions with her. What might a lawyer advise him to do?

Henry's lawyer would advise him to quickly take several steps to protect the rest of his property. If he and his wife have a safe deposit box, Henry's lawyer, or a neutral third person such as a bank officer, should inventory the box and put the contents in a new box where they will be safe until a property settlement is reached. If they have a joint bank account, Henry should ask the bank to freeze it to prevent his wife from making any further withdrawals. Since Henry and his wife both have rights to the property she took, it is unlikely that Henry will be able to get any of it back until a separation agreement or a divorce decree specifies how their property is to be divided.

George is fed up with his marriage and wants to empty all the bank accounts and cancel his joint credit cards. What will the consequences be if he does this?

If George takes all the money, he may be asking for legal and financial trouble. He could be charged with nonsupport, or forced to return a substantial amount to his wife later, when a property settlement is reached. The court may also view his actions as evidence of bad faith, and compensate his wife accordingly in the property settlement.

As far as the credit cards are concerned, George can cancel only those for which he has sole legal responsibility. If they are joint accounts with both able to sign for charges, his wife will still be able to use them.

My wife and I never went through any legal proceedings when we decided to separate. How much responsibility do I have for supporting our children while we are separated?

Your legal duty to provide necessities for your minor children continues even when they live apart from you. The extent of your obligation depends upon several factors: your income and health, the number of your dependents, and the needs of your children. It may not be sufficient to provide just the bare necessities—your obligation may also extend to college tuition if this is a reasonable expense in terms of your income.

Sally is thinking about getting a divorce. Can she legally make her husband leave their home until the divorce is final?

If Sally's husband agrees to the divorce, she can try to get him to move out as part of a separation agreement. If Sally can prove there is actual danger of physical or mental harm, she may be able to have the judge grant her exclusive occupancy of their home on a temporary basis. She may also be required to show that she is not guilty of conduct that provoked the danger, and that her husband can afford to live elsewhere.

If Sally believes conditions exist that warrant exclusive occupancy, she should tell her attorney about this during the initial consultation, because she will need help with the legal process. Sally will be required to sign a sworn statement about the dangerous conditions, and she may be required to testify about them in court.

Does it cost a lot to get a divorce?

Divorce costs vary widely. Each state or county sets its own court fees for filing for divorce; these are generally less than $100. Attorneys' fees also vary. They are based on the time and effort involved and the circumstances of the case. Many attorneys charge by the hour, but there are a growing number who set fees for specific services. You should be sure to understand the fee and the billing procedures before you hire an attorney.

Contested divorces generally cost more than uncontested ones. They take more time and frequently require fees for witnesses, mediators, and appraisers. The more difficult the divorce, the greater the cost.

We want a civilized divorce. Would it be a good idea for both of us to use the same lawyer?

No. No matter how civilized a divorce may be, it is never a good idea for both people to use the same lawyer. A lawyer's job is to protect his client's interests, and it is difficult, if not impossible, for one attorney to protect the interests of opposing people in a lawsuit. All too often, friendly divorces encounter unexpected areas of disagreement and become unfriendly. Even if your case is simple and uncontested, two lawyers won't cost much more than having one for both spouses, and each of you will have the benefit of having your own attorney's undivided loyalty.

I am unemployed and want to get a divorce. Is there any way to have my wife pay for my lawyer?

The court will consider awarding attorney's fees to you if you request it. Whether or not you are successful will depend on your need and your wife's income and assets. Payment of fees may be denied, however, if you are guilty of conduct that provides grounds for the divorce.

If my husband files for divorce and I can't afford to hire a lawyer, what should I do?

You should ask your local legal aid society for help. Legal aid societies throughout the country provide legal assistance to those who cannot afford it. Your legal aid society will accept or reject your case on the basis of your financial need; so you will have to provide documents—such as income tax returns and titles to property—that show your income and assets. If you are turned down, ask to be referred to a lawyer who might handle your case for a minimal charge, or who would be willing to accept as payment any fees the court might obtain from your husband.

Does it make a difference who files for the divorce?

Filing itself gives neither spouse any legal advantage or disadvantage in a divorce proceeding. But the person who files may have to pay the filing fees, and it will be necessary for that person to appear in court.

Can I file for divorce without my husband's knowing?

Yes, but when you file, you must give the court your husband's last known address. He will then be served with a summons notifying him that you have filed a divorce action. If your husband cannot be located, the court will advise him of the divorce through a notice published in a newspaper. However, you will not be able to obtain alimony or child support unless your husband is served with a summons.

How soon can I remarry after I am divorced?

You may not remarry until the court issues the final divorce decree ending your current marriage. In addition, some states also have a waiting period following the decree—ranging from one to six months—before you can remarry.

Separation

Marie and Richard are having marital problems and have agreed to separate. Should they get a separation agreement?

Yes. Couples who work out separation agreements have a better chance of avoiding misunderstandings over their rights and obligations and preventing long and costly court battles to settle child custody and property disputes.

Each spouse also benefits from the protection a separation agreement provides. For example, if Richard agrees to give Marie $300 a month for support, a separation agreement could make this a legal obligation, enforceable in court, if necessary, rather than leave it to his good intentions. Richard is likewise protected if Marie decides to demand $400 instead of $300.

When children are involved, a separation agreement is even more important because it can spell out in detail each spouse's continuing rights and obligations.

Do I have to go to court to get a legal separation?

No, not if your spouse agrees to the separation. There are two types of separation: separation by agreement and judicial separation. The two types are similar in content and effect.

A separation by agreement requires only the agreement of both husband and wife to separate. Although it is not legally necessary,

What to Include in a Separation Agreement

Separation agreements start out by giving the names, addresses, birth dates, and other facts about the husband, wife, and children. The agreement then describes each person's rights and obligations during the separation. To cover these points, separation agreements are in writing and usually include:

- ☑ A statement in which the husband and wife agree to live apart.
- ☑ A list dividing personal property.
- ☑ An agreement about who will hold title to any real estate.
- ☑ An agreement about who will pay financial support, the amount to be paid, and if the amount can be changed.
- ☑ An agreement about who will have custody of the children.
- ☑ A schedule of visitation rights for the noncustodial parent.
- ☑ A provision detailing the children's financial support.
- ☑ An agreement on who will pay medical, dental, education, and other special expenses.
- ☑ An explanation of insurance benefits and premium payments, and who is responsible for them.
- ☑ A statement of whether joint or single income tax returns will be filed and who is responsible for the payments and the paperwork if joint returns are necessary.
- ☑ A description of debts owed jointly and individually, including legal fees, and who will pay them.
- ☑ A statement of whether there are limitations on the right of each spouse to inherit from the other.

couples should have a written agreement drawn up by their attorneys that specifies each person's rights, obligations, and property interests during the separation.

If your spouse won't agree to this procedure, you will have to go to court and get a judicial separation. This second type of separation is also called a legal separation or limited divorce. It requires court action and is used when one spouse will not agree to a separation. One spouse files a petition for separation much like applying to the court for a divorce. If the court rules in favor of granting the petition, it will order the separation and issue a decree.

Laura and Dennis plan to draw up a separation agreement on their own. What risks are they taking by not consulting lawyers?

Laura and Dennis are taking a big risk in drawing up their own separation agreement. State laws concerning separation agreements tend to be very technical. If their contract does not meet the requirements of their state laws, they may find it unenforceable. Without good, sound advice Laura and Dennis also run the risk of inadvertently giving up some of the legal rights that each of them has.

Many states require separation agreements to be in writing and to use specific legal terms. Some states even require that the agreements be witnessed and the signatures notarized.

After a separation agreement has been signed, can either spouse date other people?

Yes, but they should be careful to avoid situations that could complicate their divorce proceedings. A serious relationship or sexual relations with a person other than one's spouse may provide grounds for divorce for adultery. Overnight guests and prolonged absences from home could weaken a spouse's ability to get the best property, support, and child custody settlements.

My husband moved out when he decided to divorce me. Although he still wants to go through with the divorce, he is continually asking me to let him move back. What effect would it have on the divorce if I did so?

If you allow your husband to move back in with you and you resume relations as husband and wife, the divorce may be denied. The judge may decide that this proves the marriage has not broken down irretrievably. The law isn't as clear if your husband moves back but you don't resume relations as husband and wife. In about half the states, the divorce could be rejected for this reason alone; in the other half your husband moving back in would be considered one of many factors in granting or denying the divorce petition.

My wife signed a written agreement to move out of our home. When she left, she took a lot of property that we had agreed was mine. Can I have it returned to me?

A separation agreement is a contract that can be enforced like any other contract, and you can sue her for violating the terms of your agreement. If you file for divorce, you can request the return of the items when the property is divided.

Sheila wants to buy a new car. Would her husband, Steve, have any claim to it as marital property if they were legally separated?

No. Sheila and Steve have a legal separation; thus the car belongs to Sheila. In many states, property acquired by a spouse after a couple separates is considered separate property even if there is no legal separation agreement in effect. Since not all states observe this rule, a written separation agreement will give both spouses more protection for property acquired after their separation.

My wife and I are legally separated. Am I responsible for her credit card purchases?

It depends on whose name the account is in. You are not responsible for credit cards in your wife's name only, but you and your wife are responsible for all purchases made on joint accounts in both your names. You can avoid misunderstandings over credit cards by working out a separation agreement that clearly states which financial obligations you are each responsible for.

When my husband died, we were legally separated and living apart. Am I entitled to any of his estate?

Most states will allow you to inherit from your husband's estate. Under the law, you are considered legally married until a final divorce decree is issued. Therefore, you are entitled to inherit as though you had been living together. However, if you had given up your right of inheritance in a separation agreement, you would not be able to inherit.

Mark and Maxine got an annulment from their church. Are they legally free to remarry?

No. There are two types of annulments: a legal annulment and a church annulment. A legal annulment is a court order ruling that the marriage never existed. A church annulment is a declaration by a church authority that the marriage never existed. Church annulments are not legally binding; thus Mark and Maxine would also have to get a legal annulment in order to remarry.

How does an annulment differ from a divorce?

An annulment denies that a marriage ever existed. A divorce acknowledges the existence of a marriage and then terminates it. An annulment also differs from a divorce because there are generally no provisions for support of the dependent person.

What legal reasons can Beth use to prevent Dave from having their marriage annulled?

There are several defenses that Beth may use to contest an annulment.

Grounds for Annulment

An annulment is a judgment by the court that a marriage was not legal to begin with. Grounds for annulment vary from state to state; the most common grounds are:

- *Duress*—A threat of serious consequences, such as revealing a drug addiction, unless the couple marries.
- *Fraud*—An intentional deception affecting the foundation of the marriage in order to lure a person into marrying. Some examples:
  - —Concealing homosexuality
  - —Concealing impotence, venereal disease, serious health problems
  - —Concealing a previous marriage, divorce, or children
  - —False claims of pregnancy
  - —Hiding or lying about a pregnancy by another man
  - —False claims of wanting to have children
- *Mental incapacity*—Inability to understand the marriage contract at the time of the wedding ceremony.
- *Underage*—Failure of either spouse to have reached the age of consent required by the state, usually from 15 to 21 years of age.

One defense is the statute of limitations. If Dave fails to request an annulment within a specified time limit (which varies widely from state to state), the annulment will be denied.

If Dave is seeking an annulment based on fraud—claiming, for example, that Beth did not tell him she had been married before—Beth can prevent the annulment if she can prove that Dave really was aware of these facts before the wedding.

Another defense is ratification. If Dave has been aware of the grounds for an annulment but has done nothing about it and has continued with the marriage, he has lost the opportunity for an annulment even though there might have been grounds for annulment earlier in the marriage.

Apart from Beth's defenses, Dave must prove his grounds in court. If he fails to do so, the annulment will be denied.

My husband and I want to get an annulment. Does this mean our six-month-old son will be illegitimate?

No. If you get an annulment, your marriage would be void but your son would be legitimate. All states have laws that allow children of annulled marriages to be considered legitimate.

Types of Divorce

What is a no-fault divorce?

In a no-fault divorce, neither spouse must prove that the other is guilty of wrongdoing that is grounds for divorce. Some form of no-fault divorce is now available in all states and is granted for incompatibility, irretrievable breakdown, breakdown of the marriage relationship, or irreconcilable differences. These terms have the same meaning—that the marriage has failed and no reconciliation is possible. Some states also recognize living apart according to a separation agreement as grounds for a no-fault divorce. Many states have changed the term *divorce* to *dissolution of marriage* in their statutes.

Can I choose between a fault and a no-fault divorce?

It depends on your individual circumstances. If you have evidence to prove grounds for a fault divorce (such as cruelty or desertion) you can choose between the two types of divorce. But without such grounds, you'll have to seek a no-fault divorce based on incompatibility. A decision about which route to follow involves both legal and financial considerations and should be made only after a thorough discussion of your specific situation with your lawyer.

Are no-fault divorces quicker than traditional divorces?

Yes. Traditional divorces based on fault—even uncontested ones—require proof of the grounds for divorce. This proof usually consists of testimony from both spouses and other witnesses. Uncontested no-fault divorces require only one spouse's testimony that the marriage is over.

Won't Alison get more in a property settlement if she accuses her husband of wrongdoing instead of getting a no-fault divorce?

Not necessarily. There is no general rule about taking a spouse's wrongdoing into account when property settlements are made. Some states require a judge to consider it; others forbid him to.

However, Alison's willingness to proceed with a divorce based on her husband's misconduct may strengthen her negotiating position with him. The prospect of going through and paying for a trial in which embarrassing private information is made public may encourage her husband to give her a better property settlement in exchange for a no-fault divorce. On the other hand, Alison's husband may not be swayed by the possibility of a divorce trial, and Alison will have the sometimes difficult and expensive task of proving his wrongdoing without any guarantee of receiving more property in the settlement.

Jean wants to get a no-fault divorce. Will her husband's infidelity have an effect on the divorce proceedings?

It may. If Jean files for the divorce and her husband contests it, Jean may be required to give proof of his infidelity in order to get the divorce. But if Jean and her husband agree to the divorce, his infidelity should have no effect on the divorce proceedings.

Do Mexican mail-order divorces have any kind of legal standing in the United States?

At one time, mail-order divorces could be obtained through attorneys in Mexico without either spouse's becoming a resident there. If challenged in a U.S. court, such a divorce was not recognized as legally binding. These divorces are no longer available since Mexico added a residency requirement to its divorce laws.

Types of Divorce

My husband says he can fly to another country and get a divorce by remaining there just 24 hours. Is this true?

A divorce obtained in another country will not be recognized in the United States if neither spouse lives or has lived in that country. A quick visit is not enough to establish residency.

I've read about emergency divorces. What are they? How do I go about getting one?

Emergency divorces occur when a waiting or cooling-off period in a pending divorce is waived to resolve an urgent situation—to enable one of the spouses to marry right away, for example, so that a baby will be born legitimate. There are few legal guidelines about what constitutes an emergency; it is up to the judge to decide. Emergency divorces are rare.

Can I have a jury trial for a divorce?

Yes, if your state allows it. But you have no constitutional right to a jury trial in a divorce.

Jury trials are rarely requested because most divorcing couples are more comfortable discussing their marital difficulties before a judge who has tried many divorces than they are in front of a jury. In addition, the time and cost of a jury trial are much greater than in a trial conducted before a judge only.

Are do-it-yourself divorce kits a good idea?

There are a number of risks involved in using do-it-yourself divorce kits. Frequently, the kit you buy is not tailored to your individual circumstances or to the specific requirements of your state. For example, states often require the use of certain words to describe the reason you want a divorce. No matter how carefully you express the idea, your case will be dismissed if you don't use the language required by law. Another example: Some kits do not make it clear that, in some states, if you fail to ask for support at the time of the divorce, you can never ask for it.

Even when divorce kit forms do get you into the courtroom, technical rules of evidence and court procedure must be followed once you are there. Few nonlawyers are able to cope successfully with these technicalities. When there is so much to lose, the ultimate price you pay for a poorly handled divorce could greatly exceed the cost of retaining a lawyer to help you right from the beginning.

There is a group in town that helps people with* pro se *divorces. What does* pro se *mean?

The literal meaning of *pro se* is "for oneself." When a spouse acts as his own attorney in a divorce, he is trying to obtain a divorce *pro se.*

Many legal aid societies conduct *pro se* clinics, providing forms and instructions to help people handle simple, uncontested divorces without a lawyer. But this is risky; going into a divorce case without a lawyer could result in an unsatisfactory settlement of such matters as child custody, visitation, and division of property.

The Divorce Process

I was just served with divorce papers. What do I do now?

You should consult an attorney at once. There is a time limit in which you must officially respond to the papers you were served. If you don't respond within the time limit, you may forfeit your right to claim property that you want to keep or to contest the divorce.

My wife's lawyer has recommended a divorce attorney for me. Would it be OK to hire him?

You should hire the attorney who is best for you, regardless of what your wife's attorney says. If you have trouble finding a good divorce lawyer, call your local bar association for a list of qualified ones.

My wife and I can't seem to agree on anything. Are there services available to help us reach a settlement that will satisfy both of us?

Yes. Many couples find mediators very helpful in reaching a settlement. Mediators are professionals trained to work with couples who have decided to divorce but cannot agree on property distribution or child custody. Since mediators cannot give legal advice or prepare legal documents, you and your wife should hire attorneys before you begin the mediation process. They can refer you to experienced mediators.

Do I have to appear in court to get a divorce?

If you are the spouse who has filed for the divorce, you must appear in court for the hearing or your case will be dismissed. If your spouse has filed for the divorce and you do not wish to contest it, you are not required to appear. But if you don't attend the court hearing, the divorce will usually be granted by default. However, you should still consult with an attorney to make sure all your rights are protected.

Todd's lawyer explained the general procedure of a divorce to him, but he was so upset that he doesn't remember it. What, in general, are the steps you have to go through to get a divorce?

The first step in a divorce is to file a petition asking the court to grant the divorce. Once the petition is filed, Todd's wife will be served with a copy of it. She will then have a specified period of time in which to answer the petition and state what action she intends to take.

Once her answer has been filed, the attorney for each spouse will put all the facts of the case together. Sometimes this can be handled informally; otherwise it must be done through a formal procedure called discovery, in which written questions and answers are exchanged or oral testimony is given by the two spouses and, if necessary, witnesses. When all the necessary information has been assembled, the attorneys will conduct negotiations to work out any unresolved issues. If Todd and his wife—and their attorneys—are able to work out all the issues, a fairly simple court hearing will be scheduled for a final resolution of the case. If any issue is contested, there will be a formal trial in which a judge will settle the issues in dispute.

If I don't want a divorce, can I stop it?

In some states, judges will grant no-fault divorces when one spouse indicates that the marriage is over. In these states it is unlikely that you could prevent a divorce. In other no-fault states, if one spouse contests the divorce, the other is required to prove grounds for the divorce. Your ability to stop the divorce in this case would depend on whether your spouse can prove grounds for the divorce to the court's satisfaction, or whether you have a valid defense.

My husband left me about two years ago, and now I want to marry someone else. How long will it take to get a divorce?

The more complex the case, the longer it will take. Contested cases, where the spouses cannot agree on property settlements and child custody, take longer than uncontested ones. And the more divorce cases before the court, the longer each must wait for proceedings to begin. Uncontested cases are generally scheduled on a separate court calendar

Steps in Getting a Divorce

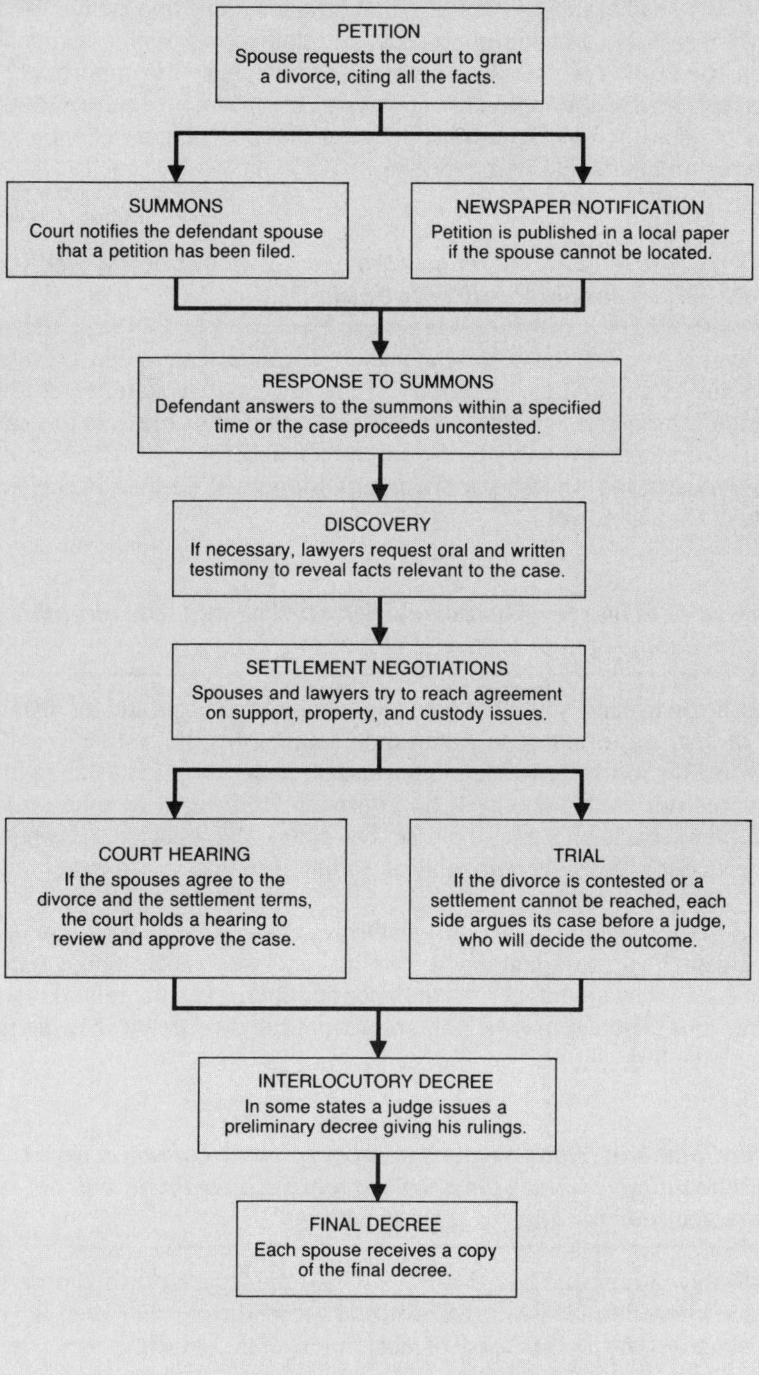

PETITION
Spouse requests the court to grant a divorce, citing all the facts.

↓ (to Summons and Newspaper Notification)

SUMMONS
Court notifies the defendant spouse that a petition has been filed.

NEWSPAPER NOTIFICATION
Petition is published in a local paper if the spouse cannot be located.

↓

RESPONSE TO SUMMONS
Defendant answers to the summons within a specified time or the case proceeds uncontested.

↓

DISCOVERY
If necessary, lawyers request oral and written testimony to reveal facts relevant to the case.

↓

SETTLEMENT NEGOTIATIONS
Spouses and lawyers try to reach agreement on support, property, and custody issues.

↓ (to Court Hearing and Trial)

COURT HEARING
If the spouses agree to the divorce and the settlement terms, the court holds a hearing to review and approve the case.

TRIAL
If the divorce is contested or a settlement cannot be reached, each side argues its case before a judge, who will decide the outcome.

↓

INTERLOCUTORY DECREE
In some states a judge issues a preliminary decree giving his rulings.

↓

FINAL DECREE
Each spouse receives a copy of the final decree.

and are heard more quickly than contested ones. State statutes may also affect the total time needed to get a divorce. Some require a cooling-off period, usually ranging from 30 to 60 days after one spouse has filed a divorce petition. In addition to providing time for a possible reconciliation, the waiting period also allows the other spouse the opportunity to get legal advice and to prepare an answer. Some states require a waiting period, usually 6 to 12 months, between the interlocutory (temporary) decree and the final divorce decree.

When Clyde left Beverly six months ago, he moved to another state. Where should the divorce be filed?

A divorce may be filed in any state where one spouse has been a resident for the length of time required by the law in that state. Most state residency requirements for a divorce are six months or less. In this case, the divorce can probably be filed in either Beverly's or Clyde's state. If child custody is an issue, a divorce petition must be filed in the state where the child lives.

I know of at least one instance when my husband was unfaithful. Is this enough grounds for a divorce?

Yes, if you live in a state that recognizes adultery as a ground for divorce, as the majority of states do. At one time, some states allowed a husband to divorce his wife for just one adulterous act, while giving a wife the right to divorce her husband only if he consistently engaged in a pattern of adultery. This is no longer the case. The states that recognize adultery as a ground for divorce require only one adulterous act, regardless of which spouse committed it.

However, whether a divorce will be granted also depends on your own behavior. If you have condoned your husband's actions by failing to raise the issue or by voluntarily resuming or continuing marital relations with him, your husband may be able to prevent the divorce by showing that you have forgiven him.

If my husband wants to move to an area of the country where I will be unlikely to find the work for which I'm trained, will he have grounds for divorce if I refuse to go?

Probably. A husband has traditionally had the legal right to choose the place where he and his wife will live, and a wife who did not move with her husband could be accused of abandoning him, which is considered

Grounds for Divorce

Grounds for a no-fault divorce exist when a married couple agree that they can no longer live together in peace and harmony. Some form of no-fault divorce is available in every state on one or both of the following grounds:

- *Incompatibility, irreconcilable differences, irretrievable breakdown, breakdown or dissolution of the marriage*—These terms mean the same thing and are used interchangeably in different states.
- *Separation*—Living separately according to the terms of a separation decree or agreement for a period ranging from 60 days to 5 years.

Grounds for a traditional divorce exist when one or both spouses are guilty of marital misconduct. Traditional grounds vary widely from state to state. Among the most common:

- *Adultery*—Voluntary sexual relations outside the marriage. This is usually difficult to prove to a court's satisfaction because most adulterous acts are committed in private.
- *Physical cruelty*—Violence by one spouse that endangers the physical safety of the other.
- *Mental cruelty*—Conduct that embarrasses or humiliates the spouse or impairs the spouse's mental or physical health.
- *Alcoholism or drug addiction*—The addiction must have started after the marriage, have continued for one to five years, and be serious enough to disrupt family life.
- *Abandonment or desertion*—Leaving home and staying away for a long period without a valid reason or without the consent of the other spouse. Abandonment cannot be claimed if there is an agreement to separate, if a spouse is forced to leave because of abuse, or if there is no intent to desert, such as leaving to comply with military orders.
- *Insanity*—Mental illness that is severe enough to prevent a normal marital relationship. In most cases, it must be shown that the mental illness is incurable and has existed for a period of time.
- *Imprisonment*—Conviction of a crime and sentencing to prison.

grounds for divorce in most states. If your only reason for not moving is that you will not be able to find a particular type of employment, your husband could seek a divorce.

Bill was an alcoholic when we married, but I didn't understand the seriousness of his drinking problem then. Can I use this as grounds for divorce?

A number of states allow a divorce when one spouse is habitually drunk. But in many of these states it must be shown that the alcoholism developed after you were married. If you live in a state in which it is not possible to divorce Bill for alcoholism, you may still be able to do so on other grounds, such as cruelty. Or you could file for a no-fault divorce on the grounds that the marriage has irretrievably broken down.

I don't know where my husband is, and I want to divorce him. How long must my husband be gone before I can get a divorce? Can I divorce him without his consent?

In a no-fault divorce, there is no specific length of time for your husband to be absent in order to obtain a divorce. But if you file for a divorce using desertion or abandonment as grounds, the time will range from 60 days to 5 years, depending on the law in your state. The most common length of time is one year.

No state requires a spouse's consent for divorce. However, there must be some attempt to inform him about the divorce, by either serving him with notice of the divorce or publishing the notice in a local newspaper.

If Gary dates Barbara while his divorce is pending, will it affect the divorce or his request for custody of his children?

If Gary and Barbara are dating casually, there will probably be no effect on his divorce or request for child custody. However, if Gary and Barbara are involved in a serious relationship, the court, in determining support, custody, and visitation, will certainly consider whether this relationship is harmful or beneficial to Gary's children.

Brian and June have been living together for 20 years in a state that recognizes common-law marriage. Does Brian have to divorce June before he can marry Alice?

Yes. If Brian and June have lived together as husband and wife and have met the requirements for common-law marriage in their state, Brian must go to court and get a divorce in order to marry Alice.

At my divorce trial, the judge was totally unaware of what was going on. He was running for reelection at the time, and now his decisions don't make any sense to me. Can we have a retrial with a different judge?

A retrial may be obtained only if an appeals court rules that an error was made by the judge in your case. For example, if the judge ignored important evidence presented at the trial in reaching his decision, an appeals court could grant a new trial. If so, your attorney could request a different judge. Some states allow a judge to reconsider his decision if you request it. In these states the judge can revise his own rulings if he finds he has made a mistake.

Can a divorce decree be set aside?

Many states allow a divorce decree to be set aside if both spouses request the court to do so within a specified time—generally one to six months after the divorce. This usually occurs when a divorced couple has reconciled. When the divorce decree is set aside, it is as though no divorce had occurred.

Tim and Louise rewrote their wills before they divorced. Does the divorce affect the wills?

If Tim and Louise are included in each other's wills, those portions of their wills are revoked by the divorce. This could change the intent of the entire will of each; thus Tim and Louise should consult their attorneys and rewrite their wills as soon as possible.

Division of Property

Alvin and Marcia are involved in a very bitter divorce. Who will decide how the property is to be divided?

If Alvin and Marcia and their attorneys are unable to reach an agreement on a fair division of their property, the judge who handles their case will divide the property according to the laws of the state in which they live. There are two general methods of dividing property used in the United States. The most common method is called equitable distribution, whereby property is divided according to such factors as the length of the marriage and the spouses' income, employability, and need, as well as their financial and nonfinancial contributions to the marriage. For example, a wife who stayed at home to raise children would be entitled to part of the value of the family's home, even if she never contributed any money toward its purchase.

The other method of dividing property, commonly known as community property, prevails in Arizona, California, Idaho, Louisiana, New Mexico, Nevada, Texas, Washington, and Wisconsin; these nine states divide equally all the property earned or acquired during the marriage, excluding inheritances. In these states any property acquired prior to the marriage will usually remain the property of the spouse who owned it before the marriage took place, unless there is a prenuptial agreement to the contrary.

Before we got married, I signed a prenuptial agreement prepared by my husband which stated that I would take only $10,000 if we ever divorced. After our marriage, I found out that he owned real estate valued at over $200,000. Will I have to settle for the $10,000, or can I get more if I go to court?

Since your husband did not reveal all his assets at the time of your marriage, it is likely that the judge will rule that the prenuptial agreement was unfair. But this will not necessarily bring you a larger property award. The judge will still divide the property according to the standards imposed by the laws of your state.

After 20 years of marriage, Bill decided to divorce his wife. The deed to their house is in his name only. Does this mean his wife will be forced out of her home after the divorce?

In most states, Bill's wife will not be forced out of the home because the deed is in Bill's name. Only three states, Mississippi, South Carolina, and West Virginia, use the name on the deed as the sole factor in deciding who will get the property.

My wife and I agreed on how to divide our property. Can a judge change our agreement?

Yes. Every property division agreement must be approved by a judge. If the judge believes that the way you want to divide your property is unfair to either of you, or that it is inconsistent with the state law, he has the right to change it.

My husband is hiding assets and making a property settlement difficult. How do I find out how much we really have?

First, start your search by examining all the financial records to which you have access, such as bank statements and income tax returns. If you and your spouse filed a joint income tax return, you can ask the Internal Revenue Service for a copy.

Second, your attorney can use a formal legal procedure, called discovery, to ask your husband questions under oath and force him to produce such records as personal or business income tax returns, financial statements, loan applications, and pension plans.

When Diane was going through her divorce, all she could think about was getting it finalized. Now she believes she should have received more in the property settlement. Can Diane have the settlement changed?

Probably not. A judge will not revise a property settlement that a spouse

The Search for Hidden Assets

People who are otherwise honest sometimes become deceptive during a divorce and try to hide assets so that the court won't give them to the other spouse. Hidden assets can include such things as bank accounts, investments, valuable personal property, or real estate. When hidden assets are suspected, there is a legal procedure called discovery that can be used to bring the assets to light.

In a discovery procedure, the attorney will ask your spouse to produce all relevant financial records. These might include:

- Personal and business tax returns
- Checking and savings account statements
- Dividend and interest statements
- Real estate records
- Loan applications
- Gift and inheritance tax returns of parents and other relatives
- Expense accounts submitted to an employer

By checking and comparing the information in these documents, your attorney can get a better picture of your spouse's financial situation. If your spouse has not provided a full accounting of his assets, your lawyer can then send him *interrogatories*, which are written questions that must be answered in writing under oath.

If hidden assets are still suspected, your lawyer can proceed to *depositions*, in which your spouse is questioned under oath with a court reporter recording the answers. Bank officials, your spouse's employer, business associates, and others who know about his finances may also be asked to provide depositions. Those who do not cooperate can be served with subpoenas, directing them to answer questions and produce papers. The discovery procedure can be expensive and is called for only when valuable assets might otherwise go unnoticed as a settlement is worked out.

agreed to and had approved by a court unless there is a very good reason, such as evidence to prove that a spouse lied to the court about the couple's assets. It is most unlikely that the judge will find Diane's dissatisfaction sufficient reason to change her settlement.

My husband and I own and operate a small printing shop. He says that if we get divorced, he will get the business because it is in his name. We used my inheritance to make the down payment when we bought the shop. How is this property likely to be divided if we get divorced?

You should get credit for the amount of your inheritance that you invested in the business. The remaining value of the business will be divided in the same manner as your other marital property, and your contributions to the business should be taken into consideration.

I inherited a substantial amount of money while our divorce was pending. Can my wife get any part of it?

Virtually every state recognizes an inheritance as the sole property of its beneficiary, not subject to division with a spouse. Your inheritance is protected in two ways. First, an inheritance is generally considered separate property no matter what the status of your marriage. Second, property acquired after separation is considered separate property.

When I married, I had a car. We sold it, and I took over the use of my husband's car. Can I get him to give me his car or buy me another one now that we are divorcing?

The value of property brought into a marriage is only one factor that is considered when property is divided. You will not necessarily leave the marriage entitled to an automobile.

My husband and I each want to keep our prize cocker spaniel after the divorce. How will the court decide the matter?

Because this issue is not going to seem as important to the court as it does to you, your attorneys will try to seek some compromise. If they are unsuccessful, the court will review information about the past care of the pet, the original motive for acquiring it, and similar details to determine who should keep it.

My wife has built up hefty charges on several store credit cards. Will I have to pay these debts if we get divorced?

Maybe. If the credit card accounts are in joint names or if you cosigned the credit agreements, you and your wife are equally liable for the charges. On the other hand, you could be liable even if you didn't sign the credit agreements. Debts are divided along with assets in a property settlement. The court will divide these credit card charges on the basis of your ability to pay, the nature of the items purchased, your wife's motives in making the charges, who benefited from the charges, and other relevant information.

Amy received legal notice that her husband had filed for divorce. She discovered on the same day that he had also withdrawn all the money from their joint checking account, leaving no balance to cover the checks she had just mailed to pay the household bills. What can Amy do?

Amy can request a court order to prevent her husband from spending the money from the account and to make good on the outstanding checks. Although Amy probably will not be reimbursed immediately for her part of this money, her husband's actions will be taken into account when their property is divided. Obtaining a court order in a situation like this involves many legal technicalities; Amy should retain an attorney to handle the matter for her.

When I got divorced, my ex-husband's attorney was supposed to have the deed to our house recorded in my name. It has been six months now, and I haven't received the recorded deed. The attorney won't return my phone calls. What should I do?

Ask your attorney to contact your ex-husband's attorney. If he still won't cooperate, you may be able to have the court certify the portion of the final divorce judgment that deals with the real estate and then have it recorded in the same office as the deed. This would have the same effect as a recorded deed.

My doctor's wife quit college to support him while he finished medical school. Now they are getting divorced. Is she entitled to a share of her husband's future earnings?

This is a rapidly changing area of law. Many states now have some way of compensating the wife for her efforts. An award to her of a share of his future earnings is only one method that has been developed to accomplish this purpose. Other methods include granting her higher alimony, a larger share of marital property, and repayment of expenses invested in his professional education.

My husband's sole source of income is his pension from the government. If we decided to get a divorce, would any part of that pension be paid to me?

Your husband's federal pension will be included as part of your marital assets. The court considers all income and assets in working out a property settlement in a divorce case; your husband's federal pension is one of the assets that will be divided.

My husband and I were married for more than 35 years before divorcing. Do I have a right to receive Social Security benefits based on his work record?

You may be eligible for benefits, since you were married for more than 10 years. But you must also meet age and other requirements. Contact your nearest Social Security office for detailed information about requirements and application procedures.

Scott and I were married for nine years, and then we got divorced. He died last month. Am I entitled to survivors' benefits under Social Security?

No. The Social Security Act requires that a marriage last for at least 10 years before you are entitled to survivors' benefits or any other Social Security payments based solely on your spouse's record.

Support for Spouse (Alimony)

Under what conditions is a woman usually granted support?

The goal in granting support is to enable a woman to become self-supporting at a standard of living reasonably comparable to the one she enjoyed during the marriage. Support is granted at the discretion of the court; it may continue until a woman becomes self-supporting or remarries, or it may continue indefinitely if it is clear that there is no possibility of self-support.

Linda's lawyer told her that she may be awarded maintenance. Is this the same as alimony?

Yes. The word *alimony* is gradually being replaced by the terms *maintenance* and *support.*

Does a wife ever have to pay support to her ex-husband?

The factors that justify support payments to a former spouse apply equally to men and women. If, for example, a wife has been the main source of support in her family, the court may order her to make support payments to her ex-husband.

Tim and Cathy have filed for divorce. Cathy did not work outside the home for 12 years while she was raising their four children. Will the court make Cathy find a job? Will Tim still have to pay support? If so, how is the amount determined?

Courts vary widely in awarding support to spouses. Cathy will certainly need to seek employment, and Tim will very likely have to pay her some support. The amount will be determined by comparing Tim's ability to pay with the amount Cathy needs to live on and the time it will take her to become self-supporting.

At the time of their divorce, Lisa did not ask Roy for support. Can she request it now?

Probably not. Generally if spousal support is not requested at the time of the divorce, it cannot be granted later.

My ex-husband is four months behind in his support payments. What can I do to make him pay what he owes me?

Your ex-husband is violating a court order (your divorce decree); you can request that the judge enforce the order and make him pay.

I heard from some old friends that my ex-husband recently received a big raise. Can I get my support increased?

Possibly. You will need to prove that your husband is now able to pay more. And you will also have to convince the court of your own need for the increased support.

Support for Spouse (Alimony)

Larry pays Kay support. Can Larry use this as a deduction on his income tax? Is Kay required to report it as income?

Larry's support payments are taxable as income to Kay, and Larry can deduct the payments on his income tax returns. However, since there are specific tax rules and exceptions relating to support payments, Larry and Kay would be wise to consult with specialists about their situation before filing their tax returns.

When Betty and Joe divorced, Joe agreed to pay support for 10 years. A year after the divorce, he was killed in an accident. Joe's will left his entire estate to his new wife, Marianne. Can Betty seek the rest of her payments from Joe's estate?

She can try to get the payments from Joe's estate, but she probably won't be successful. Unless their divorce decree included a provision instructing Joe's estate to continue Betty's support, Joe's death will terminate any obligation to support his ex-wife.

Child Custody

Robert and Mary tried to stay together because of their children, but divorce now seems inevitable. They are concerned about their children's welfare. If they agree on custody and support issues, will their wishes be followed? Who makes the final decision?

The judge will make the final decision. Since Robert and Mary agree on custody, support, and visitation issues, the court will probably accept their wishes if they are reasonable and consistent with the laws in their state. However, the judge would not accept what Robert and Mary had worked out if it were not in the best interest of the children.

What factors does a judge consider when deciding what is in a child's best interest?

The judge takes many factors into account before making a decision. He will consider the wishes of the child and the parents; the age, health, and sex of the child; the home environment offered by each parent, the character and lifestyle of each parent, and their financial circumstances. In some cases, the judge may appoint a social worker to investigate these issues and make a recommendation.

Do courts still give preference to the mother in awarding custody?

The traditional view has been that the best interests of young children, female children, and children in poor health were served by giving custody to the mother. The trend today, however, is to give mothers and fathers equal preference in custody cases.

Chris and Nancy both want custody of their children. Will the judge follow the children's wishes when making his decision?

Whether the judge will follow the children's wishes depends on their age and maturity—he is less likely to follow the wishes of a three-year-old than those of a teenager. The judge will also consider many other factors in designating the custodial parent. He will not grant custody to an unfit parent even if the child requests it.

Joanna and Tom are in the process of getting a divorce, and Joanna has temporary custody of their children. If Joanna lives with another man, will the court deny her custody?

The court will not deny Joanna custody if it finds that her conduct has no harmful effect on the children. The court will limit its examination of a parent's conduct to its effect on the child's welfare and will weigh other factors, such as the age of the children and Joanna's relationship with them, in making its final determination.

Jeff and Sarah were recently divorced, and Sarah was given custody of their two children. If Sarah decides that she is going to move out of the state and take the children with her, what can Jeff do to prevent the children from going?

Sarah must notify Jeff or the court of her plan to move the children. If Jeff objects, he can request that the court prevent the move. In making its decision the court will consider the expense of visitation, the children's standard of living in the new state, and the closeness of the children's relationship with Jeff. The judge will also determine whether or not the move is planned for the sole purpose of denying visitation.

If a custody fight becomes especially hostile, can the judge take the children away from both parents?

Yes. Custody decisions by the court are always guided by what is in the best interests of the child. The courts prefer that custody remain with one of the natural parents, but if the court determines that both parents are unfit because of the extreme hostility between them, it has the power to assign the custody of the children to a third person.

Roger and Cynthia both want custody of their children. A friend told them that they should ask for joint custody when they go to court. What is joint custody?

Joint custody is an arrangement in which both parents share legal and physical custody of their children after a separation or divorce. Roger and Cynthia would participate equally in reaching major decisions concerning their children, and the time spent with each parent would be more nearly equal, unlike the time allocated in sole custody.

Joint Custody Arrangements

Many divorcing couples feel that joint custody is the best way for each parent to have meaningful contact with the children as they grow up. Joint custody also relieves the children of the responsibility for choosing which parent to live with and helps prevent them from feeling that one parent doesn't want them.

There are two parts to joint custody: legal and physical. Legal custody requires the parents to make decisions together about the children's education, health, and overall welfare. Physical custody establishes the amount of time each child spends with a parent. Courts generally require divorcing parents who want joint custody to submit plans detailing aspects of both legal and physical custody. Courts will agree to a wide variety of physical custody arrangements as long as they are fair, workable, and in the best interests of the children. Here are some typical divisions of parental custody time from a list developed by the Joint Custody Association in Los Angeles:

- Alternate 3½ days with each parent.
- Alternate workweek with one parent, weekends with the other.
- Alternate one or two weeks with each parent.
- Alternate one month with each parent.
- Alternate two or three months with each parent.
- Spend school year with one parent, summer vacation with the other.
- Child remains at home and parents alternate according to a prearranged schedule.
- Child moves freely between two parental homes, with parents getting approximately equal time.

My wife and I don't get along or communicate with each other very well. However, we would both like to be involved in the care of our children. Would joint custody work in our situation?

Joint custody works best when the parents cooperate and work together on the issues concerning their children. If you and your wife can overcome your problems when dealing with the children, joint custody may be a good arrangement for you. If not, you should explore other custody options before making your decision.

Once custody has been awarded, does the court then leave all decisions about the child's welfare to the parent with custody?

It is the custodial parent's responsibility to make decisions regarding the child's care, discipline, education, religion, and health. The court will defer to the decisions of the custodial parent, as long as they are in the child's best interest.

My ex-husband, who lives in another state, just remarried. He has told me that he and his new wife want sole custody of our son. I haven't remarried, and my ex-husband says the court will give him custody so our son can live in a "real family." Will the court award custody to my ex-husband?

As a general rule, the fact that your ex-husband has remarried is not reason enough to make a change in custody. He would have to go to court and present convincing evidence that there have been changes in your circumstances which are harmful to your son. If he cannot do this, custody will not be changed.

Ray and Melissa were divorced several years ago. Melissa was granted custody of their two young children and has recently remarried. Can she change the last name of her children to that of her new husband?

Many states require the approval of both parents when changing a child's name. Other states will grant a request by one parent for a name change as long as the other parent does not object to it. In determining whether a name change should be granted, the court considers the child's welfare as the most important factor. Generally, a court will not grant a change of name over one parent's objection merely to save the other parent or the children from the inconvenience or embarrassment of having different last names. There must be substantial evidence that the name change is best for the children.

My ex-wife was given custody of our daughter when we were divorced. She has now remarried, and her new husband is an alcoholic. My daughter is afraid of him. Can I get the custody order changed so my daughter can live with my new wife and me?

The courts are usually reluctant to change custody orders. But since your daughter is afraid of her stepfather, you may be able to get the custody order changed. The court will look at the evidence that you can provide to show that living with your ex-wife's husband may have a harmful effect on your daughter. The judge will consider all the factors and award custody to the parent who can provide the best care for the child.

What should I do if my ex-husband disappears and takes the children with him?

Since your ex-husband's actions would be considered a crime in most states, you should contact the police right away. Be prepared to give a detailed description of your children and your ex-husband, and provide the names and addresses of people that he is likely to contact. Recent photographs of your children can also be very helpful to the police.

If you remain calm and gather as much information as you can for the police, you have a better chance of finding your children quickly. After

Parental Kidnapping: What to Do If Your Child Is Abducted

This information on what steps to take when a child has been abducted by his other parent is based on material prepared by the National Center for Missing and Exploited Children in Arlington, Virginia.

1. If you believe your child has been abducted, contact your local police department and file a missing persons report. Give the police a complete description of your child and ask them to enter this into the FBI's National Crime Information Center (NCIC) computer. Provide any information you can on the abductor, his vehicle, and where they may be.

2. Call the hotline for the National Center for Missing and Exploited Children, 1-800-843-5678, for information on local parental support groups that can help. Call the central directory at 1-800-555-1212 for telephone numbers of additional groups that may be able to provide assistance.

3. Double-check with the local police one day later and make sure that your information has been forwarded to the NCIC computer. If not, call the nearest FBI office and ask them to do so.

you have notified the police, you should contact your attorney to see what further legal action should be taken once the children are found.

When Alice and Allen were divorced, Alice was awarded custody of their children. Allen left town five years ago and has not been seen or heard from since. Can Wayne, Alice's new husband, adopt Allen's children without Allen's consent?

Wayne can adopt the children without Allen's consent only if Allen's parental rights are terminated. Termination of parental rights occurs when a parent has abandoned a child or is judged to be unfit to be a parent. Specific grounds for termination are spelled out in each state's laws. The court would very likely find that Allen's five-year absence is sufficient to terminate his parental rights.

My husband adopted my child from a previous marriage. Now I want a divorce. Will my second husband have any rights to the child he adopted?

Yes. By adopting your child, your husband was granted the same parental rights and duties as a biological father. In awarding custody the court will consider him, as well as you in determining which of you will serve the child's interests best.

4. Start court proceedings to obtain legal custody of your child, if you do not already have it. This will strengthen your position if you need to file criminal charges against the abductor. You will need an attorney to help you get a custody decree.

5. Meet with your local prosecuting attorney to consider filing criminal charges against the abductor. If the abductor has fled the state, ask the prosecutor to apply to the local U.S. attorney for an unlawful-flight-to-avoid-prosecution warrant. If a federal warrant is issued, the FBI can then assist in the search for the abductor.

6. When your child is found, immediately send a certified copy of your custody decree to the family court in the town or county where your child is located. Then ask the police there to help you enforce the decree and get your child back.

7. If the police will not help you without a local court order, petition the family court where the child is found to enforce your custody decree.

8. After your child is returned, ask your own family court to limit the abductor's visitation rights. Also ask the judge to add provisions to your custody decree to prevent a repeat abduction.

Child Custody

If I let my ex-wife's new husband adopt my children, do I still have to pay child support?

No. If your ex-wife's new husband adopts your children, your parental rights would end and you would be relieved of any further financial obligations to the children.

This is a very serious decision, and it should be carefully weighed, because any and all legal relationships to the children will be ended when they are adopted. You will no longer be able to visit the children or have any say in their upbringing.

Sue is divorced and has custody of her daughter. Can anything be added to her will to make sure her ex-husband will not regain custody if something should happen to her?

No. Sue can put a paragraph in her will stating her wish that her ex-husband not be given custody of their daughter, but such a provision will have no legal effect.

Visitation

For further information on grandparents' rights, see "Rights of Grandparents" in Chapter 2, *Marriage and Family*.

Can a wife refuse to let her husband see their children while their divorce is pending?

No. Parents have a legal right to visit their children, even while a divorce is pending. However, if this visitation turns out to be harmful to the children, a court order may be obtained that will limit or end the visitation rights.

My ex-wife is now remarried and lives in a different state. Can I get my visitation rights changed so I can have my child with me for a whole month during the summer?

You may ask the court to modify your visitation rights. The judge will consider the child's age and what effect a one-month absence from the mother might have on the child. Other considerations are the child's wishes, and any previous restrictions that may have been imposed on your visits. Modifications of visitation rights are common when a child lives in another state.

Visitation for Grandparents

One of the cruelest blows that grandparents can suffer is the loss, through no fault of their own, of any chance to visit with their grandchildren. Suppose, for example, a former daughter-in-law wins custody of the children and refuses to let her ex-husband's parents see the youngsters. Or she marries a man who adopts the children and then refuses to allow the natural grandparents to visit the children. In the past, grandparents had no legal right to visit their own grandchildren, no matter how close they might be.

Happily, the law now provides a solution. In all 50 states there are statutes guaranteeing grandparents the right to petition the court for visitation rights. Although each case is judged individually, the court generally views it as in the children's best interest to have friendly relationships with their grandparents. If there is no evidence to prove that such visits would have a harmful effect, the judge will specify the terms of visitation in much the same way they are spelled out in custodial agreements between divorcing couples.

My son and daughter-in-law are getting divorced. Will I have visitation rights to see my grandchildren?

In the past, grandparent visitation was not even an issue considered by the courts. However, recent trends recognize a grandparent's right to visit if it is in the child's best interest. If you have a close relationship with your grandchildren, you can be granted the right to visit them.

Do I have to let my children have overnight visitation with my ex-husband if he is living with his girlfriend?

If the court has ordered overnight visitation, you must abide by the order. If you believe that your children are being harmed by overnight visits with their father while he is living with his girlfriend, you may ask the court to change the visitation arrangement. You may be required to prove harm to the children when they visit their father, such as physical or verbal abuse by the girlfriend or serious neglect when she is present.

My ex-wife has custody of our two children, and I was given visitation rights. Now my children say they don't want to see me. Is there anything I can do?

If your children's refusal to see you is without good reason, or if it's the result of coercion by the custodial parent, the court will enforce your visitation rights. If the decision is theirs alone, however, and if they are old enough to understand their actions, forcing them to visit you may increase their feelings of resentment. You should be sure to remain in contact with them so that they are aware of your affection for them. Later on, many children decide on their own to see the noncustodial parent.

Mike is three months behind in child support payments. Is there any way that Sandra can prevent him from seeing their children until the payments are made?

No. As a general rule, visitation rights may not be withheld to enforce child support obligations. If Sandra continues to prevent Mike from seeing their children, Mike can ask the court to enforce his rights, or change the custody and support order in his favor.

Child Support

If the husband gets custody of the children, will the wife have to pay child support?

The court is not required to order either parent to make child support payments. But it is common for the court to require the noncustodial parent to pay for child support, regardless of whether this parent is the father or the mother.

Martha has temporary custody of her two-year-old son, Wally. Can she get child support payments while her divorce is pending?

Martha has a good chance of getting some help if she requests it. Most courts will not force one parent to bear the financial burden alone while a divorce is pending.

Can a court force a parent to go into debt to pay child support?

No, but when a court orders support payments, they must be made. If a parent has trouble making the payments, he may have to cut back on other expenses, lower his standard of living, take a second job, or sell some assets. If all this fails, he may have no other choice but to go into debt.

In the past, the amount of child support was left to the discretion of the judge in each individual case. Today, every state has guidelines for determining child support. These guidelines estimate how much the support should be—based on the cost of raising a child, the number of children involved, and the total family income; in most states the amount of child support is given as a percentage of the noncustodial parent's gross income, and does not consider his other financial circumstances.

Joan has a child by her boyfriend, Brent. Can Joan get child support from him?

Joan may collect child support if the court finds that Brent is the father. The amount will be based on Joan's need and Brent's ability to pay. It will be computed similarly to child support in a divorce.

What age does a child have to reach before child support payments can stop?

Child support payments stop when the child reaches the age of legal adulthood, which is 18 in most states, 21 in others. In some cases, the court may extend support payments beyond the age of adulthood so that the child can continue his or her education.

My ex-husband isn't paying his child support on time, and we need the money. I have contacted him about this many times. What is my next step?

It depends on how late your ex-husband is with the payments. If he doesn't actually miss payments and is only a week or two late with them, you may not want to antagonize him with a court action. If the late payments are a hardship for you, your options are the same as if he didn't make payments at all: You will have to take him to court.

Norman's ex-wife has missed several child support payments. Can her wages be garnisheed in order to get payment?

While it is possible to garnishee her wages, child support laws now allow wage assignments, which make the collection of support payments much easier. With a wage assignment, the court orders Norman's ex-wife to allow her employer to deduct the child support amount directly from her wages if she falls behind in support. The wage assignment may be activated on Norman's request or when his ex-wife falls behind a set amount in payment. There is a growing trend toward ordering wage assignments at the time the amount of child support is determined rather than waiting for the payer to fall behind.

Child Support

Can I get a cost-of-living increase with child support?

Yes. Many courts will approve automatic increases in child support to match an increase in the cost of living. If your court order does not do this, you should request it. You may request an increase if other costs of supporting your children also go up. The most common reasons for higher costs as the children grow older are clothing, transportation, and education. A child with special health or education needs may also increase your expenses substantially.

I lost the job I had when I was married and now have a new one that pays less. Can I go to court and get my child support payments reduced?

A reduction in income will be considered as a reason for reduced child support payments. However, the court will also look at several other factors. For instance, you may be able to make child support payments from resources other than wages, such as income from savings, investments, or real estate. And if the child's needs have increased, the court may feel that this circumstance overrides your reduced ability to pay.

What to Do When Your Ex-Spouse Won't Pay Child Support

Having a judge award support doesn't guarantee that your ex-spouse will send the payments you are entitled to each month. But since the enactment of the federal Child Support Enforcement Amendments in 1984, you have a much better chance of collecting. The following procedures should help extract payments from a delinquent ex-spouse:

- Automatic withholding of support payments from paychecks.
- Withholding past due amounts from income tax refunds.
- Seizing real estate or personal property.
- Reporting the delinquent individual to credit agencies.
- Requiring a cash bond or other type of security as a deposit with the court to guarantee that payments will be made.

The details for putting these procedures into effect vary from state to state, but the first step is the same: contact the nearest Child Support Enforcement Agency office, listed under your state department of social services. This office will help you obtain your child support payments and will advise you about ways to avoid the problem in the future.

If I am laid off and cannot make my child support payments, can I be put in jail?

A court has the power to jail anyone who willfully fails to abide by its orders. If you are unable to meet your child support obligations because of changes beyond your control, the court may consider modifying the amount of the award rather than putting you in jail.

My divorce decree requires me to pay $200 a month for our daughter's care. My ex-wife and I now agree that $150 a month is enough. Can we just write out a new agreement and sign it?

You can, but you may encounter some problems by writing your own agreement. (1) You may unintentionally alter other provisions in the original support order. (2) You may have to obtain a court order to modify a provision of a divorce decree. (3) You may have to file the new agreement in court, which sometimes requires a court hearing. (4) The new agreement may have no legal effect if you don't follow the correct legal procedures. You should have an attorney help you draw up the new agreement in order to avoid these problems.

When Chuck and Debbie divorced, Chuck told his son, Bob, not to worry about college tuition. Bob is 18 and will begin college in the fall. Chuck recently said he wouldn't pay Bob's tuition. Can Bob sue Chuck to force him to pay?

Possibly. While Chuck's statements at the time of the divorce are not legally binding, the terms of the divorce judgment may require him to pay Bob's college tuition. And at least one state, Illinois, now requires the supporting parent to pay for a child's college education, or professional or vocational training, even after the child reaches the age of 18, when the supporting parent has the financial resources to do so.

Floyd and Donna have filed for divorce. Donna will have custody of the children, and Floyd has agreed to pay child support. Donna would like to have the children stay on Floyd's health insurance policy. Is this possible? Can Donna remain on the policy?

Responsibility for health care expenses is an important part of child support. Since Floyd currently has a health insurance policy, the court would probably order him to maintain the children on his policy. Whether Floyd would be required to keep Donna on his health insurance policy depends on her health and her ability to carry her own insurance or pay her own health care costs.

Child Support

The clerk of the court keeps a computer record of my support payments. It is in error. How do I go about correcting it?

You should notify the clerk of the court immediately of this error. Ask him if the error can be corrected without an order from the court. If it cannot, then it will be necessary to schedule a court hearing to prove that an error was made and to request an order correcting it.

Does Bill have to continue making his child support payments if both he and his ex-wife marry again?

Yes, the payments must continue. However, if Bill feels that his remarriage has added financial obligations that make his child support payments a heavy burden, he may ask the court for a reduction in the amount. Likewise, he may also request a reduction if his ex-wife's remarriage has made it easier for her to help support the children.

Can the court make my husband take out a life insurance policy to cover child support payments in case he dies? Who would pay the insurance premium?

There are no set rules about insurance coverage for child support payments. If requested, the court could order your husband to carry a life insurance policy on himself, naming the children as beneficiaries.

CHAPTER
4

Your Home

Renting a Home

I am about to rent an apartment. What precautions should I take before signing the lease?

Thoroughly inspect the property you will be renting, especially if you have seen only a model apartment—your own unit might not be as well situated or as well maintained as the model. Note on the lease any repairs or improvements the landlord has agreed to make. Initial these notes and have the landlord initial them when he signs the lease.

Make sure that the apartment is vacant or will be vacant by the date you want to move in. You may want to check up on your new landlord by calling the Better Business Bureau and your local or state consumer protection agency and asking if any complaints have been registered against him. Your community's building inspector can tell you if there is a history of building code violations. Have an attorney review the lease before you sign it if there is anything in it you don't understand.

Greg has found the perfect apartment, but there is something in the lease he doesn't like. Can he do anything about it?

If he can get the landlord to agree, Greg can cross out the objectionable provision, then initial the margin of the lease next to the omitted clause and have his landlord do the same.

Are there circumstances in which a landlord can rightfully refuse to rent a house or an apartment to someone?

Yes. The law generally permits a landlord to refuse to rent property to someone as long as that refusal is not based on sex, religion, race, or national origin. He might, for example, refuse to rent to someone with insufficient income or an unstable work record.

My husband and I are having a difficult time finding an apartment. Most of the places we like won't accept children. Is this legal?

Probably not. Federal law prohibits housing discrimination against families with children, except in certain senior citizen communities that meet strict federal guidelines. You should contact your local housing authority to report a landlord who refuses to rent to you because you have children.

The Briscoes put down a deposit of one month's rent on an apartment that the landlord said would be vacated within two

weeks. Four weeks have passed, and the apartment is still occupied. The landlord refuses to return the Briscoes' deposit, stating that if they don't wait until the apartment is vacated, they will forfeit their deposit. What legal recourse do the Briscoes have?

In some states, the Briscoes can either void the lease or sue the present tenants for staying in the apartment after their lease has expired. Some other states would make the landlord liable to the Briscoes on the grounds that it is the landlord's duty to make sure that the premises are vacated and to evict the present tenants before the Briscoes' term begins.

The apartment I want to rent requires a six-month lease. The landlord says I don't need anything in writing because the lease is for less than one year. Should I still request a written lease?

Yes. While the law does not generally require a lease for a period of less than a year to be in writing, a written lease is always preferable. In the event of a dispute, a written lease provides reliable proof of the terms of the agreement. If your landlord refuses to give you a written lease, however, there is no way you can force him to do so.

Adam never signed a lease when he rented an apartment near the college he attends. What are his rights?

Even without a written lease, certain basic rights and responsibilities are implied in the agreement between Adam and his landlord. Adam is entitled to the quiet enjoyment of his apartment. This means he should be free from unreasonable interference from his landlord, as well as from other tenants. In most states, Adam's landlord would also have to provide such basic services as hot and cold water, heat, and adequate ventilation, and keep the hallways, stairs, and other public areas in good repair. Any unfulfilled promises made to Adam by the landlord can be enforced, but oral agreements are difficult to prove.

Marge has been renting the same apartment for three years. The original one-year lease was never renewed. Is it still valid?

No, it is not. Unless Marge and her landlord made a different agreement, her lease automatically expired at the end of the first year. Since Marge has continued to occupy the apartment, however, and the landlord has continued to accept her rent, a month-to-month tenancy has been created, and will end only when either Marge or her landlord provides advance notice of an intention to terminate it. A notice of one month is generally adequate.

Renting a Home

At the end of a one-year lease, Joe continued to pay the same rent, without talking to his landlord about renewing the lease. Three months later, Joe's landlord increased the rent. Can he do this?

Yes, but the landlord must give Joe adequate notice of the proposed increase so that he has the option of moving out. In most states, the notice must be given at least 30 days before the increase takes effect.

What should we look into before signing a lease or rental agreement in a mobile home park?

Check the local zoning ordinances to find out if there are any restrictions on what you plan to do with your mobile home—some communities, for example, will not let you build an addition to your mobile home once it has been set up. Look into the requirements for foundations, tie-downs, and connections to electric, gas, water, and telephone lines. Find out whether you can hook up to the local sewer system or must provide your own septic system. Find out if the fees the landlord is charging you include utilities, garbage and snow removal, laundry facilities, and entrance and exit fees. Ask if there are any limitations on the number of occupants, children, pets, fences, or landscaping. Look for the same things in your lease that you would if you were renting an apartment, being particularly wary of provisions that will allow sharp rent increases.

Craig has found a beautiful new apartment for a reasonable rent, but to get it he has to move out of his old apartment before his lease is up. Can he sublet his old apartment?

Yes, unless his lease prohibits it. But Craig should choose his subtenant carefully. When he sublets his apartment, Craig in effect becomes the landlord for the subtenant, but he is still responsible to the original landlord for making rent payments according to the terms of his lease. If the subtenant fails to pay the rent, Craig may have to pay it.

Can Blanche sublet her apartment even if the lease says no?

If she does, her landlord can get a court order prohibiting the subtenant from using the premises. If the subtenant has already moved in, the landlord may begin eviction proceedings against Blanche and the subtenant. In either case, Blanche would probably have to pay the rent for the remainder of the lease. Instead of trying to sublet the apartment in violation of her lease, Blanche would do better to ask her landlord to amend the lease.

Mack is having trouble making ends meet and wants to have a friend move in with him to help share expenses. Can his landlord prevent him from taking in a roommate?

Probably. A landlord can usually restrict occupancy to the number of persons named in the lease. In some cities, local zoning laws limit how many people can live in an apartment. If the landlord allows Mack to take a roommate, he can legally increase the rent to compensate for the additional wear and tear on the premises.

My roommate, Penny, and I agreed to split our bills 50-50, but Penny hasn't paid her share for several months. If we don't pay last month's rent, the landlord will throw us out. Is there some way to make Penny pay?

You can pay Penny's share of the rent and then take her to court to get it back from her, but it can be very difficult to live with someone who is your opponent in a court case. If your landlord begins eviction proceedings, you may use Penny's failure to pay as a defense against your eviction. There is a possibility that the court might then order Penny to pay her share of the rent to the landlord.

However, if your name is on the lease, most courts will hold you fully responsible for paying the full amount of the rent when it is due. In any event, both you and Penny would be allowed to remain in the apartment until the proceedings came to an end.

Erica's landlord slipped a note into her mailbox stating that her rent would go up $10 per month beginning with her next payment, which is due in three weeks. Must Erica pay the increase?

Yes, if her lease states that three weeks is adequate notice for a rent increase. But if her lease has no provision about the amount of notice, the law in Erica's state will apply. Most states require that notice of a rent increase be given at least one month in advance of the effective date. State or local law may also require that notice of a rent increase be sent to the tenant by certified mail.

Must I give my landlord notice before I move out of my apartment?

Not if you leave on the date your lease expires. If your lease allows you to leave before its expiration date, however, you must give the amount of notice specified. If you are in a month-to-month tenancy following the expiration of your written lease, most states require you to give one month's advance notice of your intention to move.

Renting a Home

After signing a one-year lease, Terence was transferred to a different city. Can he break the lease?

A lease can always be broken, but Terence should be prepared to pay the price for doing so. In most cases he would only have to forfeit his security deposit. But the landlord may refuse to terminate the lease and instead rerent the apartment on Terence's behalf. If he does so and the new tenant moves out, Terence may still have to pay the rent during the remainder of the lease. However, since Terence has a good reason for breaking the lease, he should try to negotiate with his landlord for a release from the remaining term, or find a subtenant for the landlord. If Terence anticipates another job transfer, he should seek a clause in his next lease that would permit him to terminate it when his company relocates him.

After Jill rented a house, a disco opened nearby, causing her many sleepless nights. Can she break the lease?

There is a good chance she can. A lease agreement, like any other contract, is subject to a legal doctrine called frustration of purpose. If the benefit Jill received from renting the house (peace and quiet) was destroyed as a result of the disco, and the disco's opening was totally unforeseeable by Jill when she signed the lease, she may claim frustration of purpose and break the lease without having to pay the rest of the rent.

I replaced some of the light fixtures in my apartment with my own chandeliers. Now that I'm ready to move out, the landlord claims that he can keep the chandeliers. Is this legal?

If your lease includes a provision that permits your landlord to keep any equipment or other improvements that you make to his property, he can legally keep your chandeliers. If your lease contains no such provision, your right to take your chandeliers will be determined by what a reasonable person would believe that you and the landlord intended. Courts in most states would probably presume that a reasonable person would not expect a tenant's chandeliers to become part of a landlord's real estate.

Greta recently moved out of her apartment, leaving it in good condition, but her landlord refuses to return her security deposit. How can she make him return it?

Many states have specific procedures governing the return of security deposits. Generally, the landlord must return a tenant's deposit or the proper portion of it within 30 days after termination of the lease, and in some states he must also give you any interest earned on the deposit. The landlord may keep any or all of the deposit for damage done to the apartment only if he gives the tenant written notice within the same time period. If Greta believes that the landlord has no right to withhold her security deposit, she should file a complaint with her local housing authority. She may also go to small claims court to recover her money.

Is a rent strike legal?

In some cases. In a rent strike, a group of tenants collectively withhold rent in order to force certain concessions from their landlord. The rents are placed in an escrow account, and when the landlord agrees to the concessions, the money is forwarded to him. A rent strike is almost always the last resort of a group of frustrated and angry tenants. Although some states permit rent strikes to correct substantial health and safety problems, they should never be started without the advice of an attorney.

Stan was mugged in the lobby of his apartment building. Can the landlord be held liable because of poor security?

Most states require landlords to exercise reasonable care to keep the common areas of apartment buildings safe for tenants and their visitors. But what constitutes reasonable care has been interpreted in different ways by different states. Increasingly, however, landlords are being held liable for poor building security of which they should have been aware.

Landlord Difficulties

I've had no heat in my apartment for more than a week. Although I've tried repeatedly to get the landlord to do something about it, all he says is that he's working on it. Can I move out without still being obligated under the lease?

Yes. If you can prove that your landlord knew about the furnace malfunction and failed to have it repaired within a reasonable amount of time, you will be considered to have been "constructively evicted." Most states have laws requiring landlords to maintain all major building systems, including heating. Even in states that have no such laws, landlords have a duty to see to it that their tenants have the "quiet enjoyment" of their apartments. If your landlord's failure to repair the furnace interferes with the reasonable enjoyment of your apartment, you may be relieved of your duty to remain there until the end of the lease.

Landlord Difficulties

My landlord keeps promising to fix my toilet, but it still doesn't work. Can I hire a plumber to fix it and have him bill the landlord?

No. In most states, a tenant is not authorized to obligate the landlord to pay for repairs. Most leases specify who is to make repairs. If your landlord is responsible for fixing your toilet, you should give him written notice of the need for repairs. Send the notice by certified mail and keep a copy of it. If the landlord doesn't have the repairs made within a reasonable length of time, hire your own plumber, pay him yourself, and then send a copy of the paid bill to your landlord, requesting reimbursement. If he refuses to pay the bill, deduct the expense from your next rent payment. If the landlord sues you for back rent or tries to evict you, his failure to make necessary repairs will serve you as a valid defense.

If your landlord is consistently irresponsible about keeping essential equipment in good working order, you may report him to the local board of health or building inspector. When deciding whether or not to do so, consider how eager you are to remain on friendly terms with him.

Approximately how long does it take to evict someone?

As little as a week or as long as several months. It depends upon the law in a particular state, the circumstances of the individual case, and the tenant's willingness to contest the eviction.

YOUR HOME

The Rights of Tenants

Suppose you've just signed a lease that you believe to be fair, right down to the small print, and you are now preparing to move into the place you will call home. There is no better time to make a mental checklist of your rights as a tenant. Even though your landlord seems to be a reasonable sort of person, it is comforting to know that the law provides some solid support for you, the tenant, if you ever need it.

- You have the right to the "quiet enjoyment" of your rented home. So long as you respect the terms of your lease, and do not break any laws, you may entertain anybody you choose, or do anything you please, in your home. And if, despite your polite reminders, your neighbors won't stop making too much noise, you have every right to inform your landlord and expect him to talk to the noisemakers.
- You have the right to refuse to let your landlord come into your home without your permission except in extraordinary circumstances: to make emergency repairs, for example, or to demand rent that is overdue.

Grace is two months behind on her rent because she lost her job. Two days ago the landlord went into her apartment and took her TV and stereo equipment. He says that he is holding them until Grace pays the back rent. Is this legal?

Probably not. At one time a landlord had the right to take a tenant's personal property and hold it until the overdue rent was paid. Now most states have laws that either abolish or restrict the landlord's right to seize a tenant's property without notice. These states require the landlord to petition the court for a warrant. After petitioning the court, he must give the tenant notice and make a final demand for payment. Unless the tenant pays the rent or disputes the landlord's claim in court, his property can be sold by the county sheriff. The proceeds of the sale would be given to the landlord to pay the overdue rent and, in many places, to pay the landlord's court costs and the expenses of running the sale. If any money is left over, it will be returned to the tenant.

Violet's landlord keeps coming into her apartment unannounced or while she's at work. Isn't the landlord required to notify Violet of when he plans to come in?

Generally, a person who rents an apartment has the right to keep other people from entering. Even the landlord must have permission to enter. Violet should review her lease, however, because it may allow her landlord to come into the apartment to inspect the premises for such

- You have the right to a livable property, or in legal terms, to a "warrant of habitability" from your landlord. The walls, windows, floors, and ceilings must be safe and in good repair, and the plumbing must work.
- You have the right, if you live in an apartment building, to be provided with certain services, such as heat, hot and cold running water, garbage collection, pest control, and locks and keys that work—unless the lease says you are responsible for such services. If you rent a single-family house or, in some cases, space in a multiple-family house, your lease usually makes you responsible for at least some of these services.
- You have a right to install temporary fixtures, such as pictures, room dividers, shelves, and light fixtures, unless your lease states otherwise. When you move out, you generally have a right to keep such equipment. If you damage the property while taking out your equipment, however, the landlord probably has the right to deduct the cost of repairs from your security deposit. To be sure of where you stand, always insist that your landlord give you a receipt for the security deposit and a statement detailing the conditions under which the deposit will be returned to you.

purposes as making emergency repairs, or to show the apartment to prospective tenants as the term of the lease draws to an end. If Violet's lease contains such a provision, it may also require the landlord to notify her before coming into her apartment. If he doesn't give her adequate notice, Violet can ask a court to order him to abide by the terms of her lease. She might also be able to recover money damages from her landlord for the intrusions.

My previous landlord said I could keep a cat in my apartment. She sold the building, and the new owner says the cat has to go. Does it?

If there is a written provision in your lease allowing you to keep a cat in your apartment, that provision is legally enforceable. But if the agreement with your landlord was merely an oral one, your right to keep your cat is more than likely a privilege that your previous landlord allowed you. That privilege, or "license," was probably revoked at the time of the sale of the apartment building.

Eloise wants to have cable TV installed in her apartment, but her landlord won't let the cable company hook it up. What are Eloise's legal rights?

Eloise will probably have to live without cable television unless her lease specifically says she may have it installed. However, cable television is often regulated by local ordinances; the ordinance in Eloise's community may require her landlord to allow her to have wiring installed for cable television. Eloise should check with her local government office.

The apartment building where I rent is going condo. I don't want to buy. What are my rights?

While every state has laws regarding condominium ownership, your rights are probably spelled out in a city ordinance. Many cities have laws requiring that written advance notice of the developer's plans be given months before you are required to move. You may be permitted to break your lease without penalty if you find another apartment.

Some cities require the condominium developer to compensate tenants of converted buildings for part or all of their relocation expenses or to provide low-income families with monthly rental assistance payments. Because these laws are so local in nature, you should call city hall or your local building inspector or office for citizen information to find out about the laws in effect where you live.

As I was entering the house that I rent, I slipped and fell on the icy front steps and hurt my back. Is my landlord liable?

Probably not. Local law generally places the responsibility for clearing the steps of a rented house upon the tenant; in addition, the landlord may have assigned this duty to you as one of the terms in your lease. However, if your landlord has agreed to keep the steps free of ice, and you can prove that he knew about the icy condition and failed to live up to his agreement, he can be liable for your injuries. You might also have to show, however, that you did not know that the steps were icy.

Wes broke his leg when he tripped over some frayed carpet outside Sid's apartment door. Wes wants Sid to pay his medical bills. Sid thinks the landlord should pay. Who's right?

Sid's landlord has a duty to keep the common areas of the building safe. For Sid's landlord to be liable for Wes's injury, the landlord must have known that the carpet was frayed and that it presented a danger.

A fire started in Brenda's apartment because of faulty wiring. Most of Brenda's belongings were destroyed, and her insurance did not cover all the contents of her apartment. Can she make the landlord pay for the losses not covered by her insurance?

Probably not. Brenda's landlord can only be held liable for the fire if he either caused the faulty wiring or failed to fix it once he knew about it. Unless either of these alternatives can be shown to have been true, most courts would consider the fire an act of God, and Brenda would have to accept the resulting loss.

Buying Your Home

I'm buying a house. At what point should I consult a lawyer?

It's a good idea to have a lawyer involved from start to finish. He can be invaluable in helping you to negotiate the purchase, draft the purchase agreement, perform the title search, and arrange for an appraisal, and can provide advice on financing and represent you at the closing.

Of course, you can complete the purchase of a home without the services of a lawyer, but it may not be in your own best interests to do so. Buying a home is probably the largest investment you will ever make, and you owe it to yourself to obtain expert advice so that you get everything that is due you in the transaction.

Buying Your Home

What's the difference between a binder and a purchase agreement?

Generally, a *binder* is a paper you sign indicating that you have put down a small amount of money to have a house taken off the market because you intend to buy it. The money paid at this time may also be called a binder, a deposit, or earnest money. It differs from the full down payment, which is a percentage of the cost of the house that is payable at the closing. You can withdraw your offer to buy the house if you have signed only this type of binder, but you will probably have to forfeit the deposit.

But be aware of what you sign. Some people in some parts of the country use the term *binder* for purchase agreements. A purchase agreement—also called a sales contract—is an agreement that puts you under a full legal obligation to buy the house and sets the conditions of the sale. It should be reviewed carefully before signing.

If I need an extension of time on my purchase agreement, must I get it in writing?

Yes. Every state requires a contract for the sale of real estate to be in writing; any modifications to such a contract must also be in writing.

The Browns have a growing family and need to buy a larger house, but can't afford to unless they sell their old house first. Can they have a provision put into their sales agreement making the purchase of the new house contingent on the sale of their old one?

Yes, as long as the seller agrees. Since few people can afford the cost of financing and maintaining two homes at once, most buyers insist on including a provision of this type in their offer to purchase a home. Although the seller may resist at first, he will probably agree to the provision in the end or risk not selling his house at all.

Irma and Brian are buying a house. If the house burns down after they sign the purchase agreement but before the closing, who is responsible for the loss?

In some states, such as Indiana, Iowa, and New Jersey, the risk of any loss passes to the buyer once the purchase agreement is signed. In these states, the buyer can and should insure the house when he signs a purchase agreement. Other states, such as New Hampshire and Massachusetts, take the opposite position, holding that the loss falls upon the seller until the closing. In any event, if Irma and Brian's purchase agreement says that the seller will be responsible for the loss, the seller will be responsible no matter what the state law holds. State laws, in such cases, apply only when the terms of the contract are not clear.

How do we make sure that the house we are buying has no outstanding liens or other unpaid surprises hidden somewhere?

Arrange for a title search—a detailed investigation of public records concerning the history of ownership of a piece of real estate. The title search will show whether or not the seller has full title, or rights of ownership, to the property. In effect, it will confirm the seller's right to sell the house and determine the existence of any other claims to it, including outstanding liens or mortgages.

At the end of a title search an abstract of title is prepared, summarizing all sales, transfers, judicial proceedings, recorded liens, and similar transactions involving the property. If something threatens to interfere with your full use of the property or requires payment of bills or taxes, have the current owner resolve these problems before the closing. A bank or other lender will probably require you to have a title search done before approving mortgage financing.

My attorney is concerned about a clear title to the home I'm buying because the current owner recently had some remodeling done. What is he talking about?

In most states, if a contractor has not been paid for work he did on a house, he is given a claim against the house in the form of a lien. This mechanic's lien puts a cloud over the title to the house—in other words, the contractor's claim would cast doubts upon your ownership rights because the contractor could have the house sold to get the money to pay him for his material and labor. To make sure you have a clear title (one that is not subject to a mechanic's lien), your attorney will probably require verification from the current owner that the contractor and his subcontractors have been paid in full.

Lucille is about to buy a house. Should she get title insurance?

It's advisable. Even when a title search—a thorough investigation of a property's history—is conducted, incidental transactions may not show up in the local land record office. Title insurance will provide Lucille with protection against someone's turning up after she buys her home, and claiming to have better title (ownership rights) to the property.

For example, suppose Tom, a 17-year-old whose parents had just died, sold his family house to Rick, and Rick sold it to Lucille. The fact that Tom was a minor at the time he sold the house will not appear in the land records. But because he is a minor, most courts will let him cancel his contract, and so Rick's sale of the house to Lucille would be invalid. This means, in effect, that Tom could demand the house back from Lucille. If Lucille had title insurance the insurance company would refund her money. Otherwise, she would have to sue Rick for a refund and hope he had the money to pay her when she won her case.

Meg and Jerry are newly married and want to buy an old house that they can fix up and move into. They keep seeing ads for houses that have been seized by the government, and the price for these houses is listed as only $1 and up. Should they buy one?

They should be very wary of ads of this type. Although the federal government does sell houses when federally guaranteed mortgages have been foreclosed, they are usually sold at their fair market value. The ads Meg and Jerry saw may require them to pay a fee in order to obtain lists of foreclosed homes for sale by the government. But this information is generally available from local real estate brokers at no cost. In some cities, urban homesteading programs have been established that permit first-time home buyers to purchase a house for a minimal fee, usually $1. These programs then require the buyer to restore the house and occupy it for a specified period of time. To obtain information about these programs, contact your city's housing department.

Should a husband and wife put their home in both names?

For most married couples, it's a good idea. With this type of joint ownership, called tenancy by the entirety, neither the husband nor the wife can sell the house without the other's permission, and when one spouse dies, the ownership of the property is automatically transferred to the surviving partner. Tenancy by the entirety usually results in fewer problems—especially at the time of bereavement—and in lower estate and inheritance taxes for the surviving spouse.

Without this type of deed, if husband or wife died without a will, the property might go to their children, who, if they so chose, could sell the house and force the surviving parent to move out. However, in many states even if one spouse is the sole owner, the surviving spouse may be entitled to at least partial ownership of the house.

Two or more persons who are not husband and wife may also share ownership in a house. This type of joint ownership is called joint tenancy instead of tenancy by the entirety, but it gives the owners all the same benefits and restrictions.

Terms of a Real Estate Sales Contract or Purchase Agreement

The sales contract, or purchase agreement, is the most important document you sign when buying a home. It should include the following:

- ☑ A detailed description of the land and dwelling, including any restrictions or special rights (such as to water or timber).
- ☑ A list of furnishings the seller has agreed to leave, such as draperies, oven, and lawn equipment.
- ☑ The purchase price, method of payment, and any special financial arrangements, including taxes, legal fees, and contingencies if the buyer cannot obtain financing within a specified time period.
- ☑ The amount of the deposit (earnest money), the name and address of the escrow agent, and a statement of who pays for the escrow agent and under what circumstances the deposit can be returned.
- ☑ Requests for satisfactory termite and engineering inspections.
- ☑ Who will pay for repairs if the property fails inspection or is damaged before the closing.
- ☑ Whether title is to be free and clear.
- ☑ The kind of deed to be delivered.
- ☑ Provision for a title search and title insurance to show the extent of your ownership rights (title) to the property and to protect you in case someone claims rights to the property at a later time.
- ☑ Time and place of the closing.
- ☑ Date of occupancy.

When I set out to buy a house, I was bewildered by the variety of deeds available. What are the major differences between these deeds, and which is the best to have?

Basically, there are three major types of deeds: (1) full covenant and warranty; (2) bargain and sale; and (3) quitclaim. From the buyer's point of view, the full covenant and warranty deed is the most desirable. It guarantees the buyer that no one else has a claim to the property and that the buyer can sue the seller if someone later claims part or full ownership, or appears with a lien on the property or a right to use part of it. In some instances a seller may be unable to give this type of deed. While this does not necessarily mean that someone is likely to turn up with a claim on the property, it would be wise to consult an attorney to determine exactly what type of deed the seller is willing and able to give you.

The next safest type is a bargain and sale deed with a covenant against the seller's acts. A deed of this type guarantees that the seller has done nothing that would interfere with the buyer's quiet enjoyment of his property, but the seller cannot be held responsible for anything that may have been done by a previous owner that he knows nothing about.

The least desirable type of deed, the quitclaim deed, gives the buyer only as much right to the property as the seller has. Avoid it if you can.

Warren has the opportunity to buy the house he has always wanted, but the seller says he can only give him a quitclaim deed. Should he take it?

No. A quitclaim deed would give Warren only as much right to the house as the seller had in it. If the seller's title is not valid, Warren can lose the house. If the seller is only half owner, Warren may have to share the house with the co-owner. If the house has liens against it, Warren will have to pay them off or lose the house. In short, Warren would be taking a very great chance in buying the house with a quitclaim deed, and he would find it difficult if not impossible to find financing for such a deal.

What happens at a closing?

The closing is the formal meeting between the buyer and the seller to complete a real estate transaction. At the closing, a financial accounting is made, detailing all of the costs associated with the sale and specifying who will pay for them. All expenses must be accounted for, from the price of the house, through the payment of the electric bill up to the day of the closing, to the fee for filing the deed.

The formal signing of all necessary documents to transfer ownership of the property also takes place at the closing. These documents include a deed, a mortgage or deed of trust, and any others associated with the financing of the sale. In some communities, the buyer and seller and their attorneys meet together; in other communities, each side meets separately with a settlement officer—an employee of the lender or the title company—to complete the transaction.

What do closing costs cover?

Closing costs, also called settlement costs, consist of the expenses over and above the price of your new home; they must be paid before the property can be turned over to you. Depending on your local real estate laws, closing costs may include appraisal and credit report fees, points (a one-time fee paid to the lender), the buyer's attorney's fees, fees for preparation and recording of mortgages and other documents, and reserve funds for insurance and property taxes.

Since 1974 most real estate closings must be conducted in accordance with the federal Real Estate Settlement Procedures Act. Under this law, when you apply for a mortgage, your lender must give you an estimate of closing costs and a copy of *Settlement Costs: A HUD Guide*, a booklet from the Department of Housing and Urban Development. In this way, you will have some idea of the additional money you will need at closing.

Why do I have to prepay interest at my closing?

In some cases, there is a period of time between the settlement or closing date, and the date when your first mortgage payment is due. The interest that is paid at closing covers the time between these two dates.

We're closing on our house next week. Is there anything that could go wrong at this point?

Although the great majority of closings are conducted without any problems, there are various things that could go wrong at or before the settlement. To help things move smoothly, see that all of the necessary papers are prepared correctly, including any documents your lender may require, such as policies for title insurance and property insurance.

A few days before the scheduled date, call the person who will handle the closing to find out if all is in order. If you are represented by an attorney, have him review all the documents a few days ahead of time. On the day of the closing, inspect the premises to make sure that everything is as it should be. Check that the seller has left the furnishings he agreed to leave and that he has completed the repairs he agreed to make.

What can I do if the seller does not turn the property over to me at the closing of a real estate deal?

First, determine why the seller won't turn the property over. If you have met all of the conditions specified in your purchase agreement, there should be no reason for him to renege on his agreement. If he refuses to complete the sale, you will have to take him to court. You may be entitled to damages for expenses incurred in connection with the purchase, in addition to the return of your deposit. Situations of this type are extremely rare, but they do happen.

Emily and Daniel are thinking of buying a condo. What are the major differences between owning a condo and owning a house?

A condominium is a special form of ownership. Not only do you own your own apartment, or unit, but you—together with the other condominium owners—also own a portion of the land and certain common areas of the building. These common elements generally include lobbies, hallways, laundry rooms, stairways, elevators, the exterior of the building, sidewalks, parking areas, and the other open spaces.

While you are solely responsible for the upkeep of your own unit, you are jointly responsible with the other owners for the upkeep of the common elements. All the owners of the individual units form an association, which elects officers and a board of directors. The association either manages the land and common areas directly or hires professional managers to do so. Condo owners pay a monthly assessment, or maintenance fee, to cover the running and upkeep of the complex.

We have found a condo we like very much with a monthly assessment fee that is at least 25 percent less than comparable units we have seen. Is this too good to be true?

It may be. If the monthly assessment is not high enough to cover all the expenses of the condominium complex, you will probably be faced with unanticipated bills after you move in. While the assessment fee varies from complex to complex, it should be enough to cover all the expenses, including taxes, maintenance and upkeep of the common areas, salaries of employees, and insurance. It should also be large enough to include a reserve fund for major repairs and the replacement of such structural elements as the roof or central heating and air conditioning. Generally, the more common elements, such as elevators and swimming pools, there are to maintain, the higher the monthly assessment will be.

Our condo association voted to install a swimming pool. I can't afford to pay my share, which is $2,000. Can they evict me?

You cannot be evicted from your condominium, but the condominium association could get a lien against your property, requiring you to pay the $2,000 pool assessment before you could sell your unit, or it could start foreclosure proceedings against you, which could have the same end result as an eviction. In either case, you could stop the process only by paying the assessment.

Is a cooperative apartment a greater risk than a condominium?

Yes. Each cooperative owner shares in the payment of the mortgage of the entire complex. If one or more owners default on the payments, the remaining owners must make up the difference. A condominium owner is responsible only for the mortgage on his own unit.

Reggie and Myrna want to buy a lot in a community they like and put a mobile home on it when they retire. Are there special laws or regulations governing mobile home lots?

Yes. Virtually every community in the country has zoning regulations and restrictions dealing with mobile home lots. Typically, these regulations provide for minimum lot sizes, adequate sewage treatment and sanitation facilities, minimum health and safety standards, and requirements for tying down the units. Some areas prohibit mobile homes. Because regulations vary widely from one community to the next, Reggie and Myrna should check with their local zoning board to determine exactly what regulations and restrictions apply in that community.

Questions to Ask When Buying a Condo

Before signing a contract to purchase a condominium, read the following documents thoroughly: the prospectus, also called the offering plan; the bylaws; the operating budget; an engineer's report; and the management agreement. Although the following questions will help uncover potential pitfalls, you should have all the documents reviewed by an attorney to make sure you are fully protected.

- ☑ Who holds the major interest in the building or complex—the developer or the residents?
- ☑ What is the developer's reputation? Does the Better Business Bureau have any information about him?
- ☑ Does the developer have sufficient funds to complete the project without your down payment?
- ☑ Are the residents in other condos built by this developer satisfied?
- ☑ Who owns the land underneath the buildings and the air rights above them? Who owns the parking and recreational facilities?
- ☑ Can you inspect the actual unit or location where you'll be living?
- ☑ Does there seem to be a high turnover rate of owners?
- ☑ Has the value of the units increased or decreased? (To check this and the turnover rate, ask local realtors or call the nearest municipal or county offices and ask where you can see title transfer records.)
- ☑ How is the monthly assessment computed? (A percentage of occupied units is more expensive than a percentage of total units.) Is the assessment reasonable for the services it covers? (If it's too low, you may be faced with a drastic increase after you move in.)
- ☑ Is the development's reserve fund adequate to cover major repairs?
- ☑ How is the reserve fund financed?
- ☑ Can young children in your family visit or stay over?
- ☑ Will you be allowed to keep pets or plant flowers or bushes?
- ☑ Can you rent or sell your unit without special restrictions or the association's approval?

Buying Your Home

What papers are required by law to be delivered along with a new mobile home?

You should receive a certificate from the manufacturer declaring that your mobile home complies with the standards set by the National Mobile Home Construction and Safety Standards Act of 1974. Generally, these are minimum standards for plumbing, heating, electrical work, fire safety, and the like. You should also be provided with a bill of sale for the mobile home, copies of the manufacturers' warranties, and any documents dealing with the financing of your mobile home.

Where should I keep the deed to my land?

The best place to keep your deed is in your safe-deposit box.

Buyer Beware

When buying a house, how can I make sure that the seller will leave me the refrigerator, stove, and drapes as promised?

See to it that the purchase agreement includes a list of the furnishings that are to be left by the seller. Make the list as specific and thorough as possible. Using a cover-all term like *furnishings* is not good enough, because what you consider furnishings may be quite different from what the seller does. Some sellers have been known to go so far as to remove built-in dishwashers, ovens, light fixtures, and other items that would normally be considered part of the house. To make sure this doesn't happen to you, inspect the premises just before the closing to be sure that the agreed-upon furnishings have been left in the home.

The Brewsters bought a home six months ago. Everything seemed OK until they received a notice of a lien on the property from a plumber who is threatening to sue them for his unpaid bill. What can the Brewsters do, since they didn't agree to pay for his work?

Generally, once the purchase of a home is completed, the buyer is responsible for any outstanding bills or taxes. If the Brewsters were given a full covenant and warranty deed, they can sue the seller for the amount of the lien. If they have title insurance, they can file a claim with their insurance company for payment. Otherwise, their only recourse is to pay the bill themselves.

The Thompsons have discovered that the roof of their new house leaks. Can they sue the broker who assured them that it didn't?

Yes, but only if they can prove that the real estate broker intentionally misrepresented the condition of the roof. The broker may claim that his comments about the roof were merely overstatements, or puffing. Most courts would not hold him responsible if he could show that he had no prior knowledge of the leak. If the Thompsons won their suit, however, the court would award them money to compensate for the leak and might let them cancel the contract of sale. It is best to avoid such problems by having an engineer inspect the house before you sign the purchase agreement.

When Nick agreed to buy Colin's property, the purchase agreement they signed included some warranties by Colin about the condition of the house. When the deed was drafted, these warranties were not included. If problems arise later, will Nick be able to force Colin to honor the warranties?

No. Once the buyer and seller sign the deed, the purchase agreement is no longer in effect. The provisions in the deed take over.

The seller has assured me that the house I want to buy doesn't have termites. Should I take his word on the subject?

No. Even if the seller is the most honest person alive, he may be mistaken. To be sure, insist on a mechanical and structural inspection. Your purchase agreement should specify that if the inspection shows a major flaw, the seller will fix it or the buyer can back out of the deal and have his deposit refunded. A thorough inspection should cover the basement, plumbing, hot water heater, electrical system, heating and cooling system, and foundation. Some states have laws that require a termite inspection, but even if your state doesn't, insist on one anyway.

My condominium complex has been occupied for a year, and the landscaping still hasn't been finished. What remedy do I have?

In a condominium development, there is usually a condominium association, led by a board of directors. Your first step should be to contact the board to find out when the landscaping work is to be completed. If the work will not be finished in the time period that was promised, and if you can show that the value of your unit has diminished as a result, you can sue the developer. In some cases, however, the association itself might be responsible for completing the landscaping, in which case you would in effect be suing yourself, since you are a member of the association.

Building a New Home

Gladys bought a lot—primarily because of its trees—and gave her contractor specific instructions to save them so that they would shade the house when it was built. She was shocked when she discovered that the lot had been leveled. What can she do?

Because she gave specific instructions to the contractor to save the trees, Gladys can sue him. The amount of the damages would not be based on Gladys's feelings about the trees, however, but on the dollar amount by which the value of the property is judged to have decreased because the trees were cut down. If the court decides that the value is significantly decreased, Gladys may be able to cancel her agreement with the contractor.

Who is responsible for making sure our house will comply with local zoning restrictions?

The primary responsibility rests with you, your architect, and your building contractor. Zoning restrictions are designed to protect property values in a given area. Before you begin construction, check with your zoning office to make sure that your plans comply with local regulations.

Buying an Undeveloped Lot

Many of us dream about buying a piece of land where we can build a permanent home, a vacation house, or a retirement retreat. The sale of undeveloped lots is a multi–billion dollar business, and unfortunately it has attracted a few unscrupulous operators who may try to sell you practically worthless land at hugely inflated prices. There are federal and state laws against such shady practices, but the wheeler-dealers are experts at staying just inside the law. Your best protection is to be very alert and very cautious when you read or hear about what seems to be an incredible, once-in-a-lifetime opportunity to buy a dream property.

Jokes abound about people who have bought, sight unseen, a lot described as an earthly paradise and later found it was in a swamp or desert, or on a cliffside or mountaintop. Unfortunately, many of these stories are true, so never buy property you haven't seen. Ideally, you should see it at all seasons of the year, wet and dry, hot and cold. If you don't know about the area's weather extremes, ask the local residents. Once you have seen the place, if you still want it, there are a number of additional questions to consider:

- How does the price compare to that of similar lots in the area?
- What financing arrangements are offered, and how do they rate against others available in the area?

How can I be sure that the contractor is following the plans we agreed on and obeying all the local building codes?

In most communities, the local building department requires contractors to submit plans and specifications for new houses before construction begins. While construction is under way, the building department makes periodic inspections, and when it is completed, the building inspector issues a certificate of occupancy, which states that the house conforms to the local building code.

To be on the safe side, make sure that your agreement with the contractor includes a clause that permits you to withhold some of your payment until a certificate of occupancy is issued. It is easier to get a contractor to cooperate if he has not been paid in full.

Gene's contractor did not conform to the local building code when he wired the house. What should Gene do?

Contact the office that grants building permits. Once this office finds the wiring unsatisfactory, they will order the contractor to correct the situation. If he does not, Gene can have the work done by another contractor and then seek reimbursement from the first contractor.

- Is the lot you saw the one you are actually going to get?
- Will the seller or developer give you a chance to read sample copies of the contract and other legal papers you will be expected to sign *before* you make the decision to buy?
- Will the seller give you a property report, which is a statement of pertinent information about the lot, to study before you sign anything? (In some situations the seller is breaking a federal law if he doesn't give you this document; but even when the seller isn't required to let you have a property report, you can get the basic information you need by asking the rest of the questions in this list.)
- Where are the nearest communities? Are there paved roads?
- Are there mortgages or liens on the property?
- If you make a deposit, will your money be put in escrow until you close on the property?
- If recreational or other common facilities are promised, where are they and when and how can they be used?
- Are the water supply and sewer systems operating?
- What are the projected utility services and charges?
- What percentage of the planned homes in the development are currently built? Currently occupied?
- Have you seen a report of the site's soil and foundation conditions?
- What title (ownership rights) will you get to the site, and when will you receive it?

Building a New Home

The contractor has promised to finish painting the interior of my house after the closing. How can I protect myself?

Have your attorney draft an agreement between you and the contractor that specifies exactly when the painting will be completed. At the closing, sign the agreement and have the contractor sign it. The money for the painting can be placed in escrow until the contractor completes the project. If he doesn't finish the job within the agreed time, you can use the escrow money to have the work done by someone else.

When Justine had her house built, she specified that her contractor was to use a certain brand of ceiling tile, but he used a cheaper brand that looks the same on the surface. Does Justine still have to pay him the full price?

No. As long as Justine specified the brand and quality of tile to be used, her contractor is required to refund the difference in price. Depending on the local laws, Justine might also be able to have the tile replaced with the brand that she originally specified. Her contractor might be required to do the work at no additional cost, or he might be required to pay another contractor to complete the work to her satisfaction.

We are having problems with our newly built house. The windows leak, the floors sag, and there's a crack in the foundation. Isn't the contractor responsible for making the necessary repairs?

Probably. Nearly every contractor who builds new houses provides warranties for materials and workmanship. In most cases, these warranties apply for up to a year after the house is completed. In some areas, you may be able to purchase an extended warranty for an additional cost.

Financing a New Home

For homeowner's insurance, see "Insuring Your Home" in Chapter 8, *Insurance.*

Sal is about to marry his childhood sweetheart, and he is buying a new house for them to live in. But he can only make a 5 percent down payment. The bank told him that because his down payment is so small, he must buy MGIC insurance. What is this?

MGIC refers to the Mortgage Guaranty Insurance Corporation, one of the nation's largest private insurers of home loans. A lender may require a buyer to be covered by this type of insurance if he is only making a very small down payment on the home being purchased. Since the lender is at greater risk if the buyer defaults on the loan, this insurance protects some or all of the lender's money.

Generally, private mortgage insurance will cost about 1 percent of the mortgage, paid at the time of closing, plus an additional annual premium equal to about 0.3 percent of the mortgage. In most cases, this insurance can be dropped after the borrower establishes a good payment record and builds more substantial equity in his home.

Albert and Cora have a mortgage at 9 percent interest. They are selling their house, and they want to transfer the mortgage directly to the buyers. Can the bank raise the interest rate?

Yes. Unless the mortgage contract states that the mortgage can be passed on to subsequent buyers at 9 percent, the bank can raise the interest rate to the level prevailing at the time of the sale.

Jon wants to sell his house to Elliot and have him assume the mortgage. When Elliot read over Jon's mortgage, he noticed a due-on-sale clause. Will this have any effect on their agreement?

Yes. A due-on-sale clause requires the homeowner to pay the balance of the mortgage upon selling the house, thus preventing a buyer from assuming the loan. Jon and Elliot can ask the bank to modify the mortgage agreement, but it is not required to do so.

Our buyer would like us to finance part of the purchase price. Should we do this?

While there is nothing wrong with becoming a lender, there are risks involved. The major risk is that the buyer will not be able to make his payments to you. This becomes even more serious when a bank holds a first mortgage on the property. If the buyer defaults, the bank would be paid first. In some cases, there might not be enough money left to pay you.

There is a further disadvantage to this type of transaction. Instead of getting a lump sum of cash at the time of the closing, you will be receiving small portions of this money over a long period of time. To a certain extent, you can compensate for this by charging the buyer interest. But if interest rates rise over the course of the loan, you will lose any extra income you might have earned had you been able to invest the lump sum at the higher rate. Financing part of the purchase price may still be worthwhile, however, if it makes the sale more attractive to potential buyers and if you can realize a higher purchase price on your home.

Financing a New Home

Two years ago Maurice sold his house to the Morgans, who assumed his mortgage. The Morgans ran into some financial problems and couldn't make the payments. Now the bank that holds the mortgage says Maurice is responsible for making the payments. Can this be true?

It depends on what the deed says. If it clearly states that the buyers "assume the seller's mortgage," the Morgans are fully responsible, and there is no liability on Maurice's part. On the other hand, if the deed says that the Morgans bought the home "subject to the mortgage," Maurice will probably be liable for making the payments. If he refuses to make them and the house is sold at foreclosure, he may be liable to the bank for any shortfall that arises from the sale. For example, say that the house was valued at $90,000 at the time of the sale and the Morgans bought it subject to Maurice's mortgage of $70,000. After making only $2,000 in payments

Types of Mortgages

When you buy a new home you will probably pay for most of it with a mortgage loan—money lent to you against the value of your home by a bank or other financial institution. The lender will put up the money to pay for the house (less the down payment you make at the closing), and you will get the deed to the property. In return, you will sign a loan (mortgage) agreement that says you will give up your home to the lender if you default on paying back the loan. This means that the lender can sell the house to get the money you owe him. Following are the types of mortgages you can choose from:

- *Conventional mortgage*—The buyer pays the lender back in equal monthly installments, including interest at a fixed rate.
- *Purchase money mortgage*—A conventional mortgage in which the seller, rather than a bank or other financial institution, is the lender.
- *FHA mortgage*—The mortgage is insured in whole or in part by the Federal Housing Administration. Should the buyer default, the lender is protected against losing his money. FHA-backed mortgages have low interest rates and are available to anyone who has a good credit record and can afford a relatively low down payment.
- *VA mortgage*—Much like the FHA mortgage, the Veterans' Administration mortgage guarantees payment if the buyer defaults, but it is available only to eligible veterans of the U.S. armed forces.
- *Variable-rate mortgage*—The lender can raise or lower the interest rate in response to changes in money market rates and the demand for mortgage loans. Typically, the adjustment is made annually; but it can be

against the principal, the Morgans defaulted, and the bank foreclosed. If the house has depreciated in value over the two years the Morgans had it, and it sells for only $62,000, Maurice will have to make up the $6,000 difference. This is an extremely complicated area of real estate law; Maurice should contact an attorney immediately.

When I bought my house, I used financing that requires small monthly payments for five years and then a single large balloon payment at the end. The balloon payment is coming up in a few months, and I won't be able to pay it. What can I do?

Try to arrange new financing for this mortgage right away. Under the terms of a balloon mortgage, if you are unable to refinance the loan or make the final payment on time, the lender can foreclose. If you have a good payment record, you may be able to have your lender refinance the loan himself or grant an extension until you can arrange a new mortgage.

made after a shorter or longer period. In most cases, a variable-rate mortgage specifies both the minimum and the maximum interest rate that can be charged and the amount the mortgage payment can increase in a given year.

- *Graduated-payment mortgage*—The buyer's monthly payment gradually increases over a number of years according to an agreed-upon schedule. Usually, payments rise annually over a period of three to five years, and then level off. This type of loan is often attractive to people who expect to have higher incomes after a few years.
- *Balloon mortgage*—The buyer's monthly payment consists almost entirely of interest, with only a small fraction being repayment (amortization) of the actual amount borrowed (principal). These payments are made over a specified number of years, and then a single large payment, or balloon payment, is made to pay off the loan. Over the life of this kind of loan, interest is higher than on conventional mortgages because the principal remains high. Generally when the balloon payment comes due, the buyer can refinance the loan in order to get the money to pay it.
- *Installment contract*—As in a purchase money mortgage, the buyer makes payments to the seller, but the seller need not deliver the deed until the last payment is made. In theory, missing one payment on an installment contract permits the seller to declare the buyer in default and repossess the house. In practice, however, many courts treat an installment contract in much the same way as a conventional mortgage. The seller must begin foreclosure proceedings, and the buyer can redeem the property at any time during the proceedings.

Financing a New Home

Is it more difficult to get a mortgage for a condominium when the majority of the units are occupied by renters?

In some cases. Mortgage lenders are very much interested in the amount of risk they take when making a loan. They want to be sure that the real estate involved will maintain or increase its value, and renters generally do not take care of property as well as property owners.

The Crawfords have a mortgage on their home. Can they rent the house without permission from the mortgage holder?

Many mortgage contracts require the buyer to obtain the permission of the mortgage holder before renting the property. The Crawfords should check the mortgage contract to see if such a provision is included.

I cosigned a loan when my father bought his house. If I declare bankruptcy, will my father lose his house?

No. If you are just a cosigner and not part owner of your father's home, your bankruptcy petition will not affect your father's ownership. As long as your father makes his payments, the lender has no right to foreclose.

Home Improvements and Repairs

What kind of home improvements usually require a permit?

Improvements that involve major structural work, such as adding a room to a house, require building permits. Many communities also require permits for projects that involve electrical or plumbing work, such as converting a walk-in closet into a half-bathroom. If a contractor does the work, have him obtain the necessary permits. If you do the work yourself, get the permits from your local building inspector or housing code office.

When I put a new roof on my house, I carefully followed the city building codes. Today some homeowners' association I've never heard of wrote to me saying I have to use different, more expensive material. Who are they? Can they force me to replace my new roof?

Restrictions on building materials and even architectural styles for residential structures are not always limited to those of the city's building code. In residential subdivisions and planned communities especially, many deeds contain building restrictions that require uniformity with neighboring architectural styles in order to protect the property or the value of the property of neighboring landowners. These restrictions are generally overseen by homeowners' associations that operate within the area. Even if you didn't know about the homeowners' association or its restrictions, a court may say that it was your obligation to be diligent in discovering such restrictions.

How much responsibility do I have if workers are injured while remodeling my house?

If the workers are employees of a contractor, the basic responsibility falls on the contractor. Most states require licensed contractors to have workers' compensation insurance to cover such situations. If you are directing the remodeling yourself, however, you may be personally liable for any injuries suffered by workers. Before beginning a project that you will supervise yourself, check with your insurance agent to determine the amount and type of liability insurance you should have.

Arthur talked to two contractors about remodeling his house. One of them said that he is bonded. What does this mean?

It means that he has bought surety bonds that operate as a kind of liability insurance. These bonds provide payment for any loss or damage that may result from the contractor's work. For example, if the bonded contractor fails to complete the project in accordance with the terms of Arthur's contract, Arthur can seek payment from the bonding company for any additional costs he incurs. Many states require contractors to obtain bonding in order to be licensed, and set the amount of the bonding they must have.

I hired a contractor to add an attached garage to my house and gave him $2,000 as a down payment for the job. He worked for one day and then did not return. It's been three months now. What can I do?

Notify the contractor in writing that unless the garage is completed by a certain date, you will cancel your contract and hire someone else to finish the job. If the original contractor has not actually completed $2,000 worth of work, you can sue him for the amount you overpaid. In addition, the original contractor may also be liable for damages you suffered by his not completing the work he agreed to do. You may also be able to collect the amount you must pay a new contractor over the price you agreed to pay the first one.

Home Improvements and Repairs

Sue hired George to add a family room to her house. George had several subcontractors help him. When the job was finished, George gave Sue a bill. Should she pay it in full?

Before she does she should check to see if George has fully paid all his subcontractors and suppliers. If he fails to do so, they may be able to obtain mechanics' liens, forcing Sue to pay them or lose her house. In effect, Sue would be paying twice for the same work. To avoid this predicament, Sue should ask the subcontractors to sign releases waiving their rights to mechanics' liens. This is a fairly common practice in the construction industry, and they should be willing to do so.

Earl had his basement paved a few months ago, and it is already cracking. Can he force the pavers to redo the work?

If he has a written contract with the pavers, the terms of that agreement will apply. Most reputable contractors provide some warranty of their materials and workmanship. If Earl has no written contract, however, the situation may be somewhat different. Ordinarily a new cement floor should not crack after a few months, but there may be some defenses that the contractor could raise concerning the quality of his work. The variables of weather and the condition of the basement floor at the time it was paved might have made it impossible to do a better job. Without a written warranty, a court would have to decide whether or not the contractor had performed in a reasonable manner.

Priscilla's house did not turn out the way the interior decorator said it would. Does she have any legal recourse?

It all depends upon the contract Priscilla had with the decorator. If the decorator agreed to decorate the house to Priscilla's satisfaction, and she was not satisfied, she would have the right to sue him no matter how much her tastes differed from his own. However, if there was no agreement that the decorator would specifically satisfy her tastes and he did everything he promised up to a reasonably professional standard, Priscilla has no legal right to complain.

We've heard many stories about escalating contractors' bills. Won't a written agreement prevent this from happening to us?

Generally, a written agreement can do whatever it was intended to do, including limiting escalating building costs. However, if you're having a

How to Hire a Contractor

If you decide you want to remodel part of your house, or add a room or even a wing, you will probably hire a contractor to do the job. Naturally you want to avoid any legal headaches that may arise from having the contractor and his workers in your house—and you want the work done expertly. Getting the right contractor is a matter of asking the right questions. Here are the basic ones:

- ☑ Is the contractor licensed by the city or county?
- ☑ Does the Better Business Bureau have a record of any legitimate complaints against the contractor?
- ☑ Will the contractor give you the names and addresses of satisfied customers you can contact?
- ☑ Does the contractor have a street address or just a post office box number, which may make it hard for you to find him if needed?
- ☑ How long has the contractor been in business?
- ☑ Will the contractor show you copies of his insurance policies, including workers' compensation and liability insurance? Is the coverage adequate?
- ☑ Has the contractor obtained a surety bond, requiring a bonding company to fulfill all the contractor's obligations if he fails to do so?
- ☑ Will the contractor obtain necessary permits and give you copies?
- ☑ Will the contractor guarantee materials and workmanship?
- ☑ Will the contractor request your written approval before making changes or substitutions in materials and workmanship?
- ☑ If he is late in completing the work, will the contractor pay a penalty until the job is done?

house built, make sure that you understand the terms of the contract and make sure that the agreement says what you want it to say. Usually the advice of an attorney is necessary.

Contractors typically use what is known as a cost-plus provision, which allows them to pass increases in construction costs on to the owner. These provisions are legal and allow the contractor to charge extra for increases in the costs of materials and supplies, wages of the workmen, salaries of supervisors, accident and indemnity insurance, and anything else needed, but perhaps unanticipated, for the job. Contractors also charge for changes that you request in the original plans, and so it is wise to discuss the extra costs of any changes you may want before telling the contractor to proceed with them.

Usually, if the cost-plus term exists in the contract, you are bound to pay these charges. On the other hand, courts have not usually allowed contractors to bill their cost-plus customers for increases in office expenses or for redoing work that was not done properly the first time.

Home Improvements and Repairs

I hired a painter to paint my living room for $400. When he finished, he demanded an additional $200. He claimed that the $400 was for the walls alone, and that when I told him to paint the doors and windows, that changed the price, even though he'd said nothing about a change in price at the time. Do I owe him the additional $200?

It depends on the terms of your original agreement with the painter. If you agreed to pay him $400 for painting the walls of your living room, that is all he was required to do to satisfy his part of the contract. If you then asked him to do additional work, he is entitled to compensation for the extra work and materials. If, however, your agreement stated that the painter would paint "your living room" for $400, you may not have to pay the extra $200, since a court would probably rule that it was reasonable to assume that doors and windows would be included in the job, or that the terms of the painting trade would include doors and windows in the phrase "living room."

Connie's house painter accidentally broke her favorite lamp. Can she rightfully deduct the cost of the lamp from his fee?

Not unless the painter agrees to it, or the terms of their agreement permit it. Otherwise, most courts would require Connie to pay the house painter in full and file a separate claim with the painter's insurance company for the damage to her lamp. If the painter has no insurance and refuses to pay for the damage, Connie can sue him in small claims court.

Rex and Regina hired a tree trimmer to trim a number of the shrubs around their house. When they came home, they found that all their bushes had been destroyed by excessive trimming. Can they make the trimmer pay for new bushes?

Yes. If the tree trimmer disregarded their specific instructions, Rex and Regina are entitled to collect damages. The court would probably order the trimmer to pay for replacing the bushes he destroyed.

I want to plant a tree outside the front door of my condominium. Do I need permission?

If the spot where you want to plant the tree is part of a common area, you will need permission from the condominium association. Check your condo's regulations and covenants to determine how to obtain approval.

You and Your Neighbors

For information on neighbors who borrow, see "Borrowing and Lending" in Chapter 5, *Your Personal Property*. For information on intrusive neighbors, see "Your Right to Privacy" in Chapter 12, *Your Individual Rights*.

What can I do if my neighbors blast their stereo at 2 A.M.?

Your first step should be to contact the neighbors personally and ask them to turn down the stereo. If this proves unsuccessful and the noisemakers are tenants in an apartment building or house, your next step is to bring the noise to the attention of your landlord. You have a legal right to the quiet enjoyment of your home, and your landlord has a legal obligation to see to it that this right is not disturbed by other tenants. Finally, if the noise continues unabated, you can call the police, whether you rent your home or own it. Unreasonable noise at an early hour of the morning is a breach of the peace and is against the law. A visit from a uniformed police officer usually puts an end to this kind of problem.

My neighbor's tree has grown so much that one of the branches hangs over my roof. Can I cut the limb off at the property line?

Although the tree branch is technically trespassing on your property, it may not be in your best interest to cut it off yourself. If you cut the branch improperly, destroy the tree, or in any way cause damage to your neighbor's property, you could be held liable. If your neighbor will not arrange to have the offending branch removed, you can go to court and sue him for trespassing.

Larry bought his house because it commanded a clear, sweeping view of the river. Now his next-door neighbor has put up a fence that blocks his view. Can Larry force him to take down the fence?

Probably not. Larry is asking for an easement—a right to limit someone's use of his property in some way. In most parts of the United States, easements cannot be granted for light, air, or view without some written agreement. If Larry doesn't have such an agreement, he will have to live with his neighbor's fence.

Archie has painted his house orange, and his neighbor Elvira thinks this lowers the value of her house. Can she force Archie to repaint his house?

Not unless Archie's deed restricts the colors he may paint his home or grants a right of approval to a homeowners' association. Esthetic values differ from individual to individual, and courts are reluctant to make decisions on the basis of personal tastes. If Elvira can prove that the value of her property has been diminished by the way Archie has painted his home, she may be able to recover for the lost value of her property. But any damage she suffers must be substantial and beyond speculation. In other words, it is not enough that she thinks her neighbor's orange house has reduced her property's value; she must also be able to prove it.

My neighbor had his driveway repaved, and now the rain runs into my basement. He says he is not responsible for the damage. If he's not, who is?

No matter what your neighbor says, he is probably responsible for the damage to your basement. Legally, any use by your neighbor of his property that interferes with your right to enjoy your property is called a nuisance. If you can prove that the water leaking into your basement is caused by the way your neighbor repaved his driveway, you should be able to recover for the damages you have suffered.

Tom has lived at his present address for 10 years. The land next door was purchased by Jack, who began to build a house. After the basement had been dug and actual construction had begun, Tom's basement walls settled and cracked. Tom wants Jack to pay for needed repairs to his home. Is Jack liable?

He may be if Tom can show that the settling and cracking in his basement were caused by construction activity on Jack's property. This may not be an easy matter to prove, since foundation settling can occur for a number of reasons. An engineering report may be needed to determine the cause of the damage. If the construction work is the likely cause of the settling, Jack may go to court and seek restitution from his contractor for any damages he must pay to Tom.

Gary just bought a tract of land alongside a country road. One of his neighbors drives over the tract every day to get to the road. She says that it is the only way she can get to her house. Can Gary make her pay a fee every time she drives over his land?

No. Because the neighbor has no other way in which to reach her property, she has a right to cross Gary's property. This is called an easement by necessity. Even though there may be no written agreement that allows Gary's neighbor to cross his property, a court would be unlikely to permit him to charge her a fee. If Gary can show that his neighbor has some other way to get to her house, he can seek a court order prohibiting her from driving across his land.

Pierce owns a house on a lake. Can the other property owners on the lake keep him from sailing his boat over the entire lake?

Probably. If the lake is owned as a common area by all of the property owners, there is probably an association that regulates access to and use of the lake. When Pierce purchased his lakefront home, he most likely agreed to abide by these regulations. Pierce should check his deed for any restrictions regarding lake use. If the lake is publicly owned, state and local laws may restrict his ability to sail across the lake. Such laws are often enacted to protect wildlife areas, provide undisturbed fishing spots, and limit noise and pollution.

What can I do about a neighbor who is gossiping about me?

Not very much, unless your neighbor's gossip has damaged you in some way that a court could measure. For example, if you lost your job or were denied credit because of your neighbor's gossip, you could sue your neighbor for slander. In a number of states, if your neighbor accused you of a serious crime or of having a disease that is held in "some special repugnance" by the general public, such as a venereal disease or AIDS, you could also bring suit. But slander is hard to prove, and any financial loss may be even harder to connect to your neighbor's gossip. Additionally, you would probably have to prove that your neighbor was the original source of the gossip about you.

Homeowners' Problems

For information on household accidents, see "Inside Your Home" and "Outside Your Home" in Chapter 13, *Accidents.*

Does a homeowner need a permit to rent out a spare room?

In many places, yes, and these places may demand that certain health and safety requirements be met before issuing the permit or license. For example, the homeowner may have to provide the boarder with a separate entrance or bath.

Even if his area has no licensing requirement, a homeowner should check with his local zoning authority before advertising for a boarder. Many cities and towns have ordinances that require all those living in a single-family home to be related to one another.

Homeowners' Problems

Jason is thinking of using part of his home as an office. What steps should he take before doing so?

First, he should decide what percentage of the space in his house he will use as an office and check with his local zoning authority to make sure that he would not be violating a zoning regulation. For example, he should find out if the type of work he plans to do is permitted in his neighborhood, if he will be permitted to display the signs or advertising he wishes, and if there will be enough parking space for his customers or clients.

Second, Jason should discuss the matter with his accountant. Using his home as an office may provide a tax deduction. His accountant can let him know the extent of his tax savings.

Finally, he should contact his insurance company to make sure that he is covered for liability. In the event of an accident or injury to a visiting customer or client he should be covered.

Does Aunt Sophie have to buy workers' compensation insurance to cover the houseman who cleans her house once a week?

Probably not. Workers' compensation insurance is governed by state laws that limit the numbers and types of employees who are covered. Generally, household and domestic workers are excluded from workers' compensation coverage. An employer must have a minimum number of employees before he is required to provide coverage. Furthermore, if Aunt Sophie employs her houseman through an agency, the agency will be responsible for providing workers' compensation insurance, if required. However, Aunt Sophie, like anyone else, should have liability insurance in the event that someone is hurt while in her house, whether she owns the house or rents it and whether she has anyone working for her in the house or not.

Am I responsible for shoveling snow off the sidewalk in front of my house and keeping it clean?

Yes. Even though the sidewalk may belong to the city, the law makes you responsible for keeping it free of ice, snow, and debris. Failing to shovel a snow-covered sidewalk within a reasonable time after the snowfall stops may make you liable for injuries suffered by passersby.

Jed planted a beautiful maple tree in his backyard. Over the years, the tree flourished, and Jed loved to sit in its shade. Then one day Jed came home to discover his tree being cut down by a

crew of workers from the power company. When Jed protested, the crew foreman just shrugged and said the tree was getting tangled in the overhead lines. Can Jed sue the power company for cutting down his tree?

Probably not. Most modern deeds give utility companies the use of private property for installing, maintaining, and repairing their lines and equipment. If Jed planted the tree where it would interfere with the lines, the power company was justified in cutting it down.

The city has announced plans to put sidewalks across the lots on Laura's block. Who has to pay for the paving?

In most cities, the owners of the property adjoining the new sidewalks have to pay. The justification is that since the owners receive a direct benefit from the improvement, they should pay the cost. Laura's local property tax authority will issue a special assessment, requiring her to pay for her share of the sidewalks. She and her neighbors may be able to challenge the city's decision to install sidewalks if they can show that the sidewalks are unnecessary. If the sidewalks would benefit the entire community and not just Laura's neighborhood, she and her neighbors could demand that the sidewalks be paid for with money from the property tax fund.

When the city widens the street in front of my house, can I make them replant the hedge and move the fence?

No. When the city uses its power of eminent domain to take part of your land, it must compensate you for its fair value, including the cost of improvements such as fences and hedges. Because you are paid for the loss of these items, you bear the responsibility for replacing them yourself. Of course, if the street was widened without the necessity of taking any of your property, the city has no obligation to you at all.

When the Johnsons bought their house, the developer showed them a map that indicated that the whole area was reserved for single-family homes. Now the developer is planning to build a shopping center across the street from the Johnsons' house. Can the Johnsons keep the shopping center from being built?

Yes, if they can show that a common development plan existed that prohibited the use of this area for anything other than single-family homes. In many states, the Johnsons would be required to show that the deed they received from the developer restricted the lots in question to single-family homes. A promise of this type is called a covenant and is enforceable by any of the owners in the development. But even without such a covenant in the deed, the court might decide that the absence of the shopping center from the maps that were given to prospective buyers is enough reason to restrict the developer's right to build one.

The county has recently announced plans to convert an old school in my neighborhood into a halfway house for drug addicts, many of whom have prison records. Can I stop the county from doing so?

Courts will generally permit a property to be used in any lawful and reasonable way until it becomes clear that an actual threat to the safety, health, and welfare of the community exists. Because a halfway house for hardened drug addicts can cause apprehension and fear in a neighborhood, property values might decline if one is opened. Whether or not this will be enough to prevent the opening of the halfway house is open to question, since courts have ruled that fear about declining property values is not enough to justify their interference in the way neighboring property is to be used. Once the halfway house is opened and damages can be proved, however, the court might order the facility closed.

How do I contest an increase in property taxes?

By appearing before a board of review to explain why you think the new tax rate is unfair or illegal. The most common reason for objecting to a tax increase is that it is disproportionate to the tax assessed on similar homes in your area, or that your home is being assessed at more than its actual value. If the board of review refuses to reduce the tax increase, you can appeal the decision in court.

When Hank bought his land, the neighborhood was very rural and quiet. Now some of his neighbors are operating a saw mill. The noise is horrible, and Hank's property has become less valuable because of it. What can he do to remedy the situation?

First, he should check the current zoning ordinances, and if they do not permit his neighbors to operate this kind of business, he should notify the local zoning authorities. If the zoning ordinances are not being violated, he should seek a court order prohibiting or limiting the noise at the mill on the grounds that it is unreasonable or excessive. While Hank can proceed alone, he might do better to join together with other irritated neighbors in pursuing this matter in court.

Theo and Alice's land is part of a former state-supervised landfill project. A high level of carcinogens has been found in the water and soil. What is Theo and Alice's legal recourse?

Theo and Alice should contact the Environmental Protection Agency office in their area. If the EPA determines that the high level of carcinogens is a result of the improper disposal of hazardous waste, they will move Theo and Alice and their neighbors out of the area and do what they can to detoxify the damaged soil and water.

The EPA may also pay for the cost of relocating Theo and Alice and their affected neighbors, besides compensating them for the loss of their property. Whether or not they will be compensated for any physical

Challenging Real Estate Tax Assessments

If you think your real estate tax assessment is too high, you may be able to have it lowered. The assessed value of your home should be in proportion to its relative value in the community; the taxes on a $50,000 home should be about half of those on a $100,000 home. Mistakes can be made, however, especially when assessors are required to do a great deal of work in a short time.

As soon as you get your assessment, check the information the assessor's office used to determine your property's value. Some of the figures may have been typed incorrectly, such as the number of square feet of livable area or the year the house was built. Be sure that the assessor did not overestimate the grade of the materials used in constructing your house or the quality of the workmanship or the desirability of the neighborhood. And watch out for the "obvious" mistake: Did the assessor claim you have two bathrooms when you have only one, or report your narrow carport as a two-car garage?

The assessment is usually accompanied by a notice about your right to appeal. Read this notice carefully. In some areas you have as little as 10 days from the time you receive your assessment to begin the appeal process.

As soon as you can, contact the assessor's office and set up an appointment. Go to this meeting armed with specifics and figures. Your chance of success depends on how well you can document your claim. If the assessor agrees that you have a valid complaint, he may be able to make an acceptable adjustment then and there; but you may have to take your appeal to an assessment review board—sometimes called a board of appeals or a board of equalization. There, you'll be required to present your case for a lower assessment all over again.

Finally, if the board won't see things your way, you can file suit in the court that hears assessment cases in your state. Those proceedings will be very formal, and you'll almost certainly want an attorney with you.

injury they have suffered will depend on the law in their state. In some states the time in which this type of lawsuit can be brought is limited to a few years after the pollution begins. If the hazardous material was dumped many years ago, Theo and Alice may be unable to sue. In other states the time period within which suit may be brought begins when the pollution is actually discovered. Even then, it may be difficult to determine who was responsible for dumping the cancer-causing material in the first place.

Ronald and his family live on a small farm near the county airport. Planes fly low over Ronald's property as they approach the runway. The noise has made outdoor activity unbearable for the family and has frightened the chickens so badly they have stopped laying eggs. What can Ronald do?

When noise causes actual physical discomfort and prevents a property owner from using and enjoying his property, it may legally be considered a nuisance. Ronald should seek a court order prohibiting the airplanes from flying over his property. If he can convince the court that any reasonable person would be harmed by the amount of noise the planes are making, the court will either prohibit further flights over Ronald's land or restrict them to certain hours.

Ronald might even be compensated for the damage done to his chickens and the loss of the income from the eggs. In one case of chicken trauma, the court ruled that the farmer was entitled to the difference between the price obtained for the chickens that no longer laid eggs and the price of the chickens he had to buy to replace them.

Can I shoot a burglar who is looting my house?

Only if he threatens to kill or seriously injure you or someone else. You cannot shoot an intruder simply because he is trespassing. Even if you discover a burglar stuffing the family silver into a shopping bag, you are not justified in shooting him if he offers no threat of bodily danger.

A burglar generally presents a threat to your property only, and deadly force cannot be used solely to protect property, no matter how valuable. Furthermore, in many states, you must warn an intruder to leave before using any force at all, as long as it is practical to do so. If you have good reason to believe that you or your family are threatened with serious injury or death, however, you can use any force, even deadly force, in self-defense. But if you are tempted to use force, be careful. The intruder may be able to sue you for unreasonable injuries you inflict upon him, and if you kill him there is a chance you may even be found guilty of homicide.

Ways You May Lose Your Home

David and Christine bought a house in an adults-only community. They are now expecting a baby. Do they have to move?

No. Federal law now prohibits housing discrimination against families with children, except in certain senior citizen communities, which must meet strict guidelines to remain exempt from the law. As a result of this legislation, many communities that at one time prohibited children or restricted them to certain areas must now fully accept families with children as residents. Failure to comply with the law may result in prosecution for the homeowners association, developer, management company, or others who try to prohibit children in the community. If David or Christine feel they are being pressured to move because of their new baby, they should contact their local housing authority, which will investigate the situation to determine if the law is being violated.

Jesse just learned that the state is planning to build a highway through his land. Jesse's family has lived on this land for three generations, and Jesse doesn't want to move. Can he be forced out?

Yes. Every level of government has the power to take private property for a public use, such as building highways, creating parks, or clearing slums to construct low-income housing. This is known as the power of eminent domain, or condemnation, and it is permitted on the principle that benefits to the public outweigh the rights of individuals. But the power of eminent domain is not unlimited. Property may be taken only for a public use. Jesse must be fairly compensated for his land, and he has the right to contest the condemnation in court.

The city plans to take over the land on Anna's block in order to build a school, and is offering Anna $60,000 for her house. Anna feels that her house is worth at least $75,000. Must she accept the price the city is offering?

No. Eminent domain laws in every state require the government to pay the fair market value for any property that it takes. If Anna can prove that her property is really worth $75,000 on the open real estate market, she will receive that amount for her property.

But there's a catch. Contesting eminent domain, or condemnation, proceedings can take months or even years, and during that time the value of Anna's property will probably decrease, since the cloud of condemnation hangs over it. The amount Anna will receive for her property will be its fair market value at the time the condemnation proceedings are final.

Ways You May Lose Your Home

What can I do if I can't make my mortgage payments?

Contact your lender immediately. You may be able to renegotiate the terms of your loan so that foreclosure will not be necessary. For example, you may be able to extend the period of payment, which will reduce the amount of your monthly payments.

Even if foreclosure proceedings begin, you can redeem your property by bringing your mortgage payments up to date at any time before the foreclosure sale. And in some states, the law allows you to redeem your property even after it has been sold at foreclosure.

If you have a VA or FHA mortgage, ask the bank to assign the mortgage to the federal government and work out a new payment plan with the government agency involved. If the mortgage in question is a second mortgage, have your lawyer check for violations of the Truth in Lending Act. For example, did the lender fail to notify you of the true effective annual interest rate or change how penalties are computed? If there are any violations, you may be able to have the mortgage cancelled entirely.

Finally, if you have a steady income, you may be able to take refuge in the plan provided by Chapter 13 of the federal bankruptcy law. An alternative to traditional bankruptcy, this law allows you to keep your property by developing and following a plan for the full or partial payment of all your bills over an extended period of time. (See "Bankruptcy" in Chapter 7, *Your Money*.)

What happens if the bank forecloses on my house?

Most commonly, the lender begins a court proceeding in which he must prove that you have defaulted on the mortgage agreement. If he succeeds, the court will issue an order allowing him to sell the property. At a foreclosure sale, the property is sold to the highest bidder.

The proceeds of a foreclosure sale are applied against the amount owed on the mortgage plus court costs and expenses incurred in the sale; if the lender receives a greater amount from the sale than you owe him, he will have to turn the excess amount over to you. But if the property sells for less than the amount you owe, your lender can return to court and sue you for the difference.

George and Mary are facing a foreclosure on their house. How much time will they have before they have to move out?

Once the foreclosure sale is held, they will no longer have the right to remain in the house. However, some states give homeowners the right to remain in their home during the redemption period. But George and Mary should not move out just because they have been threatened with foreclosure. They should contact an attorney immediately; it may still be possible to save their home before foreclosure.

I have lost my job and can't pay my real estate taxes. Is there any way to keep from losing my house?

In most states, the only way to prevent a tax sale is by paying the overdue taxes before the property is sold. As in foreclosure sales, some states permit you to redeem your property even after a tax sale has taken place. In these states, you must pay not only the back taxes but also any penalties and the expenses of conducting the tax sale.

To avoid such situations, most mortgage lenders insist that you pay a portion of your real estate taxes along with the monthly payment of your loan. In order to protect their interest, mortgage lenders may even pay the overdue taxes in order to avoid a tax sale. Of course, you will ultimately be responsible for reimbursing your lender for this expense.

Doris invited her cousin Rachel and her daughters to live with her in her new condominium. Doris defaulted on the payments, and the condominium association has repossessed the apartment and is threatening to put Rachel in jail for trespassing. Can it do that?

While the condominium association may be able to sue Rachel for trespassing, it is more likely to begin eviction proceedings. Because Doris defaulted on the mortgage, she no longer owns the apartment, and Rachel and her daughters have no legal right to stay there. Rachel might try to rent the apartment for herself and her daughters, but the condominium association is under no obligation to let her do so.

Selling Your Home

I'm going to sell my house, and I don't know whether to hire a real estate agent, a broker, or a realtor. What's the difference?

A broker is a person who is licensed to sell real estate in exchange for a fee. A realtor is a broker who is a member of the National Association of Realtors, a nationwide trade association. A real estate agent is someone who sells real estate under the authority of a broker or realtor, but who is not allowed to earn a commission on his own. All three must be licensed, and the licensing laws impose a high standard of conduct upon them. In most states they must undergo special training and pass qualifying examinations in order to practice their profession, although the training and exams for agents are generally less rigorous. Realtors, brokers, and agents work solely for the seller who hires them, and are strictly obligated to represent the seller's best interests.

What services do real estate brokers generally provide?

The broker's primary responsibility is to find a buyer who is ready, willing, and able to purchase the property on terms and conditions the seller finds acceptable. Additional duties and responsibilities of a broker are set forth in the listing agreement, which is the contract between the broker and the seller. Usually, the broker advertises and shows the owner's property. When a buyer is found, the broker often acts as an intermediary, arranging for inspections and the like. He may even act for the seller in determining the terms and conditions of the contract for sale. But he is not a lawyer and should not be relied upon for legal advice even if he is well versed in the customary real estate practices in his area.

Vern is hesitant about using a broker to sell his house. He feels that a broker may switch his allegiance to the buyer if doing so will help him sell the house and get his commission. Is it legal for a broker to give the prospective buyer a deal that would be to the detriment of the seller?

Although a real estate broker may seem to represent both the seller and the buyer, he cannot do so legally, because the seller and the buyer have conflicting interests: the seller wants to get the highest possible price; the buyer wants to pay the lowest. Therefore, a broker hired and paid by the seller is considered to be the seller's representative and must always look after the seller's best interest. Buyers' brokers, paid by the purchaser, are offering their services in an increasing number of states.

Any real estate broker Vern hires must get his approval or authorization before making promises or accepting or rejecting an offer to buy Vern's home.

When I told my neighbor that I was putting my house up for sale, he offered to find a buyer. If he does, do I have to pay him a broker's commission?

No. Unless you have a contract with your neighbor, you may sell your house to the prospect he has located without owing a commission—even if your neighbor is a broker. In some states it would be illegal to pay him a commission unless he were a licensed broker.

What is the most important thing to do when working with a real estate broker?

Establish the terms under which you want the broker to sell your home. Decide whether he will be the exclusive broker or one of several. Set the price of the property and the size of the broker's commission and put a limit on how long the agreement with the broker will last. Be sure the broker knows the condition of your property and its special features so that he will make no misrepresentations to prospective buyers.

Is a real estate broker's commission firmly fixed, or can it sometimes be negotiated?

Like any terms of a contract, the broker's commission is subject to negotiation. While most brokers will try to persuade you that their commission is firmly fixed, you may be able to negotiate a lower one. For example, if your home is in a very popular area where houses sell quickly, the broker will have little work to do, and it is reasonable to pay him a smaller commission. Similarly, a home that commands a large selling price will also bring the broker a large commission; you may be able to negotiate his commission percentage downward. On the other hand, if your home is in an area where houses sell very slowly, your broker may be less willing to negotiate the commission rate.

Do I have to make any repairs to my house before I put it on the market, or can I sell it as is?

You are under no obligation to make repairs to your home before you put it on the market. However, in most states, if you don't tell a buyer about needed repairs, when he discovers them, he can sue you to cancel the contract. Many homeowners make minor improvements to their property before putting it up for sale, since these may increase the price a buyer is willing to pay. A fresh coat of paint and some fertilizer on the lawn can return many times their cost.

We listed our house with a real estate broker, who found a buyer for it at the price we wanted. Now we've changed our minds about moving. The broker insists that we pay his commission. Why?

When you signed the listing agreement, you agreed to pay a commission to the broker when he found a ready, willing, and able purchaser. Having done so, the broker has performed his duties and earned his commission even though you have changed your minds. He has a right to expect you to live up to your end of the agreement by paying him for his work.

Kurt's real estate broker found a buyer who put down a deposit, then backed out before the closing. The broker claims that he should get his commission anyway. Is he right?

It depends on the terms of the listing agreement. If the agreement states that no commission is earned until the closing of the sale, Kurt's broker is not entitled to a commission. The terms of the listing agreement should indicate when a broker is owed a commission, but if they fail to do so, state law takes over.

In some states a broker is not entitled to a commission until the closing. In other states the broker must be paid when the buyer signs a purchase agreement, even if he backs out later. If Kurt lives in one of these states, and the buyer is unable to complete the purchase because of financial difficulties, Kurt may still be able to avoid paying the broker's commission by proving that the broker did not provide a buyer who was "ready, willing, and able."

Jessica signed a 90-day agreement with a real estate broker to put her house on the market for $80,000. Her broker found a buyer, but he offered only $72,000. Jessica initially turned down this offer, but four months later agreed to sell. Does she still owe the broker a commission?

Probably, if her listing agreement contained an extender clause, which obligates the seller to pay a commission when the buyer is located by a

Types of Real Estate Broker Listings

If you are planning to sell your house, you should be aware of the various types of listings that brokers use, and try to get the one that is most likely to work for you. Each type of listing has its advantages and disadvantages.

- Under a *multiple listing arrangement,* you make an agreement with a single broker or agency, who in turn makes the information about your property available to other brokers in the area. These brokers are generally organized into a cooperating group that shares information about all of the properties they have available for sale. The broker who actually finds the buyer for your home splits his commission with the broker you hired. However, you may have to pay the commission even if you locate a buyer yourself without the help of a broker; check the contract for such a provision before deciding to sign it. In most areas of the country, multiple listing arrangements are the most common and the most successful.

broker even though the sale is agreed to after the listing agreement expires. The extender clause protects brokers from being deprived of their commissions by buyers and sellers who agree to wait until the listing agreement expires before making a sales contract. Since Jessica's buyer was located by the broker's effort during the listing agreement, the broker is entitled to his commission on the sale.

A real estate broker appraised Lois's home for $95,000 and was able to sell it at that price to the first prospective buyer. Later Lois found out that houses in her neighborhood were selling for much more, and that she could easily have found someone to buy her house for $115,000 or more. Does she have any legal recourse against the broker?

If she can prove that the broker knew that $95,000 was significantly less than the actual value of her house, Lois may be able to recover the difference between the amount she received from the sale and the actual value of the house. Brokers have a duty to protect their clients' interests and to use their best efforts to get them the highest possible price. A broker who does not fulfill his duty may be accountable for any loss the client suffers as a result.

In addition, Lois might be able to recover the commission she paid the broker on the grounds that he did not earn it in accordance with the accepted practices of other brokers in the community. In any event, if Lois decided to sue the broker, the case would be a difficult and involved one because it would be hard to prove that the agent really knew the true value of the house.

- In an *open listing agreement,* a real estate broker has the right to sell your property, but you can list your property with other brokers as well or sell it yourself. The broker who actually finds the buyer gets the entire commission. If you sell the property yourself, you don't owe anyone a commission. However, you may find it difficult to convince a broker to agree to an open listing, because he may spend time and energy in advertising and showing your home, only to receive no commission at all.
- If you agree to an *exclusive agency listing* with a broker, you promise not to list your property for sale with any other broker while the agreement is in effect. Because the exclusive listing agreement gives only one broker the right to earn a commission, it theoretically increases his incentive to find a buyer, but your home may not be shown to as many potential buyers.
- Be wary of contracts that give the broker an *exclusive right to sell.* Although they are similar to exclusive listing arrangements, there is one important difference. If you sell the property yourself, you must still pay the agent a full commission, even if he had nothing to do with the sale.

Selling Your Home

Bea, who is getting married, is selling her house on June 1, but she wants to stay in it until the wedding on June 29, when she will live with her new husband. How can she arrange this?

Bea will have to negotiate an agreement with the buyer in order to remain in her home after June 1, since she no longer has a right to be in the house after the closing. Agreements of this type are not unusual. Generally, Bea would be required to pay rent for the extra month and possibly contribute to the new owner's insurance, taxes, and utility expenses; some buyers might request an adjustment in the purchase price. Any agreement of this sort should be written into the sales contract.

Dawn wants to sell her condominium, and she has just found out that her condominium association has a right of first refusal. What does this right involve?

It means that the association has the option to purchase Dawn's unit before she can sell it to anyone else. If Dawn puts her condominium up for sale and receives a written offer from a buyer, she must offer the condo to the association before accepting the buyer's offer. The association must at least match the price offered by the prospective buyer. If they agree to meet this price, Dawn must sell her condo to the association. If they don't match the buyer's offer, Dawn can sell the condominium to the person who made the original offer.

CHAPTER
5

Your Personal Property

Owning Personal Property

I have heard it said that possession is nine-tenths of the law. What does this mean?

The saying is an exaggeration, but it illustrates an important point: Anyone who claims to own property that another possesses must have a very good case to take that property away. In most instances, a person who already has property in his possession will be able to defeat the claim of anyone except the true owner.

Our lawyer asked us to draw up a list of our real property and personal property. What's the difference?

Real property is the legal term for real estate. It includes land and anything erected or growing on the land, such as houses, garages, storage buildings, and gardens. *Personal property* is everything else that may be owned, such as automobiles, clothing, furniture, appliances, pets, and money, including stocks and bonds.

Are crops considered personal property?

It depends on whether the crops are growing in the field or have already been harvested. If the crops are still growing, they are considered part of the land, and are therefore considered real property. If the crops have already been harvested and are in storage, however, then the law considers them personal property.

Our banker asked us to make a list of our tangible personal property. What is this?

Tangible personal property includes things that are valuable in themselves, such as furniture, appliances, automobiles, and pets. Intangible personal property, on the other hand, consists of things that represent something of value, such as stocks, bonds, copyrights, and patents.

Harry leased some farmland from George and built a workshop and shed on it. Who will be the legal owner of these buildings when the lease expires?

Generally an improvement, such as the addition of a physical structure, becomes the property of the landlord. The workshop and shed will belong to George when the lease expires.

Susan put Jeff's favorite hunting coat out with the trash. Wayne came along, found the coat, and put it on. Jeff saw Wayne wearing his coat a few days later and asked him to return it. Who is entitled to keep the coat?

If it came to a court case, Wayne would be allowed to keep the coat. Once property is abandoned, anyone may claim it. The only way in which Jeff would be able to force Wayne to return the coat would be by proving that Susan did not have the authority to dispose of it. But if Susan had regularly disposed of old things this way, a court would probably find that Jeff had granted her the authority to act on his behalf.

One of my neighbor's children stole my son's brand-new bicycle. What should I do?

Your first step would be to approach your neighbor and ask him to have his child return your son's bike. If this fails, your next step is to contact the police. In addition, you may be able to sue your neighbor in small claims court. While parents cannot be prosecuted for what happens as a result of their children's carelessness or accidents, in some states they can be held liable when their children intentionally do something wrong.

Pets as Property

My daughter just received a puppy as a birthday gift. Do we have to get a license for it?

Yes. Nearly every state and many municipalities require that a dog be licensed. Dog licenses serve two purposes. They protect the health of the public, since the pet usually must be immunized against rabies and distemper before a license can be issued. Licenses also act as a means of identifying a pet that has strayed from its owner. Courts have consistently upheld the right of cities and states to require licenses for dogs.

My son wants to keep a turtle he found at a public pond. If he does, will he be breaking the law?

It is against the law for your son to keep the turtle unless your state has a statute that specifically permits him to do so. Your state is considered the legal owner of wild animals located on public property. Courts have held that this ownership is really a trust, whereby the state acts to preserve wild animals for the benefit of all the people. For further information on the status of wild animals, contact your state conservation department.

Pets as Property

One of our neighbors goes away for long periods of time and leaves his dog outside, unfed and untended. The dog comes around begging for food during the day, and then it howls and whimpers all night. How can I put a stop to this?

Report the problem to the local police. The dog's owner could be charged with two offenses: (1) cruelty to an animal, because he does not feed the dog or provide adequate shelter, and (2) maintaining a nuisance, because the dog's howling and whimpering deprive you of the use and enjoyment of your property. You can also sue to obtain a court order requiring the owner of the dog to stop the noise.

My dog dug under the fence and destroyed our neighbor's vegetable garden. Do I have to pay for the damage?

If your dog is normally well-behaved and has never done anything like this before, you probably will not be liable. However, if your dog had previously dug under the fence, and you made no effort to restrain him or prevent him from doing so again, you might have to pay for the damage to your neighbor's garden.

Ingrid raises AKC champion Labrador retrievers. Gerald, her neighbor, owns a scraggly mongrel. Gerald's mutt burrowed under the fence and had a brief but passionate relationship with one of Ingrid's female Labradors. The Labrador is now pregnant. Can Ingrid sue Gerald?

She can try, but she probably won't have much luck. Historically, a dog owner has not been held liable for damages unless he knew beforehand that the dog was mischievous or vicious. As long as Gerald was unaware of his dog's amorous intentions, Ingrid will be unable to sue Gerald successfully for damages.

I want a dog to help safeguard my home. If I post a Beware of Dog sign, will I be liable if the dog hurts someone?

Posting a Beware of Dog sign may actually work to your disadvantage, since it would be an admission that you were aware of your dog's vicious temperament. If you acquire a dog that you know is vicious or dangerous, you must restrain it to prevent it from injuring anyone, including trespassers. There are a few states, such as Florida and Arizona, that limit liability if a dog owner posts an easily readable sign calling attention to

The Legal Responsibilities of Your Veterinarian

Veterinarians, like physicians and other professionals, must conduct their practices according to a set of ethical principles. These principles, adopted in 1960 by the American Veterinary Medical Association, direct veterinarians to prevent and relieve the suffering of animals, to give proper medical attention to their patients and never neglect them, and to render service during emergencies to the best of their ability. Veterinarian ethics include an obligation to treat lost animals that are brought in when sick or injured, although the person who brings such an animal for veterinary care must be prepared to pay the bill just as he would for his own pet.

Veterinarians, like other doctors, cannot guarantee cures for their patients. Many factors beyond their control—such as age, the seriousness of an injury, or a previous illness—can affect the health and well-being of an animal in their care. Although veterinarians are not subject to the same malpractice laws that apply to physicians, they can be held responsible for the suffering, injury, or death of an animal if it results from: (1) a negligent diagnosis, (2) an unskillful operation, (3) poor care in feeding and housing the animal, (4) neglecting or abandoning the case, or (5) the actions of an unskilled or negligent employee. For example, it might be a case of poor care if you left your cat overnight for routine shots and it caught an infectious disease from another cat. A veterinarian might also be held responsible if your dog fell off the examining table and injured its head because the animal wasn't secured properly, or if the vet's assistant forgot to lock the cages at night and your dog was attacked by a larger one.

A veterinarian who is guilty of negligence may be suspended from practice and could be liable for civil penalties. However, an owner who sues a veterinarian can usually recover no more than the actual dollar value of the animal.

the vicious dog. Even in these states, however, you may be held liable if your dog injures someone who is not able to read the sign.

Is it true that a dog is entitled to one bite before its owner is liable for damages?

Not really. The owner's liability is not based on the number of people that the dog bites, but on the owner's knowledge of the dog's general behavior around people and its tendency to bite. The "one bite" rule is merely a shorthand way of indicating that a dog owner will not be liable for unexpected and unpredictable injuries if he has no prior knowledge of his dog's vicious tendencies.

Pets as Property

Ellen's dog bit a neighbor's boy who had climbed over the fence to retrieve his ball. Does the fact that the boy climbed over the fence relieve Ellen of liability?

It may. A dog that would not harm someone who entered through the gate might react unexpectedly to a person climbing over the fence. In addition, Ellen may be relieved of liability if she can show there were ways the boy could have avoided the dog, such as going after the ball only when the dog was tied up or in the house.

Max's next-door neighbor refuses to put a leash on his dog even though Max is expecting a visit from his young nephews. Max is afraid that one of his nephews may be harmed. What can he do?

Max could report his neighbor's refusal to leash the dog to the police. Most cities and towns have statutes that make it illegal to allow dogs to run at large. Under these leash laws, animals that wander at will, unrestrained by their owners, can be impounded and sold or destroyed if not claimed by their owners. Max's neighbor may also be subject to criminal penalties for violating these laws.

Am I liable if my dog runs out into the street and causes an automobile accident?

If you knew your dog habitually ran into the street to chase cars and you failed to restrain it, you would be liable for injuries or damage caused by the dog. You might also be liable if a statute or ordinance made it unlawful for you to allow your dog to roam unrestrained on public streets.

Our dog was killed by an automobile. Can I sue the driver?

Yes, but you would be required to show that the driver had failed to use reasonable care—such as driving slowly enough to stop in time—to avoid killing the dog. The driver would not be liable if your dog suddenly darted into the street in front of his car.

I hit my neighbor's dog by accident as I was backing my car out of the garage. Am I responsible for paying the veterinarian's bill?

A court will not hold you responsible unless there is evidence that you were negligent in driving your car. You would be guilty of negligence, for example, if you failed to look behind you as you started backing out of the garage, or if you saw the dog but failed to anticipate its behavior.

On her way home from work Peggy ran over a cat. The cat had no identification on it. Does Peggy have to do anything further to try to find the owner, or can she just drive off?

Since the cat had no identification, the law would presume that it was either a lost or an abandoned animal. Peggy is under no obligation to make further efforts to find the owner unless she wants to. However, state or local laws may require that she report the accident to the police.

I was riding down a bicycle path when a large dog ran into me, causing me to fall and hit my head. The dog owner's insurance company will pay for my hospital bills, but not for the two months I was out of work. Can I expect to get any additional monetary compensation?

Since the dog owner's insurance company accepted liability for your hospital bills, it may also be required to accept liability for other losses or damages that you incurred as a result of the accident. You should submit an accounting of your lost income and insist on payment.

Our neighbor Steven keeps a full-grown alligator in a pond on his property. We consider this a danger to our children. Can we force Steven to get rid of this creature?

Many states and cities have laws that prohibit a person from owning a dangerous animal. If it is against the law in your area, contact the police, and they will arrange to have the creature removed. Ownership of a dangerous animal may also make Steven fully liable for any injuries it causes, even if someone provokes it or is trespassing on his property.

Entrusting Property to Others

Jeff took his best suit to the dry cleaner. When he picked it up, he found unsightly streaks on the trousers. What can Jeff do?

Jeff should first return the trousers to the cleaner. This places the cleaner on notice that Jeff is dissatisfied with the quality of the work, and it gives the cleaner the opportunity to rectify his mistake. In most instances, the cleaner will attempt to undo the damage by recleaning the garment. If this second cleaning proves unsatisfactory, the cleaner will be liable for the damage, unless it was caused by a defect or flaw in the garment itself. If the cleaner is at fault, he will be required to reimburse Jeff for the cost of the trousers less depreciation over the time Jeff owned them. Jeff is not entitled to the price of a new suit.

The cleaner laundered my cotton slacks instead of cleaning them, and now they've shrunk. Am I entitled to a reimbursement?

Yes, since the cleaner failed to exercise ordinary care in handling your slacks. This does not mean, however, that the cleaner must buy you a new pair of slacks. Instead, the cleaner would be required to reimburse you for the amount of value left in them. For example, if you paid $50 for the slacks when you purchased them a year ago, the dry cleaner might pay you only $25, an amount based on the cleaner's estimate that the one-year-old slacks had a life expectancy of two years.

I can't wear my raincoat because the cleaner lost the matching belt. Shouldn't he give me the money to buy a new one?

Yes. The cleaner should give you a reasonable amount of money to buy a new matching belt, but he does not have to buy you a new raincoat.

If the Cleaner Ruins Your Clothes

You go to the dry cleaner to pick up the silk dress you've worn only twice, and you find that the buttons have melted into the fabric. Your dress is ruined. What do you do now?

The dry cleaner may want to try to fix the damaged garment; legally, he has a right to do so. But if the garment is beyond salvation and the damage is clearly the cleaner's fault, you are entitled to be reimbursed. However, you are not entitled to the amount you paid when the item was new. All clothing has an estimated life span. While you may be reimbursed in full for a brand-new dress, you may receive, for example, only one-half the original cost of a raincoat that is 1½ years old and still in good condition.

The majority of cleaners provide very reliable service, and since they depend on repeat business and word-of-mouth advertising, your cleaner will prefer to reach a satisfactory agreement with you and keep you as a satisfied customer. But if all else fails, you may still sue in small claims court to recover the current value of the garment.

The laundry promised Matthew his dress shirt would be ready on Tuesday, when he needed it for a meeting. When Matthew went to pick it up, it wasn't ready. What legal recourse does he have?

While the laundry's failure to return Matthew's dress shirt on the date promised may have caused him considerable annoyance and inconvenience, there is not much legal recourse available. Matthew's best course of action would be to file a complaint with the Better Business Bureau and not use this particular laundry anymore.

Janet was going through some old clothes when she found a claim check for a suit she had taken to the dry cleaner six months earlier. When she went to claim the suit, the cleaner told her that it had been sold and pointed to a sign on the wall that read: "Not Responsible for Items Left Over 90 Days." Can Janet sue the cleaner for selling her suit?

Yes. Many courts have held that a posted notice disclaiming liability carries no weight unless it is called to the customer's attention before he hands over his property. Unless the cleaner can prove that he called Janet's attention to the sign when she brought the suit in, she should be able to recover the suit's depreciated value in small claims court.

Lenny left his coat in an unattended checkroom in an expensive restaurant. When he went to get the coat after dinner, it was gone. Does the restaurant owe Lenny a new coat?

No. Since the checkroom was unattended, Lenny took his chances in leaving his coat there. If the checkroom had an attendant, the restaurant would be liable for the loss.

I left my fur coat in the checkroom at a restaurant. On the ticket stub was a statement limiting the restaurant's liability to $500. If my coat had been stolen, could I have recovered only $500?

Yes. As long as the limitation is reasonable and clearly spelled out to the public, there is nothing to prevent the restaurant from setting an upper dollar limit to its liability. The restaurant should also have a conspicuous sign stating the $500 limitation of liability in order to fully carry out its duty to its customers.

Julie left her hand luggage with the bell captain of a hotel while she paid her bill. She did not ask for a receipt, since she was

leaving in a few minutes. When she went to pick up her luggage, the bell captain could not find it. Is the hotel responsible for compensating Julie for her luggage?

Yes. The hotel is responsible for the reasonable value of the luggage and its contents. The bell captain is the hotel's authorized recipient of its customers' property, and he should have made certain that Julie's belongings were adequately protected.

Is my employer liable if my purse is stolen while I'm at work?

Usually not. As an employee you are expected to be aware of the general level of security at your workplace and to take care of your personal property. However, there are two exceptions to this general rule. (1) If your employer requires you to keep your personal property in a specific place, such as a locker room, he may be liable if it is stolen from that place. (2) If you can show that the theft of your purse was due entirely to your employer's negligence, he may be held responsible for your loss. An example of negligence might be allowing strangers into an office without having them check in with a receptionist.

After putting on a new pair of jeans in the dressing room of a clothing store, Ned went to search for a mirror. When he returned, he discovered that his old jeans were missing, along with his wallet. Is the store liable for Ned's loss?

Since Ned had to take off and set aside his old jeans in order to buy new ones, the store is liable for the loss of the old jeans—but not the wallet. Stores have a general obligation to see that no harm that can be reasonably avoided will occur to their customers while they are on the premises. This obligation extends to a customer's personal property that has to be laid aside while transacting business. But since it was not necessary to set aside the wallet—Ned could have carried it with him—the store is not liable.

Henry took a watch to the jeweler for repairs. The jeweler went bankrupt, and all of his assets and all the property in his shop were frozen. How can Henry get his watch back?

Henry will have to work through the bankruptcy court in which the case is pending. If he does so, he will be listed as a creditor of the bankrupt jeweler, and he will receive notice of his right to file a proof of claim. This proof of claim, which the bankruptcy court's clerk can assist Henry in completing, is a formal notice to the bankruptcy court that Henry claims ownership of the watch.

After the bankruptcy is settled, which may take several months, the watch will be returned to Henry. If it has been repaired and Henry has not yet paid for the repair, he must pay the amount due to the federal trustee responsible for the case.

Ellen shipped an antique table to Jim by an interstate trucking company. When the shipment arrived, the crate was smashed and the table severely damaged. Who is responsible for repairing or replacing the table?

The trucking company is liable for the damage, provided that Ellen packed the table properly before it was shipped, marked the package

The Law of Bailments

When you give another person temporary custody of your personal property, you create a legal relationship called a *bailment.* You are the *bailor*; the person with temporary custody is called the *bailee.* Bailments are involved in numerous day-to-day activities. Leaving a car at a garage, dropping your shoes off at a repair shop, boarding a pet, borrowing a bracelet from a friend—all are examples of bailments. In fact, bailments are so common that a special set of legal principles has evolved to deal with them.

The liability of another person for loss or damage to your property varies according to your reason for turning the property over to him. If the transaction is for the sole benefit of the other person—lending your guitar to a fellow musician for a concert, for example—he will have to care for your property with extra diligence and return it in exactly the same condition it was in when he received it.

If the bailment is for the mutual benefit of both persons—you deliver an original painting to a frame shop for cleaning and remounting—the other person must use ordinary care in handling and safeguarding the property you entrust to him.

Finally, if the bailment is solely for your own benefit —you leave your coat in an unattended checkroom—the bailee is liable to you only if he acts in bad faith or is grossly negligent in caring for your property.

Bailees often try to limit their liability by printing a notice on a claim check or receipt, or by posting a sign in their place of business. For a limitation of this type to be effective, the notice must be conspicuous to a reasonable person or be called to his attention before he leaves his personal belongings.

clearly to indicate that it was fragile, and gave the company specific instructions about how the package was to be shipped and handled.

When we moved cross-country recently, a delicate mirror was smashed so badly that it could not be repaired. Are the movers responsible for what it would cost to replace the mirror today rather than what I paid for it 10 years ago?

Since your move was across state lines, your moving company must adhere to the regulations of the Interstate Commerce Commission. These regulations allow movers to limit their liability for damage to only 60 cents per pound. If your mirror had an actual value of $1,000 and weighed 20 pounds, you could collect only $12. Most moving companies will offer you two types of additional insurance coverage: (1) added-valuation protection, which permits you to recover losses or damages based on the current replacement cost of an item minus depreciation, and (2) full-value protection, which covers the entire cost of replacement or repair at its current value.

We plan to move out West sometime during the next few months. Is there some way we can get a binding estimate of how much it will cost to move our household goods to another state?

Interstate moving companies are not required to give estimates, but most of them will do so if requested. There are two types of estimates: nonbinding and binding.

Nonbinding estimates must be in writing, and there is no guarantee that the final cost will not be more than the estimate. However, the mover cannot require you to pay more than the amount of the original estimate plus 10 percent at the time of delivery. You will then have at least 30 days to pay any remaining charges. The law does not permit movers to charge a fee for nonbinding estimates.

When you receive a binding estimate, you cannot be required to pay the mover more than the amount specified in the estimate. Binding estimates must also be in writing, and the mover is permitted to charge a fee for providing this service.

What is a bill of lading? Why is it so important?

A bill of lading is the contract between you and the mover stating the terms and conditions that apply to your move and who is responsible for the goods while they're in transit. It is legal proof that you are the

If You Buy Stolen Property by Mistake

Sometimes a bargain isn't really a bargain. Consider the case of the $100 videocassette recorder. It came in a factory-sealed carton, and it was bought from a man who parked his car in the company lot. At retail, the recorder sold for nearly five times the $100 price. The purchaser thought he'd made a great deal and had also helped a stranger who "needed to raise cash in a hurry."

A few weeks later, however, the great deal went sour when two police officers arrived at the purchaser's door. Several recorders had been stolen from a warehouse. The serial number on the warranty card the purchaser had mailed back to the manufacturer matched the number of one of the stolen machines. Although no criminal charges were filed against the purchaser, the police took the video recorder and returned it to its rightful owner. The innocent purchaser was out $100, and there was nothing he could do about it.

To avoid buying stolen property, law enforcement agencies suggest that you: (1) purchase goods from reputable outlets only; (2) question bargains that seem "too good to be true"; and (3) never purchase anything without first noting the seller's identification.

If you buy or accept property that you know was stolen, you could be convicted of a crime and subject to a fine or even imprisonment. Going to jail is no bargain either.

owner of the goods in case they're lost or damaged en route. Don't sign a bill of lading until you're satisfied that it describes the service you want.

I bought a gold watch for $200 at Bud's Pawnshop. Yesterday a police officer came to my house and told me that the watch had been stolen by the man who pawned it. Can I get my $200 refunded?

Yes. The pawnbroker would be required to return your $200. Because pawnbrokers have often been used by criminals to dispose of stolen goods, every state and many cities strictly regulate this business. Regulations usually require a pawnbroker to restore stolen property to its original owner and to refund the purchase price to an innocent buyer.

The pawnbroker sold my antique jewelry box before I returned to pay for it. What are my rights?

If you returned to pay your debt before the time limit was up, you can sue the pawnbroker and recover the fair market value of the jewelry box.

Entrusting Property to Others

When Pat went to the pawnbroker to pay for his saxophone, he learned that it had been lent to someone to play in a band, and he couldn't have it until the next day. What are Pat's legal rights?

Personal property left with a pawnbroker is considered collateral for a loan. A pawnbroker may not use the collateral for his own benefit or lend it to others. A pawnbroker is required to return pawned property when the loan is paid off. Pat is entitled to sue the pawnbroker for lending out his saxophone; but as a practical matter, a lawsuit may be pointless if the saxophone is returned the next day.

Borrowing and Lending

If a friend borrows my emerald bracelet to attend an out-of-town wedding, is she responsible for replacing the bracelet if it's stolen from her hotel room?

Yes. The privilege of borrowing an item, especially a valuable one such as an emerald bracelet, carries with it the responsibility of replacing the item if it is lost or stolen. Your friend would also be responsible for repairing the bracelet in the event of its being damaged.

My neighbor, who is much heavier than I am, borrowed our best patio chair. While he had the chair, the seat caved in. Who is responsible for getting it fixed?

Your neighbor should pay for having the patio chair fixed. A person who borrows property has a legal responsibility to repair or replace any broken parts and to return the article to its owner in the same condition it was in when he received it. You might be held liable, however, if you knew that the patio chair was defective, but did not tell your neighbor about it at the time he borrowed it.

Hal's brother-in-law borrowed Hal's old lawn mower without his permission. It wouldn't start, so he had it repaired without telling Hal. Hal had planned to get rid of the mower and had already ordered a new one. Must Hal reimburse his brother-in-law for the cost of the repairs?

No. A person who borrows personal property may not make repairs or improvements to that property without first receiving authorization from the owner. If repairs or improvements are made without the owner's consent, the owner has absolutely no obligation to pay for them.

Mabel lent her skis to Jessie, who damaged them in a fall. Jessie wants to replace them with secondhand skis, but Mabel wants new ones. Who is right?

If the skis Mabel lent Jessie were new, Mabel would be justified in demanding new ones as replacements. But if the skis were old and worn, a court would require Jessie to replace them only at their depreciated value. The intent of the law is to restore the value the property had immediately before it was damaged. Even if Mabel had to buy expensive new skis to replace the lost ones, the court would require Jessie to pay only the price of secondhand skis.

Fred borrowed Richard's wheelbarrow a little over a year ago. When Richard went to get the wheelbarrow, Fred said that since Richard hadn't claimed it within a year's time, it had become Fred's property. Is this really true?

Absolutely not. When no specific time is stated for the return of loaned property, the law requires the borrower to return it as soon as he has finished using it, or within a reasonable time afterwards. If matters reach the point where Richard has to demand the return of the wheelbarrow, Fred must comply immediately.

What steps should I take if a friend borrows an item and then refuses to return it?

If your friend ignores your first request to return the item, you should present him with a second request in writing. If he still refuses to surrender your property, you can sue him in small claims court. Although you may not wish to go so far, you could also file criminal theft charges at your local prosecuting attorney's office.

Morton lent his boat to Gary. One of Gary's friends fell down on the boat and was injured. Is Morton liable?

He may be. The injured friend could sue Morton for negligence (1) if Morton had entrusted the boat to Gary, knowing that Gary was incompetent, inexperienced, or otherwise incapable of using it safely, or (2) if the injuries were caused by defects in the boat that Morton knew about but failed to correct before he lent the boat to Gary.

Gift Giving

Tom told Diane that he would give her his old station wagon. The next time Tom visited Diane, she asked him to turn the car over to her. However, Tom had recently changed his mind and had decided to give his car to Wayne. Is Diane entitled to the car?

No. There are only two ways a gift can become another person's possession. The first way is to transfer possession of the property to another by actually turning it over to the other person. The second is to have the transfer of ownership legally recorded, such as by signing over the title to the car. Until one of these two steps is accomplished, the gift has not been given and may be revoked by the donor at any time.

If a husband gives his wife an anniversary gift, such as a videocassette recorder, does the item belong to her, or is it considered joint property?

The videocassette recorder belongs to the wife and is considered separate property because it was a gift from her husband.

For a long time, my neighbor Marlene has helped me take care of my mother as she has grown older and more feeble. As a token of my appreciation, I gave Marlene an antique doll my father had given me when I was a child. I just found out that the doll is worth a lot of money. Can I make Marlene give it back?

No. Under the law a gift between two persons is irrevocable. You have no legal right to force Marlene to return the doll.

Barbara was near death in the hospital. When Betty visited her on Wednesday night, Barbara gave her a sapphire ring as a gift. Barbara died the next morning. Can Barbara's family make Betty return the ring?

Probably not. This gift falls into a category that the law defines as a gift *causa mortis*. A *causa mortis* gift occurs when the donor expects to die soon, makes a gift of personal property, and then actually dies.

Causa mortis gifts differ from other gifts in that they can be revoked at any time prior to the donor's death, and they are automatically revoked if the donor does not die as expected. In this instance it appears that the legal requirements for a gift *causa mortis* have been met, so Barbara's family cannot force Betty to return the ring. If Barbara had lived, however, Betty would have had to return the ring if Barbara had asked her to do so.

Lost and Found

I found a wallet containing $100 in the street. There was no identification in it, and no one was around when I picked it up. Can I keep the money?

No. You should turn the wallet and money over to the police department in your community. If no one claims it within the waiting period provided by law—usually 90 days—the police will return everything to you, and you may keep the money. The finder of lost goods acquires a right of ownership to the goods that will stand up against the claim of anyone except the true owner.

While driving along the road to our county dump, I spotted a large shopping bag. Inside were 20 brand-new shirts. They were all tagged with the name of the store, but there was no sales receipt. The shirts were all my size. Can I keep them?

No. You should take the shirts back to the store whose name appears on the tags. The store will check its sales records to see if the shirts had been sold to anyone. If so, the store will notify the rightful owner that his property has been found. If the shirts had not been sold but had been stolen, for example, or inadvertently thrown out, they would remain the property of the store.

Joyce liked to cut across Mary Anne's property on her way to work. One day, she noticed under a bush a sack with several pieces of jewelry in it. Who should be allowed to keep the jewelry?

Mary Anne has a better claim than Joyce. The owner of land is considered to have possession of everything on the property even if the owner is unaware of its presence. However, Mary Anne will have to give up the jewelry if the true owner is ever found.

When Doris's old car had engine trouble, she decided to leave it where it stopped. If Frank finds the car, can he tow it away and legally claim ownership?

It depends on what Doris's intentions were when she left the car. If she planned to come back for it, Frank has no legal right to tow the car away, since he is not the owner. The law would continue to recognize Doris as the owner as long as she retained the registration or the title certificate. However, if Doris decided to abandon the car and relinquish her ownership, Frank could claim it, since it would then not be owned by anyone else. Since Frank has no way of knowing what Doris's intentions were, he must locate the owner of the car before towing it away.

I bought three rings from a souvenir shop for $5 each. When I looked at them later, I discovered that one was 14-carat gold. Do I have a duty to return the gold ring?

You are under no obligation to return the ring. However, if the shopkeeper discovers that a valuable ring has been mistakenly turned over to you instead of a $5 one, he has a legal right to sue you in order to recover the ring or its value.

Norman gave Hannah an old trunk and told her that she could have what was in it. Hannah found a bank book of Norman's with a $5,000 balance. Can Hannah keep the money in the account?

No. Even though Hannah is in possession of Norman's passbook, the bank will not permit her to make a withdrawal from his account, since her signature does not appear on the bank's records. Hannah would be committing a crime if she attempted to withdraw any money from Norman's account.

Selling Personal Property

I am planning to sell my television for $150. Should I prepare a written agreement for the buyer and me to sign?

A written agreement is not required. The act of exchanging the television for payment shows that the buyer and seller made a legally binding contract. However, it is always a good idea to put such transactions in writing; if there is a dispute later, a written document will make it easier to prove your case.

Is it true that some types of contracts for buying and selling are required by law to be in writing?

Yes. Each state has a law, called the statute of frauds, that describes what kinds of contracts must be in writing to be enforced. A contract for the sale of land, for example, must be in writing. Contracts that cannot be carried out within a year of their signing must also be written. Contracts covering the sale of goods whose price exceeds a specified dollar amount—$500 in most cases—also require written contracts.

I gave Elaine $50 not to sell her video camera until I decided whether I wanted to buy it or not. I finally concluded the camera was going to cost too much, and I asked Elaine to return the $50 deposit. She refused. Can she rightfully keep my money?

Probably. When you gave Elaine the $50, you created what is called an option contract. In other words, you paid Elaine to keep her offer to sell open; in return Elaine promised not to sell the camera to anyone else. Elaine lived up to her part of the bargain, and she is therefore entitled to keep the money.

Mary agreed to buy my stereo for $400. Later she reneged on the deal, and I was forced to sell it to someone else for only $200. Can I sue Mary for the difference?

Yes. Even if you didn't have a written agreement with Mary, you are entitled to take her to court for reneging on the agreement. In most states, a contract for the sale of goods for less than $500 does not have to be in writing to be enforceable.

Kevin, Leon, and Mike, who live on the same block, pitched in to buy an expensive new power mower for all of them to share. When Kevin's family decided to move, Kevin demanded to be bought out of his share. Do Leon and Mike have to pay Kevin?

Leon and Mike have both a moral and a legal obligation to pay Kevin for his share of the power mower. However, they are only required to reimburse Kevin for one-third of the mower's remaining value. This value can best be determined by asking a dealer for an estimate based on the item's age and condition.

June found a Tiffany lamp at a bargain price at a garage sale. She gave the owner a check for the lamp and told him she'd pick up the lamp later. In the interim, the owner sold the lamp to someone who offered more money. June got her check back but wonders if she has any further recourse in this situation.

June could go to court and sue for breach of contract. But the money damages she would receive would be limited to the difference between the regular price she would pay for the lamp and the bargain price that was agreed to at the garage sale. However, some courts would rule that June is not entitled to receive any damages at all, because she canceled the contract when she accepted the return of her check.

Bill and his brother Brad have shared a stamp collection since they were children. Can Bill sell any of the stamps and keep the proceeds without Brad's permission?

Bill can sell only those stamps that belong to him. An individual cannot sell the property of another without the owner's consent. If Bill did sell any of the stamps that the brothers acquired jointly, Brad would be entitled to half their value from Bill.

Rosemary agreed to sell Judy an original Norman Rockwell painting. When Judy came to pick up the valuable artwork, Rosemary informed her that she had changed her mind. Can Judy force Rosemary to sell her the painting?

If they had nothing in writing, it would be difficult for Judy to force Rosemary to sell the artwork. Most states will not enforce oral contracts involving $500 or more, and most original Rockwell paintings are worth much more than that. If Judy and Rosemary had a written contract, on the other hand, Judy could sue for breach of contract, and she would have a good chance of getting the painting.

I inherited some gold jewelry from my grandmother, and I would now like to sell it. Do I need any kind of papers to prove that I own the jewelry in order to sell it legally?

Personal items such as jewelry can usually be sold without written proof of ownership. You may have received a written report of the assets in your grandmother's estate at the time you received the jewelry. This report, or other estate papers that identify the jewelry, would be helpful to a buyer concerned about the legitimacy of your ownership.

Eddie's father bought him a new bicycle for his 10th birthday. Eddie sold the bike for $20 to the boy up the street. Can Eddie's father get the bicycle back?

Yes. Eddie's father can either get Eddie to ask for it back, or he can go and retrieve it himself. In either case, the $20 will have to be returned to the boy who bought the bike from Eddie. While the law does permit children to enter into oral purchase agreements such as this, it also permits children to get out of them without being penalized for breach of contract. The purpose of this is to protect an immature person from being victimized by an unfair agreement. Eddie's father may act on his son's behalf to set this oral contract aside and get the bicycle back.

Can I sell or give away property that has a lien on it?

Yes, but there are conditions relating to liens that may make this undesirable. You should not make such a sale or gift unless you fully understand these conditions. When you sell or give away property that has a lien on it, the recipient also becomes subject to the lien. The person or company holding the lien now has a legal claim against both of you. If you defaulted on a car loan, for example, and you then sold the car, both you and the buyer would be liable for the loan.

There may be specific conditions in the lien itself that restrict or prohibit you from selling or giving away the property. If you transferred the property anyway, the lienholder could demand that the transaction be canceled and either claim the property himself or accelerate the debt, making the balance due immediately.

Can my creditors ever take my personal property and sell it without my knowledge?

Your creditors cannot take your property and sell it without first contacting you and going through a legal process to enforce whatever rights they possess. However, one very important exception occurs when you specifically grant a creditor the right to repossess your property as part of a written loan agreement. This is a common practice in automobile loans and means a creditor can take your car away without having to tell you in advance when he will do so.

Patents, Copyrights, Trademarks

While tinkering with some machinery in my basement, I invented a device that could be very profitable. How can I protect my invention from being stolen?

You should apply to the U. S. Patent and Trademark Office in Washington, D.C., for a patent. A patent prohibits others from making, using, or selling your device without your permission for 17 years after the patent is issued. Once the patent expires at the end of this term, anyone will be free to use your invention without your permission. It cannot be renewed.

To obtain a patent, you must first submit an application to the U.S. Patent and Trademark Office. The application must include a description of the invention; an oath affirming that you are the inventor; drawings that illustrate the invention's unique features; and the required application fee. You do not have to supply a model of the invention. If your application is approved, you will be issued a patent number and a document containing the government's grant of the patent rights to you.

While it is possible for you to file your own patent, the process is complicated, and the language used in the application must be legally correct in order to completely protect the invention. So most people are well advised to hire a patent attorney to handle their application. The only attorneys allowed to do this are those who are specially qualified and admitted to practice before the U. S. Patent and Trademark Office.

I have just purchased a new tool that is marked "pat. pending." What does this mean?

The term *pat. pending*—short for *patent pending*—indicates that an application for a patent has been filed with the U. S. Patent and Trademark Office. This term has no legal effect, since an item is not protected until a patent is assigned and a patent number issued.

Can my wife obtain a patent on an artistic design that is for decorative purposes only?

Yes. A new, original, and ornamental design may be patented, as long as it is intended for eventual use on some manufactured article. A design patent is usually issued for a period of 3½, 7, or 14 years. The term is selected by the applicant; the patent fee varies with the term selected.

Pam has an idea for a new board game. Can she patent her idea?

No. Ideas alone are not patentable. However, Pam can protect her game by developing a prototype and having it copyrighted. She may obtain a copyright by filing an application with the Copyright Office of the Library of Congress in Washington, D.C. She will have to send a fee and two copies of her game to the Copyright Office along with her application.

Pam's game would be copyrighted as both a literary and an artistic work—the instructions and other written material would qualify as literary work, and the board design and any drawings or pieces would be considered artwork.

What is the difference between the kinds of things that can be patented and those that can be copyrighted?

Patents protect new inventions and improvements to existing mechanical devices; copyrights protect artistic works. Some broad categories of things that can be copyrighted are: (1) literary works, such as books, poems, and magazines; (2) musical works, including accompanying lyrics; (3) plays and their musical scores; (4) audio records and tapes; (5) motion pictures, videocassettes, and other audiovisual works; (6) visual art, including lithographs and sculptures; and (7) pantomime and choreography. A copyright protects the work for the lifetime of its author or creator plus 50 years.

Does Richard need to copyright the manuscript of his book before sending it to a publisher?

No. The act of setting down his thoughts in tangible form in a manuscript is sufficient to establish and protect his copyright while it is in the hands of a publisher. To protect his work after it is published, it must carry a copyright notice.

My PTA is preparing a cookbook as a fund-raising project. We have been told that we can reprint a small number of recipes from other cookbooks without permission from the publishers. Can we?

No. The owner of a copyright has the exclusive right to print, publish, copy, and sell the copyrighted work. He also has the right to prepare derivative works based upon the original material. In order to reprint the recipes in your PTA cookbook, you must receive written permission from the copyright holder.

How can I tell if something is in the public domain?

A work that has been published without a copyright notice or one whose copyright has expired is said to be in the public domain. This means that anyone is free to copy, print, publish, sell, or use it without infringing the rights of another. Under the terms of the copyright law that took effect on January 1, 1978, a work copyrighted after this date is protected from the date of copyright until 50 years after the death of the author. Works copyrighted before 1978 are protected for 28 years and are entitled to an additional 47 years of protection if the copyright owner applies for renewal at least one year before the copyright is due to expire. Copyrights owned by a publishing company expire 75 years after publication of the work or 100 years from the date the work was created, whichever is less.

Patents, Copyrights, Trademarks

Is it legal to use a copying machine to copy pages from a copyrighted book without obtaining the publisher's permission?

Whether or not you must seek the publisher's permission depends on whether the copying complies with the 1978 copyright law. This law permits copying parts of a copyrighted work for such purposes as scholarship, research, criticism, comment, or news reporting. Teachers are also permitted to make multiple copies of a work for classroom use. However, copying for commercial purposes, such as making reprints for resale, is illegal.

I run a videocassette store, and I know that some of my customers are renting videocassettes and copying them on their VCR's at home. This is illegal, isn't it?

Yes. The systematic reproduction of copyrighted works to obtain permanent copies without purchasing them is prohibited. Most videotapes carry warnings about the legal consequences of copying, in addition to the standard copyright notice.

Leslie designed an emblem to identify her wood carvings. What can she do to make sure no one else uses this design?

Leslie can register her emblem as a trademark at the U. S. Patent and Trademark Office. A trademark is a symbol that distinguishes one brand of goods from similar items made by others. However, if Leslie's emblem resembles one already in existence, her application will not be approved.

Robert has obtained a trademark for the line of office products he manufactures. What kind of protection does this provide?

Robert has the exclusive right to use his trademark for at least 20 years. In order to notify the public of his ownership of the trademark, he must display it with the words "Registered in the U. S. Patent Office," "Reg. U. S. Pat. Off.," or the letter R enclosed in a circle following the word or phrase he uses for a trade name. If he fails to provide this notice, he will be unable to collect damages from anyone who uses the same trademark.

CHAPTER
6

Your Car

Buying a Car

Leon obtained a car loan based on a price quoted to him by the salesman. When he returned to pay for the car, the manager of the dealership said he wouldn't sell the car for the price quoted by the salesman. What can Leon do?

If Leon's agreement with the salesman was in writing, he can sue for breach of contract. If the lawsuit is successful, the court will require the dealer to fulfill the contract, and Leon will get his car at the price originally quoted. But if Leon and the salesman had only an oral agreement, Leon would have no recourse: Contracts involving more than $500 must be in writing to be enforceable.

What are my rights if I put down a deposit on a car and then the dealer sells it to someone else?

You are entitled to a refund. If you have a written contract with the dealer, and he sells the car to someone else, you can cancel the contract and get back the money you left as a deposit. However, the dealer may have the right to replace the car with an identical one, depending on the fine print in the contract. If you did not have a contract but left a deposit to show that you intended to return later and work one out, you are still entitled to get your money back.

Alexander lives in state X. He bought a car in state Y. In which state does he pay the sales tax?

Alexander will pay sales tax in state Y, where he bought the car. However, if he plans to register his car in his home state, Alexander may also have to pay a use tax on the car. States impose use taxes to recover some of the tax revenue they lose when people go to another state, as Alexander did, to make a major purchase.

Jackie's car dealer sold the car she traded in before the loan was approved for her new car. Does a dealer have the right to do this?

Probably not. Most contracts to purchase new cars are contingent upon financing. This means that if the buyer can't get a loan, the contract is canceled. If Jackie's contract was contingent upon financing, the dealer had no right to sell her trade-in because title to the car had not yet passed to him. In essence, he sold a car that still belonged to someone else. If Jackie's contract was not contingent upon financing and she had transferred the car's title to the dealer, he did have the right to sell it.

A car dealer wanted me to subtract 20,000 miles from the odometer statement on the car I was trading in. I wouldn't do it. Should I report this incident to someone? What might have happened to me if I had signed this statement?

You should report the matter to your state attorney general's office and to the nearest office of the National Highway Traffic Safety Administration for possible prosecution. Tampering with an odometer, or issuing a false odometer statement, is a federal offense that can be prosecuted in both criminal and civil courts.

If you had gone ahead and signed the statement, you could have been charged with a federal crime. In addition, the buyer of your old car could have sued you in a civil court for three times the amount the price was inflated as a result of the false statement, or $1,500, whichever was greater. The person suing could also have recovered his attorney's fees and other costs from you.

Fred is frantic. His car has been in the repair shop four times since he bought it 10 months ago, and he's written to the manufacturer three times, but the car is still not running right. What can he do?

Under consumer lemon laws, Fred is entitled to a refund or a replacement car if the defect cannot be fixed in four tries or if the car is out of service for 30 days within the first 12,000 miles or 12 months. Fred's next step is to submit a formal complaint to an arbitration panel set up by the manufacturer; his car owner's manual will tell him how. Fred can request a copy of the arbitration panel's procedures. He can also ask for copies of whatever evidence the dealer or manufacturer submits that disputes his claim. At the same time, Fred can write to the manufacturer's zone manager and ask for any service bulletins about the model of his car. If other new car buyers have had the same problems, this will strengthen his case.

Arbitration panels are generally required to reach a decision within 60 days of the date the complaint was filed. In most states, Fred would have the right to reject the arbitrator's decision if he weren't satisfied with it. He could then sue the manufacturer in court.

Some states, including Connecticut, Massachusetts, New York, Texas, Vermont, and Washington, D.C., have their own arbitration panels. Check with your state attorney general's office about the laws in your state.

Edith has taken her new car back for service five times in two months, and each time she had to rent a car. Can Edith get the dealer or manufacturer to reimburse her for the cost of the rentals?

Yes. Under most lemon laws the manufacturer is liable for additional costs when a new car is defective.

Buying a Car

Can I withhold payments on a new-car loan if the car is a lemon?

It depends upon who arranged the loan. If you personally arranged the loan with a bank or other lending institution, you may not withhold payments. The loan is between you and the bank, and whether or not the car works, the bank is entitled to repayment. On the other hand, if the car dealer arranged the financing for you, you may be able to withhold your payments. However, before doing so, you should consult an attorney to be advised of your full rights and responsibilities.

I bought a new car six months ago and haven't had any problems with it. But this model is now being recalled. Should I worry about the safety of the car? Can I force the dealer to take it back?

If you comply with the recall and take your car in for inspection and repair, your car should be safe to operate when you get it back. Recalls are initiated when a safety problem shows up in a group of cars of the same make, model, and year. If a defect is discovered when you take your car for inspection, it will be corrected free of charge. If you've had no trouble with your car, and the recall prevents a future problem, you cannot force the dealer to take the car back.

What to Do If You Bought a Lemon

Most states have lemon laws that keep you from getting stuck with a new car that keeps breaking down no matter how many times it's been to the shop. Under these laws, you are generally entitled to a refund or a replacement car if your new car has a substantial defect that cannot be fixed in four tries, or if the car is out of service for 30 days within the first 12,000 miles or 12 months. For updated information about lemon laws in your state, contact your state consumer protection office or attorney general's office, or the Center for Auto Safety, 2001 S Street NW, Washington, D.C. 20009. If your state does not have a lemon law, you may be able to sue under the Magnuson-Moss Warranty Act, a federal law that protects consumers who have purchased defective merchandise. In any case, if you think you have a lemon, you should:

- Bring the car in for repair before the warranty period ends. This will ensure your right to have the defect fixed even after the warranty runs out. It will also guarantee you other legal options if the problem persists.
- Keep accurate, detailed records. Give the dealer a written list of what needs to be fixed every time you take the car in for repair. Always keep a copy for yourself. Save all copies of the dealer's bills and repair orders.

One morning Jay discovered that his car was missing. He reported it stolen but later learned that the bank had repossessed it. Is it legal for a bank to repossess a car in this manner?

Yes. If Jay missed a payment, and the car was collateral on the loan, the bank has the right to send a "repo man" to take the car. Most banks don't notify delinquent borrowers that they're coming to claim the car, because it's so easy to hide a car by moving it somewhere else. Most repossessions take place at night to avoid unpleasant or hostile confrontations, since repossessions must take place without disturbing the peace.

Loretta's car was repossessed when she couldn't keep up her payments. An officer from the bank that lent Loretta the money to buy the car told Loretta that she still owes the bank $1,000. How can she owe anything when the bank has the car?

Once the bank repossessed the car, it had the right to sell it to pay off Loretta's debt. When a car is repossessed and sold, if the resale price is less than the amount outstanding on the loan, the borrower must pay the difference. So if Loretta owed the bank $6,000 on the car loan when she defaulted, and the bank sold the car for only $5,000, Loretta would still owe the bank $1,000. If the bank had sold the car for more than the amount due, however, Loretta would have received the difference.

- Report the defect to the Auto Safety Hotline. (Call 1-800-555-1212 for the hotline's toll-free number.) If there are enough complaints about a specific problem, the manufacturer will have to issue a recall for that model and fix the defect.
- Notify the manufacturer in writing about your problems before you take the car in for the fourth repair attempt or before the car's 30th day out of service. The address for this notice is listed on your warranty. Manufacturers are legally entitled to one final attempt to fix the car before these deadlines. Follow your manufacturer's instructions; you may be asked to take the car to a different dealer.
- If the defect still isn't fixed, submit a complaint following the procedures described in the manufacturer's warranty in your owner's manual. This will set in motion an arbitration process in which the manufacturer will try to resolve your problem without your having to go to court. The arbitration panel will usually reach a decision within 60 days of the date you filed the complaint.
- If you do not agree with the arbitration panel's decision, consult a lawyer about further action. In most states, you can reject the panel's decision and file a lawsuit against the manufacturer. If you win your case, the manufacturer can be made to pay your legal costs.

Buying a Car

Many married couples put their homes in joint ownership. Should we do the same with our car?

If you title the car as joint owners with right of survivorship, you will have equal rights to it. Neither spouse will be able to sell the car without the other's consent. In the event of a divorce, the court will decide who keeps the car if you are unable to reach an agreement. If either of you dies, title to the car will automatically pass to the surviving spouse.

I bought a used car from a dealer whose ad said the car was "never wrecked." A mechanic told me later that the car had indeed been in a major accident. What can I do?

Sue the dealer for fraud. Since you based your decision to buy the car on his fraudulent statement, you can sue him even if you bought the car "as is."

Pete bought a used car from a dealer who said that the car was in fine working condition. What can Pete do if the car keeps stalling?

When the dealer told Pete the used car was in "working condition," he made a warranty, or promise, that the car would operate properly. If the dealer can't repair the car, Pete is entitled to have it fixed elsewhere and obtain reimbursement from the dealer for the repair work.

Calvin bought a used car from Carl, but he has not been able to register the car because the title doesn't match the vehicle registration number. What should Calvin do?

Calvin has the right to return the car and get a refund. When Carl sold Calvin his car, he made a promise, or warranty, that he was transferring a valid title to Calvin. Carl has breached that warranty.

Renting or Leasing a Car

The car rental people told Audrey that for a little extra, she could get a "collision damage waiver." Should Audrey have taken it?

The waiver would protect Audrey from liability for damage to the rental car if she were involved in a collision, regardless of who was at fault. If Audrey rejects the waiver, she may have to pay for any collision damage to the rental car. However, since many automobile insurance policies also cover the use of a rental car, Audrey should check her own policy—if she is already covered, she doesn't need the collision damage waiver.

In Illinois, the sale of collision damage waivers is prohibited by state law, and a renter's liability for any damage to a rental car cannot exceed $200 in most cases.

What happens if I have an accident while driving a rental car?

Your liability depends on your own automobile insurance and the type of agreement you sign with the car rental agency. Some car rental agreements would make you liable for everything; with others you would be responsible up to a fixed dollar amount. The car rental agency cannot hold you liable if (1) you paid extra for collision and bodily injury coverage, or if (2) your own automobile insurance covers you for an accident with a rental car.

After signing a lease agreement with John's Auto Leases, Joe and Julie realized they couldn't afford the payments. A friend told them that they had a three-day grace period in which to cancel the contract. Is this true?

No. Unless their lease agreement specifies a three-day grace period, Joe and Julie cannot cancel it. Their friend was probably thinking about consumer protection laws that allow a three-day cooling-off period in which a buyer can change his mind after signing a purchase agreement with a door-to-door salesperson.

Marlene leased a car that turned out to be a lemon. Is she entitled to turn the car in and get a new one?

Yes. The federal law that protects consumers who have purchased lemons, the Magnuson-Moss Warranty Act, protects both the original purchaser and anyone to whom the automobile is leased.

Harvey leased a car for a five-year period. Two years into the lease he was given a company car for his own use. Can he get out of the three remaining years of his lease?

It depends on the terms of Harvey's contract. If the contract includes conditions and penalties for terminating the lease, Harvey will have to abide by them. If there are no such provisions, the dealer can sue Harvey for any losses he suffers if Harvey breaks the contract.

Renting or Leasing a Car

I leased a vehicle last year, but I can't afford the payments now. The leasing company is demanding payment as usual, regardless of my personal circumstances. What can I do? Can I sell the car?

Do not try to sell the car you're leasing; it does not belong to you. Selling a leased car is as illegal as selling an apartment you rent. Read your lease agreement to see if it includes procedures for terminating the contract. You may be able to cancel the lease by returning the car and paying a penalty. However, not all leases provide for termination. If you break the lease by turning in the car and defaulting on your payments, the leasing company can sue you to recover any monetary losses it incurs.

Selling a Car

What records do I need in order to sell my car?

You must have a certificate of title and a valid registration. You may also be required to give the buyer a bill of sale. Every state has its own regulations regarding the transfer of vehicles; you should contact your local department of motor vehicles to find out the proper procedures.

What steps should Laurie take to sell a car on which she has an outstanding bank loan?

First, she should check her loan agreement. It may not allow her to sell the car without the bank's permission. If it's all right with Laurie's lender to sell the car, she is still obligated to pay the balance due on the loan or keep her monthly payments up to date. Laurie must tell the buyer about the loan because if she defaults on it, the bank can repossess the car from the buyer. Finally, many states require that outstanding loans on a car be listed on the title certificate. If Laurie's state is one of these, she should make sure her title certificate has this information on it.

Last week, Lloyd sold his car to his 15-year-old neighbor. The boy came to Lloyd's house today and said he no longer wanted the car. Does Lloyd have to give him back his money?

Yes. Children who have not yet reached the age of adulthood, usually 18 or 21 years of age, are considered legally incompetent to make a valid contract. Selling a car involves a contract, either written or oral, and in this case it is not binding because of Lloyd's neighbor's age.

Precautions to Take When You Sell Your Car

Selling your car instead of trading it in often means a higher profit for you and a better bargain for the person who buys the car. But there are precautions you should take, or the sale might end up creating legal problems for you. Here are some of the steps you should take when you put your car up for sale.

- Contact your state motor vehicle department before you sell the car and find out how to make sure that the transfer of ownership will conform to all your state's required procedures.
- Check with your town or city government before putting a For Sale sign on your car. Many communities restrict the size of these signs or prohibit them entirely.
- Be accurate in what you say in newspaper advertisements and in any notices you put up on community or office bulletin boards. Buyers have used exaggerated or false statements about a car's condition to have the sale voided later in court.
- Ask for a nonrefundable deposit if the buyer can't pay in full at the time you make the deal. This will eliminate people who are not serious about buying and will help compensate you for taking the car off the market and losing other customers if the original buyer changes his mind or never shows up again.
- Give the buyer a written receipt for the deposit; it should include the buyer's name, a description of the car, the total price to be paid, the amount received, and the date when the car will be put back up for sale if the buyer does not complete the deal. The receipt should state that the buyer understands the deposit is nonrefundable if the sale isn't completed by the date indicated. Keep a copy for your records.
- Have two copies of a bill of sale completed when the car is turned over to the new owner. (Standard bill of sale forms can be obtained at office supply or stationery stores, or you can prepare your own.) Include the year, make, model, identification number, and engine number of the car, names and addresses of buyer and seller, and total selling price on the bill of sale. Include a statement that the car is being sold "as is" with no guarantees of any kind.
- Federal regulations require an odometer statement whenever ownership is transferred. You must indicate the mileage on the date the car is sold and declare that the odometer has not been turned back nor the car driven while the odometer was disconnected.
- If the car is being purchased by a minor, have his parents sign the bill of sale. Otherwise you have no legal recourse if the young person changes his mind.
- Even if you know the buyer, ask for payment by certified check, money order, or cash.
- Hand over the car title or registration only when you have the cash or certified check in hand.

Selling a Car

If I sell my car to a friend, do I have to give any warranties? She knows that it barely runs and is paying me only $50.

You are not required to give a warranty when you sell a used car. Make it clear that you are selling the car "as is" by writing this on the bill of sale. This lets your friend know that you are making no promises about how the car will perform. By taking the car as is, she is accepting it in whatever condition it is in.

When Albert bought a new car, he sold his old one to Hank, his best friend, for $400. After Hank had the car for two weeks, the transmission gave out. Hank wants his money back. Does Albert have to return Hank's money?

It depends on what Albert said at the time of the sale. If he made any promises about the car's performance to persuade Hank to buy it, Hank may be able to get his money back. For example, if Hank bought the car relying on Albert's assurance that the transmission would be good for another 10,000 miles, Hank is entitled to a refund. But if Hank bought Albert's car "as is," Albert owes him nothing. When someone buys a car as is, the seller need not make any promises about the car and is released from responsibility for any defects or problems.

Car Warranties

Norman and Lenora bought a new car last year. About six months after the purchase, they had to take it to the car dealership for repairs. Two days after the one-year warranty was up, the same problem occurred. The dealer refused to honor the warranty. What can Norman and Lenora do?

Norman and Lenora can insist that the dealer correct the problem because it first developed while the warranty was still in effect. Although the one-year period is over, this does not mean the dealership is absolved from all further responsibility. A warranty guarantees that defects arising during the warranty coverage will be fixed by the dealer.

What is the difference between a full warranty and a limited one?

A full warranty, which is unusual, must meet several requirements. It must state its duration clearly and agree that defects will be repaired within this period without charge and within a reasonable time. If a defect cannot be repaired within a reasonable amount of time, or after a reasonable number of attempts, the manufacturer or dealer offering the full warranty must replace the car or refund the purchase price.

If a warranty does not meet all these standards, it is a limited warranty, the most common type of coverage for a new car. Typical limitations require that you pay the labor costs when defective parts are replaced, or that you pay for renting a car while yours is in the repair shop. Some items—such as spark plugs, filters, hoses, belts, and other maintenance parts—may not be covered by a limited warranty. Tires and batteries usually have their own separate warranties.

When Sheldon bought his used car, the dealer gave him a warranty that included free repair or replacement for a limited time. Who makes the final decision to replace or repair the defective part, Sheldon or the dealer?

The dealer has the right to decide whether to repair or replace a defective part, and Sheldon has no choice but to go along with the decision.

Whenever I pick up my car after warranty work, I always have to pay some charge or other. Is this legal?

If your repairs are covered by a full warranty, you should not have to pay anything. If you have a limited warranty, which is usually the case, it may require that you bear part of the cost. Read your warranty carefully to make sure that you are not being charged for costs that should be paid by the dealer or the manufacturer.

Nearly every car salesman I've spoken to has told me about the benefits of purchasing an extended warranty. Are extended warranties as good as they say?

The value of a warranty depends on its terms and its cost. If you want protection for situations not covered by your warranty or if you want repairs guaranteed after your warranty runs out, consider buying an extended warranty. But before buying a warranty, compare it to the warranty that comes with the car you are buying. If the extended warranty contains too many restrictions, conditions, or limitations, or if it provides little more than the original warranty, it may not be a good investment.

Sandy sent in a claim under her extended service plan for repairs she had done on her station wagon, but she was turned down

because she had not had the work done by an authorized dealer. Isn't Sandy entitled to be reimbursed for the cost of the repairs?

No. Sandy's problem illustrates the difference between warranties and service plans. Under a service plan, the manufacturer has the right to limit coverage to its own dealers whether or not one is readily available when needed. A warranty, on the other hand, guarantees performance of the car's parts. A warranty can ask the consumer to use authorized dealers, but only if such a dealer is readily available when and where the car breaks down. If Sandy's car had broken down in an isolated area and she wasn't able to get to an authorized dealer, she could have been reimbursed for the cost of the repair work if her warranty had still been in effect, but not under her service contract.

Car Repairs

Andrea's mechanic said he couldn't fix her car until he did a thorough inspection, so he asked Andrea to sign a blank order for repairs. Is this OK?

No. Never give a mechanic a blank authorization for repairs. If the mechanic is unscrupulous, you could end up with a bill for thousands of dollars. By signing a blank authorization, Andrea would be agreeing to let the mechanic do anything he wanted and charge her for it.

A mechanic is entitled to charge you only for work that you authorize. You have the right to insist on an explanation of all repairs he thinks are necessary plus a written estimate of the costs of those repairs. In some states, such as California and New Hampshire, a mechanic is required by law to give a written estimate.

Marvin took his car to have an oil leak repaired. The mechanic went ahead and made other repairs without his permission. Must Marvin pay for all the repair work?

No. Marvin is obligated to pay only for the repairs that he authorized. The mechanic has no legal ground to demand payment for any work that Marvin did not approve.

A service station fixed Dorothy's car for $1,250 without first getting her approval. It took her six months to save up enough money to pay this bill, but when she tried to pay it yesterday, she

was told they were charging an additional $180 storage fee for the six months they kept the car. Is Dorothy responsible for paying the storage costs?

Dorothy does not have to pay for repairs that she did not authorize, and the service station had no right to keep her car or charge her storage costs. However, if she signed a blanket authorization form, it might have required her to pay storage costs if the repairman had to keep the car in order to collect his bill.

When Charles took his car for repairs, the mechanic did a poor job. Charles doesn't want to give the mechanic a chance to make things right, and he doesn't want to pay for bad work. Does he have an alternative?

Charles's best strategy is to pay the bill and then consider suing the mechanic for the amount it will cost to have someone else do the work. Otherwise, under the state's mechanic's or artisan's lien law, the mechanic is allowed to keep the car and sell it if Charles does not pay him—even if the mechanic's work is unsatisfactory.

Gabrielle took her car to a repair shop and was told that the engine needed to be rebuilt and that it would cost $800. The actual bill came to over $2,000. What can she do?

If Gabrielle did not get the estimate in writing, she is legally obligated to pay the bill. However, if the final cost of the work greatly exceeds the estimate, as it does in this case, Gabrielle may be the victim of a type of fraud called lowballing. Lowballing occurs when a mechanic gives you an estimate that is extremely low in order to persuade you to authorize repairs. The repairman knows the work cannot be done at that price and has no intention of honoring his estimate.

Gabrielle's best course of action is to pay the inflated repair bill and then sue the mechanic for fraud. If she wins her case, she will get her money back and may also be awarded punitive damages—a sum of money the court will order the mechanic to pay her as a punishment for committing the fraud.

If I take my car in for minor repairs and the repairman causes further damage, can he be held responsible?

Yes. When you leave your car with a repairman, he is required to take proper care of it, just as a dry cleaner is expected to care for your garments and not damage them when you entrust the garments to him. In this situation, the mechanic is required to repair the additional damage to your car or reimburse you for the expense of having someone else do it.

After Phyllis had her car's carburetor repaired, she drove 50 miles and stopped for lunch. When she got back into the car, it would not start. A tow truck took her to the nearest town, where a mechanic told her that a minor part on the carburetor was stuck, and fixed the problem. Can Phyllis collect from the first mechanic?

Yes. If Phyllis's carburetor failed because the first mechanic was negligent and did not do the job properly, he must reimburse Phyllis for the cost of having her car towed and repaired a second time.

Melanie's car bumper fell off four months after it was repaired at Brewster's Body Shop. Has too much time passed for Melanie to claim that the repair shop is responsible?

No. Melanie has every right to insist that the shop correct the problem at no cost to her. If the bumper fell off because Brewster's mounted it

How to Avoid Car Repair Rip-offs

Having your car in the repair shop is always an inconvenience, but even worse is the discovery that you have been charged for unnecessary or incompetent work, or for work that was not done at all. Here are some practical ways to make sure you get your money's worth when you take your car in for repair:

- Understand the procedure your mechanic uses to make estimates. Many states require written estimates, which list the costs for parts and labor separately and indicate if parts are used, rebuilt, or reconditioned. If major work is recommended, get a second opinion.
- Check the items on the work or repair order; they should describe exactly what you want done. When you sign a work order it becomes a legal contract between you and the repair shop. Do not sign it if it is incorrect or too vague. Do not sign a blank work order. If you do, you will be authorizing the mechanic to make any repairs he wants to, and you will have to pay for them whether or not they were necessary.
- Find out about the shop's warranty for parts and labor; it should be in writing somewhere on the work order. If you don't find it, ask someone at the shop to give you a copy of their warranty policy, or have them write it on the work order. If the shop will not give you its warranty in writing,

improperly, Melanie should inform the shop immediately; delaying too long may weaken her case for having them fix it at their expense.

A tire store rotated and balanced Eugene's tires for $25. Four days later, one of the wheels came off, and the car was ruined in an accident. Is the tire store responsible?

Yes. If the wheel came off because of defective work at the tire store, the store is responsible for all the resulting damages.

While Gilbert's car was in the repair shop, his brand-new golf clubs and fishing tackle were stolen from the trunk. Is the repair shop responsible?

If Gilbert informed the shop manager that his sports equipment was in the trunk, the manager was required to protect it as he would his own property in the shop. If the shop was locked and the thief disconnected a burglar alarm to get in, the shop owner is not responsible for the loss, because he took reasonable steps to protect Gilbert's property. On the other hand, if he left Gilbert's car behind the shop with the keys in it, he did not exercise proper care and is responsible.

you should seriously consider taking your business elsewhere. Unless the warranty is in writing, you have no recourse if the work is unsatisfactory.

- Ask about the policy regarding the return of your car's replaced parts. You may want to have another mechanic examine them if you believe unnecessary work was done. You generally have the right to keep these parts unless they are under warranty and have to be returned to the manufacturer or dealer. There is usually a box on the work order that you can check to indicate whether or not you want the replaced parts. If not, have your request written on the work order.
- If the shop calls and recommends additional repairs, go back to the shop and sign another work or repair order. If you don't authorize the new work in writing, you may end up being billed for unnecessary work.
- If, after two or three days of normal driving, it is obvious that the repair work is not satisfactory, return the car to the shop and insist that the shop live up to its warranty and fix the problem.
- If you are out of town, try to find a full-service dealership that sells and services your type of car. If you belong to an automobile club, ask the local office to recommend a repair company.
- Always deal with a company that you know well or that a knowledgeable friend has recommended. To be on the safe side, pay with a credit card, so that you can stop payment if a dispute over the work arises.

Licenses and Registrations

If I allow my son to drive the family car for practice before he gets his learner's permit or driver's license, will I be given a summons if he is caught?

Yes. In most states it is illegal to allow an unlicensed driver to use your car, even if you accompany him. The penalties for doing so range from fines to imprisonment. If an unlicensed driver has an accident with your car and causes damage or injury, you too will be liable. In most states a would-be driver may practice only after he receives a learner's permit.

Why do some states require a new road test and written exam when someone moves to that state with a valid driver's license from another state?

Each state wants to ensure that its residents can drive safely. Some states will accept proof in the form of a valid license from another state. Others will not. These states want to make sure that a new driver understands the traffic laws, which vary from state to state.

Kim is going to attend college in another state. Will she have to get a new driver's license and new license plates in that state?

Probably. Many states require out-of-state residents to obtain driver's licenses and new registrations if they will be driving their cars extensively in the second state. Since Kim will be in the state nine months each year, she will probably have to obtain a new driver's license, register her car in the new state, and pay the required fees and taxes.

Does Roger need a special license to drive a delivery truck?

Yes. Most states require that a person who drives for a living have a chauffeur's license. Truck drivers, delivery men, bus drivers, and taxi drivers are among those who must have a chauffeur's license. If Roger's job requires him to drive only once in a while, however, he may not need the special license.

Reggie has been driving with an expired driver's license. What can happen to him if he gets caught?

He can be fined and even sentenced to jail. In some places his license can be suspended, and he wouldn't be eligible to get a new one until the end of the suspension period. If you are caught driving with an expired license, you should renew your license before you appear in court. The judge may be more lenient if you show him that you are now complying with the law.

Can the state suspend my driver's license if I am in an accident?

Yes, if you have violated a law in connection with that accident. If you leave the scene of an accident or have been driving under the influence of alcohol or drugs, it may result in an automatic suspension of your license. Your license may be suspended if you have accumulated several moving violations, or points, on your record, or if you don't carry the insurance your state requires. The U. S. Supreme Court has ruled, however, that the state must hold a hearing to determine if an uninsured driver is liable for damages before his license can be suspended.

James was driving with an expired driver's license when he was in an accident. James was not at fault. Will his expired license prohibit him from collecting damages?

No. The fact that James's driver's license had expired does not make him responsible for the accident. He should be able to collect damages for personal injury and property damage.

What is the difference between having my license suspended and having it revoked?

When your license is suspended, you are deprived of driving privileges for a certain period of time, usually 30, 60, or 90 days. Afterward, your license can be reinstated. In some cases, you may have to take the written test or the road test again. When your driver's license is revoked, you are permanently banned from driving. However, some states—such as Illinois, Tennessee, and West Virginia—will allow you to apply for reinstatement after a specified period of time, usually one to five years.

How many tickets must I receive before my license is suspended?

Each state sets its own standards for suspending or revoking a license. Licenses are often suspended when a driver has accumulated a certain number of violations in a stated period of time, usually one or two years.

Some states use a point system to determine when a license should be suspended. Driving through a stop sign might be a one-point offense, and reckless driving might be four points. When a driver exceeds the allowed number of points within the period specified by the laws of his state, his license will be suspended. In addition, such offenses as leaving the scene of an accident and driving under the influence of alcohol or drugs automatically result in a suspension of driving privileges in most states.

Ray works in my store. If his license is suspended for one year but he is given a permit that allows him to drive to work, can he drive company vehicles for purposes that are work-related?

No. Ray must comply exactly with the conditions imposed on him when his license was suspended. If he is caught violating any of these conditions, he could be subject to severe penalties, including jail.

Since I was away several months, I was unable to renew my car registration before it expired. Will they give me an extension?

Your state may allow a 30-day grace period in which you can renew your registration after it expires. Call your state department of motor vehicles for information. If there is no grace period, it is illegal for you to drive your car once the registration has expired, regardless of the reason why.

Eric has been restoring an old car and had to replace the engine. A friend told him he had to let the motor vehicle department know he was doing this. Is this correct?

Yes. In most states you must file a special registration form when you replace a car's engine. Eric should contact his motor vehicles department.

Tickets and Violations

Jennifer parked her car at a two-hour meter. When she returned an hour later, one of the car wheels had a "boot" on it—a metal device that locks around the tire to prevent the car from being driven away. It took her several hours and cost her $50 to have the boot removed. Jennifer thinks that she is being punished without the opportunity to defend herself. Isn't this unconstitutional?

No. Most people who find boots on their cars have several unpaid parking tickets. This is one method cities use to catch *scofflaws*—people who ignore parking tickets. Courts have consistently ruled that using boots and towing away illegally parked cars are not unconstitutional.

Kenneth was arrested and spent the night in jail for 17 unpaid parking tickets. Is this legal?

Yes. Most traffic tickets are also summonses, which require the driver to appear in court. If you don't pay a ticket or appear in court in answer to the ticket summons, a warrant may be issued for your arrest.

A police officer ticketed Agnes last night because the taillight on her car had burned out. Shouldn't she have received a warning instead of a summons and a fine?

In most states it is illegal to drive with defective equipment. Thus the officer was right to issue the ticket. As a practical matter, a judge may not fine Agnes if she brings proof to court that she replaced the light.

If I'm stopped by a police officer and my passenger is not wearing a seat belt, as required by law, who must pay the fine?

Most statutes requiring the use of seat belts make each individual responsible for himself. However, the driver is often held responsible for making sure that any children in the car are wearing their seat belts.

Will Charlene be fined if she lets her baby ride on her lap instead of in his car seat?

Yes, if she is driving in a state that requires children to ride in car seats. If she cannot afford to buy a car seat for her child, many hospitals have programs that lend car seats to parents who need them.

Oliver's state has a mandatory helmet law for motorcycle riders. If Oliver allows his daughter to ride a motorcycle without a helmet, can he be fined?

No. Oliver's daughter, not Oliver, would receive the citation for driving or riding without a helmet. Not all states or cities have helmet laws, and these laws have created considerable controversy over the proper role of government intervention in our daily lives. Courts in Alabama, Arizona, Arkansas, Colorado, Florida, Hawaii, Kansas, Maine, Texas, Utah, and other states have ruled that helmet laws are valid because of the government interest in promoting the health, safety, and welfare of its citizens. At least one state court, that of Ohio, has taken the opposite view: Since helmet laws only protect the rider from himself, there is no public interest to be served, and they are, therefore, unconstitutional.

Tickets and Violations

When I walk downtown, I have difficulty crossing the street because cars come around the corner too fast. Don't pedestrians have the right of way?

Yes. Pedestrians do have the right of way at crossings. If cars are not yielding the right of way at an intersection, inform the police so they can monitor the intersection for traffic violations and unsafe conditions.

Is it against the law to hitchhike or pick up a hitchhiker?

Yes. Most places make it illegal to solicit a ride, and prohibit drivers from picking up hitchhikers. These laws are not enforced in emergency situations such as accidents.

May went through an intersection on a yellow light. A police officer saw this and gave her a ticket for failing to obey a traffic control signal. Should May have been given the ticket?

Yes. May was required to stop before entering the intersection when the light was yellow, unless she could not do so safely.

Dennis came to a stop sign and stopped. He saw another car approaching on the main road and knew that if he moved quickly, he could get across the intersection safely. He did so, but a police officer gave him a ticket for not yielding the right of way. Dennis insists that he is not guilty, because he obeyed the stop sign. Is Dennis right?

No. Dennis was required to yield the right of way to any approaching traffic at the intersection. This does not mean that he had to wait until every approaching car passed, but that he had to use reasonable care in determining if he could cross the intersection without a collision. If Dennis had to hurry to get across, or if the approaching motorist had to hit his brakes or swerve to avoid a collision, the police officer was correct in ticketing him.

Maurice received a ticket for speeding. The only evidence against him was the radar reading. Is this sufficient for a conviction?

Yes. In most states radar readings are considered reliable measurements of actual speed. The prosecutor must establish, by testimony of the police officer or state trooper who took the reading, that the radar equipment was set up properly, was in good working order, and had been tested for accuracy before and after the reading. Maurice may be able to contest the reading's accuracy if the officer acknowledges that there was other traffic between the radar equipment and Maurice's car.

When Laura was stopped for speeding, the police officer told her that her speed was calculated by timing how long it took her car to travel a measured distance. How does such a method work?

A police team measures a section of highway, marks its boundaries, and times the cars as they enter and leave the measured section. Knowing the distance and the time it takes to cover the distance, they can easily calculate a car's speed. At least one state (California) has declared, however, that evidence obtained this way is inadmissible in court.

Jodi's speedometer shows a speed lower than her actual speed. Is this a good defense if she gets a speeding ticket?

No. The fact that Jodi didn't intend to speed is not an adequate defense. Many judges, however, will excuse offenders like Jodi if they submit proof that the speedometer was faulty and that it has been repaired.

Seventeen-year-old Brandon was stopped for speeding in a school zone. What penalties is he subject to?

Brandon will probably receive a fine, and the judge may require that he attend a driver education or driver improvement course. The fact that Brandon is 17 will have no impact on the punishment he receives; most traffic courts treat teenagers and adults the same way. In addition to the fine, Brandon's speeding violation will be counted against his driving record; too many violations in a certain time period could cause him to lose his license.

Mitchell was driving home when he saw the flashing lights of a police car at a roadblock. As Mitchell slowed down, a police officer waved him over and asked to see his driver's license and registration. After a few minutes, the officer sent Mitchell on his way. Did the stop violate Mitchell's rights?

No. The police in many states use license and registration checks at roadblocks to detect drunk drivers. These roadblocks are also referred to as sobriety checkpoints. For a number of years, the courts disagreed on whether these roadblocks violated a driver's Fourth Amendment rights to be free from unreasonable searches and seizures. Finally, in 1990 the United States Supreme Court held that sobriety checkpoints are permissible and do not constitute an unreasonable search or seizure, because the government has an important interest in finding drunk drivers, and because the stop is usually a short one for sober drivers.

When my son pleaded guilty to reckless driving, he was fined $200 and placed on probation, his driver's license was suspended for six months, and he has to go to driver education classes. Isn't this a severe penalty for careless driving when there was no accident?

Traffic code violations are divided into infractions, punishable by fines, and more serious violations, punishable by fines, jail, or such other sentences as driver education or improvement courses, suspending and revoking driving privileges, community service, and one or more weekends in jail—commonly called shock probation. A judge can order any or all of these punishments.

Can I be arrested if I have unpaid traffic tickets in another state?

Yes. Every state has the right to request another state to arrest someone who has committed a crime and then left the state. That person can be extradited, or returned, to the state where the crime was committed. It is unlikely, however, that a state would go through a complicated extradition procedure for someone who is only wanted for unpaid traffic tickets.

Rita was given a ticket for not yielding the right of way, and will have to appear in traffic court. Should she hire a lawyer?

No, unless she has so many moving violations, or points, on her record that her driving privileges could be revoked if she is convicted. In such an event, a lawyer could try to persuade the prosecutor to let Rita plead guilty to a lesser charge so that she wouldn't lose her license.

Do I have a right to a jury trial for a traffic violation?

Not in most cases. Traffic violations are usually petty crimes and carry penalties of no more than six months in jail. Some violations, though, such as drunk driving, carry more serious penalties. Defendants involved in these more serious charges would have the right to choose a jury trial.

What will happen if Lindsay cannot pay her traffic fine?

If Lindsay gives the judge good reasons why she is unable to pay, he may change the penalty and sentence her instead, for example, to attend a driver's school. Some judges will give her additional time to pay the fine. However, if Lindsay does not pay the fine within the specified period, she will be in contempt of court, and the judge can issue a warrant for her arrest and sentence her to jail.

Drinking and Driving

What can a policeman legally do to determine if a person has been driving while intoxicated?

If a police officer has a reasonable suspicion that you are driving while intoxicated, he has the right to stop you. The officer's suspicion must be based on his observations. Generally, police officers watch for erratic driving or other signs of impaired judgment, such as not turning on your car lights while driving at night.

If you are stopped and you appear intoxicated, or if there is a strong odor of alcohol about you, the officer may ask you to perform a field sobriety test. This consists of one or more physical tasks such as walking a straight line, picking something up from the ground, and extending your arms and leaning backwards.

The police officer may also ask you such questions as "Have you been drinking?" "How many drinks have you had?" and "When did you start and stop drinking?" Finally, the officer may ask you to take a chemical test of your breath, blood, or urine to determine the amount of alcohol in your blood. The breath test is given at the time a driver is stopped. Blood and urine tests are administered at the police station or at a medical facility.

Beverly's father has great difficulty keeping his balance and flunked the field sobriety test. Does that mean he will be convicted of drunk driving?

No. The court will consider many factors, along with balance, in determining if a driver was intoxicated. The court will take into account the driver's physical condition at the time of the arrest. Were his eyes red or glassy? Was he disheveled? Was there an odor of alcohol about him? If he was given chemical tests, did they show a high blood alcohol content?

The court will also consider his behavior and attitude. Was his speech slurred? Did he admit to drinking too much? Was he able to speak rationally, or was he incoherent? Was he belligerent or cooperative?

Drinking and Driving

Can I be convicted of drunk driving even though I passed a roadside breath test for alcohol?

Yes, if the amount of alcohol you have consumed has affected your ability to drive as demonstrated by the results of a field sobriety test.

A policeman stopped Bill's car because he suspected that Bill had been drinking. Does Bill have to submit to a roadside breath test? Can he talk to an attorney before it is conducted?

Bill does not have to let the police give him a breath test to determine if he is intoxicated, but under the laws of most states, if he refuses, his license could be suspended or revoked. Bill's license could not be suspended or revoked if he refused to take a field sobriety test, such as walking a straight line or picking up a coin. However, such a refusal is almost certain to result in the police officer's asking Bill to submit to a roadside breath test or some other chemical test.

The question of Bill's right to consult an attorney before consenting or refusing to take a breath test has been answered differently in different

How Many Drinks Make You Legally Drunk?

In most states anyone with a blood alcohol level greater than .10 percent is considered legally drunk. The number of drinks it takes to make you drunk varies from person to person and depends on such factors as the amount of alcohol you've consumed, how much food you've eaten, your individual tolerance for alcohol, your age and weight, whether you're taking medication, and whether you are male or female. (Females tend to be more susceptible to alcohol because of their body chemistry.) The chart below is a guide to the effect of alcohol on your ability to drive.

	Drinks in a Two-Hour Period †		
BODY WEIGHT	CAUTION ADVISED	ABILITY IMPAIRED	LEGALLY DRUNK
100–120 pounds	2	3	4 or more
140–160 pounds	2	3–4	5 or more
180–200 pounds	3	4–5	6 or more
220–240 pounds	4	5–6	7 or more

† A drink is 6 ounces of wine, 1½ ounces of liquor, or 12 ounces of beer.

states. Courts in Alaska, Iowa, Minnesota, New York, Vermont, and Washington have ruled that a driver does have the right to talk to an attorney before deciding whether or not to take the test. Courts in Arizona, California, Colorado, Hawaii, Kansas, Kentucky, Louisiana, Maine, Michigan, Nebraska, Nevada, New Hampshire, Oklahoma, Oregon, Pennsylvania, South Dakota, Utah, and Virginia have held the opposite—that there is no constitutional right to consult an attorney in such situations.

Joanna rode home from a party with her boyfriend. She knew he had been drinking, but she didn't think he was drunk. If he had been arrested for drunk driving, could Joanna too have been arrested for letting him drive?

In some states—such as California, Kansas, North Carolina, and Texas—a person can be found guilty of a crime if he lets a person who is intoxicated drive. If Joanna gave her boyfriend the keys to her car and asked him to drive her home, she too could be arrested, if she lives in one of these states. However, if the intoxicated boyfriend was driving his car or another over which Joanna had no control, she could not be arrested for merely riding with him.

Is it legal to have an open beer in my hand while driving?

Many states, including Kansas, Illinois, and California, prohibit open containers of alcohol in cars and other vehicles. In those states, you can be arrested for driving with an open beer in your hand. You could also be arrested for having an open beer—or any other alcoholic drink—on the seat beside you or on the floor.

After traveling a few blocks, Cliff realized he was in no condition to drive. He parked his car on the street, shut off the engine, and went to sleep. He woke up to discover a policeman at his window. After a brief conversation, Cliff was arrested for drunk driving. Was Cliff's arrest justifiable, since he was not driving when he was arrested?

Yes. If Cliff admitted to the police officer that he had driven a few blocks before pulling over, he could be arrested for driving while intoxicated. It is more likely, however, that he was arrested for having control of a motor vehicle while intoxicated. Cliff was in the car, had the car keys with him, and could have started driving again at any time; therefore, he was considered to be in control of his car. Most states make it illegal for an intoxicated person to have control over a vehicle, even if that person is not operating it at the time.

Drinking and Driving

Doug's son, Allen, was arrested for drunk driving. It was his first offense. Will his license be suspended?

It could be. Many states automatically suspend a driver's license if the driver is convicted of drunk driving. However, Allen may qualify for a diversion program offered by many courts. If so, he would plead guilty to the drunk driving charge, but the judge would put him on probation until he completed a special program, usually requiring attendance at an alcohol education course. If Allen did not complete the course, or if he were arrested again for drunk driving, his probation would be revoked and he would be sentenced for drunk driving. If Allen completed the course, however, the drunk driving charge would be dismissed at the end of the probationary period. His driving record would not reflect a drunk driving conviction, and his license would not be suspended.

Does Anne have the right to a lawyer if she is arrested and charged with drunk driving?

Whenever a person is charged with a crime that carries a possible jail sentence, he has the right to be represented by an attorney. In most states and cities, drunk driving is punishable by jail. If Anne cannot afford to hire an attorney, the court must appoint one for her.

My son-in-law was in a car accident after drinking too much liquor in my home. Can the people injured in the accident sue me?

Until 1984, no court would have held you responsible. The courts felt that the person who consumed the alcohol, not the person who furnished it, was responsible. However, a person who furnished liquor to a minor in his home would be held responsible if the minor then had an accident.

Since 1984, courts in Indiana, Iowa, and New Jersey have ruled that a host who serves liquor to an obviously intoxicated person, knowing that person intends to drive, is also liable if that person causes an accident. These rulings may signal a trend that other states will follow.

If a tavern serves me several drinks and I have an accident on the way home, can I sue the tavern?

In most states, dramshop laws make a tavern owner responsible if he serves alcohol to an obviously intoxicated person who then causes injuries or property damage. However, only those who are injured or whose property is damaged by an intoxicated person can sue the tavern

Penalties for Drunk Driving

Drunk driving, or driving while intoxicated (DWI)—the terms mean the same thing—has aroused so much public concern that state laws are getting tougher and the punishments more severe. Probation and suspended sentences, once common penalties for first offenders, are no longer the rule. Although the types of sentences a judge can impose for drunk driving vary from state to state, they tend to be similar. They include the following, often in combination:

- Fines.
- Confinement in jail for several days to several months.
- Suspending or revoking a driver's license.
- Community service work.
- Participation in a rehabilitation program for alcoholics.

Some states have enacted mandatory sentences, even for first-time offenders. If a person has been guilty of drunk driving before, usually within five years, the sentence is more severe. Repeat offenders face longer jail terms, higher fines, and a loss of driving privileges for a greater period of time.

In many states, drunk driving that kills or seriously injures someone is a felony. It is also a felony for a drunk driver to leave the scene of an accident. Conviction for a felony usually results in much heavier fines and longer terms of imprisonment.

owner. If you cause an accident after drinking too much in a tavern, the people you injure, or whose property is damaged, could sue both you and the tavern keeper.

While Victor was traveling through another state, he was arrested and convicted for drunk driving. Can his license be suspended?

Yes. When an out-of-state driver commits a traffic violation, it is common practice to send proof of the conviction to the agency that issued the driver's license. So Victor's violations will count against his license just as if they had been committed in his home state.

Gwendolyn was driving home from a party despite the fact that she was drunk. She was involved in an accident that caused an injury, but the accident was not her fault. Will the fact that she was drunk affect her liability?

If Gwendolyn's intoxicated condition did not cause the accident, she will not be liable. For example, if Gwendolyn had been waiting for the traffic light to turn green at an intersection and a station wagon hit her from behind, she is not responsible for the accident, and therefore not liable, regardless of her physical condition. However, Gwendolyn could still be arrested for drunk driving.

Alex was involved in an accident with Carl and is now being sued in two separate lawsuits. One charges him with driving while intoxicated; the other seeks damages for Carl's injuries. What's going on here?

If Alex was driving while intoxicated and the accident was his fault, his actions have both criminal and civil consequences. He will be prosecuted in criminal court for breaking the law against driving while intoxicated. The case against him will be prosecuted by the state or local government; he can be punished by a fine, jail, or probation with special conditions such as alcohol counseling or community service.

Carl's lawsuit for damages against Alex will be heard in a civil court. In a civil case, it is the person who has been injured who files the lawsuit, not the government. The goal of the civil case is to determine if the injuries or property damages suffered by Carl were Alex's fault, and if so, how much Alex should compensate him.

At the Scene of an Accident

Do all accidents have to be reported to the police—even minor fender benders?

If an accident injures someone or causes damage to someone's property in excess of a certain amount—usually \$100 to \$200—it must be reported to the police.

On his way to work, Patrick witnessed a car accident. But he was in a hurry and didn't stop. Did Patrick have a legal obligation to stop or to notify the police and make a statement?

No. Patrick was not required by law to stop at the scene of an accident in which he was not involved, nor was he required to report the accident to the police. But if he thought his testimony as a witness could be helpful later in court, he should have stopped and identified himself to the people involved in the accident or to the police.

A child was hit by a car in the alley behind my house. I wanted to help so I picked her up, carried her into my yard, and wrapped her in a blanket. Later, I was told that I should not have moved her. Can I be held liable?

You are not required by law to assist anyone in distress unless you caused their predicament or have a special relationship with that person, such as parent-child or employer-employee. Once you decide to help an injured person, you must use reasonable care so that you don't make the person's condition worse. Your actions will be judged in the light of your knowledge or training and the circumstances of the accident, but you will not be held to the same standard of care as a physician or paramedic.

Every state has some type of Good Samaritan law, which protects people who aid accident victims from liability for any further injuries they cause while assisting the injured. Some state laws only protect doctors; others protect all trained medical personnel; and still others protect anyone who comes to the aid of another person.

While driving, Eleanor accidentally ran off the road and damaged an unoccupied parked car. What should she do?

Eleanor should leave her name, address, and telephone number affixed to the damaged car so the owner will know whom to contact. She must report the accident to the police, and give them the license number of the unoccupied car so they can help her trace the owner.

Keith was driving on a foggy night and killed a deer that was crossing the road. What should he do?

Keith should not move the deer unless it is blocking the road, and he should absolutely not load it into his car and take it home. That is illegal. Keith should report the accident to the police and then contact the nearest office of the state conservation or fish and game department. In some states, Keith would be allowed to take the animal home after the authorities had examined it.

It was raining as Carole drove along the expressway at the speed limit. Suddenly she saw that cars were stopping up ahead. She hit the brakes, and her car spun around. The cars behind piled into one another to avoid hitting her, but her car was not touched. What should she do?

Although Carole's automobile wasn't struck, she is still part of the accident. She should contact the police, or make sure that someone else

At the Scene of an Accident

does so, then stay at the scene and follow the instructions of the police when they arrive. If Carole drives away, she can be charged with leaving the scene of an accident, a serious criminal offense punishable by fines, jail, or loss of driving privileges.

When Jan's car was hit in the middle of a busy intersection, she refused to move it until the police arrived on the scene. This created a terrible traffic jam. Would it have been OK for Jan to move the car out of the way?

Yes. If Jan was able to pull her car over to the side of the road or off the road completely, she probably should have done so. By blocking the intersection, she could have caused further accidents and even more damage to her own car. If Jan was concerned about preserving evidence and giving the police an accurate version of what had happened, she should have taken down the names, addresses, and telephone numbers of witnesses to the accident. Their statements, plus an analysis of damage to the cars, marks left on the pavement, and debris from the accident, will help the police reconstruct the event.

Liability for Automobile Accidents

For information on automobile insurance, see Chapter 8, *Insurance*.

In automobile accident claims, what is the difference between negligence and liability?

You are negligent if you do something you should not have done, or you fail to do something that you should have done. If you run a red light, for example, you are negligent. If you fail to use your headlights after sunset, you are negligent. If your negligent act results in an accident, you become liable for any personal injury or damage that you cause. Liability means you are obligated to compensate the person who is injured, or whose property is damaged as a result of your negligence.

If I am innocent of negligence in an automobile accident, can I still be liable for damages?

No, unless someone else causes an accident while driving your car. You might be held liable if you allowed someone in your family to use the car when you knew it had a serious defect, such as bad brakes or faulty signal lights, and the person caused an accident. If you own a business, you might be held liable for damages caused by an employee while he was driving a company vehicle—or his own car—on company business.

If Priscilla lends her car to a friend who is visiting her for the holidays, who will be responsible if her friend has an accident with the car and injures someone or causes property damage?

Priscilla's friend is liable if she is negligent. In some cases, the injured person may sue Priscilla as well. If Priscilla's friend was intoxicated, or didn't have a driver's license, or was unfit to drive for any other reason, Priscilla could be held liable for entrusting the car to her.

Can the passengers in my car sue me if I have an accident and they are hurt?

You have a duty to take reasonable care to protect all your passengers from injury. If your passengers are injured because of your negligence, or because you didn't use reasonable care, they may sue you.

Because the street in front of my apartment is very steep, I always set my emergency brake when I park. Last night the car rolled down the hill and struck another parked car. Will I have to pay for these damages?

Everyone is required to use reasonable care when parking a vehicle. When you park on a steep hill, you are expected to angle your front wheels in toward the curb and set the emergency brake. If you don't do these things, you will probably be held responsible for the damages. Some states have a "safe brake" statute, which requires you to maintain adequate brakes on your car. If your state has a law like this, you might be considered responsible if your car rolled down the hill because the brakes didn't hold.

Edna's car was damaged by a shopping cart that rolled downhill in the supermarket parking lot. She wasn't there when it occurred, so she doesn't know how it happened. What can she do?

Not very much. Unless Edna can find a witness who saw the accident and can tell her who was responsible for it, her best recourse is to submit a claim to her insurance company. The supermarket would not be liable for the damage done to the car unless Edna had evidence that it was negligent in managing the parking lot and that this negligence led to the damage to her car.

Liability for Automobile Accidents

Nell's car was damaged in an automatic car wash. Isn't the car wash liable for the repairs?

Yes, if the damage was caused by defective equipment or a negligent employee, or if the instructions for operating the car wash were wrong, misleading, or incomplete. On the other hand, if the damage occurred because Nell disregarded instructions or acted recklessly, the car wash would not be liable.

Adam's car was vandalized while it was parked in a commercial garage. Is the garage owner responsible for the damage?

If the garage is one where Adam parks his own car, locks it, and keeps the keys, the garage owner has no duty to protect Adam's car and is not responsible for the damage done to it. Adam is considered to be renting or leasing space from the garage owner. On the other hand, if Adam gives his car keys to an attendant who parks the car, the law expects the garage owner to care for Adam's car in the same way he would care for his own property. For example, if the owner left the garage unattended and the vandals came in during that time, or if an attendant vandalized Adam's car, the garage owner would be responsible for the damage.

The person who stole Russell's car was involved in an accident. Is Russell liable?

No. Russell is not responsible for damages caused by a thief—or anyone else—who uses his car without permission.

What happens if both drivers involved in an automobile accident are at fault?

In the past, if an automobile accident was due to the negligence of both drivers involved, neither could sue the other for his injuries or for the damage done to his car. This rule was called contributory negligence, and its effects were sometimes unfair. For example, if an accident was 95 percent driver A's fault, driver B still could not collect monetary compensation, since he was 5 percent responsible.

Because of the unfairness caused in applying the rule of contributory negligence, courts and lawmakers have been replacing it with the rule of comparative negligence. Under this much fairer rule, financial responsibility for an automobile accident is divided according to the degree of fault of each driver.

If someone is injured because his car was in my blind spot, can I be held responsible?

Yes. You are responsible for being aware of all blind spots.

I hit a pothole and needed $200 worth of repairs. Is the city liable?

Yes, if the pothole was wide and deep enough to be dangerous and if the city was aware or should have been aware that this dangerous condition existed. Cities have a duty to be aware of the condition of their streets and to keep them reasonably safe.

Is there something special I should do if I am involved in an accident with a city or state vehicle?

If the accident was due to the other driver's negligence, and you were injured or your property was damaged, you should consider suing the city or state. Some people may claim that you can't sue the state or that it is protected by sovereign immunity. These concepts came into the American legal system from English common law and date back to the time when the king was the government. The king could do no wrong, so you could not sue the government or any government official or employee. In the United States, *sovereign immunity* came to mean that you, a citizen, cannot sue the government or a person acting for the government unless the government consents to the lawsuit. This seemed so unfair that many states passed laws making it possible to sue state and local governments without their consent. Even in states where such laws have not been passed, the courts have ruled that an individual can sue the state or city government when one of its employees is accused of negligence.

It is not a simple matter to sue the government. Most cities and states have time limits within which a claim can be filed. They also have special requirements for the form of the claim.

Stephanie was driving to the grocery store at night when she hit a truck that had stopped in front of her. The truck's taillights were not working. Shouldn't that relieve Stephanie of any obligation to pay for the damage done to the truck?

Stephanie would not be liable if it had been impossible to see the truck and avoid hitting it. This would be the case, for example, if the truck had been stopped on the highway right below the crest of a hill, far away from a streetlight. But if the truck was easy to see even without its taillights and Stephanie hit it because she wasn't paying enough attention to the road, she would be responsible.

Liability for Automobile Accidents

I was injured in a four-car accident. How can I tell who is responsible for my injuries if I don't know which car hit me?

In a chain reaction accident, one or several drivers may be responsible for your injuries, regardless of who hit you. If one driver started the events that led to your part in the accident, he is responsible even if his car never touched yours. If several drivers contributed to the accident by their carelessness, they are all responsible. You don't have to find out which of the four cars actually hit you; the important thing is to determine which car caused the accident.

When Ben had his car accident, he was ticketed for running a stop sign. Does this mean he can't collect damages?

If Ben caused the accident by running the stop sign, he will probably not be able to collect damages; in fact, he will probably be liable for the damages suffered by the others involved in the accident. If Ben was not the main cause of the accident, however, he may be able to collect some damages from the person who caused it. If Ben's traffic violation had no bearing on the accident, he would be able to collect from the person who caused the accident.

Harry was involved in a minor traffic accident in which the other driver was at fault. But immediately after the accident Harry jumped out of his car and cried, "Oh no, it's all my fault. Look what I've done!" By the time the police arrived, Harry had regained his composure and denied responsibility. Can Harry's first statement be used against him?

Yes. Such a statement can be used if Harry becomes involved in a court case. However, his statement is not enough, by itself, to shift the blame for the accident to him. The other driver will have to offer evidence, beyond Harry's statement, that the accident was Harry's fault.

Angela received serious injuries in an automobile accident. If she had been wearing her seat belt when the accident occurred, she might not have been injured so badly. Could Angela's failure to fasten her seat belt prevent her from recovering damages from the other driver?

Possibly. Lawyers have often argued that the driver who causes an accident is not responsible for the full extent of the other person's injuries

What to Do If You Are in an Accident

The first few minutes after an accident are critically important in getting medical assistance for the injured and in establishing exactly what happened. The following steps can help you later if there is a dispute about an insurance settlement:

- ☑ Check for injuries among drivers and passengers.
- ☑ Call the police; request an ambulance if necessary.
- ☑ If you can, move your car out of the traffic and turn on its flashing hazard lights to warn other drivers.
- ☑ Get the names, addresses, and telephone numbers of witnesses before they leave the scene.
- ☑ Write down the other driver's name, address, telephone number, make and model of car, license plate number, driver's license number, and the name and address of his insurance company and its local agent.
- ☑ Limit your remarks about the accident; don't discuss who is at fault or the extent of your insurance coverage.
- ☑ Note the time of the accident, the weather, and the road conditions.
- ☑ If possible, take pictures or make sketches of the scene of the accident. Record skid marks, the point where the cars collided, damage to the cars, and the location of any road signs.
- ☑ Take pictures of your car showing all damage in detail.
- ☑ See your doctor immediately, even if you don't seem to be hurt. You may have a serious injury and not know it right away.
- ☑ Keep a diary after the accident, especially if you are injured. It will help you recall specific events if you need to testify later.
- ☑ Don't sign anything hurriedly. Harmless-looking forms may include statements in which you agree not to make any claims against the other person, or in which you accept liability for the accident.
- ☑ Notify your insurance agent of the accident as soon as possible.
- ☑ If there are personal injuries or extensive property damage that might exceed your insurance coverage, consult an attorney.

if the injured person was not wearing a seat belt. This defense has been used successfully in Florida, Illinois, New Jersey, and New York. Courts in other states, such as Iowa, Maine, Minnesota, Tennessee, and Virginia, have rejected it, ruling that the accident was caused not by the injured person's failure to wear a seat belt, but by the other person's recklessness.

After an accident, the other driver offered to pay me $1,000 if I would sign a release from further liability. Is this a good idea?

No. Never sign a release until you know the extent of your injuries and the amount of damage to your property. Signing this type of release usually will prevent you from suing the other driver later if you discover more injuries or greater damage to your car. Get a complete physical examination from your doctor to determine if you have any injuries and how serious they are. Be sure to get estimates for all work necessary to repair your automobile. If your personal injuries and the damage to your vehicle will be covered by $1,000, you may want to consider signing the release. But don't be in too big a hurry; some injuries do not show up until many days after an accident. If you do sign the release, be sure you understand all its legal ramifications.

Gene's car was hit from behind while he was making a left turn into a parking lot. The other driver, who was tipsy, waved his checkbook at Gene and offered to pay him $750, which would more than cover Gene's repair bill, if he didn't report the accident. Should Gene accept the offer?

Definitely not. There are several reasons why Gene should not accept the other driver's offer. First, Gene is required by law to report the accident if the damages exceed a certain amount—usually $100 to $200. Second, although Gene's quick assessment at the scene of the accident leads him to believe that $750 will cover his damages, he may have injuries that he has not discovered yet, or the cost to repair his car may be more than he thinks. Finally, Gene has no guarantee that the other driver's check is good. By the time Gene discovers that the check is worthless, it will be difficult, if not impossible, to locate witnesses.

Christie was involved in a minor fender bender in which no one was cut or bruised. Should she see a doctor anyway?

Yes. Many times people suffer physical injuries in automobile accidents that are not immediately apparent. So she should see her doctor as soon as she can, even if she thinks she is all right. If the doctor discovers an injury that might give her trouble later, this will provide the evidence she needs to make a claim against the other driver. If she waits too long to see a doctor (or if she agrees to a settlement with the other driver before she discovers her injury), she may be unable to make a claim.

Al was severely injured by a hit-and-run driver. Will he be stuck with all of his medical bills from this accident?

If the police can't find the hit-and-run driver, Al will have to pay his bills himself unless his own insurance covers him for this situation. Some states have indemnity funds to compensate the victims of hit-and-run or uninsured drivers. Since it is a crime to leave the scene of an accident, a state fund that compensates victims of crime might cover Al's accident. If he is not adequately covered by insurance, he should write to his state legislator asking if there is a state fund that could help him.

Abigail asked her neighbor for a ride to the grocery store and got hurt when the neighbor ran a stop sign and hit another car. The neighbor says Abigail can't sue a Good Samaritan. Is this true?

No. Abigail's neighbor is confused. Good Samaritan laws protect people who help victims of accidents. They offer no protection to someone simply because she was doing the victim a favor when the accident occurred. Abigail has the same right to sue her neighbor as any other passengers involved in an accident would have to sue their driver.

My wife was driving, and I was asleep in the back seat, when she ran off the road and hit a tree. I was seriously injured. My neighbor said I should sue my wife. What would I gain?

You might get a much higher payment from your insurance company to cover medical expenses and loss of income. If you don't sue, all the insurance company will pay is what is due under the medical payments clause of your policy. But if you sue, you may be awarded damages up to the full amount of your personal liability coverage.

In the past, spouses were not able to sue each other for injuries in a situation like this. But the law is changing, and now many states will allow you to sue your spouse for negligence. These states include Alabama, Colorado, Connecticut, Idaho, Kentucky, Maryland, Massachusetts, Michigan, Missouri, Nebraska, New Jersey, New York, North Carolina, Rhode Island, Tennessee, Virginia, Vermont, and Wisconsin.

While out driving two years ago, Tom hit a child who was riding his bike in the street. The police and paramedics were called to the scene, but the child appeared to be fine. Now Tom is being sued for injuries to the child. What should he do?

Tom should contact his automobile insurance company or the one he had at the time of the accident. If his policy covers this type of claim, the insurance company will provide an attorney to defend Tom. If Tom's insurance does not cover this accident, he should consult his own attorney right away. He has a limited amount of time to respond to the lawsuit, and there are complex legal rules that he must comply with or run the risk of damaging his case.

Liability for Automobile Accidents

A year ago Robert had an accident and had to pay the other driver a large sum. At the time, Robert suspected his car had some defect. Now he has received a notice that it is being recalled. Shouldn't the manufacturer be responsible for the money Robert had to pay because of the defect?

The fact that Robert's car is being recalled is not proof that the accident was due to a possible defect. However, if the recall discovers a defect that could have caused or contributed to his accident, he may have a case against the manufacturer. Robert would have to prove that the accident would not have happened if the defect hadn't existed or that, even if it was not the only factor, the defect contributed to the accident.

Janet has agreed to drive eight neighborhood children to school, since she has a van. Are there agreements or releases that Janet should get from the other parents?

Janet should consider having the parents sign a release agreeing not to sue her if she has an accident that injures the children. However, such a release may not hold up in all courts. Some courts will not recognize agreements protecting someone against suits for injuries that have not yet occurred. If Janet is at fault in an accident, she may be faced with a lawsuit regardless of what papers the parents signed.

CHAPTER

7

Your Money

Financial Institutions

My friend Dudley advised me to switch my money from a savings bank to a regular, or commercial, bank because I will get more services and be charged lower fees. Is he right?

Not necessarily. The only way to know for sure is to check the specific services and fees of your bank against those of other banks. Also compare the minimum balances required, and interest paid, by the banks on their various kinds of accounts. Until banking deregulation was enacted by Congress in the 1980's, savings and regular banks were quite different. Now any bank can offer checking and savings accounts, safe-deposit boxes, money orders and cashier's checks, traveler's checks and credit cards, loans, and financial advice.

There seem to be so many kinds of banks—"national" banks, state banks, savings and loan associations. Is my money just as safe in one kind of bank as it is in another?

The federal government insures deposits in most banks and savings and loan associations up to a maximum of $100,000 per account. The Federal Deposit Insurance Corporation (FDIC) insures your account in a qualifying bank through its Bank Insurance Fund. Since 1989, deposits in qualifying savings and loan associations have been insured by the FDIC through its Savings Association Insurance Fund. This fund replaces the Federal Savings and Loan Insurance Corporation. To qualify for deposit insurance, institutions must meet federal standards and submit to regular examinations of their records.

Some states also have laws that protect deposits up to a specified amount. Check the laws of your own state.

If you are worried about the stability of your institution, ask a bank officer for proof of government insurance. You can also investigate your bank's financial health by examining the various financial reports on file in most large libraries. For more information about how the government insures your accounts, you can contact the FDIC, Office of Consumer Affairs, 550 17th Street, NW, Washington, D.C. 20429.

Rose's bank was closed by the federal government. Will she get her money back? How long will she have to wait?

If Rose's bank was insured by the Federal Deposit Insurance Corporation (FDIC), her account is protected up to $100,000. Payment must be made by the FDIC within 10 business days after her institution is closed, either by giving her a cash payment or by transferring her account to another financial institution.

Is a credit union a safe place to put my money? Will I be able to make withdrawals without restrictions?

As in banks or savings and loan institutions, the safety of your money in a credit union depends upon such factors as its management, its loan policies, and the state of the economy in general. Many credit unions also enjoy the security of having their accounts insured by a federal agency, the National Credit Union Administration.

Generally, a credit union allows you to withdraw all or part of the balance in your account at any time, except, of course, if your account is pledged as collateral for a credit union loan.

Is it legal to have a Swiss bank account?

Yes, provided that the account is not being used to hide income from the Internal Revenue Service, or to launder money (that is, hide its original source) obtained from illegal activities. Interest earned in any foreign account, like that from a U. S. bank account, must be reported on your income tax return.

Is it legal for Jack's bank to deduct more in service charges than it pays in interest on his account unless he increases the balance to a figure named by the bank?

Yes. Since the mid-1980's, banks have been relatively free of government regulations that set the interest rate they could pay and the minimum balance upon which they would pay it. Since the cost of handling small accounts is about the same as that of handling large ones, many banks no longer wish to handle accounts below a certain minimum. If Jack doesn't like his bank's requirements, he should look for another bank that will give him a better deal.

I was charged a $2 transaction fee when I made a withdrawal from my savings account. How can the bank charge me for access to my own money, especially since the bank makes money by lending out my money?

In order to bring in more money for their stockholders or owners, many banks now charge their customers for services that once were free. Before federal deregulation of the banking industry in the mid-1980's, federal laws restricted what banks could demand in terms of fees, penalties, minimum balances, and the like. Since deregulation, banks have added many new charges and increased their fees for such special services as stopping payment on depositors' checks.

Financial Institutions

I suspect that the bank has added some illegal charges to my account. Where can I go to file a complaint?

Start with your state banking department. Although banks are permitted to make reasonable charges for their services, state laws set limits on such fees. The banking department may launch an investigation into your bank's practices if the bank has a history of complaints.

Mike has had a dispute with his bank for months about his account balance. The bank will no longer discuss the problem with him. What is Mike's next step?

After making sure his facts are absolutely correct, Mike should report his problem to the banking department in his state, which will investigate the complaint. If Mike's bank is a member of the Federal Reserve System, he should first call the Federal Reserve Bank in his area, which is overseen by the Federal Reserve Board in Washington, D.C.

My most recent bank statement shows that I have $1,000 more in my account than my own calculations say. Can I keep this money?

Not if the $1,000 was credited to your account by mistake. If you try to withdraw the money, criminal charges could be filed against you. Notify the bank immediately if you think an error has been made.

Amy has an arrangement with her bank to have her bills paid automatically. What happens if the bank makes a mistake?

The bank is required to correct its mistake. Amy should call the error to the attention of a bank officer as soon as possible. If her credit rating has suffered because of late payments, the bank may be held liable. However, most banks make every effort to rectify their mistakes immediately; and they will generally explain the situation to a creditor if asked to do so.

Last Friday I put a $500 cash deposit in my bank's automatic teller machine. It took the money, but it didn't give me a receipt. What should I do?

You should contact your bank on the next business day. Federal law requires that customers receive proper receipts for transactions made at automated teller machines. While failures are rare, they can occur.

Deposits from automatic teller machines are balanced daily, and your bank will provide you with a receipt as soon as your deposit is verified. In addition, many automatic teller machines print and retain duplicate receipts; your bank may be able to give you a copy of this duplicate.

Debbie gave Curtis a check. When Curtis tried to cash it eight months later, the bank refused to pay. Is this legal?

Yes. Under the Uniform Commercial Code (UCC), a set of laws governing business transactions, a bank is under no obligation to pay a check that is more than six months old—although the bank may pay it as a matter of good faith. Most states follow the UCC rules.

Safeguards for Paperless Banking

While the cashless society isn't here yet, advances in technology bring it closer every day. You can have your payroll or pension check deposited at your bank, make loan and credit card payments, pay utility bills, even buy groceries, and never use (or see) a dollar's worth of cash or write a single check.

New technologies bring new problems for consumers, however. The electronic machines can malfunction, receipts can be lost, and transaction cards can be misplaced or stolen. Here are some tips to take the glitches out of paperless banking:

☑ Keep a record of each transaction you make. It's easy to forget to subtract a withdrawal or fund transfer unless you enter it in your checkbook immediately.

☑ Check your statement as soon as you get it and make sure its balance agrees with your records. If it doesn't, contact your bank immediately.

☑ Memorize your personal identification number (PIN) and keep it in a file at home. Never write it on your transaction card, or on a piece of paper in your wallet. If you forget or misfile your PIN, ask your bank to locate it in your records.

☑ Give your PIN only to a bank officer in person. Never tell your PIN, or lend your card, to anyone. A common scam is for a phone caller to claim he is from your bank and ask for your PIN for "verification." Hang up and notify your bank immediately of the phone call.

☑ When using an automatic teller machine (ATM), be sure you have your receipt and your transaction card before walking away. Never leave an ATM before your transaction is complete.

☑ Be cautious when using an ATM at night, or in an out-of-the-way location. You could be prey for a robber lurking nearby.

☑ If you lose your transaction card, notify your bank within two business days. Up to $500 could be charged to your account if you wait longer; otherwise, your liability is limited to $50.

Financial Institutions

Edmund deposited his paycheck on Friday afternoon. That night, he wrote a check to a department store for a new suit. The check bounced despite his deposit. How could this happen?

Edmund's bank, like most others, requires customers to wait a certain number of days before they are allowed to draw against checks deposited in their accounts from other banks. The banks feel that they must wait to see if a check is good before letting a customer draw against it. As a general rule, the more distant the bank on which the check is drawn, the longer the wait will be.

Because of public irritation with unreasonably long delays, Congress passed the Expedited Funds Availability Act to guarantee bank customers quicker access to their deposits. Banks must now clear local checks in two business days or less, and nonlocal checks must be cleared within five business days of being deposited. As a special courtesy, some banks will cash paychecks or accept them for deposit as if they were cash.

Henry discovered that $500 was missing from his money market account because of a bank error. However, the statement reads: "If you do not object within 30 days, this statement will be presumed correct." If more than 30 days have passed, does Henry have any recourse against the bank?

Yes. Although Henry's bank says it limits the time during which he may object to an error, it cannot profit from a mistake in its favor. It must credit the $500, plus the interest it would have earned, to Henry's account.

When I bought my car, the salesman said he would only accept a check if it were certified. Why?

In some ways, a certified check is as good as cash. When a bank certifies a check by having one of its officers stamp "certified" across its face, it immediately freezes that amount in your account and holds it until the check is presented for payment. A certified check means the bank guarantees to cash it for the payee.

What is the difference between a certified check and a cashier's check, or a bank check?

A certified check is one that is drawn on a depositor's account and upon which the bank stamps the word *certified*. This statement is a guarantee that there are sufficient funds on deposit to allow the check to be cashed.

A cashier's check, or bank check, on the other hand, is drawn by the bank on itself and issued by an authorized bank officer. The bank makes sure it has your money behind its cashier's check in one of three ways: (1) it transfers the necessary amount from your account to its own, or (2) you give the bank cash (usually plus a fee) to cover the amount of the check, or (3) you write a check to the order of the bank for the necessary amount. A cashier's check is usually considered as good as cash.

Is it true that I can't stop payment on a certified check?

Yes. A certified check guarantees that payment will be made to the person legally entitled to it. Unless the person who wrote the check dies before it is presented for payment, a certified check must be honored by the bank upon which it was drawn.

How do I go about getting my bank to stop payment on a check I have written?

Call the bank immediately and be prepared to give them your account number, the check number, the amount of the check, the date of the check, and the name of the payee. In addition, your bank will require you to fill out a stop payment request form within a certain time period, usually 10 business days. A written stop payment order is binding for six months; it must then be renewed to remain in effect.

Because of the cost to the bank in complying with your request, it may charge you a fee for stopping payment. If your bank should honor a check after you have entered a stop payment order, it must make restitution to your account. But if the check was paid before the bank received your stop payment order, the bank is under no obligation to repay you.

Sylvia is thinking about purchasing a rubber stamp to endorse checks. Is this legal?

Yes. The law allows a person to endorse a check in a variety of ways. Generally, any symbol that a person adopts with the intention of making it an endorsement can be used. This includes using a rubber stamp.

My father is always telling me not to endorse my paycheck with just my name. What is the problem with doing it that way?

When you endorse your paycheck by signing your name on its back, you have created a blank endorsement, which means the check can be cashed by anyone. If you intend to deposit your paycheck into a checking or savings account, you might add the words *for deposit only* beneath your signature. If the check is then lost or stolen, nobody can cash it, and it can only be deposited in your bank account.

Sally received a check from her cousin and wants to endorse it over to a coworker. Can Sally make sure she is not required to pay the coworker if the check bounces?

Yes. Sally should endorse the check with her signature followed by the words *without recourse*. By adding these words, Sally disclaims any responsibility to her coworker if the check is not honored by the bank upon which it is drawn. If a check endorsed in this way does bounce, Sally's coworker will have to recover the money from the person who originally wrote the check.

My sister added my name to her checking account so that I could pay her bills if she ever became disabled. She died suddenly. Can I use the money in her account as I wish?

If you and your sister were both listed as owners of the checking account, you held this account as joint tenants. As the surviving owner, you are entitled to use the funds in the account in any way you wish.

Can someone gain access to my safe-deposit box if I give them a written note?

Probably not. The possibilities of fraud, forgery, or duress in getting you to sign such a note present too great a risk for your bank. However, a notarized statement authorizing access to your safe-deposit box might be sufficient for some banks. Check with your bank.

If a husband dies and the wife wants access to the property in a joint safe-deposit box, does she need a court order?

In many states, a safe-deposit box that is held jointly is sealed when one of the owners dies, and can be opened only after obtaining an order from the probate court or the state tax authority. Any unidentified items such as cash or jewelry are considered the property of the first owner to die. If you want access to a safe-deposit box that is owned by your spouse, your bank can give you a form that grants you access to the box, even though you are not a joint owner.

Record-Keeping Tips

Good record keeping is simply a matter of putting the right papers in the right place, and disposing of what you no longer need. For example, the original of your will should not be kept in a safe-deposit box. The bank may seal the box when the boxholder dies, and open it only when authorized to do so by the probate court or the state tax authority. You should leave the original of your will with your lawyer or someone else you trust; keep copies at home and in your safe-deposit box, with notes attached stating who has the original. The following chart is a guide to efficient record keeping.

ITEM	WHERE TO KEEP	HOW LONG TO KEEP
State and federal income tax returns	Home file	Indefinitely (along with canceled checks of tax payments)
Social Security cards	Home file	Indefinitely
Canceled checks and bank statements	Home file	Six years
Warranties	Home file	Until after expiration
Deeds, mortgages, titles, agreements	Safe-deposit box	Until property is sold
Stock certificates	Safe-deposit box	Until sold
Insurance, pension, retirement plans	Home file	As long as in force
Paycheck stubs	Home file	Until compared with annual W-2 form
Birth and marriage certificates	Safe-deposit box	Indefinitely
Divorce papers and other court decrees	Safe-deposit box	Indefinitely
Military service records	Safe-deposit box	Indefinitely
Adoption and citizenship papers	Safe-deposit box	Indefinitely
Credit card numbers	Home file	Until card canceled
Inventory of personal property	Safe-deposit box	Indefinitely
Burial instructions	Home file	Indefinitely

Financial Institutions

I wrote a check for $80. Someone changed the amount to $800, and the bank cashed it. What should I do?

Notify your bank immediately. Most banks will agree to charge your account only for the amount you originally intended to pay—$80, in this case. To recover the additional $720, the bank would have to sue the person who altered the check. If your bank refuses to credit you with the $720, you will need to decide whether or not to sue the bank.

However, if the alteration was possible because you were negligent in writing the check—for example, if you left space for the alteration to be made—you may be held responsible for the entire amount.

Jeannie was on vacation for three months. When she returned, she went through her bank statements and noticed her signature had been forged on two checks. Is she liable?

The law requires that you notify your bank within 14 days of discovering a forged check. Once the bank is notified of a forged signature, it must bear the loss for the forgery. Since Jeannie was away for three months and without access to information about her account, she should not be liable for the checks that were forged during her absence.

Martin lost the check Doris had given him. When he asked her for a replacement, Doris replied that the check had already cleared. Someone must have forged Martin's signature. If Doris refuses to write him a new check, what can Martin do?

Not much. A bank is protected when it pays a check even if the check has been lost or stolen, as long as it acted in good faith and in accordance with customary and reasonable banking practices. Doris is not required to pay Martin twice to compensate him for his own negligence. In short, Martin can't recover the amount of the check from anyone but the forger.

A counterfeit $50 bill turned up in the day's receipts from Jim's bar and grill. However, it was so authentic-looking that Jim didn't notice it. When the bank teller saw the bill, he kept it and refused to credit the $50 to Jim's account. Why did he do that?

Because to credit the counterfeit money to Jim's account would be a fraud on the bank. The teller is the bank's agent, and the law requires that he must inform the bank of the counterfeit money. The bank, in turn, is legally required to notify the police.

Establishing Credit

How do I establish credit for the first time?

For a great many people, credit begins with the opening of a charge account at a store in their hometown or at college. By promptly paying the store's monthly bills, you start building a solid credit history.

Getting your first loan from a bank can prove much more troublesome than opening your first charge account. Evidence of steady employment, good references, even a checking account at the same bank, may still not be enough to sway the bank's loan officer. He may ask that someone cosign—in effect, take equal legal responsibility for repaying—your loan. Many first-time borrowers turn to their parents or other older relatives and friends to serve as cosigners; but cosigning does carry a financial risk that many people, no matter how much they like and respect you, may not wish to take on.

There is one almost surefire way of making certain that you can get a bank loan in the future—if and when you need it. Borrow a small amount of money from a bank where you have opened a savings account, and let the bank hold your savings account as collateral. Then make all of the monthly payments on time. This will help you establish a credit history. What should you do with the money you borrow? If you have no other use for it, put it in a savings account at another bank. The interest you earn will help offset the interest you must pay on the loan, and will reduce the cost of establishing credit.

What kinds of things affect my ability to get credit?

A number of factors, including your employment history and income; the amount of time you have lived in the community; whether you have accounts at local banks or other financial institutions; whether you own real estate or other valuable property; and previous credit history. Factors that can adversely affect your ability to borrow are tax liens, records of arrest and conviction, loans and credit accounts that are seriously and repeatedly delinquent, and lawsuits or court judgments filed against you. If a creditor reports that you have been more than 30 days late on an account, that information can stay on your credit report for at least 7 years; information on a bankruptcy might remain for 10 years.

When a woman with credit established in her maiden name gets married, what happens to her credit history?

It stays the same. In 1974, Congress passed the Equal Credit Opportunity Act. Under this law, a creditor may not take action against a woman's account merely because she has changed her marital status. When a woman marries, she has an option to keep her own credit history, using either her maiden name or her married name, or to start a joint credit history with her husband. In fact, her past credit record may be a plus when she and her new husband apply for credit.

Is it difficult for a woman to establish credit in her own name after a divorce?

It should be no harder for her than it is for anybody else. Under the Equal Credit Opportunity Act, a creditor cannot refuse to consider such income as alimony, child support, or separate maintenance in deciding whether or not to grant credit.

In addition, federal regulations require a creditor to consider the good payment record of an ex-husband when a divorced woman's credit history has been "hidden" under her ex-husband's name. A divorced woman who is denied credit because of her ex-husband's poor credit history can also show that such a record does not reflect on her own ability to borrow money and pay it back on time. A divorced woman can follow the usual steps of establishing credit, such as opening a department store charge account or taking out a small loan with a savings account as collateral, and making the required payments promptly.

Betsy receives $1,600 a month from her ex-husband in alimony and child support. She applied for a credit card, but her application was rejected. Is this illegal?

It could be. Under the Equal Credit Opportunity Act, alimony or child support must be considered as regular income in determining a person's creditworthiness if it is listed as income on the person's credit application. If the credit company would give a card to someone earning $1,600 a month from other sources, it is illegal for the company to deny a card to someone like Betsy, who receives an equal amount in alimony and child support payments.

What is Bea's legal recourse if she feels she has been denied credit because her sole income is from alimony and support payments?

First, Bea should make every effort to get satisfaction from the company or bank, by talking directly with its representatives and even writing a letter to its president. If this course of action is not successful, Bea could report the situation to the Federal Trade Commission and follow its recommendations. As a last resort, if Bea thinks she can prove that a creditor has discriminated against her, she may sue. If she wins, the court may award her court costs and a reasonable amount for attorney's fees.

Can a college student get his own credit card if he has no previous credit rating?

Some credit card companies will issue cards to college students because the companies' research indicates that, by and large, a college student is an acceptable credit risk.

Arnold is 70 years old and has a full-time job. Can he be denied a credit card simply because of his age?

No. The Equal Credit Opportunity Act prohibits such discrimination. Under this law, a creditor can consider an applicant's age only to give him a benefit for being an older person, or to extend a particular kind of credit to him because he has reached a certain age. For example, organizations of retired people may offer credit cards to people past 55 years of age, but not to younger ones; or a bank may consider 40-year-olds as better credit risks than those in their twenties.

Andy's company is transferring him to its home office. Will he have trouble establishing credit in a new city?

Probably not, if he already has a good credit history, because credit bureaus around the country can and do exchange information. However, if Andy is worried, he has several options to consider: (1) He can ask his employer for a letter of recommendation describing his work record and salary level. (2) He can request a credit report from the bureau in the city he is leaving. This report will have the most up-to-date information about Andy's credit history. (3) He can apply for a credit card at a major department store in the new city. (4) He can open a checking or savings account, or both, at a local bank.

Paul and Lois are divorced. Lois has since remarried, and she usually goes by her new husband's last name. But when she wants to obtain credit, she uses Paul's last name because he has a better credit rating than her new husband. Is this illegal?

Yes. It is fraud for Lois to use Paul's name without his permission in order to obtain credit. Fraud is a crime, and it is also grounds for a civil suit. Paul has the right to sue Lois if he loses money, if his credit rating is damaged, or if he is sued by someone else because of her actions.

Establishing Credit

A few years ago Nick and Diana fell way behind on their bills because Nick was laid off for four months and Diana was sick. Now that their financial troubles are over, how do they go about reestablishing their ability to get credit?

Nick and Diana should explain in a letter to each of their lenders that the difficulty in paying bills was temporary and that their tough times now seem to be over. Under the Fair Credit Reporting Act, they are guaranteed the right to have their explanatory statement made a part of their credit report. At the same time, Nick and Diana should make absolutely sure that they make the required payments on outstanding debts on or before the dates due. If they need more time to pay off past balances and bring payments up to date, they should see if their creditors will accept reduced payments. If the bad credit rating is based on debts owed by only one of

What Credit Bureaus Do—and Don't Do

If you have established credit with a store or bank (called a *credit grantor*), certain information about you has probably been passed on to a *credit bureau.* A credit bureau is in the business of collecting information about your borrowing and bill-paying record and supplying this information, for a fee, to stores and banks that are considering whether or not to grant you credit. To find out the names of credit bureaus in your area, check the telephone book. Some call themselves credit agencies or credit-reporting bureaus (or agencies, or services).

A credit bureau summarizes the information it has about you into a *credit report*, which may also be called a credit record or credit profile. In addition to basic information about you (name, address, age, Social Security number, employer if known, and so on), the credit report contains your *credit history*, which shows problems you may have had paying your creditors regularly and promptly.

Using the credit report, a credit grantor will assign you a *credit rating*, which determines whether or not the bank or store will grant you credit, and if it does, how much—a dollar figure that is often called your *credit line.* Thus, a credit rating is a judgment by one specific store or bank. It is not an absolute or universal grade set by a credit bureau; and if one credit grantor gives you a poor rating, another may not.

You are entitled to see a copy of your credit report. You may have to pay a small fee for it, but if you have been denied credit in the last 30 days because of a credit report, you can get a free copy. Your credit report will include the name of any prospective employer who obtained information about you in the past two years, as well as the name of anyone else who saw your report in the last six months.

them, Nick and Diana might consider applying for credit in the other's name. For example, if the overdue debts were in Nick's name, they could try applying for a loan in Diana's name.

A final point to remember is that the passage of time will eventually improve a person's credit rating. In general, the older credit problems are, the less they will bother potential creditors and lenders. Legally, credit problems that occurred more than 7 years ago (10 years in the case of a bankruptcy) cannot in most cases be used to deny you credit.

Do I have the right to see my credit report?

Yes, although in some areas you must make a written request to the credit bureau, rather than just walking in. If you have been denied credit in the past 30 days because of a report from this agency, it must give you the information at no charge. Otherwise, you may be charged a small fee.

Jill believes her credit report contains misleading information. What can she do?

She can ask the credit bureau to reverify the information from the lender or include an explanatory statement in the file. Adding an explanatory statement may be a good idea even if the information in the file is technically correct. If, for example, Jill fell behind on payments last year because of heavy medical expenses, her explanation of why she was late might lead a creditor to overlook her past payment problems.

Remember, though, that more than one credit bureau may serve your area. A problem with one may mean that the same information is in your file at another, where you may have to repeat your explanatory statement. If you can't find the names and addresses of local credit bureaus in the telephone book, ask your bank's lending officer for help.

After I submitted a credit application to buy a new car, the bank told me that a credit report showed I had a slow payment record at Ella's Electronic Bazaar. I believe that's inaccurate. What can I do to get this statement removed from my credit report?

Ask the bank or the electronics store for the name of the credit bureau that reported you as a slow payer. Write a letter to the bureau explaining why you think the information is not correct. Ask it to investigate. If the information does prove to be inaccurate, the credit bureau will delete it from your file. It will then notify any person you designate that the information has been deleted—if that person has received a copy of the earlier report within the past six months. If you don't know who has seen the report, you have a legal right to get the names from the credit bureau.

Credit Cards and Charges

For disagreements about merchandise and services that you have purchased, see Chapter 9, *Consumer Rights*.

Charlotte wants to apply for a bank card, but she is confused about the difference between a credit card, a debit card, and a travel and entertainment card. Aren't they all the same?

No. Although different kinds of cards are often lumped together in the category of credit cards, there are significant differences. A credit card enables a person to obtain credit from an organization, such as a bank or department store. Most bank cards fall into this category. However, some banks also provide their customers with a debit card, which enables them to withdraw or deposit money in automatic teller machines. In addition, some bank debit cards can be used at stores that have a point of sale terminal, which allows the merchant to deduct the amount of a purchase directly from a customer's account.

Travel and entertainment cards were once used primarily to pay for travel, hotel rooms, and restaurant meals, but are now accepted by a variety of merchants. Some of these cards may not offer extended repayment terms; the amount charged to the card must be paid in full upon receipt of the statement.

Is it wise to shop for credit cards?

Yes. Different credit card issuers charge different fees and interest rates. For example, one bank may charge as much as 10 percent more interest than another bank. Some banks charge an annual fee for their cards; others don't. And some cards charge interest from the very first day of a purchase, while others give you up to a month of interest-free days (called a grace period) after you make a purchase.

A friend told me that the credit card I received from Graham's Department Store was for a revolving account, or "open-ended" account. What does this mean?

This kind of account permits a buyer or borrower to purchase goods or obtain loans on a continuing basis. It can be used indefinitely as long as the outstanding balance on the account does not exceed a certain predetermined limit. With a revolving account, loans are repaid and new loans are granted in a continuing cycle.

I recently went into a local department store to apply for credit. They handed me a two-page application with lots of personal

questions that seemed unrelated to my ability to pay. Isn't there a limit to the kinds of questions a creditor can ask?

Yes. A credit application may ask only for information that directly relates to your credit history and your ability to repay your debts. The federal Equal Credit Opportunity Act prohibits discrimination on the basis of a credit applicant's race, color, religion, national origin, sex, or marital status. If you feel that a question on the department store's application is discriminatory, unnecessary, or improper in some way, ask the credit manager to explain why it is included. If you find his answer unsatisfactory, leave the answer blank. If the store rejects your application for credit, you have the right to know the reason. If the rejection is discriminatory, you have the right to complain to the Federal Trade Commission office in your area. You may also be entitled to sue the department store.

Mary was in a hurry when she applied for a department store credit card, and roughly estimated the balances due at several other stores. Will this create a problem if the department store discovers that she underestimated the amounts owed?

Probably not. Because many people have a number of credit cards with varying balances, they may be unable to accurately state the amount owed on each card at any given time. If you are not in a position to know the exact balance due on an account, a reasonable estimate is usually acceptable to a creditor.

I applied for a credit card three months ago, but I have not received it yet. What can I do to find out why it's taking so long?

You should contact the card issuer. Generally, an issuer has 30 days to notify an applicant whether or not the application has been accepted or rejected. You should also contact the credit card company for another reason: if your application was approved and a card mailed, it may have been lost or stolen in transit. If the issuer is notified that you have not received your card, it can cancel the lost card and issue a replacement.

Are there facts that a credit card holder must be told?

Yes. Under the Truth in Lending Act, a credit card issuer must disclose the annual percentage rate, the monthly rate of interest, and the method by which finance charges will be calculated. Additional information about the monthly statement and the legal rights and responsibilities of the card holder and issuer are optional, but are usually included as well.

Credit Cards and Charges

When I charge purchases at some national department stores, my charge slip includes a "security agreement." Does this mean they can repossess what I bought if I fall behind on my payments?

In most cases, a security agreement means that if you do not pay your account as agreed, the creditor may take the secured property in order to pay the debt. As a practical matter, a store may repossess such larger items as furniture and appliances, but smaller personal items or clothing are generally of no value to the creditor.

Ada has a well-known credit card and always pays her bills on time. However, she does not make a habit of asking the merchant for the carbon paper from the charge slips. One day, she got a statement showing a number of purchases made in a state she's never been to. What is her legal liability or recourse?

She should notify the card issuer immediately. Under the Fair Credit Billing Act, she is permitted to challenge the incorrect billing information, but she must notify her credit card issuer in writing within 60 days from the date that the incorrect statement was mailed.

In her letter, Ada should describe the items in question, give her reasons for questioning them, and decline to pay for the items. When it receives her letter, the credit card issuer must investigate the problem. If the charges were not incurred by Ada, the company will have to credit the entire sum, plus any interest charged on it, to her account.

A department store has told Barney that the recurring error on his bill is "a computer problem." What recourse does he have?

He has the right to withhold payment of the amount in dispute. Generally, the Fair Credit Billing Act requires the credit card issuer to rectify the billing problem within 90 days of notification. The fact that it is a computer error does not change this obligation. The law also prohibits a creditor from sending or threatening to send bad reports to a credit bureau while the overdue amount remains in dispute. If the store cannot resolve the matter to Barney's satisfaction, he can contact the Federal Trade Commission office in his area.

What should I do about my credit cards if I lose my wallet?

You should always keep a list of your credit cards and account numbers in a safe place away from the cards themselves. If your wallet is lost or

Protecting Your Credit Cards

Credit card fraud is a multimillion-dollar business. While federal law limits your liability for fraudulent credit card use to $50 per card, the loss of 5 or 10 cards means you could be liable for $250 to $500.

To protect yourself, experts suggest that you:

- ☑ Sign your credit cards immediately upon receipt. An unsigned card can easily be forged and used.
- ☑ Cut old credit cards into pieces before throwing them away.
- ☑ Carry only the cards you need. A wallet or purse bulging with credit cards makes an inviting target for a thief.
- ☑ Cancel cards that you don't use. A card from a store in a city you once lived in might disappear without your knowing it—until you receive the monthly statement for goods you haven't purchased.
- ☑ Examine your monthly statement as soon as you get it. Report any suspicious charges immediately.
- ☑ Keep a list of your accounts and the phone numbers for reporting lost or stolen cards. Don't keep this list in your wallet or with your credit cards; put it in a safe and easily accessible place.
- ☑ Never give your account number over the phone unless you are certain of the person's identity and affiliation. Several years ago, a number of people received phone calls telling them they had won a prize but that the caller needed a credit card number to verify them as winners. The winners never received their prizes, but they did get some large credit card bills.

stolen, call the issuer of your credit card immediately (your credit card statement shows the number to call to report a missing card) and be sure to follow up your phone call with a letter. If you do not alert the card issuer immediately, you may be liable for up to $50 of unauthorized charges per card. You will not be liable for any charges made after you notify the issuer.

I keep getting advertisements in the mail for credit card protection plans. What do these plans do? Are they legitimate?

Credit card protection is a form of insurance. You give a list of all your credit card account numbers to the plan's operator, and if your cards are lost or stolen at some time in the future, you call a toll-free telephone number to report the loss. The plan operator then notifies the individual credit card issuers, and reimburses you for any unauthorized charges.

There are many legitimate credit card protection plans, but if you have questions about the legitimacy of a particular plan, contact your local Better Business Bureau or the consumer protection division of your state attorney general's office.

Personal Loans

For mortgages, see "Financing a New Home" and "Ways You May Lose Your Home" in Chapter 4, *Your Home.*

Ryan wants to borrow enough money to take his wife on a cruise. Should he admit this when he fills out the loan application, or should he say he's borrowing to make home improvements?

He should tell the truth. A false statement will be considered fraud; if it's discovered, the bank may declare the entire loan due at once, and Ryan may be subject to civil and criminal penalties as well.

Now that Shirley's loan for a new roof has been approved, what should she look for before signing the agreement?

She should pin down the exact amount of credit she is being granted and find out the annual percentage rate (APR) that she will be charged and the total amount of interest she will pay over the life of the loan. The Truth in Lending Act requires a lender to give her all this information in writing before she signs a loan agreement. In addition, Shirley should find out if there are penalties for prepaying her loan, what rights the lender has if she defaults or is late with a payment, and what penalties she may incur if she is late with a payment.

What can I do if I signed a loan agreement, and later realized I misunderstood the terms?

Most courts will presume you understood the terms and agreed to them when you signed the document. However, if the creditor failed to make the disclosures required by the Truth in Lending Act (finance charges or dates payments are due, for example), you have a right to sue.

Does* payable on demand *mean that the lender can demand complete payment at any time for any reason?

Yes, unless there are conditions in the loan agreement that restrict when a creditor can do so.

Under what conditions can a bank demand full and immediate repayment of a loan or take possession of collateral?

This drastic step is called accelerating a loan, and your bank can take this action if you default (don't make a payment), if you fail to pay off the entire amount when it is due, or if you fail to meet other conditions stated in the loan agreement. However, most lenders are reluctant to accelerate loans, for the simple reason that they derive valuable income from the interest payments.

State and federal laws may limit a lender's right to accelerate a loan when the debtor can easily correct the condition upon which the acceleration is based. For example, a court would probably not enforce a loan agreement that calls for acceleration if the borrower fails to notify the lender immediately of any change of address, since all the borrower would have to do is give the lender his new address.

When Mitchell decided to pay for his new camper on an installment plan, the dealer explained that if he missed even one payment, the company could demand that the entire loan be paid immediately. As it turned out, Mitchell missed two payments, and the dealer wrote to demand full payment. Mitchell offered to make three payments to bring his account up to date. Can the dealer reject his offer and insist on full payment?

Yes, but if Mitchell refuses to pay in full, the issue will most likely have to be decided in court. A contract provision that permits the lender to demand full payment if a debtor misses one or more payments is called an acceleration clause. In most cases, these clauses are not enforced unless nonpayment has been extensive and continuous. In this case, the dealer can enforce the contract only by taking Mitchell to court. However, a court will probably order the dealer either to repossess the camper or to reinstate Mitchell when he brings his payments up to date.

Can a minor use the money in his trust fund as collateral to get a college loan?

It depends to a large extent on the terms of the trust agreement and the duties and powers given to the trustee. However, most student loans are offered on an unsecured basis—no collateral is needed.

Shortly after I applied for a loan, I received notice that my request had been turned down. The bank offered no explanation for this. Am I entitled to one?

Yes. If your application for credit is rejected, you must be told why. The Equal Credit Opportunity Act requires that the lender give you the reason at the time of rejection. If you're not given a reason, contact the nearest office of the Federal Reserve Bank (if the lender is a member) or contact the Federal Trade Commission or the Federal Deposit Insurance Corporation.

Personal Loans

Michelle was turned down for a personal loan at her bank. Should she try another bank, or will they turn her down as well?

Michelle should try again. While most lenders use similar systems to evaluate applicants, there may be differences that would affect the outcome of a loan request. For example, some lenders give great weight to home ownership, while others consider a stable job history and regular wage increases just as important. Moreover, lenders use different credit reporting agencies. The bank that rejected Michelle's application may have used a credit report that contained negative information about her credit history that would not appear in another agency's report.

Two years ago Ben lent me $500 to help pay some unexpected hospital bills. Now Ben says he is willing to forgive his loan to me. Should I get this agreement in writing?

Yes. Forgiving a loan means the lender no longer requires repayment of the loan. In order to avoid future disputes, a forgiveness agreement should always be written.

What exactly is loan-sharking, and is it legal?

Loan-sharking generally refers to the practice of lending money at very high interest rates to borrowers who are unable to obtain credit through the usual outlets. These loans may carry interest charges that are as high as 100 percent a week, and the borrower soon finds himself unable to make the necessary payments. As a result, the unfortunate borrower is never able to repay the loan. While most states have laws that prohibit loan-sharking, the practice has proved difficult to eradicate.

Mark signed an agreement to repay $4,000 at 10 percent interest. When the loan company typed up the papers, they indicated the finance charge was $510. Mark thought the finance charge was the interest he was going to have to pay—$400. Where did the extra $110 come from?

A finance charge is the total of all the charges that you are asked to pay to obtain credit. While interest is the largest component of this charge, it also includes such items as loan application fees, service charges and "points," fees for obtaining a credit report, premiums for credit life insurance, and any amount paid as a discount. Mark should ask the loan officer to explain these additional charges in detail. If he feels that the explanation offered is either unclear or unsatisfactory, Mark may wish to consult an accountant or an attorney before signing the loan agreement.

How can I find out whether or not a personal finance company has a good reputation?

First contact your local Better Business Bureau or the consumer protection division of your state attorney general's office. Since the personal finance industry is subject to federal regulations, you might also want to get in touch with the nearest office of the Federal Trade Commission if you need any additional information.

Betty Lou inherited some money from her uncle. She wants to use it to pay off her auto loan ahead of time. Can she expect to have the finance charges refunded?

No. Betty Lou is responsible for repaying the principal remaining on the loan and all interest charges that have accrued until the day that the loan is repaid. However, she is not required to pay any future interest that would have come due if the loan had run its full course.

Sean chipped a tooth during a softball game and found himself confronted with a $300 dental bill. He asked his friend Jonathan for a loan, for which Sean said he would give his friend a written IOU. Jonathan said he'd prefer a promissory note. What's the difference between the two?

An IOU is a document given to the lender by the borrower; written on it are the letters IOU (for "I owe you"), the amount owed, and the borrower's signature. A promissory note usually contains the wording "I promise to pay" (the amount borrowed) by a certain date, to a certain person. If Jonathan has to sue Sean to collect the money, some courts would consider a promissory note stronger evidence of Sean's obligation to pay because it specifies a deadline for repayment. Both IOU's and promissory notes should be kept in a safe-deposit box. They should be marked "paid in full" by the lender and returned to the borrower when the debt is paid.

I know I'll be unable to make a loan payment on time. What should I do?

Contact your lender as soon as possible. In many cases, the lender will either extend the time for payment or allow you to make a reduced payment. If your past record with this lender has been a good one, he

The Language of Loans

Your loan application has been approved; the bank's check is there on the desk—but before you get it, the loan officer says, there's "just a little paperwork" to do. He hands you a pen and the loan contract, which appears to be in English, but you can't decipher much of it.

While many states have laws requiring a loan contract to be in "plain English," the language can still be almost unintelligible to anyone but bankers and lawyers. The Federal Trade Commission has alerted consumers to a number of standard clauses that frequently appear in loan contracts. Here are translations of some of them:

WHAT IT SAYS:	WHAT IT MEANS:
To secure payment hereof, the undersigned jointly and severally irrevocably authorize any attorney of any court of record to appear for any one or more of them in such court in term or vacation, after default in payment hereof and confess a judgment without process in favor of the creditor hereof for such amount as may then appear unpaid.	If you sue us because we haven't paid, we agree to let you win—even if we have a good reason for not paying. In fact, your lawyer can represent us.
WHAT IT SAYS:	WHAT IT MEANS:
This note is secured by a security interest in all of the following described personal property and proceeds thereof: If checked at left, consumer goods consisting of all household goods, furniture, appliances, and bric-a-brac, now owned and hereafter acquired, including replacements, and located in or about the premises at the debtor's residence (unless otherwise stated) or at any other location to which the goods may be moved.	If we don't pay, you can take all our household goods.
WHAT IT SAYS:	WHAT IT MEANS:
Each of us hereby both individually and severally waives any or all benefit or relief from all exemptions or moratoriums to which the signers or any of them may be entitled under the laws of this or any other state, now in force or hereafter to be passed, as against this debt.	If we don't pay, you can take even the personal belongings state law would allow us to keep.
WHAT IT SAYS:	WHAT IT MEANS:
Default in the payment of any installment of the principal balance or charges hereof or any part of either shall, at the option of the holder hereof, render the entire unpaid principal balance hereof, at once due and payable.	If we miss a payment, you can make us repay the whole loan immediately.

WHAT IT SAYS:	WHAT IT MEANS:
The undersigned, jointly and severally, agree that the lender may at its option communicate with any persons whatsoever in relation to the obligation involved, or its delinquency, or in an effort to obtain cooperation or help relative to the collection or payment thereof.	If we don't pay, you can tell all our friends and relatives.

WHAT IT SAYS:	WHAT IT MEANS:
We severally hereby authorize and direct our said employers or any future employers or either of them to pay (a part) of salary, wages, commission or other compensation for services to the said assignee and release such employers or any future employers from all liability to us on account of any and all monies paid in accordance with the terms hereof. We severally give and grant unto the said assignee, full power and authority to demand, receive, and receipt for the same or any part thereof in any of our names.	If we don't pay, just have one or both of our bosses deduct the money from either paycheck. We won't argue about it—even if we've got a good reason for not paying.

WHAT IT SAYS:	WHAT IT MEANS:
In consideration of the making and acceptance of the within note . . . undersigned cosigner jointly and severally unconditionally guarantees to the said creditor and to any assignee of said creditor, the payment of all monies due or to become due under said note . . . and also the full performance by the said debtor of all the promises and covenants on his or their part therein contained. . . . The undersigned cosigner hereby consents to all extensions of time for the making of any or all payments by the debtor and further guarantees the payment of all said payments due by reason of said extensions. Notice of acceptance of this guaranty, notice of nonpayment and nonperformance, notice of amount of indebtedness outstanding at any time, protest, demand, and prosecution of collection, foreclosure, and possessory remedies are hereby expressly waived.	If we don't pay, you can collect from a cosigner without trying to collect from us first. You don't even have to warn our cosigner we've fallen behind in payments.

WHAT IT SAYS:	WHAT IT MEANS:
If this agreement is referred to any attorney for collection due to any default or breach of any promise or provision hereunder by debtor, debtor agrees to pay an attorney's fee of 15% of the total of payments then due, plus court costs.	If you sue us, we'll pay for your lawyer.

should be willing to work with you to resolve the problem. A late payment can have a negative effect on your credit rating, but the fact that you anticipated trouble and asked for a payment extension or reduction may preserve your good credit history.

Genevieve has agreed to lend Mary Jane $1,200, and Mary Jane will put up her computer as collateral. What's the best way to formalize this loan agreement between the two friends?

First, Mary Jane should give Genevieve a promissory note for $1,200 that states the agreed-upon repayment date. They should also draw up a document called a security agreement and file it with the Secretary of State in the state where Mary Jane lives. If Mary Jane defaults, Genevieve would have the right to sell the computer to collect the balance of the debt, any unpaid interest, and any expenses incurred in selling the computer. Mary Jane must still pay any remainder on the debt.

Sarah borrowed $250 from Clarence and gave him a promissory note saying she would repay it by January 1. In mid-December, she asked Clarence for another month to repay. He said, "Sure." Should Sarah ask Clarence to sign a statement agreeing to this one-month extension?

Yes. It is always preferable to obtain an extension in writing. This is especially important when the original loan agreement is also in writing. If Clarence changes his mind a week later and demands payment on the original due date, Sarah will need the written extension as evidence of their new agreement.

Two years ago I lent a friend $3,500. I have phoned him several times, but he always says he is too busy to talk, and never calls me back. What can I do to get my money from him?

Notify your friend in writing that you are demanding payment of the amount he owes you. Your letter should include these specifics: the date you lent him the money; the amount of the debt; the date that repayment was due; and a demand that he make payment to you by a certain date. Send the letter by certified mail, return receipt requested, and keep a copy for your records.

If your friend neither responds to your letter nor makes payment by the date you set, he leaves you little choice but to sue him in order to collect the debt. If $3,500 exceeds the limit for the amount that can be recovered in small claims court, you may want to consult an attorney and find out what he would charge to represent you in a court proceeding.

Victor would like to lend his daughter Susan $5,000 to help with the down payment on the new house Susan and her husband want to buy. How should Victor protect his interest?

He should have his daughter sign both a mortgage and a promissory note. If the property will be owned jointly by Susan and her husband, he too should sign the documents. The mortgage and promissory note should then be filed in the land records office of the county in which the house is located. By filing these documents, Victor gives notice to others that the house is being used as collateral to secure the $5,000 he is lending his daughter. Consequently, the home could not be transferred or sold without repaying Victor the $5,000.

Is it possible for two or more people to help shoulder the responsibility of a loan?

Yes. However, remember that each joint applicant may be held solely liable for the entire amount of the debt. If one of the borrowers is unable to pay his share, the other will be required to pay the full amount.

Should Lloyd cosign a loan for his sister?

Only if he is reasonably confident that his sister will pay the loan as agreed, and is willing to pay the debt for her if she doesn't. If a borrower fails to make payments, the lender will look to the cosigner to pay.

I cosigned a loan for my son. He was late with one payment, and now they want the entire balance from me. Do I have to pay?

Probably. Most loan agreements allow lenders to do a number of things if a payment is late, including making a demand for payment from cosigners. States that have adopted the Uniform Consumer Credit Code (UCCC) require the lender to provide a cosigner with a separate written notice that identifies the debt the cosigner agrees to guarantee and reasonably informs the cosigner of his obligation if the borrower defaults. The cosigner should also receive a copy of the underlying loan agreement. If your state follows the UCCC and you didn't receive the required documents before you cosigned for your son, you may not have to pay. If you did receive them, or live in a state that doesn't require them, you may still be able to work out a more realistic repayment schedule with the lender.

Personal Loans

I'm being sued for $3,000 I owe on a car loan, and my car has been repossessed under the terms of the loan agreement. What can I do about this?

First, you should insist that the lender tell you if he has sold the car and, if so, for how much. He is entitled to recover the balance of the loan, plus any unpaid interest and the reasonable expenses incurred in selling the car and collecting the debt. Although the lender may sell your car at either a public or a private sale, he must try to sell it for a fair price. For example, if the car was worth $5,000, but was sold for $500, the lender may not be entitled to collect the remaining balance of the loan.

Payment Problems

For default on a mortgage, see "Ways You May Lose Your Home" in Chapter 4, *Your Home*.

Virginia cannot make the monthly minimum payment on several charge accounts. Can she have her payments reduced?

Some stores will agree to a temporary reduction or delay in payments. If Virginia takes the initiative in contacting the store, it may be more willing to accommodate her, since she has demonstrated that she does not take her indebtedness lightly.

Leon has some huge debts, and his payments are falling further and further behind. Is a debt consolidation loan the solution to Leon's problems?

It could be, if Leon is sure that he can meet the payments. A debt consolidation loan is one large loan for the purpose of paying off many smaller loans and debts. In most cases, this will result in lower monthly payments because the repayment period for a debt consolidation loan is usually longer. However, a longer repayment period means more total interest over the life of the loan. Because Leon's debts are very large, he might consider a Chapter 7 or 13 bankruptcy petition, explained in further detail in the final section of this chapter.

Martha, an elderly neighbor, is behind on her gas bill. Can the gas company legally turn off the heat without notice?

No. In all states, a public service (or utilities) commission prohibits utilities from shutting off fuel supplies without prior notice. Furthermore, most states require utility companies to notify a relative of the resident or a government or social service agency before turning off service for unpaid bills. This allows someone else to arrange for payment before the service is terminated. Most utilities offer payment plans that spread the cost of winter heating over the full year; many states give special consideration to senior citizens faced with shutoffs.

I was a little late paying my phone bill, and now they want a $100 deposit, or they will terminate my service. What can I do?

Contact your state's public service commission to determine the maximum deposit permitted in your state for your type of service. If $100 is within the allowed limit, you may have to pay it to keep your telephone service. However, you may be able to persuade the telephone company to waive the deposit if a onetime emergency, such as sickness or a death in the family, caused you to be late with your payment.

Some states have regulations that restrict a telephone company's right to disconnect service to certain people, such as the elderly or handicapped, who are unable to pay their bills. Contact your public service commission to check if these lifeline rules apply in your state.

Gene called in a pledge to Friends of the Sick telethon. The following week, Gene lost his job. Can the charitable organization make Gene fulfill his pledge?

Perhaps. Some courts might order Gene to pay if the charity could show it had initiated some project or activity (such as making a down payment on a new ambulance) as a result of Gene's promise.

Sherry is being sued in small claims court because she hasn't paid some bills. Can her creditors demand that she turn over all or part of her Aid to Families With Dependent Children check?

No. An AFDC check is considered support for children, not for the parent.

My doctor is suing me for medical bills that I owe him. His lawyer said that they were going to seize my property. Can they do this?

Yes, if he wins his lawsuit. That is why you should make every effort to avoid reaching this point, by trying to work out a reasonable solution with the doctor—or with any creditor. For example, he may delay suing you if you send him small good faith payments toward the full amount. If he does sue, he will seek to collect from you through a court judgment called an execution. If he obtains the judgment, the doctor becomes known legally as a judgment creditor; he will ask the court to issue a writ of execution, which the court will deliver to the sheriff or another officer, directing him to seize enough of your property to pay the debt.

The law varies from state to state regarding the kind of property that can be seized and in what order. For example, in some states, personal property must be seized before real estate. And many states exempt certain property from seizure, such as your family home.

The only asset Dick owns with any value is a life insurance policy. The cash surrender value is $1,800. Can creditors force Dick to cash in the policy if he defaults on a loan?

No. Dick's creditors must first sue and win a court judgment against him. Furthermore, Chapter 7 of the Federal Bankruptcy Code protects the cash value of a life insurance policy if it is needed for the debtor's support. (For more on bankruptcy, see the final section of this chapter.)

If Stella buys a microwave oven on credit and it breaks before it's paid off, does she have to continue making payments?

Not necessarily. Under the law certain warranties are stated or implied for nearly every purchase that a consumer makes. These warranties say that a product should perform the function for which it was purchased. In this case, if the microwave doesn't perform the functions that a person would reasonably expect of a microwave, the seller must repair or replace the oven or refund the purchaser's money.

Before Stella stops making payments, she should inform the seller in writing of the problem with the oven. She must then give him an opportunity to repair the unit or replace it with a similar one. If the seller does neither, not only can Stella stop making payments, she can also demand a refund of the payments she has made.

Duncan bought a carpet on credit, with installation included, but the installers did a bad job laying it. Duncan refused to pay until it was repaired. Two years later, after calling the carpet company many times, he received a summons notifying him that the company was suing for payment. What should Duncan do?

He can countersue the company for breach of contract. When Duncan purchased the carpet, he was entitled to have it installed properly; the carpet company failed to live up to its obligation.

Jenny made a small down payment at a health club and signed a membership contract that said the club had a right to assign her promissory note. Then the club went out of business, and Jenny made no more payments. Now a collection agency demands she pay the full amount of her membership. Must she pay?

Because she signed the contract allowing the club to assign her promissory note—sell it to another company for collection—Jenny is technically liable for the full payment. However, Jenny may be entitled to withhold payment, since the health club breached its contract with her when it went out of business.

The first thing Jenny should do is write a letter to the collection agency informing them that the health club has closed down. She should also find out if her state has specific laws regulating the health club and spa industry. These laws may permit her to discontinue payments without penalty, and may even permit her to be reimbursed for the money she has already paid. Jenny should contact the attorney general's office in her state for more information.

How to Recognize Debt Trouble

Is there a way to know if your debts are climbing toward the danger level? Financial advisers who study the problems of consumers say to watch for these warning signs:

- You can't ever seem to reduce the balances on your department store credit cards.
- You make smaller down payments on new purchases, and only the minimum payments required on your installment loans.
- You begin to get regular reminders from your creditors that payments are past due.
- Your credit card and installment payments use up a larger and larger percentage of your income.
- You take a debt consolidation loan, and soon find yourself taking on even more credit card debt.
- You use cash advances on your credit card to pay everyday expenses such as food, rent, and utility bills.

If you are receiving some or all of these danger signals, you can do two things that will cost you little or no money. (1) Contact your creditors and ask if they can work out new payment schedules that allow you to make smaller monthly payments over a longer period of time. (2) Contact the nearest Consumer Credit Counseling Services office. There are more than 200 of these nonprofit community service agencies across the United States, and they are listed in most telephone books. For no charge or a nominal fee, they will advise you on handling your credit problems and getting out of debt.

Payment Problems

Harry bought a freezer on a 12-month installment contract. The appliance store then sold Harry's note to a finance company. The freezer doesn't work. Can Harry refuse to make payments?

Yes. Harry can refuse to pay until the appliance store either repairs or replaces his freezer. At one time, the sale of the installment contract to a finance company would have put Harry in the unenviable position of having to make full payment for his defective freezer; but now federal and state laws protect the consumer in such situations.

Can my creditors keep selling my installment contracts to other companies for collection?

Yes. The practice is common with every type of installment contract, including mortgages, and is legal as long as the company that buys your contract does not ask you to make higher payments or to put up additional collateral.

My friend Chester is diligently trying to pay off some old debts, but the people at one collection agency keep calling him at all hours. Last night one of them called him after 10:00 P.M. Chester blew his top. Will this just make it tougher for him?

The law is on Chester's side. Under the Fair Debt Collection Practices Act, a collection agency is not allowed to call Chester between 9:00 P.M. and 8:00 A.M., unless he agrees. Furthermore, it cannot contact his boss and ask him to make Chester pay a debt. It cannot threaten prosecution for a crime or use other harassing methods to collect.

Chester should keep a written record of the collection agency's harassing techniques. This documentation will be essential if Chester decides to take the collection agency to court. More information about the limits placed on bill collectors is available from your regional office of the Federal Trade Commission, or from an attorney.

If I am delinquent in my payments, can a creditor garnishee my wages (arrange with my employer to have automatic repayments taken out of my paycheck) without going to court?

No. Unless you have given him written permission to do so, a creditor cannot garnishee your wages without a court judgment. In fact, some states do not allow garnishment of wages at all. Other states limit the amount of money that can be taken from your paycheck.

Your Investments

For information about investing for retirement, see "IRA's and Keogh Plans" in Chapter 15, *Pensions, IRA's, Social Security*.

Should married couples put their investments in both names?

A simple yes or no answer is impossible. Many couples like the fact that jointly held property, such as stocks or real estate, passes directly to the surviving owner when the other dies and thus avoids the occasionally lengthy delays of probating the will. The surviving spouse can sell the property immediately, if necessary. In some states, joint ownership can reduce or entirely avoid estate and inheritance taxes.

On the other hand, a court judgment against one owner may be applied to the joint assets of both. Another drawback is that, since jointly held property passes to the surviving owner, it may end up being distributed in a way that the deceased spouse never intended. For example, a deceased husband may have meant an investment to be used for the eventual benefit of the couple's children, but the surviving wife may remarry and place the property in joint ownership with her new husband, who may not wish to pass it on to his stepchildren. Because no two family situations are exactly alike, it is a good idea to discuss the pros and cons of joint ownership, as they relate specifically to you, with your accountant, financial planner, or attorney.

A company Felicia owned stock in went bankrupt. Will she be able to get her money back?

It's possible, but not likely. Stockholders are among the last to be paid when a company goes bankrupt, and the company's assets are usually gone before the stockholders are reached. However, Felicia should still file a claim with the bankruptcy court. If the claims are small enough or if the company is sold or remains in business, she may recoup some of her investment.

I have lost a stock certificate. Can it be replaced?

Yes. Contact a broker and notify him of the missing certificate. He can advise you about the forms you'll need to fill out.

What would happen if the brokerage I use went out of business?

The Securities Investor Protection Corporation (SIPC), created by the Securities Investor Protection Act of 1970, would step in and seek a court order to protect the firm's customers. The court would then name a trustee to liquidate the brokerage. This would involve settling customers' claims and returning to them the securities and cash held by the firm. However, the amount of protection for investors' accounts afforded by the SIPC is limited to a total of $500,000 in securities and cash, of which no more than $100,000 can be in cash.

Do I have the same protection on funds invested through a discount broker as I do on funds invested through a regular broker?

Yes, if the discount broker is a member of the Securities Investor Protection Corporation. All stockbrokers registered with the Securities and Exchange Commission are automatically SIPC members. However, brokerages that deal exclusively in mutual funds, insurance, or investment advice may not be SIPC members.

Can I sue a stockbroker for giving me bad advice?

It is unlikely that you could win a lawsuit because the broker made an honest error in judgment or offered poor advice. However, a stockbroker is considered a fiduciary, a person who has a legal duty to act in your best

How to Avoid an Investment Swindle

Investment opportunities that sound too good to be true usually are—but that doesn't keep thousands of people from getting stung by con artists. That's why some experienced investors, when they get a call from a salesperson they don't know, say flatly that they never make such decisions over the phone, and hang up. Other people can't resist hearing at least a little about a "once in a lifetime deal." If you're that curious sort, here are seven questions designed to expose a fraud. Any one of the questions might deter a dishonest person—but all of them together won't daunt an honest one. This list is adapted from recommendations by the Chicago-based National Futures Association, a professional self-regulatory organization of firms and individuals that buy and sell commodities (such as metals, foods, and oils) for investors.

- Can I see some literature about your company and the investments you are selling, including the names of stockholders and directors? This won't stop a con artist from giving you false names, but it will serve notice that you are the kind of person who checks details. If there is no written material, or the salesperson explains that the deal is so hot that there hasn't been time to prepare any, you are probably being conned.
- Will you mail me a copy of your proposal? Crooked operators hate to

interests. If he put your money into inappropriately risky investments, or made trades without your authorization, you might be able to win a lawsuit against him. But because lawsuits can be expensive and take years to complete, most brokerage agreements give you the right to seek binding arbitration of claims against your stockbroker.

Bud's stockbroker has him buying and selling stocks every week. Despite all this activity, Bud's account isn't making money. What should he do?

Bud should put a stop to all the buying and selling and look into the possibility that his broker is "churning"—that is, making numerous stock transactions solely for the purpose of generating commissions. As a fiduciary, a stockbroker must act in his client's best financial interest. Buying and selling securities without a reasonable basis for doing so is a violation of this duty. Under federal and state securities laws, a broker found guilty of churning may have his license revoked, and faces other criminal and civil penalties as well.

If my stockbroker tells me that he can recommend investing in Nifty Computer Software Company because his friend, who is

hear this question for four reasons: (1) It takes time, and a crook would prefer to have your check at once. (2) The extra time allows you to think over the details of the proposal and change your mind. (3) A written proposal could be evidence in court. (4) Using the mail means the con man could be charged with breaking federal mail fraud laws.

- Could I meet with you at your office? Most likely, an unscrupulous salesperson won't want you to see the phone-filled "boiler room" from which he calls "mooches" (as the victims of investment scams are called in slang).
- How can I liquidate (sell for cash) my investment? In most honest securities transactions, this can be arranged in a matter of minutes.
- How many dollars or what percentage of my money would go for commissions, management fees, and the like? Don't settle for such glib answers as "These will be negligible compared to your profits."
- What government agency or professional association monitors your firm's dealings? Few things stop a fraudulent salesperson faster than the thought of being visited by an investigator from a regulatory agency or professional association.
- Would you mind describing your investment proposal to my attorney, accountant, banker, or investment adviser? If the salesperson says he would be happy to do so if there were more time, or insinuates that you should make your own investment decisions, your best bet is a quick good-bye.

chairman of the board of Nifty, has given him some reliable information, can I be charged with insider trading?

Yes. It is illegal to buy or sell a stock because you have information that is undisclosed outside the corporation. Insider trading is forbidden whether it is done by an officer of the corporation, by a stockbroker who possesses inside information, or by an investor who receives a tip from a corporate insider. Any profit you made from such a transaction would be subject to forfeit, and you might also be subject to other penalties.

Can I buy stocks through my bank?

Yes. Federal law permits banks to act as stockbrokers, but they are not required to provide this service.

Since U.S. Treasury Bills are guaranteed by the government, does this mean I can't lose money in them?

A Treasury Bill will always pay you its face amount if you cash it in at maturity, which ranges from three months to one year from the date you purchase it. Treasury Bills are backed by the full faith and credit of the United States government, which means that you could lose all your money if the United States defaulted on payments to its creditors. While this is possible, it is extremely unlikely.

After Ed's grandmother died, he found some old savings bonds in a metal box in her attic. Will the government redeem them?

Yes, but not necessarily for Ed. If they were owned jointly, they belong to the surviving owner. Otherwise, the savings bonds are now part of his grandmother's estate, and only its executor or administrator has the legal authority to redeem them on his grandmother's behalf.

A traffic accident left Ron in a coma, but he is expected to recover. What happens to Ron's investments while he is incapacitated?

If prior to his accident Ron had arranged to give someone a power of attorney—a document drawn up by a lawyer that gives someone the authority to act in another person's behalf—that person could manage Ron's financial affairs. If he had given no one power of attorney a probate judge would probably appoint someone to manage Ron's financial affairs after consulting with Ron's close relatives. The court-appointed guardian or conservator would be legally obligated to protect Ron's financial interests. Once a guardian or conservator is selected, he may be required to post a bond, although some states waive this requirement when the conservator is a bank or other financial institution. The guardian will manage Ron's property until a court determines that Ron is again capable of managing his own affairs.

I've been seeing a lot of ads in newspapers and magazines lately that describe services provided by financial planners. How should I go about looking for one?

Because this is a relatively new and unregulated field, nearly anyone can claim to be a financial planner. Before hiring any financial planner, you should interview several. Be sure you understand what fees, charges, and commissions you may have to pay, as well as if the financial planner is paid by any company for recommending its products or services.

Income Taxes

A friend of mine says the federal income tax is unconstitutional, and therefore he doesn't pay it. Is my friend correct?

No. Over the last 70 years, a number of attempts have been made to challenge the constitutionality of the federal income tax. All of these challenges have proven unsuccessful. Therefore, anyone who does not pay federal income tax when it is due is subject to criminal penalties, including fines and imprisonment.

If Ida's accountant, David, fills out her income tax form and he makes an error, can Ida be held responsible? What if the person who fills out her form is not an accountant?

The final responsibility for an individual's income tax form lies with the taxpayer. Therefore, no matter who fills out Ida's tax return, she is ultimately responsible for paying the correct tax and will be held liable for interest and penalties if less than the correct amount is paid. However, Ida has the option of suing the accountant for the money she had to pay because of the accountant's mistakes in preparing her return. An accountant is a professional and is held to a high standard of responsibility. In the case of an error made by a friend or relative, who is not held to the same standards as an accountant or attorney, it would be unlikely that Ida could recover the interest and penalties.

Income Taxes

My mother and father are thinking about selling their house but are afraid taxes will take most of the money. Isn't there a special tax rule that helps people in their situation?

Yes. If your parents qualify, federal tax law permits them to keep, tax free, up to $125,000 of the profit from selling their house. To qualify for this tax break, (1) either the homeowner or his spouse must be age 55 or older on the date of the sale; (2) the house must have been the owner's principal residence for three out of the past five years; and (3) neither the homeowner nor his spouse can have taken the exclusion before.

Do I have to report garage sale proceeds on my income tax return?

Generally, you must report income from the sale of an item when it results in financial gain. In most cases, items sold at a garage sale bring in less than what was originally paid for them, so there is no income to report.

My grandfather gave me $5,000 as a gift. Should I report it as income on my tax return? Will my grandfather have to pay a gift tax?

Neither you nor your grandfather will have to pay tax on the $5,000 gift. You needn't report the amount on your tax return, because gifts are not considered part of your gross income, but you will have to report and pay taxes on any dividends or interest you receive from investing the money.

Your grandfather will not have to pay a gift tax, since the value of the gift is less than $10,000. Tax laws permit your grandfather to give gifts to you and to others without paying federal gift taxes as long as he doesn't give more than $10,000 in cash or property each year to one individual.

Our daughter earned $700 last year by babysitting. Must she file a federal tax return?

Yes. Anyone whose income from self-employment is $400 or more must file a return. However, your daughter would not owe any tax on the $700 if that were her only income during the calendar year.

Julia pays her housekeeper in cash and doesn't withhold Social Security taxes. Is this legal?

It depends. If Julia hired her housekeeper through an agency, the agency usually takes responsibility for withholding and paying Social Security taxes. However, if the housekeeper is not represented by an agency and Julia pays her more than $50 in a calendar quarter, then Julia must withhold Social Security taxes from the housekeeper's wages, and pay an equal amount as an employer's contribution. Forms and information concerning these payments are available at Internal Revenue Service and Social Security Administration offices.

Can I deduct all lawyer fees from my income tax?

No. Until 1987, if you itemized your deductions, you were allowed to deduct legal expenses that you incurred to produce taxable income. This included legal fees for advice on the tax aspects of your investments; for contesting tax liability; and for collecting taxable alimony payments. However, under the Tax Reform Act of 1986, this is no longer the case. Such legal expenses must now be combined with the other deductions you list under "miscellaneous" if you itemize on your tax return; and they are deductible only to the extent that the total of your miscellaneous deductions exceeds 2 percent of your gross income.

What will happen if I don't file my taxes by April 15?

You may be subject to a penalty for late filing, interest on any tax due, and a possible penalty for late payment. If April 15 is approaching and you know you will not be able to fill out and mail your tax return in time, get the automatic four-month extension form from your nearest Internal Revenue Service office (also sometimes available at banks and post offices), fill it out, enclose a check for the amount of taxes you estimate you will owe, and mail it by the April 15 deadline. This will save you the penalty for late filing of a return, but it will not save you the penalty and interest for late payment *unless* the amount you pay by April 15 is equal to or exceeds the tax you actually owe.

Eric waited until the last minute to figure out his taxes and discovered he owed the government $950, which he doesn't have. What should he do?

He should seriously consider taking out a loan to make the $950 payment by the April 15 deadline. While it's easy enough for Eric to file the automatic four-month extension form, this does not change the deadline for payment of taxes due. Not only will Eric eventually have to pay the $950 he owes plus interest on that amount, but he may be subject to a penalty for failure to pay as well. These charges, applied from the April 15 due date, will probably exceed the interest Eric would have to pay on a loan from a bank.

Income Taxes

If Nathan owes back income taxes, is it true that the Internal Revenue Service has the power to garnishee his entire paycheck?

No. Nathan can keep 75 percent of his net wages or 30 times the federal minimum hourly wage, whichever is greater.

The IRS called me in for an audit. Why did they single me out?

Usually a taxpayer is selected for an audit by a computer program developed by the IRS to analyze returns. The computer looks for items that indicate possible error or fraud, such as deductions that are extremely large in proportion to the reported income. If you are in a high income bracket, you are more likely to be audited than someone with a lower income. In addition to returns that seem suspicious, a sample of returns is selected every year for audit under an IRS program for research into taxpayers' characteristics. To prevent tax evaders from escaping audits, the IRS jealously guards the exact criteria its computer uses in selecting a return for audit. Not every return selected by the computer is actually audited—that decision is made by IRS employees who review the returns selected by the computer.

What happens at an IRS audit?

Audits are conducted in several ways. Some are done by letter: these *correspondence audits* require the taxpayer to supply requested information by mail. Usually, however, an audit is conducted at an IRS office. Most often this *office audit* is limited to one or more issues or items selected by the IRS in advance. The taxpayer is notified by letter which items are in question and will be requested to bring documentation relating to these items. A *field audit* usually takes place at the taxpayer's home or place of business. It is generally very comprehensive, and may require that you give the auditor access to nearly all of your financial records. An attorney or certified public accountant, or both, may represent you at an audit, but it is not required.

What recourse do I have if I disagree with the outcome of a tax audit and do not want to pay additional taxes?

You have several avenues of appeal. After an office audit, you may request an immediate meeting with the auditor's supervisor. If you can't reach an agreement with the supervisor, the IRS will send you a letter stating the amount it regards as the tax you owe and notifying you of your right to an administrative appeal if you act within 30 days. If you choose to make this appeal, it will be conducted at the local IRS office.

You may challenge the results of an IRS audit in one of three federal courts: the U. S. Tax Court, the U. S. District Court for your district, or the U. S. Court of Claims. The Tax Court is a good forum for disputes under $10,000, since it uses simplified hearing procedures. If you go to Tax Court, you will not be required to pay the disputed amount in full before your hearing. Decisions of the Tax Court are final and cannot be appealed.

You can obtain detailed information about tax audits and appeals by writing to the Internal Revenue Service and requesting Publication 556, *Audit of Returns, Appeal Rights, and Claims for Refund.*

If the IRS audits my federal return, will my state tax office find out and audit my state and local returns?

It depends. If the audit indicates that you owe additional federal income taxes, the IRS will report this information to the state, since it almost always affects your state tax liability. However, the IRS does not automatically inform the state tax office when it conducts an audit.

How long should I keep income tax records?

Under federal law, your tax return can be challenged within six years of filing. After six years, even the IRS usually destroys copies of your returns. If you are missing one of your last six years' tax returns, you can obtain a copy from the IRS for a moderate fee.

One argument for never throwing away tax returns and basic tax information is that occasionally errors occur in recording payments to your Social Security account; your income tax records enable you to correct such errors. It is a good idea, anyway, to check the accuracy of your Social Security account every three years. This can be done through your nearest Social Security office. They will provide you with a postcard to fill in and mail. Upon receipt of this card, the Social Security office will forward a record of your payments to the present time.

Personal Bankruptcy

Barry makes a good salary, but he's overextended himself and owes $10,000. He has been making regular payments on all his bills, but can't get out from under. Should he think about bankruptcy?

Yes. America's bankruptcy law gives a person like Barry a fresh start by eliminating the pressure of existing debts. Before resorting to bankruptcy, however, Barry should consider some alternatives: (1) See if his creditors will accept smaller payments over an extended period of time. (2) Contact the Consumer Credit Counseling Services (a national nonprofit group) or some other financial counseling group. (3) Ask his creditors to accept a smaller amount than the total debt he owes. Under a plan called a *composition with creditors,* he would have to pay some percentage of the total amount due.

If his state permits debtors to make an *assignment for the benefit of creditors,* Barry could turn his property over to a trustee who would sell it and pay the creditors with the proceeds. However, this is a poor alternative to bankruptcy, because if the proceeds of the property are less than the amount owed, the creditors still have a claim for the remaining amount.

Before deciding to pursue bankruptcy or an alternative to it, Barry should see an attorney. He might also check state and local bar associations, which sometimes have free booklets explaining bankruptcy law.

If Bill declared bankruptcy, would he lose everything?

No. The fresh start concept of the bankruptcy law allows a debtor to keep certain assets and possessions, which are called *exempt* property. The property a debtor must give up to pay off creditors is called *nonexempt* property. What is nonexempt property in one state may be exempt in another. To find out what property his state permits him to keep, Bill should ask his state attorney general's office or bankruptcy court.

Suppose Fay decides to declare bankruptcy. What happens then?

She begins by filing a voluntary petition of bankruptcy in federal bankruptcy court. The court then sends notices to the creditors listed in her petition, ordering a halt to collection efforts against her and setting a date for her first meeting with all her creditors, usually held several weeks after the filing. At the meeting, creditors will question Fay about her property, debts, and other facts relating to her bankruptcy; a trustee may be appointed to supervise the sale of any assets that must be sold to pay her debts. The proceeds from this sale are divided among Fay's creditors according to priorities set out in the bankruptcy laws. Finally, a judge will formally grant Fay a discharge of all the debts listed in her petition.

Is there more than one kind of bankruptcy?

Yes. The two types used by individuals, as opposed to companies, are covered by Chapter 7 and Chapter 13 of the Federal Bankruptcy

What You Can Keep If You Go Bankrupt

Neither of the two main types of personal bankruptcy, covered by Chapter 7 and Chapter 13 of the Federal Bankruptcy Code, leaves you penniless. Under Chapter 13 you can keep all your property while you try to pay off your debts in full over a three-to-five-year period. Under Chapter 7, even though you are not required to pay your debts in full, federal or state bankruptcy laws allow you to keep certain property that will help you make a fresh start. What you can keep is called *exempt property;* what must go to pay your debts is called *nonexempt property.* Exempt property under Chapter 7 of the federal code includes:

- Up to $7,500 interest in the property used as a residence by the debtor or a dependent, or in a burial plot, and up to $400 ($3,750 if you do not own a home) in any other property.
- Up to $1,200 equity in a motor vehicle.
- Up to $500 worth of jewelry.
- Personal and household items, including clothes, books, appliances, musical instruments, and animals—up to $4,000 per household, with no one item to exceed $200 in value.
- Up to $750 worth of professional books and tools of your trade.
- If needed for support of the debtor and dependents, support payments resulting from a divorce decree and benefits from pensions, annuities, and life insurance.
- Benefits from Social Security, disability, and unemployment compensation.

Federal exemptions are more generous than those granted under state laws. State exemptions vary widely and can be rather curious: In Vermont, for example, your automobile is nonexempt, but one yoke of oxen is exempt. In general, state exemptions are more generous in the Southwest, more restrictive in the Northeast. While federal law allows debtors to use the exemptions allowed under state law, most states require that only their own exemptions be followed.

Code. A Chapter 7 bankruptcy, sometimes referred to as a straight bankruptcy, requires a debtor to sell his property to satisfy debts; the proceeds are divided up among the various creditors, who may get only a fraction of what they are actually owed. A person can file for Chapter 7 regardless of whether or not he has a regular income.

In a Chapter 13 bankruptcy, a debtor pays off his creditors over an extended time period—up to five years—out of future income as well as from the sale of property. To file a Chapter 13 bankruptcy, a debtor must have a regular source of income. Chapter 13 allows the debtor to keep his property and gives him one last chance to pay off all his debts according to a schedule set by the court. In contrast, Chapter 7 calls for the debtor's assets to be sold at once and the proceeds used to pay his creditors.

Does Perry's employer have to know if he files for bankruptcy?

If Perry files for Chapter 7, his employer will not necessarily be notified, unless the court-appointed trustee requires additional information about Perry's wages. If Perry chooses Chapter 13, his employer will probably be notified, since the trustee may ask that a portion of Perry's wages be paid directly to him. In either case, it is illegal for the employer to discriminate against Perry because he has filed for bankruptcy.

Can a person file for bankruptcy more than once?

Yes. Somebody who can't meet the payments under a Chapter 13 can then file for a Chapter 7. And a person who has gone through a Chapter 7 can file for a Chapter 13 anytime later. However, somebody who is discharged of debts under Chapter 7 cannot file again for a Chapter 7 for six years.

Leroy went bankrupt eight years ago. Can he be refused credit?

Yes. Under the Fair Credit Reporting Act, a bankruptcy can remain in a person's credit history for up to 10 years, but he is legally entitled to have his written explanation of the circumstances made part of his credit record. A past bankruptcy may not deter creditors, especially if it was a Chapter 13 and the debtor met the required schedule of payments. If Leroy stays out of financial trouble, it may not take 10 years for creditors to start lending to him again.

Can Jerry be turned down for a job because he had his debts discharged in bankruptcy court?

No. It is illegal for either the government or private employers to discriminate against an individual because he previously filed for bankruptcy. In addition, it is illegal for a federal, state, or local government agency that grants licenses and permits to discriminate against someone who has gone through a bankruptcy proceeding.

CHAPTER
8

Insurance

Is there a difference between what an insurance agent and an insurance broker can do? Does either one have to be licensed?

An agent is an employee of an insurance company and represents that company in making legally binding contracts. A broker is a self-employed individual who locates suitable coverage for persons seeking insurance. Generally, a broker cannot legally bind an insurance company to a contract: the contract is between his client and the insurance company.

Both agents and brokers must meet state licensing requirements, which typically include a period of residency in the state, a passing grade on a written exam, references and other evidence attesting to the applicant's good moral character, and in some states the posting of a bond that insures clients against default or fraud by the agent or broker.

Roy's mother asked him to look over her insurance policies, but he found he couldn't understand some of them. Don't insurance policies have to be in plain English?

Many but not all states require that insurance policies be written in plain English so that the meaning is not obscured. Even in states without such laws, plain English versions of policies may be available.

If Roy is unsure what certain words or phrases mean, he should call the insurance company and ask for a brief, clear outline of what is and is not covered in the policies. If he still isn't satisfied, he should put his specific questions in a letter to the company.

Wendy paid the premium when she filled out an insurance application. Will she be covered if something happens before she receives the actual policy?

Many insurance companies issue a binding receipt, or binder, when the first premium is paid. A binder would protect Wendy for the few days it takes to process her application and payment. If her application is rejected, Wendy would be entitled to a refund of her premium payment.

I gave some incorrect information on my insurance application. Should I correct it now?

Yes. Insurance companies have many ways of verifying the information you give. If you make a claim and the company discovers misinformation on your application, your claim may be denied and your policy voided.

With life insurance, if the insured dies within two years after buying a policy, an untruthful application (one that neglects to mention a family history of heart disease or diabetes, for example) can prevent the payment of proceeds to the beneficiary, because of fraud. If the misinformation on a life insurance application relates to age, the claim won't be denied, but the amount the beneficiary receives will be adjusted to reflect the insured's actual age. Suppose, for example, that Clarence's age on his life insurance policy is 10 years younger than his actual age. If he dies and the insurance company discovers the truth, it will compute the additional premiums that Clarence would have paid as an older person, and subtract that amount from the money his beneficiary is to receive. Don't wait until you have a claim to see if the erroneous information on your application will be used against you. Write to your company or agent immediately, giving the correct data.

Questions to Ask When Buying Insurance

A common misconception about insurance is that all companies sell essentially the same coverage at a similar cost. The fact is that you can get more protection for your money by careful inquiry. If you ask the following questions, you will challenge an insurance agent or broker to find you the very best coverage at the lowest cost:

- ☑ If I need immediate coverage, can I get a binder that protects me while my application is being evaluated?
- ☑ Is there a waiting period before I can receive benefits?
- ☑ How does this policy's premium compare with the premiums paid by other policyholders with similar coverage from this company? How do this company's premiums compare with those of other insurers?
- ☑ To exactly what date is the policy in effect?
- ☑ Is there a grace period for late premium payments?
- ☑ On what grounds can the company cancel my policy?
- ☑ If I decide to cancel, how much of a refund can I expect?
- ☑ Can I get a policy the company guarantees is renewable and that cannot be canceled by the company?
- ☑ How soon must I submit claims and report accidents, damage, injuries, death, or illnesses?
- ☑ When I make a claim, what documentation and what procedures are required to show proof of loss?
- ☑ How soon will an adjuster investigate my claim?
- ☑ How long does it take to settle the average claim?
- ☑ Can you tell me what percentage of claims by policyholders end up in court and how this percentage compares to the average throughout the insurance industry?
- ☑ Will rates be raised after a claim is paid, regardless of the amount, or will they be raised after a set number of claims?
- ☑ Does this policy duplicate coverage I already have?

If I can't pay the full premium that is coming due, will I still be covered if I pay part of it?

No. Generally, most insurance contracts require premiums to be paid in full to keep a policy in force.

Two days after Farley filled out an insurance application and paid the first month's premium, he had second thoughts about the cost. If he cancels the policy, is he entitled to a refund?

Yes, but whether it is a full or partial refund depends on where he lives and what kind of insurance is involved. More than half the states have laws mandating a "10-day free look," or cooling-off period, for health and life insurance policies (but not for auto and homeowners insurance), with the promise of a full refund if the buyer decides to cancel the agreement within 10 days.

Farley can expect at least a partial refund no matter where he lives and what kind of insurance is involved; he should read his policy to find out his cancellation and refund rights. If Farley calls the company and is told that his application has not yet been approved, he can withdraw his application and request a full refund. If Farley isn't sure if his state has a "free look" law, he can find out by contacting his state department of insurance (sometimes called the state insurance commissioner's office).

Warren's insurance agent cashed one of his premium checks but did not send the money to the insurance company. If Warren makes a claim, will the company pay it?

Yes. The company authorizes its agents to act on its behalf. If a broker, and not an agent, were involved, Warren's risk of losing his money would be greater, since a broker does not legally represent the company. If the insurance company did not honor Warren's claim, his only choice might be to sue the broker.

I'm having trouble finding a company that will insure me or my property. What can I do?

There are many private and government-backed programs available for hard-to-insure people. For health and life insurance, group policies are generally available through your own or your spouse's employer and don't require medical examinations. Fraternal, trade, religious, and alumni associations may also offer health and life insurance policies that don't require medical examinations, but such policies can be expensive in proportion to the benefits offered. Some states offer pooled-risk health insurance to individuals who would not otherwise be able to get coverage. Florida, Indiana, and Minnesota, for example, have health insurance plans for residents who have been turned down by two or more private insurance companies.

If you are having trouble getting homeowners or tenants property insurance because you live in a high-crime area, you may qualify for state or federal programs that offer coverage. If your problem is auto insurance, you may be eligible for your state's assigned risk plan, although you will pay higher rates than the average. For further information, contact your state insurance department or commissioner's office.

Can I buy insurance from the government?

Yes. The federal government offers flood, crop, and crime insurance for some areas. Many states offer pooled-risk health insurance, and all states have auto insurance programs for high-risk drivers. All of these programs insure people who would otherwise be without coverage. Some private insurance companies have names that imply government involvement, such as *National, Federal, State, Veterans,* and *Republic.* If you aren't sure whether a program is private or governmental, call the organization or check with your state insurance department.

Joel thought he was buying the same health insurance policy that his friend had; but when he received his policy, it had several riders attached. What should Joel do?

Riders can be used to limit or eliminate coverage offered in a standard policy. In Joel's case, after the company reviewed his medical history, it may have decided not to give him coverage for certain conditions, at least not right away. For example, if Joel had recently recovered from an ulcer, one of the riders might state that he would not be covered for ulcer treatments for three years from the date the policy was issued.

If Joel is not willing to accept the conditions imposed on the policy by the riders, he may demand a refund and look elsewhere for coverage. Or he can negotiate further with the company to try to get one or more riders altered or removed, or his premium reduced.

Is it legal for insurance companies to charge women rates that are different from those that men are charged?

Yes, in most states. Generally, because they are expected to live longer, women are charged less for life insurance than men are, but women pay more for health insurance. The insurance industry's use of sex-based criteria for setting rates has been challenged in several court cases, but there is no federal law prohibiting it. As of 1987, Montana was the only state to prohibit rates based on sex in any insurance policy. Other states, including Massachusetts, Michigan, and North Carolina, prohibited setting auto insurance rates on the basis of sex.

When I submit a claim, how fast must my insurance company act?

It depends on where you live. Some states require that the insurance company act within a reasonable time, but leave the specific amount of time for the court to decide in each case. For example, a court might rule that the company should send an adjuster within a few days after receiving a claim and that a month was unreasonable. Other states require action within a specific period of time. For example, some states with no-fault auto insurance programs require insurance companies to pay a claim—or give a reason for denying it—within 10 days.

When Constance bought her insurance, the agent said a particular item was covered. Now that she has put in a claim, the company says the item isn't covered. What can she do?

First, Constance should present her case in writing to the insurance company; if necessary, to the company's president. If the company still refuses to pay her claim and she doesn't agree with its explanation, she should send a complaint and copies of her correspondence to her state commissioner (or department) of insurance, whose address she can get by calling her state government information number. Constance also has the option of suing for fraud. Her chances of winning depend on whether she can prove that the insurance company or its agent or the broker deliberately misled her about the policy.

On what grounds can an insurance company cancel a policy?

Grounds for cancellation are spelled out in your policy. The most common ones are (1) not paying your premiums; (2) misrepresenting or concealing important facts on your application; (3) failing to report accidents, claims, or other important information; and (4) not cooperating with your insurance company as specified in your contract.

Auto insurance may be canceled for any reason (or no reason at all) during the first 60 days of coverage unless you have already made a claim. Auto insurance may also be canceled if your driver's license is suspended or revoked. The insurance company must notify you when your policy is canceled, and the cancellation is not effective until the company does so.

Some states that have compulsory auto insurance limit the grounds for cancellation to not paying a premium, suspension of a driver's license, or false information on an application.

What are my rights if my insurance policy is canceled?

You must be notified in advance that your coverage will be canceled and told the reasons for canceling it. Most states define how many days in advance are required, but the exact number of days varies from state to state and with the kind of insurance. If you believe the company had no right to cancel your policy, you can contest the cancellation. If your policy is canceled during a period for which you have paid the premium, you are entitled to a refund of a portion of the premium you have paid.

Eva's husband canceled their insurance. Can she get it reinstated?

Many policies allow reinstatement within a certain period of time if past premiums, plus interest, are paid. Eva may need to provide evidence that she and her husband are still insurable. If their policy does not allow reinstatement, she will probably have to seek new coverage.

What can I do if I have a complaint about either my insurance policy or the company that issued it?

First, send a letter to the person who sold you the policy. If he does not resolve the problem, write a letter to his supervisor and, if necessary, work your way up to the head of the company. If you are still dissatisfied, contact your state insurance department or commissioner of insurance. The commissioner can impose fines or other sanctions on companies that follow unfair practices. Finally, if you believe the insurance company has acted illegally, you can hire an attorney to help enforce your rights.

Life Insurance

Gerald bought a life insurance policy two years ago. He now has a job that gives him a large amount of life insurance. Will his beneficiary be able to collect on both policies?

Yes. Life insurance contracts do not prohibit double coverage. Gerald may buy as many policies and as much protection as he wishes.

Life Insurance

As a nonsmoker, am I eligible for lower premium rates than those charged to smokers?

Yes. Most insurance companies offer reductions of up to 50 percent for people with healthful lifestyles. Generally, to qualify for this reduction, you must take a medical examination that shows you have normal weight, blood pressure, and cholesterol levels. You may also be asked to verify that you exercise regularly and use a seat belt when driving.

Edwina keeps getting letters urging her to buy credit life insurance. Does she need it?

Credit life insurance is a type of insurance that guarantees the payment of a debt, such as a mortgage or personal loan, after a person's death. Usually this insurance is known as decreasing term because its benefit decreases over the period that the owner is paying off the debt. For example, assume Edwina bought credit life insurance to cover a new car loan that had a four-year schedule of payments. If she dies during the first year, the amount the policy pays will be much greater than the amount it

How to Shop for Life Insurance

The life insurance industry is full of fancy-sounding policies with elaborate features. But don't let the complexities intimidate you. Stick to the basics, as suggested by the following three questions, and you'll make life insurance decisions that are right for you.

- *How Much?* When deciding on the amount of coverage you need, total your short-term debts (car loans, credit card balances) and figure how much your dependents will need to settle these accounts and pay your funeral and burial expenses. Then estimate your dependents' costs of continuing to live as they do now. Include their rent or mortgage, food, clothing, and education expenses. Measure this against the financial resources that will remain after your death: your spouse's salary; life insurance you already have; stocks, bonds, savings accounts, and other income-producing investments; real estate or other kinds of property your dependents could sell if they chose. The National Insurance Consumer Organization recommends that the head of a family with two young children should be covered by life insurance with a face value five times his annual salary; but financial experts differ about any "right amount." Your best course is to get several opinions (from friends, family, and colleagues, as well as from insurance people), then make up your own mind about how much is enough.

will pay if she dies during the fourth year. Although a lender can legally require that Edwina have some type of insurance to cover a debt, the lender can't require that she buy a particular type or that she buy it from a particular company. Most experts advise having a standard term policy to protect heirs against being saddled with a large debt.

Can I buy insurance that will pay me at a later date, rather than pay a beneficiary after my death?

Yes. This type of insurance is called endowment insurance or retirement income insurance. The face value of the policy is paid to the insured if he is still alive at the date specified in the policy. The beneficiary is paid the face amount if the insured dies before reaching the age specified.

Uncle Harry bought a life insurance policy even though a court had declared him incompetent. Is the insurance policy valid?

No. Contracts signed by persons who have been declared legally incompetent are void. However, contracts made with people who are mentally ill, but not legally incompetent, can be voided only by the ill person.

• *What Kind?* You will need to weigh the pros and cons of two kinds of life policies, permanent and term. Permanent insurance is known by many names, such as *straight life, ordinary life,* and *whole life*, which may add various features to the basic plan. Premiums usually stay the same for the duration of the policy. Unlike term insurance, permanent life accumulates what is called a cash value. Part of each premium goes into a fund that is a type of savings. This amount, or cash value, grows with each premium payment and earns interest at a rate set by the company. The cash value is available to you if you want to borrow all or part of it (for which you are charged interest) or if you cancel the policy.

Term insurance has no cash value and offers protection for a certain period of time, called the term. If you die during the term, your beneficiary receives the proceeds. If not, the policy terminates and you must renew it or buy a new policy. Term insurance is almost always less expensive than permanent insurance. However, the premiums for term go up as you get older. Many people buy renewable term (such as ART, or annual renewable term). This means the insured doesn't have to requalify for insurance when renewing the policy.

• *Which Company?* Premiums and policy provisions vary greatly from company to company, and some comparison shopping is a must to find what's best for you. Various publications that rate insurance companies are available at most public libraries.

Life Insurance

Is it possible to borrow against the cash value of an insurance policy in order to pay the premiums?

Yes. Many life insurance policies have a feature known as the automatic premium loan, or the extended term provision, that allows the insurance company to use the cash value of the policy to pay past due premiums. Remember, however, that this is a loan: you will be charged interest on it; and if you die owing money on your policy, the loan amount will be deducted from the proceeds paid to your beneficiary.

My ex-husband and I had life insurance policies on each other's lives when we were married. Does our divorce automatically cancel this insurance?

No. If you die while the policy is in effect, your ex-husband will collect the proceeds. As the policy owner, you can cancel the coverage or change the beneficiary unless your divorce decree prohibits you from doing so.

My grandparents bought an accidental death policy believing that it was a standard life insurance policy. My grandfather died recently, and the insurance company won't pay my grandmother anything. Does my family have a case?

Probably not. If your grandparents were simply confused or mistaken about the type of insurance they were purchasing, they have no recourse against the company. The insurance company is obligated to pay only if your grandfather's death was due to an accident. However, if the company's agent misled your grandparents into believing they were buying a standard insurance policy, your grandmother could sue the company for fraud, and a court could rule that the death benefit be paid.

Beneficiaries

For information on other kinds of beneficiaries, see "Naming Your Heirs" and "Establishing Trusts" in Chapter 16, *Wills and Estates*.

Can I name anyone I choose to be a beneficiary of an insurance policy on my life?

Yes. However, if you want a child to get your life insurance proceeds, you may wish to establish a trust as the beneficiary and name a trustee or guardian to manage the money until the child reaches adulthood.

If You Are a Life Insurance Beneficiary

In most cases, it is a simple process to collect the benefits to which you are entitled under a deceased person's life insurance policy. Inform the company that issued the policy, or its agent, of the insured person's death. The company will send you the necessary forms and instructions for submitting your claim. Complete the forms and return them by certified mail, along with any documents that the company may request, such as the death certificate and the policy itself. If you cannot find the policy, notify the insurance company, and it will send you a lost-policy receipt.

Before paying, the insurance company will probably ask you to choose between several settlement options. The lump sum option pays in one check. Under the interest, or deposit, option, all the money is left with the company until a later time, and only the interest earned on that amount is paid to the beneficiary for the time being. Under the fixed, or installment, option, the money is left with the company, where it earns interest, and is paid out in fixed amounts to the beneficiary until it is all disbursed.

Sometimes—for example, when the insured person died during the contestability period (usually two years after purchasing the policy)—the company may delay paying. If you are notified that your claim is being investigated, you can help yourself by (1) finding out the claim number that the company has assigned to your case and using the number in all contacts with the company; (2) keeping a log of all telephone calls (including the dates and times of the calls), the names of persons to whom you spoke, and the substance of your discussions; (3) sending the company a letter that summarizes each phone conversation; and (4) keeping copies of all correspondence.

Not only will such records help you remember names, dates, and details, but they could also prove useful if you later feel you must take the matter to your state insurance commissioner or decide to challenge the insurance company's decision in court.

Richard owes his friend Ellen $10,000. Can Ellen take out a policy on Richard's life naming herself as beneficiary?

Yes, if she gets Richard's permission. Ellen has what is known legally as an insurable interest in Richard in the amount of $10,000. To have an insurable interest in someone means that, if the person died, you would be harmed in some way or suffer some kind of loss. Ellen could lose $10,000 if Richard died and his estate did not have enough money to pay her and other creditors. The legal concept of insurable interest also applies to a close relative whose death would deprive the beneficiary of companionship and emotional support. Thus, ties such as a parent-child, brother-sister, and wife-husband are considered insurable interests.

Rhonda's uncle Ned died six months ago, and Rhonda thinks he named her as the beneficiary of his life insurance policy. She has heard nothing. What should she do?

Rhonda should ask to look through her uncle's checkbooks and other financial records, contact his previous employers, and talk with family and friends. If her uncle was a veteran, she should check if the policy was issued under National Service Life Insurance, which she can reach by calling the Federal Information Center, whose number is listed in the phone books of major cities or can be obtained from the operator.

Another avenue of inquiry for Rhonda is the American Council for Life Insurance, headquartered in Washington, D.C. Its information service unit helps people who think they may be the beneficiaries of a deceased person's lost or destroyed life insurance policy. Rhonda would complete an application about her late uncle, which would be sent to some 100 life insurers with the greatest amounts of ordinary life insurance in force. These companies would then search through their records to see if they issued a policy to Uncle Ned.

When Jessica and Nathan divorced, the court awarded Jessica the right to the proceeds of a life insurance policy Nathan had bought while they were still married. Jessica is afraid that Nathan will change his beneficiary. Can he do this?

This is one of the few situations in which the owner of a life insurance policy is severely restricted in controlling it. If Nathan tried to name a new beneficiary, and the court found out, he would probably be held in contempt of court, since the divorce decree gave Jessica the right to the proceeds of the policy. Furthermore, if Jessica was named as irrevocable beneficiary, Nathan couldn't name another beneficiary without her consent, nor could he cash in the policy or borrow against it. If he refused to pay the premiums and the policy lapsed, the court could order him to compensate Jessica for her financial loss.

If someone who owns a life insurance policy dies, and the beneficiary is also dead, who gets the proceeds?

The proceeds are paid to the insured person's estate and then distributed, either according to the insured's will or according to state laws if the insured died without a will. To prevent your life insurance from going to someone you didn't select, you can add contingent (alternative) beneficiaries to your policy.

How does my last will and testament affect the disposition of my life insurance?

If you have named your estate as beneficiary of your life insurance proceeds, the money will be distributed according to the terms of your will. Otherwise, payment would not be affected by the will and in almost all circumstances would be made directly to the beneficiary. For an exception to this, see the next question and answer.

Can a creditor claim the proceeds of a life insurance policy to cover unpaid debts?

Generally, the beneficiary of a life insurance policy receives the proceeds free of creditors' claims. However, if the insured person pledged the policy as collateral for a loan, the creditor would have a legal claim on the proceeds for the amount of the debt. If the insured person named his estate as the beneficiary, the proceeds would be used, like any other asset, to pay debts.

My aunt named me a beneficiary of her life insurance. She died this month. Do I have to report the insurance proceeds on my income tax return?

No. The proceeds of a life insurance policy are not considered taxable income unless you paid the insured to name you as the beneficiary.

Paulette's husband disappeared three years ago. Can she have him declared legally dead so she can collect his life insurance?

To have her husband declared legally dead, Paulette must show he has been absent, without explanation, for a certain period of time, ranging from 4 to 10 years; most states set the period at 5 or 7 years. To check the requirement in her state, Paulette should contact her state attorney general's office. She must also show that she has made a diligent search for her husband.

Stella's husband, Trevor, had a terminal illness. He committed suicide to avoid a slow and painful death. The insurance

company says that Stella cannot collect the proceeds from his life insurance. Is this true?

Not necessarily. So long as there is no clause in the policy that specifically excludes coverage in the event of suicide, the company is required to pay, with one possible exception. If Trevor died before the end of the policy's contestability period, the company can contest its obligation to pay.

During the contestability period, which usually lasts one or two years after the purchase of the policy, the company can investigate the insured to verify the information on his application. If, in the case of a suicide, the insurance company should discover a history of mental illness that was not reported by the insured, this omission could be legal grounds for refusing to pay on the policy.

Health and Disability Insurance

For more on medical charges, see "Paying the Bills" in Chapter 14, *Your Medical Rights*. For Medicare and Medicaid, see Chapter 15, *Pensions, IRA's, Social Security*.

Can my medical insurance coverage be canceled if I get sick?

No. Illness is not a valid reason for an insurance company to cancel your medical insurance. If your policy is guaranteed renewable, the company cannot refuse to renew your policy when its term is over.

Kevin wants to make sure that his health insurance policy won't be canceled. Are such policies available?

Yes. Kevin could buy an individual policy that is noncancelable during its term of coverage and guaranteed renewable at the end of the term. These policies will cover Kevin to a particular age, or for life. If Kevin opts for enrollment in a group health insurance plan through his employer or an organization to which he belongs, he cannot lose his coverage unless the insurance company cancels its policy for the entire group.

What's the difference between major medical policies, catastrophic illness insurance, and standard health insurance?

Generally, *major medical* and *catastrophic illness policies* are different names for the same protection. This coverage may be combined with *standard health insurance* and sold in a *comprehensive policy*. The major medical plans cover serious illnesses that require long hospital stays and

Key Questions to Ask About Health Insurance

With the staggering costs of medical care it is important that you protect your family and yourself with both standard health insurance, to help pay the ordinary medical costs that most people face over the years, and major medical insurance, for the huge expenses associated with serious, long-term illness. These two kinds of health insurance may be sold together in a comprehensive policy. To obtain the best possible coverage, ask your insurance agent these questions before buying:

- ☑ How soon will I be insured under the policy?
- ☑ Will the policy cover everyone in my immediate family?
- ☑ To what age are my spouse and I insured? When either of us reaches 65, can the policy be converted to one that supplements Medicare?
- ☑ To what age are my children covered?
- ☑ Can the company cancel the policy, and if so, for what reasons?
- ☑ Are there diseases or conditions that the policy does not cover?
- ☑ How does your company define preexisting conditions, and does the policy cover them?
- ☑ Does the policy pay for medical costs resulting from both illnesses and accidents?
- ☑ Am I covered for diagnostic tests, whether or not they are performed in a hospital?
- ☑ How large are the deductibles, and how long is the waiting period before benefits are paid?
- ☑ What is the most I will be left to pay on any medical bill? (Generally, after the deductible is met, policies cover a percentage of the cost, leaving the patient to pay the rest.)
- ☑ How many hospital days are covered per year, and how much per day will the policy pay?
- ☑ Are hospital services (such as nursing, lab tests, X-rays, medications, use of operating room) fully, or just partially, covered?
- ☑ How does the maximum per-day coverage compare with the actual amount charged by hospitals in my community?
- ☑ Is there a complete list of exactly how much (as a percentage or dollar amount) the policy will pay for different kinds of surgery?
- ☑ Do surgical payments realistically reflect the fees charged by surgeons in my area?
- ☑ What is the maximum payable under major medical provisions?
- ☑ Does the major medical maximum apply to each separate illness, or does it apply to all illnesses?
- ☑ After recovery from an illness, is there a waiting period before the maximum amount of benefits again becomes available for a recurrence of that illness?
- ☑ Does the policy have a stop-loss provision that limits the maximum amount of medical costs I must pay?
- ☑ Is the company that would issue the policy licensed by the state department of insurance?

expensive surgery or other costly treatment and care. These policies typically pay 75 to 85 percent of the covered costs, after the deductibles are met. Standard health insurance, on the other hand, pays part of the cost of less serious, shorter-term medical problems, usually including visits to the doctor for diagnosis and treatment of illnesses, as well as prescription drugs. Major medical plans are designed to come into effect when, because of prolonged illness, the benefits available under a person's standard health insurance are exhausted. The term *major medical* does not necessarily mean that all major illnesses are covered; that depends on what the policy states.

Is it legal for an insurance company to reject me for a health policy because I may have had a certain serious disease?

Yes. It is not against the law for an insurance company to decline to sell health insurance to a person who has had a particular disease. However, if you are rejected by one company on the basis of your medical condition or history, another company might very well accept you.

Emma has seen advertisements for policies that cover specific diseases. Should she think about purchasing one?

Most experts on health and medical insurance consider the so-called dread disease policies a poor value because they have high premiums and usually cover a person for just one disease, such as cancer. Before buying such a policy, Emma should carefully weigh its coverage and cost against more traditional policies, such as a comprehensive policy that includes both major medical and standard health insurance.

My father saw a television commercial stating that anyone over 65 years old can get a health insurance policy without a physical exam, and the policy can't be canceled for any reason. Is there a catch to this?

Yes. The catch to many of these policies is that there is a long period (sometimes as much as two years) before your coverage actually begins. Additionally, this type of policy is usually expensive, and the benefits are sometimes inadequate to meet the standard costs of health care.

Four months ago, Rhoda took out a health insurance policy. When she turned in a claim for treatment of her bad back, the

company refused to pay because it was a preexisting condition. How can they do this?

Most individual health insurance policies exclude coverage for preexisting conditions. A preexisting condition is a health problem that began before you bought the insurance policy. If Rhoda previously suffered from a bad back, the company probably has the right to refuse her claim. If Rhoda had a group policy, her preexisting condition would have been covered. (Group policies, however, may exclude coverage for a preexisting pregnancy by not paying for childbirth costs until a woman's policy has been in effect for nine months.)

I've heard alcoholism referred to as an illness. Does this mean it would normally be covered under a general health policy?

Most health insurance plans include coverage for the treatment of mental health problems and alcohol and drug abuse; and most states require by law that insurance companies provide this type of coverage. However, many policies cover only short hospital stays (or none at all) and limit payments for outpatient treatment.

Tom asked his insurance agent if he should include a one-day hospital stay, three years ago, on his application. The agent said, "Don't worry about it." Six months later, Tom required major surgery. The insurance company refused to pay, claiming that Tom had lied on his application. Does the company have legal grounds for not paying?

Tom has been the victim of a practice known as clean-sheeting, in which an agent knowingly leaves out health information that may result in an application's rejection, because it would prevent the agent from earning a commission. Tom's insurance company can claim that he attempted to defraud them, because he signed and verified the application. However, since the company's agent knowingly submitted the incorrect application, a court may rule that the insurance company cannot use the application to deny coverage.

Is it possible to keep my group medical insurance coverage after I quit my job—or even if I'm fired?

Yes. Federal law requires most employers to offer employees the option of coverage under the group health policy for up to 18 months (up to 36 months for widows and divorced spouses and their dependents) after you leave your job, unless you have been fired for gross misconduct. This law does not apply to group plans covering fewer than 20 individuals and church plans. However, many states require employers to extend group coverage beyond the federal limits: check with your state department (or commissioner) of insurance. When the group coverage ends, you have the option to convert your group policy to an individual one.

Marty is now clear of all signs of cancer, but no company will give him health insurance. Is this legal?

Yes, but Marty should not give up trying to find insurance. If he is no longer in treatment, he may be able to buy insurance coverage at a higher rate, or he may be able to buy a policy that will begin after a six-month to one-year waiting period. Marty should contact a knowledgeable broker or agent who may be able to find coverage for him. If Marty is unable to purchase health insurance from a private company, he should check his state insurance plans. Many states offer pooled-risk insurance to people who are unable to find health insurance because of their medical history.

Sue was injured in a car accident in which the other driver was at fault. Her insurance paid the medical bills. In her settlement with the other driver's automobile insurance company, she was paid for pain and suffering and her medical expenses. Does she have to reimburse her insurance company?

Yes. Sue's insurance policy probably has a subrogation clause, which means that her insurance company, once it has paid Sue's medical expenses, has the right to recover those expenses from the other driver's insurance company. Sue's insurance company does not have a claim on the money she was awarded for pain and suffering.

Jane has medical insurance for her $5,000 hospital bill. However, six months have passed, and the insurance company has not paid. The hospital is now suing Jane. Is it legal for the hospital to do this when Jane is clearly not at fault?

Yes. The hospital has the right to sue Jane because it is her bill that remains unpaid, regardless of who is supposed to pay it. Jane should contact an attorney and ask that the insurance company be named as a defendant in the lawsuit. If the insurance company does not have a valid reason for not paying the bill, Jane can request that the company be ordered to pay her legal fees as well as punitive damages as a penalty for acting in bad faith.

Gus and Trudy's baby needs a liver transplant. Their major medical insurer refuses to pay for the operation even though the child will die without it. What can Gus and Trudy do?

Gus and Trudy should have a lawyer review their policy to verify that liver transplants are excluded. If they are not, the lawyer will demand a review by the insurer's legal department. If the company claims the transplant is experimental, is an unacceptable medical practice, or is not medically necessary, Gus and Trudy may have to sue to compel the company to pay.

Do I need disability insurance if I have a steady, full-time job?

Most insurance experts recommend it strongly. Disability insurance provides benefits while you are unable to work because of illness or an accident. Workers' compensation and Social Security may not be available to you or adequate for your needs.

The ABC's of Disability Coverage

The purpose of disability insurance is to provide income if you cannot work for an extended time because you are seriously ill or injured. Insurance companies generally insure you for up to two-thirds of your gross salary. Some key points to remember when you are considering disability insurance include:

- The definition of disability varies from company to company. Most experts say the best policies are those that define disability as being unable to perform in your *usual occupation,* not just inability to perform any job.
- Depending on the policy, benefits can start anywhere from a week to more than a year after you are disabled. The longer the waiting period, the lower your premiums should be.
- The period of time in which benefits are paid varies with the company and the policy. Some policies cover only 13 weeks of disability, while others pay until your 65th birthday, or even for life.
- Many companies offer noncancelable and guaranteed renewable coverage. Ask for it.
- The best policies include coverage for disability from both accidents and sickness; watch out for those that don't.
- You may already have some form of disability insurance, from your employer or union or military service. Furthermore, in the sixth month of a disability that is expected to last for at least 12 months, you may become eligible for Social Security benefits.
- Some companies offer a rider called a cost of living benefit (for which you pay more), under which the amount you are paid if you become disabled may be increased to offset the effect of inflation.

Insuring Your Home

For information on title insurance, see "Buying Your Home" in Chapter 4, *Your Home*.

How much homeowners insurance should I buy?

Many experts advise homeowners to insure their homes for 100 percent of the replacement value, but 80 percent is often considered full coverage—because even if your home burns to the ground, you will not have to replace the foundation, the basement, and the land on which the house stood. Your replacement cost may be greater than the purchase price you paid for your home, or greater than its current value. You can hire a professional appraiser or work with your insurance company to determine the replacement cost.

If you wish to insure the contents of your home at their replacement value, you will want to think about purchasing a replacement cost endorsement. Without the endorsement, you will probably recover only the actual value (replacement cost less depreciation) of your home's contents in the event of a loss.

In buying homeowners insurance, as in making most purchases, the more you pay, the more you get. For example, a policy that insures you against a greater number of perils costs more than one that covers fewer perils. Most policies are issued for one or three years, with a discount from the full annual premium usually available on the three-year policy. At renewal time, you may change the amount of insurance you carry to reflect the new value of your house.

The Standard Five of Home Insurance

There are five standard kinds of homeowners insurance, including policies for tenants and co-op and condominium dwellers. As in the list below, these five are commonly identified in the insurance business by an HO (homeowner) number, followed by a brief word or phrase.

Many people find that the amount of protection for personal property included in these policies is less than adequate. To insure valuable items, they purchase floaters that cover specifically described property for its full value. Another kind of coverage, called an umbrella policy, adds liability protection (usually $1 million or more) if you or a family member is responsible for injuring someone or damaging his property.

- *HO-1 (Basic).* Covers your home and its contents against losses resulting from: (1) fire and lightning; (2) windstorms and hail; (3) explosions; (4) riots; (5) aircraft; (6) vehicles not owned or operated by persons covered in the policy; (7) smoke; (8) vandalism and malicious mischief; (9) theft; (10) glass breakage; (11) volcanic eruption (but not loss caused by earthquake).
- *HO-2 (Broad).* Expands coverage of the HO-1 policy by protecting

Hal and Linda's house is worth $100,000. Their agent advised them to insure it for $120,000 with replacement cost insurance. A fire destroyed the house. How much must the company pay?

The insurance company is obligated to pay all the costs necessary to restore the house up to, but not exceeding, $120,000. If the costs are only $110,000, this is all the insurance must pay. Hal and Linda will not get a $10,000 bonus for overinsuring their house. Were that true, the temptation to commit arson would be very great.

If I take out two policies on my house, can I collect from both if something happens?

No. Most homeowners policies exclude double coverage so that you cannot collect twice for one loss.

If I rent my house to another family, will my homeowners policy cover accidents, theft, or damage during the rental period?

No. Property that you own and rent to another family is usually excluded from coverage under homeowners policies because those policies cover your residence. You may want to consider purchasing a policy designed to protect your property while it is rented.

against losses from six additional risks: (1) falling objects; (2) weight of ice, snow, and sleet; (3) sudden accidental rupturing, cracking, burning, or bulging of a steam or hot-water heating system or of appliances for heating water; (4) accidental leakage or flow of water or steam from a heating, plumbing, or air conditioning system or household appliance; (5) freezing of a plumbing, heating, or air conditioning system or household appliance; (6) damage to electrical appliances, devices, fixtures, and wiring caused by short circuits or other accidentally generated currents.

- *HO-3 (Special).* In addition to risks covered in HO-2, this policy protects the dwelling (but not its contents) against damage or loss from all perils, except flood, earthquake, war, nuclear accident, and any other risk specifically excluded. If the HO-15 endorsement is added to this policy, coverage against all perils (except those excluded) is also extended to the contents of the home, making this policy the broadest.
- *HO-4 (Tenants and Co-op Dwellers Contents, Broad).* Provides the same protection for home contents as HO-2, but excludes the actual dwelling, which should be insured by whoever owns the building.
- *HO-6 (Condominium or Unit Owners).* Similar to HO-4, but includes limited coverage for the dwelling.

Insuring Your Home

Carolyn has decided to rent a small house. What type of insurance should she purchase to protect her furniture and other personal property after she moves in?

The standard tenants policy will protect most of Carolyn's personal property from losses due to fire or lightning and many other common perils. Carolyn may wish to purchase specific coverage for certain items of personal property that are only partially covered under the basic standard policy. This kind of coverage, which can be added to a standard policy in the form of attached statements called floaters, is often used for jewelry, furs, cameras, musical instruments, artwork, antiques, deeds, stocks and bonds, and stamp and coin collections.

A spark from the fireplace ignited Karen and Bob's carpet, causing a smoky fire, which the fire department had to put out. Will their losses be covered by their homeowners insurance?

Yes. All standard homeowners policies cover losses due to hostile fires, which are defined as fires that are not where they are supposed to be. Damages due to friendly fires are not covered. Friendly fires are those burning where they are supposed to burn, for example, in a fireplace. When the spark left the fireplace, it became a hostile fire. Smoke damage and losses caused by fire fighting, such as water damage, are also covered by the standard homeowners policy.

Our neighbors were burning leaves, and the sparks set our roof on fire. Our neighbors do not have insurance, but we do. Who should pay for the damage?

Your insurance company should pay you for the damage caused by fire. The company may then seek reimbursement from your neighbors, since they were responsible for the damage.

If my house is damaged by fire, does the insurance company have to pay me for the cost of temporary quarters until my home is made livable again?

Homeowners policies usually cover the additional living expenses that you incur while your home is being repaired (up to 10 or 20 percent of the coverage on your house). If you are living in a motel and must eat all your meals in a restaurant, the company will pay the amount in excess of your usual housing and food costs. Some insurance companies will advance funds so you don't go into debt for living expenses while waiting for the final settlement check. However, some companies will reimburse you for these costs only when the repairs are complete. This can pose a big problem if the repairs take a long time. Some families rent trailers or move in with relatives to keep their expenses down.

Victor's roof was damaged in a hailstorm. His insurance company is rejecting his claim because his premium payment was overdue. What can Victor do?

If Victor's roof was damaged while the payment was overdue, his coverage lapsed, so he'll have to pay for the expenses himself. If the damage occurred after the company accepted his late payment and reinstated his coverage, the insurance company must pay his claim.

If Conrad's home is damaged by a flood, will his homeowners policy cover his losses?

If bursting pipes caused the flood, many home insurance policies would cover the damage. If the flood was from natural forces such as a heavy rainfall, the answer is probably no. Every standard homeowners policy excludes this type of flood damage from its coverage. Conrad may be eligible to purchase flood insurance through the federal National Flood Insurance Program. For more information, he should contact his local insurance agent or the Federal Insurance Administration, Washington, D.C. 20472. This insurance is offered to communities that have taken steps to minimize the effects of future floods. A few private insurance companies offer flood protection at higher rates.

Our second car was not being driven; so we stopped insuring it. A tree fell on it while it was in our driveway. Will our homeowners insurance pay for the damage?

No. Homeowners policies usually exclude cars from coverage.

Insuring Personal Property

For information about personal property, see Chapter 5, *Your Personal Property*.

I lost a valuable ring. Will my insurance company pay for it?

Only if the ring is specifically covered by a floater policy. Standard homeowners policies usually do not cover the loss or the unexplained disappearance of a piece of jewelry, although there is limited coverage when valuable jewelry is stolen. With floater insurance, you can protect valuable property such as jewelry and artwork. For each item covered, you must give a specific description and value. A bill of sale or professional appraisal is usually required to prove the item's value. Floater insurance covers mysterious disappearance and loss as well as theft.

George recently inherited his grandfather's stamp collection. Should he have it valued separately on his insurance policy?

Since the standard homeowners policy offers limited protection, George should purchase a floater policy to protect the collection for its full value.

Will floater insurance cover a guest's personal property?

No. Floater insurance covers only the items specifically described and valued by the policyholder. However, if you have standard homeowners insurance, it may cover the loss of a guest's personal property. Check the terms of your policy.

To what extent would my homeowners insurance reimburse me if a thief stole my jewelry or other personal property?

Most homeowners policies will cover losses if your house is burglarized or if property is stolen from a temporary residence, such as a motel or dormitory room or other place you stay or stop outside your home. Many homeowners policies also cover thefts from your automobile if there is evidence, such as a broken window or door, that your car was entered by force. Standard homeowners policies do not cover the theft of credit cards, but you can add this coverage to your policy, usually for a few extra dollars. None of these policies cover the loss of cash.

Most homeowners policies cover the homeowner and members of the household. If you don't have a homeowners policy, some insurers will sell you a policy to cover your losses due to theft. If you have floater coverage for specifically listed items, the theft of these items is covered as well.

No company will give me theft coverage because I live in what is reputed to be a high-crime area. Isn't this discrimination?

One federal court has found this practice, known as redlining, to be a violation of the Fair Housing Act. There is a federal crime insurance program: to find out if you qualify, start with a call to the nearest federal information center, whose number is listed in the telephone book in many areas or is available through the operator. Some states have similar programs; call your state insurance department for information.

When Clara's home was burglarized, the thieves broke a window and ransacked the house. Will the damage to her home be covered by her homeowners insurance?

Yes. Standard homeowners policies cover vandalism and malicious mischief in addition to theft.

A burglar entered our house through a window I left open. Will I be able to collect insurance even though the company claims I was negligent?

It depends on the terms of your homeowners policy. Some policies specify that there must be visible evidence that a burglar had to use force in order to enter your home. If your policy contains such a provision, you may not be able to collect.

While I was in the dentist's chair having a tooth filled, someone took my mink coat from the waiting room. Can I recover from my insurance company?

Yes. Your homeowners policy will cover the theft of your personal property while you are away from home. Unless the coat was brand-new, you will be reimbursed for the replacement cost of the coat, less depreciation. If the coat was several years old, you may not receive very much from your insurance company.

Jan left her pocketbook in the car while she ran into the nursery school to pick up her child. Will her insurance cover the loss if her purse is stolen?

Many insurance companies require evidence of forced entry into an automobile before they will cover the loss of property. If the thief broke a window or lock to get to Jan's purse, the company will cover the loss. If the thief opened an unlocked door, the company may refuse to pay.

After Jim's house was burglarized, the insurance adjuster seemed to be determined to value everything as if it were at a flea

market. Jim wants full value so that he can replace the stolen items with new ones. Who is correct?

Neither Jim nor the adjuster. Unless Jim had a replacement cost endorsement on his homeowners policy, he is not entitled to the full cost of replacing all his stolen items with new ones. Jim is entitled to the actual cash value of the lost property, which is usually defined as the replacement value of each item, less depreciation.

If my home is burglarized and I don't have receipts or an appraisal for all the items, how will the insurance company establish what it will pay me?

Most insurance companies have tables to help them arrive at standard depreciation values for personal property. It will be a fairly simple task to determine the replacement cost of each item and then subtract the depreciation value to arrive at the actual cash value.

If you believe that the amount the insurance company comes up with is too low, you may refuse the settlement and negotiate further with the insurance company. If you cannot reach a settlement, your next steps are to present your case to the state insurance commissioner and, as a last resort, to sue the insurance company for breach of contract.

Will a homeowners policy cover property that is stolen or missing if I rent out my home?

No. Homeowners policies do not cover dwellings that are being rented to others; neither do they cover the property left in those dwellings. What you need to get is a multiperil policy; with it the house you rent out will be covered for fire and other losses, and you will have medical and liability coverage for persons injured on the premises.

My insurance company refuses to compensate me for property stolen from my house. What can I do?

First find out why the insurance company is not cooperating. If it requires proof of loss, you can use photographs, receipts, warranties, canceled checks, credit card statements, and witnesses to prove you owned the property you lost. If the insurance company does not believe that the property was stolen, use the police investigation and report to substantiate your claim. If the insurance company is refusing payment that is clearly due you under your policy, you may sue for breach of contract.

Documenting Your Personal Property

If your home is struck by fire or burglarized, you'll be better off if you have taken the time to prepare a room-by-room, itemized inventory of the contents of your house and, in doing so, marked valuable items with an identifying number. The inventory will help substantiate your claims for personal property losses under your homeowners insurance policy and on your income taxes, while the identifying numbers prove your ownership. Here are specific how-to suggestions:

- For each item in your inventory, give all the pertinent information available, including its manufacturer and its serial number, if it has one. A physical description (size, color, etc.) or a photograph could turn out to be extremely useful if the item is destroyed. Keep a copy of this list in a safe-deposit box; update it as necessary, at least every few years.
- Keep all proofs of ownership (warranties, receipts, bills of sale). If you have very valuable items, such as jewelry, works of art, or antiques, get written appraisals of their value, and update them every few years.
- If you have valuable items that you don't need or use at home, keep them in a safe-deposit box.
- Put your Social Security or driver's license number on your property so you can identify it if it is recovered after a burglary. Many police departments will lend you the marking and etching equipment.

My home was burglarized. After my insurance company paid my claim, the police recovered my stolen property. Will I have to repay the company?

Yes. You are not allowed to keep both the property and the money that the insurance company paid you for the loss of the property. That would be paying you for something you hadn't lost.

Liability for Personal Injury

If a pedestrian trips and falls over the buckled sidewalk in front of my house, and suffers a badly sprained wrist, will my homeowners insurance pay his medical bills?

Yes, up to the limits stated in your policy. However, because an injured person's claims may exceed the limits of a standard policy, some homeowners purchase additional medical insurance or an umbrella policy that offers up to $1 million or more of protection for situations like the one you describe.

Liability for Personal Injury

Mildred hired Tommy, the 15-year-old son of a neighbor, to mow her lawn and do other odd jobs around her house and grounds. What kind of insurance should Mildred have in case Tommy is injured on her property?

Mildred's standard homeowners policy will cover a limited amount of medical expenses if Tommy is injured on her property. If Tommy's injuries are Mildred's fault, she may be personally liable for expenses that exceed her policy limits. Since medical bills and jury awards for pain and suffering frequently amount to tens of thousands of dollars, Mildred should consider purchasing an umbrella policy to supplement her insurance. Umbrella policies usually give up to $1 million or more of liability protection. If Tommy works for Mildred on a regular basis, several days a week, Mildred's homeowners policy will not cover medical payments if he is injured on the job; she should talk with her insurance agent or broker about the possiblity of other coverage.

The owner of the house next door was injured while swimming in my pool while I was away for the weekend. Do I have to pay for his medical bills?

If you invited him, you are not liable for injuries he received while using your swimming pool unless there was an extremely dangerous condition in the pool that was hidden in some way. If your neighbor was using your pool without your permission, you are liable only if you caused his injury by doing something extremely reckless or malicious, like having broken glass all around the pool.

The law is somewhat different if a child sneaks into your pool and injures himself. Legally, your pool is considered an attractive nuisance, and you can be held liable unless you have made an effort to keep children from using it, such as by putting a fence around the pool. It is not a good idea to allow children to use your pool while you are away, since you may be charged with negligence if you are not there to supervise the children and make sure they follow basic safety rules.

Should I report all injuries or property damage at my home to my insurance company?

Yes. Most policies require that you report all losses or possible claims immediately. Check your homeowners policy to find out the time limits for reporting injury or damage. If you wait until someone injured on your property says you are responsible for paying his medical bills, you may find that your homeowners policy will not cover the claim.

A friend invited me to take the wheel of his high-powered cabin cruiser, and I did. What if I had caused an accident?

If you have an umbrella policy, it would probably cover your liability for personal injuries while skippering the boat. However, umbrella policies have large deductibles, and they don't cover all watercraft. If your friend invites you again, ask him if his insurance policy covers guests who operate the boat at his invitation. If it doesn't, don't play skipper.

Diane just bought a boat. Does she need to buy a special policy?

Diane should buy a policy that covers damage to her boat and liability as well. Some experts advise purchasing $300,000 worth of standard coverage plus an umbrella policy for further protection against catastrophic, high-liability situations.

Insuring Your Car

For information on who is liable in an automobile accident, see "Liability for Automobile Accidents" in Chapter 6, *Your Car.*

What kinds of insurance do I need for my car?

Almost every state requires that car owners carry liability insurance, which covers damage that you cause while driving your car, whether it is an injury to a person or damage to another's property. Umbrella policies can be purchased to augment your auto liability coverage.

You may buy collision and comprehensive protection as well. Collision covers losses to your car due to your own negligence, such as backing into a telephone pole. Comprehensive is a catchall term that means you have coverage against theft, vandalism, storms, fire, falling or hurtling objects, explosion, earthquake, flood, riot, and collisions with wildlife. Some people choose to forgo collision and comprehensive coverage if they drive an old car with little value. You may also buy uninsured motorist coverage. This covers accidents in which you cannot recover from the driver who is at fault because he is uninsured or underinsured, or because he drove off and cannot be identified.

What is no-fault insurance?

No-fault insurance is a system in which people involved in accidents are paid for their injuries by their own insurance companies. The system is called no-fault to contrast it with the traditional system, in which the person at fault and his insurance company are legally required to compensate all others involved in the accident. Thus the traditional, or fault, system has led to the payment of some huge awards by one driver and his insurance company.

Under the fault system, the victim or victims of a negligent driver can collect for damages, medical expenses, lost wages, and pain and suffering from the negligent driver's insurance company. The major issue in a fault system is establishing negligence, and this can involve many months or years of legal arguments and court proceedings.

Under the no-fault system, the victim of a negligent driver is restricted to recovering his medical expenses and a percentage of his lost earnings from his own insurance company. The victim is not compensated for his pain and suffering, although some no-fault programs allow lawsuits for pain and suffering. Under the no-fault system, the negligent driver also collects from his own insurance company. At least 21 states have no-fault insurance in some form.

Ernest says auto insurance is a waste of money for his 11-year-old station wagon, and he's going to stop paying for insurance on the car. Can he do this?

Not if he intends to drive his car anywhere. Some states require proof of liability insurance before issuing vehicle license plates. Other states make it a crime, punishable by fines or imprisonment, to drive without liability insurance. Finally, other states will suspend or revoke the license of an uninsured driver who causes an accident.

Are there guidelines that will help me decide how much insurance coverage I need?

All states legally mandate the minimum amount of liability insurance you must carry. However, the minimum amount may not afford you adequate protection if you are involved in an accident. Most experts advise that you carry at least 100/300/50 liability coverage. This means up to $100,000 for each injury with a maximum amount of $300,000 per accident, and $50,000 to cover property damage in an accident. If you buy an umbrella policy as well, it will provide $1 million or more of liability protection.

The amount of collision and comprehensive damage you should carry depends on the value of your car. Some experts advise car owners to drop their collision and comprehensive coverage if the car is more than five years old because of the decline in the car's value.

Finally, you may be offered uninsured motorist or hit-and-run coverage to pay your medical bills if you are struck by either an uninsured or a hit-and-run driver. Before you decide to purchase this type of coverage, check the health and disability coverage that you already have. Such coverage may be adequate if you are the victim of an uninsured driver.

What will happen if someone sues me for a great deal more than I am insured for?

If someone successfully sues you for an amount that exceeds your policy limits, you will be held personally liable for payment of the difference between the amount of money the court awards and your insurance coverage. This means that the person who wins the lawsuit has a claim on your personal assets.

Many states are developing standards for insurance companies to follow when the insured's liability exceeds his policy limits. The law requires that the insurance company act in the interest of its policyholder and try to settle within the limits of his policy. If the company disregards the policyholder's interest and he finds himself facing a huge payment ordered by the court, he may sue the company for breach of good faith and fair dealing.

If you are being sued for more than your insurance coverage, the insurance company's attorneys will handle the lawsuit. However, you should hire your own attorney, who will be responsible for protecting your interests alone.

Denise was involved in a serious accident. Does the fact that she lives in a state that has no-fault insurance mean Denise can't sue the other driver, even though he ran a red light?

Depending on her state's no-fault laws, Denise may be able to sue the other driver. Many no-fault insurance laws allow the victim of a negligent driver to sue for negligence in certain circumstances, such as if death, disfigurement, or a permanent disability resulted from the accident.

While Sara was waiting at a stop sign, another driver hit her from the rear, throwing her young son into the dashboard. The insurance company refuses to pay the boy's medical bills because he was not wearing a seat belt. Must the insurance company pay?

The "seat belt defense" has been used successfully to limit liability in Florida, Illinois, New Jersey, and New York. Its proponents argue that the injured person would have suffered less injury had he been wearing a seat belt. However, most states do not recognize this argument, and some states—such as Iowa, Maine, Minnesota, Tennessee, and Virginia—have rejected it completely. It is most likely that the insurance company will be required to pay the boy's medical bills.

Insuring Your Car

Is there a maximum amount an insurance company is allowed to pay under no-fault insurance?

Under some no-fault plans, payment for medical expenses and lost wages is limited to a set amount, which can be as low as $2,000. To recover losses above this amount, the injured person must file a lawsuit against the other driver, just as in the fault system. Under other no-fault plans, an injured person may recover up to the limits in his policy.

Mary was driving home from work when one of her front wheels came off. She ran off the road, damaging her car. She has collision but not comprehensive coverage. Does her insurance company have to pay?

No. Collision protection, as the name implies, generally covers damages caused by collisions with other cars or objects or by overturning. Since the damage to Mary's car was not due to a collision, she is not eligible to recover under her policy.

Can I collect insurance for an accident or damage from poorly maintained roads, such as ones with potholes?

If you have comprehensive coverage, your policy may cover damage to your car from potholes, if the deductible is met.

My car was stolen and recovered later in another city. Will my insurance company pay to transport it back and have it repaired?

Yes, if you have comprehensive coverage that protects you against all damages related to a car theft. Transportation and repair costs, in this case, are considered damages caused by theft. However, some policies specifically exclude the cost of transportation.

Is my insurance in effect if I drive in another country?

Many automobile insurance policies give coverage while you are driving in another country. Before leaving on your trip, read your policy carefully to make sure this coverage is not excluded. If the coverage is excluded, you can purchase travel insurance that will cover you.

No American policies are valid in Mexico. You must purchase your coverage from a Mexican insurance carrier.

My son is under 18 years of age. If he has an accident, will my insurance cover the liability?

Probably, if your son still lives at home. Most automobile insurance policies extend liability protection to all relatives who live in the insured's household. Some states require that this coverage be included in every automobile insurance policy.

If I have an accident and the other driver is at fault, is his insurance company obliged to pay for a rental car while mine is being repaired?

Yes. Most liability insurance policies will cover some of the extra expenses resulting from your accident. The expenses associated with being without your car are called consequential damages.

Will Griffith's insurance cover him if he has an accident while he is driving a rental car?

Probably. Most policies cover a person while driving a rented car under the "use of other automobiles" clause. However, some policies specifically exclude coverage for property damage by the driver of a rental car. If Griffith's policy excludes this coverage, he should read his rental agreement; many rental fees include the cost of insurance coverage. For an additional fee, Griffith may purchase insurance through the rental company. This is usually called the collision damage waiver. Most umbrella policies cover the use of rental cars as well.

If someone destroys my car and the insurance check does not completely pay off my car loan at the bank, can the other person be required to pay the balance of my loan?

Probably not. If you live in a no-fault state, your insurance company will reimburse you for the value of your car, but it is not required to pay the balance of your car loan. Under the no-fault system, you will probably not be allowed to sue the other driver.

In a state without the no-fault system, when you accept a check from the negligent driver's insurance company, you are usually required to sign a release forgoing further claims. Once you have settled your claim, you may not later ask for more money to cover your car loan.

James had a 1957 Thunderbird in mint condition. Another driver hit it from the rear, causing damage amounting to an estimated

$2,500. The insurance company says the value of the car is only $1,000 and refuses to pay more. How can this be right?

The insurance company is trying to declare James's car a total loss. A car is totaled if the cost of repairs exceeds the value of the car prior to the accident. To arrive at car values, most insurance companies use published guides, which can usually be consulted at public libraries or at car dealers. If James can prove that the actual value of his car is more than $2,500, he has the right to insist on payment sufficient to restore his car to its condition before the accident. If he cannot prove that its actual value is more than the guidebook figure, the insurance company can declare the car a total loss and limit its payment to $1,000.

Is it legal for my insurance company to cancel my policy if I am involved in an accident?

Yes, if that's what your policy says—but it must first cover the losses incurred in the accident. If your insurance policy does not say anything about cancellation in the event of an accident, the company cannot cancel your policy. However, it can decline to renew your policy when it expires. Many no-fault states, and states with compulsory liability insurance laws, allow an insurance company to cancel your policy only if you don't pay your premium, if you misrepresent facts on your application or on a claim you submit, or if your driver's license is suspended or revoked.

If I don't report an accident and later get sued, will my insurance cover me if I lose the lawsuit?

Many insurance policies require you to report accidents, losses, and possible claims within a specified time. Check your policy. Your insurance company may be able to use your failure to report the accident as grounds not to pay claims arising from the accident.

There is another reason to report accidents immediately. It is easier for your insurance company to investigate the accident, contact witnesses, and prepare a defense for you immediately after the accident.

If I have an accident and am at fault, can I pay the other person directly and not report it to my insurance company?

It is not illegal, but it is extremely risky. If the other driver later discovers more damage to his property or greater personal injury, he may then decide to file a lawsuit against you to get more money. Your insurance company may, at that point, decline to cover you because of your failure to comply with the reporting requirement stated in your policy.

Car Insurance Rates

If I have an accident with only minor damage, would it be a good idea not to make a claim to avoid a rate increase or cancellation?

Perhaps, if you can be sure there is only minor damage. Insurance companies usually base premium increases on the number of chargeable claims made by a customer, rather than on the amount of any single

How Insurers Set Car Premiums

Automobile insurers commonly consider various factors when setting premium rates. The most important factor is the amount and type of coverage you select. If you carry comprehensive, collision, and uninsured motorist coverage in addition to a high level of liability insurance, your rates will be much higher than someone who carries only the minimum coverage required by law. If your policy has no deductibles or very low ones, your rates will be higher. Many people choose to reduce their premiums by carrying high deductibles. Among the additional criteria used by insurers are these:

- *Your Driving Record.* You'll pay higher premiums if your record shows moving violations, such as speeding. Some offenses, such as drunk driving, may cause your insurer not to renew your policy. If your license is suspended or revoked, your insurance can be canceled.
- *Your Claims.* Many insurance companies raise your rates in proportion to the number, not the dollar amount, of claims you submit. For example, if you have made several claims because of fender benders or vandalism, you may have to pay higher premiums than someone who actually received more money from the insurance company but submitted just one claim following a bad accident.
- *Your Car.* The more expensive your car, the higher the premium tends to be, as a general rule.
- *Your Age and Sex.* In many states, males under 25 years of age may be charged more than others for automobile insurance.
- *Your Address.* City dwellers sometimes pay higher rates than residents of rural areas.
- *Members of Your Household.* If you have teenage drivers in your family, your rates will be higher than those who don't.
- *Discounts.* Some companies may have discounts available for senior citizens, nondrinkers, and people who have not had an accident for many years. Most insurers also give two-car families a break by reducing the premium on the second car.

claim. A chargeable claim is one for losses above a certain amount (usually $200 to $300). If you can afford to pay for the damage and if you doubt that you'll be sued, it may be a good idea to avoid making a claim. However, if your policy requires you to report all accidents to the insurance company and you fail to comply, the company may use this as a valid reason to avoid paying later claims. You may be best advised to report the accident without making a claim.

Beryl's insurance company raised her rates after an accident that was not her fault. Is this legal?

Yes. Insurance companies may base their rates, in part, on the number of claims the insured makes, regardless of who was responsible for the damage or injury. Consequently, victims of hit-and-run drivers, vandals, and thieves often find their rates higher after turning in a claim.

If my insurance company finds out that I have been charged with driving under the influence of alcohol, will my premiums go up?

Being charged with driving under the influence of alcohol will not affect your auto insurance rates, but a conviction for this offense will cause you to be classified as a high-risk driver. Your insurance company may then raise your premiums or refuse to renew your policy.

While Wilma was shopping, her parked car was hit by another car. Her insurance company paid the damages, but then added a surcharge to her premium. Is this permitted?

Wilma should request an explanation from her insurance company. Usually, a surcharge is a one-time fee imposed on drivers who are at fault. Unless Wilma's manner of parking contributed to the accident, she was not at fault and should not have to pay the surcharge.

Hit-and-run and Uninsured Drivers

Stephanie was crossing the street on foot when she was struck by a hit-and-run driver. Who should pay Stephanie's medical bills?

If Stephanie has health insurance (which should cover injury from accidents) or hit-and-run and uninsured driver's coverage, these policies will pay her medical bills up to the policy limits. Many states have a fund to pay the victims of hit-and-run or uninsured drivers. If Stephanie's insurance coverage is inadequate, she should see if she qualifies for reimbursement from her state's fund.

Shelly bought the maximum insurance coverage for her brand-new sports car. While waiting at a red light, she was struck from behind by Dave, whose old car has the minimum insurance coverage allowed. How can Shelly be properly compensated for her personal injuries and the damage to the car?

If Shelly lives in a no-fault state, she can collect from her own insurance company. If she lives in a state where the traditional fault system is in effect, she can also collect from her own company, depending on her medical and disability coverage and on whether she has uninsured motorist coverage. Although Dave was not actually uninsured, many insurance policies and state laws provide that an underinsured driver is to be considered the same as an uninsured driver for purposes of collecting from one's own policy or from the state uninsured motorist fund. Finally, if Shelly wins a lawsuit and is awarded damages for her injuries in excess of Dave's insurance coverage, she can hold him personally liable for the difference. This means that Dave's assets (real estate, stocks and bonds, car, furniture, bank accounts, wages) can be used to pay Shelly's expenses.

I was involved in an accident with someone who had no insurance. My insurance company fixed my car, but I had to pay the $250 deductible and rent a car. Can I recover my losses?

Yes. If the accident was the fault of the other driver, you can sue him in small claims court for your deductible and the car rental fees. You may also qualify for compensation from your state's uninsured motorist fund.

What happens if I am in an accident and I don't have insurance?

If you caused the accident and have no insurance, you will be personally liable for the damages suffered by the others in the accident. This means that if a court orders you to pay the victims' expenses and damages, you will have to do so out of your own assets and income.

In many states, you could be subject to a fine, imprisonment, and the loss of your driving privileges if you operate a motor vehicle without liability insurance. Before getting your license back, you may be required to post a bond to cover the other driver's damages and provide proof of insurance. This would not be required if the accident was not your fault.

Hit-and-run and Uninsured Drivers

Jim's car was struck by a van that sped off before Jim could get its license number. His insurance company won't pay the claim. What are Jim's options?

If Jim's insurance policy covers him against uninsured and hit-and-run drivers, or if he lives in a no-fault state and his company doesn't seem to have a valid reason for refusing to pay his claim, he should sue the insurance company. He may win money, called punitive damages, from the company. If he has a health insurance policy, his medical bills should be partially covered. If Jim is not covered under his own insurance policies, he should see if his state has a fund for which he qualifies.

Adjusters and Settlements

Jeff filed a claim with his insurance company after a minor traffic accident. The company said it would send an adjuster to look at the damage. What does an insurance adjuster do?

Insurance adjusters are employed by insurance companies to investigate claims, establish the claims' value, and negotiate settlements. In Jeff's case, the adjuster will examine Jeff's car, give an opinion on how much repairs will cost, and offer Jeff a check in payment.

If Your Insurance Company Won't Pay a Claim

If your claim has been denied, and the insurance company has told you its decision is final, your reaction may be to get an attorney—and sue the company. First, however, you should ask yourself these questions: (1) Does the policy state that the claim should be covered? (2) Did you report the loss within the time limit allowed? (3) Did you make accurate and complete statements in your application? (4) If you are being sued, did you keep the company fully informed of all legal actions and notices and follow its instructions?

If you can answer yes to these questions, you are in a strong position to challenge the insurance company's denial of your claim. You should file a complaint with your state commissioner of insurance and contact an attorney. Many states have laws that prohibit such unethical claims procedures as misrepresenting facts or policy provisions; failing to investigate or pay claims within a reasonable time; settling a claim for much less than a reasonable person would expect; and failing to promptly provide a reasonable explanation for denying a claim.

After my accident, an insurance adjuster called and asked me to give my version of exactly what happened. Should I discuss the accident with him?

No. Never make a statement or even talk about the accident with anyone who could conceivably use what you say against you, without first consulting a lawyer. The adjuster, for example, could use your statements to deny you benefits. Do not tell anyone that the accident might have been your fault, and don't say that you have no injuries until you have been thoroughly checked over by a doctor. Do not sign a release until you are certain that all your injuries are known, even though it may take several months or more for a full and final medical diagnosis. If you have been in an accident, many lawyers will talk to you about your case at no charge. Such lawyers often advertise, "No charge for the first consultation in personal injury cases."

If Gary accepts the insurance company's check to settle his claim for a knee injury suffered in a car accident, can he get more money later if complications arise?

Probably not. Settlement checks are usually presented after a release is signed. If Gary signs a release that says he is accepting the check in payment of all his claims, he gives up the right to pursue claims for injuries that he was not aware of at the time he signed. For this reason, it is best for Gary not to accept a settlement until he has consulted his physician and an attorney.

Should I sign a release or accept a settlement check for an automobile accident if I am pregnant?

No. Wait until your child is born to see if he has suffered any injuries from the accident. If you sign a release, you may give up the right to seek compensation for your child's injuries.

Is it legal for insurance investigators to question business associates and friends about my personal habits while trying to settle a claim for an accident I had?

Yes. Insurance adjusters may conduct investigations to verify the information you have given them regarding the accident or your injuries, or on your application for insurance. In some cases, your personal habits are relevant to your claim or your application. For example, if you made false statements about your drinking habits in your application, the insurance company may have the right to void the policy and deny your claim.

Adjusters and Settlements

Rupert's car was sideswiped by a truck, and the insurance adjuster has offered him $800 for the damage. Rupert does not think that's enough. How does he go about challenging the offer?

He should contact the adjuster's supervisor, or the insurance company's legal department, or its president. If he can't get these company officials to increase the payment, and Rupert still feels he is right, he should contact his state insurance commissioner or department of insurance to find out how to take his complaint further. Most states have an arbitration procedure for the settlement of disputed insurance claims.

An adjuster offered Elise $3,000 for the damage to her car, but warned her, "If you get an attorney, I will withdraw all offers." Isn't this against the law?

California is the only state that has a law specifically forbidding an adjuster to advise or induce a person to forgo consulting an attorney. However, almost half the states have statutes that prohibit the use of unfair practices in settling claims. These states include Arizona, Arkansas, Illinois, Indiana, Kansas, Missouri, Nebraska, New York, Pennsylvania, and Texas. Under these laws, the adjuster who advised Elise not to see an attorney could face fines ranging from $500 to $5,000.

Even in states without such laws, it is unlikely that the adjuster will actually withdraw his offer. There is no question about Elise's right to seek legal advice in this situation.

If my car is damaged in an accident, do I always have to get more than one estimate?

Not all insurance companies require repair estimates. Those that do usually require at least two signed estimates from body shops. If estimates aren't required, getting at least two would be advisable in order to be fully informed about the cost of repairing your car when your claims adjuster offers a settlement.

Must I use the body shop recommended by the adjuster?

No, but if you don't you may find that your repair bills exceed the check the insurance company has issued to you. Insurance adjusters frequently base their estimates on the rates charged by body shops with which they do business. These shops usually charge lower rates in order to get the insurance company's business.

CHAPTER
9

Consumer Rights

Nora saw an advertisement for a product that promised long, beautiful fingernails in 10 days. Can she assume that the product works, or else it would be against the law to advertise it?

No. Although the Federal Trade Commission Act and many state laws prohibit false advertising, there is no federal or state agency that reviews advertisements before they are broadcast or published. Typically, government agencies investigate the accuracy of an advertisement only after the product has been on the market for a while and complaints have been lodged against it. Consequently, some ads may contain false promises.

Ads for Coldchaser Capsules say that the product is guaranteed to cure the common cold. Is this false advertising?

Yes. Although laws against deceptive advertising do not keep a manufacturer from expressing an opinion about his product—such as "Bonnie's Bonbons are as sweet as a loved one's kiss"—they do prohibit a manufacturer from making claims that can't be substantiated. In the case of Coldchaser Capsules, the manufacturer would have to prove that his product cures the common cold. This would be extremely difficult to do, since medical experts claim that no cure has yet been developed for the common cold. Colds are cured by Mother Nature or Father Time whether the person consumes medicine, hot toddies, chicken soup, garlic, vitamin C, or nothing at all.

The manufacturer of CleanAir claims that his product kills germs. Can he be required to retract the statement if it proves false?

Yes. This claim can be easily tested and proved true or false. If it is false, the Federal Trade Commission (FTC) will order the manufacturer to stop making the claim. The FTC can also require the manufacturer to initiate "corrective advertising" to inform consumers that the product does not have the qualities falsely attributed to it.

How can Fred find out if a product advertised to promote new hair growth is effective?

Fred should discuss the product with his family physician or dermatologist before buying it. He might also ask the manufacturer for copies of any scientific studies that back up the company's claim. In a case involving a nationally known pain reliever, its manufacturer was required to support its claims of superiority with two clinical studies.

Laws Against False Advertising

The advertising industry is regulated by the Federal Trade Commission (FTC), and a consumer who is harmed by dishonest advertising can report it to the FTC, but he can sue only under the laws of his state. Although many states have modeled their false-advertising laws on FTC rulings, not all of them have adopted precisely the same regulations. Following are some typical state laws against false advertising:

- A store cannot advertise goods without intending to sell them as advertised. For example, a video shop cannot advertise tapes at low prices when there aren't enough tapes on hand to satisfy a reasonable demand, unless the ad clearly states that the supply is limited.
- When specially advertised items run out, a store must take orders or give rain checks.
- A merchant may not advertise a product at a low price and then tell his customer that the model is sold out and try to sell him a more expensive one. This illegal practice is called bait and switch.
- It is illegal to mark up the price of an item and then show a "reduction" to make it appear that the item is a bargain.
- A seller may not misrepresent used goods as new.
- A manufacturer may not misrepresent the quality, usefulness, reliability, or durability of his product.
- A vocational school may not make false or misleading claims about the quality of its instruction or about its job-placement services.
- An advertisement may not falsely claim that a product is sponsored or approved by a professional group. For example, a company cannot legally claim that their stop-smoking program was approved by the American Cancer Society unless the society had specifically approved it. It is not enough to reason that the society would approve because it actively campaigns against smoking.

Fred can find out from the Food and Drug Administration if it has approved the product for sale to consumers. The consumer protection agency in Fred's state can tell him if dissatisfied customers have filed complaints about the product.

One of the shops in town advertises itself as a discount store, but its prices are about the same as, or sometimes higher than, those in other stores. Isn't this illegal?

No. It is not illegal for a store to use "discount" in its name unless it tries to mislead the public by making specific—and false—claims about its prices. For example, it would be illegal to falsely claim that its prices are 20 percent lower than those of competitors or to misrepresent the prices of its competitors to make its own prices appear lower.

Deceptive Advertising

Connie paid $120 for a six-week computer course, advertised as a "hands-on learning experience." But she was allowed to operate a computer for only 30 minutes. At the end of six weeks, Connie demanded her money back. Is she entitled to a refund?

Yes. State laws against deceptive sales practices apply to vocational schools as well as businesses that sell goods and services. In most states, Connie would be entitled to a refund, and she could sue the school to enforce her right to it.

In some states, Connie could sue for two to three times the amount she paid for tuition. In a few states, she would have to complain to the state consumer protection agency (usually part of the attorney general's office), which would enforce her right to a refund.

Larry tried to take advantage of a sale on humidifiers at a local appliance store, but was told that the advertised models were no longer available. The store refused to give Larry a rain check. Is there anything he can do?

Yes. He can ask that a similar humidifier be sold to him at an equivalent reduction in place of the rain check. If the store refuses, Larry can warn the manager that he will inform the state attorney general's office that the store is advertising sales merchandise that is not available.

Gordon saw a newspaper ad for a tool set at the local hardware store for $9.95. When he went to buy it, the cashier told him the price was really $99.95, and that the newspaper had made an error. Can Gordon get the tool set for $9.95 as advertised?

No. There is a difference between an honest error and a deceptive sales practice. Since the price in the paper was the result of a printer's error, and the store had no intention of deceiving its customers, a court would probably not force the store to sell the tool sets at the lower price.

If a store displays an item in its window at a sale price, is it required to sell the item at the advertised price?

Probably. In most states it is illegal to deliberately misrepresent the price of an item in order to lure customers into the store. Unless the price of the item in the window is an honest mistake that is immediately corrected when employees learn of it, the store cannot charge a higher price than is shown on the item in the window.

While shopping, I found a suede coat with a price tag of $19.99. When I went to pay for it, the clerk said it cost $79.99. Doesn't the store have to sell me the coat for the price marked on the tag?

No. If the coat was mistagged, the store is not required to sell you the coat at that price. However, if the coat was deliberately advertised and tagged at $19.99, the store is required to honor the price.

When Russell bought his compact disc player, the salesperson told him that he couldn't find a better model anywhere. Less than three months later, the player needed extensive service. Does Russell have any claim based on the statements the salesperson made about the equipment?

No. The salesperson was giving a sales pitch, or engaging in what is known in the trade as "puffing." The law assumes that all consumers know that sellers will claim that their products are of good quality—Russell would not expect the salesperson to tell him that the disc player was mediocre and that it would give him nothing but trouble if he bought it. On the other hand, if Russell received a warranty or guarantee that promised to fix any defects or replace the disc player within the first 90 days or more, he does have a valid claim.

Reggie purchased a used vacuum cleaner at his neighbor's garage sale. The neighbor said it ran like new, but in fact, it didn't run at all. Since Reggie couldn't try the vacuum out before purchasing it, can he get his money back?

Yes. His neighbor's statement that the vacuum cleaner ran like new led Reggie to believe that the vacuum cleaner worked. His neighbor made a promise or warranty that the cleaner would run. Reggie has the right to a refund, based on the neighbor's breach of warranty.

When I bought a used motorboat, the salesperson told me to look it over carefully. I couldn't see anything wrong with it. After our first ride, the motor conked out completely. The salesperson said there was nothing he could do because he had given me a chance to inspect the boat before I bought it. Is this true?

No. When you purchase a complex machine, such as a boat, a simple inspection may not uncover all its defects, and so the law allows you a reasonable amount of time to find any defects. Your discovery of the

Scams, Shams, and Swindles

Uninformed consumers make inviting targets for con artists and swindlers. Knowing a little about how these rogues operate may keep you from being fooled by their schemes. Some of their most common shady deals follow, along with tips on how not to get taken. One precaution that always applies is never to do business with someone you don't know anything about—check the reputation of an unknown company with the Better Business Bureau or chamber of commerce.

If, despite all precautions, you are bilked by an illegal scheme, get in touch with your state attorney general. If the deal involved the mail (even if you only paid by mail), inform the local postmaster. Sometimes the publicity generated by a letter to the consumer reporter of a local radio or television station will help you get what you paid for—or a refund.

THE SCAM	HOW TO AVOID BEING TAKEN
Unlucky Winner: Someone phones and says you have won a vacation or other gift, but to be sure you are the correct person, the caller needs to know your credit card number. If you give it to him, you get nothing and the caller goes on a shopping spree with your credit card number.	Never give your credit card number over the phone unless you have initiated the call. Ask the names, addresses, and phone numbers of unknown callers, verify the information, and call back. If you inadvertently give out a credit card number, contact your card company immediately.
Work at Home Holdup: An ad says that you can earn money at home (generally by stuffing envelopes or doing some other fairly easy job), but first you must buy something and give the names of other people who might be interested.	Make sure you understand all the terms of any agreement you sign. If you suspect that the business is a fraud, do not involve others in it, or you will risk investigation by the U. S. Postal Service.
Art Scam: A reproduction of an artwork is passed off as an original, or a lithograph is said to be signed by the artist but is not, or is signed in the stone, and so is of lesser value.	Check the dealer's credentials with an art museum. Get a certificate of authenticity and a receipt describing the artwork and stating its price.
Fake Final Sale: "Going Out of Business" banners announce big sales, but the store is not closing, and its goods are inferior and overpriced.	Comparison shop before buying. Get details about returns, refunds, warranties, and service in writing.

THE SCAM	HOW TO AVOID BEING TAKEN
Mismatched Mates: A dating service promises to introduce you to lots of perfect partners, making a show of cataloging your likes and dislikes and even videotaping you, but in the end the people who are sent are few and far between or woefully inappropriate.	Get a written contract complete with the costs, the dates the service is in effect, the number of introductions guaranteed, and the qualifications you request in a partner (such as age and education). Avoid lifetime contracts for large sums of money.
Franchise Frame-up: The promoter promises you will earn enormous profits if you buy a franchise or distributorship, and pumps you for the names of others he may be able to sell to. He makes money; you don't.	Ask the seller for credit references and contact people who have already bought franchises. Find out what the franchise fee covers and doesn't cover and how the agreement can be terminated. Get everything in writing.
Health Club Hazard: Preopening discounts are offered for health club memberships, but the club never opens, or extra charges are added for essential services, or the swimming pool or other facilities can be used only at specified—usually very inconvenient—times.	Ask if there is a trial period that can be applied toward your membership. Find out if use is restricted in any way. Ask about cancellations and refunds. Get everything in writing.
Job Gyp: An ad promises exciting, high-paying jobs, often overseas; you must pay to get information about the jobs, but the jobs are nonexistent. Or an ad offers to sell the names of prospective employers, but the names are simply culled from telephone directories.	Be skeptical of ads where no experience or skills are needed, or ads guaranteeing jobs, particularly abroad. Never pay in advance for job lists or employment advice.
Miracle Cures: An ad promises that a bracelet cures arthritis or a diet pill results in instant weight loss, or a face cream keeps complexions young forever, but the products don't work, and they may cause some serious health problems.	Ask the manufacturer for supporting evidence and names and addresses of satisfied users. Check with your physician before using any product that may affect your health.

Continued on page 354

Scams, Shams, and Swindles *(continued)*

THE SCAM	HOW TO AVOID BEING TAKEN
Unfair Repair: A repairman takes your TV or appliance in for service, and because of "lowballing"—giving an artificially low estimate—charges a far higher price than he first quoted, and bills you for work you did not agree to have him do.	Get a written estimate of the repairs and costs and insist on approving any repairs not on the original estimate. If used or rebuilt parts are supplied, make sure the invoice says so—and have the replaced parts returned to you.
Charity Fraud: You are asked to donate to a charity that doesn't exist. The charity's name may resemble that of a well-known one. Your solicitor demands cash, and pockets the money himself.	Get the charity's name, address, and phone number. Check that the solicitor works for the charity. Pay by check, made out to the charity, not to an individual.
Trade School Trap: Promotions for a trade school promise good jobs to graduates, and the school offers a free aptitude test on which applicants are told they scored very well; but after graduation, there are no jobs.	Ask local employers if they hire graduates of this school. Find out if the school is recognized by the U. S. Department of Education. Ask if you can pay in installments instead of paying in full before starting. Find out if there is an extra charge for its placement service and how long after graduation you may use it.
Prize Disguise: A letter informs you that you have won a prize, such as a VCR or a stereo. But to claim it, you must either visit a condominium or time-share development or attend a meeting at which great sales pressure will be applied to get you to buy property. Complicated paperwork is required before you get the gift.	Get the exact procedure for claiming the prize in writing before agreeing to anything and ask for the makes and models of merchandise being offered. If you want to buy the real estate, don't pay until you inspect the land or dwelling, check the seller's references, and have a lawyer look over the contract.
Last-Chance Loan: Borrowers rejected by banks and other lending institutions are assured that they can get a loan if they first pay a fee, but after they pay, no loan is forthcoming and the fee is lost.	Never pay fees in advance. Deal only with lenders whose backgrounds and reputations you can verify. Avoid lenders whose only address is a post office box number.

defective boat motor after the first ride is reasonable. You can demand that the dealer repair the motor or replace it. If you bought the boat "as is," however, you have no right to repairs or a replacement.

Chuck recently purchased a fishing rod that broke in two places right after he had paid for it. The rod was on sale and marked "as is." Can he get his money refunded?

No. The term "as is" means that the manufacturer or dealer does not promise that the product is of good quality or won't break. You buy at your own risk. Although Chuck is not legally entitled to a refund, he should call the matter to the store manager's attention. The manager may give him a refund to maintain customer goodwill.

Eric ordered a microwave oven that the appliance salesperson assured him would fit into the space he had built for it. It doesn't. The salesperson won't exchange the microwave or give Eric a refund, since he had to place a special order to get this particular one. Is Eric stuck with an appliance he can't use?

No, because he bought the oven relying on the salesperson's assurance that it would fit into his space. An implied warranty is created whenever a buyer relies on a seller to supply a product that meets the buyer's requirements. If Eric gave the correct dimensions of the space, the salesperson must replace the oven with one that fits or give Eric a refund.

Darren signed an order for a new dishwasher after the salesperson took $100 off the price. Afterward, the store manager informed Darren that the salesperson wasn't allowed to offer discounts, and Darren would have to pay the extra $100. Does he have to pay?

No. Darren may cancel the agreement and demand a refund of the money he has already paid, or he may sue the store for breach of contract. The salesperson, acting as the store's agent, made a contract with Darren that was legally binding on the business.

Can Deborah demand a refund if a table she bought at an auction turns out to be a reproduction rather than an antique, as was stated in the catalog?

Yes. Just as it is illegal to label used goods as new, it is illegal to label a reproduction as an antique. Deborah has a right to a refund because her decision to buy the table was based on the seller's misrepresentation.

Buying by Mail

I received some cosmetics in the mail even though I had never ordered them. If I keep them, do I have to pay for them?

No. Under federal law and most state laws, you do not have to pay for unordered goods or return them. You may treat them as a gift. It is illegal to send consumers unordered merchandise unless it is a free sample, or a gift from a charitable organization, used to encourage donations.

Are chain letters legal?

Generally, yes, but any chain letter that requires you to send anyone money or something else of value violates a federal law prohibiting the use of the mail for lotteries.

Janet doesn't want the forthcoming selection of the record club she belongs to, but she has missed the time limit for notifying the club. Must she pay for the record?

Yes. Under federal law, if her record club mailed the announcement so that she had at least 10 days to accept or reject the record, the company may insist that she live up to her part of the bargain. Janet can write to the company, explaining her situation. The company is not legally bound to honor her request, but it may do so to maintain good customer relations.

A mail-order catalog stated that an offer for fishing tackle would expire July 1. I sent in my order in early June, but received a form letter stating that the offer had been canceled. Can they do this?

No. The mail-order company cannot cancel its offer after you have accepted it by ordering the tackle. Had the company notified you that the offer was canceled before you placed your order, the cancellation would have been effective. In this case, the cancellation is a breach of contract.

Corky saw a bedspread she liked in a mail-order catalog and ordered four of them to give as gifts. She sent her check with the order. When the spreads arrived in the mail, two of them were of substitute patterns, which she didn't like. Can Corky return the substitute spreads and get her money back?

Yes. If the merchandise shipped did not conform to Corky's order, she has the right to return the items for a complete refund.

It took two months to receive the merchandise I ordered from a mail-order catalog. By then, it was too late to give the items as gifts. Do I have a right to return the merchandise even though there was nothing wrong with it?

Yes. If you were not notified that the delivery would take two months, you had the right to expect delivery within 30 days. However, if you were notified in advance that delivery would take two months, and you did not, at that time, cancel your order, the company had the right to assume that you had no complaint about the delay, and you have no right to a refund.

Alexander bought pills by mail to lose weight. The pills turned out to be vitamin C tablets. A friend suggested that he report it to the U.S. Postal Service. What good will that do?

When the Postal Service receives a customer complaint about business transacted through the mail, it contacts the firm involved and requests that it investigate and resolve the complaint. The Postal Service may conduct its own investigation as well and, if necessary, may prosecute the company for using the mail for fraudulent purposes. If the company is found guilty of mail fraud, the Postal Service may stop delivering its mail, and the guilty persons may be subject to fines or imprisonment.

The cookware Sherry bought through the mail was guaranteed to be burn-proof and tough enough to last a lifetime. The first time she used one of the pans, it warped and turned black. She wrote to the distributor, whose only address was a post office box number, but her letter was returned, marked "Addressee Unknown." What can she do?

Sherry can track down the distributor by getting his business address from the postmaster in the city where the post office box is located. This information is available to the public if the post office box is being used to conduct a business. Once she has the distributor's address, Sherry can write and demand a refund. Many experts advise consumers not to place orders with a business that does not give a street address.

Emil ordered a food processor by mail. His check was cashed, but the merchandise never arrived. Phone calls and letters have gone unanswered. How can Emil get either the merchandise or a refund?

Emil should contact the Federal Trade Commission, the U.S. Postal Service, and his state consumer protection agency to report this possibly fraudulent practice. Emil can also sue the firm for breach of contract or, in most states, for violating consumer protection laws. In many states, if a consumer can show that a mail-order company was engaging in fraudulent, unfair, or deceptive practices, he can collect two to three times the money he lost in dealing with the company.

I ordered a set of china figurines by mail, but I'm afraid they may get damaged in shipping. If any pieces are broken when the merchandise arrives, what should I do?

When the figurines arrive, unpack the carton carefully. If you discover a piece that is damaged, unpack no further, but replace everything you have already unpacked, and reseal the carton. Then contact the company—many have toll-free telephone numbers—and ask for instructions on returning the merchandise.

Some companies will guarantee the return postage, while others will arrange for pickup. Make sure that the company will bear the expense for the return one way or the other.

If you are asked to mail back the figurines, send them return receipt requested. Be sure to return them promptly. Some companies have time limits on money-back guarantees. If you delay several weeks, you may lose your right to return the damaged items.

Door-to-door Sales

Several people have come to my door selling jewelry, vacuum cleaners, cosmetics, vitamins, and other products. Are they required to have some type of permit or license?

Many cities and states have laws requiring door-to-door salespersons, or peddlers, to be licensed. Peddling without a license can result in fines, imprisonment, or both. Some cities have laws, called Green River Ordinances, that keep people from going to a person's home to make a sale unless invited to do so.

A door-to-door salesperson pressured Francis into buying monthly supplies of food supplements. When the bill arrived, before any of the supplements, Francis decided he could not afford the program. Can he cancel the order?

Only if it is within three days of the sale. Under a regulation of the Federal Trade Commission and laws in most states, consumers have the right to a three-day cooling-off period in which they can reconsider and cancel certain transactions, including those with door-to-door salespersons. Under the FTC regulation, the salesperson should have given Francis written notification of his right to cancel his order. If Francis did not receive this notification, he can cancel the order even after the three-day cooling-off period has passed.

Jay and Sue bought a $2,000 burial plot from a salesperson who came to their home. They wrote a check for $100 as a deposit, then

Guarding Against Door-to-door Sales Schemes

Although underhanded door-to-door sales practices have often been the focus of exposés, legislation, and public outrage, some fast talkers are still making a good living by promising what they can't deliver and trusting the consumer won't complain. Here are some things to look out for:

- Beware of any door-to-door solicitor who claims he doesn't want to sell you anything. The offer of a free inspection of your furnace, roof, or plumbing is often a ploy to sell you repairs that you do not need.
- Don't invite in anyone who says he is taking a survey, or you may find yourself listening to a high-pressure sales pitch and at a loss as to how to get your "guest" to leave.
- If someone appears with a free gift and asks you to sign a receipt for it, read the receipt carefully. It may be a contract to purchase the "gift" at an inflated price.
- If a salesperson is trying to sell you something from a catalog, look carefully at the picture of the product, noting that the product will be photographed in its best light or made to look even better than it actually is. Remember that the words *simulated, faux,* and *reproduction* in the context of jewelry, art, and antiques mean that the item is not genuine or original.
- Read the disclaimers on the order form or sales contract. They might state that you will have to pay excessive shipping charges or that delivery will take 8 to 12 weeks.
- Pass up offers good for "this day only." This is a ploy used by sales people to create the false impression that you are being offered a once-in-a-lifetime deal. If the salesperson doesn't want to give you time for reflection, there's probably a good reason.
- Be wary of contractors who are "working in the neighborhood" and have extra materials on hand that they can use to fix your house at a special discount rate. They may do a poor job on work you really didn't need at an inflated price, and you will not be able to locate them afterward to fix the problems they have created.
- Take advantage of the three-day cooling-off period. Under a Federal Trade Commission regulation you may cancel transactions with a door-to-door salesperson within three days of the sale. (You do not get this protection when you buy from a television ad or by telephone.)

on reflection, they decided that they didn't really want the plot. Can they just stop payment on the check to get out of the deal?

No. Stopping payment on the check will not automatically cancel their order. If the salesperson stopped at their home without an invitation, Jay and Sue can cancel the order in writing within three days. If Jay and Sue requested a sales presentation in their home, they do not have the right to cancel the order unless the terms of the sales agreement allow it.

A door-to-door salesperson claimed that the ring he sold me was 18-karat gold, but it was only dipped. Can I get my money back?

Yes, because the salesperson lied about the gold content of the ring. If your money is not returned, you can sue the salesperson for fraud.

Telephone and TV Sales

Brenda received a telephone call from someone selling magazines, and she accepted the offer, which at first sounded terrific. After the call was over, she calculated that she had agreed to pay more than the cover price for five years! Can she cancel the order?

No. The three-day cooling-off period allowed for sales made by door-to-door salespersons does not apply to solicitations over the telephone.

How can I check on the reliability of a firm selling by telephone?

Look in your telephone directory to see if the firm has a street address. If not, you may wish to forgo dealing with it. You will not be able to enforce your rights if you have a complaint, unless you can locate the firm. If the company has an address, contact your local Better Business Bureau and state consumer protection agency to see if any complaints have been filed against the firm. Finally, ask the company for references.

Eileen always uses a credit card when she places a telephone order because she feels it offers her more protection than paying by check. Is she right?

Yes. If Eileen has a dispute with the seller on a charge of $50 or more, she may withhold payment (1) if the transaction occurred in her home state;

(2) if it occurred within 100 miles of her current mailing address; or (3) if she used a credit card issued by the seller, such as a department store credit card. If Eileen does withhold payment because of a dispute with the seller, the seller may not notify credit bureaus that the disputed amount is delinquent until the dispute is resolved.

If I order merchandise from a TV ad, do I have less protection than if I order from a printed ad?

No. Both televised and printed ads are subject to regulation by the Federal Trade Commission. However, if you have a dispute about the truth of claims made in the advertisement, it will be easier to prove what a printed advertisement claimed, unless you have recorded the commercial on videotape.

Gracie saw a television commercial for a set of exercise equipment that she wanted, but the merchandise could only be ordered by telephoning an 800 number. If Gracie orders the equipment in this way, will she have any protection if it doesn't arrive or is not as advertised?

Yes. Gracie will be protected against false and deceptive trade practices under the Federal Trade Commission Act and under state consumer protection laws, but she will be missing out on broader protection. Some sellers take orders only by telephone to avoid the U.S. Postal Service regulations that govern the fraudulent use of the mails, and to cheat buyers out of the rights that they would have in a mail-order sale: for example, Gracie would not be able to cancel the order if the merchandise were not delivered within 30 days. Before ordering, Gracie should make sure that she is dealing with a reputable company.

Owen bought a diamond pendant he saw on a television ad, which promised he would get his money back if he were not completely satisfied. The stone turned out to be much smaller than it appeared on the screen. What can Owen do if the company refuses to refund his money?

Owen can report the company to the Federal Trade Commission and his state consumer protection agency, which is generally a division of the attorney general's office. If Owen's state has a law similar to one in Massachusetts that requires a company advertising money-back guarantees to make full refunds, Owen may be entitled to sue the company for double or triple the price of the ring. If Owen's state does not have such a law, he can sue the company for not honoring the money-back guarantee.

Prizes, Gifts, and Rebates

Do they really award all those big cash prizes that you see advertised so often?

Yes. The Federal Trade Commission (FTC) and the U. S. Postal Service regulate contests and sweepstakes to ensure that the sponsors make no false claims about awarding prizes. Most experts agree that sweepstakes sponsored by nationally known companies are on the level. Under FTC guidelines, the sponsors of sweepstakes are not required to award all unclaimed prizes. However, to keep the goodwill of their contestants, many of them do hold "second chance" drawings in order to ensure that all the prizes that they promised are awarded.

I find it hard to believe that I don't have to make a purchase to be in the running for a sweepstakes prize. What is the law on being eligible for such prizes?

The law prohibits requiring you to purchase anything to be eligible to enter and win a sweepstakes drawing. If you are required to fill out a special entry form, the sponsor of the sweepstakes must provide the form free of charge. If entry forms are included inside the product's container or printed on its wrapper, the sponsor must give you an alternative way of getting entry forms without buying the product. It is illegal for the contest sponsor to shift the odds of winning to those who have ordered or purchased a product.

Kathy received a letter informing her that she had won one of three attractive prizes. In return for receiving the prize, her only obligation would be to listen to a 30-minute sales presentation about a vacation time-sharing program. How can Kathy find out if this is a legitimate offer?

Kathy can check with her local Better Business Bureau and state consumer protection agency to see if any complaints have been made about this company. Most promotions of this type are legitimate, but the prize announcements can be misleading. For example, some motorboat winners have found that their craft was only an inflatable raft with a tiny motor. Others have won vacations to Florida, then discovered that their food and transportation costs were not covered and their lodging was in a hotel where they had to listen to another promotional pitch. Still others, on going to collect their prizes, have been told that their prize was temporarily out of stock, and were then offered a cheap substitute.

Because many of the prize announcements are deceptive, at least one state, New York, requires land promoters to tell their winners, in advance, exactly what they have won. The law also requires that the promoters pay the transportation costs for those who wish to collect their prizes.

Ramona received a notice in the mail that she had won a three-month membership in a fitness club. When she went to claim her prize, she was told she would have to pay equipment rental charges and locker-room fees. Is this legal?

If the health club normally charges separate membership, equipment, and locker-room fees, this promotion would not be viewed as deceptive or misleading by the courts. If, however, these fees are never assessed separately and have been added just for the purpose of the promotion, the "prize" may be viewed as a deceptive sales practice.

I was promised a free TV for listening to a sales pitch for lake-front property, but the TV never arrived. What can I do?

Contact the land promoters. If they are unwilling to give you your promised gift, inform them that you will report them to the state attorney general for conducting a fraudulent promotion. In many states, you may sue the promoter for this deceptive business practice.

Are there laws regulating rebates?

Yes. Federal law prohibits a seller from rebating part of the purchase price of goods to a buyer with the understanding that the buyer will not buy or use a competitor's goods. Most states prohibit "secret" rebates that are not paid to all customers on like terms. They also prohibit insurance agents from rebating portions of their commissions to their clients. The purpose of laws governing rebates is to prevent price discrimination among different groups of customers and to eliminate trade practices that stifle competition among businesses.

Jan sent for a $3 rebate on a hair dryer. She never received her rebate. What can she do about it?

Jan can write to the customer service department of the company, telling them when she made her purchase and when and how she complied with the terms of the rebate offer. She should give the company a reasonable time to comply with her request for the rebate, setting a deadline for action. If she receives no response, she should write again, sending her letter by certified mail, this time informing them that she will contact the state consumer protection agency if she does not receive her rebate.

Consumer Contracts

Chip, aged 17, purchased a stereo on the installment plan. After making a few payments, he decided to return the stereo. Does the store have to accept the returned equipment?

Yes. Under the law, minors are considered to be incapable of making binding contracts. Until he reaches the age of adulthood (18 years in most states, 21 in others), Chip will be allowed to back out of his contracts. On the other hand, the store does not have the right to cancel the contract.

Marcie signed a printed-form contract when she purchased her washer and dryer. Will the fact that it was a form contract put her at a disadvantage if there is a problem after the sale?

No. If a dispute arises over the terms of Marcie's agreement with the store and the written provisions of the form contract are unclear, a court will interpret the contract in Marcie's favor. If a court finds the form unreasonably unfair to customers, it will not enforce it.

What should I do if the furniture dealer won't delete a clause I object to in a contract to purchase a dining room set on time?

Take your business elsewhere. Generally, courts will not step in and force buyers or sellers to accept or delete particular terms in contracts.

What does it mean when an installment payment contract gives the seller the right to assign the contract?

It means that the seller may sell the right to collect payments to another company. This arrangement is typical of health club contracts. The clubs usually assign their contracts immediately to a finance company, which then collects the payments.

When Jay bought his VCR, he signed a note agreeing to make payments for 18 months. The video store then sold the note to a finance company. The VCR has stopped working. The finance company claims that Jay has to continue making payments or they will repossess the VCR. Are they justified in doing this?

No. Under a Federal Trade Commission regulation and many state laws, you have the same rights to withhold payment as you would if the video store had not sold the note.

According to her sales contract, if Evelyn missed one payment on her mink coat, the furrier could demand the remaining balance on her loan. Evelyn missed two payments, and the furrier wrote to demand full payment. Evelyn offered to make three payments to bring her account up to date, but the furrier refused. Can he legally enforce this clause?

Yes. Many contracts contain acceleration clauses, which state that if a payment is missed, the seller can demand that the buyer make all the remaining payments immediately. The furrier does not have to accept the late payments. If Evelyn can't pay off the balance of the loan in a lump sum, the furrier probably has the right, under their contract, to repossess the coat and resell it. If the sale price is not equal to the balance Evelyn owes, the furrier may sue her for the difference. Evelyn may wish to obtain a loan from her bank for the balance due if she wants to keep the coat.

A salesperson offered to reduce the price of a computer by $500 if Eva would give him the names of six friends who might be interested in buying one. Is this part of Eva's contract enforceable?

If the salesperson alters their contract, in writing, or fills in the price to reflect a $500 reduction, Eva can feel fairly confident that a court will enforce the terms of the contract. Eva should be wary, however, if the salesperson offers to reduce the price only if the contacts she gives him result in sales. The salesperson may have no intention of contacting the other people, or if he does one or more may not buy, leaving Eva to pay $500 more than she expected.

The sales contract for my new furnace states that if I sue the seller because of defects, I will have to pay the seller's attorney fees. This doesn't sound right to me. What should I do?

Request that the dealer delete the clause from your contract, initialing and dating the change. If the dealer refuses to do so, consider taking your business elsewhere. In some states this type of clause is illegal, and the courts would not enforce it even if it remained in the contract.

After signing the order for a new living room set, the Morgans discovered that Mrs. Morgan was going to have a baby. Without Mrs. Morgan's income, the couple can't afford the new furniture. Can they cancel their order before the merchandise is delivered?

Not unless their contract lets them cancel. However, even if they cannot cancel the contract, the Morgans should notify the seller immediately that they cannot pay for the furniture and will not accept delivery. By refusing to accept delivery, they are limiting the seller's losses and the amount they may have to pay for breach of contract. The seller may be limited to suing for his lost profit rather than the full price of the set.

Six weeks ago, I took my stereo in for repairs. The repair shop gave me an estimate of $30. When it was ready, the bill came to $150. I refused to pay anything. Can the repair shop keep my stereo if I don't pay?

Yes. The repair shop has a right to keep your stereo until you pay your bill and may even, under state law, be entitled to sell the stereo to cover repair costs. To keep them from doing so, pay the bill, noting on the receipt that you are paying under protest. You can then sue the shop to get back the amount you were overcharged.

When Elaine enrolled in dance school she signed a contract to make monthly payments for a year. The next day, she changed her mind and called to cancel. She was told that there was no problem and that the membership would be canceled. Three months later, Elaine began to receive collection letters from a finance company for the membership fees. Does she have to pay?

Under some contracts, cancellations must be made in writing to be valid, and so Elaine's attempt to cancel her contract by phone may have been ineffective. However, if a cancellation must be in writing, the contract should say so. If the contract Elaine signed did not say that cancellations had to be in writing, Elaine's cancellation was valid, and she does not have to pay the fees.

Cecilia, a dressmaker, agreed orally that she would make Tina's wedding gown for $450. When Tina returned for a fitting, Cecilia said she was too busy to sew the gown. Does Tina have any rights in this situation?

Yes. Because Cecilia had agreed to make Tina's gown for less than $500, Tina had an enforceable contract. If Tina must pay another dressmaker more money to have her gown ready in time, or must purchase a ready-made gown at a higher price, Tina may sue Cecilia for the extra money it costs her. If the agreed-upon price had been more than $500, however, Tina would have no enforceable rights against Cecilia. Contracts for goods or services for over $500 must be in writing to be enforceable.

I went to a health club that advertised a free initial visit, and was pressured into signing a contract for a three-year membership, payable every month. Can I cancel my membership?

Many health club contracts allow a member to cancel and get a refund for the unused portion of his membership, although some allow a member to cancel only if he moves out of town or becomes disabled. Read your contract to find out what your cancellation rights are. At least 20 states regulate health clubs and give the customer the right to cancel a new contract within a three-day cooling-off period. Some states also prohibit clubs from signing up members for more than one year at a time.

Ronnie and Paula signed a time-share agreement in a nearby vacation retreat because it could be "swapped" with other properties around the country. After signing all the papers, they discovered that there were only three other places they could swap for, and none were in areas they wanted to visit. Do they have the right to break their contract?

Only if they were misled by a sales pitch and promotional materials into believing their swapping options would be more extensive than they actually are. If the promoter sues Ronnie and Paula for money due under the contract, they may use his unfair and deceptive advertising as a defense. They should also report the matter to their state attorney general. At least one promoter has been successfully prosecuted for leading people to believe they could vacation in Hawaii, when actually only one-fifth of the time-share units were located there, and thus many members had to settle for less desirable locations.

Warranties and Service Contracts

For warranties on automobiles, see "Car Warranties" in Chapter 6, *Your Car.*

What is the difference between a warranty and a guarantee?

Both words describe promises that a manufacturer or dealer makes about a product. A warranty can be either *express* or *implied.* An express warranty is a specific promise about the product—for example, that it is of a certain quality, is made of a particular material, will do a certain job, or will last a specified period of time. A seller or manufacturer obligates himself to repair, replace, or refund the price of a product that does not live up to its warranty. If there is an express warranty it must be available to the customer to read before buying if the product costs more than $15.

An implied warranty is an unstated promise, assumed by the law in most sales transactions, that the product will be of at least average quality and will do what the average customer would expect it to do. For example, a toaster should toast bread and a vacuum cleaner should pick up dirt. As with an express warranty, the manufacturer or seller must remedy the situation if the product is unusable or defective.

A product is covered by an implied warranty unless a disclaimer is specifically made—for example, by using the words "as is." In some states, including Kansas, Maryland, Massachusetts, Mississippi, and West Virginia, an implied warranty cannot be disclaimed. Other states, including California, Maine, Minnesota, and Vermont, regulate the seller's ability to eliminate the warranty.

When Matt bought a color television set, the manufacturer included only a partial warranty for the picture tube, but a full

Understanding Warranty Terms

Not all warranties are printed on tags or in booklets that are packaged with the products you buy. Some are contained in advertisements and promotional materials. Others are never stated, but are implied. All can be enforced by law. To be fully aware of your rights as a consumer, you should understand the terms most commonly applied to warranties:

- *Express warranty*—A specific promise, which may or may not be in writing, that the manufacturer or seller makes about his goods or services. "Rustproof," "14-karat gold," and "parts guaranteed for 90 days" are all express warranties.
- *Implied warranty of merchantability*—An unstated promise that the product you buy will work and will be of average quality and will do what it's supposed to do. In its most basic terms, it means a sewing machine will stitch, a refrigerator will keep food cold, and a teakettle won't crack.
- *Implied warranty of fitness for a particular purpose*—An unstated promise that a product will fit your needs. This warranty is created in only some situations. If you go to a hardware store and tell the salesman that you need water-resistant paint for an outdoor swing set, you are informing him that you need a product for a particular purpose. If the salesman then sells you some paint, knowing your purpose, he has created a warranty—even if he makes no spoken promises. He has warranted that the paint won't wash off in the rain, and if it does, you are entitled to a refund.
- *Full warranty*—An all-inclusive written warranty. Under federal law, defective products or parts covered by a full warranty must be repaired or replaced without charge; the buyer should not even have to pay shipping costs. If the defect cannot be fixed after a reasonable number of attempts, the buyer is entitled to choose between a replacement and a refund.

warranty for all the other parts. How can this be? If there's a full warranty on the set, doesn't it have to apply to everything?

No. Under federal law, a product can be covered by more than one warranty. In such a case, some parts can be covered by a full warranty, which absorbs all costs, including the price of replacement parts, labor, and shipping; other parts can be covered by a limited warranty.

Two weeks after Amanda bought a new toaster, she discovered that the warranty card should have been returned within 10 days of purchase. If Amanda sends the warranty card in late will she still be protected?

Not necessarily. A dealer or manufacturer may require that a warranty card be returned within a certain time to guarantee coverage. However, to

- *Limited warranty*—A written warranty that covers some defects or problems, but not others. For example, a warranty on a video recorder may include replacement of all defective or worn parts except the recording heads or may cover the cost of new parts but not labor.
- *As is*—A warning to consumers that the product carries no warranties, either stated or implied. When you buy something "as is," you have no legal grounds to expect that it will be of any particular quality, will last any length of time, or will work at all.
- *Consequential, or incidental, damages*—Losses that are indirectly caused by a defect in a product. For example, if a defect caused your new oven to explode, ruining your kitchen walls, and you had to miss work to have the walls redone, the damage to the walls would be considered direct damages, and would be covered by the warranty, but your lost wages would be consequential, and not covered. Under federal law, consequential damages can be excluded from a full warranty only if a statement of this fact is conspicuously placed on the first page of the warranty. No limitation on consequential damages will be enforced if personal injuries are involved. A few states, such as Kansas and Maryland, prohibit warranties on consumer goods from excluding consequential damages even if no personal injuries are involved.
- *Customer misuse*—A statement that damage that results from a customer's misuse of a product is not covered by a warranty. If you have used a product in a careless manner or have not followed the manufacturer's instructions, the seller is not obligated to repair the product without charge.
- *Unauthorized repairs*—A statement that repairs may be made only at authorized shops or that only a certain brand of parts may be used in repair work. This requirement is valid only if the services or parts in question are provided free under the warranty.

keep their customers' goodwill, some dealers honor warranties even when this requirement is not met. Amanda has nothing to lose by returning the card late.

In the warranty booklet that came with my clothes dryer I noticed the words "repair or replace." Do I determine whether the dryer is to be repaired or replaced—or does the manufacturer?

The manufacturer. However, if after a reasonable number of attempts, the manufacturer has been unable to repair the clothes dryer, you may demand a replacement dryer or a refund.

The warranty on Mark's coffee maker does not apply to damage caused by neglect, abuse, or mishandling. If the coffee maker needs to be repaired, will Mark have to prove that the damage was not caused by his misuse?

No, unless the manufacturer sees signs that Mark has misused the appliance. If there are no such indications, the manufacturer must honor the warranty without dispute.

Eddie bought a lawn mower from a local discount store. After numerous engine problems while it was still under warranty, Eddie tried to return it. He discovered, however, that the store was out of business. Is Eddie stuck with paying for the repairs out of his own pocket?

No. Eddie's warranty was probably provided by the lawn mower's manufacturer. If so, he can contact the manufacturer about repairs.

My grandmother bought a dishwasher and, for an extra charge, signed a service contract. When I looked over the fine print I realized that she wasn't going to be getting much service for her money. Isn't there some law that requires limitations and disclaimers in service contracts to be in bold print?

The federal Magnuson-Moss Warranty Act requires that the terms of service contracts be fully, clearly, and conspicuously disclosed. However, *conspicuously* does not refer to the size or kind of type used in printing the contracts: It is perfectly legal to put important provisions in small print. (In contrast, the act does cover type size in warranties.)

Deciding on a Service Contract

If you've bought a major appliance lately, the salesperson has probably tried to sell you a service contract to cover it. A service contract is an agreement to maintain and repair a product for a set period of time. A service contract serves, in some ways, the same purpose as a warranty, but it should not be confused with one. A warranty is a promise that the merchandise you buy will meet certain standards of quality or performance. If those standards are not met, the buyer may demand repairs, replacement, or in some cases, a refund. A service contract, on the other hand, is a form of insurance. Necessary repairs or maintenance, if covered by the contract, will be performed at no charge or for a reduced fee.

Some service contracts are well worth having, while others are not. Before investing in a service contract, examine its terms and see if they will really benefit you. Here are some questions to ask:

- Is the coverage substantially more than what you are given free of charge by the warranty? Will it extend beyond the life of the warranty?
- Are minor defects covered as well as major ones?
- Are repairs for routine wear and tear included?
- Are you offered routine maintenance at no charge?
- Are all parts and labor supplied at no extra charge? (Some service contracts charge a nominal set fee each time the product is serviced.)
- Are there any deductibles involved? (Some service contracts have deductibles like those of insurance policies.)
- Does the contract cover service calls at your home or include provisions for moving the product should it need repairs at a service center?
- Will repairs be made even if the damage resulted from misuse—your not following the manufacturer's directions when using the product?

If I didn't fully understand a service contract when I signed it, can I get out of it or have it amended?

No. The law will presume that you read and understood the contract before signing it. If there was no fraud or deception involved, you will not be allowed to cancel without penalty unless the contract says you can.

Darlene bought a service contract for her freezer. The unit broke down, but the repairman won't come to her home. What can she do?

If the contract states that it does not cover service calls or transportation for the freezer, Darlene will have to get the unit to the repair center herself. If the contract is ambiguous or if Darlene was led to believe that it included service calls, she can sue for deceptive sales practices.

Defective and Unsafe Merchandise

Eunice bought a defective ice cream maker. Should she complain to the store or to the manufacturer?

She has the right to complain to both because both are responsible for defects in the products they sell or make. As a practical matter, however, it would be much more convenient for Eunice to seek a refund, repairs, or a replacement from her local store.

A canned ham that Penny bought at her local supermarket was spoiled. When she brought it back for a refund, the store manager told her to return it to the supplier, who in turn told her to return it to the store. What are Penny's rights?

The supermarket should either give Penny a full refund or exchange the ham for an unspoiled one of the same weight and quality. Shoppers have the right to expect that the food they purchase at a supermarket will not be spoiled. The store manager is responsible for seeing to it that the food he sells is fresh, and he cannot shift that responsibility to the supplier, even though the supplier is also responsible.

Nicholas bought a new digital phone from a department store. When he got home, he discovered that the plastic case was badly cracked. What are his rights?

He has the right to return it to the store for a replacement or a refund, provided he did not crack the case himself. He may not be entitled to anything, however, if he knew when he bought the phone that it was cracked, or if it was sold as a factory second or marked "as is." In such cases, it would have been assumed that he took the chance of getting damaged goods in exchange for paying a low price.

If I don't have time to try on a suit and later discover it is defective, do I have any recourse?

Yes. Generally, you may return the suit for a refund or replacement, especially if the defect is one that could not be easily discovered. However, if you were aware that the store had a no return policy, you had a duty to inspect it closely before purchasing it.

Anna bought a silk dress at a designer discount store. When she got home, she discovered that the dress had a hole in it. She tried

to return the dress, but the store owner pointed out a sign that stated "No Returns, No Refunds." If Anna sued the store, would she get a refund in spite of what the sign says?

When a store displays a "No Return, No Refund" sign, or when the price of an item has been greatly reduced, it is assumed that a shopper has been alerted to the possibility that the goods may be irregular or damaged. The shopper in such situations has the responsibility of carefully inspecting the goods before purchasing them. If, however, the "No Refund" sign was in small letters or in a spot where it was difficult to read, a court may decide that Anna had the right to believe she could return the dress, and may enforce her right to a refund.

My new air conditioner did not cool properly, so I called the store I bought it from and told them to pick it up and give me a refund. They offered to replace the machine but refused to give me back my money. Don't I have the right to a refund?

No. If you buy defective merchandise, the seller has the right to try to fix the defect by repairing the item or replacing it with an identical item that works properly. If he can't do this within a reasonable amount of time, you then have the right to a full refund.

Sarah purchased a home computer, but it is defective, and she wants to return it for a refund. The salesman says that Sarah will be charged 20 percent of the purchase price if she returns the computer. Is this legal?

No. The seller cannot charge you for returning defective goods; but in most situations, if an item is defective, the seller or manufacturer has the right to replace or repair it rather than give you a refund.

Jeff bought a new tape deck. After using it for a week to play back prerecorded tapes, he tried to tape a business meeting, and found out that the recording function didn't work. Can he return the tape deck despite the fact that he used it?

Yes, because the defect was one that he would not necessarily have discovered upon inspection or on first use. However, if Jeff continues to use the deck after discovering the defect, he will lose his right to return it.

John bought a new battery for his expensive 35mm camera and carefully installed it. The battery leaked, and the acid corroded

the camera to such an extent that it cannot be repaired. Can John sue the battery manufacturer for the cost of the camera?

Yes, as long as the battery was new and properly installed in the camera, John could sue for the amount the camera was worth just before he installed the defective batteries. However, if the battery was not used according to the instructions for the camera or the batteries, John does not have a valid claim.

My husband and I are expecting our first baby and want to be sure the furniture and toys that we buy are safe. Where can we get information on product safety?

From the Consumer Products Safety Commission. Call their toll-free hotline—dial 1-800-555-1212 to get the current number—or write to them. The commission's main office is in Washington, D.C., and there are regional offices in Atlanta, Boston, Chicago, Cleveland, Dallas, Denver, Kansas City (Missouri), Los Angeles, Minneapolis, New Orleans, Brooklyn, Philadelphia, San Francisco, and Seattle.

If a child is injured while playing with a toy, can the parents successfully sue the manufacturer or the retailer?

Yes, they may sue both if the injury is due to a defect in the toy or if the toy is inherently unsafe for children. The injured child's parents may sue the manufacturer for producing a defective or unsafe toy and the retailer for a breach of the implied warranty of merchantability—a toy that injures the child who plays with it does not work as one would expect a toy to work.

A week after I started to use a new brand of makeup, I developed a serious skin condition. Can I sue the manufacturer even though I can't prove that he was negligent in making the product?

Yes, the manufacturer is responsible for any harm his product does when used according to directions, whether or not you can prove that he was negligent. In the past, a consumer could sue a manufacturer only if he was negligent or if the product did not live up to its warranties. In the 1960's the theory of strict liability was developed to protect consumers who could not prove negligence or breach of warranty.

To win your case, you would have to prove that your skin condition resulted from your using the makeup. You would have to show that you did not contribute to the skin condition by failing to read or follow the manufacturer's instructions. For example, if the makeup contained an ingredient that you are allergic to and it was listed on the label, a court might not hold the manufacturer responsible. Similarly, if you disregarded specific instructions to test the makeup on your arm before using it on your face, a court might not make the manufacturer pay you anything.

Lorraine let Bella, her hairdresser, talk her into lightening her hair. Bella left the solution on too long because she was busy with other clients, and when she removed it, Lorraine's hair was bright orange. Although Bella quickly corrected her mistake, Lorraine's hair was damaged. Can Lorraine sue Bella?

Yes. Hairdressers can be held responsible for any damage they do by carelessly or negligently applying hair bleaches or dyes. They can also be held responsible for damage caused by the careless use of hair waving machines or solutions. The amount Lorraine will be able to sue Bella for will depend on how severely her hair was damaged.

When I lifted my new luggage down from a closet shelf, the handle came off, and I fell, injuring my back. Can I sue the manufacturer?

Yes, if you can establish that your injury was the direct result of the defective handle and that the defect was caused by the manufacturer and not by ordinary wear and tear.

Your Rights at a Restaurant

Lyle went to a restaurant that advertised "All you can eat for $7.95." When he asked the waitress for a third helping of shrimp, she told him he could have chicken, but there was a limit of two servings of shrimp. Would Lyle be justified in reporting the restaurant to the FTC for false advertising?

Probably not. The restaurant did not advertise unlimited shrimp; rather, it advertised unlimited food. The restaurant would be guilty of false advertising only if it had advertised "All the shrimp you can eat for $7.95."

Shirley went to a restaurant that advertised the best fried chicken in town. Is she entitled to a refund if she doesn't like the chicken?

No. The law recognizes that no merchant would claim that his goods are just mediocre or passable. Therefore, the use of such words as "best," "top," or "finest" is not interpreted by the courts as a specific promise or warranty. Although Shirley disagrees with the restaurateur's opinion that his fried chicken is the best in town, she is not entitled to a refund.

Is it true that if I'm dissatisfied with the service at a restaurant, I don't have to pay?

No. Dissatisfaction with the service, when the food itself is of adequate quality, does not give you the right to refuse to pay for the meal. Poor service is grounds for leaving a small tip or no tip.

If, however, the poor service results in food that is cold, spoiled, or otherwise unsatisfactory, the customer has the right to request that it be prepared again or to cancel the order.

Arnold was turned away from a restaurant because he wasn't wearing a jacket and tie. Doesn't this violate his rights?

No. Generally, the manager or owner of a restaurant is not required to accept anyone as a customer and may refuse to serve men not wearing jackets. A restaurant may not refuse to serve customers on the grounds of race, color, religion, or national origin, but these are the only restrictions that are forbidden by law.

Can I be forced to sit at the counter in a restaurant when I'm dining alone?

Yes. The manager or owner of a restaurant may seat you or any other customer anywhere he wishes, whether you are alone or not, provided he does not do so because of your race, color, religion, or national origin.

An incompetent waiter spilled sauce on Amy's dress, and the cleaner can't get the spots out. Is the restaurant responsible for reimbursing Amy for the cost of the dress?

Yes, but it is not responsible for the full purchase price of the dress unless it was brand-new. Since clothing has a limited life span, the restaurant will take into consideration the garment's wear and tear since Amy bought it, and she will be reimbursed for the present value of the dress, rather than the full purchase price—for example, she might be reimbursed only one-half the purchase price of the dress if the garment is 1½ years old and still in good condition.

Carole purchased a sandwich from the corner deli. She took the sandwich back to work, ate part of it, then noticed that there were hairs in the sandwich. What is Carole entitled to?

She is entitled to a new sandwich or a refund. All states have laws prohibiting the sale of unwholesome or contaminated food. Carole should take the sandwich back to the deli immediately, show it to the manager, and tell him whether she prefers another sandwich or a refund.

After I bought a soft drink from a store, I discovered a small bug in the bottle and got sick. Can I sue the manufacturer or the store?

If you drank from the bottle before discovering the bug and your illness is due to the bug, you can sue both the manufacturer and the store. The manufacturer can be held liable for the negligence that allowed the creature to get inside the bottle. The store can be held liable for breaching the implied warranty of merchantability—that is, you can sue the store for selling you something that wasn't fit to be sold. Everyone in the chain of distribution, from the manufacturer to the retailer, is responsible for supplying a safe product.

While eating at a restaurant, I found a piece of glass in my food. The food was quickly replaced, but later that night I became very ill. What are my rights?

If you can prove that your illness was caused by the glass in the food, you may hold the restaurant responsible for your medical bills, lost wages, and pain and suffering. The lapse of several hours before the onset of the illness does not destroy your claim.

Travel Troubles

When I flew from Seattle to St. Louis last month I had to change planes in Minneapolis. Just after my plane landed in Minneapolis, the airport was closed because of heavy snow, and I had to sit up in the airport all night waiting for the weather to clear. Shouldn't the airline have put me up for the night at their expense?

Not necessarily. Although some airlines do provide overnight accommodations and meals for passengers in such circumstances, they are not required by law to do so. Most airlines provide telephone service to help stranded passengers notify those who are expecting them of the delay; but again, they are not legally bound to do so.

Travel Troubles

Nancy bought a ticket for a charter flight to Hawaii and paid for it three months before the day of departure. Two days before the flight, she was notified that the price of the ticket had been increased $100 and she had to pay the balance. Can they make her pay?

No. Although charter airlines can raise their rates as late as 10 days before departure, passengers must also be notified of the rate change 10 days before departure. Nancy cannot be forced to pay an additional $100, because she was not notified of the increase at least 10 days before.

Harry made airline reservations several days before he was due to leave on a business trip. When he checked in for his flight, he was told it was overbooked. What are Harry's rights?

If Harry is bumped from his flight because of overbooking, the airline must try to get him to his destination within one hour of his original arrival time. If Harry arrives between one and two hours late, the airline must pay him the price of a one-way ticket, up to a maximum $200. If his delay is over two hours, that amount is doubled. At least one federal court has also given bumped passengers the right to file suit.

Stephanie was bumped from her flight to Europe because it was overbooked, and so she was late arriving. As a result, the hotel canceled her reservation. The only available room was much more expensive. Shouldn't the airline pay the additional expense?

Courts in New York and Montana have held that overbooking is a breach of the passenger's contract with the airline, and allowed the bumped passenger to sue for damages. However, airlines are allowed to limit their liability for problems indirectly caused by late departures, such as the loss of hotel reservations, by printing a notice on the ticket itself. Many travelers protect themselves from this type of inconvenience and extra expense by purchasing traveler's insurance, which covers extra expenses caused by delays in travel arrangements.

Cloudway Airlines lost my luggage several months ago, and no action has been taken. What should I do?

File a claim against the airline. You can get a claim form from the airline's passenger service representative. If your flight was a domestic one, you are entitled to up to $1,250 for lost or damaged luggage and its contents, excluding cash, jewelry, cameras, or very fragile items that were packed in your luggage. If you were on an international flight, you are entitled to up to $9.07 per pound for luggage that was lost or damaged by the airline.

On future trips, you might consider buying additional protection in the form of baggage insurance, especially if your luggage and its contents are valuable. Travel experts advise that you never leave jewelry, cameras, cash, or other valuables in your luggage. You should keep these items with you on the airplane.

I planned a vacation near a very popular amusement center and made reservations at a motel two months in advance. When I arrived, the motel had overbooked, and I had to stay 25 miles away. Can I sue?

Yes. In a similar case, vacationers who had confirmed reservations at a hotel in Hawaii sued when the reservations were not honored because of overbooking. The court declared that the hotel had breached the contract with the couple, and awarded damages for their distress and disappointment as well as for their extra expenses.

Ray and Virginia prepaid a travel agency for a package trip that proved to be unsatisfactory. Their rooms were not ready on time, and they lost three days of sightseeing because of trouble with their charter flights. Do Ray and Virginia have any recourse?

Yes. Ray and Virginia can sue the travel agency for breach of contract. The court may order the travel agency to compensate them for their fares for alternative transportation, the cost of their meals for the extra three days, inconvenience, and the value of the three days lost traveling.

When You Have a Complaint

Vivian bought a sofa bed from a furniture dealer, but the store never delivered it. What steps should Vivian take?

Vivian should contact the dealer to determine if there's been a mistake or unavoidable delay in the shipment. She should ask the dealer for assurance that the sofa bed will be delivered in a reasonable amount of time. If the dealer cannot make such a guarantee, Vivian has the right to cancel the sales contract and demand a full refund.

A repairman charged my next-door neighbor, Alice, $125 to fix her dishwasher. Less than two hours after he left, the appliance

flooded again. Alice stopped payment on her check, and now the repairman is threatening to take her to small claims court. Is this the right place to settle their dispute?

Yes. Small claims courts handle simple lawsuits for small amounts of money—ranging from $150 to $3,000, depending on the state. Procedures for filing and presenting cases are not complicated, and neither the repairman nor Alice will need a lawyer. For more information see the section on small claims court in Chapter 18, *Going to Court.*

I asked my hairdresser for a trim, but he lopped off two inches instead. I'm furious. I complained to the salon manager, but he just shrugged his shoulders. What can I do?

A hairdresser or barber can be held responsible for damage done to a customer's hair through negligence. If your hairdresser was behaving

When You Have a Complaint

Most of us have had a complaint ignored or pushed aside by an unconcerned merchant or manufacturer. When faced with a defective product, we may alternate between wanting to give up because complaining is not worth the trouble, and threatening to take the case "all the way to the Supreme Court" on principle. The most sensible attitude lies between these extremes. If you have a problem, try these steps:

1. Contact the merchant or manufacturer as soon as possible. If you phone, ask for the name of the person with whom you are speaking and keep a record of the time and date of all calls, as well as the nature of your conversation. If you write, keep several copies of your letter. Give the merchant or manufacturer the following information:

—Your name, address, and daytime telephone number.

—An exact description of the product. Include the model name, dimensions, and color.

—The date and place of purchase and the manner in which you paid for the product (check, cash, or credit card).

—An accurate description of the nature of the defect. Be specific. ("This clock radio is garbage" is not a specific complaint. "The alarm on this clock radio does not ring when it should" is.)

—What you expect the merchant or manufacturer to do. Do you want the product repaired or replaced, or do you want a refund? If you simply state, "I demand satisfaction," you are not telling the merchant or manufacturer what you want him to do.

negligently, in disregard of your express instructions, you may consider suing in small claims court. However, if you were vague or unclear in your instructions, the court may not hold the hairdresser responsible. You may also file a complaint with the agency that licenses barbers in your state.

Which government agencies handle what consumer complaints?

To find out what federal agencies might be able to help you, call the Federal Information Center, whose number is listed in the phone books of most major cities or can be obtained from the operator. Generally, the Federal Trade Commission handles complaints about false advertising, mislabeled goods, unfair pricing, and problems with bills, credit, and warranties. The Food and Drug Administration handles complaints about misbranded or adulterated food, drugs, and cosmetics. The U.S. Postal Service investigates complaints about mail fraud, and the Consumer Products Safety Commission handles complaints about unsafe products.

Almost every state has its own consumer protection agency to enforce state laws against unfair business practices. Generally, the agency works

2. Wait three weeks. If you don't receive a response in that time, send a certified letter, return receipt requested. Refer to your first call or letter of complaint, repeat the information presented in it, and add a brief statement of why you believe you are entitled to the resolution you are requesting ("This defect is a breach of my written warranty" or "I relied on your advertised claim that this fabric was machine washable, but it shrank and faded in the wash"). Follow this with a brief statement that you expect the complaint to be resolved within a specific period of time ("I trust that you will send instructions for returning this defective hair dryer for a replacement by April 15"). Finally, let the merchant or manufacturer know that, if necessary, you will take further action ("If I do not hear from you by April 15, I will take all actions necessary to secure my right to a refund or replacement").

3. If there is no response to your letter, send a warning, also by certified mail. In it, refer to your earlier correspondence and list the steps you will take if your complaint is not resolved ("If I do not hear from you by June 1, I will assume you do not intend to rectify this problem, and I will institute legal proceedings" or "I will report you to the attorney general's office and the Federal Trade Commission").

4. If this letter of warning produces no result, decide whether or not you want to sue. If the problem involves a small amount of money, you can sue in small claims court. If the business was acting fraudulently or a large amount of money was involved, you may wish to see an attorney about bringing a lawsuit or, if you can, get a consumer protection group or agency to sue on your behalf.

directly with the state attorney general's office. Every state has a board or agency that licenses lawyers, doctors, insurance and real estate agents. Your state representative can direct you to the appropriate agency if you have a complaint against a member of one of these professions.

Is the Better Business Bureau an effective place to make a consumer complaint?

You would do better to use the Better Business Bureau before you make a purchase, rather than afterward when you have a complaint. The bureau collects information on local businesses. By calling the bureau, you can find out how long a business has operated, what type of complaints have been made against it, if any, and how the complaints have been settled.

The Better Business Bureau may not be as helpful to you once you have a complaint. It does not have the power to force settlements between consumers and merchants or to issue orders that are legally binding. But you might try the bureau anyhow. In some cases it acts as an arbitrator.

Allen wants to complain to the manufacturer about a defective product. Should he do it by phone or by mail?

Many product labels carry a toll-free number for complaints or questions about the product. If the manufacturer has provided one, Allen should telephone first. If his phone call does not produce results, or if the manufacturer is located out of town and doesn't provide a toll-free number, Allen should write to the manufacturer. He should keep copies of his correspondence and make a log of his telephone calls.

Marie is writing a complaint to the manufacturer of the defective skates that caused her son's injury. Should she threaten to sue?

If Marie's son's injuries are so serious that she is considering a lawsuit, she should hire an attorney and leave all the correspondence to him. If the injuries are minor and Marie does not intend to hire an attorney, she should write a polite but firm letter of complaint, stating how the product was responsible for her son's injuries and how she would like the company to resolve her complaint. She should let the manufacturer know that she feels certain that he will resolve her complaint. Threatening a lawsuit in her first communication may antagonize the manufacturer and prompt him to refuse to cooperate. If Marie receives no response or a negative one, she can then write a letter warning of the possibility of legal action.

CHAPTER
10

Your Job

A help-wanted notice in our local newspaper advertised security guard openings for "men, ages 20–28." Is it legal for an employer to restrict applicants like this?

No. Age restrictions of this kind are illegal unless an employer can show that most people above the specified age cannot adequately perform the tasks required by the job, as might be the case with fire fighters. The advertisement may also be illegal because it prohibits women from applying. However, if there is a justifiable reason for restricting the applicants to men—if the security job is in a prison for men, for example—the ad would not violate sex-discrimination laws.

I have heard radio ads for flight attendants for a major airline. The qualifications include height and weight limits. Can an airline rightfully impose such requirements?

Yes. Federal law permits an employer to establish height and weight requirements for a job, but only if they are necessary for the safe and efficient operation of the business—as is the case with flight attendants. In most circumstances, though, height and weight requirements are prohibited because they tend to discriminate against women and ethnic groups whose members are, on average, shorter or lighter in weight.

After driving a school bus for 12 years, Russell applied for a job with the city bus system. He was rejected because he is 52 years old—two years over the city's maximum age of 50 for a bus driver. Is this legal?

A maximum age of 50 is legal as long as the city bus system can prove that this restriction is reasonably necessary to conduct its business. If challenged, the city would have to show that the physical skills needed to drive a bus decrease as a person gets older, and that there is no practical way to determine the rate at which such skills decrease with age. Courts have recognized that jobs such as those of airline pilots, bus drivers, and police officers require physical skills that are affected by age.

Anne's application for a nursing position was not considered, because she has a hearing disability. Does she have a basis for challenging this decision?

Yes, if her impairment is a minor one or if it can be corrected with a hearing aid, and it does not interfere with her job performance. However,

Job Interview Questions You Don't Need to Answer

Both federal and state antidiscrimination laws limit the types of questions an employer may ask during a job interview or in a written job application. As a general rule, employers may only seek information that will help them evaluate a person's ability to do the job. If a question is personal or seems irrelevant to the requirements of the job, the prospective employee is not required to answer it. A job applicant should not be questioned about the following:

- Marital status or future marriage plans.
- Spouse's or parents' occupations or job titles.
- Number of children, their ages, or plans for having children.
- Babysitting arrangements.
- Whether a spouse would agree to overtime work or business travel.
- Age or date of birth.
- Feelings about working for someone younger.
- Place of birth. (But a foreign-born person seeking employment may be required to prove he is in the United States legally.)
- Race or national origin.
- The origin of a surname.
- Religion or what religious holidays are observed.
- Handicaps, unless they relate to the job.
- Political views or political party preference.
- With whom a person lives.
- Home ownership or rental status.
- Debts and who the creditors are.

if her disability would interfere with her doing the job or endanger the health and safety of her patients or others, the employer would be within his rights in turning her down.

While interviewing me for a job, a personnel director asked if I was married and whether my husband approved of my working. What should I have said to the interviewer?

It is illegal to ask these questions during a job interview; all questions must pertain to your qualifications for the job. You have three options in such a situation: (1) ask why these questions are relevant; (2) refuse to answer the questions and remind the interviewer that they should not be asked; or (3) answer the questions. If you don't get the job and you can show that your replies were used to disqualify you, you will have a valid reason to sue the employer.

Applying for a Job

On her job application, Amy listed her last employer as a reference. But Amy's former boss refused to comment on her job performance, and Amy did not get the position. Does she have any recourse against her former employer?

No. As a general rule, an employer is not required to give references for former employees. In fact, many employers provide only factual information about former employees—date hired, salary, job title, or last position held—because they are concerned that comments about job performance could lead to a lawsuit for defamation of character.

Margaret was expecting to land a new job, but was rejected because she received poor references. Does she have a right to find out what was said and who gave the appraisals?

There is no general legal requirement that applicants be given the details about former employers' comments. However, in Texas, Margaret has the right to receive a copy of any letters from her former employer to her prospective employer. And in several other states, including Maine, Missouri, Montana, and Nevada, Margaret has the right to request a letter from her former employer stating the reasons why she is no longer employed with that company. In still other states, Margaret has the legal right to see her personnel file, and she could indirectly find out what information was sent to prospective employers, since most references are based on material in the personnel file.

Ned failed to mention a physical impairment on his application form. Can the firm discharge him if they later discover he withheld this information?

If Ned's impairment affects his job performance, his failure to mention it could be grounds for discharge. Employment applications often state that if false information is given, the employee will be dismissed.

When I applied for a job, the company required a physical examination, which revealed an old back ailment that could lead to future problems. I didn't get the job for this reason. Can the company legally do this?

Yes. Employers are allowed to require medical tests to determine whether an applicant is physically able to carry out a job. These tests must be given to all applicants, and the same criteria must be used to evaluate all applicants' ability to do the work. Discrimination may be indicated if the employer does not consistently require physical examinations or if he uses them to hide the real reason for rejection—such as the applicant's race, color, religion, sex, age, or national origin.

Adam's interviewer asked him to sign a waiver allowing the Dynamic Data Processing Company to delve into his medical history. Must he sign this waiver?

No. Adam does not have to grant access to this information unless the interviewer can show a direct connection between the job and Adam's medical history. Medical histories are a legitimate area of investigation only when a job requires definable physical strength or skills.

The manager who interviewed Wendy said he would hire her only on an at-will basis. What does this mean?

An at-will agreement means that the employer-employee relationship may be terminated at the will of the employer for any reason, at any time; it usually applies when there is no written job contract. Today, however, there are a number of federal and state laws that restrict an employer's right to dismiss at-will employees. These laws forbid dismissals because of race, color, religion, sex, or national origin. Nor may employees be fired in retaliation for reporting safety violations, for taking time off for jury duty, or for having just one garnishment against their pay.

I was promised a job at a specified wage and starting time. When I went to work on the agreed-upon date, they told me the job had been filled by someone else. Do I have any legal recourse?

Possibly. If you and the employer had signed a contract that contained a clause specifying the date you were to start working for him, you could sue the employer for breaking the contract. If there was no written agreement, however, a legal solution to your problem becomes more difficult. You may be able to sue the employer if you relied on his promises and quit another job.

Can I be denied a job for which I am qualified if I refuse to be photographed and fingerprinted?

In most states, yes. Only some states restrict the use of photographs and fingerprints. Colorado does not allow employers to photograph job applicants before hiring them, while New York generally prohibits fingerprinting both applicants and employees. California law allows employers to fingerprint and photograph individuals once they have been hired. As a practical matter, however, employers do not usually ask applicants for photographs before hiring them, because photographs can be used as evidence if an unsuccessful job applicant brings a lawsuit for racial or sex discrimination.

George applied for a job and was told he would be hired if he took a lie detector test. Must George take this test?

Probably not. In 1988 Congress enacted the Employee Polygraph Protection Act to restrict the use of so-called "lie detector" tests by employers. Under the terms of this law, most employers are now prohibited from requiring that job applicants submit to polygraph tests. The use of voice stress tests and psychological stress testing devices is also prohibited.

An employer who violates the provisions of the act can be subject to a penalty of up to $10,000 for each violation. In addition, the act allows the affected job applicant to sue the employer for civil damages.

What are my rights if an employer wants to give me a psychological test as part of the application process?

Under the Employee Polygraph Protection Act, most employers are prohibited from requiring job applicants to submit to psychological stress testing. These tests have been outlawed because they often have no relation to the job applied for, and because evaluations of the test results were often incorrect or subject to different interpretations. However, employers may legally test potential employees' ability to meet legitimate job requirements, so long as the tests are not used to eliminate applicants on the basis of race, color, religion, sex, age, or national origin.

When my daughter applied for a job, the receptionist handed her an application that asked if she had ever been arrested or convicted, and if the answer was yes, to supply details. Does a potential employer have the right to ask about such matters?

Questions about convictions can be asked if there might be a connection between the job's responsibility and a crime. For example, an employer would be justified in finding out if someone applying for a job as an accountant had ever been convicted of embezzlement; and the employer would be within his rights in rejecting an applicant if there had been such a conviction. An employer may also ask about arrests, but can be sued if an applicant is turned down for this reason, since an arrest does not always mean that the person was convicted. Some states, including Connecticut, Massachusetts, Minnesota, New York, and Rhode Island, prohibit or restrict requests for arrest information.

Belinda has always wanted to work for the federal government. Are there special requirements for a civil service position?

Yes. Belinda will be given a numerical rating based on her education, training, experience, and written test score, if a test is required. When a position opens up in a federal government agency, the names of those interested in the job are given to that agency in the order of their numerical ratings.

When I took a civil service test, the examiner told me that extra points would have been added if I had had military service. I am upset that someone with military service could be given a higher score this way and get a job for which I might be more qualified. Why is this practice allowed?

Congress enacted the GI Bill of Rights and the Veterans' Preference Act in 1944 to help World War II veterans readjust to civilian life and to compensate for their loss of educational or vocational experience. The benefits to veterans include preferred status when applying for a civil service job, job training assistance (including up to four years of college education), job placement services, and career counseling. These benefits have since been extended to veterans of the Korean and Vietnam wars and other military campaigns and to anyone who becomes disabled as a result of military service.

Victor received a dishonorable discharge from the army. Can he still get veterans' preference if he applies for a civil service job?

No. Anyone with a dishonorable discharge from military service is not eligible for veterans' preference.

Seth's interview at the Grand Old Insurance Company was arranged by an employment agency. He didn't get the job at the time, but five months later the insurance company offered him the position. Must Seth pay the agency's fee?

Yes. The agreement Seth signed with the agency probably states that he must pay the agency its fee if he obtains a job within one year. Even if the agreement does not contain such a provision, an agency is usually entitled to payment for its services if its efforts directly or indirectly result in a client's being hired.

Lester accepted a job through an employment agency, but before he started he was offered a better job at another company. Does he have to pay the agency its fee if he takes the better job?

Yes. Once the agency fulfills its obligation by finding a job that the client accepts, it is entitled to payment.

I found a job through an employment agency but was fired two weeks later. Do I have to pay the rest of the agency fee?

Most agency agreements call for payment of the full fee as soon you accept a job. However, some contracts may allow the fee to be reduced if you are fired. State law may also limit your obligation to pay. For example, in Pennsylvania an employment agency can collect only a percentage of the fee if the client loses the job within 10 weeks of being hired.

On the Job

Can my job description be changed without my approval?

Yes, unless the change is so drastic that it creates a totally different job. Job descriptions often include a general statement that says an employee must "perform any other tasks as may be assigned," which allows employers to revise job duties as the needs of the business change.

My supervisor and I disagreed about my job performance, and I'm sure she put negative reports in my personnel file. Do I have a right to see these reports?

A number of states, including California, Connecticut, Illinois, Maine, Michigan, Oregon, Pennsylvania, and Wisconsin, have passed laws that allow an employee access to his personnel file. However, not all of these states permit an employee to copy the file or to include a written statement in it. Connecticut, Illinois, Michigan, and Wisconsin are among the states that allow you to contest information contained in your file. If you don't agree with what's in the file, you may add a signed statement of your version of the facts. This becomes a permanent part of your file. Federal employees have the right to read and make copies of their files, and to challenge information that they contain.

Sydney worked for Harold during the day as a carpenter, and at night he worked as a clerk at a convenience store. When Harold learned about this, he demanded that Sydney quit his second job. Does Sydney have to submit to this demand?

The general rule is that an employee may spend his off-duty hours any way he wants to, including working at a second job. However, if Sydney's second job is adversely affecting his performance on his first job, he might have a problem. For example, if Sydney is making costly mistakes, taking unnecessary safety risks, or otherwise jeopardizing the quality of his employer's work because he is overtired, Harold has the right to ask Sydney to quit the second job.

Can my employer legally forbid me to moonlight for a competitor?

Yes. Every employee has a legal duty to promote his employer's best interests, and helping a competitor is not compatible with this duty. In addition, if you and your employer agreed, when you were hired, that you would work exclusively for him, moonlighting for a competitor could be considered a breach of this agreement.

When Dorothy was promoted, her boss asked her to sign a new contract that prohibited her from working for a competitor for three years if she should quit or be fired. What will happen if she signs the new contract, and then quits a year later to join a competing company at a much better salary?

If Dorothy lives in a state that permits such a contract, she could be sued by her former employer. But before a court would prohibit Dorothy from working for a competitor, her former employer would have to prove that she knew trade secrets or other confidential information that, if imparted to competitors, would cause him substantial harm.

As manager of a local fitness center, Betty developed an aerobic training manual for new employees. She was laid off, but they are still using her manual. Can't she get some remuneration for this?

No. Betty developed the manual as part of her job, and any material prepared as a part of a person's job becomes the employer's property.

On the Job

What can I do if my boss tells me to do something illegal?

This is a difficult situation. If you follow your boss's orders, you will be guilty of committing a crime. If you don't follow your boss's orders, you run the risk of being fired. However, if you are fired, you can sue. Since you were dismissed for refusing to break the law, a court would view this action as a violation of public policy.

Barney, a school custodian, knows that his boss signs for supplies that are never delivered, and suspects his boss is getting a kickback. Can Barney lose his job if he reports this misconduct?

It depends on the state in which Barney lives. Some states, including Arizona, California, Connecticut, Massachusetts, Montana, and New Hampshire, have laws that protect whistle-blowing employees from being fired. If Barney's state doesn't have such a law, he can be fired, but he is not without legal recourse. Since it is against public policy to fire an employee for reporting illegal activities, Barney can sue to get his job back and to be compensated for being wrongfully dismissed.

When Bruce was passed over for a promotion, he filed a lawsuit against the company for age discrimination, and his attorney has asked Eric, a coworker, to testify on Bruce's behalf. Is Eric protected if he testifies against the company?

Yes. The Age Discrimination in Employment Act prohibits employers from retaliating against those who testify or assist in investigations, proceedings, or lawsuits, as well as those workers who file the charges.

Judy routinely expresses her political views to other employees and frequently distributes political literature. Her boss has ordered her to stop these activities. Is he permitted to do this?

Judy's boss can restrict Judy's political activities only if she's neglecting her job, disrupting others' work, or jeopardizing her employer's business.

Can Georgette be ordered not to smoke at her desk?

Yes. A growing number of states have enacted clean indoor air laws, including Montana, Oregon, and Utah. These laws require that public places and government offices designate areas as either "smoking" or "nonsmoking." If Georgette works for a government agency or an office open to the public, she will have to comply with the state law.

Georgette would also have to comply if her city had an ordinance restricting smoking in offices or if her employer had established reasonable rules to safeguard the health and safety of the employees. If Georgette cannot accept these rules, she may be dismissed.

Can my boss search my desk looking for stolen property?

Yes. When property has been stolen, an employer has the right to look in desks and other areas if he suspects an employee might be the thief. The search should involve only those areas where the stolen property might reasonably be found. For example, if a typewriter has been stolen, an employer cannot search a desk drawer.

Because there has been a series of recent thefts involving expensive company property, my employer hired a security guard to search

Reporting Job-Related Crimes

As you get ready to leave work one night, you notice that a coworker is putting typewriter ribbons and a package of typing paper into her tote bag. You know she never takes work home, so you suspect that the supplies are for her personal use. Do you say something to her, forget about it, or talk to someone else in your department?

This predicament is not uncommon. Taking office supplies is just one of many unlawful activities that plague businesses throughout the country. Using company property—such as copying machines—for personal purposes, falsifying time sheets or expense accounts, forging signatures, and embezzling company funds cause billions of dollars of losses to American business each year, according to the U. S. Chamber of Commerce.

Since it is impossible, and undesirable, for employers to monitor each employee's actions, they must rely on coworkers to report thefts and other business crimes. Most companies have established procedures for reporting theft or misconduct. Find out what steps you should take if you know about illegal activities in your company. If your company does not have a reporting procedure, talk to your supervisor or boss. You must let someone in a supervisory or management position know about what you have observed or risk disciplinary measures yourself for not reporting the illegal activity. This is not just a matter of personal choice—courts have ruled that employees who fail to report a job-related crime may be fired.

employees' packages and purses as they leave the building. Can I be fired if I refuse to let the guard search my purse?

Yes. Your employer has the right to combat the thefts by searching your possessions, and to dismiss you if you refuse. However, the search must be conducted in a reasonable manner. If employees are detained for too long, or the search is conducted in the presence of customers or outsiders, you could refuse to submit to the search and would have a good case against your employer if you were discharged.

Patricia was working at a department store and was asked by her manager to take a lie detector test to see if she knew anything about some recent thefts. Does she have to take the test? What happens if she refuses to take it?

Generally, under the federal Employee Polygraph Protection Act, employees may only be asked to take a polygraph test as part of an ongoing investigation of economic loss suffered by the employer, such as theft or embezzlement. Only employees who would have access to the missing property may be tested. The store must show that it has a reasonable suspicion that Patricia is involved in the thefts, and she must be given at least 48 hours prior notice. Patricia should consult with an attorney familiar with employment law before agreeing to be tested.

Can my employer require that I submit to a drug test?

Yes, if the test relates to your ability to do the job or if the safety of coworkers or the public is involved, as is the case with airline pilots and bus drivers. Before conducting a drug test an employer must (1) have a reasonable suspicion of drug use; (2) give notice that testing will be carried out as part of company policy; and (3) keep the information about who is tested and the test results confidential. If you belong to a union, this issue may have been negotiated with your employer as part of the union contract.

If my car is vandalized in the company parking lot, is my employer responsible for the repair bill?

Usually, no. However, if your employer has provided specific security measures, such as guards or locked gates, or if you are required to give your car keys to a parking attendant, the employer will have to assume some responsibility for damage to your car.

Andy wants to start his new job as soon as possible. Does he have to give his current employer a certain number of days' notice?

There is no general rule about when Andy must tell his employer he is leaving. If Andy signed a contract when he was hired, it may specify how far in advance he must notify the company.

Pay and Benefits

For information on employee medical insurance, see "Health and Disability Insurance" in Chapter 8, *Insurance*. For pensions, see "Pension Plans" in Chapter 15, *Pensions, IRA's, Social Security*.

If I am hired as a salaried employee, can the company convert my status to that of an hourly employee without my consent?

If you have a written contract, your employer cannot change your method of compensation without your approval. To do so would be a breach of contract. If you don't have a contract, your employer could change the way you are compensated, but if you lose fringe benefits, such as pension plan eligibility, you may have legal grounds to challenge this action.

Vivian works for JKL Foods, a company that sells frozen pizza. She makes $2.50 an hour. Doesn't the company have to pay the federal minimum wage?

Not necessarily. JKL Foods is required to pay the federal minimum wage if its business involves interstate commerce (if any product involved in making or selling the pizza crosses state lines). However, if she is a trainee, apprentice, or full-time student, she may be paid less than the minimum wage. To be allowed to do this, JKL Foods must get permission from the Wage and Hour Division of the U. S. Department of Labor. If Vivian should have been paid the minimum wage and hasn't been, she can sue JKL for twice the amount they owe her plus court costs and attorney fees. If JKL Foods is not engaged in interstate commerce, the company must meet state standards for minimum pay.

When Monica applied for a job as a manicurist, the manager of the shop said her pay would be at the minimum wage rate reduced by the amount of money she receives in tips. Is her employer allowed to do this?

Yes, but federal law limits how much Monica's boss can deduct from her wages for tips. First, Monica must regularly make more than $30 per month in tips before her employer can reduce her pay. Second, the deduction for tips cannot be more than 40 percent of what she would earn under the minimum wage. Monica should also check with the state department of labor to see if her state's laws give her any additional protection in this area.

I thought everyone who worked more than the normal hours got overtime pay. My new employer tells me he doesn't pay overtime. Is this legal?

It depends on the type of work you do. The federal Fair Labor Standards Act, which regulates overtime pay, exempts many categories of workers from overtime coverage, including those in executive, administrative, or management positions; professionals, including teachers; salespeople who work off premises; most farm workers; workers in firms employing fewer than 15 people; and employees of small retail or service businesses whose transactions are all within one state.

If you are not guaranteed overtime pay under federal law, you may still qualify for it under state law. Check with your state department of labor, or whatever agency is responsible for monitoring wages in your state. Their offices should be listed in the telephone directory under state government offices.

Can I be forced to work overtime?

Yes, but if overtime pay is guaranteed for the type of work you do, your employer must pay 1½ times your hourly wage (or 1½ times your hourly rate computed from a weekly, monthly, or annual salary). However, some federal and state laws and labor contracts set a maximum number of hours that you can put in during a week in certain jobs, including those of airline pilots, fire fighters, and police officers. Your state department of labor can tell you what the law is in your state. If you are a union member, your union representative should have this information.

Carolyn works as a seamstress and is paid by the number of garments she sews. For the last month, Carolyn has been putting in 45 to 55 hours each week to fulfill an order. The supervisor refuses to pay her overtime; he says it isn't required, since she is paid by the garment. Is he right?

No. Carolyn is entitled to overtime pay for the hours that she worked in excess of 40 hours a week. Piece-rate workers are covered by the overtime provisions of the federal Fair Labor Standards Act. Carolyn's employer must first determine her hourly rate by dividing the pay she receives for the pieces she completes in a typical week by the number of hours she works to complete those pieces. He must then multiply this hourly rate by 1½ to get Carolyn's overtime rate. Let's assume Carolyn typically worked 50 hours and received $200. Her hourly rate would then be $4 ($200 divided by 50 hours), and her overtime rate would be $6 (1½ times $4). Since Carolyn worked 10 hours overtime, she should get $60 overtime pay and $160 regular pay ($4 times 40 hours) for a total of $220 for the 50-hour week.

Troy works for a company that has a standard workweek of 37½ hours. He worked 45 hours last week. When he got his paycheck, it showed only 5 hours of overtime pay. Shouldn't Troy be paid for 7½ hours of overtime?

No, unless his contract or state law specifically says so. Under federal law, overtime is only paid for time worked in excess of 40 hours per week. Although Troy's standard workweek is 37½ hours, federal law requires his employer to pay overtime only for the 5 additional hours he worked.

Valerie's boss asked her to work late several evenings in a row, and mumbled something about comp time. What is comp time?

Federal law permits Valerie's employer to give her compensatory time off rather than pay her overtime, if this comp time is granted during the same pay period in which Valerie worked overtime. Comp time is calculated at the same 1½ rate as overtime pay. If Valerie worked 8 hours overtime, she would be entitled to 12 hours off as compensatory time.

What can I do if my employer doesn't give me my pay?

You should try to get help from your state department of labor or employment or from a similar agency. Most states require that wages be paid at regular intervals, such as every two weeks or once a month, regardless of how your wages are calculated—by the hour, by piecework, or on an annual basis.

The company Hennessey worked for went out of business without paying him for work he had done. What can he do?

He has the right to sue for any wages due him. If his employer has declared bankruptcy, Hennessey is protected under federal bankruptcy law. Wages earned within 90 days of the employer's closing of the business, up to a total of $2,000, are given priority status. This means that Hennessey will be paid ahead of some other creditors when the bankrupt business's assets are distributed. Hennessey can also get help from such government agencies as the Wage and Hour Division of the U. S. Department of Labor and his state labor or employment department.

Elmer works as an assistant manager for a department store that has eight locations across the state. His salary is lower than that of a woman who holds the same position at one of the store's other locations. Doesn't the store have to pay all its assistant managers the same salary?

Not necessarily. Different salaries may be justified because of differences in living costs or the competition for qualified people in different locations. Federal law also allows different wages to be paid to employees of different sexes if the wages are based on a seniority system, on a merit system, or on quantity or quality of production.

When I was hired, the company promised it would give me a raise after six months. Seven months have passed, and the raise hasn't materialized. Doesn't the company have to keep its promise?

Yes, unless the increase in pay was dependent on your doing satisfactory work. If you received a poor evaluation, the company is not required to raise your salary.

Bonnie dropped and broke a computer terminal while moving it from one desk to another. Can her employer dock her pay to cover the cost of repairing or replacing the terminal?

Yes, but the amount deducted cannot reduce Bonnie's pay below the federal minimum wage. State laws also outline what deductions can be made. For example, Wisconsin law requires that deductions for property damage are allowable only when the employee has agreed to the deduction in writing, or a court has found the employee liable, or the employer and a representative, chosen by the employee, agree that the employee is responsible for the damage.

Stuart got a part-time job at a gas station. At the end of Stuart's shift one night, his boss informed him that $100 was missing from

Part-time Workers' Benefits

Anyone considering part-time work should be aware that wages, fringe benefits, and other employee prerogatives may not be the same as those of a full-time job. Although part-time workers are protected by the same antidiscrimination laws and receive the same workers' compensation coverage as full-time employees, there are a number of areas in which they can be treated differently, including the following:

- *Wages*—State minimum wage laws do not always cover part-time employees. Some state laws exclude work "at irregular times" from minimum wage coverage. As a general rule, time spent at work on a regular basis, such as every other afternoon, is covered by minimum wage laws. The federal minimum wage law generally covers part-time employees who would qualify for coverage if they were working full-time.
- *Group health insurance*—Part-time workers may be excluded from coverage. Many company policies only cover employees who work a specified minimum number of hours each week.
- *Pensions*—Coverage will depend on the number of hours worked each year as specified in the company's retirement plan.
- *Unemployment benefits*—If a person does not work the minimum time set by his state, he may not qualify for unemployment benefits.

the cash register. The boss said that he would dock Stuart's pay $100. Is it legal for Stuart's employer to do this?

Yes. Stuart's pay can be docked as long as this doesn't bring his pay below the minimum wage rate. But different states have different laws about docking an employee's pay. In California, for example, an employer must have proof that the loss was due to the employee's dishonesty or gross negligence. In Hawaii, Stuart's pay couldn't be docked unless he was the only employee with access to the cash register and he was regularly required to give an accounting of the money in the register at the beginning and end of his shift.

Doesn't a company have to give the same benefits to everyone?

Some fringe benefits, such as pension plans, group life insurance, and accident and health insurance, must be offered to every employee to comply with federal and state laws. But other benefits, such as company cars and expense accounts, do not have to be offered to all employees. However, no company may offer a benefit on the basis of race, color, religion, sex, age, or national origin.

Pay and Benefits

I'm entitled to two weeks' vacation, but my boss says he can't spare me. It's been a year now, and I really need a break. Doesn't he have to let me go?

If there is no urgent business reason why you can't be spared, your boss should grant the vacation. On the other hand, if he has a good reason for not giving you time off when you want it, you can't leave without risking being dismissed. You may have to make a formal, written request or invoke seniority to get the vacation dates you want.

When Paula resigned from her job, she had accumulated 30 hours of unused sick leave and 40 hours of vacation time. Her employer would not pay her for these days. Is this legal?

Yes. Employers are generally not required to reimburse employees for unused fringe benefits such as holidays, sick leave, or vacation hours. There would have to be a written company policy about paying for this time, or it would have to be covered in an employment or union contract.

I injured my back while lifting a crate at work, and my doctor advised me to rest in bed. The company has a group disability insurance policy that protects employees' pay while they're out sick, but they said I wasn't eligible, and now I have no income. What can I do?

Since your injury occurred while you were doing your job, you should apply for workers' compensation. It is not unusual for an employer's group insurance policy to exclude work-related accidents or illnesses, since these are covered by workers' compensation programs.

Does Danielle have a right to her old job when she returns from maternity leave?

Yes. Companies with 15 or more employees must comply with the federal Pregnancy Discrimination Act and treat pregnancy as they would any other disability. If Danielle's coworkers have had their jobs held open when they were disabled for other medical reasons, Danielle's job must be held open for her until after her baby is born. Many states also have laws protecting the jobs of pregnant workers. The U. S. Supreme Court upheld a California law requiring employers to provide up to four months' disability leave for pregnant workers and to reinstate those workers in the same jobs if possible.

My neighbor was told that her three-month maternity leave would be without pay. Complications developed, and she was absent one week longer than anticipated. Should her employer's health plan pay sick leave benefits for this one-week period?

Yes. Illness and disability caused by pregnancy and childbirth must be treated like any other illness. If the company health plan covers paid sick leave for workers who develop complications from other illnesses, your neighbor must receive the same benefits.

Workers' Compensation

Dennis was injured the second day he was on the job. Is he covered by workers' compensation?

Yes. The fact that Dennis was on the job only two days does not affect his ability to receive benefits. His right to workers' compensation began when he was hired. However, not all workers are entitled to workers' compensation. Usually, farm and household workers are exempt from coverage, as are workers of a company with fewer than the minimum number of employees specified in the state's workers' compensation law.

Can I get reimbursed for my medical expenses and lost wages if I'm injured on the job?

You should notify your employer immediately that you were injured on the job. In some states, the notice must be in writing, while in other states, you can simply tell your employer about the injury. Your employer will then submit a claim to the appropriate agency in your state. The benefits under workers' compensation consist of (1) medical benefits, including payment for doctor and hospital bills, recuperative aids such as crutches, medication, and other necessary treatment; and (2) disability benefits, which compensate workers for lost earnings. The amount of the disability benefit is based on several factors: the extent of the injury (partial or total), how long the worker will be disabled (temporarily or permanently), and how much he would be earning if he were not disabled.

Norman was injured while working at an auto repair shop. His employer has made a workers' compensation claim. Can Norman also sue his employer for his injuries?

Probably not. Workers' compensation is generally recognized as the only remedy available to injured workers. However, some states permit an employee to sue the employer even though workers' compensation benefits are being paid if the injury was caused by a deliberate violation of a safety standard or the employer concealed hazardous or dangerous working conditions.

Woody aggravated an old back injury by lifting some heavy cartons and needed three weeks to recover. Will workers' compensation cover him even though he had a previous injury?

Yes. Although Woody's disability is due to a preexisting condition, it will not automatically disqualify him from benefits. But Woody would have to prove through expert medical testimony that lifting the file cartons aggravated the previous injury.

Can a worker who suffers a nervous breakdown because of job-related stress collect workers' compensation?

Some states won't allow it, but many others do—including Louisiana, Massachusetts, Michigan, Oregon, Pennsylvania, and Wyoming. But to collect compensation for a nervous breakdown in these states, an employee must establish, by expert medical testimony, that the breakdown was caused by extraordinary or unusual work-related stress. Ordinary job stress affecting all employees of the company is not enough.

Debbie volunteered to go to the bakery shop and buy coffee and rolls on her break because she also wanted to pick up a few items to take home. She was injured on the way. Is she covered by workers' compensation?

Probably. An employee's eligibility for workers' compensation is determined, in part, by whether the injury "arises out of and in the course of" employment. Since Debbie did go to the store on behalf of her employer, as well as for personal reasons, a court would probably give weight to the business reason for her trip and allow her to receive workers' compensation benefits.

I broke my finger at the company softball game. Will workers' compensation pay for the medical bills?

Many states would cover your injury if you were compelled, pressured, or strongly encouraged to take part in the game, or if the employer derived some benefit from it. Some courts have decided that activities such as company softball games improve employer-employee relations, and these courts would be likely to approve a workers' compensation claim. Other courts have denied benefits because improved employer-employee relations is too vague and speculative a concept.

Hilda was injured as the result of a coworker's prank. Is she eligible to collect workers' compensation?

Possibly. For many years, workers' compensation did not cover injuries caused by pranks or practical jokes, because they were considered an unauthorized activity. The trend now is to look at the facts of each case. For example, Hilda may be awarded benefits if she did not participate in the prank, but was attending to her duties at the time she was injured. Or she may receive compensation if her employer knew that his employees were engaging in horseplay or pranks and took no steps to discourage or prevent this activity.

Greg slipped on the ice around the gas pump one December night and broke his leg. When his boss heard that Greg had filed a workers' compensation claim, he fired Greg, stating, "Nobody is going to collect any money from me for getting hurt on my time!" Isn't it against the law for Greg's employer to fire him in this way?

This firing would be illegal in some states, including Alabama, Kentucky, Maine, and Oregon, where workers' compensation laws prohibit discrimination against employees who file claims. If Greg lived in one of these states he might be reinstated in his job, and he might receive back pay and other benefits, plus reimbursement for his legal fees.

In a few of the states that do not have antidiscrimination provisions in their workers' compensation laws, courts have rejected an employee's claim for being fired in situations similar to Greg's. These courts recognize no exceptions to the doctrine that an employee without a contract can be discharged at any time for any reason.

Two employees had an argument over an assignment and got into a fist fight. Both of them landed in the hospital. Is either one of them covered by workers' compensation?

Compensation would probably be awarded to both employees, regardless of who started the fight. At one time, the aggressor would have been denied benefits, but the trend now is to disregard who threw the first punch. However, if it turns out that the underlying reason for this fight was personal, the benefits will probably be denied.

Workers' Compensation

Barry was injured on the job and missed several months' work. When he returned, he was supposed to be given a light-duty assignment. He wasn't, and he was fired because he was unable to do the work. Can Barry still collect workers' compensation?

Yes. In order to persuade a court that Barry has lost his eligibility for workers' compensation, his employer or insurance company would have to prove not only that a job was offered to Barry, but that he was able to do the job in his weakened condition. Since Barry was unable to do the work, he is still entitled to receive workers' compensation benefits.

How long is a person entitled to receive workers' compensation?

It depends on what state the worker was injured in. Payments are usually made weekly, and either continue for the number of weeks specified in the state law or, in the case of a permanent disability, until a maximum amount, such as $100,000, is reached.

Can an employee receive both disability insurance payments and workers' compensation at the same time?

Yes. Benefits from other sources, such as pensions and disability insurance, usually do not prevent the payment of workers' compensation benefits, nor do they reduce these benefits. Social Security disability payments are an exception, however. Under federal Social Security law, a person may receive Social Security disability and workers' compensation payments at the same time—but the Social Security disability amount will be reduced according to a formula that takes into consideration the workers' compensation benefits.

Unions and Strikes

There is going to be a union election at my plant next week. If the union wins, will I have to become a member?

It depends on the type of agreement the union works out with your employer. Under a *union shop agreement*, employees must join the union and remain as members as long as the agreement is in effect. If an *agency shop* is established, you do not have to join the union, but you may be required to pay fees to the union for the benefits you receive—such as a higher pay scale—as a result of its efforts.

Our company is not unionized. If I circulate a petition among my fellow employees suggesting that we choose a union to represent us, can I be fired?

No. Your employer cannot use any kind of pressure, such as firing you or other pro-union employees, to discourage you from affiliating with a union. You and your fellow workers have the right to circulate petitions and to meet with coworkers about unionizing without fear of retaliation.

Hank applied for a job at a union shop. Does he have to join the union if he accepts the job?

Yes. If union shops are legal in his state, Hank will have to join the union after being on the job for a certain length of time, usually 30 days. However, about half the states, including Alabama, Georgia, Iowa, Kansas, Nebraska, South Carolina, and Wyoming, have right-to-work laws prohibiting union shops.

I'm getting a lot of pressure, including phone calls at home, to join a union I don't want to belong to. What should I do?

You should consider filing a complaint with the National Labor Relations Board. The decision to join a union should be made without any force, intimidation, or pressure of any kind. The National Labor Relations Act prohibits unions from using these tactics to increase membership.

Our factory is becoming automated, and many of us will be losing our jobs. Will our union be responsible for seeing that we are retrained for other jobs?

Your employer, not the union, will probably be responsible for retraining workers, since it was management's decision to automate that created the loss of jobs. A federal law, the Worker Adjustment and Retraining Notification Act, may also apply to the layoffs at your plant. Your union representative can provide more details.

Janet felt her employer treated her unfairly in a disciplinary matter. Will the union help her, even if she never joined?

Yes. When a union is authorized to represent a group of employees, it must represent all employees, even if someone in that group is not a member of the union. Failure to do so is an unfair labor practice. Janet should contact the union representative for help in handling her problem.

Unions and Strikes

Lauren was fined by her union. Is she required to pay the fine?

Yes, as long as certain procedures were followed. Union members have the right to a fair review of their problems whenever they face discipline by the union. Lauren should have been given a written notice of the charges against her; a reasonable amount of time to prepare her defense; and a fair hearing before a panel of union members or officials. She does not have to pay the fine if any of these procedures were not followed.

Do I have to observe a picket line if I'm not a union member?

No. Both nonunion and union members may cross a picket line and continue working if a strike has been called. However, union members can be fined if they work during a lawful, union-authorized strike.

If I am a union member and I am fired by my company, what does the union have to do for me?

The union must first conduct an investigation to ascertain why you were fired and whether the proper dismissal procedures were followed, and

If You Go on Strike

The rights of workers who go on strike are protected under federal and state laws, provided the strike is a legal one. Illegal strikes—such as sit-downs, wildcat strikes (ones not authorized by a union), or strikes that violate a no-strike clause in a union contract—result in the loss of all protection under labor laws for the strikers. The points below illustrate some of the general principles governing the rights of workers and employers during a legal strike:

- *Wages and unemployment compensation*—You are not entitled to wages for the time you are out on strike or to unemployment compensation (except in some states, such as New York and Rhode Island, where strikers may apply for unemployment benefits). However, you may be paid some money by your union to replace lost income.
- *Picketing*—Picketing is allowed if it is done by small groups of strikers; mass picketing is illegal. Picketing must be peaceful and must not continue for more than 30 days unless a petition for a longer period has been filed with the National Labor Relations Board. If you are a union member, you have a duty to honor the picket line during a lawful strike; if

then set in motion a grievance procedure for challenging your dismissal. If the union fails to handle the matter properly, you could sue it for violating its collective bargaining agreement.

Can a union get new benefits and provide them to the active members but withhold them from retirees?

Yes. There is no legal requirement for active members and retirees to receive the same benefits. Whenever negotiations take place, the union has a duty to represent all members fairly. But this does not mean that equal benefits must be obtained for each member. Unions often make concessions that affect a few members in exchange for benefits that apply to a majority. However, the union may not bargain away pension benefits that have already been vested or guaranteed to their members.

If the union orders a slowdown, must I comply?

No. Union members have a right to strike, but they do not have a right to organize or participate in a slowdown. A strike is defined as a complete work stoppage. Anything less than a full strike is illegal. Union members who participate in work slowdowns are not protected by labor laws, and they may be fired.

you cross the picket line, you can be fined by the union or subject to some other disciplinary action.

- *Violence*—Strikers are prohibited from blocking the entrance to a plant, destroying property, or threatening employees, the public, or management. If property is damaged or destroyed during a strike, the individuals involved, and the union, may be held liable. The union may also discipline or expel members who take part in violent activity.
- *Discrimination*—An employer is prohibited from discriminating against employees while they are lawfully out on strike or after they have returned to work.
- *Reinstatement*—If the strike was called to protest unfair labor practices, such as intimidating workers, the strikers are entitled to be reinstated in their jobs, even if the employer has already hired replacements. Those hired to fill the vacancies must be dismissed. If the strike was called for economic reasons, such as higher pay, strikers are not entitled to have their jobs back. However, the employer is required to put their names on a preferential hiring list for future jobs. Many union contracts require the employer to dismiss replacement workers and rehire strikers, regardless of the reason for the strike.

Unions and Strikes

What happens if a judge orders strikers back to work, and the union votes not to go?

Defying a court order or an injunction to return to work can result in contempt of court charges and fines against the union. Injunctions are often issued to stop illegal strikes, or those that threaten the health or safety of the public, such as strikes by the police.

Job Discrimination

For more information on discrimination, see "Equality Under the Law" in Chapter 12, *Your Individual Rights.*

Hundreds of people showed up to take the employment test at a local manufacturing plant. Cathy and 10 of her women friends failed the test; all but one of her male friends passed. Cathy wonders if the test is biased against women in some way. What would she need to do to prove bias?

Cathy will have to prove that the test was designed to exclude substantially more women than men. Since hundreds of people took the exam, Cathy needs to find out what the failure rate of all the women was in comparison to the failure rate of all the men, rather than just how her friends did on the exam. She will also need to find out why the employer required the test and how the scores were used in selecting employees. She may have to get a court order to make the employer provide this information.

Sarah learned that the new man hired in her department makes as much as she does. Their responsibilities are the same, but Sarah has three years' seniority. Is this discrimination?

Possibly, but the equal pay of the new man does not automatically mean that Sarah is a victim of sex discrimination. Employers consider many factors in deciding how much to pay their employees. The new man in Sarah's department may have more experience, training, or education.

I am the only woman in the packing department of my company, and I am sure my salary is lower than that of my coworkers. Whom should I call? If I report it, will the company know?

The agency that you should contact depends on whether your employer must comply with federal or state laws regarding equal pay and sex discrimination. If your employer has 15 or more employees, he must comply with federal laws. Contact the nearest office of the federal Equal Employment Opportunity Commission or the Wage and Hour Division of the U. S. Department of Labor. If he has less than 15 employees, state laws apply. Contact your state department of labor, department of employment, or wage and hour office. In many cases, you have the right to have your name withheld from your employer if you make a complaint, but you must make a specific request that this be done.

Evelyn's allegation of unequal pay for equal jobs is currently being investigated by the Equal Employment Opportunity Commission. If Evelyn wins her case, how much back pay could she expect to receive?

Evelyn could receive back pay for up to two years before the time she filed the complaint with the Equal Employment Opportunity Commission. An additional amount, called liquidated damages, may also be awarded. This compensation could equal the back pay she receives.

I notified the Equal Employment Opportunity Commission of possible discrimination almost two years ago. Should I wait to learn what they determine before filing a lawsuit?

No. You should not wait for the commission to finish its investigation, because there are deadlines you must meet if you want to file your own lawsuit. You should contact the Equal Employment Opportunity Commission for a status report of its investigation, request a right-to-sue letter, and proceed with your lawsuit as soon as possible. You must have a right-to-sue letter before you can begin your own legal action, and you have 90 days to file your lawsuit after receiving the letter.

Several promotions have opened up during the six years Jackie has worked in the shipping department, but Jackie's boss has consistently refused to recommend her for any of them, claiming that she would not like supervising 20 men. Jackie disagrees. What are her options?

If Jackie's company has a grievance procedure (either union-run or company-run), she should comply with it to try to resolve her problem. If there is no grievance procedure, Jackie should take her problem to the company's personnel department or to her boss's supervisor. She should prepare a written statement of her complaint, and should follow up her conversations with management with memos about what those conversations covered. She should also keep an accurate record of the key events in the case, the dates they took place, and the names of witnesses. This documentation will be important if a sex-discrimination claim is made.

If Jackie's efforts within the company do not produce satisfactory results, she should consider taking her case to the Equal Employment Opportunity Commission or to the agency in her state that handles sex-discrimination claims. She should also consider retaining a lawyer who specializes in these matters to help her, as this kind of case can sometimes become very complicated.

My company won't add a separate locker room for women only. Isn't this illegal?

A company must have appropriate facilities available for both men and women. But your company does not have to build a separate facility—it could divide the existing facility in two or establish separate hours for men and women. However, your employer cannot use the lack of separate facilities as a reason for not hiring women. Some have tried to do this, but courts have rejected this argument.

I was passed over for promotion to division supervisor 2½ years ago. I was pretty sure the decision was influenced by my age, but it has taken me all this time to assemble the facts. Is it too late to do something about it?

Almost. You had 180 days to file an age-discrimination complaint with the Equal Employment Opportunity Commission, or 300 days if you live in a state with its own age-discrimination law. This 180- or 300-day filing period started the day you were informed that you would not get the promotion. Although you have missed the deadlines for filing a complaint with the Equal Employment Opportunity Commission, you may still be able to file your own civil lawsuit against the company. If you are alleging that your employer willfully violated the federal Age Discrimination in Employment Act, you have three years to begin your lawsuit.

Can I be forced to retire at age 62?

Usually not. Under the federal Age Discrimination in Employment Act, employers with more than 20 employees cannot set a mandatory retirement age, but exceptions can be made when age is a bona fide qualification for the job. If the Age Discrimination in Employment Act does not apply to the company in question, an employee may still be protected by state legislation prohibiting mandatory retirement.

Francine's religion requires her to observe the Sabbath on Saturdays. Can she be fired for refusing to work on Saturday?

No. The law requires Francine's boss to make reasonable accommodations for her religious practices. This includes finding someone else to trade shifts with her and letting her work longer hours on other days. If he did not take these steps before firing her, the charge of religious discrimination is justified. However, Francine's employer may successfully defend himself by claiming that it would be an undue hardship on the business to accommodate her religious practices.

Am I being discriminated against if I have to use up a vacation day to observe a religious holiday?

No. The law requires an employer to make reasonable accommodations to allow employees to practice their religion. However, if your employer can establish that rearranging schedules, changing payroll records, and finding other employees to perform your job would create an undue hardship, you may have to use vacation time to observe this holiday.

Sexual Harassment

My supervisor repeatedly makes lewd comments and uses foul language, which I find offensive. What can I do to make him stop?

Your first step is to tell your supervisor that his comments and language make you uncomfortable, and that if he continues, you will discuss the matter with his boss. If this first step fails, you may file a complaint or sue for sex discrimination. Unwelcome verbal or physical contact that is sexual in nature and creates an offensive, intimidating, or hostile work environment constitutes sexual harassment, which is against the law.

One of Nancy's male coworkers often makes sexually suggestive remarks when he comes to her desk. She reported this to her employer, but he refuses to do anything. What can Nancy do?

If the company employs more than 15 people, Nancy's employer is bound by the federal discrimination laws, and Nancy could file a complaint with the Equal Employment Opportunity Commission. Since Nancy informed her employer of the problem and nothing was done, Nancy's employer could face charges that he violated federal sex-discrimination laws. If Nancy's company employs fewer than 15 people, Nancy may be able to file charges under her state discrimination laws or her union contract if there is one.

Sexual Harassment

When no one else was around, Holly's boss told her that she had to have sexual relations with him if she expected to get ahead in the company. She refused, but now she is worried that she'll be fired, since there were no witnesses. What should she do?

Holly should immediately write a detailed account of her boss's conduct and statements so she will have some documentation of the incident. Demanding sexual favors in exchange for a promotion, raise, or other type of job benefit is a violation of federal and state sex-discrimination laws. If Holly is fired or denied a promotion or other job benefit, or if her boss continues his demands, she should seek legal advice.

My supervisor has been pressuring me to go out with her, but I have refused. I want to keep my job but don't want to put up with any more harassment. What should I do?

You should write down every comment and action of your supervisor's. This will help you later if you need to file charges against her or your employer. Your next step is to discuss the situation with your personnel manager or follow established grievance procedures, if your company has them. Although you want to keep your job, you may choose to resign if the situation becomes intolerable. You may then file a complaint with the Equal Employment Opportunity Commission (or, if the company employs fewer than 15 employees, with the state agency that handles sex-discrimination cases), alleging that you have been constructively discharged. This means that although you quit, your supervisor really forced you out. If the EEOC upholds your complaint, it may order that you be reinstated in your job and be allowed to collect back pay. It may also issue an injunction against the company prohibiting further harassment.

Hazardous Work Conditions

Frances works in a warehouse with 100 other employees. Several fire exits are blocked by boxes. The company has never held a fire drill or distributed written instructions about procedures to follow in the event of a fire. How should Frances report this?

Frances should first report this safety hazard to her personnel manager or the plant safety manager, preferably through her supervisor. If she receives no response within a reasonable time, she should contact the local fire department and inform them that the fire exits are blocked. This should prompt an inspection that will solve the problem. Most cities have fire codes that require exits to be open and escape plans posted. As an alternative, she could contact the state or federal agencies responsible for occupational health and safety. The primary federal agency regulating health and safety in the workplace is the Occupational Safety and Health Administration (OSHA). The act that created this agency requires all employers to furnish a safe workplace. OSHA regulations specifically require that every fire exit be clearly visible or the route to reach it plainly marked. Fire exits must also be unobstructed.

Conditions at the plant where I work have become so unsafe that I have not reported to my work station for the last three days. Can my employer refuse to pay me for those three days when it was his fault that the place was dangerous?

No, not if the plant was really dangerous. You are protected by the regulations of the Occupational Safety and Health Administration if you walk off the job because: (1) the danger to your health or safety was serious and imminent; or (2) you notified your employer of the problem and, if time allowed, notified your nearest Occupational Safety and Health Administration office, and nothing was done. If you refused to cooperate when your employer asked for your help in eliminating the problem, offered to have you work temporarily in another area while the condition was corrected, or asked you to do your job in some other way to reduce the chances of injury, you would not be protected against loss of pay.

My husband works in a room with no windows and poor lighting, and as a result he has been getting terrible headaches. Can he sue the company for making him work under hazardous conditions?

No. The Occupational Safety and Health Act does not allow workers to sue employers for safety and health violations. Your husband would have to notify the Occupational Safety and Health Administration office in your area. This office will investigate his complaint and impose any penalties on his employer if it finds violations.

Your husband should also file a claim for workers' compensation. If it is determined that his headaches are work-related, he could be reimbursed for medical costs and for loss of income.

Warren has noticed several unsafe practices at his factory, but he is afraid to report them because of possible retaliation. Will his employer be told who filed the complaint?

No. Under the Occupational Safety and Health Act, an employee does not have to sign his name when he makes a complaint against his employer for safety violations. Even if an employee does sign his name, he can request that it be deleted from the employer's copy of the complaint as well as from any records made available by OSHA investigators.

The molding machines on the shop floor have been modified so that the safety gates don't close. The foreman says this increases output. Can I be fired if I call the government safety inspector?

No. The Occupational Safety and Health Act specifically prohibits an employer from firing, suspending, demoting, or discriminating in any way against a worker who files a complaint with an OSHA office or assists in an investigation. If your employer retaliates, contact your nearest OSHA office immediately. If proof of retaliation is found, OSHA will see that you are reinstated and that lost wages and benefits are paid to you.

If You Lose Your Job

When Allen arrived at work, his boss told him he would be out of a job at the end of the week, but he wouldn't tell Allen why. Doesn't Allen have the right to know why he's being fired?

Only if there is a specific law in the state where Allen works that requires an employer to tell an employee why he has been fired. Among the states that have such laws are Maine, Missouri, Nevada, and Texas. Allen should give his employer a letter requesting this information, since some state laws require disclosure only if the employee asks. Even though the employer may not have to tell Allen why he was dismissed, Allen may still find out if he applies for unemployment compensation. The employer is required to state the reason for termination if he disputes an employee's right to receive unemployment benefits.

My company's employee handbook states that people will be fired only for cause. If my supervisor fires me during an argument at a party, can I get my job back?

It depends on where you live. In some states, including Arizona, California, Michigan, and Oregon, you would have a good chance of sucessfully challenging your dismissal, because failure to follow company policy for dismissal outlined in employee handbooks may be grounds to appeal a supervisor's action. In a few other states, employers are required by law to deal fairly with all employees and not fire them arbitrarily.

What are my rights if I am fired for no reason?

Most workers are called at-will employees because they are hired and fired at the will of the employer. At-will employees can be fired for any reason except discrimination—or for no reason at all. However, if you have a written or union-negotiated contract, you may be able to sue your employer for breach of that contract. You may also be able to sue him if your state recognizes employee handbooks as part of an employment contract and your company has a handbook that states that employees will be fired only for cause—such as excessive absences or drinking or using illegal drugs on the job.

One July night Bert arrived for work at the restaurant wearing a flowered Hawaiian shirt, Bermuda shorts, and fluorescent orange sneakers. The owner told Bert that since he was dressed for a vacation he could take a permanent one. Can Bert be fired for the way he was dressed?

Probably. Employers generally have the right to establish dress codes for their employees as long as these codes are for a reasonable purpose and apply equally to all employees. To challenge his dismissal, Bert would have to show that the restaurant did not have a dress code that he was aware of, that the restaurant owner did not routinely fire others for inappropriate attire, or that the restaurant owner generally warned or suspended employees before firing them for inappropriate attire.

On his job application, Roger said he had a degree from a local college. He got the job and earned excellent evaluations. In a random check by the personnel department, they discovered he was not a college graduate. Can Roger be fired for cause?

If the employer has a policy of terminating all employees who are found to have made false statements on their applications, Roger is probably out of a job. Applications often contain notices indicating that any false statements will result in dismissal. The employer has a strong case if Roger's falsification related directly to job qualifications. This could be interpreted as a deliberate attempt to mislead the employer, whereas an unintentional mistake in dates of previous employment or college attendance would not be so serious.

What are Laura's rights if she is fired for being habitually late?

Habitual lateness is generally accepted as a valid cause for dismissal. However, Laura might have a good argument for reinstatement if the company had guidelines for disciplining employees, but did not follow them in her case. For example, if company policy said that being late would result in a warning, a loss of pay, suspension, and finally dismissal, and Laura had never been reprimanded, she could ask a court to order her employer to reinstate her.

My employer fired me on payday and stated that since my work was inferior, he was not going to pay me. What can I do?

You should ask the wage and hour division of your state labor department to help you get the money your employer owes you. All states require that terminated employees receive all the wages they have earned either on the day they are dismissed or on the next regular payday thereafter.

I was fired because I accidentally destroyed some of the company's computer files. What can I do?

There is not much you can do if the company has a general policy of discharging employees who damage company property. However, if other employees have had similar accidents and have not been fired, you may want to pursue legal action against the company for discrimination.

Bernie had major surgery and missed eight weeks of work. Was it legal for his boss to fire him?

Yes, the company is justified in firing Bernie if its policy is to dismiss employees who have been out sick for eight weeks, and all employees in the same situation are fired.

I was called for jury duty. My boss told me to try to get out of it, but I served anyway. When I returned to work he fired me. What can I do to get my job back?

You can sue your employer for wrongfully dismissing you. The federal Judiciary and Judicial Proceedings Act prohibits an employer from dismissing employees who serve on juries. The majority of states, including Arizona, Indiana, New Mexico, Texas, and Wisconsin, also have laws requiring employers to allow employees time off for jury duty. Even if your state does not have a statute prohibiting your dismissal, you may be able to sue on the grounds that public policy has been violated: society has a strong interest in having citizens serve on juries.

When Can You Be Fired?

In the past, employees who worked without contracts—that is, most workers—had to live with the possibility that the boss could fire them for little or no reason at any time. They had no right to challenge such firings. Today, although employers still have broad discretion in dismissing employees, their right to fire at will is being restricted by laws and court decisions. Employers should follow the company's disciplinary procedure before dismissing an employee, and they generally must be consistent in disciplining employees for the same violations. If you believe that you have been fired unjustly, you can bring the matter before a court. Below are some guidelines, based on previous court decisions, to help you decide whether or not you have a good case. Bear in mind, however, that the law in each state is different as are the circumstances of each case.

You Can Be Fired For:	You Cannot Be Fired For:
Sleeping on the job.	Unsatisfactory work unless your employer warned you that your work was inadequate and gave you guidelines about what was considered acceptable work.
Leaving early without permission.	Your race, color, religion, age, national origin, sex, or handicaps.
Failing to learn the job after considerable training has been provided.	Being pregnant.
Mistreating customers.	Taking time out for jury duty.
Permitting personalities to interfere with getting the job done.	Participating in union activities.
Using company property without getting permission.	Asserting your rights under wage and hour laws.
Falsifying attendance records.	Filing for workers' compensation.
Making negative comments about the company's policies, performance evaluations, and equal opportunity goals.	Refusing to do something illegal.
Endangering the health and safety of coworkers.	Reporting unlawful activities, such as payoffs and kickbacks.
Using sick leave to be interviewed for another job.	Reporting unsafe working conditions.
Failing to meet a sales goal.	Testifying against the company in a lawsuit.
Moonlighting in violation of company policy.	Having your wages garnisheed for the first time.

If You Lose Your Job

Can an employee be fired if he refuses to accept a transfer to a different job in another city?

Yes, if that is his employer's general practice. However, if other employees have declined transfers and have not been fired, or if the transfer is being made to retaliate against an employee who has reported a company violation to the authorities, he can sue his employer to get his job back or to be compensated for his loss. If the employee has a union contract or a company employment contract that protects him from transfers that are undesirable, or if he has an employee handbook that does so and his state makes such handbooks legally binding, he can sue his employer for breach of contract.

Can a company fire me if I'm three years away from retirement?

Only if there's a good reason. If the company is firing you in order to deprive you of your pension, however, it is violating the Employee Retirement Income Security Act (ERISA). If the company is dismissing you solely on the basis of your age, then it is violating federal or state age-discrimination laws.

Can Elaine be fired if she occasionally needs to stay home with her children?

Whether Elaine can be fired or not depends on the employer's policy on personal leave. If Elaine's employer allows other employees to stay home periodically with their children when needed, the employer would be discriminating against Elaine if he fired her. On the other hand, an employer is not required to grant employees leave for child care. If Elaine is taking off too much time or doing so during times when the work load is heavy, the employer may be justified in dismissing her.

I was fired because customers said they preferred to deal with a white beautician. Do I have grounds to sue?

You do if the business has 15 or more employees. In that case, it comes under the federal Civil Rights Act, which prohibits discrimination based on race or color. An employer cannot defend himself against a charge of racial discrimination by claiming that customer preference requires him to hire only people of a certain race. If the business has fewer than 15 employees, your state law may protect you. Check with your state attorney general's office.

Can I be fired for being a homosexual?

Yes, unless some state or local law or some court ruling specifically prohibits discrimination based on sexual preference. The state of Wisconsin, as well as a number of cities and counties, has passed a law banning this type of discrimination. Some large corporations include this prohibition in their personnel policies, as do many union contracts. If you work for the government you may also be protected. Courts have overturned public school board policies that prohibited the hiring of homosexuals. Title VII, which is part of the federal Civil Rights Act that protects workers from job discrimination, prohibits sex discrimination among men and women, but this is not the same as discrimination based on sexual preference.

Can an employee be fired for drug or alcohol abuse?

Yes. It is generally recognized that employees have an obligation to report for work sober and free from the influence of drugs. However, an employee fired for this reason could challenge the dismissal if he can prove that the company did not follow established procedures (such as giving him a warning) or that he was unaware of company rules or that the company does not routinely dismiss all employees who drink or use illegal drugs on the job.

My cousin's employer told her to do something illegal at work. When she refused to carry out his order, she was fired. Can she do anything about it?

Yes, she can sue her employer to get her job back. Although traditionally employees working without a contract could be fired for any or no reason, society does not want to punish citizens for obeying the law. Consequently, as a matter of public policy, an employer cannot fire anyone for refusing to break the law. Your cousin should also check with her state attorney general's office. The law in her state might allow her to sue her employer to compensate for her wrongful dismissal.

Bill saw his supervisor stealing from the company warehouse but did not report it to anyone. When the owner discovered the theft and learned that Bill had known about it, Bill was fired, too. Can his employer do this?

Yes. Many union contracts, company procedure manuals, or employee handbooks contain provisions that require employees to report a co-worker who steals.

If You Lose Your Job

Can an employee who resigns or is fired continue to receive group medical coverage until he finds another job?

Yes. Under federal law, group health plans for companies that have 20 or more employees must allow medical coverage to continue for 18 to 36 months if the employee wishes to pay for it himself. Other companies are covered by state law.

Unemployment Compensation

Tim's supervisor was browbeating him for several months. The situation became so tense that Tim finally quit. Is he entitled to unemployment benefits?

Only if he can show that his supervisor's actions created a situation that was so unbearable that he was justified in quitting. Unemployment compensation laws distinguish between employees who leave voluntarily with good cause (such as unsafe working conditions or being asked to do something illegal) and those who leave voluntarily without good cause. An employee who leaves voluntarily without good cause is ineligible for unemployment benefits or must wait a certain period of time—usually several weeks—before benefits can begin.

Mindy was fired from her job for misconduct. Can she still collect unemployment insurance?

Probably not. Misconduct is generally understood to mean more than just one incident. If Mindy repeatedly ignored her employer's policies or intentionally destroyed her employer's property, she may not receive unemployment benefits. On the other hand, if her work was unsatisfactory but involved no misconduct, or her dismissal was based on inefficiency, she has a better chance of receiving benefits. Mindy's work record and the circumstances surrounding her dismissal would be taken into account when deciding her eligibility for benefits.

Another employee has been harassing me at work. I brought this to my boss's attention, but he didn't do anything to correct the situation. Can I collect unemployment if I quit?

Only if you can show that you quit for good reasons. The duration, type, and seriousness of the harassment are important considerations. Unpleasant or angry remarks by a coworker may not be considered good reasons, while sexual harassment or threats of physical harm could justify your leaving. The fact that nothing was done when you reported this harassment will also help your case.

When Mike's labor union was unable to negotiate a new contract, the employer locked the factory gates. Mike and his coworkers continued to show up for work, but the gates remained locked. Are Mike and his coworkers eligible for unemployment benefits?

Employees who are out of a job because of a labor dispute are often ineligible for unemployment benefits. Michigan and Texas are among the states that include lockouts as part of their definition of a labor dispute. However, several states, including Minnesota and Pennsylvania, recognize that there is a difference between labor disputes in which employees voluntarily decide to stop working and those in which the employer's actions bring about the unemployment. Mike and his coworkers would have a good chance of getting unemployment benefits if they worked in one of these states.

Lola's company has been forced to close down several branch offices. The company has offered to transfer Lola to another branch, but she does not want to commute 60 miles each day. Would Lola's refusal to transfer affect her eligibility for unemployment benefits?

It depends on the facts in Lola's case. In larger urban areas with extensive public transportation, a 60-mile commute might be considered reasonable. If Lola refused to transfer to another branch when reasonable commuting was available, she would not be eligible for unemployment benefits, because her unemployment would be voluntary. On the other hand, a 60-mile commute in a rural area might not be reasonable. She might be able to get unemployment benefits in this situation because she would be unable, through no fault of her own, to accept the new job the company offered her.

Harry was laid off when the company closed the Texas plant he worked in. He believes his job prospects are now better in Arizona. Can he collect unemployment in one state even though his last job was in another state?

Yes. Every state participates in the Interstate Reciprocal Benefit Payment Plan. This plan allows Harry to file for unemployment benefits in Arizona. However, he must meet the eligibility requirements for his old state,

Texas, not those for Arizona. The amount of his benefits and how long he receives them will be based on Texas law. Harry will have to register for work in Arizona and follow that state's requirements for reporting to the unemployment office.

Can a person receive unemployment benefits while enrolled in a job-training program?

Yes. While benefits are generally denied if a person is not available for work, many states recognize that job training will help unemployed workers find new employment, and they will grant benefits if someone is in an approved job-training program.

My husband has been out of work for two months. He is depressed and spends his unemployment checks gambling. Is it possible for me to receive his unemployment benefits?

No. Your husband is the only person who can collect these benefits. State laws prohibit unemployed workers from assigning or pledging their unemployment benefits to anyone else.

CHAPTER
11

Your Own Business

Starting a Business

Can anyone start his own business?

Yes. All you need is something to sell. A business can be built on any kind of service or product. A climbing guide, who sells the service of leading people up and down dangerous mountains, is as much in business as the owner of a company that manufactures jet engine parts. Of course, what you sell and how you sell it must be permitted by federal, state, and local laws. Your local chamber of commerce is a good place to find out how and where to check on the legality of a new venture.

Does starting my own business mean I will automatically become a corporation, with **Incorporated** *after my business name?*

No. You have a choice of three basic forms of business, only one of which, a corporation, entitles you to use *Inc.* In a *sole proprietorship,* you own and run the business and are personally responsible for its income and expenses, assets and liabilities. The same is true when you form a *partnership,* except that you share responsibility with one or more partners. When you form a *corporation,* you separate the business from your personal assets and create a new legal entity that has its own rights and responsibilities and acts, in effect, like an independent person.

Is buying a franchise like starting any other kind of business?

Yes, from a legal standpoint. You can buy and operate a franchise as a sole proprietor, partner, or corporation. However, a franchise often obligates you to a close working relationship with the franchisor.

Do I need special licenses or permits to start a business?

It depends on the kind of business. State and local governments, in their role of acting in the public interest, have broad powers to regulate business. For example, restaurants, barbershops, dry cleaners, day-care centers, and nursing homes must pass inspections and obtain licenses before opening their doors to the public. Plumbers, electricians, house painters, and contractors must meet licensing and bonding requirements and are subject to having their work inspected. Doctors, lawyers, dentists, accountants, pharmacists, and veterinarians must all pass examinations and receive licenses before practicing their professions lawfully.

If you can't find out what regulations apply to your business by calling your local and state government offices, ask the Better Business Bureau, or someone who already runs a similar business. Some businesses are also regulated by federal laws. To reach the proper agency, call the federal information center (for its number in your area, check the phone book or call information).

If Janice operates a small upholstery business in her basement, does she need a special license?

It depends on where Janice lives. Some states and towns prohibit a resident from operating a business in the home. Even if this isn't the case in Janice's community, she may be required to purchase a business license or seller's permit; and since her business is one that often necessitates moving bulky furniture in and out of her house, she may encounter problems with zoning laws that restrict businesses in residential areas. Such laws commonly ban a business that changes the residential character of the house and its grounds, and limit the number of employees or the percentage of square footage that may be devoted to the business. Some ordinances require off-street parking and prohibit displaying signs in the yard. Other state or local laws may prohibit objectionable noise, odor, or waste.

Does starting a mail-order business pose special legal problems?

Yes. The Federal Trade Commission has truth-in-advertising regulations, with which you must comply or risk federal prosecution for unfair business practices, and it mandates the shipment of merchandise within 30 days of receiving a customer's order, unless you inform the customer that you cannot do so and give him a chance to cancel. Businesses involving chain letters, lotteries, or pornographic material are illegal and can result in fines and imprisonment. In addition, the U. S. Postal Service has the power to investigate suspected frauds against consumers, and to seek criminal penalties for fraudulent use of the mails.

Do I need to apply to the post office for a permit before I start a mail-order business?

No. The U. S. Postal Service does not require permits or licenses for mail-order businesses.

If Victor starts a business that will do frequent large mailings, how can he get a bulk rate discount?

Victor should ask at his local post office which branch office will accept bulk mailings; not all stations are equipped to do so. From that branch, he can obtain an application, called a postal permit for bulk rate. Other, separate permits are required if Victor wants to distribute postage-prepaid, business-reply cards or use precanceled postmarks.

Is it legal to have a post office box number as a business address?

Yes. However, when you apply for your post office box, you will be required to give a street address. The postmaster will thus have a record of the actual location of your business.

My wife and I have always dreamed of buying a restaurant. We have found one for sale that we like very much. The current owner is asking $90,000. How can we determine if this is a fair price?

There are many formulas for determining a fair price for a business. One formula says the price should be approximately five times the business's annual profit; another equates a fair price with the amount of gross sales for 100 days; a third suggests the value of the inventory plus one month's gross receipts. None of these formulas guarantees that you will arrive at a perfect price or buy a profitable business.

The most you can hope for is to arrive at a reasonable figure, and to do so you should ask for and review the following documents: a prospectus of the business; the current owner's business plan, income tax returns, and balance sheets for the past several years; records of accounts, contracts, and leases; and legal documents in any pending lawsuits. If the current owner can't or won't produce many of these documents, your suspicions should be aroused. Have an experienced accountant or lawyer review the documents to evaluate the strengths and weaknesses of the business before you commit yourself in any way.

Albert saw a magazine ad offering to get him started in a profitable business that he could operate from his home. How can he find out if the company is legitimate?

Albert should call the nearest Better Business Bureau, as well as the attorney general's office or the consumer protection agency in his state and the state where the company is located. Their staff members can tell him if any complaints have been lodged against the company. If no complaints are on file, Albert should then contact the company itself and ask for more details about the business opportunity described in the magazine ad. If the company's answers seem suspiciously vague or evasive, he would be best advised to seek other ways of earning income at home. Albert should be especially careful about companies that offer to sell him equipment and materials and promise to buy articles that he produces. Some of these firms afterwards refuse to purchase the completed items—or simply disappear. Extreme caution is also advised when a company claims that it will buy back your unsold inventory or promises huge profits with minimal risks.

I have a van and most of the tools I need to start my own plumbing business. My uncle is willing to put up $10,000 to tide

Sole Proprietorship: The Business Is You

The simplest form of business is called a sole proprietorship, in which you earn money from selling goods or services on your own. You can become a sole proprietor with no legal formalities whatsoever. You may even be one without knowing it; many self-employed people, such as freelancers and independent contractors, are sole proprietors.

A person can be both a company employee and a sole proprietor at the same time. For example, suppose you made $20,000 last year as an assistant office manager and $3,000 from your at-home business of making hand-painted napkin rings. Working a few hours a week and earning a few thousand dollars a year, you are just as much the sole proprietor of a business as a luncheonette owner who makes $50,000 a year.

- *Legal steps*—No legalities are necessary to form a sole proprietorship except obtaining any licenses or permits required by local and state laws. If you decide to do business under a name that isn't your own, you will have to register the name with the secretary of your state.
- *Tax treatment*—Income and expenses are reported on your individual federal return. Your business income will be taxed at your federal individual rate. You may also have to pay state and local taxes as an unincorporated business, either a percentage of the business's income or on some other basis.
- *Control of the business*—You alone make all the decisions, and negotiate and approve all agreements that concern your business, which is completely dependent on and legally inseparable from you.
- *Your personal liability*—Because a sole proprietorship has no legal identity apart from you, the courts consider your business and personal assets and obligations to be one and the same. If you default on a loan you have taken for business purposes, the creditor may take your personal property to pay the debt; and if you cause a car accident through negligence or carelessness, and an injured person wins a lawsuit against you, he can force you to sell your business assets to pay for his medical bills, if they exceed your insurance coverage.

me over while my business gets established; but he would like to have some sort of protection for his investment and also to be sure that my creditors won't sue him if I can't pay my bills. What kind of arrangement can we make that will be fair to us both?

If your uncle is content to be a lender, not your business partner, he can make you a personal loan, and you can put up $10,000 worth of collateral. With such an arrangement, your uncle would not be liable for any of your business debts.

If your uncle wants part ownership of the business in return for his $10,000, you and he can draw up an agreement that makes him a limited partner. This means that he will have a financial interest in your business but will not participate in any other way. Although your uncle, as a limited partner, could lose his $10,000 investment, he would not be personally liable for any business debts. His home and personal belongings could not be seized by an unpaid creditor of the business.

Vanessa has been a computer programmer for six years. Now she would like to start her own computer programming firm, but she is worried that her current employer will sue and put her out of business. Could this happen?

Yes, but only under certain conditions. If Vanessa signed an agreement that prohibits her from competing with her employer in specific ways for a period of time after she leaves the company, and she breaks this agreement, her employer can sue her for breach of contract. However, most courts require that such no-competition agreements be reasonably limited in scope. For example, an agreement never to operate a competing business anywhere in the United States would probably be too broad to hold up in court, while an agreement saying that Vanessa could not open a competing business in the same state for two years after she left the company would quite likely be upheld.

The Laughlins are planning to open a linen shop and hire three employees: one full-time and two part-time. Are the Laughlins obligated by law to furnish and contribute to such benefits as health insurance, life insurance, and pension plans?

Generally, no employer is required to offer these kinds of fringe benefits, although a great many do. However, the law does require employers such as the Laughlins to offer such basic benefits as Social Security contributions and workers' compensation insurance to both their full-time and part-time employees.

Must an employer pay Social Security taxes for everyone his company employs?

Yes, as a rule. An employer must match the Social Security deductions for all his regular employees, whether full-time or part-time. Exceptions are people who work for the company but are technically self-employed, such as independent contractors or freelancers; students in particular jobs at their schools; spouses who work for each other; and minor children working for their parents. An employer must pay Social Security for household workers who earn more than $50 per quarter, and for farm workers who earn more than $150 per quarter. Self-employed persons are legally responsible for making their own Social Security contributions.

Kate has just hired three employees to work full-time for her. What deductions is she required to make from their paychecks?

Kate must withhold certain amounts for federal income taxes, and—depending on where she operates her business—perhaps for state and municipal income taxes. These amounts can be calculated from government tax tables. She must send the money withheld, at regular intervals, to the proper taxing authority, which for federal taxes would be the Internal Revenue Service. Kate will also be required to withhold, and match, amounts to be forwarded to the Social Security Administration for old age, disability, Medicare, and survivors' benefits.

My wife and I set up an answering service. We were told by the IRS that we needed an employer identification number, although we do not intend to hire any employees. Is this correct?

Perhaps not. An employer identification number, or EIN, is assigned to your business by the Internal Revenue Service. One of its purposes is to identify businesses that withhold taxes from their employees and forward the money to the IRS. If you have no employees and are, therefore, withholding no taxes, you do not need an EIN. However, if you are self-employed and wish to set up your own retirement plan, you may need to obtain an EIN, even with no employees, to help the IRS identify your plan.

When he started his investment business, Wendell figured he would save money by not incorporating. Now his accountant tells him he must pay an unincorporated business tax. Do all unincorporated businesses have to pay this tax?

No. Only some states and municipalities levy this kind of tax. Depending on where Wendell lives, an unincorporated business tax may be imposed

Starting a Business

on the value of his business property (such as machinery, equipment, or inventory), or it may be a certain percentage of his sales in the state.

Warren has a degree in landscaping and would like to go into business for himself. In the past he has fallen behind in making credit card payments and the installments due on a personal loan. Will these personal credit problems affect his ability to establish a new business?

Yes, if Warren has to borrow money to get started. If his new business is a sole proprietorship or a partnership, his personal credit will be very important to prospective lenders, since his business and personal finances would be mingled. Even if Warren is considering incorporating the business, so that his business and personal assets would be treated separately, creditors may insist that Warren give a personal guarantee for loans. If his personal credit history shows problems, they may decline to lend him money for the business.

Forming a Partnership

Stan and Frederick want to set up a business. Are there advantages in forming a partnership instead of a corporation?

The major advantage of a partnership over a corporation is simplicity. Each partner's share of the profits and losses is reported on his individual income tax return. Unlike a corporation, which must pay taxes on its profits and whose shareholders must also pay taxes on the dividends the corporation pays out of profits, partners are taxed only once on the income generated by their business. The main disadvantage of a partnership is that each partner is personally liable for business debts.

What should be spelled out in a partnership agreement?

It should contain the name of the partnership and the names of its members; a description of the type of business to be conducted; a statement of the financial contribution of each partner; a description of the duties and powers of the partners, along with any restrictions on their power to act for the partnership; the method of dividing profits or losses; procedures for withdrawing from the partnership or admitting new members; steps to be followed in the event of the death of a partner; and procedures and conditions for dissolving the partnership. Some agree-

Setting Up a Partnership

In many ways a partnership is like having two or more sole proprietors running the same business. They are known legally as *general partners,* which means they manage the business, share in its profits, and assume personal responsibility for its loans and obligations. *Limited partners* are restricted to investing money and sharing in the profits. A limited partner is not personally liable for partnership debts so long as he stays completely clear of any management role.

• *Legal steps*—The general partners should check state and local laws for permits or licenses needed for their type of business; and they must register the partnership name with the secretary of their state. In addition, they should prepare a document setting out the purpose of the partnership, its members, the business and accounting methods to be used, the rights and duties of each partner, and the method of distributing profits and losses among the partners. A formal agreement is not legally required; however, when one doesn't exist, most courts would assume that all partners were meant to share equally in the profits and losses and to have equal voices in management.

• *Tax treatment*—Each partner reports his share of the partnership income on his federal individual income tax return. Federal tax rates are the same as for personal income. State and local governments also tax partnership income or assess fees.

• *Control of the business*—Unless there is an agreement that states otherwise, (1) each general partner may make decisions and negotiate contracts on behalf of the partnership; (2) the death or resignation of a general partner dissolves the partnership.

• *Your personal liability*—If the partnership defaults on a loan, the creditor can hold you (and other general partners) personally responsible. Thus, if the partnership can't repay a business loan on time, the lender can sue each of you and you face the risk of losing personal property. Carelessness or negligence by one partner may also result in a lawsuit against the partnership, raising the possibility that you may be held personally liable.

ments also stipulate the methods to be used for resolving disputes that arise among the partners and even the amount of insurance to be carried for the partnership.

Can a partnership exist legally without a written agreement?

Yes, but having only an oral agreement could well be a source of trouble in the future. If the partnership is to last one year or longer, the agreement must be in writing to be enforceable. As a practical matter, it is best to have such a serious and important agreement in writing and to make sure each of the partners fully understands its terms and how they will apply.

Becky wants me to be her partner, but I'm not sure we'll get along. Can we set up a trial period for the partnership?

Yes. Your agreement can limit the duration of the partnership. For example, your agreement can state that the partnership will last three months, with an option to renew at the end of that period. You may also include the right to dissolve the partnership.

Lloyd, Matthew, and Lawrence formed a partnership two years ago. Now Ian would like to join the firm as the fourth partner. Lloyd and Matthew approve; Lawrence does not. Can Ian be made a partner despite Lawrence's objection?

No. As a general rule, new partners must be approved by all current partners. Unless the partnership agreement states otherwise, Ian may not join as a partner over Lawrence's objection.

Veronica and Elaine are experts in the clothing business. Shirley and Heather are investors with no experience in this field. When they draw up their partnership agreement, can they stipulate that Veronica and Elaine will make all management decisions?

Yes. This arrangement is usually known as a limited partnership. A limited partner agrees to contribute financially to the partnership, but to leave the management of the business to the other partner or partners. The advantage to the limited partners is that they are not personally liable for partnership debts. A creditor cannot have their homes or personal belongings seized and sold to pay business debts. The disadvantage is that limited partners cannot participate in running the business. If they do, they become general partners and, as such, become personally liable for partnership debts.

Simon and Joe are going into business as partners. Would Joe's home, which he owns jointly with his wife, be protected from a creditor if the partnership defaults on a loan?

No. Joe's interest in his home could be used to pay a creditor who successfully sued the partnership for an unpaid debt. The court could order that the house be sold, even though it is jointly owned, and that the proceeds be used to discharge the loan. However, the creditor can take only Joe's interest in the house (one half of the proceeds) and must reimburse Joe's wife for her interest. If Joe's half is greater than the debt, the creditor must give Joe the difference. A lawyer can advise Joe if filing for bankruptcy would protect a greater share of his interest in his home.

One of my partners was involved in an automobile accident. A lawsuit names him as the defendant. If he loses the case, can the court force him to pay damages out of our firm's assets?

No. If the accident had nothing to do with your firm's business, the court cannot take the partnership's assets. However, the court can require your partner to use his share of partnership earnings to pay damages.

Earl is going to retire from his firm at the end of the year. What steps should he take to make sure he isn't liable for business conducted by his partners after he leaves?

Earl should send a letter to all the partnership creditors and clients, informing them that he is leaving the firm and that as of December 31 he is no longer authorized to act for the business, or liable for business debts. If he doesn't do this, he could remain liable for partnership debts.

Incorporating

My son, Ira, wants to set up his own business as an auto mechanic. Is it necessary for him to incorporate?

No. A business need not be incorporated. Ira can operate as a sole proprietor, or he can form a partnership with one or more other persons.

Can I start a corporation of which I am the only shareholder?

Yes. There are no requirements that a corporation have a minimum number of shareholders. You may own all the stock issued by your corporation. Some state laws, however, require that your application for a charter as a corporation (called articles of incorporation) name at least three incorporators. You may wish to have friends or relatives serve as incorporators. You must be very careful, however, to keep personal assets and those of the corporation separate or you will lose the protection of your personal assets that a corporation gives you.

Incorporating

Sybil started out doing some part-time word processing on her computer at home. This has become a very profitable full-time operation, but she has never incorporated. Now that she is so successful, should she?

Not necessarily. Although by incorporating she would escape being held personally responsible for her business liabilities, Sybil could also find herself paying more taxes and putting more time, paperwork, and expense into meeting state requirements for certifying her corporation. Sybil would be well advised to seek legal and financial advice before she makes such a decision.

Do I need an attorney to incorporate?

Yes. Although almost anyone may file articles of incorporation with the secretary of his state, and have them approved, this will not guarantee that your corporate status will stand up in court. If your corporate status is later challenged for some reason by a creditor, the court might find that you did not incorporate properly, and it could therefore hold you personally responsible for the debt.

Incorporation: Business With a Life of Its Own

A corporation has an independent legal existence, distinct from that of its owners. Like a person, it pays taxes; can buy, own, and sell property; can sue and be sued; can commit crimes and be tried and punished for them. To raise money, most corporations issue stock that is bought by the public: you become part owner of a corporation when you buy one or more shares. Creating a corporation requires certain procedures.

- *Legal steps*—A corporation cannot exist without the permission of state government. *Articles of incorporation* must be filed with the secretary of your state. In most states, this document must give the names and addresses of at least three *incorporators*, the name and address of the corporation and its purpose, the number and type of shares of stock to be issued, and the amount of capital the corporation has to work with. After approving the document, the secretary of state will issue a certificate of incorporation, or charter, at which point *Incorporated* or *Corporation,* or their abbreviations, must be added to the company name. Once the corporation is chartered, it is responsible for obtaining the licenses, permits, and registrations required for its business activities.
- *Tax treatment*—Net profits are subject to corporate income tax rates, which are generally higher than rates for individuals.

YOUR OWN BUSINESS

Art calls his business Art & Sons, Inc., even though it isn't incorporated. Is this legal?

No. Art misrepresents his firm's legal status if he uses *Inc., Corp., Incorporated,* or *Corporation*. Only the state can grant corporate status.

If I form a corporation, can my business creditors take my house if they sue me and win?

No. If you have not mixed your personal affairs with corporate business affairs, your personal assets, such as your home, car, or bank account, cannot be seized by business creditors. Corporate creditors may take your personal assets only if you have given a personal guarantee for debts or offered your personal assets as collateral for a business loan.

I have just incorporated, and I am trying to lease a store in a mall. The owner's agent asked me to sign a personal guarantee. What legal effect does this have? Can they require me to sign it?

Your personal guarantee will make you personally liable for money that the corporation may owe the mall in the future. For example, if the

• *Control of the business*—The first job of the incorporators is to call a meeting of the shareholders. The shareholders will vote on the rules (bylaws) by which the company will be run, and elect a board of directors, which has overall responsibility for the major decisions and direction of the corporation. The board then names officers—the president, treasurer, vice presidents, secretary, and so on—to take charge of the day-to-day management of the business. Ultimate control of the corporation rests with the shareholders, who can vote to keep, add, or replace directors; however, there is no law against incorporators, directors, officers, and large shareholders being the same persons. In practice, an individual who owns just a few shares of stock has little direct control over the decisions of the corporation.

• *Your personal liability*—A corporation limits the personal liability of its shareholder-owners, and even of its officers and directors, if the corporation defaults on a loan or is sued for some careless, negligent, or criminal act. For example, creditors of the corporation cannot take the personal assets of a corporate director or officer or those of a shareholder to pay corporate debts. However, if an officer or director participates in a wrongful act—such as signing a check knowing that there are no funds in the account—that officer or director could be held personally liable for his actions.

corporation cannot pay the rent, and the mall's owner sues and wins, he may have your personal property seized and sold to pay the overdue rent. The owner may legally require such a guarantee, and creditors of new or struggling corporations often demand it. However, by signing, you lose a chief advantage of incorporating—protection of your personal assets.

Hugh and Vera have been running a small bakery for the past two years. Is it too late for them to incorporate?

No. They may change the form of their business at any time—from or to a sole proprietorship, partnership, or corporation.

Juliana wants to lend money to her corporation to help it through some financial difficulties. Is this legal?

Yes. However, Juliana should be sure that her roles as owner and creditor do not become confused. This loan should be treated like any other and entered in the corporate records. The corporation should not give preference to Juliana over other creditors, and she should not repay herself out of corporate assets in a way that other creditors cannot.

I've noticed that many companies are incorporated in the state of Delaware. Would it be better for me to incorporate my company in my own state or to set it up in Delaware?

Many businesses incorporate in Delaware because it has low taxes and allows corporate charters that place relatively few restrictions on how a corporation conducts its business. For example, Delaware does not require that incorporators reside in the state, or that stockholders or the board of directors conduct their meetings there. However, many states have followed Delaware in creating a favorable environment for corporations, and you or your attorney should compare your own state laws with Delaware's to determine where it would be best for you to incorporate.

The local high school has asked Claudia to set up and head a small nonprofit corporation to raise funds for a scholarship program. Is a nonprofit corporation set up differently from a profit-making one? Can Claudia get paid for this work?

Generally speaking, a nonprofit corporation is organized in much the same way as a for-profit corporation and is granted a charter by the state to conduct business. There is no law against a nonprofit corporation's hiring salaried employees, and thus Claudia can be paid for her services.

If we form a nonprofit corporation to publish a consumer newsletter, do we have to file tax returns for it?

Yes. Even nonprofit corporations with tax-exempt status must file information returns with the Internal Revenue Service. Corporations set up for religious, charitable, scientific, literary, artistic, or educational purposes, or for the prevention of cruelty to children or animals, generally qualify for tax-exempt status. An organization must apply for exemption to the Internal Revenue Service.

Willard says he set up his business as a Chapter S corporation. What's he talking about?

Formerly known as Subchapter S corporations, Chapter S (or simply S) corporations take their name from a provision of the Federal Tax Code that allows some corporations to elect to be taxed as individuals (not corporations). In order to gain this federal tax treatment, S corporations accept certain restrictions. For example, only domestic corporations with 35 or fewer shareholders are entitled to Chapter S status; and none of the stock of an S corporation can be held by other corporations or partnerships. An S corporation can issue only one class of stock. Most states follow the federal lead in granting S corporations a tax break.

I own a small business that is incorporated. While driving to work in my personal car, which I often use for business purposes, I caused an accident. Am I personally liable for any damages?

Yes. If you caused the accident through carelessness or negligence, you can be held personally liable for any injuries. Even if corporation business was the sole reason you were driving, you would not be relieved of liability; however, the corporation might share liability with you.

Elliot operates his catering business as a sole proprietorship, and one of his vans was in an accident. If he files for incorporation immediately, will he be protected from personal liability for injuries resulting from the accident?

No. In determining whether Elliot can be held personally liable for damages, a court would consider the status of his business at the time of the accident, not at the time of the trial.

Incorporating

Can Herbert incorporate his failing business, have it file for bankruptcy, and thus protect his personal assets?

No. Herbert cannot dodge his debts by changing the form of his business. He will still be personally liable for all preincorporation business debts.

Judd has a criminal record for something he did over 20 years ago. Can he incorporate and run a business?

Yes, but he may have problems getting a license or permit to run certain types of businesses, depending on his offense. For example, if Judd was convicted of illegal gambling, the state might refuse him a license to sell lottery tickets. If it was a weapons offense, the state might not allow him to sell guns. Judd's conviction, however, is only one factor that the state or local government would consider when deciding to grant the license.

Buying a Franchise

Randy is thinking about starting his own fast-food restaurant. He has read about a national group offering franchises. Would Randy own the business if he purchased a franchise?

No. He would own only the right to sell or distribute the franchisor's product or service. Randy would pay a franchise fee that covers many of the costs involved in setting up the business, and then he would have to pay royalties to the franchisor based on the amount of his sales. Many franchise licenses (or contracts) expire after a number of years. At that point, Randy would have to negotiate a new contract to stay in business.

If I buy a franchise, how much control will the franchisor be able to exert over me legally in telling me what I can and cannot do in operating the business?

It depends primarily on the contract you sign. Many franchisors make it a policy to discourage innovation because they feel that the key to their success is familiarity and predictability. They exert tight control and strictly regulate day-to-day operations. A typical franchisor will select the exact site for a franchise, build the outlet according to standard plans, purchase or lease all the necessary equipment, dictate the quality and appearance of all supplies used at the outlet, and provide training for the employees and managers.

At a Start Your Own Business fair, Sean and Vicki found a franchise deal that promised big profits, and the salesman said it was easy to run. How can Sean and Vicki check up on the franchisor's claims before they invest the required $20,000?

The Federal Trade Commission requires that a franchisor disclose certain information about the franchise—including the owner's identity and the franchise's history, costs and expenses, and contractual obligations—at least 10 days before entering into an agreement with a potential franchisee. Once they get this information, Sean and Vicki should look it

What You Get When You Buy a Franchise

A franchise is a license or permit to operate a business that sells a product or service developed by the franchisor. You, the franchisee, pay a fee and royalties to the franchisor in exchange for the right to sell the product or service. As a franchisee, you are in some ways the owner of your own business, but your autonomy can never be complete because of your relationship with the franchisor. Some franchisors exercise strict control over all aspects of the business, while others give their franchisees great freedom. The terms used for the different types of franchises reveal the amount of control the franchisor wields:

• *Turnkey operation*—The franchisor has full control of the business, and all the new franchisee must do is turn the key in the lock and open his door to begin business. The franchisor chooses the site for a new outlet after extensive marketing and traffic-flow studies; builds the outlet and furnishes it according to a standard plan; and trains the manager and employees. Once in business, the franchisee must follow the franchisor's instructions: where to set up displays, when to offer specials, what uniforms the employees must wear, how to enter items in his ledger, what hours he may operate, and from whom he may buy supplies. If the franchisor distributes coupons or runs a promotion or contest, the franchisee may be required to participate. The franchisee may also be required to lease equipment from the franchisor and pay rent on the outlet, thus making his financial obligation to the franchisor more than paying royalties.

• *Trade name franchise*—The franchisee sells a product already manufactured by the franchisor. Gas stations, auto parts stores, and specialty clothing stores are examples.The franchisee is granted the exclusive right to distribute the product in a certain area. In return, the franchisee operates his outlet according to the franchisor's guidelines and pays royalties to the franchisor.

• *Business format franchise*—Goods or services are produced by the franchisee at his outlet, such as at a fast-food restaurant. The franchisor provides instructions and equipment to ensure consistent quality.

over and ask a lawyer or accountant to do the same. Then they should do some further investigating. They should talk to current franchisees—in person to those near them, and by telephone to those at a distance. They should ask if the franchisor is supportive of his outlets, if the training and advertising offered are adequate, and if the franchisor is honest and fair in dealing with the franchisees.

Russell and Amanda want to buy a franchise from the current owner. How can they make sure the business is as profitable as the owner claims?

Russell and Amanda should ask the owner for a detailed financial statement and then have their accountant evaluate it to make sure that the owner's claims of profitability are valid.

Maria inherited some money and would like to invest it in a franchise that is considering opening another outlet in her town. What risks does she face?

Most statistical studies show that franchises have a better survival rate than independent single-person small businesses. This better-than-average success rate is attributed, in part, to the already established reputation and goodwill of a franchise and its resources for marketing studies and advertising. For many inexperienced people, franchising is the safest way to start their own business.

However, the franchise formula does not guarantee success. Some franchisors overextend themselves and are unable to continue to offer the advertising and training programs they promised. Sometimes their marketing studies err, and they try to open an outlet in a location already adequately served. And while most franchisors are fair and honest, some sell used equipment to franchisees at inflated prices; others divert advertising fees to their own general funds. Maria's best protection is to do a thorough investigation of the history, financial status, and reputation of the franchisor.

What should I do if the company from which I purchased a franchise tells me it is going out of business?

If your franchisor is unable to fulfill his obligations under your agreement, you may sue for breach of contract. In such a lawsuit, you will need to prove the amount of your loss. If the franchisor has few assets, or if he files for bankruptcy, you may not be able to collect your full loss.

I want to open an appliance store. Are there any guarantees that I'm required by law to offer my customers?

The law does not require you to give, either orally or in writing, any specific guarantees on items you sell. However, there are guarantees that the law considers implied in every sales transaction. Of these implied warranties, the most far-reaching is the *implied warranty of merchantability*. It guarantees that the item is of average quality and will do what it is supposed to do—for example, a new toaster will toast, a can opener won't break on first use, and a new dress won't have a broken zipper.

There is also an *implied warranty of fitness for a particular purpose.* This applies if a customer asks you for a product that will do a particular job or fit a particular space, then purchases the product you recommend. In this case you have, in effect, guaranteed or warranted that the product will work in the way the customer has described. If the customer asks you for a food processor that will knead dough, for example, he can return the machine he buys from you if it does not do the job properly.

In some states, you can avoid these two warranties by alerting customers that you are selling a product "as is," without any express or implied warranties.

Olivia, age 65, responded to our ad for a new cashier. Will I be guilty of age discrimination if I reject her application?

It depends on why you reject her. The Age Discrimination in Employment Act—a federal law that applies to businesses engaged in interstate commerce (anything involved in making or selling a product that crosses state lines)—protects employees and job applicants between the ages of 40 and 70. Under this law it is illegal to make employment decisions based solely on age. You will be breaking the law if you reject or refuse to consider her application solely because she is 65. If you reject Olivia's application because you have another applicant who has more experience, you will not be violating the law.

Peter would like to run a small consulting business after he retires. He plans to have the firm buy him a car, cover some of his lunch expenses, purchase his life insurance, and even absorb some of his living expenses. Is this possible?

Yes. Peter can establish a corporation, which can hold title to his car, authorize an expense account, purchase life insurance as a benefit, and pay him a salary. Peter must be very careful, however, to keep his personal and corporate assets separate. He should not, for example, charge a birthday gift to his wife on his expense account. If Peter mingles his personal and corporate money, a court may decide that there is really no corporation separate from Peter, and he will be personally liable for corporate debts.

How can I keep someone else from using my business's name?

Generally, a state will not allow two businesses to register under the same name. A name must be registered with the secretary of the state if the business is a corporation or if the name does not identify the proprietor or partnership—Up-and-up Wares, for example.

If you are the first to use a name, and another business uses it, you can stop its use through an injunction. (An injunction is a court order to halt a particular activity.) If you feel another company illegally used your name to its gain and your loss, you can sue that company for money to compensate you for your loss; a court will decide whether or not to award you the money you demand in your lawsuit.

To avoid the headache of inadvertently using another business's name, many firms employ a service that makes name searches. Your secretary of state's office can tell you how to locate such services.

Because Glenn's business has expanded, there are a lot of orders to fill. Will he be violating any laws if he has his employees work 10 to 12 hours a day to meet his deadlines?

No. However, the federal Fair Labor Standards Act requires all businesses engaged in interstate commerce (that is, if anything involved in making or selling their product crosses state lines) to pay a minimum hourly wage for hours worked up to 40 per week, and overtime compensation (time and a half) for hours in excess of that. Under the federal statute, some employees, such as farm workers and executive, administrative, and professional personnel, are exempt from the overtime requirement, as are businesses with fewer than 15 employees and ones that are not involved in any way in interstate commerce. Because state overtime regulations may differ from federal law, Glenn should also check with his state department of labor on the legality of his overtime policy.

I'd like to hire Todd as a clerk in my store, but my partner doesn't trust him. How can I check on Todd's trustworthiness?

You can ask Todd's former employers and his references about his honesty and reliability. Generally, you are not allowed to question Todd himself about his personal finances or whether he has ever been arrested. However, any criminal convictions would be in the records of the county where Todd lives or used to live. You may wish to have Todd bonded by an insurance company to protect your business against potential theft or embezzlement.

Although at one time some employers required job applicants to take a polygraph examination, a federal law, the Employee Polygraph Protection Act, now prohibits you from requiring Todd to submit to a lie detector or voice stress analysis test. If you violate the provisions of this law, you may be prosecuted by the U. S. Department of Labor, and you could be fined up to $10,000. In addition, Todd could also sue you for damages in civil court.

Sherman has a valuable customer who keeps falling way behind in paying his bill. At what point would it be advisable for Sherman to sue the customer for payment?

Sherman should first ask the customer why he hasn't paid and when he expects to be able to pay. Perhaps they can work out a new payment schedule. Sherman can freeze the customer's account, allowing no further credit until the payments are brought up to date. If it still appears that the customer cannot pay his debt, Sherman has the option of suing to make him pay what is owed.

I operate a used clothing business in a suburban shopping plaza. My lease prevents me from placing items on the sidewalk in front of the store. However, the tenant next door displays his items on the sidewalk. How can he do this when I can't?

Your landlord is not required to negotiate identical leases with each tenant. However, if your lease says no other tenants can display goods on the sidewalk, you may sue the landlord to enforce this term of your lease and collect damages for the losses your business incurred.

Will Gabrielle need to purchase liability insurance for the business she is about to start?

Most companies need some type of liability insurance. Exactly what type depends upon the nature of the business. Public liability insurance covers accidents to customers on the company's premises. If Gabrielle is going to manufacture merchandise, product liability insurance may be a good idea. This covers injury or damage caused by the manufacturer's negligence in designing, producing, or marketing the product or instructing customers about how it should be used. If Gabrielle will have employees, she will probably be required to contribute to the workers' compensation fund to cover job-related injuries. Finally, she may wish to buy liability coverage for injuries or damage caused by her employees. Corporations routinely buy liability insurance for their officers and directors, in case they are sued by stockholders or regulatory agencies, for example.

When I start my business at home, will my existing homeowners and liability insurance be sufficient to protect me, or will I need additional coverage?

Homeowners policies often exclude losses related to the commercial use of your home, and while covering personal property, may not protect business inventory and equipment. They do not cover job-related injuries to your employees. Personal liability or umbrella policies seldom cover

If the Business Fails: Your Choices

Every year in the United States thousands of businesses, great and small, come to a point where their liabilities exceed their assets, and the only reasonable course is to consider bankruptcy. For sole proprietors, the choice is one of two types of personal bankruptcy, as discussed in Chapter 7, *Your Money*. For corporations and partnerships, bankruptcy law offers a choice between reorganization (Chapter 11 of the Federal Bankruptcy Code) and liquidation (various other chapters of the Code). However, if the owner of the business has given a personal guarantee in order to get a loan for his corporation, as some creditors request, his personal assets as well as business assets would be used to pay creditors.

- *Reorganization*—The key element for a reorganization, or "rehabilitation," bankruptcy is a repayment plan. The typical steps are:

1. The business files a Chapter 11 petition in the bankruptcy court.
2. The court issues a stay (stop) against creditors' lawsuits and specifies which assets the owner can continue to use to operate the business.
3. The owner has 120 days from the date of filing his petition to negotiate a repayment plan with his creditors. Usually, creditors accept a reduction in the amounts due and a three-year period for repayment.
4. If all the creditors agree to the plan, it is sent to the court for approval. If the creditors don't agree, the owner can ask the court to impose a plan on them. In some cases, after 120 days, a creditor may propose his own repayment schedule.
5. After the court approves a plan, the company continues to do business while paying off its back debts. The creditors may not sue or attempt to collect more than is due them under the plan.

business activities, most notably malpractice and product liability. Depending on the nature of your business, you may wish to purchase fire and explosion coverage, public and product liability coverage, burglary coverage, fraud and credit insurance (to cover bounced checks and bad debts), and floater insurance for your inventory. If you are engaged in a profession such as medicine or dentistry, you should certainly consider malpractice insurance.

Ryan owns a small business. He asked his clerk to drive to the stationery store to pick up some envelopes. On his way back, the clerk was involved in an auto accident in which he was negligent. Can Ryan be held responsible?

Yes. Since the employee was carrying out his employer's directions when the accident occurred, Ryan can be held responsible.

6. If the business pays off its creditors on schedule, the court's records show a successful reorganization under Chapter 11.
7. If the business cannot meet its obligations under Chapter 11, it may convert to a straight bankruptcy proceeding.

• *Liquidation*—Straight bankruptcy, or liquidation, gathers up and disposes of all the business's assets (except for certain exempt property) to pay creditors either partially or in full. This process can take months or even years, but at the end of it the partnership or corporation is rid of all its debts. Here in brief is how a straight business bankruptcy works:
1. The company or its creditors file a bankruptcy petition in federal court, reporting the business's debts, property, and operations in detail.
2. All business property is placed in the custody of the bankruptcy court.
3. The court issues a stay (stop) on lawsuits by creditors. (This stay can be challenged by a creditor and may, in some circumstances, be lifted.)
4. The court notifies the firm's creditors about the petition and the stay, and sets a date for the first creditors' meeting.
5. Creditors file their claims and, at the meeting, may question the firm about its assets and liabilities. If the court has not named a trustee to handle the bankruptcy, the creditors can elect one at this meeting.
6. The trustee sells the firm's assets and uses the proceeds to pay the creditors' claims, following guidelines set by federal and state laws. Priority debts include administrative and legal fees incurred in the bankruptcy and back wages owed the employees of the firm. Creditors who are not near the top of the list may get nothing. Back income taxes are almost never excused or reduced.
7. When all the proceeds have been distributed, the court declares the business free of the creditors' claims against it.

Running a Business

My friend Vincent has opened a car repair shop. Last week, someone drove in and asked one of Vincent's mechanics to give his car a tune-up and check the brakes. Right after the customer drove his car out of the shop the next day, he was involved in an accident that was caused, he claims, by faulty brakes. Can Vincent's Auto Shop be held liable for damages?

Yes. If an employee of Vincent's Auto Shop was responsible for the faulty brakes or reported that the brakes were repaired when they were not, the business could be held liable. If Vincent's is incorporated, the corporation would be responsible. If the business is a sole proprietorship or partnership, the owners would be held personally responsible.

As the president of my company, I signed a contract that said I would deliver certain equipment to the Bellwether Grape Company. I have two employees out sick and can't deliver when I promised. Does Bellwether have grounds for a lawsuit?

Yes. Your failure to deliver on time, no matter what the special circumstances that prevented you from doing so, is a breach of contract, one of the most common reasons for lawsuits in business. If your company is incorporated, only the corporation will be liable for damages. If you are the sole proprietor or a partner of an unincorporated business, you may be held personally liable for breaking the contract.

Dan's company has a big order of giant stuffed pandas to deliver to a chain of stores in time for the Christmas buying season. One of his fabric suppliers just had to close down because of a strike and can't deliver the necessary material. What are Dan's legal responsibilities?

Dan must still live up to his contractual obligations to the chain of stores. If he does not deliver the toys on time, he may be sued for breach of contract. Dan should make every possible effort to get the material he needs from other suppliers. If he must pay higher prices for the material and suffers a loss, Dan can sue his supplier for breach of contract and for the losses he suffered.

Josephine has been operating a custom furniture-making business in a building next to an apartment complex. Several tenants have complained about the noise of her power saw. They say the noise is a public nuisance and a health hazard to them.

Can they prevent Josephine from operating a power saw on her own premises?

Yes. Josephine's neighbors could obtain a court order, or injunction, against her if the court decides her use of the power saw is a public nuisance or if its operation is prohibited by local zoning laws. In deciding if Josephine's use of the saw is a public nuisance, the court would consider how the surrounding property is used and how much inconvenience, discomfort, or harm Josephine is actually causing her neighbors.

Our business is about to hire an employee who must use a wheelchair to get around. What changes must we make to comply with the laws and regulations about handicapped accessibility?

A federal law, the Americans With Disabilities Act, passed in 1990, requires employers to make reasonable accommodations to a disabled employee that would enable him or her to perform a particular job. Reasonable accommodations, which are defined as those that do not create undue business hardships on the employer, might include modifying access to the work site, rest rooms, lunchrooms, and parking; for someone in a wheelchair, this might require installing ramps and nonskid surfaces. For the hearing impaired, lights can be used to supplement sound signals, such as fire alarms; and for the blind, bells and Braille make elevators less difficult.

Nellie and Penelope incorporated their real estate business last year. Is it important for them to have a stockholders' meeting every year and write up the minutes of these meetings?

Yes. Most state laws require corporations to hold annual stockholder meetings; and Nellie and Penelope must keep minutes of these meetings in their corporate records. It is very important that a corporation act like a corporation to keep the protection that incorporation offers: If it appears that Nellie and Penelope mingle their personal assets with corporate assets, or don't observe the formalities required of corporations, a court may decide their business is conducted more like a partnership or sole proprietorship than a corporation, and they will find themselves personally liable for corporate debts.

As a stockholder, can I be personally liable in any way for the actions of the corporation?

No. Although you are a part owner of the corporation, you cannot be held personally liable for corporate actions. The corporation, not its stock-

Running a Business

holders, will be sued. However, you would lose this immunity if, for example, you were a stockholder of a family corporation and used corporate assets for personal purposes.

If Ruth Ann is named a director of a corporation, will she have to put her corporate responsibilities ahead of her personal interest?

Yes, in some respects. As a director, Ruth Ann must act in the best interest of the corporation, even if that conflicts with her personal interest. She cannot use information she has learned as a corporate director for personal gain or against the interests of the corporation. According to the law, Ruth Ann is in a position of trust (a fiduciary), and must act with diligence to protect the corporation's interests.

To fulfill this duty, Ruth Ann should attend directors' meetings and keep informed about corporate business by reviewing material provided by the corporation, including past minutes of the meetings, agendas, proposals, financial statements, and stockholder reports. If the other directors propose a course of business that she thinks is wrong, she should make her objections, on the record, at the directors' meetings. If Ruth Ann doesn't act in the corporation's best interest and neglects its affairs, she can be sued by the corporation's shareholders for not fulfilling her fiduciary duty.

Selling or Ending a Business

Julian wants to begin turning over his construction company to his sons. Would forming a partnership be a good way to proceed with the transfer?

A partnership may be best if Julian's sons would gain tax advantages from it. Julian and his sons should consider the corporate form as well, with its limited liability. Whichever form the business takes, Julian and his sons will have to agree on how to share ownership and management and how to resolve disputes if they arise. They should also decide how long Julian will continue to play a role in the business; what that role will be (for example, officer, director, or consultant); and how much he will be paid for his services and for what length of time.

Van wants to retire from the day-to-day management of his business and has offered it to his cousins at an attractive price. Since they don't have the cash right now to buy him out, Van is

willing to stretch their payments over a number of years. How can he protect himself if his cousins fail to make the payments?

There are several ways that Van might transfer control of his business while protecting his ownership until his cousins could buy him out. He could lend them the purchase price and accept the company's assets as collateral for the loan. His cousins would own and manage the business and he would have the right to take all the business assets if they defaulted on the loan.

Or Van might incorporate his business and name his cousins as officers and directors. As officers, they would receive salaries, and they could buy shares of stock in the business from Van according to an agreed-upon schedule. Such an arrangement would allow the cousins to manage the business while gradually acquiring ownership from Van. If they did not buy stock on schedule, the cousins' percentage of ownership would increase at a slower rate.

When our family formed a corporation, we signed an agreement to keep it always within the family. Now I want to sell my shares of stock to Brett, who is not a family member. Can my relatives prevent me from doing this?

Yes, if your corporate bylaws or an agreement with other family members prohibits you from selling your stock to an outsider. However, in many cases, the bylaws or the agreement will let you sell your stock outside the company if you first get the consent of the corporation's board of directors or other shareholders or if you offer the shares to the corporation or the other stockholders before offering them to an outsider.

Felix and I are friends, and I want to sell half of my existing business to him. The selling price is $50,000, but Felix has only $10,000. How can we both be protected?

If Felix can get a bank loan, be sure that he offers personal collateral, such as his home, car, or personal bank account, rather than his interest in the business. Otherwise, if he defaults, the partnership assets may be seized by the bank to pay the loan. Likewise be certain that Felix does not obtain the loan as a loan to your business. If Felix defaults on a loan made on behalf of the business, the lender could seize your assets, both partnership and personal, to pay the debt. If a bank will not lend Felix $40,000 to buy into your business, you may not want to do so either.

Randall worked for several years as an employee in his uncle's bookstore. When his uncle died, Randall inherited the store and

tried to run it as the sole proprietor and only employee. Business is bad and getting worse. Can Randall close the shop and collect unemployment compensation?

No. Randall is not considered an employee under unemployment compensation systems, which are funded by state and federal unemployment taxes paid by employers. Self-employed people do not pay these taxes.

I am running a sole proprietorship. I don't have any children, and my husband does not seem to be interested in the business. What will happen to it when I die?

A sole proprietorship is a personal asset, just like your home or bank account, and would therefore become a part of your estate, to be passed on or divided according to the instructions in your will. In most cases similar to yours, the surviving spouse or executor of the estate sells the business, uses the proceeds to settle claims against the estate, and then passes the remaining funds along to the owner's survivors or the beneficiaries of his will.

CHAPTER

12

Your Individual Rights

Our Rights as Citizens

When I went to my attorney, he kept talking about my legal rights. What did he mean?

When we think of rights, we generally think of such things as freedom of speech, freedom of the press, freedom of religion, and the right to a fair trial. These basic rights are protected by the first 10 amendments to the U. S. Constitution, also known as the Bill of Rights. Further rights are protected by other constitutional provisions and by statutes, regulations, and ordinances. They include your right to vote, to marry and raise a family, to work, to own property, to expect adequate heat and plumbing when you rent an apartment, to get compensation if you are cheated by others or hurt because of their negligence, and to leave your property to your loved ones when you die.

Does the Bill of Rights apply to state governments?

Yes. But when the Bill of Rights was written, the intention was to restrict the role of the federal government, and the states were not specifically required to uphold the basic rights described in the Constitution. It was not until the passage of the 14th Amendment, after the Civil War, that courts began to apply the provisions of the Bill of Rights to state governments. The 14th Amendment specifies that "no State shall make or enforce any law which shall abridge the privileges or immunities of citizens of the United States."

Does the Bill of Rights apply only to U.S. citizens?

No. The protection provided by the Bill of Rights also applies to aliens—as people who are not U. S. citizens are legally called. There is one exception, however; the right to bear arms, which is found in the Second Amendment to the U.S. Constitution, does not apply to aliens. All of the other personal rights guaranteed by the first 10 amendments to the Constitution apply to anyone who is in the United States, whether a citizen, resident alien, or visitor.

Can our rights as citizens ever be taken away without our consent?

Yes, but only temporarily during an emergency. After a riot or disaster, state and local authorities have the right to declare a state of emergency and impose restrictions on the people, such as a curfew, in which businesses are ordered to close early and citizens are ordered to stay off the streets. The most extreme restriction is martial law, which may be

What Is the Law?

Perhaps the best definition of the law is the simplest one: it is the set of rules we live by to maintain order in society. As our society has grown in complexity, however, so has this set of rules. Over the centuries, it has evolved into an elaborate legal system made up of the following:

- *Constitutional law*—The basic law upon which our government is founded as set forth in the U. S. Constitution and in the individual state constitutions. Constitutional law does not provide detailed directives on the subjects it addresses, but states general principles and establishes a foundation of law and government. Our federal and state constitutions dictate how laws can be made and enforced, and name the basic rights of the people that may not be violated, such as freedom of speech and religion, and the right to vote and to own property.
- *Statutes*—Laws passed by the U. S. Congress or state legislatures, which specify what a person can and cannot do to keep within the bounds of legality. Statutes cover every area not declared outside their power by the Constitution. Among other things, statutes set requirements for marriage, put limits on interest rates and other business practices, prohibit fraud, establish minimum wages and minimum standards for contracts, protect inventions through patents, and define crimes and give guidelines for punishing criminals.
- *Regulations*—Orders enacted by public administrative agencies to supervise or control various matters that affect the general public. These agencies—such as the Social Security Administration and the Environmental Protection Agency—are set up by the U. S. Congress and state legislatures, which give them the power to make and enforce regulations. Among other things, regulations bar discrimination in hiring, set radio and television broadcasting standards, and establish safety standards for food and drugs. Violating a regulation is essentially the same as violating a statute. Violators can be subject to a variety of disciplinary actions, including fines and having their licenses revoked.
- *Ordinances*—Laws enacted by a municipal legislature, often called the city council. Rules relating to the health, safety, and welfare of residents—such as those involving parking, littering, or snow removal—are examples of ordinances. Since cities and towns derive their powers from the state in which they're located, they cannot pass ordinances that contradict or violate state laws.
- *Uniform codes*—Model laws drafted by scholars in particular fields, such as commercial law or family law, which may be adopted with or without modification by the states. The Uniform Commercial Code and the Uniform Probate Code are examples of such codes.
- *Common law (also known as case law)*—A body of principles based on earlier court decisions in similar cases. When no specific statute or regulation applies to a particular case, the principles of common law are applied by the court.

declared only if our country's system of law or government has completely broken down. Martial law must end when it is possible for the civil government to resume power.

After a bad flood, our governor declared a state of emergency and ordered the National Guard into the most devastated areas. What gives him the right to do this?

All states have laws that authorize the governor to declare a state of emergency and to call out the National Guard. Events that may trigger this emergency authorization are earthquakes, floods, fires, airplane crashes, riots, rebellions, invasions, and war. The governor is authorized to give whatever power and authority he deems necessary to the National Guard to protect people's lives, liberty, and property. This might include enforcing curfews to keep people safe and out of the way of emergency workers, as well as evacuating residents, safeguarding property, and directing the activities of organizations participating in the relief effort.

Ray, a sergeant in the army, is facing a court-martial. Does he lose any of his basic rights as a citizen because he will stand trial before a military court?

The sergeant—along with everyone else in the U. S. armed services—is subject to the Uniform Code of Military Justice, and his rights under this code closely resemble the rights of nonmilitary citizens, especially in the area of criminal law. Ray has the right to an attorney and to a fair hearing, and to appeal the verdict, but he does not have the right to trial by jury.

Why don't all the states have the same laws?

The U. S. Constitution leaves to each state the power to pass its own laws in matters where there is no overriding national concern. For example, states have the exclusive right to determine what requirements must be met for an individual to marry or to get a divorce.

Our city has an ordinance prohibiting trucks from traveling on boulevards. This includes pickup trucks used for personal transportation. Can we get this ordinance changed?

Yes. City ordinances are enacted by your local city council, or the equivalent governing body. Legislation to change an ordinance must be proposed by a member of the council. You may ask your city councilman to introduce legislation to abolish the ordinance or amend it to exclude pickup trucks used for personal transportation. If you are unable to persuade your city council member to propose such legislation, circulating a petition among local residents may help your cause. If presented with a petition, signed by a large number of voters, the council member might be more inclined to act on this issue.

You might also appeal directly to the mayor, or if your city has a street department or traffic-planning division, you might want to ask them to study your city's need for truck traffic on boulevards. Many cities rely on the advice of transportation officials for recommendations about ordinances regulating traffic.

U.S. Citizenship

How does a person become a U.S. citizen?

A person becomes a citizen by birth or by naturalization. You automatically become a citizen if you are born in one of the 50 states, the District of Columbia, the Commonwealth of Puerto Rico, or one of the U. S. territories. You are also a citizen if you are born in a foreign country but you have at least one parent who is a U. S. citizen and a report of your birth is filed with the U. S. consulate in the country of your birth. If you are born at a U. S. military medical facility, this report, called a consular report of birth, is filed automatically by the military.

Naturalization is the legal process used by those who do not qualify for citizenship by birth. The applicant for citizenship must meet several eligibility requirements, file a petition, go through a hearing to examine his qualifications, and take an oath of allegiance to the United States.

Is it possible for an American to have dual citizenship?

Generally no, but there is an exception. If a child is born in the United States but both of his parents are citizens of another country, or if he is born abroad and one or both of his parents are U. S. citizens, he may have the rights and responsibilities of citizenship in the United States as well as those of citizenship of the other country.

What is a green card?

It is a card that identifies a person as a legal immigrant who is living permanently in the United States in anticipation of becoming a naturalized citizen. It is named for its traditional color (although most of these cards are still green, white ones are sometimes issued). The green card is issued by the Immigration and Naturalization Service (INS) when it grants immigrant status to an incoming foreigner. Temporary visitors, such as tourists, students, businessmen, and crew members of airplanes and ships, do not qualify for green cards.

I have the opportunity to hire a highly qualified woman from another country as a nanny for my child. What steps must I take to get her into the country legally?

You, the employer, will have to file a petition with the Immigration and Naturalization Service (INS). If your nanny will be employed in the United States only for a time and then expects to return home, you will have to file a petition with the INS for a nonimmigrant visa, which will allow her to come for a certain period—one or two years with possible extensions. If

Becoming a U.S. Citizen

Each year thousands of immigrants become U. S. citizens through the process of naturalization. Generally each person applying for citizenship must meet six eligibility requirements. He must:

1. Be at least 18 years old.
2. Have been admitted as a permanent resident in the United States at least five years before filing an application for naturalization and have been physically present in the state where the petition is filed during the six months before applying.
3. Show that he is a person of good moral character. Convicted murderers and gamblers, those connected with narcotics or prostitution, those convicted and jailed for as much as 180 days, and habitual drunkards will not be granted citizenship.
4. Renounce allegiance to his former country, promise to obey the laws of the United States, and—unless there is an objection on religious grounds—agree to serve in the armed forces or perform other services as required by the government.
5. Be able to speak, read, write, and understand the English language. Some exceptions are made for older applicants.
6. Know the history of the United States and understand how the government operates. Citizenship classes in these subjects and in the English language are often given by schools and other community agencies, and textbooks are available from the federal government and civic organizations.

the employee is coming to the United States permanently, then you will have to file a special visa petition, called a Form I-140. In both cases, you will have to obtain a certificate from the U. S. Department of Labor stating that the skill you require is in short supply in the United States. To obtain this certificate, you will have to advertise for a U. S. worker to fill the job at a reasonable wage, and then show that you were unable to fill the job. The entire process takes from four to six months to complete.

Can an American ever lose his citizenship?

Yes. Any American can lose his citizenship if, by his own choice, he (1) serves in the armed forces of another country, (2) serves as an official of another country, (3) becomes a naturalized citizen of another country, or (4) renounces his citizenship and declares allegiance to another country. A naturalized citizen may lose his U.S. citizenship if it is discovered that it was obtained by fraud, such as by concealing a criminal record in his native country.

If a person meets all of these requirements, he is ready to begin the naturalization process. The first step in the process is to complete the Application to File Petition for Naturalization and fill out a biographical information form and a fingerprint card. The forms are available free of charge from any immigration counseling agency or office of the Immigration and Naturalization Service (INS) or from the clerk of the naturalization court. The completed forms should be mailed to the INS or taken to the nearest INS office.

The second step in the process is the examination. After receiving the application, the INS office will schedule an appointment, which because of the backlog of applicants, may be several months later. Two witnesses should accompany the applicant to this appointment to verify that the applicant has been a resident of this country for five years and that he is a person of good moral character. The INS examiner will take the testimony of the witnesses and question the applicant in English about U. S. history and government. If the INS examiner determines that the applicant has met all the requirements, he will send the application to the clerk of the court. The clerk will prepare the formal petition for naturalization and give it to the applicant and the two witnesses to sign. A small filing fee must be paid at this time.

The third step is a personal appearance at the final hearing. This will not take place until at least 30 days after the petition is filed. The judge conducting the final hearing will make sure that everything is in order, administer an oath of allegiance, and issue the Certificate of Naturalization to the new U. S. citizen.

Your Right to Vote

Who determines if a person is eligible to register to vote?

Each state establishes the eligibility requirements for its voters. However, these requirements must not violate three amendments to the U.S. Constitution: the 15th Amendment, which prohibits voter discrimination based on "race, color, or previous condition of servitude"; the 19th Amendment, which prohibits discrimination based on sex; and the 26th Amendment, which lowered the voting age from 21 to 18.

Can state governments require residents to pay their taxes before allowing them to vote?

No. The U. S. Supreme Court has ruled that requiring a person to pay his taxes as a precondition to voting is unconstitutional. States may not impose poll taxes, and cities may not require residents to pay real estate or personal property taxes before voting in a municipal bond election.

Carla's parents live in one state, but she goes to college in another. In which state should Carla register to vote?

Carla can choose either state. If she wants to vote in her college town, she may have to establish that she no longer considers her parents' residence her home and that she intends to make the college town her legal residence for the time she is a student.

Bernice moved to another state where a gubernatorial election was to be held a month later. When Bernice tried to register to vote in that election, the clerk told her she was ineligible because she had not lived in the state long enough. Was this legal?

Yes. A state can establish residency requirements for its voters, as long as the requirements are not excessive. States have residency requirements ranging from a few days to as much as 50 days before an election, but courts have ruled against 1-year and even 90-day residency requirements.

Had the election Bernice wanted to vote in been a presidential election, she would have been able to vote despite the residency requirement. It is a violation of the Voting Rights Act to deny anyone the right to vote in a presidential election because he or she did not meet a residency requirement. In order to vote in a presidential election without being registered, a person need only complete an application at the polling place or file a certificate of an intent to vote. Each local board of elections has its own procedure.

Are criminals who have served time allowed to vote?

It depends on state law. The U. S. Supreme Court has ruled that the Constitution does not prohibit states from excluding convicted felons from voting; thus each state establishes its own restrictions. In Texas, for example, convicted felons must be pardoned, wait two years after completing their probation, or receive a discharge from the board of pardons and paroles before they are eligible to vote.

I plan to be on a cruise to the Caribbean on election day, and I want to cast an absentee ballot before I leave, but the board of elections won't let me. Do they have the right to refuse me?

Yes. Absentee voting is regarded as a privilege, not as a right. While most states have laws permitting absentee voting for primaries and regular elections, they often require that the voter's absence be truly unavoidable. Generally, you can get an absentee ballot if your work will take you out of town on election day, but you may or may not be able to get one if you are on vacation, depending on the law in your state.

Freedom of Religion

Prayer is important to me, and I believe that our children should be encouraged to pray. Why can't the state pass a law requiring public school children to say a simple, nondenominational prayer together each morning to start off the school day right?

The courts have consistently held that time set aside for prayer in the public schools violates the First Amendment to the U. S. Constitution. No law or regulation can require a student to participate in a religious activity such as prayer, even a nondenominational or silent prayer.

Andrea is an officer of a campus church group at the state university. When she tried to reserve a room at the student union for a church service, the manager refused to let her have the room. Is he justified in doing this?

No. The manager probably thinks that allowing a church group to use a state facility violates the constitutional prohibition against the government's promoting one religion over another. This is not the case here, however. The university can allow church groups to meet on its premises as long as it treats all church groups equally—it cannot allow one group to meet in the school but refuse another.

Freedom of Religion

Under a state law, Arthur is required to close his card shop on Sundays, but he would rather stay open on Sundays and close on Saturdays, when his religion celebrates the Sabbath. Would Arthur be successful if he challenged this law as violating his First Amendment right to freedom of religion?

Probably not. Courts have consistently upheld store closing laws because their purpose is to establish a uniform day of rest, rather than to conform to a religious practice. However, Arthur might challenge the law if it discriminates against certain types of businesses or if it is vague—courts have overturned laws that were so vague that it was hard to determine which stores must close on Sundays and which need not close.

Joe had four wives at the same time and was found guilty of polygamy. He claims that his religion encourages polygamy and the state is interfering with the practice of his religion. Is he right?

No. Though the Bill of Rights includes the freedom to practice one's religion, a person may be prevented from performing a specific religious practice if it violates the law. Courts have consistently ruled that society is better served by state laws that make polygamy illegal than by exceptions that would allow it.

As parents, do we have the right to prevent our children from receiving medical treatment that is contrary to our religion?

No. When a child's health—or the health of the public—is at stake, courts have consistently ruled against parents who have tried to deny their children medical treatment for religious reasons. Vaccinations and blood transfusions are two examples of medical treatment that courts have ordered against the wishes of the parents.

Freedom of Speech

If my coworkers and I want to protest our employer's practices, do we have the right to carry signs of protest?

Yes. The freedom of speech guaranteed by the First Amendment is not limited to oral communications. Opinions expressed in signs and on bumper stickers, buttons, and T-shirts are equally protected. However, the messages on your signs must not incite people to cause a disturbance or break the law. If you belong to a union, there may be additional guidelines or restrictions on how your message can be expressed. Your union representative can advise you about the legal requirements.

Can an irate customer picket a store without getting a permit?

Probably, as long as he doesn't get his friends together to picket in a group. The right of free speech includes the right to picket, as long as the picketing does not intimidate customers or result in violence. Generally, a permit is required only when a group of people are planning a demonstration.

If I get angry and call my boss a crook, can he sue me?

Only if the incident amounted to slander. Calling someone a crook does not automatically qualify as slander. The circumstances and the effect of the statement on your boss's reputation would have to be considered. If you made your statement in the hearing of others and in such a way that someone who heard it interpreted it to mean that your boss was really dishonest, or if the remark resulted in your boss's being ridiculed, he may have a legitimate claim for a lawsuit. If your boss sues you, he will have to show that someone besides the two of you heard the remark and that the remark caused harm or was meant to harm his reputation.

In a speech Senator McFibbert made in the state legislature about a bill to regulate home remodeling companies, he called Jerry's Builders "a bunch of crooks" led by "a man who has been convicted of fraud." No one at Jerry's has ever been convicted of fraud. Can the owner sue the senator for slander?

He can, but he doesn't have a very good case. As a general rule, legislators cannot be sued for statements they make while acting in their official capacity. Both the federal and state constitutions protect legislators from lawsuits or criminal charges for what they say or do during a legislative session. However, this protection would not apply if the senator distributed copies of his speech about Jerry's Builders to the general public.

Deborah's pastor named her as a sinner in a Sunday sermon. Now no one from her church will speak to her. Can she sue her pastor?

Depending on what precisely her pastor said, Deborah might be able to sue him for defamation of character or for invasion of privacy. Speaking from the pulpit does not give a clergyman any special legal privilege or protect him from being sued. Lawsuits have been brought against clergymen for disclosing private facts to the public and for intentionally inflicting emotional distress. To win her case, Deborah would have to show that the pastor said something about her that would be highly offensive to an average person and did not simply make some general remark about all of us being sinners, "like you and Deborah and me."

Our Patriots' Club would like to propose a new state law that would require all schoolchildren to salute the flag and recite the Pledge of Allegiance or be suspended from school until they agree to do so. Would such a law be valid?

No. Courts have ruled against schools that require every student to salute the flag and recite the Pledge of Allegiance. Schools may not even require students to stand in silence or leave the room if they do not want to participate in this ceremony. As long as a student does not disrupt class when the Pledge of Allegiance is being said, he cannot be punished.

Freedom of the Press

Can a judge keep news reporters from attending a trial?

Yes, if there is an overriding reason for excluding them. Though reporters have a general right to attend criminal trials, a judge can deny them access if he feels their presence would make it difficult for the defendant to get a fair trial. A judge might keep reporters from covering a civil trial if he felt they might publish testimony that revealed a company's trade secrets or private matters discussed by a couple seeking a divorce.

Chad was interviewed on videotape by a television reporter. The tape that was aired later had been so edited that it changed the meaning of what he had said. What can Chad do to force the television station to air a more accurate version of the interview?

Chad should contact the reporter or the station manager and ask him to broadcast the unedited tape or broadcast a statement correcting the false impression that was made by airing the edited tape. If Chad believes that the television station intentionally misrepresented or distorted his comments, he can notify the Federal Communications Commission (FCC). The station may have violated FCC regulations.

Since publicity that places a person in a false light is considered an invasion of privacy, Chad may be able to sue on these grounds. Chad would not have to establish that his reputation had been damaged, as he would if he sued for slander. But he would have to show that an average person would have thought the broadcast was highly offensive.

A newspaper article said that a nationally known singer and the owner of a local business—whom it specifically named—had been seen in a nightclub with a man "suspected of having organized crime connections." Would either the singer or the businessman have a good case for suing the newspaper for libel?

Possibly. Both the singer and the businessman would have to prove that their reputations had been damaged. But courts distinguish between public figures, such as the singer, and private individuals, such as the businessman. The singer would have to establish that the statements were made with malice—that when the statements were printed, the newspaper knew they were false or had reason to believe that they might be false, but made no effort to verify them.

The businessman may not have to prove malice; most states require a private individual to show only negligence—that the newspaper failed to acquire the facts. The other states do require private individuals to show malice or gross irresponsibility—disregarding the standards ordinarily used by journalists to gather and disseminate information.

Derek, a reporter for a big city newspaper, has been given information about a new military weapon. The government has told Derek that the information must not be published. Isn't this a violation of freedom of the press?

No. The courts have recognized that there is a legitimate interest in keeping some sensitive government information from being published. The government could seek an injunction to halt the publication of this information. However, it would first have to prove that national security would be threatened if the material were published.

Our county commission has established a review board for all motion pictures shown in our area. Doesn't this infringe on my right to decide what I want to see in the theater?

No. The state has a legitimate interest in limiting the availability of obscene materials. Therefore, the state or its subdivisions may adopt procedures to review and rate movies. However, a review board cannot block the showing of a movie on its own, but must convince a court to issue an injunction against showing the film on the grounds that it is obscene, corrupts morals, or incites people to commit crimes.

Your Right to Have Firearms

Chris, who does a lot of hunting, claims that a proposed gun control law in his community would be unconstitutional because it would restrict his right to own and use guns. Is he correct?

No. The Second Amendment to the U. S. Constitution deals with the right of the American people to keep firearms, but it does not prohibit gun control laws. What the amendment says is that the people have a right to keep and bear arms in case they ever need to form a militia to protect themselves. Courts have interpreted the Second Amendment to mean that the people as a group rather than as individuals have the right to keep society safe and secure. Similar provisions in state constitutions have been interpreted in the same way. State and local governments are allowed to pass gun control laws to protect the public health and safety.

There have been several burglaries in our neighborhood recently. Are we allowed to keep a handgun at home for self-defense?

Check with your local police department. State and local gun control laws often prohibit handgun ownership. Even if you are allowed to keep a handgun, you may have to register the weapon and get a license for it.

When Ronald went to the gun shop to buy a shotgun, the store owner made him fill out a registration form. Then he had to wait one week before he could pick up the gun. Doesn't the U.S. Constitution allow Ronald to buy a gun without going through all of this annoying paperwork and waiting?

Not necessarily. States and cities may require the registration and licensing of guns at the time of purchase without violating the Constitution. Licensing requirements frequently include a waiting period that gives the police time to check the applicant's background—anyone who has been convicted of a crime involving the use of a gun will generally not be given a license. The waiting period also allows a person who is angry or upset time to cool off and reconsider his reasons for buying the weapon.

Is it legal to carry a high-powered hunting rifle in the trunk of a car?

Probably. While it is illegal in most instances to carry or transport a concealed weapon, state laws often make an exception if the gun is in the trunk of a car. But you may have to meet special state requirements. West Virginia law, for example, allows someone to transport firearms used for hunting, but only if the person has a state hunting license.

Jesse is an antique gun collector. Does he also have to comply with licensing and registration laws in his state?

Some states, including Indiana and South Dakota, exempt antique firearms from licensing or registration requirements. Other states require that antique guns be altered so that they cannot be fired.

Equality Under the Law

For information on job discrimination, see "Job Discrimination" in Chapter 10, *Your Job*.

Lawyers in civil rights cases frequently talk about the equal protection clause. What is this, and where is it found?

The equal protection clause is found in the 14th Amendment to the U. S. Constitution, and says: "No state shall . . . deny to any person within its jurisdiction the equal protection of the laws." This clause ensures that no law will be enacted that discriminates against a particular group of people. It also ensures that laws will not be enforced in a discriminatory manner.

However, there are some circumstances in which courts have upheld laws that single out or exclude groups of people; examples are laws that exclude felons from voting, and laws that require men, but not women, to register for the draft.

Rex is concerned that a lot of highway accidents have involved 18-to-21-year-old men who were drinking and driving. Would it be legal to pass a law raising the drinking age to 22 for men and leaving it at 18 for women?

Probably not. The Supreme Court has already declared a similar law to be unconstitutional because it denied equal protection of the laws to 18-to-21-year-old men. The Court noted that if a state could demonstrate that traffic safety would be substantially benefited by having a different drinking age for men and women, such a law might be upheld. But the statistics offered in the 1976 Supreme Court case did not prove this point.

The people in our neighborhood are concerned about the noise of the summer rock concerts at a nearby park and the rowdiness of many of the people attending them. Could we get the city commission to pass an ordinance allowing the police to deny permits to rock bands?

No. A restriction of this kind would probably be unenforceable. While the courts recognize that limits on the time, place, and manner of noisy performances may be needed, the city would find it difficult to justify an ordinance against all rock bands. Prohibiting access to a public forum to one segment of society is a denial of the equal protection of the laws guaranteed by the Constitution. The city would be in a better position to enforce an ordinance that required all park activities to end at a certain time or that restricted the use of loudspeakers.

Bart and his twin sister, Blanche, just celebrated their 18th birthdays. Bart will have to register with the Selective Service, but his sister will not. Isn't this discrimination?

No. The Supreme Court has ruled that laws requiring only men to register are not discriminatory. Since the primary purpose of registration is to obtain a list of names of people available for combat duty and military policy bars women from combat duty, there is no need to have women's names on a registration list.

Rights of Nonsmokers

Although a person who smokes tobacco has a legal right to indulge his personal habit without government restriction, the well-being of society in general must also be considered. Because scientists and medical researchers have established that the smoke from other people's cigarettes can harm us, many cities and states have enacted legislation to protect nonsmokers without seriously curtailing the rights of smokers. The typical law does not completely prohibit smoking. Instead, it designates areas where smoking is permitted and where it is not. Violations of no-smoking laws are usually misdemeanors, and are generally punishable by fines. Here are some typical restrictions:

- Retail stores, restaurants, schools, theaters, and other buildings open to the public must reserve specific areas for smoking and no smoking.
- Smoking is prohibited in elevators, trains and buses, restrooms, health facilities, libraries, and courtrooms.
- Under a regulation of the Federal Aviation Administration, airlines must seat smokers apart from passengers who do not wish to smoke.
- In Maine and New Hampshire, employers must develop a written policy about restrictions on smoking at work, and in other states, many companies are doing this on their own without being compelled by law.
- In Rhode Island, employers must either ban smoking totally in the workplace or provide reasonable accommodations for nonsmokers.
- In Nebraska, employers must ask a worker to stop smoking if a coworker requests it.

Angela, president of the PTA at our public high school, is upset because one of the new teachers admitted, when asked, that she is a lesbian. If Angela manages to get the teacher fired, will the dismissal stand up in court?

Probably not, unless Angela can show that the teacher is no longer competent to carry out her school duties. Public schools are run by the government, and the government may not engage in discrimination. Teachers have successfully challenged school board policies that prohibit the hiring of homosexuals; and courts have ruled that being a homosexual does not mean that a person will or will not be an incompetent teacher.

A large number of refugees have moved into our city recently, and a few of them have applied for positions as teachers in our local schools. Can the school board legally refuse to hire them?

Not if the applicants are certified to teach in your state. However, states have the right to require teachers to be U. S. citizens before they can be certified. Among the states that have such a requirement are Illinois, Massachusetts, North Dakota, Pennsylvania, Texas, New York, and Washington. However, these states also allow qualified teachers who are not citizens to be certified if they declare their intention of becoming citizens.

Can a state limit professional licenses to U.S. citizens?

Not generally. Any law that automatically excludes foreigners can be challenged in court. In the past, foreigners have won cases against laws that prohibited them from becoming attorneys or engineers. However, courts have upheld citizenship requirements for some educational or government workers, such as teachers, state troopers, and probation officers.

After joining a fraternal organization in town, I learned that it excludes people because of their race. Isn't this illegal?

No. A fraternal organization is a private club, and is free to establish any membership qualifications it wants. This means an individual can legally be denied membership, even for a discriminatory reason. Courts cannot force a private club to accept someone as a member. However, many private clubs that once restricted membership to a certain race or sex have yielded to the pressure of public opinion and have dropped such restrictions.

Faith wants to join a nationally recognized organization that is very well known for its charitable activities. Her application for

membership in the local chapter was denied, and she was told that only men were accepted as members. What can Faith do?

Faith could file a lawsuit against the organization for sex discrimination, but since private clubs are allowed to restrict their membership, Faith would have to show that this organization could not be considered a private club. If it administered projects that served the public, had ties to local or state government or business, or had activities in which nonmembers participated, a court might rule that it must open its membership to women as well as men.

My Aunt Hazel is confined to a wheelchair. What are her rights of access to public buildings and public transportation?

A number of federal laws require better access for the handicapped to public buildings and transportation. The federal Architectural Barriers Act states that all federally financed buildings should be designed, constructed, or renovated so that physically disabled people can gain access to them. The Urban Mass Transit Act makes similar requirements for mass transit systems that receive federal aid. Amendments to the Airport and Airway Development Act require all new airport terminals and existing facilities undergoing renovation to provide access to the handicapped. Where federal funds are used to improve streets and highways, ramps or curb cuts must be provided at each intersection. In addition, nearly every state has enacted legislation to prohibit or restrict architectural barriers to the handicapped.

In 1990, Congress passed the Americans With Disabilities Act, which extended requirements for accessibility to the handicapped to hotels, motels, restaurants, theaters, shops, grocery stores, schools and recreational facilities, and many other privately owned and operated builidngs.

Your Right to Privacy

A newspaper reporter interviewed me by telephone and taped the call without asking my permission. Isn't this illegal?

Not necessarily. Federal law allows the person you are having a phone conversation with to tape the call without permission. However, some states—including Georgia, Michigan, and Pennsylvania—have laws that require your consent. If the law in your state requires the consent of both persons in a phone conversation for the call to be taped legally, you could sue the newspaper and bring criminal charges against the reporter.

Can a court force a lawyer to reveal confidential information about a client? What about doctors and priests?

A lawyer cannot be compelled to reveal confidential conversations with a client. The law recognizes that a client must be able to disclose facts about a case to his attorney without fear that they will be divulged to other people.

Most states have laws protecting confidential communications between a doctor and his patient or a clergyman and his parishioner. Doctors do not have to release information about a patient unless their silence would threaten the health or safety of others; for example, a doctor may be required by law to report that a patient has a communicable disease. A doctor must also notify the authorities if a child he is treating shows signs of abuse or if he treats a patient for a gunshot wound.

Members of the clergy do not have to disclose communications made by a person seeking spiritual comfort—as in confession—or privately discussing religious matters, even if the person admits to committing a serious crime. However, this protection does not apply if the clergyman is acting as a marriage counselor.

The state attorney general has informed Guy, a pharmacist, of a new law that requires him to provide a list of all customers who purchase a particular prescription drug. Won't Guy be violating his customers' privacy if he provides such a list?

No. The Supreme Court has upheld a similar law that was aimed at minimizing the misuse of dangerous drugs. Although pharmacy customers have a right to privacy in personal matters, such as what medicines they buy, the Court noted that a state's duty to protect the public health is great enough to justify a limited intrusion into individuals' rights to privacy.

Brandon would like to know what information the FBI and other federal agencies have gathered about him. How can he find out?

Brandon should write to each agency and request the information he wants. The Freedom of Information Act requires federal agencies to release information in their files unless it is confidential for reasons of personal privacy (someone else's medical records, for example) or classified because of national security. Under the Privacy Act, a person may review the files an agency has on him, correct any mistakes, and even add new information. Since these two acts differ in terms of deadlines, the right to demand or amend a file, and the right to appeal, Brandon should refer to both of them in his letter of request.

Since there is a fee for copying information, Brandon might state that if costs exceed a certain amount, he would like to review the material before it is copied. This will help him avoid paying for copies he does not want.

Your Right to Privacy

Can a person's photograph be used in an advertisement without his consent?

No. The unauthorized commercial use of a photograph in which a particular person can be clearly identified can be an invasion of privacy. In one case, a customer successfully sued a photo studio because after having taken some photographs of her, it used one, without her permission, to promote the studio.

While André was picketing at a gay rights rally in a nearby city, a reporter took his picture and published it in André's hometown paper. André was clearly recognizable in the photo, and as a result, he has been teased and harassed by his neighbors and coworkers. Can André sue the paper for invasion of privacy, since they didn't get his permission to publish the picture?

No. Courts recognize that the right to privacy must be balanced against the guarantee of freedom of the press. When an event is of public interest, such as a political rally, a newspaper can publish articles including the names and pictures of participants, without getting the permission of the individuals involved.

My son ran away from home when he was 12 years old, and I had to ask the police to help find him. Will the records of this incident be kept confidential?

Yes. In many states, including Connecticut, Maryland, Minnesota, Missouri, and Washington, police records on juveniles are kept confidential and cannot be read or obtained by the general public. In other states, such as North Carolina, juvenile records must be kept in a separate file, and access to them is limited to the prosecutor, the juvenile himself, and his parents or legal guardian.

Percy lives in a boardinghouse where the mail for all the residents is left on a table in the entrance hall. Someone has been opening Percy's personal mail. What can he do about it?

Percy should report his problem to the local postmaster. It is a crime to tamper with someone else's mail, and it makes no difference whether the mail is still in the hands of the Postal Service or left on a hall table. Anyone convicted of tampering with the mail can be fined up to $2,000 or given a jail sentence of up to five years.

Ever since I bought my videocassette recorder I have been receiving ads for X-rated films. I don't want this type of mail coming into my house. Is there anything I can do about it?

Yes. You should contact the post office and request that your name be placed on the Postal Service list of persons who do not want to receive sexually oriented advertisements. When you fill out the required form, you can also include the names of your children so that mail is not addressed to them either. It is a federal crime to mail such advertisements to people on the Postal Service list.

How can I put a stop to obscene phone calls?

Report an obscene call to the telephone company as soon as possible; the number to call should be listed in the front of your telephone directory, along with information about the best way to handle such calls. The telephone company is often able to track down the source of obscene phone calls and can take legal action to put an end to them. Under the federal Communications Act, anyone making obscene phone calls can be punished by a fine, imprisonment, or both. Laws in many states, including Georgia, Indiana, and Kansas, also prohibit obscene comments, suggestions, or proposals over the telephone.

Nora, a neighbor of ours, sometimes wanders outside our house at night, climbing through the shrubbery and peering in through our windows. Although we really have nothing to hide, we feel uneasy about being watched. Isn't this an invasion of our privacy? How should we handle this matter?

You might try talking with Nora and telling her that you will call the police the next time you see her looking into your windows. If this doesn't work, notify the police. State and local laws in most places make it a misdemeanor to look through people's windows in order to pry into their private lives.

A group of people in our town want to reserve a part of the local beach for nude sunbathing. Can we stop them?

You would have to contact the mayor or city council about enacting an ordinance prohibiting nudity on public beaches and in other public areas. Courts have upheld this type of ordinance as a valid way for town residents to ensure the peaceful enjoyment of public property. Your state may also have a law against people's exposing themselves in public. If so, the law can be enforced to keep people from sunbathing in the nude.

Dealing With the Police

For arrests, see "Rights of the Accused" in Chapter 17, *Victims and Crimes*.

A stranger was walking up and down our street late the other night, and two police officers stopped and frisked him because he "looked suspicious." Wasn't this illegal?

Yes, unless there was some reason to suspect that the stranger had committed a crime or was about to commit one. For example, if the stranger had been walking up and down the street in a high-crime neighborhood, giving the impression that he was casing a house to rob, the police would have been justified in stopping him.

They could also have frisked him if they believed their personal safety was at stake, but the frisk, or pat-down, could have been done only to search for weapons.

Can a store detective stop me from leaving even if I haven't done anything wrong?

Yes. A store detective has the right to stop a customer if he has reason to believe that the customer has stolen something, as long as the detective does not mistreat the customer or detain him for an unreasonable length of time. A number of states—including Florida, Michigan, Ohio, and Oklahoma—have laws that protect store owners from liability for unlawful detention if it turns out that a customer who was stopped had done nothing wrong.

Ira came to Gordon's home while the police were searching it for evidence of a robbery. Can the police search Ira?

No. The police can only search those areas specified in the search warrant. Unless they have reason to believe that Ira has also committed a crime, there is no legal justification for searching him.

The police searched Adrian's car while it was parked in front of his house. Was this legal?

Only if they believed that there was some evidence of a crime hidden in the car, such as stolen goods. Generally, the police must get a search warrant that specifically describes a car before they can open and search it without the owner's permission. However, they may not need a search warrant if there isn't time to get one: Courts make exceptions to the warrant requirement if there is reason to believe that the evidence will be destroyed or the car will be moved before a search warrant can be obtained.

When the Police Can Search Without a Warrant

Most searches of a person or his property are considered illegal if they are conducted without a warrant that describes the person or place to be searched and the things that can be taken. Evidence found during an illegal search cannot be used in court. There are several special situations, however, in which the police can legally carry out a search without a warrant:

- *A consent search*—The police may make a search without a warrant if the person involved gives his consent without being coerced. However, the search must be confined to the area the person authorized. For example, if someone agrees to a search of his living room, the police cannot open a file cabinet in his den without a warrant.
- *A plain-view search*—Police may seize evidence that is out in the open or that comes to light as they search for something else for which they have a warrant. But evidence obtained this way cannot be used in court unless: (1) the police were lawfully at the location where the item was found, (2) it was obvious that the item was evidence of a crime, and (3) the discovery was accidental. For example, if the police are searching a suspect's hotel room for a gun, and unexpectedly uncover a cache of counterfeit money, they may take the money and use it as evidence against the suspect, even though it was not mentioned in the warrant.
- *A stop and frisk*—If a police officer believes he is in danger, he may stop and frisk, or pat down, a suspect to find a concealed weapon.
- *A search incident to arrest*—When making an arrest, a police officer may search the suspect and the area within the suspect's immediate vicinity for weapons or evidence of the crime that has been committed in order to protect himself from bodily harm and to keep the evidence from being lost or destroyed.
- *An inventory search*—When the police impound cars or take into their possession other personal property that belongs to a suspect, they may search the property to make a list of everything impounded. This is permitted to protect the suspect's property and to protect the police from claims that they have stolen something and from possible dangers, such as explosives hidden in a car.
- *Emergency searches*—The police may search without a warrant if they have a good reason, or probable cause, to believe that they will find evidence that could be moved, hidden, or destroyed—burned or flushed away, for example—before they could return with a warrant. This often occurs when officers are chasing a suspect who enters a building.
- *Vehicle searches*—If the police have probable cause, or good reason, to believe that evidence of a crime will be found in a car, truck, boat, or other vehicle that could easily be moved elsewhere before they could obtain a warrant, they may search the vehicle on the spot. For example, if the police have good reason to believe that a car is carrying illegal drugs, they can stop it and search it on the highway.

Dealing With the Police

In an effort to crack down on the use of drugs in our local high school, the principal agreed to let the police conduct random drug tests of students. Is this legal?

No. Drug tests are a type of search, and the police cannot conduct searches unless they have what the law calls probable cause to believe there is wrongdoing. Probable cause is a set of circumstances that would give an ordinary person reasonable grounds for believing that the law is being violated. Courts have ruled against random drug tests by government agencies, stating that there must be a reasonable suspicion about a particular person before a drug test can be required. However, courts have upheld drug testing of persons in jobs that affect public safety, such as fire fighters and air traffic controllers.

Can a male police officer search a woman who is suspected of hiding illegal drugs under her clothing?

No. The body search should be conducted by a female officer. The procedure for these searches may be regulated by state law—as in Illinois, Iowa, and Kansas—or by the local police department's regulations.

I was walking downtown the other day when a man ran toward me. A policeman across the street shouted to me, "Stop that guy!" I didn't, and the police officer arrested me. Can he do that?

Yes. You have an obligation to assist the police when they seek help, and in many states, you could be charged with a misdemeanor for refusing. If you live in South Dakota, for example, you could get 30 days in jail and a $100 fine for failing to help a police officer.

CHAPTER
13

Accidents

Accidents Inside Your Home

For car accidents, see Chapter 6, *Your Car.* For auto insurance, see Chapter 8, *Insurance.* For information on other types of accidents, see "Liability for Personal Injury" in Chapter 8, *Insurance,* and "Workers' Compensation" in Chapter 10, *Your Job.*

Lydia's bridge club met at her house while it was being remodeled. Since there were pieces of wood scattered all over the floor, Lydia warned her guests to be careful, but Madge tripped and fractured her elbow. Is Lydia liable for Madge's injury?

Probably not. A homeowner is not automatically liable for every injury that results from an accident in the home. As a hostess, Lydia has a duty to tell her guests about any dangerous conditions that are not obvious. Since pieces of wood scattered all over the floor would be clearly visible, and since Lydia warned the bridge players to be careful, she fulfilled her legal responsibility.

If a burglar breaks into my home, slips on my son's roller skate, and fractures his collarbone, can he sue me for damages?

No. When a burglar trespasses on your property, he assumes full responsibility for whatever hazards he may encounter. You are not liable for any accidental injuries a burglar receives while on your property.

Winning an Accident Case

You will not necessarily win a lawsuit just because you were injured or had your property damaged in an accident. Accidents occur even when everyone involved takes the proper precautions. To win an accident case, you must show that the person who caused the accident was negligent—he did something he shouldn't have or he didn't do something he should have. For a court to decide that someone was negligent, three basic conditions must be met:

1. *The person had a duty to use reasonable care to protect an individual from harm in a particular situation.* For example, if someone lights firecrackers to celebrate the Fourth of July, he should do so in a safe place and not in a crowded area. In some circumstances, a person has a duty to protect an individual because he has a special relationship or responsibility to him. For example, building owners have a duty to keep their buildings safe for tenants and visitors and to warn them of any danger. If the marble floor in the lobby of a building has just been washed and is still wet, the owner of the building has a duty to put up a notice saying Slippery When Wet. But if you see someone drowning in a motel

When Hank came into Joyce's home, he slipped on a throw rug in the hall and injured his back. Joyce helped Hank up, saying, "I really should move that rug. Everyone falls on it." Could Joyce's statement hurt her case if Hank decides to sue her?

Yes. Joyce's statement indicates that she knew the rug was a hazard. The court would take this into account when considering whether she had a legal duty either to warn Hank about the rug or to minimize the risk by using a rug with rubber backing.

During a party at Skip's house, Cheryl tripped over an extension cord and cracked two ribs. Afterward, some of the guests remarked that Cheryl had had too much to drink. Cheryl is now threatening to sue Skip for her medical expenses unless he pays her $5,000. Should he pay?

No. The fact that Cheryl was injured in Skip's home does not mean that he is automatically responsible. If the extension cord could be seen, Skip had no responsibility to warn his guests about it. On the other hand, if the danger were not clearly visible, a court would have to decide if Skip should have warned Cheryl.

The court would also consider whether Cheryl contributed to the accident by drinking too much liquor. It would then allocate a percentage

swimming pool, you have no legal duty to rescue him—even if you are an experienced swimmer—unless you are the lifeguard on duty or the motel owner or manager.

2. *The person failed to use reasonable care.* To determine what reasonable care is, courts ask the question, Would an ordinary person have acted in the same manner under similar circumstances? For example, in a case in which your neighbor's house accidentally caught fire, the court would consider whether an ordinary person would burn leaves near his neighbor's house on a windy day.

3. *The person's actions or failure to act caused the accident.* For example, if a customer dies in a fire because a store owner has blocked the exit with cartons of merchandise, the owner's action caused the customer's death; if you visit your neighbor and fall into a hole he dug in his yard, your neighbor caused the accident because he failed to cover the hole or warn you about the danger. However, a person is only liable for consequences that can be foreseen, and not for anything unpredictable. For example, a person can foresee that leaving his car keys in the ignition might result in the theft of his car, but not that the thief might then have an accident and injure someone.

of fault to both Skip and Cheryl. In some states, such as Wyoming, Utah, and North Dakota, Cheryl could collect only if she was less than 50 percent at fault. In other states, such as Washington, New York, and Rhode Island, she could collect even if she was more than 50 percent at fault. A few states would deny her any monetary compensation if she were at fault in any way.

While entering the lobby of my friend's apartment building, I pushed against the glass panel of the door because the push bar was missing. The glass broke, and I cut my arm. Can I sue the apartment building owner?

Yes. A landlord has a duty to keep his building's common areas in good repair. Before you decide to sue, however, make sure that you will be able to prove that the landlord was negligent. For example, if you could show that the landlord knew that the door's push bar was missing but failed to make the necessary repairs, or if you could find evidence that the glass had been cracked or loose for some time, you would have a good chance of winning your lawsuit.

During the summer we rent our vacation home to our friends. Can we have them sign a release waiving any claims against us if they are injured while occupying the house?

The law in your state will determine whether you can include such a provision limiting your liability. This provision, called an exculpatory clause, is prohibited in a number of states, including Kansas, Massachusetts, Maryland, and Montana. Even if you live in a state that does not prohibit exculpatory clauses, you should be careful about having such a clause in your agreement, because courts do not like people to sign away their legal right to sue.

Accidents Outside Your Home

Several boards on Anthony's front porch were missing, and others were loose. When a salesperson stepped up to ring the doorbell to see if anyone was home, he tripped and broke his leg. Is Anthony responsible?

In some states Anthony's duty to the salesperson depends on whether or not Anthony invited him to his home. If Anthony asked him to

Legal Responsibilities of Homeowners

When you own a home, you have a legal responsibility to keep your property safe for anyone who visits you. In some states, however, the amount of responsibility you bear depends on the reason for the person's visit. The law classifies visitors into three categories: invitees, licensees, and trespassers. Homeowners are most responsible for the safety of invitees and least responsible for the safety of trespassers.

- An *invitee* is someone you ask to your home to do some work for you, such as a repairman. A delivery man, such as a letter carrier or a furniture deliverer, is also included in this category. If an invitee is injured on your property, you will be held liable if you did not take steps to make your home safe or if you did not warn your visitor about the danger. For example, if there is a weak handrail on the stairs, you should have it repaired before the invitee arrives or else warn him about it. Once an invitee is on your property, you have a responsibility to use greater care than usual when performing potentially dangerous tasks, such as backing a car out of the driveway.
- A *licensee* is someone who comes into your home for his own benefit, such as a door-to-door salesperson or a person soliciting for charity. Friends and relatives who come to visit are also considered licensees. You have a legal duty to warn such visitors about any dangers that are not apparent, such as a slippery floor, and to use greater care than usual when performing potentially dangerous tasks.
- A *trespasser* is someone who enters your property without your permission, such as a burglar or a person who is lost. You are not liable if such a person is accidentally injured while on your property. However, a homeowner owes a special duty to children who trespass. He must take extra precautions if an object or condition on his land is both dangerous and likely to attract children. If the seat on a backyard swing is broken, for example, it should be either removed or repaired. If you know that someone repeatedly trespasses—whether the person is a child or an adult—you have a legal duty to make that person aware of any hidden dangers.

come, he had a duty to make sure his home was safe and to warn the salesperson about hidden dangers. If a court decided that the missing boards made it obvious that the porch was unsafe, Anthony would not be liable. If Anthony had not invited the salesperson, he would be liable only if he recklessly or intentionally exposed the salesperson to danger.

In other states, it doesn't matter whether the person was invited, since courts decide on a case-by-case basis whether conditions were clearly dangerous. Since the porch was in an obvious state of disrepair, Anthony could have anticipated that someone might be hurt, and therefore could be held partially or totally liable for the salesperson's injuries.

Accidents Outside Your Home

Ward's neighbor, Fred, borrowed Ward's chain saw to trim some trees in his backyard. Fred had an accident with the saw and needed surgery. Can Ward be held liable for compensating Fred for his injuries?

No, unless Ward lent the chain saw to his neighbor knowing that it was defective. When you lend property to someone without charge, your only responsibility is to warn the borrower about known defects. However, Ward could be held liable if he let his neighbor use the chain saw, knowing that Fred did not know how to operate it properly.

I repaired a bicycle that belonged to my neighbor's son Barry. While he was riding down a steep hill, the front wheel loosened, and the bicycle skidded into a wall. Can Barry's parents sue me?

For you to be liable, there must be some evidence that your repairs caused Barry to have the accident. Barry's parents would have to show that your repair work was the most likely cause of their son's injuries. The amount of time that elapsed between your repair work and the accident would be important in establishing this connection.

If there is evidence to attribute the accident to your repair work, Barry's parents must also prove that you did the work negligently. As long as you made the repairs in a reasonably competent manner, you would not be liable for Barry's injuries.

Nathaniel decided to put a fence around his yard, but only got as far as digging the postholes. That night, Jamie took a short cut through the yard, fell in one of the holes, and injured his Achilles tendon. Can Jamie sue Nathaniel?

Jamie has a good case if he lives in one of the states that do not take into consideration the purpose for which one person visits another's property. A court would probably decide that Nathaniel should have realized that unmarked or uncovered postholes are a hazard, and therefore declare him liable for Jamie's injuries.

If Jamie lives in a state that classifies him as a trespasser, however, he could only recover damages if a court rules that Nathaniel was clearly irresponsible in failing to cover the postholes.

If Jamie used the shortcut regularly, he may have a stronger case. As a homeowner, Nathaniel has a legal duty to protect people who have safely cut across his yard in the past. A court might say that Nathaniel should have put up a barrier, lights, or some other type of warning to let people like Jamie know that conditions had changed.

In the process of adding a garage to their home, the Nelsons had to have several large rocks dug out from the ground. The contractor piled the rocks in a corner of the backyard. Billy, a five-year-old boy, fell while climbing the rock pile. Are the Nelsons liable for Billy's injuries?

Perhaps. As homeowners, the Nelsons have a legal duty to protect young children, even if they are trespassing, from potentially dangerous situations they might be attracted to. The Nelsons should have realized that children would be attracted to the rock pile as a place to play. Swimming pools are the most common objects covered by this legal principle, which is called the attractive nuisance doctrine.

A neighbor's son was injured when he jumped off our diving board backwards. We have repeatedly warned him not to try such dangerous stunts. Are we liable?

Possibly. Your best argument for denying responsibility is that the boy contributed to his own injuries by ignoring your warnings. But your liability may depend on the age of the child. Courts have ruled that children under a certain age—some courts say age 7, others 14—cannot be held responsible for their negligent actions. To protect yourself in the future, you should make sure a responsible adult is on guard at the pool when children are using it.

Kirk has a swimming pool in his yard. Posted near the pool is a large sign that says, "Swim at your own risk." Does this sign relieve him of liability if a young child is injured in the pool?

No. Posting a sign is of little value to children who cannot yet read or understand what the words mean. Kirk should find out from the city clerk what the legal requirements are for residential swimming pools. Local laws may require that a fence be installed, and may even specify its height and the materials to be used.

Alfred built a swimming pool in his backyard and fenced in the yard. A youngster from next door climbed the fence, fell into the empty pool, and broke his leg. Is Alfred liable?

Under the law, a homeowner is expected to use reasonable care to protect children from serious injury. The primary question in this situation is whether the fence was high enough. Since a young child was able to climb the fence, the fence may not have been adequate, and Alfred could be held responsible for the child's injury.

Accidents Outside Your Home

If ice falls off the roof of my mother's house and strikes the meter reader, is my mother liable?

No. In general, your mother has a duty to keep her home and property reasonably safe and to warn invitees, such as the meter reader, about any dangers or defects she is aware of that are not apparent. In this case, however, your mother probably did not know that the ice on the roof was a hazard, and therefore could not have been expected to warn the meter reader about it.

The postman cuts across my lawn even though I have asked him to use the walk. One day he tripped over a garden hose and broke his wrist. Am I liable for his injury?

Possibly. As a homeowner, you are responsible for keeping the premises reasonably safe and must warn guests about any hidden dangers. If the garden hose was clearly visible, you had no obligation to warn the postman that it was in the yard. If the garden hose was hidden under some leaves, however, you were obligated to remove it or to alert guests to the danger, for example, by putting up a temporary sign.

ACCIDENTS

When Sidney, a door-to-door encyclopedia salesman, was leaving Dawn's home, he slipped on a doll left on the sidewalk by Dawn's two-year-old daughter. Is Dawn liable?

Probably not. Although Dawn has a responsibility to keep the sidewalks clear and to warn invited guests about unsafe conditions that are not apparent, Dawn did not invite the salesman to her house, and the doll could clearly be seen on the sidewalk. Consequently, Dawn had no duty to warn him about its presence.

While snowmobiling at night on a farmer's land, Gil and Ross were seriously injured when they hit some barbed wire strung across their path. They had used this path before without incident. Will Gil and Ross be successful if they sue the farmer?

Since Gil and Ross have gone snowmobiling in the same area before, they have a good chance of winning their case. If the farmer knew that his land was used by snowmobilers, he would be required in most states either to warn them about hidden dangers or to remove the hazards. A few states have statutes that apply specifically to the unauthorized use of private property for recreational purposes. In Michigan, for example, Gil and Ross would be unlikely to win their case unless they could prove that their injuries were caused by the farmer's reckless disregard for their safety.

Julian was helping Pat fix his roof. Pat warned him that one rung on the ladder was weak, but Julian proceeded to climb up the ladder without testing each step first. The weak rung collapsed, and he fell off the ladder. Does Julian have a case against Pat?

No. When Pat warned Julian that the ladder was defective, Julian had the choice of either not using the ladder or climbing it with caution. Because he chose to ignore Pat's warning, Julian assumed the risk involved in climbing the defective ladder.

I hired my son's friend Marty to mow my lawn. Am I liable if Marty is injured while using my mower?

Possibly. Power mowers are considered dangerous tools. For that reason, owners and operators must take special precautions to minimize the chances that someone will be hurt. Several factors would be important in determining your liability, including (1) Marty's age, (2) whether he realized the dangers involved in using a power mower, (3) whether the mower had some defect that you knew about, (4) whether you permitted Marty to use the lawn mower, knowing that he did not know how to operate it, and (5) whether you knew there were dangerous conditions in the yard and failed to warn Marty about them.

Accidents on Public Transportation

Lena was getting into a taxi when the driver accidentally slammed the door shut on her hand. Is the driver or the taxi company liable for Lena's medical expenses?

Both are liable. Under the law, any company that transports people for a fee must exercise the highest degree of care for the safety of its customers. Lena should be able to collect for her injury.

Scott told a cab driver, "Get me to the airport in a hurry." As the cab raced away, it hit another cab. Will Scott be able to recover from the cab company for his injuries?

Yes. A cab driver cannot ignore his duty to transport passengers safely and to obey traffic laws simply because he is asked to hurry. Passengers have a right to expect that a cab driver will not exceed the legal speed limit or drive in a manner that is unsuitable for the traffic conditions.

April had just paid her fare on a city bus and was about to take a seat when the bus driver swerved away from the curb. April lost her balance and fell. Is the bus company liable for her injuries?

Probably. A bus driver has a legal duty to drive safely. By pulling away from the curb before April had a chance to take a seat or hang onto a strap, the bus driver was acting inappropriately.

I was in such a hurry that I twisted my ankle while running down the stairs of the railroad station. Is the railroad company liable?

Probably not. To prove the railroad company liable, you would have to establish that it was negligent in some way. For example, if the steps had

If You Are Injured on Public Transportation

When a vehicle transports people for a fee, such as a bus or taxi, its operator is required by law to use extreme care to protect the passengers. If you are injured in an accident and you think the driver of the vehicle was at fault, you should seek legal advice to determine whether you should file a lawsuit. It is important to do this at once if you are injured on a vehicle operated by a government agency, since many states require claims against such agencies to be filed within several months of the accident. If you're not seriously injured, make some notes about the accident right after it occurs. That way if you decide to file a claim later, you'll have all the necessary information. Here are the facts you should record:

- ☑ The date, time, and location of the accident.
- ☑ The weather conditions.
- ☑ The vehicle's license number and line number.
- ☑ The driver's name, his driver's license number, and his identification or badge number.
- ☑ The names, addresses, and telephone numbers of other passengers who were injured.
- ☑ The names, addresses, and telephone numbers of witnesses.
- ☑ The condition of the vehicle, road, traffic lights, and warning signs.
- ☑ The physical appearance of the drivers involved.

not been cleared of debris or if their skid-resistant coating had worn off, you might have a claim against the company. But in this situation, you yourself were the cause of the accident.

Accidents in Public Places

As Marilyn was running to catch the bus, she tripped on a broken area of the sidewalk and hurt herself. Can she sue the village?

In many states, sovereign immunity—the principle that the government cannot be sued without its consent—protects cities and towns from such lawsuits. Even if Marilyn lives in a state that permits lawsuits against the government, she will have to file her claim within a certain period after the accident, and the form of the claim will have to meet special legal requirements. However, if an ordinance makes landowners whose property is adjacent to the sidewalk responsible for keeping the sidewalk in good repair, Marilyn could sue the landowner rather than the village. If Marilyn is able to sue, she will have to prove that she did not contribute to the accident by rushing to catch the bus. Furthermore, if Marilyn used this sidewalk regularly, a court could reason that she knew about the broken patch and should have avoided it.

Doreen slipped and fell on an icy sidewalk in front of a local shop. Is the store owner liable for her injuries?

Not necessarily. In areas where there are frequent winter storms, business owners cannot be expected to keep sidewalks clear at all times, so people must accept the risks involved in walking on icy sidewalks. But this does not mean that the store owner is not liable for her injuries.

If Doreen wants to sue the owner, she should consider the following factors: (1) Whether it was snowing or sleeting at the time she fell. If it was, this would favor the owner, since he cannot be expected to clean the sidewalk during a storm. (2) How long it had been since the snow or sleet stopped. Property owners are given a reasonable amount of time to clear sidewalks. (3) Whether the building near where she fell had a defective drainage system. If so, the hazard was not a natural condition, but one caused by negligence. This would make Doreen's case stronger.

I was in a bar when an intoxicated customer hit me for no reason. Is the bar liable for my medical bills?

There are two ways in which the tavern owner might be responsible. First, if your state has a dramshop act, the tavern owner may be liable for serving liquor to an intoxicated person. Second, if your state requires tavern owners to oust intoxicated or disorderly customers, you may be able to show that the owner was negligent in not properly supervising the premises. Your case would be strengthened if you could establish that the owner (1) knew the customer had a tendency to get into fights; (2) allowed the customer to stay, even though he was disturbing others; (3) permitted conditions at the bar to get out of control; (4) did not have an adequate staff to supervise the premises; or (5) ignored warnings that the customer was threatening to hurt someone.

As Dale was passing a construction site, he saw a woman get struck in the head by a piece of debris. Dale ran over to the woman and tried to control her bleeding, but when she lost her pulse he panicked and left. The woman died. Does Dale face any consequences for his actions?

Dale was not legally obligated to help the injured woman, but once he made the decision to come to her aid, he had a legal duty to continue his assistance until a doctor, paramedic, or other medical professional arrived at the scene. The only valid reason for Dale to have abandoned his rescue attempt would have been if doing so did not place the woman in a worse position than she was in before he tried to assist her.

If such an incident took place in Indiana, Georgia, or another state with Good Samaritan laws that protect people who provide voluntary medical care from being sued, Dale would not be liable. But if the incident occurred in a state whose Good Samaritan law covered only licensed medical personnel, Dale might face legal charges.

On a rainy day, Sarah was hurrying into a department store. As she stepped onto the tile floor in the lobby, she slipped and fell, hitting her head. Can she collect damages from the department store?

Sarah's chances of winning a lawsuit would depend, in part, on how carefully the store had tried to keep the entrance dry. On rainy days, a store owner cannot be expected to keep the floors of his property completely dry. However, he should see to it that floor mats are placed at each of the store's entrances to prevent sliding and to absorb some of the moisture. He should also have maintenance workers mop wet floors periodically to prevent water from accumulating.

Another important factor is whether Sarah contributed to the accident by hurrying into the department store. A court might decide that Sarah should have been aware that tile floors are slippery when wet, and that therefore she should have proceeded with caution when entering the store on a rainy day. In such a case, her haste to enter the building may reduce or eliminate the compensation she could receive.

While walking down the aisle of a department store, Rosemary accidentally knocked down a pyramid-shaped display of expensive crystal. Must she pay for it?

Probably not. Store owners must display merchandise so that it can be easily removed and returned without injuring customers or breaking. If

If You Are Injured in a Public Place

If you're injured as a result of an accident in a public place, such as inside a department store or on a sidewalk, and you believe that the property owner was at fault, you may want to sue him for your medical expenses and your pain and suffering. Knowing the answers to the following questions will help you with your case:

- If the accident occurred in a building:
  —Who owns the building?
  —Who is the building's manager or superintendent?
  —In which part of the building did the accident occur?
  —Were there any obvious signs of disrepair, such as torn carpeting or loose tiles?
  —How old is the building?
- If the accident occurred on a stairway:
  —Was the lighting inadequate?
  —Which step caused you to slip or trip?
  —Did the stairs have a skid-proof coating that was worn?
  —Were the stairs covered with carpeting or linoleum that was ripped or torn?
  —Was the handrail wobbly or loose?
- If the accident occurred on an elevator or escalator:
  —Who is the manufacturer?
  —What is the name and model number of the equipment?
  —When was it manufactured?
  —Who is responsible for maintaining the equipment?
  —When was it last inspected?
  —Was the elevator automatic or run by an employee?
- If the accident occurred on a sidewalk or in a parking lot:
  —Does the sidewalk or parking lot adjoin a home or a business?
  —How far away from the nearest building were you when the accident occurred?
  —Was the lighting inadequate?
  —Does the area have a concrete, gravel, or asphalt surface?
  —Was the surface cracked, icy, wet, or muddy?
  —Do tree roots protrude from a broken surface?

goods are arranged in a manner that increases the likelihood that they will be knocked over, the store has to absorb the cost of the breakage.

Joyce went to an amusement park, where she rode the roller coaster. At the end of the ride, her car came to a sudden stop when the brakes malfunctioned. Joyce fell forward and broke her nose. Is the amusement park responsible for Joyce's injury?

Court decisions about such situations have not been consistent. In some instances, the amusement park owner has been required only to use reasonable care in maintaining the roller coaster. In other cases, the owner has been held to a higher degree of responsibility because of the serious hazards posed by such a ride. In any case, the owner has a duty to inspect and test the equipment frequently to make sure it's safe.

Annette was riding a ski lift when her seat belt unsnapped. She fell out of her seat and broke her leg. Several months later complications set in, and Annette lost the use of her leg. It's been two years since the accident. Can Annette still sue the resort?

Annette may have waited too long to file a claim. Each state sets its own deadline, by legislation called a statute of limitations, for filing negligence lawsuits. The time periods for filing such a lawsuit range from one to six years, with two or three years the most common. Annette can find out her state's time limit by calling the county clerk's office.

Lucinda shouted "Fore" before hitting a golf ball, but Janice didn't hear her and was hit by the ball. Is Lucinda protected because she has witnesses who heard her call out the warning?

Having given a warning does help Lucinda establish that she was not negligent. By checking to make sure that those people who were in the path of the ball's flight knew that she was ready to hit the ball, and then giving an audible warning, Lucinda fulfilled her duty.

I took my nephew Patrick to the zoo. As he tried to feed one of the chimpanzees, it grabbed his arm and bit him. Shouldn't the zoo pay Patrick's medical bills?

Most likely. Because some of the animals housed in a zoo can be dangerous, courts generally require zoo owners to exercise a high degree of care. Since Patrick was able to get close enough for the chimpanzee to grab his arm, the zoo might be considered negligent for not providing a better barrier, such as wire mesh, to keep the chimpanzee from reaching out. Moreover, zoo administrators know that visitors, especially children, often ignore warnings not to feed the animals, which is even more reason for providing better barriers.

When my son enrolled at camp, I was required to sign an agreement not to sue the camp if he were injured. Later in the summer he injured his knee when the trampoline he was using collapsed. Am I now prevented from suing the camp?

Not necessarily. The agreement you signed is known as an exculpatory agreement, and the court will very likely scrutinize both the wording of such an agreement and the facts surrounding your decision to sign it. In some situations, a court would uphold the agreement. In this case, however, it appears that you were placed in an unfair position—the camp would not have accepted your son unless you signed the agreement—and a court would probably void the agreement, making the camp liable for your son's injuries.

While Sean and his family were staying at a motel, they noticed a sign posted by the swimming pool, stating that it closed at 10:00 P.M. Two of Sean's children, ages 12 and 16, went out to the pool at 10:30 P.M. The 16-year-old slipped on the diving board and suffered a concussion. Is the motel liable?

Probably not. Motel owners are required only to use reasonable care to protect guests from being injured at a swimming pool. This requirement is usually satisfied by warning signs, fences, and lifeguards. Because Sean's children are 12 and 16, they are considered old enough to understand the closing sign and to know the risks involved in diving in a pool at night. These factors would probably prevent Sean from obtaining compensation for his son's injuries.

A spectator at a baseball game was hit by a foul ball. Shouldn't the baseball park be held responsible for this?

No. The law assumes that spectators at a baseball game accept the possibility of being injured by a ball that's hit into the stands. Ballpark owners are required to put up protective fencing only in the area immediately behind home plate, which is considered the most dangerous part of the ballpark. If the spectator was hit because the fencing was torn or inadequate, then the ballpark owner might be liable.

Accidents in Public Places

While Ricky was playing second base on his Little League team, a player on the other team ran into him to prevent Ricky from throwing to first base. Is the player liable for Ricky's injuries?

Yes. While a player must accept the risk of being injured during competition, that does not mean that he must assume responsibility for every injury he receives. When playing baseball, a player could anticipate being injured by a bat or a ball, but not by another player deliberately running into him. Since the player on the other team violated the rules of the game, he is fully responsible for Ricky's injuries.

Several youngsters were playing crack-the-whip at a roller skating rink even though signs were posted around the rink stating that this activity was prohibited. Shannon's arm was broken when she was accidentally pushed against the wall. Can her parents sue the rink owners?

Yes, if they can prove that the owner failed to supervise the skating rink properly. Since the owner had posted signs prohibiting crack-the-whip, he was aware that the game was dangerous for skaters. Therefore, he had a duty to monitor the rink closely and have enough attendants on hand to stop such activity.

My son injured his neck and shoulder on his school's playground equipment during recess period. Should I sue the school or the manufacturer of the equipment?

You might not be able to sue either one. The manufacturer would not be liable unless the equipment were defective in some way. To sue the school, you would have to prove that the playground was not adequately supervised or that the school failed to fix equipment that it knew needed repair. If your son attends a public school, sovereign immunity—the principle that the government cannot be sued without its consent—may limit your right to sue the school or prevent you from suing.

Betty went into Hoffman's appliance store to buy a television set. As she walked through the video department, looking at the pictures on all the TV screens, she tripped over a carton that had been left in the aisle. Does Betty have a claim against the store?

Yes. Since shoppers are expected to look at displays as they walk through a store, the store is obligated to keep its aisles clear and properly maintained. The fact that Betty was not watching where she was going should not prevent her from suing the store, even if the carton was left by another customer, rather than an employee.

Boating Accidents

Whenever I have guests on board my boat, I always provide them with life jackets and ask that they wear them from the time we leave the dock to the time we return. Does this precaution free me from liability if someone refuses to put on his life jacket and then drowns as the result of an accident?

Not entirely. A passenger's refusal to wear a life jacket may be a factor in determining the extent of your liability, but it does not mean that you will be relieved of all responsibility for a passenger's injuries or death. Generally, a court would try to determine whether the person's injuries or death could have been prevented by the use of a life jacket. The court would also want to find out if the accident was caused by your negligence in operating or maintaining the boat.

While swimming one day, I saw a boat that was being steered by a child crash into another boat. Don't you need a license to operate a boat on public waters?

It depends on where you live. Some states require boat operators to have licenses; others do not. In New Jersey, for example, the law distinguishes between boats powered by inboard motors and those powered by outboard motors. Children under 16 cannot operate the former, and children under 13 cannot get a license to operate the latter. In New Hampshire, a child may operate a boat, but only when accompanied by an adult, who is held responsible for any injuries or property damage the child may cause.

When Norman was out on the lake fishing one afternoon, another boat rammed into the left side of his boat. Do boat owners have to observe the same rules as automobile drivers when it comes to yielding the right-of-way?

There are several different sets of rules governing boat traffic. The inland rules, which apply in lakes and most other inland waters, state that a boat must yield to another boat that is directly in front of it or to its right. Since Norman's boat was to the right of the other boat, the boat's operator had a responsibility to yield to Norman.

Boating Accidents

While Gordon was sailing around the lake, he noticed a distress flag on one of the other boats. Was Gordon obligated to help?

No, unless Gordon was a lifeguard, police officer, member of the Coast Guard, or was in some way responsible for the safety of the people on board. However, boat owners frequently offer to assist a boat in distress or notify the Coast Guard about the situation.

Joe had been drinking just before he took the wheel of Leonard's boat so that Leonard could water-ski. Leonard was injured and the boat was damaged when Joe steered the boat into a rock. Can Leonard be compensated by his own insurance carrier?

It would depend on Leonard's insurance policy. Some policies require the insured person to exercise due care. If Leonard's policy has such a provision, he would not be eligible for coverage if the insurance company determined that Leonard was aware of Joe's drinking and still permitted him to steer the boat.

CHAPTER
14

Your Medical Rights

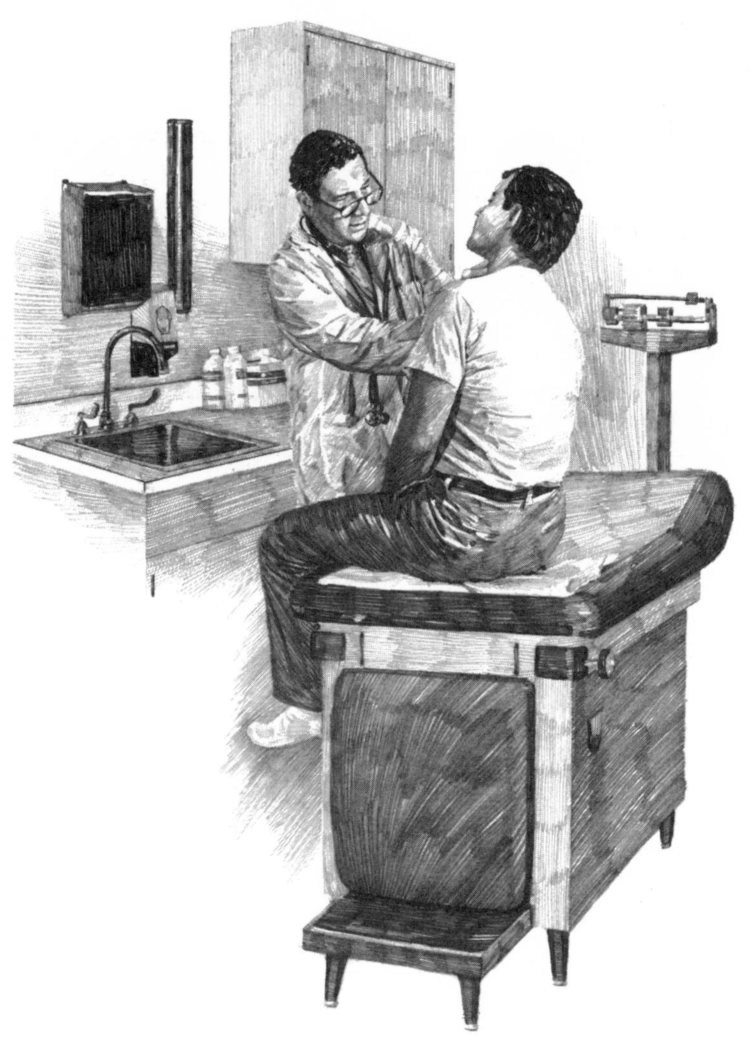

Howard's doctor has recommended surgery. How can Howard make sure this surgery is necessary?

Howard should have his doctor explain in detail why he feels that surgery is the best medical option, and what the alternatives are. Before a doctor can proceed with any type of treatment, he must have the patient's consent. This consent is valid only if all the practical methods of treatment have been explained, together with the risks involved and the benefits expected. Telling a patient only about the particular surgery or treatment that the doctor advocates is not sufficient. It is usually a good idea to get a second opinion from another doctor when surgery is recommended. In fact, some health insurance companies require it.

Does Mindy have the right to refuse laboratory tests even though her doctor believes they are necessary?

Yes. Mindy has the right to refuse any type of treatment, including laboratory tests. However, Mindy's doctor may ask her to sign a form releasing him from liability, because her refusal to take the tests may make it impossible for him to diagnose or treat her illness successfully. Mindy also has the right to refuse to sign this release. To protect himself, the doctor will note her refusals on her medical chart.

Can a teenager prevent a doctor from letting his parents know about a drug problem?

In most states, yes. Drug counseling or treatment is generally available to teenagers without parental notification. However, state law may leave it up to the doctor to decide whether or not to notify the parents. In Georgia, for example, a doctor may tell parents about a child's drug problems even if the child objects. But in Iowa, drug treatment may not be reported to the parents unless the child consents.

Do parents have the right to know if their teenage daughter gets a prescription for birth control pills from their family doctor?

No. Although parents are usually required to give their consent for the medical treatment of minor children, there are legal exceptions to this general requirement. Most states have laws that make family planning services available without regard to age, and on a confidential basis. Family planning assistance under the federal Aid to Families With Dependent Children program is also confidential, regardless of age.

A psychiatrist is treating a man who has repeatedly expressed a desire to hurt an ex-girlfriend. Doesn't the psychiatrist have to tell the ex-girlfriend or the police about his patient's intentions?

Yes. Although the doctor-patient relationship is a confidential one, there are times when other considerations are more important. If the patient is a genuine danger to his ex-girlfriend, the psychiatrist must notify her or the police or take any other steps necessary to protect her.

When Tracy's doctor explained the purpose of the medication he was prescribing, he didn't tell her that the treatment was experimental. Does Tracy have a right to know this?

Yes. For Tracy to make an informed decision about whether or not to consent to the treatment, her doctor is legally bound to explain the risks and benefits of the treatment and any alternatives. Telling her that the treatment was experimental should have been part of that explanation.

If the experiment is being financed with federal money, a number of safeguards must be followed. These include review by a committee to determine that the research is sound, clear evidence to indicate that the predicted benefits outweigh the risks, and assurance that the participants understand that they can withdraw from the experiment at any time.

When I found I needed major surgery, I got Dr. Heart, the top specialist in the state, to do it. After it was all over I found out that another surgeon had actually performed the operation. Wasn't it wrong for Dr. Heart to turn me over to someone else?

As a general rule, a physician cannot have another doctor substitute for him without notifying the patient and obtaining his permission, except in an emergency. However, the consent form you signed prior to the operation may have authorized the surgeon "or associates or assistants of his or her choice" to perform the surgery. If so, the substitution was legally acceptable as long as the substitute was fully qualified to do the surgery. If you did not give your permission in any form, you could sue Dr. Heart for abandoning you as a patient unless the substitution of doctors occurred as the result of an emergency.

A doctor agreed to treat my grandmother, but then he withdrew from the case. My grandmother refuses to see anyone else. Is there anything she can do to get that doctor to treat her?

Not if the doctor gave your grandmother sufficient time to find another doctor. A doctor has the right to withdraw from a case, just as a patient has the right to choose another doctor. However, if your grandmother's doctor withdrew so abruptly that her treatment was disrupted, she might be able to sue him for abandoning a patient.

Lorna's children are concerned about her ability to handle any bad news. Do they have the right to ask Lorna's doctor to withhold negative information?

Lorna's children may ask the doctor to withhold negative information, but the doctor does not have to comply with their request. As long as Lorna is competent to make medical decisions, the doctor is required to supply her with all the information relating to her case. However, if the doctor agreed that disclosing certain information would have a seriously detrimental effect on her, that information could be withheld.

When Nathan found out he had only six months to live, he asked the doctor not to tell his family. Must the doctor honor this request?

Yes. A doctor is generally prohibited from disclosing medical information unless the patient consents to it. However, if Nathan had a communicable disease, the doctor would have to inform the family.

Your Rights in the Hospital

Does a hospital have the right to turn away someone from an emergency room if he doesn't have medical insurance?

No. A hospital with an emergency room must provide care to anyone who comes in seeking medical assistance, regardless of the person's ability to pay. If a hospital refuses to treat someone in a medical emergency, it could face a civil or a criminal lawsuit.

When I entered the hospital, they wrote down some information about me and gave me a form to sign. I was too sick to read all of it. Did I sign away any of my rights?

Probably not. Even if the form you signed contained a blanket consent in which you agreed to any and all services of the hospital or a statement releasing the hospital and its staff from liability, you still have the right to refuse a medical procedure or course of treatment. When blanket consent forms have been challenged in court, judges have ruled against them because they don't give the patient enough information to make an informed decision. Courts also do not favor contracts that release a hospital from liability if a patient is harmed as the result of a mistake or accident. Since a patient may not be admitted to the hospital unless he signs such a release, courts have ruled that these releases place the patient in an unequal negotiating position, and will not enforce them.

Can a woman insist that she be cared for by a woman doctor in the hospital, even when Medicare is paying?

Yes. A patient always has the right to choose a physician. However, if Medicare is paying the bill and the patient chooses a doctor who does not participate in Medicare, she will have to pay the difference between the doctor's fee and the Medicare rate.

Six-year-old Jill was hit by a car. The doctor believed that Jill was all right, but he decided to keep her in the hospital overnight for observation. Does Jill's mother have the right to stay with her?

No. Parents do not have a legal right to stay overnight in the hospital with their child. However, many hospitals permit parents to stay, as long as the doctor agrees to the arrangement. If Jill's mother makes such a request and the hospital refuses, she can ask the doctor to include in his orders that she be allowed to stay overnight.

Arthur's wife, Doris, may have to have a cesarean section when their child is born. Can Arthur stay with Doris throughout the birth?

He has no legal right to do so. The decision to allow fathers in the operating room is usually based on hospital policy and the recommendation of the doctor. Even if Arthur is allowed to stay, he may have to sign a release, agreeing to leave the operating room immediately if asked to do so.

I'm having major surgery next month. Can I arrange to have an anesthesiologist, rather than an anesthetist, attend me in the operating room?

Yes. The anesthesiologist (who is a medical doctor) supervises the kind of anesthesia to be used, but does not necessarily administer it. He may leave orders for an anesthetist (who is trained and certified to administer anesthetics) to follow during the actual operation. If you want to make sure that you are tended by an anesthesiologist, let your doctor know.

Your Rights in the Hospital

When Serena's doctor came to examine her the day after her surgery, he brought six interns and residents with him. Serena was embarrassed and upset at this. Did she have the right to ask these six people to leave?

Yes. Every patient has a right to privacy and confidentiality. If Serena did not agree to the presence of medical personnel who were not directly involved in her care, her examination should have been held in private. Even in teaching hospitals, the attending physician must get the patient's permission before allowing residents and interns to observe a case.

A nurse has awakened Earl from a sound sleep the last two nights in order to give him a sleeping pill. Doesn't he have a legal right not to be disturbed?

Although the American Hospital Association's A Patient's Bill of Rights says that patients are entitled to considerate and respectful care—which includes not being awakened to take a sleeping pill—there are no actual laws prohibiting hospital personnel from waking up patients to give them medication. If Earl doesn't want to be disturbed again, he should ask his doctor to note this on his chart.

A Patient's Bill of Rights

Most hospitals include the American Hospital Association's (AHA's) A Patient's Bill of Rights—describing the level of care a hospital patient is entitled to—in the packet of information they give to patients on admission, or display it prominently throughout the building. Seven states—California, Colorado, Massachusetts, Michigan, Minnesota, Pennsylvania, and New York—have enacted their own versions of the Patient's Bill of Rights into law, and many other states have passed legislation guaranteeing specific rights, such as access to medical records. Under the AHA bill, you have a right to:

- Considerate and respectful care.
- Complete, up-to-the-minute information from your doctor, in terms you can understand, about your condition, treatment, and prognosis.
- Sufficient information from your doctor to allow you to give informed consent, including a full description of the procedure or treatment, the risks, alternatives, how long you will be hospitalized, and the name of the person responsible for carrying out the procedure or treatment.
- An explanation of the consequences of refusing treatment and the right to refuse treatment to the extent permitted by law (in extreme circumstances, a court may order you to undergo treatment to save your life).

If I'm a hospital patient, don't I have the right to see my medical chart?

Not necessarily. You have no automatic right to see your medical chart. Technically, your medical records are hospital property, and for many years, a patient could not demand to see his chart. Today, states are beginning to recognize a patient's interest in his own medical records. Oregon, South Dakota, Tennessee, West Virginia, Wisconsin, and Nevada are among the states that have enacted laws regarding a patient's access to medical information. But even in these states, a hospital does not have to hand your chart over to you immediately upon your demand. To see your chart, you generally have to submit a written request, and you may be required to state why you want to see the records.

Todd has been a patient in the same hospital for two months, and he expects to need hospitalization for an additional six weeks, but he is afraid that they will transfer him to another hospital or to a health care facility. Can they do that without his consent?

Not unless there is an emergency, or the hospital does not have the proper equipment to treat him. If neither situation exists, the hospital must explain to Todd why a transfer is necessary or desirable, notify him of the options available and the risks involved, and then obtain his consent for the transfer.

- Privacy in all aspects of your medical care. Individuals not directly associated with your care must have your permission to be present during any discussion, examination, consultation, or treatment.
- Confidential treatment of all your records and any communications pertaining to your care.
- A reasonable response by the hospital to your requests for such services as evaluation, treatment, and referral.
- Information about hospital rules and regulations that apply to you.
- An explanation detailing why a transfer to a different facility may be necessary and what, if any, alternatives there are. The new facility must accept you in advance.
- Information about the relationship between the hospital and all other health care institutions or individuals who treat you.
- Information about and a full explanation of any experimental procedure or treatment that will affect you. You have the right to refuse to participate in such experimentation.
- Continuity of care. You have the right to know when and where doctors will be available for appointments, and how continuing care will be provided after you are discharged.
- An opportunity to examine your bill and an explanation of its contents regardless of how it is to be paid.

Your Rights in the Hospital

How much notice must a hospital give before discharging a patient?

Generally, a hospital need not give a patient any particular amount of notice before discharging him. The attending physician can even sign the release order on the morning the patient is to leave. However, if Medicare is paying part of the bill, the hospital must give the patient at least a 48-hour notice in writing to allow him time to appeal the discharge decision to a review board, if he chooses to do so.

Can a hospital prevent me from leaving?

No. You cannot be hospitalized against your will. You must be allowed to leave, even if your doctor objects. The only time the hospital might be justified in trying to stop you is when you have a communicable disease or when you present a danger to yourself or others.

Rosemary, who has no family, is dying and wants to spend her last days in a hospice. But Rosemary has been told that before she can be admitted to the hospice she must designate someone else to serve as "primary care giver." What does this mean?

A primary care giver is the person responsible for handling the arrangements for a dying patient. This is usually a relative, but since Rosemary has no family, she could ask a friend to fill this role, or hire a nurse's aide or companion to attend to her needs.

Consent for Medical Treatment

At what age is someone authorized to give consent for surgery or medical treatment?

Most states set 18 as the minimum age at which a person can give consent for medical treatment. However, younger people may be allowed to give consent if they are married, pregnant, or living independently of their parents or guardians. State laws also permit minors to obtain medical treatment without parental consent for mental health problems, drug or alcohol problems, pregnancy, or sexually transmitted diseases.

Dorothy's doctor recommended that she have surgery and carefully explained the proposed procedure and why it was

necessary. Dorothy agreed to have the operation. Does the doctor have all the permission he needs to proceed with the surgery?

No. Dorothy's doctor must do more than just describe the recommended procedure and its benefits; he must explain the alternatives available to her, their risks and benefits, and how long she might be incapacitated after each alternative. Before any surgery or medical treatment is performed, the law requires a patient to give his informed consent. For Dorothy to be considered informed, she must understand the implications of her surgery, including the pros and cons of all her options.

After Wes was scheduled for outpatient surgery, a nurse gave him a consent form to sign. Can Wes revise the form if he wishes?

Yes. Wes can make changes, delete provisions, or make notations in the margins. He may find, however, that his doctor is unwilling to perform the surgery under the conditions he has indicated. If Wes has questions or doubts about any of the provisions on the form, he should discuss them with his doctor and try to work out a compromise with him.

Beverly signed a consent form when she was admitted to the hospital. Will it be valid for her entire stay?

Yes. The consent form probably does not include a termination date but is effective for the duration of a patient's hospital stay. Even so, if Beverly's condition changes significantly or if her treatment is altered substantially, she may be asked to sign a new consent form.

Max signed a consent form after his doctor convinced him of the benefits of having surgery. If Max changes his mind, can he revoke his consent?

Yes, but the doctor or hospital will probably ask Max to sign a form releasing them from liability for the consequences of his refusing surgery.

Can a patient sue a surgeon for malpractice even though the patient signed a consent form before the operation?

Yes. The consent form only authorizes the doctor (or his associates) to perform the designated operation. It generally does not include a release from liability. If the doctor didn't follow the established procedures for the operation or if he lacked the necessary surgical skills, he can be sued for malpractice.

Consent for Medical Treatment

When Howard went into the hospital for a gall bladder operation, he signed a form giving his consent to the surgery. Afterward, he learned that his doctor had removed his appendix as well as the gallstones. Did the doctor have the authority to do this?

No. A surgeon is authorized to perform only the surgery listed on the consent form. The only time a surgeon can exceed this authorization is if life-threatening complications develop during an operation. If Howard's surgeon performed any surgery that Howard did not consent to, Howard could sue him for malpractice, battery, and breach of contract.

Karen and Steve took their six-month-old daughter to a hospital emergency room. A doctor on duty recommended that the child have surgery as soon as possible. If Karen and Steve refuse to give their consent, can the doctor authorize the operation?

Only if the child's life is in danger, or if not having the surgery would seriously jeopardize her health. While parents generally have the right to make health care decisions for their children, the state will intervene, if needed, to protect the child. However, if the surgery would not prolong the child's life, or if the child would not suffer undue harm by not having the surgery, the doctor would have to accept Karen and Steve's decision.

Gloria refused to let her doctor perform the surgery he insists she needs. Her family does not agree with Gloria's decision. As relatives, can they give consent for the operation?

Not unless Gloria has been declared mentally incompetent and one of her relatives has been appointed her guardian or has a medical power of attorney. Otherwise, Gloria has the right to refuse medical treatment for herself, even if her decision jeopardizes her life; her family cannot interfere with her decision.

Rocco is divorced, and his ex-wife has legal custody of their son. If the boy is injured while visiting his father, can Rocco sign a consent form to have the boy treated?

Yes. Although Rocco does not have legal custody of his son, he is still the boy's father; as the parent, he can grant the necessary consent for medical treatment. However, if the doctors or nurses believe that the custodial parent might object to the suggested treatment, they may also seek the consent of Rocco's ex-wife.

Malpractice

My doctor gave me a written order for a prescription. The druggist who filled the order gave me the wrong dosage. He claims the doctor's illegible handwriting is to blame. Who is at fault?

Both the druggist and the doctor may be at fault. The doctor should have taken care to write clearly and the druggist should have called the doctor for clarification if he was unsure about the prescription.

When Sally called her doctor, he prescribed medication over the telephone. Wasn't it malpractice for the doctor to prescribe a medication for Sally without seeing her?

Probably not. When familiar patients call for prescriptions to alleviate common illnesses such as colds, the flu, sunburn, or poison ivy, it is not unusual for a doctor to prescribe a remedy over the telephone. As long as the doctor was familiar with Sally's sensitivity to various types of drugs and knew that she would suffer no adverse reaction to the medication he prescribed, there is no basis for a malpractice claim.

However, the doctor might be guilty of malpractice if he misdiagnosed Sally's illness because he failed to give Sally the physical examination that a reasonably responsible doctor would ordinarily make under the circumstances. For example, if Sally had called to complain about abdominal pains and the doctor had said she was constipated and told her to take a laxative, Sally could sue the doctor for malpractice if she had actually been suffering from acute appendicitis and her appendix burst.

I've heard that some people have become addicted to drugs prescribed by their doctors. Wouldn't a doctor who did this be liable to have malpractice charges brought against him?

Yes, prescribing enough narcotic drugs to create addiction in a patient may well justify charges against a doctor. Doctors must use care in selecting drugs for use by their patients and must determine whether a patient is unusually susceptible to a particular drug or likely to become addicted to it or to suffer other adverse effects from using it.

Randolph has been thinking about changing doctors. How can he find out if the new doctor has ever been sued for malpractice?

The clerk of the court keeps a register by both plaintiffs' and defendants' names of all cases filed with that court. Since the doctor would be the defendant in a malpractice suit, Randolph can ask the clerk of the court to look up the doctor's name on the register of defendants. If there are several court divisions, there may be a centralized computer system with terminals that he can use himself to find out if the doctor has ever been sued. Failure to locate any cases does not mean that the doctor has never been accused of malpractice, however. In some cases, settlements are reached before a lawsuit is filed.

When Colleen agreed to have surgery, her doctor told her it would cure her pain. She is still in agony three months after surgery. Is the doctor's statement a basis for a malpractice lawsuit?

Probably not. Doctors often express opinions about proposed surgery or try to reassure patients when discussing the benefits of a surgical procedure. Colleen could not sue for malpractice unless she could show that her doctor had given her a guarantee that the surgery would totally stop her pain, and that she had relied upon that guarantee when deciding to have the operation.

After fathering two children, Paul decided to get a vasectomy. The doctor failed to complete the operation successfully, and Paul's wife, Becky, became pregnant again. Can Paul and Becky sue the doctor for the expenses of raising the third child?

They may sue the doctor, but it is unlikely that Paul and Becky will be able to obtain a monetary award that will cover all the expenses of their third child. However, they may be able to recover some of the costs. A few courts have made awards based on the total amount needed to raise the child, reduced by an amount representing the benefit and joy the family receives while the child is growing up.

Carla miscarried because of a medication prescribed by her doctor when she was three months pregnant. Carla wants to sue the doctor for her medical expenses, pain and suffering, loss of wages, and emotional stress. What are her chances of success?

Her chances depend on a number of factors. If Carla told her doctor about the pregnancy, the doctor should have considered the possibility of the medication's causing an adverse reaction. If other doctors would not have prescribed the medication, the doctor may be liable for damages. If the doctor was not told about the pregnancy, or current medical knowledge did not indicate any potential risk to pregnant women from that particular medication, the doctor is probably not guilty of malpractice.

What Constitutes Malpractice?

Because of the many uncertainties in the practice of medicine, the law considers it impossible for a doctor to guarantee that his course of treatment will result in a cure or complete recovery from an illness. Therefore a patient cannot sue a doctor for malpractice if a treatment is unsuccessful. However, if a doctor fails to follow standard medical procedures in treating a patient, the doctor may be guilty of negligence. A charge of malpractice may be justified if a patient's condition worsens as a result of this negligence. Doctors and hospitals have been found negligent for:

- Prescribing medication that a patient was known to be allergic to.
- Failing to give a patient medication at the designated time.
- Injecting a drug into the wrong area of the body.
- Diagnosing a fracture as a sprain.
- Improperly setting a broken bone.
- Failing to provide a hospitalized patient with a call button or other device to summon help.
- Failing to put up rails to prevent senile, sedated, young, or unconscious patients from falling out of bed.
- Not checking the identification bracelet of a patient in the operating room before beginning surgery.

After my surgery three years ago, I felt fine. But last week I became ill and visited another doctor. She told me that X-rays indicated that the surgeon had failed to remove a surgical instrument. Is it too late to sue the surgeon?

Perhaps not. Even if the deadline in your state for filing malpractice lawsuits has expired, you may still be able to sue the surgeon. When you are suffering from an injury that you could not discover for yourself, and the symptoms develop gradually, a court might rule that the time limit under the statute of limitations must be counted from the time you discovered the problem.

Francine told the doctor not to amputate her foot, but the doctor ignored Francine's wishes. The surgery saved her life. Does Francine still have a right to sue her doctor?

Yes. As long as Francine was mentally competent to make the decision not to amputate, she had the right to expect the doctor to follow her instructions. Operating without consent is both battery and malpractice, even though the surgery saved her life.

Malpractice

After having a wisdom tooth extracted, I experienced considerable pain. X-rays by another dentist revealed that part of the root had not been extracted. Can I sue my original dentist?

Yes. Dentists, like doctors, can be held responsible for improper treatment. But it may not be necessary for you to sue your dentist. If you explain to him what happened and present him a bill for the costs involved, you may find that your original dentist is willing to reimburse you without going to court.

While Matilda was in the hospital, she acquired an infection that she feels was unrelated to her illness. Does she have to prove the hospital was at fault in order to sue successfully?

Yes. Matilda will have to establish a clear connection between her infection and a lack of care by the hospital staff. Every hospital must have an infection-control program with isolation and sanitation procedures to minimize the possibility that patients will acquire an infection during hospitalization. If the hospital staff was careless and exposed Matilda to a contagious disease or infection, or if the hospital allowed infection rates to become unreasonably high, Matilda may have sufficient evidence to sue the hospital and win.

A nurse gave Bret a shot. A day later, an abscess formed. Was the nurse legally liable for this injury?

Only if Bret can show that the nurse was negligent. If the nurse did not follow standard procedures—such as scrubbing the skin with alcohol before the injection and using a sterilized needle—and if the abscess formed at the point where the injection was made, Bret may have the evidence he needs to support a claim of negligence.

Ruth called a nurse to her room and showed her that there was water on the bathroom floor. The nurse went to get someone to mop it up, but no one came. Ruth couldn't wait any longer and went into the bathroom, slipped on the wet floor, and fell, injuring her back. Is the hospital liable?

It could be. A hospital is required to maintain a safe environment for its patients, and this would include keeping the bathroom floor dry. In this case, the hospital had been notified about the water on the floor and therefore had a duty to get rid of it. A court would have to decide whether the nurse was negligent in not returning immediately with someone to mop the floor or in not mopping it herself. A court would also consider whether or not Ruth was sufficiently careful in walking into the bathroom when she knew the floor was wet. Her own negligence may have contributed to the fall.

When Caroline brought her two-year-old son to the hospital, she told the nurse that he was very active and asked that extra measures be taken to assure his safety, but the nurse took no additional precautions. The boy was injured when he climbed over the side railing and fell out of bed. Does Caroline have a good case if she sues the hospital and the nurse?

Yes. Since Caroline specifically warned the hospital that her son was very active, the staff should have taken further steps to prevent injury. If she can show, through expert testimony, that other hospitals would have done more than ensure that bed rails were in place, Caroline would have a good chance of being awarded damages for her son's injuries.

Your Medical Records

Are there laws protecting the privacy of medical records?

Yes. Medical records are considered private matters subject to the same constitutional protection as other areas of our private lives. Anyone who releases medical information without a patient's consent may be charged with invasion of privacy, breach of contract, or betrayal of confidentiality, depending on the circumstances of the case. Federal and state laws also protect medical records from unauthorized release.

In certain situations, however, the law requires a doctor to release specific information, even if the patient objects. If a patient is suffering from a communicable disease or a gunshot wound, or if a child shows signs of abuse, the law may require a doctor to notify the appropriate public health or police authorities.

I asked my internist for a copy of my medical records, but he said I wouldn't understand what was on them and refused to turn them over to me. Did he have the right to do this?

The laws on this matter vary from state to state. States that permit patients to see their medical records include Alaska, California, Colorado, Connecticut, Florida, Georgia, Indiana, Maine, Maryland, Massachusetts, Minnesota, Mississippi, Nevada, Ohio, Oregon, South Dakota, Tennessee,

West Virginia, and Wisconsin. However, even in these states there may be restrictions. For example, Connecticut, Florida, and Maine permit patients to get their medical records only after they are discharged from a hospital. In Minnesota the doctor or hospital can provide a summary of the medical records. If your doctor practices in a state that does not require him to let you see your records, he is within his rights to turn down your request.

My 16-year-old daughter went to the doctor for a checkup last week. When I asked the doctor what she and my daughter talked about, the doctor told me it was confidential. Don't I have the right to know what goes on in the doctor's office?

No. Many states permit minors to make decisions about such matters as drug or alcohol abuse, mental health treatment, and family planning without telling their parents. Even if your daughter was not seeing the doctor about one of these concerns, the confidential doctor-patient relationship still exists. Unless there is some overriding reason why you should be notified, the doctor should not discuss your daughter's medical condition without her consent.

Does Teresa have a right to ask that confidential records about her illness not be released to a potential employer?

She doesn't even need to ask. A potential employer has no legal right to see Teresa's medical records unless Teresa signs a release. Access to medical records is restricted to the doctor, his or her staff, and those people (if any) that Teresa might want to designate.

To get reimbursed for medical expenses, Brad signed a release form that authorized his doctor to make his medical record available to the insurance company. Brad just learned that the insurance company was given his entire medical history, and not just the records about his recent hospital stay. Did the doctor violate Brad's rights?

Maybe. Brad should review the form he signed. If he signed a general release that did not specify which records could be forwarded to the insurance company, the doctor's office did not violate his rights. On the other hand, if he had agreed to the release of the records of his hospital stay only, the doctor exceeded his authority, and Brad could sue him for invasion of privacy.

Our family doctor died, and the executor of his estate said our medical records belonged to the estate and couldn't be released to us. What are our rights?

The executor was right in refusing to hand the records over to you. The originals of the medical records do not belong to you, but are the property of the doctor's estate. However, your family's medical records contain information that is important to you, and you can authorize the release of a copy of the file to another doctor. The executor of the estate should comply with your request, but he will probably ask you to pay for the costs of copying the records.

Paying the Bills

For medical insurance, see "Health and Disability Insurance" in Chapter 8, *Insurance;* see also "Medicare" and "Medicaid" in Chapter 15, *Pensions, IRA's, Social Security.*

Doris received a bill for lab tests in addition to the ones she had been told were being done. Does she have to pay the bill?

Doris may have to pay this bill if she signed a form giving general consent to all tests needed to diagnose her illness. But Doris should check to be sure that the test was actually done for her. Until this matter is resolved, Doris is within her rights in refusing to pay that portion of the bill.

Henry will not be able to pay his hospital bills. Can the hospital force him to leave?

No. Henry cannot be forced to leave until he is well enough to be released. If Henry were forced to leave and his condition worsened, he could sue the hospital. The hospital will have to bill Henry after he leaves, then take him to court if he doesn't pay.

On the day Ellie was to be discharged from the hospital, she refused to pay a portion of her bill. An administrator told Ellie she would not be allowed to leave until she paid her bill in full. Can the hospital detain Ellie against her will?

No. If the hospital detained Ellie against her will, she could file charges of false imprisonment—even if the administrator did not use force to keep her from leaving but only gave her reason to fear that force would be used. Moreover, there is no reason for the hospital to detain Ellie to bring pressure on her to pay the bill. The hospital can get its money by suing Ellie after her release.

Paying the Bills

On Jared's first visit to the doctor's office he had to fill out an information sheet. After looking at this form, the doctor refused to treat Jared because he was unable to pay. Is the doctor required to treat patients regardless of their ability to pay for services?

No. Doctors are not required to treat every person who comes to them for medical care. As long as Jared was not an emergency patient, the doctor could refuse to treat him and not be guilty of breaking the law. But if this had been an emergency, and Jared's condition worsened, the doctor could be held responsible for not treating the emergency. A doctor might also be guilty of professional misconduct if he used Jared's inability to pay as an excuse to reject him because of race, color, creed, or national origin.

After treating Geraldine for five months, her doctor refused to complete the course of treatment because Geraldine was three months behind in paying her bills. Does the doctor have the right to stop treatment?

No. The doctor must continue to treat Geraldine until she no longer needs medical attention, or he must give her sufficient time to find another doctor. Discontinuing needed treatment before Geraldine has had time to find a replacement is considered abandonment of a patient. Geraldine could sue the doctor if he abandoned her and her condition worsened.

Living Wills

Donald does not want medical care continued when there is no chance of surviving without life-support systems. What can he do to make sure his wishes will be carried out?

Donald should consider making a living will. In it Donald could instruct doctors not to use heroic measures to prolong his life if there should come a time when there is no hope of survival. Once he has completed the living will, Donald should give copies of it to his family, doctor, attorney, and anyone else who may be consulted about his medical condition.

My sister Jean lives in a state that does not have a living will law. Can she still make out a living will? Will it have any effect?

Your sister may still make a written declaration that she does not want life-support systems used if she is near death. Preparing this declaration could be helpful in two ways: (1) it is written evidence of her wishes so that you and other family members will know what she wants if you are ever faced with a decision about continuing life-support systems; and (2) her state legislature may pass living will legislation in the future. Some state laws grant validity to living wills signed before passage of the law.

Janice completed a living will while she lived in one state. She moved to another state last year. Is her living will still valid?

Laws regarding the proper form and execution for a living will vary from state to state. To be sure that her living will is valid Janice should complete a new living will according to the laws of the state where she now lives.

The Benefits of a Living Will

A living will instructs doctors to withhold or withdraw life-support systems if a person becomes terminally ill. It is a signed, dated, and witnessed document that states, in advance, a person's wishes about such life-extending measures as mechanical respiration and artificial feeding by tube. It relieves relatives of the need to guess the wishes of someone too ill to communicate his thoughts, and it helps doctors with the difficult decisions they must make.

Forty states and the District of Columbia have enacted legislation that sets out the requirements for a valid living will. In some states, the document outlined in the statutes must be used, while in other states, the provisions can be modified. Although a living will does not need to be prepared by an attorney, there are certain formalities that must be followed. Most states specify that a person must be at least 18 years of age to make a living will. In a number of states, witnesses to the will cannot be relatives or beneficiaries of the person's estate.

Once you have completed a living will, give copies to members of your family, as well as your family doctor, attorney, clergyman, and anyone else who might be notified of the seriousness of your condition. You should also discuss the document with them to make sure they understand what is to be done. This will also provide an opportunity to learn who might have reservations about following the instructions. If a doctor is hesitant about complying with your living will, for example, you can find another doctor who will follow your instructions.

If you want to make a living will, you should ask your doctor, attorney, or hospital or nursing home for information. They may have blank forms available for you to complete that will be valid in your state. Or contact Concern for Dying, 250 West 57th Street, New York, New York 10107, a national nonprofit organization that answers questions and provides information about living wills.

Living Wills

Ten years ago, Oscar completed a living will. Is it necessary for him to renew this document by initialing or redating it?

Yes. In fact, Oscar may have to complete a new living will periodically. Some states have expiration dates for a living will. In California and Idaho, for example, a living will expires after five years; in Georgia, it expires after seven years. Even if his state law gives no expiration date, Oscar should periodically review his living will and bring it up to date in the light of any medical advances or changes in his life.

Can Jerome's living will be made a part of his medical records?

Yes. In fact, state law may require it. If Jerome lives in Alabama, for example, his doctor must put a copy in the medical file once he is notified that Jerome has made a living will.

Edith felt strongly about the right to die with dignity and made out a living will. Over the objections of the family, the doctors have kept Edith on a respirator, even though she is certain not to recover. Can Edith's daughter "pull the plug" on the respirator without criminal responsibility?

No. Living will legislation does not allow family members to take such matters into their own hands. A living will is a directive, or communication, between patient and doctor, not between patient and family. Only a qualified doctor has the right to remove the respirator. Edith's daughter could face murder or manslaughter charges if she took matters into her own hands and disconnected the respirator.

The best course of action for Edith's daughter would be to get together with other members of the family and appeal to Edith's doctor to reconsider. If he remains firm, the family can ask him to refer Edith's case to someone who will honor Edith's wishes. If he refuses, he may be violating state law, in which case the family may seek a court's permission to disconnect the respirator without the doctor's approval.

Susan is terminally ill and has asked her husband, Duane, to help her die peacefully by taking her life. Could Duane be convicted of a crime if he does as she requests?

Yes, Duane could be convicted of murdering Susan. Ending someone's life to prevent further suffering is euthanasia, or mercy killing. But it is considered a form of murder, nevertheless.

Organ Donations

Burt wants to make his body available for organ donations or medical education. How does he go about doing this?

The Uniform Anatomical Gift Act suggests a number of ways to do this. Burt could fill in the form on the back of his driver's license, include a provision in his will, or draft a letter to keep with his personal papers. Each of these documents must be signed and witnessed. Burt should find out about the exact requirements in his state. Even though all the states have adopted the Uniform Anatomical Gift Act, many have modified it.

Can I donate my organs to science in my will?

Yes, but if you decide to use your will to express this wish, you should tell close relatives or others who will be notified of your death immediately. Time is often important when dealing with organ donations. If no one is aware of the contents of your will, the organs may be useless by the time your wishes become known. The will does not have to be probated for your organs to be donated.

Brian, a 16-year-old, wants to donate his organs to science when he dies. Would a signed and witnessed document be valid?

No. Most states follow the Uniform Anatomical Gift Act, which requires a donor to be at least 18 years old. In some states, he may have to be 21. However, Brian could let his family know his wishes. Many state anatomical gift acts list, in order of priority, the family members who can give consent for the donation of a minor's organs.

If I sign an organ donation form, will my family or my estate be responsible for the costs of removing these organs?

No. Generally, hospitals pay all costs associated with organ donations. There are also private foundations that help pay these costs in order to encourage hospitals to take part in organ donation programs.

Claire's husband signed the back of his driver's license, allowing organ donation. He was just killed in an accident. Can Claire stop the hospital from transplanting any of his organs?

Yes. If Claire gets in touch with the appropriate members of the hospital staff, they will probably follow her wishes despite the fact that her husband had completed the donor card. Doctors and other hospital personnel prefer to have authorization from the next of kin before proceeding with organ donations.

Eight years ago, Helen filled out a declaration for organ donation. She has changed her mind and wants to revoke the declaration. How should she do this?

It depends on which form Helen used originally to state her wishes. If she used the back of her driver's license, she should write "void" across the back of the card and sign and date it. If her wishes were included in her will, she should have her lawyer prepare a change, or codicil, which should be signed and witnessed. To cover all other possibilities, she should also prepare a statement revoking her previous one, sign it, and have it witnessed. Any other papers stating her wishes to be an organ donor, such as letters to relatives, should be located and destroyed.

CHAPTER
15

Pensions, IRA's, Social Security

Pension Plans

Cliff has just been hired by a company that does not have a retirement plan for its employees. Aren't all companies required by law to offer such plans?

No. However, many companies choose to offer such plans to their employees. If the retirement plan complies with the requirements of a federal law, the Employee Retirement Income Security Act (ERISA), the company's contributions to the plan are tax deductible for the company.

When Homer started at his new job he was 42 years old. The company does not permit new employees over 40 to join its retirement plan. Should Homer challenge this policy?

Yes. Under ERISA guidelines, the general rule—which applies to Homer—is that a company cannot use age as a reason to exclude an employee from its retirement plan. However, the law allows a plan to extend the retirement age for employees who start work within five years

Types of Pension Plans

Although the world of pensions and retirement plans may look jumbled and confusing at first glance, familiarity with the types of plans will help you compare the advantages and disadvantages of the various options available. Here are some of the terms used to discuss retirement plans, what they mean, and how the plans work:

- *Defined contribution plan*—The amount of contributions, or the formula for determining the amount of contributions, is preset. The amount of your benefit depends on the success of the investments made with the funds (contributions) in your account. Some defined contribution plans allow you to choose how the money in your account is invested.
- *Profit-sharing plan*—A type of defined contribution plan under which your employer's contributions are made according to a formula based on company profits or a percentage of your pay. The employer may contribute a smaller percentage or nothing at all in years when profits fall below a certain level. Under some profit-sharing plans, you may make voluntary contributions of up to a certain percentage of your income. This is known as an *incentive savings plan*.
- *Money-purchase pension plan*—Your employer's annual contributions are based on a percentage of your compensation. The employer must make these contributions every year, regardless of company profits.

of the plan's normal retirement age. For example, the plan could provide that, for such employees, retirement age would be the fifth anniversary of the employee's date of participation in the plan.

Will my pension benefits stop accumulating if I work past 65?

It's illegal for a company to stop or slow the accrual of pension benefits just because you work past normal retirement age. However, a plan may specify the number of years during which benefits can accrue.

My company's retirement plan is only for union members. Is this allowed by federal law?

Yes, if certain federal requirements are met. A qualified plan—one that allows the organization a tax deduction for its contributions—must cover at least 70 percent of all employees, as a general rule; and it must cover employees in a way that does not discriminate in favor of officers, shareholders, or highly paid employees. Union members can choose not

- *Target benefit plan*—The company sets a goal for the retirement benefit of an employee, then calculates the schedule of contributions that will be required to meet that goal. The actual benefit at retirement may be greater or less than the goal, or target, depending on the success of the plan investments, as well as on how accurately the company predicted the turnover, retirement, and life expectancy of its employees.
- *Defined benefit plan*—Your future benefit is determined in advance. It may be a set dollar amount (*flat benefit*) per month, or it may be determined by a formula, such as 75 percent of your annual income at retirement (*fixed benefit*). Contributions are based on the amount necessary to provide a certain benefit amount. You cannot direct the investment; instead, the fund is managed by fiduciaries and trustees. Some defined benefit plans multiply a set amount (called the unit) by the number of years you work to arrive at a *unit benefit* for retirement.
- *Contributory plan*—Both the employer and employee contribute. The *primary contributor* is the employer. *Noncontributory plans* are those to which only the employer contributes.
- *Salary reduction (401k) plan*—From his gross pay an employee chooses to put aside a certain percentage or dollar amount (up to a maximum set by the company). This money goes into a trust account, where it accumulates tax-free earnings. In effect this reduces the employee's take-home pay but also reduces his income tax because he is not taxed on the amount placed in his 401k account.

to participate in the plan by collective bargaining. In that case, they are not counted when measuring whether 70 percent of employees are covered. The company may choose to set up separate plans for union and nonunion employees, but the benefits must be comparable.

I have worked for the Minnow Company for 15 years. If I quit or am laid off or fired, will I lose the money that the company contributed to my retirement plan?

No. After 15 years of employment, your benefits should be fully vested. That means that all employer contributions to the plan are yours—even if you quit or are fired or laid off. Your own contributions to the plan vest immediately. They were yours to begin with.

In the past, employers could postpone vesting for as long as 15 years. Beginning in 1989, most employers must choose between two vesting schedules: one provides for complete vesting after five years of employment; the other for gradual vesting over seven years.

Is it sex discrimination for a company to pay women lower monthly pensions than it pays men?

Yes. A 1978 Supreme Court decision made it unlawful for an employer to use sex-linked actuarial tables to compute benefits for mandatory employer-funded defined benefit plans. Using these tables, the Court said, forces women to pay more than men do for the same benefits. In 1983 the Court further ruled that it is unlawful to pay women lower benefits for the same contributions to a voluntary deferred compensation plan.

In practice, many women do not receive pension benefits equal to those of men because they earn less and work fewer years. To help resolve this problem, Congress amended ERISA to lower the age for plan participation from 25 to 21 (which allowed more young women, as well as men, to start accumulating retirement benefits), to require joint and survivor annuities for married workers, and to preserve some benefits of workers who leave and then return to a company.

After 17 years with one company, where his retirement benefits are fully vested, Calvin is moving to a new company. Must he leave his pension funds with his old company until he retires?

Not necessarily. Many plans allow an employee to withdraw his vested benefits when leaving the company, whether or not he has reached retirement age. If that isn't allowed under the plan of Calvin's old company, he still should be able to take out his own contributions: ERISA regulations permit anyone who is more than 50 percent vested to withdraw his own money from a company retirement plan without forfeiting employer contributions.

Jasper's interest in his company's pension plan was vested before he became disabled as the result of a car accident. Will his disability reduce his retirement benefits?

It shouldn't. In fact, Jasper's disability may allow him to withdraw funds from his plan without penalty, even though he has not reached retirement age. He should not lose benefits because of a disability.

Can my company reduce the amount it contributes to the pension plan during periods when business is poor?

It depends. In both defined benefit and defined contribution plans, the company must make set contributions, regardless of profits, or have a fine imposed by the Internal Revenue Service. If, however, a company can show that mandatory contributions would result in a substantial business hardship, the company may be allowed to reduce the contribution without penalty. Under a profit-sharing plan, the company may forgo contributions altogether in a bad year.

If his company lays off Clark shortly before his pension rights are vested just so it can avoid paying his pension, can Clark sue?

Yes, if he can show that the company has been both (1) dismissing employees before vesting and (2) discriminating in favor of those employees who are shareholders, officers, or highly compensated. One federal court has ruled that a "break in service"—that is, leaving the company—won't affect vesting if it is for reasons beyond the worker's control, such as a layoff; and if a company closes a plant or office and all the employees there are laid off, their accrued benefits will become vested. If an employee leaves and later rejoins the company, ERISA break-in-service rules preserve his years of credit toward vesting until his break in service equals his prior period of service. (That is, if the employee had worked for two years, his break in service could be as long as two years.)

If my company goes bankrupt, will I lose all my vested benefits?

No. If the company you work for goes bankrupt, the federal Pension Benefit Guaranty Corporation (PBGC) will step in to guarantee payment of your vested retirement benefits, up to the legally established monthly limits, for life. The maximum amounts are adjusted on an annual basis. If the company is unable to pay, the PBGC will. In return, the PBGC can receive a percentage of the company's net worth to defray the cost of taking over the company's retirement plan obligations. In addition, to discourage financially troubled companies from misusing pension funds, both ERISA and the federal Tax Code impose stiff penalties on a company that underfunds its retirement plan.

Archie's retirement benefits were fully vested when he left and went to work for another company. Archie is now ready to retire and has learned that his first employer is no longer in business. Can he still get the benefits from his first job?

Yes. Archie shouldn't lose any benefits he earned just because he worked for more than one company. Even if Archie's old employer left no assets,

ERISA and Your Company's Pension Plan

The Employee Retirement Income Security Act, or ERISA, sets rules for the operation of company pension plans and gives covered employees certain rights. The effect of ERISA is to keep employees informed about their pension plan. The employee, for example, has the right to know his actual and projected benefits, and the right to receive information about the plan's assets, liabilities, receipts, and disbursements. These and other ERISA mandates, with which a company must comply in order to get a tax deduction for pension plan contributions, have helped standardize pension plans in several important respects, among them:

- *Eligibility*—The company can require only that an employee have completed one full year of service or have reached his 21st birthday, whichever comes later. (That is, if you joined the company at the age of 18, you would not be eligible until you reached 21; but if you joined at 21, you would be eligible after a year of employment.) An exception is made for plans with immediate full vesting: they can require three years of service before admitting an employee to plan participation. A company plan may not exclude older employees; but if a new employee is within five years of the plan's normal retirement age, he may be required to work a specified number of years before he can retire and begin to receive benefits under the plan.
- *Majority participation*—Generally, a plan must cover 70 percent or more of all employees, and it must cover employees in such a way that

Archie's pension funds are protected through the Pension Benefit Guaranty Corporation. Archie will receive his pension up to a specified limit per month, under the plan of the defunct company.

What happens to my pension if my company merges with another?

You are protected. The Pension Benefit Guaranty Corporation insures your benefits if a plan terminates because of a business merger. If the new organization replaces your old plan with a new one, your benefits under the new plan must be at least equal to your benefits under the old one.

Louise retired at 65, but wants to take a part-time job at a supermarket. Will her pension checks be reduced?

No. Louise's former employer may not reduce the benefit because she gets another job. There is an exception: if Louise goes back to work for her old employer, her benefit might be suspended during her reemployment.

it does not discriminate in favor of the company's highly paid personnel, its shareholders, or its officers.

- *Vesting*—Most companies must give employees either (1) 100 percent vesting after five years of service; or (2) gradual vesting leading to 100 percent vesting after seven years.
- *Joint and survivor annuities*—Plans whose benefits are in the form of an annuity must provide joint and survivor annuities for married workers, thus assuring that if the covered worker dies while receiving benefits, the spouse will receive the benefit.
- *Nonforfeiture*—Any participant who is at least 50 percent vested may withdraw his own contributions without forfeiting the entire benefit.
- *New plans*—If an employer decides to replace a plan with a new one, the participants must be entitled to benefits equal to or greater than those they had under the old plan.
- *Fiduciaries*—Pension funds must be managed by one or more fiduciaries for the benefit of covered employees. They must follow certain investment rules endorsed by the Treasury Department (such as diversifying investments), and may never use pension plan funds for their own benefit or for the benefit of the employer.
- *Summary plan description*—Every plan participant must receive a document called the summary plan description. It must be written in easily understandable language and explain each participant's rights and obligations. If the plan is modified, each participant must receive an explanation of the changes.

Pension Plans

I have the option of taking my retirement benefits in a lump sum or in monthly payments. Which would be better?

It depends on several factors. If you take all your benefits at once, your income for that year may put you in a higher tax bracket than usual, and you could lose a portion of your benefits to income taxes. In the past, 10-year income averaging could be used to soften the effects of a lump-sum settlement, but it is now available only to individuals who were 50 years old or older on January 1, 1986. Before choosing a lump sum or monthly payments, figure what each option would cost you in income taxes.

You can avoid these taxes when making a lump-sum withdrawal by "rolling over" the funds—that is, transferring the lump sum to an individual retirement plan, such as an IRA offered by a bank or mutual fund. You must make this transfer within 60 days of receiving the retirement benefit. If you are still several years away from retirement and have other sources of income, with no immediate need for funds, this may be your best option. The lump sum you put into a rollover IRA can continue to accumulate tax-free earnings until you withdraw the funds.

Will my wife receive benefits from my retirement plan if I die before she does?

Yes, if your plan is a defined benefit, money purchase, profit-sharing, or stock bonus type. ERISA requires these plans, as well as the Keogh type, to pay benefits to surviving spouses. The benefits are in the form of joint and survivor annuities, which stipulate that (1) if the worker dies while receiving payments, the benefit will then go to the surviving spouse, or (2) if the worker dies before receiving the benefit but while eligible for it (if working past the age of 65, for example), the surviving spouse will receive it as if the worker had died while receiving the benefit. If you have a joint and survivor plan, your monthly benefits will be lower than if your plan covered just your own life. This is because it is likely that monthly payments will be made for a longer time.

Is it legal for a company to withhold taxes from Katharine's pension check?

Yes. Federal tax laws require that the employer withhold taxes on pension payments, unless the employee elects not to have taxes withheld. This requirement covers payments from deferred compensation plans, IRA's, bond-purchase plans, annuities, and profit-sharing plans. Katharine's employer must notify her at least once a year of her right to choose whether or not to have taxes withheld.

What Is an Annuity?

An annuity is a contract, purchased with either one lump sum or periodic payments, that assures an individual a certain amount of money, usually paid out at fixed periods for a specified length of time or for life. Annuities that are set up to make payments at some future date, such as when you retire, are called *deferred annuities.* They are typically offered by life insurance companies, because their premium rates and benefit amounts, like those for life insurance policies, are based on actuarial data.

Many people choose to purchase an annuity contract with the benefits that have accumulated in their pension or retirement plans, thereby guaranteeing them a regular, predictable income. Annuities that provide income for the life of the worker and the worker's spouse are called *joint and survivor* contracts.

A deferred annuity is a type of savings program in which your original investment grows by accumulating interest and, if you choose, by your additional contributions. At the end of this accumulation period, the money is paid out according to the terms of the contract you signed. The major advantage of a deferred annuity is that while the money is accumulating, there is no tax on the earnings. Some deferred annuities earn interest at a set rate—these are called fixed deferred annuities. Others, called variable deferred annuities, allow the owner to change the investments in his annuity account—thus the earnings and total value of the account depend on the success of his investment decisions. The term *self-directed* is also used to describe an annuity for which the owner may choose the investments.

What is retirement insurance, and how does it work?

It is life insurance that you can convert to an annuity. If you reach the age specified in the policy, usually retirement age (55-70), you can choose to continue the life insurance coverage or receive regular payments.

IRA's and Keogh Plans

All my income is from my job as an employee of a printing company. Can I have both an IRA and a Keogh?

No. You can have only an IRA. However, if you were self-employed you could have both. An IRA is for anyone who earns income either as an employee or as a self-employed person. A Keogh is only for the self-employed person and his employees: for example, a doctor and his receptionists and nurses. Anyone with employees who sets up a Keogh plan must include all full-time employees who have worked three years or more. The employer gets a tax deduction for contributions that he makes to his employees' plans.

Nadine and her husband, Paul, who both work, want to open IRA's. Should they have separate IRA accounts?

Yes. If both husband and wife are employed, each can open an IRA and contribute up to $2,000 to the account, for a total contribution of $4,000. If one spouse were not working, the other could open a joint IRA account and contribute up to $2,250 a year.

William is 70 years old and has an IRA. He has no thought of retiring. If he works for several years more, can he continue to make contributions to his IRA?

No. William must stop making contributions to his IRA and begin withdrawing the money that has accumulated in his account by April 1 of the year following the year he reaches 70½.

Sally has opened an IRA and plans to contribute $1,000 each year. Does it matter if she makes the contribution in January or October of each year?

Not from a legal or tax standpoint, but the earlier Sally makes her contribution each year, the longer the funds accumulate tax-free interest. Over the course of 20 or 30 years, while she is saving for retirement, this extra interest can add up to a substantial sum.

Several years ago, Myrtle began making contributions to an IRA. She is now 58 and needs some money to pay off large medical bills. What are the penalties if she withdraws all or part of the money in her IRA?

If Myrtle withdraws funds from her IRA before she reaches the age of 59½, all the money in the plan will be subject to income tax and a penalty tax of 10 percent. This penalty may be increased in the future. No penalty is imposed if the person becomes disabled or dies (the money would then go to the deceased's estate). Unless Myrtle can claim a disability, she will be penalized for withdrawing her funds.

IRA's, Keoghs, and SEP's

For many Americans, retirement planning involves setting up an IRA (individual retirement account), Keogh plan, or SEP-IRA (simplified employee pension–individual retirement account). The earnings from these accounts, in contrast to those from a savings account or other investments, are allowed to accumulate tax free. Over the years, the tax exemption for these earnings can add substantially to the income later available to a retiree.

- **Who Qualifies?**

IRA—Anyone with earned income may put money into an IRA account. Generally, earned income means wages or salary, or money you make as a result of your own labor or effort. It does not include income such as rent, interest, or dividends.
Keogh—Any individual who is self-employed may establish a Keogh account with money earned through self-employment. If you are self-employed part-time, only the money earned from self-employment can be counted in calculating what percentage can go into a Keogh account. If your business has employees, you must include them in your Keogh plan. A self-employed person may have both an IRA and a Keogh.
SEP-IRA—SEP-IRA's can be established by both the self-employed and the wage earner. You may have both a SEP-IRA and a Keogh.

- **How Much Can I Contribute in a Year?**

IRA—The annual limit is $2,000 of earned income. A worker with a spouse who has no earned income can contribute up to $2,250 to a joint account annually.
Keogh—The percentage of earned income that you can contribute varies (from about 15 percent to 25 percent) with the kind of Keogh you set up; for many kinds of plans the limit is $30,000 annually.
SEP-IRA—The maximum annual contribution is $30,000 or 15 percent of earnings, whichever is lower.

- **When Must I Open My Account?**

IRA—It can be opened for a particular year as late as April 15 of the following year. Contributions may be made up to that date as well.
Keogh—To receive a tax deduction for contributions made in a tax year, the account must be opened by December 31 of that year. Contributions are deductible if made through April 15 of the next year.
SEP-IRA—Same as for IRA.

- **When Can I Withdraw My Money?**

IRA—An individual may start withdrawing funds at 59½. If you withdraw any of your money before that age, there is a penalty tax. Exceptions are made for distributions due to the death or disability of the account owner. Withdrawals must begin by April 1 of the year following the year the owner reaches 70½.
Keogh—Same as for IRA.
SEP-IRA—Same as for Keogh and IRA.

IRA's and Keogh Plans

Saul's will gives his entire estate to his wife, Florence. Should Saul name Florence as the beneficiary of his IRA and Keogh, or should he name his estate as the beneficiary?

If Saul dies before Florence, she will have the same options for receiving benefits whether he names her as beneficiary on the account or in his will. If Saul dies before taking out any of his IRA or Keogh funds, Florence may delay withdrawing money until Saul would have had to do so (April 1 of the year after he reached 70½). If Saul was already receiving money from his retirement account, Florence must follow the same withdrawal schedule that Saul set up or a faster one.

Does the law restrict where I can put my IRA or Keogh money?

Yes. If you have a self-directed IRA, one in which you make your own investment decisions, you may not invest in collectibles, such as artwork, antiques, gems, rugs, stamps, and coins (although you may invest in gold and silver U. S. coins). If you use IRA funds to purchase these collectibles, the purchase will be considered a distribution. You will be taxed on the distribution and penalized if you have not reached the age of 59½.

Where can I go to set up my own retirement plan?

Keoghs, IRA's, and SEP-IRA's can be established through banks, savings and loan institutions, insurance companies, brokerage firms, mutual funds, and other similar organizations.

Qualifying for Social Security

My brother Lonnie says that now that he has worked for two years, he is entitled to receive Social Security benefits when he retires. Is this true?

No. Lonnie must work and make the required Social Security contributions for a total of 40 calendar quarters before he qualifies for retirement benefits, although he may qualify for Social Security payments as a disabled worker or a dependent if he works for less time. Each of these quarters is three months and is also called a Social Security credit. A worker may earn up to 4 credits a year—in other words, he can accumulate the necessary 40 quarters in 10 years of continuous work. If a worker turned 21 before 1950, special rules apply: he must have worked one calendar quarter for every year after 1950 until he turns or turned 61. In no circumstances will the work requirement be more than 40 quarters.

Because of family demands, Bea has had to start and stop work several times over the past 35 years. How can she find out how many Social Security credits (quarters of work) she has earned?

A record of the quarters Bea has worked and her Social Security contributions should be on file at the Social Security Administration (SSA) headquarters in Baltimore, Maryland. To obtain the form (SSA-7004) needed to request her earnings record, or for other information, she should contact the nearest Social Security office. The address and phone number are listed in local phone books under Social Security Administration or U. S. Government.

Copies of W-2 wage statements, or of her tax returns if she was self-employed, are Bea's own records of her Social Security contributions. These papers should be kept indefinitely in a home file, in case of disagreement with the SSA about her earnings.

When can I start receiving my Social Security retirement benefits?

Assuming that you have accumulated the required number of calendar quarters, you may receive full retirement benefits if you retire at age 65. You may also choose to retire at 62, but your benefit check will be smaller. If you decide to continue working after 65, you can defer receiving Social Security checks until you retire; but you must begin receiving benefits by 70. If you work between the ages of 65 and 70, you increase your eventual Social Security retirement income by a certain percentage for each month you postpone collecting your benefits.

You also have the option of continuing to work after 65 *and* receiving your monthly benefit. However, the benefit will be reduced if you earn more than the annual limit, which may change from year to year. (Your nearest SSA office can tell you the current annual limit.) After 70, your earnings will not reduce your Social Security retirement benefit.

Is there any truth to the rumor that the legal retirement age will be raised in the future?

Yes. In fact, the law has already been passed. After the year 2000, for a period of six years, it will rise by two months every calendar year. For example, in 2001, to qualify for full retirement benefits, a worker will have to be age 65 years and 2 months; and in 2004, 65 years, 8 months. From 2006 to 2016, the retirement age will stay at 66, then it will resume increasing at the rate of two months a year until reaching 67 in 2022.

Qualifying for Social Security

Must a self-employed person pay more of his own money into Social Security than a company employee, even though they have the same annual income and can expect the same benefits?

Yes. A self-employed person in effect pays as both an employer and an employee, whereas a company employee's contribution is matched by that of his employer.

What papers do I need to take to the Social Security office to prove my eligibility for benefits?

You must take your Social Security card, a birth certificate or other document that proves your age, and your W-2 forms for the last two years (or Schedule C if you were self-employed). When applying for benefits based on your spouse's work records, you will need your marriage certificate. Your divorce decree is necessary if you are claiming on an ex-spouse's record. If you are applying for survivor benefits, you will need a death certificate for the worker who was covered by Social Security. If applying on behalf of children, take their birth certificates. If you are applying for disability, you need to bring your medical records.

When Josie's aunt applied for Social Security benefits, she was asked for a copy of her birth certificate. She was born in Poland, and her town's records were destroyed in World War II. What can she use as proof of age?

Josie's aunt may use school records, her driver's license, voter registration documents, immigration records, her passport, or applications for insurance. If there was a religious record made of her birth or baptism, she will be able to use that. She can also use the testimony of friends, relatives, or her physician. For a man, a draft registration card is another acceptable proof of age.

Mitchell was remarried last month. Should he notify the Social Security office?

Yes. Anyone covered by Social Security should report any changes in his life or in his family's that might increase or decrease benefits paid by Social Security. In addition to marriage or remarriage, events that should be reported include births, adoptions, divorces, the death of a person who is receiving benefits or who is eligible to receive benefits, and a child's becoming disabled.

Felicia has read that she should contact her Social Security office three months before her 65th birthday. If she fails to do so, does she lose her right to collect benefits?

No. But Felicia shouldn't wait too long. If her application is late, she can receive up to six months of back payments, but no more. Husbands, wives, children, and widows and widowers can get up to 12 months of retroactive benefits if they apply late. The SSA advises applying three months before age 65 because this allows time to process applications and start sending benefits as soon as the applicants become eligible.

I found a mistake in my Social Security earnings record four years after the fact. What are my rights in having this corrected?

Generally, you may have such errors corrected if less than 3 years, 3 months, and 15 days have passed since the error was made. But if no earnings were reported for a quarter in which you were working and paying Social Security, then you have the right to appeal, starting with your Social Security office and, if necessary, appealing all the way up to federal court. Because of the time limit for correcting errors, you should request a copy of your record every two to three years by filling out form SSA-7004 at your Social Security office.

Luke worked for the railroad for six years and was told that he was not eligible for Railroad Retirement benefits. If that is so, can his years be credited to his Social Security retirement account?

Yes. A railroad worker earns quarters of coverage under the Social Security system while employed by a railroad. If Luke had worked at least 10 (and up to 30) years for the railroad, he could have retired under the Railroad Retirement system with a full benefit at 65 or a partial benefit at 62. If he had 30 or more years of railroad service, he could retire at 62 with a full benefit and at 60 with a partial benefit.

Collecting Social Security

How is the amount of my Social Security retirement benefit calculated?

Your benefit is based on your income—up to a dollar limit specified by law—during the years you worked. The dollar limit increased from $3,000 in 1950 to $48,000 in 1990, with further increases likely. The money you earn annually in excess of this amount is not considered in figuring your benefit. The actual formulas for determining individual benefits, while set by law, are quite complex; but your local Social Security office can give you an estimate.

A range of minimum benefits has been established for those who have worked for very low wages. It varies with the number of years a person has worked and contributed to Social Security. There are also maximum benefits: For a worker who retired at 65 in 1990, the maximum retirement benefit was $975 per month.

Elizabeth is considering early retirement. How will that affect her monthly Social Security benefit?

If Elizabeth retires before 65, her monthly check will be less than if she waited until she was 65 or older. The amount will be lower because it is probable that she will be receiving benefits for a longer period of time. If she retires at 62, her benefits will be reduced by 20 percent. After the year 2022, retirement at 62 will result in a 30 percent reduction.

Kay has just turned 62 and is trying to decide whether to retire before age 65. How can she figure out how much her monthly benefit will be reduced?

First, Kay can obtain an estimate of her retirement benefit at 65 from the SSA by completing Form SSA-7004 and noting at the bottom of her form, "Please furnish benefit estimate." Using the SSA figure, Kay can then calculate her reduced benefit by subtracting 0.555 percent for each month before her 65th birthday (and after her 62nd) that she plans to retire. If she intends to retire at 63 (or 24 months before 65), she would multiply 24 times 0.555 percent and find that her benefit would be reduced by 13.32 percent.

Terence retired when he was 65, but wants to go back to work to help make ends meet. Will the amount he receives in his Social Security checks be reduced?

Probably. If Terence works only part-time, he may be able to continue to receive his full benefit if his earnings don't go above a certain level. This earnings limit, which Terence can find out by calling his local Social Security office, is set every year. Once his earnings go above the limit for the year, his benefit will be reduced by $1 for every $3 he earns. Benefits are reduced $1 for every $2 earned over the limit by Social Security recipients between 62 and 65; after age 70 earnings do not affect benefits.

Michael, who is 65 years old, will continue to work. He will begin receiving Social Security payments next month. Will Social Security taxes continue to be deducted from his paycheck?

Yes. As long as Michael is working, he will continue to contribute to the Social Security fund. He must pay Social Security taxes on all earnings covered by the Social Security law.

John will be receiving a company pension when he retires. Does this income affect the amount of his Social Security benefit?

No. Income from a company or personal retirement plan does not affect the Social Security amount. Neither does income from savings, investments, annuities, insurance, or inheritances. Only earned income, such as salary or wages, affects this amount.

In the past year, my mailbox has been broken open three times. I am retired and rely on my Social Security check as my main source of income. How can I make sure I get my check every month?

You should request and fill out Form SF-1199 at your bank. This form will enroll you in the Social Security direct deposit program. Instead of being mailed, your benefits will be deposited directly into your account; this will prevent the loss or theft of your checks from your mailbox.

My aunt can't handle her financial affairs and has asked me to help her. Can we have her Social Security check sent to me?

If you have evidence that your aunt is unable to handle her financial affairs, you may request that the Social Security Administration declare you her representative payee. If you become her payee, the checks will come to you. You will be expected to handle the money solely for your aunt's benefit.

Matthew's tax specialist said that Matthew would have to pay income tax on some of his Social Security retirement benefits. Could that be right?

Yes. If Matthew's income exceeds a certain amount, his Social Security benefits become taxable. Your nearest Social Security office can tell you the amount of annual income above which you must pay income taxes on your Social Security benefits.

Social Security for Dependents

What are Social Security dependents' benefits?

They are payments to help support the dependents of a wage earner who has retired or died. Among those entitled to dependents' benefits are husbands, wives, children, and in some cases, the parents of the retired or deceased wage earner.

When a wage earner retires and begins receiving Social Security, the worker's spouse may, upon reaching 65, collect half the amount of the wage earner's benefit (or a reduced amount at age 62). The spouse could forgo this secondary benefit if entitled to a larger amount on the basis of his or her own work record. If the wage earner has died, the surviving spouse, upon reaching 65, is entitled to 100 percent of the wage earner's benefit at 65. The widow or widower can collect a reduced benefit as early as age 60 or, if disabled, as early as age 50. Divorced spouses are entitled to these benefits as well, if they were married at least 10 years and if they are single when they apply for benefits.

Children under the age of 18 qualify for benefits when a parent dies or retires. These benefits will continue until the child reaches the age of 19 if the child is still in high school. A child of any age may receive benefits if permanently disabled before the age of 22. A parent age 62 or over can claim benefits on the basis of a deceased adult child's earnings if the parent was dependent on that child for at least half of his support while the child was alive.

Sharlene's husband worked most of his life outside the country and never earned Social Security credits. Does that mean he is not eligible for any type of Social Security benefit?

No, not necessarily. Sharlene's husband may receive Social Security benefits based on Sharlene's work record. His Social Security check will be half the amount of hers. He may also receive a widower's benefit if Sharlene dies before him. The same principle holds true if the situation is reversed: If Sharlene's husband had been the one who had worked and qualified for Social Security benefits, then she would be eligible for payments as a dependent or a surviving spouse.

Wilma and her husband have just celebrated their 65th birthdays. Is Wilma entitled to receive Social Security benefits based on her husband's work record?

Yes. If her husband has elected to begin receiving his benefit, Wilma is entitled to her own benefit check based on her husband's earnings. The check will be half the amount of her husband's check. If Wilma is entitled to benefits based on her own work record, she may choose between claiming her own benefits and claiming those to which she is entitled as a spouse. She should compare them to see which will give her a larger benefit. She may *not* receive both.

Laura is 65 and has been divorced from her husband for 12 years. Is she entitled to receive Social Security benefits if her former spouse has not yet retired?

Yes. An ex-spouse who has been divorced at least 2 years (after 10 years of marriage) may begin receiving reduced benefits at the age of 62, or full benefits at 65, regardless of whether the former spouse has retired.

Can I collect Social Security benefits from both a former and a current spouse's work records?

No. Such double benefits are not allowed. You may collect benefits as a divorced spouse starting at age 62 only if unmarried when applying. If you are divorced from the second spouse after 10 years of marriage, you may choose the larger of the two benefits. If your second spouse dies after at least one year of marriage, you may choose the larger of the divorced spouse benefit or the surviving spouse benefit. You can collect the larger of the two, but not both.

Helen is 68 years old and receives a widow's benefit from Social Security. If she remarries will she continue to receive this benefit?

Yes. Helen will not lose her survivor's benefit by remarrying, since she is past the age of 60. Both widows and widowers can receive benefits even if they remarry after 60 if they were unmarried when they applied. After being married 12 months to a new husband who is receiving retirement benefits, Helen will be able to choose to continue receiving survivor's benefits based on her first husband's work record or spouse's benefits based on her new husband's record.

Donna is 67 years old and receives a monthly check based on her own work record. Her husband just died. Can Donna receive both the widow's benefit and her own retirement benefit?

No. Although Donna is entitled to both types of benefits, she cannot collect more than the larger of the two benefits. She should compare the amount to which she would be entitled as a surviving widow with the amount she is now receiving and choose the bigger benefit.

Social Security for Dependents

After Fred died, his widow, Marion, continued to put his Social Security checks in their joint bank account and withdraw the money as she needed it. Is there anything wrong with this?

Yes. Marion should report Fred's death immediately to the nearest Social Security office. Not only is she obligated to return all the money she receives from Fred's checks, but she also faces charges of fraud and severe fines if convicted. Marion should request instructions for returning the money and applying for survivor's benefits.

My wife and I have two children in college, ages 19 and 21. Both of us are eligible for Social Security retirement benefits. Can our children receive monthly payments based on our records?

No. In the past, your children were entitled to receive benefits when you retired until they reached the age of 18, or until they reached the age of 22 if they were full-time students. Now, children are entitled to this benefit only until the age of 18, or 19 years of age if still in high school.

Nat died leaving two children, one adopted child, and three stepchildren, all under 18 years of age. Will they all be eligible to receive survivors' benefits?

The adopted child and Nat's two natural children are entitled to survivors' benefits. The stepchildren are entitled to these benefits if they had been living with Nat for at least nine months before his death, and if he was contributing to their support.

Do grandchildren under 18 years of age have any claim to the benefits of their grandparents?

Yes, in some cases. If the grandchild's parents (natural or adopted) are dead or disabled when the grandparents become entitled to benefits, and if the grandparents have provided support for the grandchild, that child is entitled to benefits.

Is there a time limit for claiming the lump-sum death benefit?

The surviving spouse or eligible surviving children must apply within two years for this payment, which is intended to offset the funeral and burial expenses for the deceased.

Medicare

For information on individual and group medical insurance, see "Health and Disability Insurance" in Chapter 8, *Insurance*. For problems with paying for medical care, see "Paying the Bills" in Chapter 14, *Your Medical Rights*.

My social worker told me that I wasn't eligible for Medicare, but that I might qualify for Medicaid. What is the difference?

Medicare is a health insurance program created by the federal government mainly for the benefit of people who are 65 or older. It is funded by the contributions that employers and employees make to Social Security. The federal government contracts with various private companies to administer the Medicare program in each state: for example, in Massachusetts, the provider is Blue Cross and Blue Shield; in Alaska, it is Aetna; in Idaho, it is Equitable.

Medicaid is a type of welfare program, funded by both the state and federal governments, that provides medical assistance to the poor. If you meet income guidelines and have a medical need, you may qualify to have your medical expenses paid by Medicaid.

Guy will soon be 65 years old and eligible for Medicare. Will all of his medical needs be paid for by Medicare?

No. Medicare has limits to its coverage. For example, if Guy is hospitalized for more than 150 continuous days, Medicare will not pay for his hospital charges beyond that time. Nor does Medicare cover many necessary medical expenses, such as prescriptions, eyeglasses, checkups, immunizations, dental care, and custodial care. Medicare members must also contribute a 20 percent copayment for doctors' services. Additionally, Medicare sets a maximum amount that it will pay for a doctor's services. If Guy's doctor's bill is higher than the maximum, Guy will probably have to pay the difference.

Must you be retired to have Medicare protection at age 65?

No. Once you reach age 65, you are eligible for Medicare coverage even if you choose not to retire and collect your Social Security benefits. You should apply for Medicare three months before your 65th birthday.

My next-door neighbor is 42 years old and has health coverage through Medicare. Isn't Medicare only for people over age 65?

In addition to providing health care coverage for those over 65, Medicare covers the disabled—those who have been receiving Social Security disability benefits for at least 24 months—and those who suffer from kidney disease, which, while not always disabling, may require costly and frequent treatment with dialysis machines.

What is the difference between Medicare Part A and Part B?

Part A, or hospital insurance, covers expenses associated with hospitalization, post-hospital home health care, and blood when you are hospitalized. Those entitled to Medicare pay no premiums for Part A. Those not eligible for Social Security benefits may purchase Part A coverage for a monthly premium. Details are available at Social Security offices.

Part B coverage is also known as medical insurance. All those enrolled for this coverage must pay a monthly premium. Part B medical insurance

Appealing Social Security and Medicare Decisions

The retirement and disability benefits, Supplemental Security Income (SSI), and Medicare programs run by the Social Security Administration help millions of retired, sick, or poor Americans to pay bills that might otherwise overwhelm them. Sometimes, however, people who feel they are entitled to benefits are turned down, or get less than they were expecting. When this happens, you should know that you can appeal all the way to a federal court—between 25 and 50 percent of the claims that are appealed are eventually resolved in favor of the recipient. At any stage of the appeal process, you can be represented by anyone you choose, including an attorney, paralegal, social worker, or social service volunteer. The process is similar for Social Security and Medicare benefits, and can be divided, with minor differences, into five basic steps:

1. *Difference of opinion*—If you receive a notice that your Social Security benefits have been denied, reduced, or stopped, or that Medicare will not cover a bill, call or write a letter to the Social Security office, giving the details on the notice you received, and informing them that you do not agree with the decision that has been made. If there has been a clerical or computer error, it is possible that you can have your problem resolved with no further effort.

2. *Reconsideration*—Ask for and fill out a special request for reconsideration form, including any relevant evidence (such as statements from your doctor). Your case will be reviewed by Social Security employees—but not those who originally made the decision to deny, reduce, or stop your benefits—and you will be notified of their decision by mail. You must file this form within 60 days of receiving a notice helps cover many of the expenses not paid for by Medicare Part A: doctors' bills, medical supplies, outpatient hospital care, home health care, and blood if you are an outpatient.

Beatrice is automatically eligible for Part A coverage. When she got her Medicare card, it also indicated that she had Part B coverage, with the premium being taken out of her Social Security check. Beatrice never signed up for this Part B coverage. Has there been some mistake?

No. When Beatrice began receiving her Social Security retirement benefits, she was automatically enrolled in Part B coverage. Unless she informs the Social Security Administration that she does not want to have this coverage, the monthly premium will continue to be deducted from her Social Security benefit check.

disallowing all or part of your claims for retirement or Medicare Part A benefits, or within six months of being denied benefits on Part B claims. If you are appealing the cutoff of disability or SSI benefits, you have the right to a face-to-face interview, rather than an exchange of letters.

3. *Hearing*—If your claim is denied at the reconsideration stage, you have 60 days to request a hearing before an administrative law judge, who is employed by the Social Security Administration Office of Hearings and Appeals. Your request must be made on a special form available at Social Security offices. At the hearing, you may have witnesses appear on your behalf and present other evidence concerning your eligibility for benefits. For Medicare Part A, the disputed amount must be $100 or more to request a hearing. If you are disputing a Medicare Part B payment, an employee of the insurance carrier, not a judge, will preside at the hearing and render a final decision. (This is usually the last stage of a Part B appeal.)

4. *Appeals Council*—If you do not agree with the decision made by the judge, you may file a request within 60 days for a review by the Appeals Council of the Social Security Administration. If the council agrees to review your case, it will probably focus on whether the administrative law judge followed the proper procedures and made a correct decision at the hearing. In some cases the Appeals Council will allow you or your representative to appear in person and present new evidence.

5. *Federal court*—If the Appeals Council decides against you, you have 60 days to file a lawsuit in federal court, where the decision rests with a federal judge. If you did not have the help of a lawyer up to this point, now is probably the time to consult one. If the dispute is about a Medicare claim, the disputed amount must be $1,000 or more, excluding deductibles and copayments.

Medicare

Morton is not eligible for Medicare Part A coverage. Can he still pay for Part B?

Yes, Morton can apply for Part B coverage even though he is not eligible for Social Security or Part A coverage. Morton must be 65 to apply for enrollment. Disabled widows and widowers between the ages of 50 and 65 who are not receiving Social Security disability are also eligible to apply for Part B coverage.

Mildred has never been employed and is not eligible for Social Security. She will be 65 years old next month. Can she obtain Medicare coverage?

Yes, but she may have to pay for it herself. Once Mildred reaches 65, she can purchase health insurance through the Medicare program. She will be required to pay a monthly premium for this coverage. If Mildred is married to, or the widow of, a man eligible for Social Security benefits, she will, at age 65, automatically be eligible for Medicare coverage without having to pay the premium.

In 1990 the premium for voluntary enrollment by an individual in Medicare Part A was $175 per month. The premium for Part B coverage, which every member must pay whether qualifying for Social Security or not, was $28.60 per month. These amounts are subject to change.

Am I protected under Medicare as soon as I become eligible?

You are automatically enrolled in Medicare when you apply for Social Security or Railroad Retirement benefits at age 65. If you retire at 62, you will be enrolled in Medicare when you reach 65. If you decide to continue working past 65 and not apply for Social Security, you are not automatically enrolled in Medicare (although you are entitled to benefits). You must enroll by filling out and sending in an application for benefits to your Social Security office.

Patricia, age 65, plans to continue working three more years. She has a good health benefit plan at work. Will she have to convert to Medicare coverage?

No. Patricia can continue under her employer's health insurance plan and may be required by law to do so. In certain cases, those eligible for Medicare must continue with their employer-sponsored group coverage as the primary insurer. Medicare will be her secondary insurer in that case. She may find this to her benefit, especially if her company insurance plan covers expenses not reimbursed by Medicare, such as private nursing care, routine dental expenses, and doctors' bills above the maximum allowed.

Randy has decided to work until he is 70 years old. His Social Security monthly benefits will be delayed until he retires. Does that mean Randy will also have to wait until he is 70 for Medicare coverage to begin?

No. Randy will qualify for Medicare at 65, even though he continues working and does not start receiving his Social Security benefits until the age of 70. Randy should be sure to apply for coverage, since it will not begin automatically.

My eight-year-old daughter needs an operation. Her father currently receives Social Security disability benefits. Is the child eligible for Medicare?

No. Although your daughter's father is probably eligible for Medicare coverage because he is currently receiving Social Security disability benefits, your daughter is not eligible. The only people under the age of 65 who are eligible for Medicare are those who have received Social Security disability benefits for 24 months, or those receiving benefits because of kidney disease.

When Clarence was referred to a heart specialist, he was told that the doctor was not a participating Medicare physician. What does that mean?

Participating physicians are those who bill Medicare patients for services at fees set by Medicare. The patient of a participating physician will only have to pay the 20 percent of the bill that Medicare does not pay. If a nonparticipating physician's bill is higher than the Medicare fee, the patient must pay the difference between the Medicare fee and the doctor's bill, plus the 20 percent of the charge that Medicare doesn't pay. Since the fees set by Medicare are about two years behind actual doctors' fees, Clarence will probably have to pay more for the services of a nonparticipating physician.

Ida was alone when she fell down, and she called a doctor who lived nearby. She later learned that he was not a participating Medicare physician. Would the fact that Ida used this doctor only

because she had an emergency make a difference in how much Medicare would pay for his services?

No. Medicare will pay only 80 percent of the fee it has established for her doctor's services. Ida must pay 20 percent of Medicare's set fee plus any difference between Medicare's fee and this doctor's.

Mamie, who is 69, has had the same doctor all her life. Does she have any rights if he charges her a larger amount for a service than Medicare allows?

No doctor can be forced to accept the fees Medicare sets; and no Medicare patient can be forced to consult with only participating Medicare doctors.

What recourse do I have if my nephew missed the time limit for submitting my Medicare insurance claim?

Under Medicare rules, a claim must be submitted no later than December of the year following the year that charges were incurred. This gives you, in some cases, up to two years to submit a claim: for example, a claim for services provided in January 1991 must be submitted by December 1992, as must a claim for charges incurred in July 1991.

However, if your charges were incurred in the last three months of the year, Medicare will treat them as if they were incurred in the following year. In other words, charges incurred in October through December 1991 will be treated as if incurred in 1992. Therefore, the claims could be submitted as late as December 1993. If your bills fall into this category, it may not be too late to file your claim.

My husband will be going into a nursing home next month. Will our Medicare coverage take care of his expenses?

Your husband's physician must certify that his care is medically necessary. If your husband needs only custodial care, such as assistance in getting in and out of bed, dressing, eating, and bathing, Medicare will not cover the costs. Medicare will only pay for costs incurred in a skilled nursing facility (not in an intermediate or residential care facility) that provides 24-hour nursing care, daily rehabilitative services, a physician or registered nurse on the staff, and a physician available for emergencies. Your husband must be admitted to the skilled nursing facility after a hospital stay of at least three days (in the preceding 30 days), and he must be entering the facility for treatment of the same illness for which he was hospitalized. He must require skilled nursing care or skilled rehabilitation services on a daily basis.

If he meets these requirements, Medicare will pay 100 percent of his first 20 days' expenses. From day 21 to day 100, your husband will be required to pay some coinsurance. Medicare will not pay any of the expenses incurred after a stay of 100 days.

Our grandmother, a Medicare patient in a skilled nursing home, does not seem to be receiving the same quality of care as other patients. What can we do?

Your grandmother's rights to a certain standard of nursing home care are clearly set out in most states and backed by the Department of Health and Human Services. (See the special feature, "Rights of Nursing Home Patients," in Chapter 2.)

You should report violations, or suspected violations, of these rights to the Health Care Financing Administration (a federal agency that is a division of the Department of Health and Human Services); to your state's health department; and to your state's office on aging. This should be done whether the patient's nursing home costs are paid by Medicare, Medicaid, a private insurer, or personal funds. Some patients have brought successful lawsuits to force nursing facilities to provide the required level of care.

Elsie went into the hospital on April 1 and was discharged on April 15. She was readmitted on May 22. Will she have to pay the Medicare deductible for each hospital stay?

No. Elsie will have to pay the deductible again only if she reenters the hospital in a new benefit period. The deductible in 1990 was $592 for the first 60 days. A benefit period is determined in this manner: The period begins the day Elsie enters the hospital and continues until she has been out of the hospital for 60 consecutive days. Since Elsie was out of the hospital only 37 days before being readmitted, she is in the same benefit period and does not have to pay the deductible again.

The hospital told me my private duty nurse would be partially paid for by Medicare, but Medicare rejected the entire bill. Can I appeal this if the hospital was misinformed?

Yes. In some cases, Medicare will pay for services usually not covered. You should ask Medicare for a waiver of beneficiary liability, which can be applied when the patient, because of the actions of the hospital, had reason to believe that the services being provided were covered. Medicare might rule that the hospital should pay for the private duty nurse, since it should have known these services were not covered.

Joanna's grandmother is getting to the point where she needs a lot of care, but she will not consider moving to a nursing home. Will Medicare pay any of the expenses of taking care of her in her own home, or in Joanna's home?

Medicare will probably help pay for Joanna's grandmother's at-home care if her condition is one that does not require hospitalization, but does require intermittent skilled nursing care. "Intermittent" means at least one visit a month by a skilled nurse and usually does not include round-the-clock attendance. However, Medicare sometimes covers the cost of intensive care by a skilled nurse for a limited period of time. Another criterion for these payments is that Joanna's grandmother must be largely confined to her home, although occasional trips outside will not disqualify her from Medicare coverage.

If she meets these guidelines, Medicare will cover the costs of intermittent skilled nursing care; physical, speech, and occupational therapy; home health aides; social services; and medical supplies and appliances. These services must be provided through a home health agency. Medicare will pay 100 percent of the costs for an unlimited number of medically necessary visits. Purely custodial care is not covered. If Joanna's grandmother moved into Joanna's home, the payments would continue, so long as they were for medical, not custodial, care.

I have seen a lot of ads on television about insurance policies to add to my Medicare coverage. Should I buy one?

Before purchasing a Medigap policy, designed to supplement your Medicare coverage, compare it carefully with your coverage under Medicare. Some policies advertised as supplements to Medicare merely duplicate Medicare coverage, and you cannot collect twice for the same claim. Look for policies that will cover your Medicare deductibles, coinsurance, and prescription drugs. Check to see if the policy offers supplements to both Part A and Part B of Medicare. Avoid policies that exclude preexisting conditions. Unfortunately, no policy covers everything that Medicare doesn't.

I'm retired, and my wife and I are both covered by Medicare, Part A and Part B. We are beginning to plan a trip we have always

dreamed about, a tour of the capitals of Europe. If we need medical or hospital services in a foreign country, will our Medicare coverage pay for those expenses?

No. Medicare covers medical expenses incurred in the United States only. An exception is made if you are in the United States and a Canadian or Mexican hospital is closer than the nearest American hospital that can provide the care you need.

My father, who has just retired at 65, says he and others who qualify for Medicare will never have to worry about their coverage ending. Is this really true?

No. If you qualify for Medicare because you have reached 65 and are retired, your hospital coverage will end after a hospitalization of 150 straight days. This coverage consists of a 90-day benefit period plus the 60-day "lifetime reserve." Once the 60-day reserve is used, it's gone forever—it cannot be used again. If you recover and then have to be readmitted to the hospital during a new benefit period, you will be eligible to receive benefits for another 90 days.

If you are under 65 and qualify for Medicare because of kidney disease, your benefits will end 12 months after you discontinue dialysis treatments. If you have a successful kidney transplant, your benefits will end three years after the operation.

Medicaid

My neighbor is elderly, poor, and very sick. How can I help her apply for Medicaid?

You can accompany her to the Medicaid offices and help her with the application process. Medicaid is administered with other welfare and social service programs, such as Aid to Families With Dependent Children. In fact, if your neighbor is currently receiving welfare benefits, or if she is entitled to them but not receiving them, she is entitled to Medicaid. She can also qualify for Medicaid if she is medically needy. This means she can receive Medicaid assistance even if she has enough money to live on, but has spent all her savings on medical bills, still owes more, and will need further medical treatment.

Although my Uncle Eric is receiving Medicaid benefits for his nursing home costs, I have agreed to buy him things he needs or wants. The nursing home buys these items and sends me a bill

every other month. After looking at some of the charges on my bill, I am wondering if Medicaid shouldn't be paying for some of them. How can I find out?

Part of the Medicaid benefit is a personal needs allowance, which in 1987 was $25 per month. If you believe that some of the charges billed to you should be covered by this allowance, contact the local social service or welfare agency that administers Medicaid. You can also contact local agencies that provide legal assistance for the poor, such as a senior citizen law project or legal aid.

Under current regulations, Medicaid allows you, as a family member, to pay for services it does not cover; and Medicaid recipients like your uncle can keep a certain amount of money for their personal needs in excess of $25 per month. This raises the possibility that nursing homes may charge residents or their families for services already paid by Medicaid. Thus you are wise to double-check all charges on your uncle's bills.

My Aunt Ruby has had two long hospital stays in the last year. She is worried that if she has to enter the hospital again, Medicaid won't pay. Could this happen?

No, unless Aunt Ruby's financial picture suddenly improved and disqualified her for Medicaid. Unlike Medicare benefits, which can be exhausted by a prolonged hospital stay, Medicaid payments for hospitalization continue as long as medically necessary. A Medicaid recipient is never presented with a bill for deductibles, coinsurance, or days after coverage ceases. Billing and payment are arranged between the Medicaid agency and the health care provider.

In what kinds of situations can I lose my Medicaid benefits?

Since Medicaid is based on financial need, you can lose your benefits if you no longer qualify for Aid to Families With Dependent Children, disability, or aid to the elderly benefits in your state. If you inherit a fortune or win the lottery, you will lose your Medicaid benefits, but you will not be required to pay for any past services.

Mae has been told she is no longer eligible for Medicaid benefits. Can she appeal this decision?

Yes. Mae must be notified 10 days in advance if the Medicaid agency plans to deny her benefits. She may request a hearing within those 10 days; if she does so, her coverage must continue while her appeal is pending, unless the laws governing Medicaid change. To prepare for her hearing, Mae has the right to inspect her file and other relevant documents.

She must be notified of the result of the hearing within 90 days of requesting the hearing. She has the right to request that a court review the agency's decision if it rules against her. The judicial review may be in a state or federal court, depending on whether Mae's claim relates to federal or state law. Both apply because the Medicaid program is based on federal law, but administered through state regulations.

Disability and SSI Benefits

How long do I have to work to be eligible for disability payments?

To become eligible for Social Security disability benefits, you must accumulate a certain number of Social Security credits, but fewer credits are required to be eligible for disability than for retirement. If the disability occurred before the age of 24, you must have worked for a total of six quarters in a job covered by Social Security. If disability occurs between the ages of 24 and 31, you must have worked at least half the time between turning 21 and the start of the disability. If disabled at 31 or later, you must have accumulated at least 20 credits (calendar quarters of work) in the 10 years before your disability.

Do I have to be completely disabled to receive disability benefits under Social Security?

To qualify for disability benefits under Social Security, you must suffer from a mental or physical condition that prevents you from having any kind of substantial gainful employment *and* that is expected to last, or has lasted, at least 12 months, or that is expected to result in death. There is no general agreement on the meaning of the term *substantial gainful employment*; the courts have defined it on a case-by-case basis.

Pierre is 52 and receives Social Security disability income. When he turns 65, can he receive Social Security retirement income in addition?

No. Pierre might be eligible for Social Security retirement at 65 if he worked enough quarters before becoming disabled. However, individuals who are eligible for both retirement and disability benefits may only collect one of them. Pierre should determine which benefit is larger and choose to collect that one.

Disability and SSI Benefits

What are my rights in applying for Supplemental Security Income (SSI) if I have never worked?

Eligibility for SSI benefits does not depend on a work record. If you are in financial need (as determined by your assets and income), you may qualify for SSI. The other requirements are that you be 65 or older or blind or disabled and a resident and citizen of the United States, or an immigrant lawfully admitted for permanent residence here.

Lionel learned he was eligible for Supplemental Security Income a few years after he could have received benefits. Can he apply for retroactive payments?

No. Lionel is eligible only as of the day of his application for SSI. There are no retroactive SSI benefits.

CHAPTER
16

Wills and Estates

Your Estate

My insurance agent keeps asking me to get together with him to plan my estate, but I really don't have much—a house, a car, a life insurance policy, and some other personal property. Why should I bother planning my estate?

Estate planning can give you a sense of security by assuring that your assets will be distributed the way you want. And, in many cases, good planning can produce important tax savings. Many people think that estate planning begins and ends with making a will. But it really involves much more than that. For example, property that you and your spouse own separately can be put into joint ownership to keep it from being tied up in court proceedings after one of you dies. Trusts can be created and guardians named to ensure that your children are properly cared for. Gifts can be made to reduce estate and inheritance taxes.

Taking the time now to plan for the future can prevent family arguments and enable an executor to handle your estate more smoothly. It can also reduce some of the costs involved in managing and distributing your property so that more is left for your heirs.

What types of property are included in an estate?

An estate consists of all the property a person owns. This includes assets of which the person is sole owner—such as bank accounts, jewelry, life insurance, and pension plans—and property in which he or she shares ownership with a spouse, partner, or someone else—such as a home, business, car, or joint bank account. Stocks and bonds, copyrights, patents, and any money owed to the person are also included in the estate, as are any unpaid loans, taxes, or other debts.

What can I do to be sure that my wife will have access to the money in my bank account if she needs immediate cash when I die?

You could set up a joint account, with your wife named as a joint tenant with right of survivorship. But check your state law. The entire balance may not be immediately available to her on your death. In some cases, state taxing authorities must be given advance notice before withdrawals are made so that they can compute the true value of your estate.

As an alternative, you could set up a payable-on-death account, if such accounts are permitted in your state, and name your wife beneficiary. Money in the account would then be available to your wife immediately after your death. Or you could have a bank account set up as a trust for your wife. In this type of arrangement, known as a Totten trust, the money would automatically pass to your wife on your death.

Roxanne wants her husband to inherit her house when she dies without having the matter go through any court procedures. How can she arrange this?

She can have the house put into both her name and her husband's. This type of ownership, called joint tenancy with the right of survivorship, may also result in lower estate or inheritance taxes. However, if Roxanne decided to sell the house, her husband would have to agree to the sale.

Are there advantages if my husband names me as beneficiary of an individual retirement account (IRA) instead of simply letting the proceeds from his IRA become part of his estate when he dies?

Yes. If you are the beneficiary of the IRA, the proceeds will pass directly to you on your husband's death, and you will not have to go through any court procedures to get them. Like life insurance benefits, the money would be available to you much more quickly than funds whose distribution must be approved by the probate court.

What is the difference between estate and inheritance taxes?

Estate taxes are imposed on a person's estate after his death, and are based on the value of the estate after certain deductions have been made. Inheritance taxes, on the other hand, are imposed on the beneficiaries—those who inherit an estate. The tax is usually based on the value of the property inherited and the relationship of the beneficiary to the person who died. Immediate members of the family are taxed at a lower rate than more distant relatives.

Evan gave $5,000 to Farrah as a gift six months before he died. Will she have to pay an inheritance tax on the gift?

Yes, because Evan died so soon after making the gift. Most states presume that a gift given shortly before death is made to avoid taxes—*in contemplation of death* is the legal term. Generally, the gift is taxable if it is made within one to three years before the date of death.

What are the best ways to reduce inheritance taxes?

There are several methods of reducing inheritance taxes. You can (1) make gifts of money or property during your lifetime up to the amount, and within the time limits, specified by federal and state tax laws; (2) put some of your property into joint ownership, which will automatically pass it to the other owner on your death; and (3) take out life insurance, naming as beneficiaries the people who would normally inherit part of your estate. These strategies do not reduce inheritance tax in every case, so you should consult an attorney or estate-planning specialist before committing yourself to any of them.

Geraldine has property valued at $200,000, including her $85,000 house and a $50,000 life insurance policy. In planning her estate, does she need to worry about federal estate taxes?

No. Since 1987 only estates valued at over $600,000 have been subject to federal estate taxes. However, Geraldine should consult an attorney or tax expert about state law. Being free of federal taxes does not automatically mean that her estate will also be exempt from state taxes.

Planning Your Estate

You don't have to be wealthy to plan an estate. In fact, when you buy life insurance or name a beneficiary on your pension plan, you are planning your estate. Estate planning is organizing your assets for your maximum benefit while you are alive and seeing to it that what is left after your death is passed on to the right people quickly and with a minimum of taxes and legal fees. A will is usually the cornerstone of most estate plans. But a will needs to be approved by a probate court—a process that keeps your heirs from receiving the property immediately and that involves legal fees, which may reduce the amount they receive. Consequently, many people use additional ways of leaving assets to their heirs. The most popular options are:

- *Last will and testament*—Your will states whom you wish to have what part of your estate after you die. It also names an executor to administer your estate and a guardian for minor children.
- *Joint tenancy with right of survivorship*—This special type of co-ownership is often used by married couples for their homes and bank accounts. On the death of one of the owners, the other automatically becomes sole owner of the property. In some states, however, jointly held bank accounts are frozen upon the death of one of the owners until tax authorities assess the amount of money in the account.
- *Payable-on-death accounts*—These bank accounts can be used to transfer funds automatically to a beneficiary. Also called trustee bank accounts, they can be helpful if state law requires that a joint bank account be frozen when one of the account holders dies. U. S. Savings Bonds may also be registered as "payable on death" to a named beneficiary.

If Thomas leaves everything to his wife, will she have to pay federal estate taxes?

No. Since 1981 all property left to a spouse, regardless of its value, has been exempt from federal estate taxes.

Mel has four life insurance policies on himself. Each of the policies has one of his four grandchildren named as a beneficiary. If Mel doesn't want the policies to be taxed as part of his estate, what can he do?

He should have the policies put into an irrevocable life insurance trust, naming someone other than himself as trustee. This will transfer ownership of the policies from Mel to the trust and remove the policies from his estate. However, any policies he puts into the trust within three years of his death will still be considered part of his estate.

- *Life insurance*—Policies are often purchased to provide immediate income to the beneficiaries or to pay estate taxes. But life insurance can increase estate taxes. Consult an expert on estate planning to find out how to avoid this pitfall through the use of cross-owned policies, irrevocable life insurance trusts, or other technical arrangements.
- *Gifts*—The law currently allows gifts of up to $10,000 a year to any individual without the payment of a gift tax, or up to $20,000 if husband and wife make a joint gift. Gifts between spouses do not have any limit; the marital deduction permits spouses to give an unlimited amount to each other. Gifts reduce the size of an estate (thereby saving taxes), reduce probate costs, ensure that the right person receives the property, and sometimes reduce income taxes. However, gifts that are made within one to three years of the giver's death (depending on the state) may be subject to inheritance tax.
- *Trusts*—Trusts that take effect during a person's lifetime are called *inter vivos,* or living, trusts. Those set up in a will to take effect after death are called testamentary trusts. Only a living trust avoids probate. A typical reason to create a trust is to provide for minor children or others who are incapable of taking care of themselves. By creating an irrevocable living trust (one that you cannot change), you remove the property that was placed in the trust from the estate for estate tax purposes.
- *Pensions and other employee benefit plans*—Proceeds from pensions and benefit plans are passed directly to the designated beneficiaries. However, the funds may be included in a person's estate for tax purposes if the proceeds are payable to the estate or if the proceeds result from employee contributions to the plan.

Making a Will

Why do I need a will if I am leaving everything to my wife?

Because your wife may not get all of your estate if you die without a will. Each state has its own laws governing the distribution of property when someone dies without a will. In most states, your wife would get only one-third or one-half of your estate if you are survived by any children or grandchildren—or in some states by other close relatives. By not making a will, you give up all right to say how your property will be divided.

Ken and Rita are young newlyweds, who rent a furnished apartment and own almost nothing other than their clothes, a car, and a few household items. Do they need wills?

Yes. Suppose, for example, Ken and Rita were killed in an automobile accident. Their heirs might be able to sue the driver for a large amount of money. If Ken and Rita didn't have wills, the laws of their state would determine who would get the money. A relative they dislike could get rich because of the tragedy. If they had wills, however, the money would go to the person or persons of their choice.

Can my 17-year-old son, with $3,000 in a savings account, make a will leaving his assets to me?

In most states, the answer would be no. State laws routinely set the minimum age for making a will at 18, and Wyoming sets it at 19. However, in Louisiana, a 16-year-old can make a will if he is near death, and in Georgia, a 14-year-old can do so.

Is it necessary for my husband and me to have separate wills?

No. You and your husband can draw up a joint will—one document that covers both of you. In a joint will a husband and wife usually designate the same beneficiaries and the same executor for their estates. However, joint wills are not used very often. It is usually simpler and just as economical to have separate wills.

Must an attorney write a will if it is to stand up in court?

There is no law that says that an attorney must draw up a will, but there are so many legalities involved that it is advisable to have a lawyer draft one for you. He can advise you of the latest changes in the laws, alternative ways to distribute your property so that you can leave more to heirs, and the best way to word the document to make sure that your wishes are carried out.

I saw a book that has a form in it for drafting your own will. Would this kind of do-it-yourself will be acceptable in court?

Do-it-yourself wills can work if the form complies with the latest laws in your state. However, if you fail to follow the exact legal procedures or if the language you use to fill in the blank spaces is not precise enough, the will could be declared invalid after your death, and your property would be divided according to state law instead of the way you wished.

Is a handwritten will valid?

In almost half the states, a handwritten, or holographic, will is valid, but there may be restrictions on the circumstances under which it can be written or the type of property it can cover. For example, in some states a holographic will is not valid unless it is written by someone on military duty, and even then it may not be valid for leaving real estate to someone.

Uncle Stanley turned on his video camera, sat in front of it, and outlined how he wanted his estate to be distributed. He also stated the current date and taped and named all the people in the room, who served as witnesses. Is this a valid will?

Probably not. Although legislation covering videotaped wills has been proposed in several states, by 1987 Indiana was the only state to have enacted a statute dealing with the subject. But even in Indiana a written will must be prepared at the time the videotape is made. The videotape can only be used to prove, for example, that the person making the will was mentally alert and was not under undue influence.

Last month Eli became seriously ill and told the nurses and his doctor how he wanted his property distributed. Does this oral will replace the written will he had prepared five years ago?

No. Because he already had a written will, Eli would have to revoke that will before making a new one. Destroying the old will or writing a new one are the preferred ways of revoking a will.

If Eli had never prepared a will, his oral statements might constitute a valid will. Some states recognize oral wills, but there are many restrictions. In some states, the oral declaration must be made when the person making it is in danger of dying, and the eyewitnesses must put the oral statements in writing within a certain time limit. Some states permit all property except real estate to be disposed of through an oral will.

Eileen wants to name her childhood friend, Charlene, executor of her will, but Charlene lives in another state. Is that OK?

Probably. In most states, a nonresident can serve as an executor, but there may be special restrictions. For example, if Eileen lived in Wyoming, Charlene would be able to serve as executor, but she would have to appoint a Wyoming resident as her agent to receive court orders, notices, and other documents relating to the estate. If Eileen lived in Florida, she could not appoint Charlene or any other nonresident unless the person were a close relative. But even if the state law allows it, having a nonresident serve as executor causes delays in handling routine estate matters, and it can add expenses because of the additional travel.

Peggy asked her neighbors, Al and Iris, to watch her sign her name to a document and then witness it. Do Al and Iris have to know the document is a will in order to be valid witnesses?

Most states would not require Al and Iris to verify that the document is a will. They would only have to (1) see Peggy sign the document or (2) be told by Peggy that the signature is hers.

Virginia had Sal witness her signature on her will. After Virginia died, Sal discovered that he is named in the will. Does the fact that Sal acted as a witness affect his right to receive the property Virginia left to him?

Yes. He may not receive the property Virginia designated in her will, unless he is related to Virginia and would have received the same amount even if she had died without a will. As a general rule, the law does not allow witnesses to gain by the death of the person who made the will.

My friend Kelly, who is terminally ill, had me witness her signature on her will. When Kelly dies, will I have to testify in court about the signing of the will?

It depends on the laws in your state. Some states do require witnesses to come to court to attest that all the legal requirements were followed in

What a Lawyer Needs to Write Your Will

There are many decisions to make when drawing up a will, and a lawyer needs specific information at his fingertips in order to carry out his client's wishes. If you are having a will drawn up, you can save time and money if you bring the following information to your first consultation:

- ☑ Names, addresses, and birth dates of your spouse and children, together with any disabilities or special needs they may have.
- ☑ The amount and source of your income, including interest, dividends, and your spouse's salary.
- ☑ All your debts, including mortgages, installment loans, leases, and business obligations.
- ☑ A list of your real estate, bank accounts, businesses, stocks, bonds, cars, jewelry, antiques, furniture, property owned jointly with someone else, and any other assets. Note the approximate value of the property and the person or persons named as owners.
- ☑ A list of your life insurance policies, showing who owns the policy, the company issuing the policy, the policy number, the face amount, the beneficiaries, and any loans against the policies.
- ☑ A list of sources of retirement benefits, including those from company pensions, profit-sharing plans, IRA's, and Keogh plans.
- ☑ A list of possible executors and guardians for young children.
- ☑ A list of specific items that you want left to particular relatives or friends, such as family heirlooms or things of sentimental value.
- ☑ Documents affecting your estate, including premarital agreements, divorce decrees, trust agreements, recent federal income tax returns, real estate deeds, and your current will, if any.

making and signing the will. In other states, the witnesses can sign the will in front of a notary public. These self-proving wills eliminate the need for witnesses to appear in court and validate their signatures.

How many witnesses are needed for a will?

In most states two. Vermont, however, requires three or more witnesses, and Louisiana requires three witnesses, one of whom is a notary public.

Should there be more than one signed copy of a will?

No. The original document is the only one that should be signed. Having additional signed copies could create problems. For example, if you made out a new will but did not destroy all signed copies of the old one, there could be some confusion about which will was the valid one.

Making a Will

Where should a will be kept?

A will should be kept in a place where it can be easily located by a member of the family or the executor of the estate. The best place might be in a metal strongbox at home or in your lawyer's office. In some states you can file your will with the probate court for safekeeping. Check with the court in your area. You may also store your will in a safe-deposit box in the bank, but before doing so check your state law about safe-deposit boxes. In some states, a safe-deposit box must be sealed as soon as the person renting it dies, and cannot be opened until a tax examiner makes an inventory of its contents.

Daphne moved to another state. Does she have to make a new will?

She may not need to write a new will, but she should have a lawyer review her will to see if the laws in her new home state are different. For example, Daphne may need three witnesses to her signature instead of two.

I have lost my will. How do I get a new one?

Contact your lawyer and have a new will drafted. If you still have an unsigned copy of the will you lost, you could use it as a guide in drawing up the new one. But do not just sign a photocopy of the old will; a court may declare the photocopy invalid, and your property would be distributed according to state law rather than according to your wishes. Since the lost will may someday be found, be sure to state in the new will that all previous wills are revoked.

Naming Your Heirs

Should I leave everything to my wife, or should I divide things between my wife and my children?

There are no quick or easy answers to this question, because too many factors are involved. If you feel that your wife could manage your estate and the family without help, you may leave everything to her; if you feel it would put too great a strain on her, you might set up trusts for her and your children. Before making a decision, find out what tax benefits your family might gain or lose if your entire estate went to your wife. Also consider whether or not you would want to make special arrangements in case your wife remarried.

Alice is afraid that after she dies her husband will remarry and might neglect their children. Can she put a provision in her will that states that if her husband remarries, a portion of what she is leaving him will, instead, go to the children?

Yes, but this type of restriction may not be acceptable in every state. Alice could accomplish the same result, with less risk, if she set up a trust. This trust could give her husband the right to use the interest or other earnings from the money or property in the trust during his lifetime, but keep him from touching the principal or selling the property. In the event of his remarriage, everything in the trust could be transferred automatically to the children, either directly (if the children are no longer minors) or in the form of another trust.

Both Enid and Phillip have children from previous marriages. After their deaths, they want all they own to be divided equally among their children. How do they do this?

The simplest thing for Enid and Phillip to do is have their wills state that their stepchildren shall be considered by the court to be the same as natural children. This will allow the court to interpret the phrase "to all my children, equally" to include the stepchildren whenever the phrase appears.

If Enid and Phillip have a joint will, it should state that they agree not to change the provisions relating to their children in subsequent wills. Then, for example, if Enid should die before Phillip, Phillip could not legally revise his will and cut out Enid's children.

What steps can I take to make sure that my young children will be cared for and educated properly after my death?

Decide who would do the best job of raising your children and then get that person's consent to be named in your will as guardian. Also arrange for a contingent guardian who can take over the responsibility if the first guardian dies or is unable to take care of your children for some other reason. In addition, you can establish a trust fund in your will for your children's educational expenses. You will need to select a trustee to manage the trust and make sure the money is distributed properly.

Keith wants to leave all of his property to his mother. If he puts a provision in his will stating that he is leaving nothing to his wife, will it be honored?

No. A person has the right to receive a portion of his or her spouse's estate—generally one-third or one-half, depending on state law. This is known as the spouse's statutory share. If Keith's will provides less than this statutory share, his wife can request and receive the amount she is entitled to under state law.

Adele hasn't spoken to her daughter for 10 years, and wants to cut her out of her will. Can she do that?

Probably. In most states it is perfectly legal for a parent to disinherit a child, even a young child. But if Adele wants to disinherit her daughter, she must specifically state in her will that she is knowingly and intentionally leaving her daughter nothing. If there is any doubt about the matter, a court will probably grant the daughter the portion of the estate she would have received under state law if there had been no will. Generally, courts assume that a person does not want to disinherit his own child.

However, if Adele lives in Louisiana, she may not be able to cut her daughter out of her will, no matter how specifically she states her wishes. Louisiana law permits a parent to disinherit a child for only 12 reasons, including the child's attempt to take a parent's life or a minor child's marrying without parental consent.

Vicki is a well-to-do widow with only one child, Maurice. Vicki wants to leave her entire estate to Maurice, but he is currently involved with a woman whom Vicki considers unfit for her son to marry. If Vicki writes into her will that Maurice can't have a penny if he marries this woman, will it be effective?

It may be. While courts do not favor wills that prohibit an heir from ever marrying, they often uphold a restriction against the heir's marrying a particular person.

If Vicki includes this condition in her will, she should also name a contingent beneficiary (someone who would inherit her property if her son did not). In addition, she should state how she wants her property to be redistributed if Maurice marries the woman in question after his mother's estate has been settled.

To avoid having to change his will if he has other children, Christopher wants to state in his will that "40 percent of my estate shall be distributed equally among my children." Wouldn't this guarantee that his wishes will be carried out?

Not necessarily. A court would want to know whether Christopher meant to include adopted children, stepchildren, illegitimate children, and children born after the will was made. To clearly express his wishes and avoid confusion later, Christopher's will should be as specific as possible.

What happens if a child is born after the parent's will is prepared and the child is not mentioned in the will?

Many states would allow the child to share in the estate as though the parent had died without a will. After the child's portion is deducted, the rest of the estate is distributed as much as possible according to the will.

Stan, Burt's best friend for 30 years, now lives in Europe. Can Burt leave him something in his will?

Yes, Burt can leave whatever he wants to Stan, regardless of where Stan lives. However, Burt should provide specific information on exactly

Points to Consider When Making Your Will

Wills follow a traditional format and include many standard terms. But a will also reflects its maker's wishes and his plans for providing for the needs of his family. Although it is difficult to plan for everything that might happen, here are some points to consider when drawing up a will:

- ☑ Whom do you want to serve as executor of your estate?
- ☑ Is it likely that additional children will be born or adopted?
- ☑ Do you want your stepchildren to receive a share of your estate?
- ☑ If you have young children, who should serve as their guardians and contingent guardians?
- ☑ Do you want to give your spouse complete freedom to sell or give away your property if he or she remarries?
- ☑ Who should receive the remainder of your estate after all specific bequests have been made?
- ☑ Would it be a good idea for your estate to pay off real estate mortgages before your property is turned over to your heirs?
- ☑ Do you want to cancel debts owed to you by any of your heirs, or do you want these debts to be deducted from their inheritances?
- ☑ In case assets must be sold to pay your debts, do you want to make a priority list, designating what is to be sold first and what last?
- ☑ Are there advantages in paying estate and inheritance taxes out of the assets of your estate?
- ☑ How should your estate be handled if you and your spouse are killed in the same accident?
- ☑ Do you want to waive the requirement for your executor to post a bond?

where Stan can be found so that the executor will not have too much trouble tracking him down when the time comes to settle Burt's estate.

Henrietta has definite ideas about how she wants her jewelry to be distributed after she dies. What is the best way for her to have her wishes carried out?

The best thing for Henrietta to do is to make a list of these and other specific bequests, clearly indicating who is to get what, and ask her lawyer to include this information in her will. She could also make the list itself a part of her will by describing it in her will and indicating that personal property is to be distributed according to it. However, this process, called incorporation by reference, is not recognized by all courts.

I am 87 years old and have no relatives. My only companion is my dog, Spot. Can I leave all of my property to him?

No. If you want your dog to be properly cared for after your death, you should make an agreement with someone to take care of Spot, and then leave that person enough money or salable property to carry out your wishes. You should also designate who will receive the balance of your estate after Spot dies.

I am leaving my house to my great-granddaughter. Is it sufficient to describe the house in my will by its street address?

Yes, but the more specific the description, the better. Many lawyers include not only the street address but also the number of the lot or tract of land, boundaries, distances, or landmarks.

My husband passed away seven years ago, and I inherited all his property, including our house. I recently married a widower, who sold his house to come and live with me. I want to leave my house to my three children, but I don't want them to throw out my new husband if he wants to stay. What can I do?

One way to protect both your second husband and your children is to create a life estate in your will. A life estate would give your husband the right to live in the home, but he would not own the property. When he died, the property would go to your children. However, if you do establish a life estate in your will and you have not left your husband the one-third or one-half of your estate allowed to spouses under state law, he will have the right to contest the will and receive his rightful share. Unless he signed an agreement relinquishing any right to a share in your estate, he could receive part or full ownership of the house. To avoid this possibility, you might consider placing your house in a trust that would remain in effect as long as you and your husband live. Upon your deaths, the trust would end and the property would be transferred to your children. Both you and your new husband would have to sign the deed that places the house in the trust.

Joshua owns a $60,000 house with $20,000 left on the mortgage. He also has $15,000 in a savings account, plus some stocks, a bit of jewelry, and two life insurance policies. If Joshua leaves his house to his sister and everything else he owns to his children, does his sister get the house with or without the mortgage?

She would get the house with the $20,000 mortgage unless Joshua specified in his will that the mortgage should be paid by his estate. While wills usually provide that all debts must be paid before an estate can be divided among the heirs, mortgages are an exception. Without clear directions to the executor to pay the mortgage from the proceeds of the estate, Joshua's sister would become responsible for paying it. The mortgage would not be paid by the estate.

Ben is divorced and has custody of his child. What provisions, if any, can be made in Ben's will to guarantee that his ex-wife will not be named guardian of their child upon Ben's death?

None. Ben could have a paragraph put into his will stating his wish that someone other than his ex-wife be named guardian, but it would probably have no legal effect. In most states, a child's natural parent has first priority when a guardian is selected. So the court would probably name his ex-wife as guardian.

Although his will cannot guarantee who will have custody of his child after his death, Ben can still designate a conservator—a guardian for the money the child inherits. This will ensure that someone Ben approves of will oversee how the child's finances are handled.

Abe wants his will to cancel the unpaid portion of a $10,000 loan he made to his son. What is the best way to handle this?

Abe should state in his will that the balance of the debt is canceled. If Abe doesn't do this, the debt will be deducted from whatever share of the estate Abe's son receives.

Establishing Trusts

When my wife and I talked to a lawyer about making a will, he suggested that we set up a living trust. What is that?

A living, or *inter vivos,* trust is one that takes effect during your lifetime. If you decided to create a living trust, you would transfer property or money into the fund, and appoint someone (a trustee) to administer it. The trustee, who could be a lawyer or accountant or a bank or other financial institution, would then manage and invest these assets and distribute income from the trust to the beneficiaries—the persons for whom you have set up the trust—according to the terms you have specified. Since the living trust would already be established when you die, the property placed in it would not have to go through probate court under your will.

Grandfather Johnson has set up testamentary trusts for all his grandchildren. What is a testamentary trust?

A testamentary trust is a fund established by a will and administered by a trustee named in the will. In contrast to a living trust, a testamentary trust does not go into effect until the person who made the will dies. Testamentary trusts are frequently set up to provide income or educational funds for young children and grandchildren, and in some cases they can have substantial tax advantages.

The Benefits of a Living Trust

Trusts are often included in wills to enable the maker of the will to have some control over how his property is to be used. You might want to use this type of trust—called a testamentary trust—to help manage the property you leave to your young children or to others who are incapable of managing their own financial affairs. But you may also use another type of trust—the *inter vivos,* or living, trust—which will go into effect while you are still alive. Some distinctive advantages of doing so include:

- Giving someone else the power to manage your investments or property when you no longer wish to do this for yourself. A living trust can be set up that instructs the trustee to pay you income during your lifetime and then to distribute the trust property to your family after your death.
- Protecting your property in case you become incompetent. If you become too ill to handle your affairs, the trustee will continue to manage the property in the trust while guardianship or conservatorship proceedings are held to determine who will manage your other property and your personal affairs.

If I establish a trust fund in my will, can money from that trust be made available to the beneficiaries without going through probate court proceedings?

No. All trusts created in a will must be reviewed by a probate court to ensure that they comply with state law. A living trust, on the other hand, does not go through probate; it is effective as soon as it has been signed.

Henry created a living trust for his sister, Miriam. What happens if Miriam dies before Henry?

The trust would end and the money or other assets in it would be returned to Henry. However, if Henry had named a contingent beneficiary, that person would receive the benefit of the trust after Miriam's death.

Kirk wants his nieces and nephews to inherit a large portion of his estate, but he is concerned that Marty, his youngest nephew, will spend his entire inheritance right away. Can Kirk do something to prevent this?

Yes. Kirk can establish a support trust that will release a specified amount of money to Marty at regular intervals, such as once a year. Support trusts usually contain precise instructions to the trustee (administrator of the

- Reducing income tax liability. By putting assets into an irrevocable trust (one that cannot be changed), you give up ownership of the property and may no longer be required to pay taxes on the income it produces. The trust itself—or the beneficiaries of the trust, who may be in a lower tax bracket—will generally pay those taxes.
- Reducing federal estate taxes or state death taxes. The assets of an irrevocable trust are not included in an estate. This can save both state and federal estate taxes and reduce the amount of inheritance tax your heirs will have to pay.
- Passing property to others without the delays of probate required by a will. Following the terms of the agreement, the trustee of a living trust can distribute its money or property to your heirs after your death without going through formal court proceedings.
- Keeping the details of how you divided your estate from becoming public knowledge. Probate proceedings are public records, and anyone can go to the courthouse and review a probate file to find out how an estate was distributed. But living trust agreements are private documents and are not open to public scrutiny.

trust) about the manner in which payments are to be made and the amount of money the beneficiary is to receive in each payment.

Jeremy is concerned that trust funds given to his nephew, Kyle, will be taken by Kyle's creditors. Can Jeremy keep this from happening?

By setting up a spendthrift trust, Jeremy could arrange for Kyle to get only the income from the trust, not the trust property or principal itself—for example, income from the rental of any real estate in the trust, the earnings on stocks and bonds, or the interest on money in a bank. Jeremy could also stipulate how much money he wished Kyle to receive each year, or he could give the trustee (the administrator of the trust) the authority to decide when and how much income to give Kyle. However, once Kyle receives his trust income, his creditors can obtain this money because the payment is no longer protected by the trust.

Must I decide how much money per year my family should receive from a trust fund, or can I give the trustee (the administrator of the trust) the authority to decide from year to year?

You can leave it up to the trustee, but you should give the trustee guidelines to use in determining your family's needs. Factors to be considered are the standard of living you want for your family, the provisions another person might make in similar circumstances, and how much you wish to contribute toward educational and other special expenses.

Raymond would like to establish a trust fund five years from now and have one-third of his salary put into the trust each year thereafter. Can he have the trust agreement drawn up now?

No. Raymond's expectation of future salary cannot be used to create a trust fund. A trust must contain assets that currently exist. However, Raymond could put a small sum of money into a trust fund now and reserve the right to transfer additional assets into it in the future.

Claudia never married and has no close relatives. If she sets up a trust fund, can she name friends as the beneficiaries?

Yes, but she should not just designate them simply as "friends." The beneficiaries must be clearly identified by name. If the description of the beneficiaries is too vague, the trust will not be valid.

I want to make sure that my cats are taken care of after I die. Can I establish a trust to pay for their care?

Yes, but you should find out if your state has any special requirements for this type of trust. For example, in some states a time limit is placed on the length of time a trust for the benefit of animals can last—in Missouri such a trust cannot last longer than 21 years.

If you name your cats as the beneficiaries, you also risk having the trust declared invalid because there is no human beneficiary. An alternative is to put money or property in trust for someone with the condition that the money will be distributed to that person as long as he takes care of your cats. You will also have to name contingent beneficiaries to receive the remaining trust property when your cats die.

Daniel had a trust agreement drawn up in 1981, which named Marietta as the beneficiary. He wants to change the beneficiary to Clarissa. Can he amend this trust?

Only if a right to amend the trust was included in the trust document. Otherwise, in order to make the change, Daniel would have to obtain the written consent of all persons involved, including Marietta—who may be unwilling to give up the income she would receive from the trust.

Anita did not include instructions in her trust agreement about how it could be terminated. What should she do if she changes her mind about the trust?

She would have to get the written consent of everyone involved in order to cancel the trust. Without getting everyone's consent, a trust cannot be terminated, revoked, or amended unless that power is specifically given in the trust agreement.

If a trust is set up for Monica's support until she is 18 years old, are there any circumstances in which Monica can get all the trust money outright before she is 18?

Probably not. Any attempt to defeat the purpose of a trust must be approved by the beneficiary. Because Monica, the beneficiary in this case, is not of legal age (either 18 or 21, depending on the state), she could not legally give her approval to terminating the trust. However, if Monica marries before she reaches the legal age and that marriage makes her an adult in the eyes of the law of her state, she may be able to ask the trustee (the administrator of the trust) for an early distribution of funds from the trust, and get it.

The Role of the Trustee

What is a trustee, and what are his duties and responsibilities?

A trustee is a person or a bank or other institution who has agreed to hold the property of another person in safekeeping for one or more beneficiaries named by the property owner. A trustee is responsible for administering the trust in accordance with the trust agreement. In addition to any specific instructions, a trustee must keep the trust property separate from his own property, invest the property, protect the property through insurance, keep accurate records of income and expenses, pay income to the beneficiaries, deal impartially with all beneficiaries, and seek the advice of experts in investing or managing the trust property.

How do I know that the trustee for my children's inheritance will not use some of the money for his own personal benefit?

Although you can never guarantee that mismanagement will not occur, you can minimize the possibility. Choose a trustee who has earned your confidence. If you want to be doubly sure, require the trustee to purchase a bond that would be forfeited if he didn't carry out his duties properly.

You are also protected by the law. If the trustee uses money in the trust for his personal purposes, he can be removed and charged with theft. Any profits he made by misusing trust funds would become part of the trust.

Dwight wants to set up a trust for his children. Can he name himself as the trustee?

Yes, as long as he meets the qualifications in his state. Generally, a trustee need only be competent to carry out the duties specified in the trust.

Does the trustee have to live in the same state in which I live?

No. However, state laws may require that the nonresident trustee appoint a resident agent who can be served with writs, summonses, and other legal documents. The trustee may also have to post a bond.

The trustee named in Ernie's will died four months after his appointment. Will the trust end automatically?

Not unless Ernie specifically indicated that the only person who could serve as trustee was the one he named. Otherwise, the court will appoint someone else to fulfill the duties of the deceased trustee.

When Isabel set up her trust, she named Greg as the trustee, even though she knew he never got along with her son Floyd, the beneficiary. Can Floyd challenge the appointment of Greg as trustee after his mother's death?

Floyd can challenge the appointment, but he may not be successful in having Greg removed as trustee. Tension or hostility between the trustee and beneficiary is usually not sufficient reason to remove a trustee. However, if it can be shown that Greg would be unable to administer the trust properly because of his hostility to Floyd, the court might consider denying Greg's appointment as trustee.

Robin is the beneficiary of a trust created by her father. Gilbert was designated the trustee. Gilbert sold himself some of the trust property at a price below the market value. Robin is afraid he will do this again. What can she do?

Robin should seek legal advice immediately. Gilbert has violated his duty as trustee by placing his interests above those of the beneficiary. Robin should ask that Gilbert be removed as trustee. She can also ask that the sale be voided and that Gilbert's expenses and commissions be denied. She may even get the court to make Gilbert pay her punitive damages—an amount of money over and above what he cheated her of as punishment for the wrong he did.

Can a trustee be fired for doing a poor job?

Yes. An incompetent trustee may also have to forfeit his commissions, and he may have to reimburse the trust for any losses suffered as a result of his mismanagement.

Changing or Revoking a Will

My wife and I had wills prepared about three years ago. We would like to make some changes. Is it necessary for us to write entirely new wills?

Not necessarily. If the changes are minor, you could simply have your lawyer add codicils, or amendments, to your wills. If major revisions are required, however, it is better to have the wills completely redrafted to eliminate possible confusion. If you want to cut out certain heirs, or change the amount of money an heir will receive, you should revoke the old wills and make entirely new ones.

Changing or Revoking a Will

Are there any problems involved in using a codicil to make changes in a will?

Not if it is prepared, signed, and witnessed according to the same formalities followed in drawing up the basic will. However, the codicil must be worded carefully to make clear the nature of the change—whether a provision of the will is being revoked, a new provision is being added, or an existing provision is being modified. For example, if it is not made clear that the executor named in the codicil is replacing the executor named in the will, the result could be that coexecutors will handle the estate.

An additional precaution is keeping the will and codicil together. If the two documents are separated and no one knows about the codicil, the terms of the will could be carried out without the changes designated in the codicil, and the estate would not be distributed according to the wishes of the person who made the will.

Clint made a will leaving his estate equally to his son and daughter. Because of an argument with his daughter, Clint scratched out a paragraph of his will and wrote a statement on it that he wanted his estate to go exclusively to his son. Clint died two weeks later. Is his change valid?

No. All changes in a will must be made with the same formalities used in making a new will. Whenever a part of a will is crossed out, it makes the validity of the entire will questionable. So by marking through a portion of the will, Clint risked not only having the revision disregarded, but also having the entire will revoked. Changes should always be made in a codicil, or amendment, or by drawing up a new will.

My will names my sister as executor, but she passed away last year. Do I have to write a new will now?

If you don't revise the will, the court will appoint someone else to handle your estate. But you don't have to draw up a whole new will. Instead, you could prepare a codicil, or amendment, that names the new person you want to serve as executor.

How can I revoke my will?

Every state has its own laws that specify exactly how a person can revoke his will. This applies whether the person wants to revoke the whole will or

When You Should Change Your Will

Because wills do not have expiration dates, one drawn up when a person was 20 would still be valid when he died at age 85. But life is full of changes, and a will should be reviewed every two or three years to make certain that it still reflects your wishes. You should also review your will and revise it, if necessary, when any of the following occur:

- Your marital status changes. When you marry, your will is automatically revoked unless you wrote it prior to getting married and named your future spouse in it. If you get divorced, the portions of your will affecting your ex-spouse will be invalidated.
- You have a child or adopt one. State laws may allow children to claim a share of your estate even though they are not mentioned in your will, but the state might not grant them what you would in your will.
- An executor, guardian, or trustee dies or can no longer fulfill his duties because of poor health or some other reason.
- The needs of your heirs change. For example, if one of your children marries and has children, your spouse becomes seriously ill, or an heir gets into serious financial difficulties, you may want to leave more to him or her than you originally intended.
- The amount of assets in your estate changes drastically.
- You no longer own something you left to someone in your will.
- Trusts you established for your young children are no longer needed, because the children are old enough to manage on their own.
- Changes are made in the laws governing estate or inheritance taxes.

only part of it. Generally, you can (1) prepare a new will stating that all previous wills are revoked; (2) prepare a codicil, or amendment, that revokes part of the existing will; or (3) destroy the old will by tearing or burning the original document and all copies.

Hildegard's father revoked his will by tearing it up and stating, "I want you to have everything, Hildegard. I don't want to leave anything to my good-for-nothing son, Tony." Is this a valid revocation of a will?

The act of tearing up the document was a valid way for Hildegard's father to revoke his will. Furthermore, his statement that he did not wish to leave anything to his son made it clear that destroying the will was not an accident, but was intended. However, for Hildegard to receive the entire estate, her father will have to draft a new will making this intention clear. If he does not draw up a new will that specifically disinherits Tony and leaves everything to Hildegard, Hildegard and her brother will have to share the estate.

Contesting a Will

My sister died six weeks ago and didn't leave me anything, even though I was her only remaining relative. Can I contest her will?

Not unless you have some proof that your sister was incompetent when she made her will or that someone used undue influence to make her write the will in his favor. Your status as sister does not, by itself, give you the right to challenge the will; no law requires a person to provide for his brothers or sisters in his will.

When Mortimer found out he was dying, he told his neice, Myrtle, that he would leave her his house if she would move in with him and nurse him through his final illness. She did. When Mortimer died two years later, there was no mention of her in Mortimer's will. Would it do her any good to challenge the will?

No. An oral statement cannot be used to revoke an existing will. However, Myrtle may be able to sue Mortimer's estate for the value of the services she provided him during his final illness.

Clifford's live-in housekeeper, an attractive young woman, was always very attentive to Clifford, who was a widower, but she turned him against his children. Shortly before he died, Clifford revised his will, cutting out his children and leaving everything to the housekeeper. Can the children contest the will?

Yes, but they would have to show that the housekeeper used undue influence over Clifford and that there was a connection between her influence and Clifford's decision to cut the children out of his will. For example, if the children can show that their father was so smitten with the housekeeper that he would do anything she asked and that she deliberately manipulated him into changing his will in her favor, a court may declare the will invalid.

Doreen and Timothy had a joint will prepared that provided the survivor with the use of real estate and other property for life. When the surviving spouse died, all the property would go to Annie. After Doreen's death, Timothy had a new will prepared, leaving everything to Vernon. Does Annie have any right to challenge Timothy's new will?

It depends upon the language of the joint will and the state in which it was probated. If the joint will clearly states that the surviving spouse may not revoke or amend the will, Annie can have Timothy's new will invalidated. If there is no such provision in the original will, however, the probate court will consider the intent of Doreen and Timothy in making their joint will, and base its decision on what it finds. Some states would allow Timothy to revoke the joint will, but would also allow Annie to sue Timothy for breach of contract.

After having a joint will prepared, Jed and Muriel were separated, and Jed died before revoking the will. Is the will still valid?

Yes. Separation does not invalidate a will. The marriage would have to be terminated through divorce or annulment before the will, or any of its provisions, would be revoked automatically.

My ex-husband remarried and had a child with his new wife. He died last month and left his entire estate to his current wife and their child. Aren't the children from his marriage to me legally entitled to a share of his estate?

Not necessarily. While a spouse (but not an ex-spouse) is legally protected from being cut out of a will, the law does not provide the same protection for children. If your ex-husband explicitly states in his will that he wishes to leave nothing to his children by you, the courts will probably uphold the will.

However, if your ex-husband does not mention the children in the will at all, they may be able to challenge the will on the grounds that they were unintentionally left out of it. If a court rules in their favor, they may be awarded the same amount they would have received if their father had died without a will.

Scott made a provision in his will that Beth would receive his 1986 Ferrari at the time of his death. A year later Scott traded in his 1986 Ferrari for a 1988 Ferrari. If Scott dies, does Beth get the new car?

No. Beth is not entitled to receive the 1988 Ferrari, since it is not the one designated in Scott's will. When a specific item that is given in a will is no longer in the giver's estate when he dies, the bequest is said to have been adeemed by extinction. If Scott's will had simply left Beth "my Ferrari," without mentioning the model, Beth would have received the 1988 car.

In his will, Taylor provided that his farm be sold and the proceeds divided among his three children. The remainder of his estate was to go to finance cancer research. Shortly before he died,

Contesting a Will

Taylor sold the farm for $175,000. The buyer paid Taylor $100,000, with the remaining $75,000 due in six months. Do his children have any claim to the $100,000 or to the $75,000 balance due?

Yes. The gift Taylor made to his children was not the farm itself, but the proceeds from the sale of the farm. As long as these proceeds are identifiable, Taylor's children are entitled to receive them.

While backing his car out of his driveway one night, Craig accidentally hit his elderly uncle Fred and killed him. It turned out that Fred had left $5,000 to Craig in his will. Can Fred's daughters keep Craig from getting the $5,000 because he caused the death of his benefactor?

Probably not. Although Craig caused his uncle's death, he did not do so intentionally. The death resulted from an accident. Fred's daughters could only prevent Craig from receiving his inheritance if they could prove that Craig intentionally murdered their father.

Hattie had poor eyesight and asked her brother, Gus, to help her draft a will. Gus had the will typed up, substituting himself as the main heir rather than his sister Hester. Hattie signed the will and had it properly witnessed. Can Hester challenge this will?

Yes. Gus has committed a fraud. A will drawn up as a result of fraud can be challenged and declared void.

Terry is considering challenging her uncle's will. If the court agrees that her uncle was not competent to make a will, how will his estate be distributed?

If the court declares the will invalid, Terry's uncle would be considered to have died without a will. State law would then dictate how the property would be distributed. Every state has a descent and distribution law that outlines which relatives have priority in inheriting property and what percentage of the estate they will receive.

What steps are necessary to contest a will?

The person contesting a will must go to court and file a petition stating the grounds for contesting the will, such as fraud, undue influence, or lack of competence by the maker of the will. A hearing will then be held to determine if the objections are sufficient to deny the validity of that will. Only the people affected by the will can contest it.

Some of my mother's relatives want to contest a provision in her will. Will this delay my inheritance and my being able to pay for funeral and burial expenses?

Yes. Until the court determines the validity of the will and allows the estate to be settled, no one is authorized to pay the heirs any of their inheritance. The executor of the will is usually limited to collecting debts owed to the estate and preserving property while the will is being contested. If you are the executor of your mother's estate, ask a lawyer or the probate judge what duties you can and cannot perform while the will is being contested. In Ohio, for example, the executor can pay funeral expenses even though his appointment as executor has not yet been confirmed by the court.

Dying Without a Will

Gil died without making a will. He left a wife, one son, and two granddaughters, who are the children of a deceased daughter. How will the property be distributed?

Gil's widow will receive one-third to one-half of the estate, depending on the law in Gil's state. The remaining property would usually be divided equally among his children. But since his daughter is dead, the two granddaughters will divide the share that would have gone to their mother. Thus Gil's son will get half the estate remaining after Gil's widow has received her share, and the two granddaughters will divide the other half.

When someone dies without a will, he is said to die intestate. Each state has descent and distribution laws that specify the percentage of the estate that each heir is to receive when a person dies without a will.

Sue and Ron had a child a year before they were married. When Ron died, he left no will. Can Ron's son inherit anything from his father?

State law will determine whether Ron's son will receive a share of the estate. In the past, an illegitimate child could not inherit from his father unless the father had named the child in his will. In recent years, however, most states have revised the definition of illegitimacy so that a child becomes legitimate if the parents subsequently marry. If Ron lived in one of those states, the laws covering persons dying without a will would determine what share of the estate his son would receive. Even if Sue and

Dying Without a Will

Ron had not subsequently married, Ron's son might have a right to inherit. Many states now allow an illegitimate child to inherit from his mother and also from his natural father if the father ever acknowledged paternity or if the child can prove paternity.

What happens to the estate of a person who dies without making a will and has no living relatives?

It goes to the state after court proceedings in which any possible claimants have the opportunity to present their cases.

Meg and Manny, the parents of four young children, never made a will. Both were killed recently in a car accident. Will immediate family members have custody of the children, or will the children become the responsibility of the state?

Since both parents have died, the court would try to find relatives to serve as guardians before turning to someone outside the family. The court may also split the duties of raising the children by appointing one guardian to provide daily care of the children and another to handle financial matters.

Settling an Estate

What does it mean when an estate is said to be in probate?

Probate is the process by which a special court establishes that a will is valid and legal according to state law. The probate court also oversees the administration of a deceased person's estate. It (1) grants legal authority to the executor named in the will to administer the estate; (2) supervises the executor and receives reports from him; (3) makes sure that the executor settles all bills, taxes, and other claims against the estate; (4) sees to it that the executor distributes the remaining assets to the rightful heirs; and (5) closes the estate and releases the executor from further obligations. If there is no will, the probate court must appoint an administrator to handle the estate.

Is it possible to probate a will without a lawyer?

Yes. A lawyer is not legally required to probate a will and settle an estate, and if the estate is a simple one, the executor named in the will should be

What an Executor Has to Do

Serving as the executor of an estate is a serious responsibility, involving a lot of complicated, time-consuming work. After the person who made the will has died, the executor generally accompanies the lawyer who wrote the will to probate court. Once the court has ruled that the will is valid and has authorized the executor to do business for the estate, he performs the following duties:

1. Sets up a checking account, with printed checks showing the names of both the estate and the executor. All money received by the estate should be deposited in this account, and all expenses paid from it.
2. Conducts an inventory of the contents of any safe-deposit boxes. A representative from the state tax division may have to be present at the opening of the safe-deposit boxes to make a similar inventory.
3. Obtains extra copies of the death certificate to use in processing life insurance claims and settling other legal matters.
4. Files a change of address with the post office so that all mail for the deceased person is forwarded to the executor.
5. Publishes notice of his appointment as executor in local newspapers so that creditors will know that they should present their claims against the estate to him. The law in each state determines the details of what newspapers should carry the notice and how often.
6. Obtains appraisals on real estate and valuable personal property, such as antiques, art, or jewelry, then makes sure they are adequately insured. Rents a safe-deposit box for the jewelry and other small items.
7. Processes claims for life and medical insurance.
8. Applies for any benefits to which the estate is entitled, including Social Security, veterans', company, or union benefits.
9. Reregisters stocks, bonds, and other securities in the estate's name.
10. Pursues on behalf of the estate any lawsuits or legal claims that were pending when the person who made the will died.
11. Prepares a list of the estate's assets, including cash on hand or in bank accounts, real estate, personal property, investments, life insurance, business interests, and debts owed to the person who made the will.
12. Invests funds for maximum return or sells assets to generate additional income, as required by the needs of the estate.
13. Pays all the estate's bills, including those for medical care, burial, and the expenses of administering the estate; settles any leases; and takes care of any claims presented by other creditors.
14. Prepares tax returns and pays any amounts due for federal and state income taxes, federal estate taxes, and state death taxes.
15. Submits to the probate court an accounting of all the transactions handled for the estate and a schedule for distributing the property.
16. Distributes the property and gets receipts from the heirs.
17. Applies to the court for a discharge, which terminates his authority and releases him from liability to the estate's heirs and creditors.

able to comply with probate court requirements without hiring a lawyer. Many states have simplified their probate procedures for handling small estates. For large estates a lawyer is almost a necessity.

Maxine knows that her husband prepared a will, but after his death she could not find it. What can she do?

She must prove that the will was made and what it contained. If she cannot, the court will assume that her husband revoked it by destroying it and will distribute his estate as though he had died without a will.

Evidence of the existence of the will and its contents could include testimony from the people who witnessed it and the lawyer who drafted it. Maxine will probably also have to prove that her husband did not destroy the will. One way she may do this is to establish that the will was never in her husband's possession—for example, Maxine could show that she had kept the will in a locked file in her office, where her husband never went, and that it had been accidentally thrown out with some old files.

Can a photostatic copy of a valid will be probated?

A probate court will not accept a photocopy of a will as valid unless enough evidence is presented to show that the original document was inadvertently lost or destroyed, and that a thorough search for it has been made. Whenever the original will cannot be shown in court, the law presumes that it was intentionally revoked by being destroyed.

After his father's death, Anthony found his father's will, which left everything in the estate to him. Since there are no other heirs involved, can Anthony just take possession of the property in the estate without going through probate?

No. In some states, a person who doesn't probate a will may lose the right to inherit under the will. If Anthony's father owned real estate, or had other assets that were in his name alone, a probate procedure will be required in order to transfer these assets to Anthony's name.

A widow wants to sell her late husband's car. Can she do this without going to probate court?

If the car was in her husband's name only, she will have to go through probate. But if the widow owned the car jointly with her husband with right of survivorship, the car becomes her property without going through probate. Depending on state law or department of motor vehicle regulations, the widow may be able to have the car transferred to her name by presenting her husband's death certificate and a waiver of inheritance taxes. She could then sell the car.

Our house is in both my name and my wife's so that when one of us dies it will pass to the other without going through probate. Does this arrangement also avoid estate tax on the property?

No. Taxes are levied on the gross estate, which includes whatever portion of jointly owned property (typically one-half) is actually yours. This would apply to other assets as well as your house. The proceeds from life insurance policies, for example, would be paid directly to the beneficiary, but if you owned the policy or had the right to change the beneficiary, surrender or cancel the policy, or obtain a loan using it as collateral, the proceeds would be included as part of your estate. Assets placed in a trust or gifts made up to three years before your death might also be added back into your estate for tax purposes.

My husband and I live in Michigan but spend every winter in Florida. Where will our estates have to be settled?

Since your permanent home is in Michigan, your will should go through a Michigan probate court. However, if you own real estate in Florida, that property must go through the Florida probate court unless the property was jointly owned and therefore bypasses probate. You should make sure that your wills fulfill the requirements of both states. If your wills do not meet Florida's requirements, your Florida real estate may be distributed as though you had died without a will.

If a husband and wife do not have wills and one dies, are all properties, investments, and bank accounts frozen until the matter goes to probate court?

It depends on the laws of the state. Property held in joint tenancy with the right of survivorship may pass directly to the survivor. But in some states, even jointly held property or accounts are frozen until the tax authorities have been notified and given an opportunity to assess the value of property that should be included in the estate. New Jersey and South Carolina require 10 days' notice before securities, deposits, or assets can be transferred. In these states, however, some funds may generally be transferred without waiting. In New Jersey, for example, up to $5,000 can be transferred to the surviving spouse without waiting the 10 days.

Settling an Estate

What happens if a husband and wife are killed in a plane crash and it is impossible to determine who died first?

Each person's estate would be distributed as though the other person were already dead before the accident. In other words, the husband's property would be passed to his heirs as though the wife had died first, and the wife's property would pass to her heirs as though the husband had died first. Jointly held property would be divided equally, one-half going to each estate. These issues are covered by the Uniform Simultaneous Death Act, which has been adopted by every state except Alaska and Louisiana. To avoid having their estates automatically divided this way, a couple can indicate in their wills how their property should be distributed in the event they are killed in the same accident.

How long does an executor have to settle an estate?

State laws vary in how much time they allow an executor to close an estate. In Kansas, the executor has nine months from the date of his appointment, and in Wyoming, he has one year. Because creditors must be paid before the property can be distributed to the beneficiaries, the earliest date for closing an estate is after all debts and taxes have been paid. The executor must also wait until the deadline for challenges to be filed has passed.

Is an executor required by law to be paid for his services?

Yes. The amount or rate of compensation is either fixed by state law or left to the discretion of the probate court. If he wishes, the maker of the will can specify the amount of compensation in the will itself. If the amount is reasonable, the probate court will probably approve it. However, an executor can waive his right to receive any payment.

Molly was named executor for her aunt's estate, but she doesn't think she can handle the responsibility. Can she decline to serve?

Yes. Molly should file a renunciation with the probate court, stating that she does not want to serve as executor. If her aunt named a contingent executor, he will handle the estate in Molly's place; otherwise the court will appoint someone to do it. When making a will, you should always make sure that the person to be named executor is willing to take on the job. It is also a good idea to name a contingent executor in case the named executor is unable to serve.

Can the executor buy assets from the estate?

The law limits an executor's ability to purchase assets from an estate to prevent any unfairness to the heirs that might occur when the buyer and seller are the same person. Court approval may be necessary, the heirs may have to be notified of the executor's intention of making a purchase, or the executor may be limited to making purchases at public sales only.

The executor of Meredith's estate refuses to give Alma the money Meredith left her in his will until the IRS has been paid. This might take years. Is the executor right to wait so long?

Yes. The executor should not give anything to Meredith's heirs until he has determined the amount of all the debts and taxes that need to be paid. If the executor gives the heirs what was left them and later discovers that there are insufficient funds remaining in the estate to pay debts and taxes, he could be held personally liable for the payment of these claims.

What happens if there isn't enough money in my estate to pay taxes, burial expenses, and remaining debts?

Once the cash in an estate has been used up, the executor must begin selling other assets to pay the remaining obligations. Creditors have a right to be paid before any money or property is distributed to heirs. Each state designates which debts receive top priority as well as the order in which property will be used or sold to pay these debts. Funeral expenses, the costs of closing the estate, and estate taxes receive top priority.

Can an executor ever be held liable for the estate's taxes?

Estate taxes are a high priority in terms of debts of the estate. If an executor fails to pay the estate taxes or if he pays other debts that have a lower priority and then doesn't have enough money to pay the taxes, he could become liable for paying them out of his own pocket.

Can children force their surviving parent to sell the family home to finance their share of the inheritance?

No. The executor would not sell the home just to generate cash for the children's inheritance. The children would have to settle for a reduced inheritance. For example, if a parent specified that each of his three children was to receive $10,000 and the estate only has $18,000 plus the home, the children will receive only $6,000 each.

Settling an Estate

My father's will directs his executor to sell the real estate he owned and distribute the proceeds among his children. My brothers and sisters and I have all agreed that it would make more sense financially to keep the property. Can we stop the executor from selling the real estate?

You could ask the probate court to approve a family settlement agreement. This is a document signed by all the heirs, agreeing to changes in the provisions of a will. If the judge finds that all of the persons involved have willingly agreed to keep the property, he may incorporate this agreement into the final settlement.

Herman received a bill for merchandise his father had ordered and received several weeks before he died. How should Herman handle this?

Herman should turn the bill over to the executor of his father's estate. The executor will then verify that Herman's father actually ordered the merchandise and that it was received. Swindlers have been known to send bills for or deliver merchandise that was never ordered.

After her mother died, Trisha received a notice from a life insurance company stating that one final payment was needed in order for Trisha to receive benefits. Is this legal?

Yes, but Trisha should be cautious about this type of notice; it might not be legitimate. Con men sometimes check obituaries and contact a relative about a nonexistent life insurance policy. The unsuspecting relative pays the final premium, but never receives any insurance proceeds.

Trisha should make sure that her mother had actually purchased a policy from this company. If the policy included an automatic premium loan provision, Trisha could request that the outstanding premium payment be deducted from the money she is to receive.

When Franklin died, he owed Louis $3,000. What does Louis have to do to collect this debt?

Louis will have to submit a claim to the executor of Franklin's estate. In settling the estate, the executor must publish a notice in the newspaper informing the public that he has been appointed to administer the estate and advising creditors of the deadline for making their claims. Louis should be sure that he meets this deadline.

When Douglas died, a notice was published in the newspaper informing all his creditors of the deadline for filing claims against his estate. Hamilton was out of town and did not see this notice. Can he still make a claim against the estate a year later?

Hamilton is too late. Failure to file a claim against the estate within the designated time limit prohibits a person from collecting his debt. Without this rule, an executor would never be able to settle an estate, because he could never be sure what outstanding debts remained.

If Bridget is named in Vern's will but she can't be located at the time the estate is settled, what happens to her share of the money?

If an heir cannot be found, the property is sold and the cash is held by the state treasurer. Bridget would still be able to claim this inheritance if she filed a claim within the time designated by state law. In Wyoming a missing heir has five years to claim property, and in South Carolina Bridget would have eight years to make her claim. When this time has expired, the inheritance becomes state property.

Candace's estate was closed in August after her house had been sold to Wilbur. When Wilbur remodeled the house in September of the following year, he discovered a tin box containing $10,000 in coins. Is it too late to distribute this money to Candace's heirs?

No. Estates can be reopened when new assets are discovered. Any interested person could petition the court to reopen Candace's estate. The same executor or a new one would be appointed to distribute the $10,000 in accordance with Candace's will.

Funerals and Burials

Jessica wants to make funeral arrangements now to save her family from having to do it when she dies. Can she do this?

Yes, either with the help of a memorial (burial) society or on her own. Memorial societies, which generally charge a modest one-time membership fee, provide information about funeral and burial options and costs. These nonprofit organizations may also be able to get their members reduced rates at funeral homes.

If Jessica wants to contact funeral homes herself, she should inquire about a *pre-need plan,* under which she can prepay funeral costs. Many states have laws that safeguard money that is put into pre-need plans.

Funerals and Burials

Uncle Edgar prepaid his funeral costs. He died last week, and the funeral bill is $1,200 more than he had paid. Must his estate or the family pay the difference?

Not if Uncle Edgar had a fixed-price contract. However, if his contract did not guarantee a fixed price, Uncle Edgar's family or the executor of his estate would have to pay the difference.

What happens if I prepay for my funeral arrangements, and the funeral home later goes out of business?

You should receive some or all of your money back. Laws in states such as Nevada, Ohio, South Dakota, and Washington require most, if not all, of the money paid under a pre-need plan to be placed in a trust fund. The trust would terminate if the funeral home went out of business, and the trustee would return your money to you.

Gladys wants to spare her children the expense and bother of arranging for her funeral when she dies, and she is thinking of

Letter of Last Instructions

When a person dies, the family must make a number of decisions fairly quickly about the funeral and burial. Some people include details about these arrangements in their wills. But this is not always advisable, since the will may not be read until some time after the funeral. A better alternative is a letter of last instructions, which is a private, informal statement of what arrangements you prefer. If you write such a letter, give copies to your spouse or anyone else who may be responsible for handling final arrangements. Keep the original in an easily accessible place that the family knows about. Do not put it in a safe-deposit box, since the box may be sealed until a state tax representative can make an inventory of its contents. The letter should give the following information:

- ☑ Disposition of the body—whether you prefer to have your body buried, cremated, or donated to medical science.
- ☑ Where the funeral service should be held.
- ☑ List of speakers and music for the funeral.
- ☑ The kinds of flowers preferred.
- ☑ If contributions are preferred to flowers, the names of the organizations to which the contributions should be sent.

buying insurance that will take care of all the costs. If she does, will the funeral home she selects be able to ask for direct payment from the insurance company when Gladys dies?

No. If Gladys names her estate as the beneficiary of the policy, the funeral home would present its bill to the estate's executor. In some states, including Maryland and Tennessee, insurance companies are prohibited from issuing policies that specify direct payments to funeral homes.

I want to be cremated after I die. How can I make sure that my family will carry out my wishes?

You can't. You can clearly state your wishes to the family members or friends who will be responsible for arranging your burial, but oral or written instructions about whether or not you are to be cremated are not legally binding on your family or the executor of your estate.

Who has the legal authority to arrange for a burial?

The spouse or the next of kin usually takes charge of burial arrangements and is legally permitted to do so. If no one steps forward to accept this

- ☑ Details about any funeral plan that has been purchased in advance or other funds that have been set aside for final arrangements.
- ☑ Location of the family burial plot—including the name and location of the cemetery, the lot, and the grave number—with the names of the cemetery authorities to notify.
- ☑ Names, addresses, dates of birth, and places of birth for yourself and your spouse, children, parents, brothers and sisters, and, if you are divorced, your ex-spouse.
- ☑ Name and address of your employer.
- ☑ Social Security number and the location of your card.
- ☑ Dates of service in the armed forces and your service number.
- ☑ Biographical information that could be included in an obituary.
- ☑ Policy numbers, insurance company names and addresses, and the location of your life insurance policies.
- ☑ Information on union benefits, company profit-sharing, and other employment benefits.
- ☑ Where you keep your will and who is named as executor.
- ☑ Location of your safe-deposit box.
- ☑ Location of your birth and marriage certificates, prenuptial agreements, divorce papers, trust agreements, military records, and other personal documents.

responsibility, the body will be buried, or otherwise disposed of, according to state and local laws. Later, when the appointment of the executor has been approved by the court, the executor may be required to purchase a tombstone or monument in accordance with the dead person's will.

My mother is in the last stage of a terminal illness. Can I get the information I need to compare funeral costs and procedures over the telephone without actually having to visit funeral homes?

Yes. Under Federal Trade Commission regulations, relatives are entitled to receive information by telephone about funeral plans and costs. You can also ask the funeral home to send you a written price list.

If a funeral home offers a package price, can we save money by excluding some of the services offered in the package?

Yes. The Federal Trade Commission forbids a funeral home to require the purchase of one part of a package in order to receive another. Price lists prepared by the funeral home must include a statement that, even though a package is offered, you can select only the options you want.

Do undertakers and funeral directors have to be licensed?

Yes. Each state has licensing requirements, and applicants must pass a written examination. In addition, professional organizations, such as the National Selected Morticians and the National Funeral Directors Association, monitor the business practices of the funeral industry.

Brandon lives in Massachusetts but wants to be buried in his family plot in Delaware. Are there legal regulations about transporting a body?

Yes. Various kinds of state laws require permits to transport a body into or out of the state. The necessary permits are usually obtained by the funeral home at the same time as the death certificate. The funeral home should make sure that the laws of the states involved are followed. Nevada, for example, imposes a fine on anyone who tries to move a body out of the state without a permit; and it is illegal to bring a body into Idaho unless a permit is obtained. In some states and municipalities, a certificate from the health department is needed to move a body, and regulations stipulate the type of container that must be used.

While my wife and I were on an around-the-world cruise, one of our fellow passengers died. Would it have been legal for the ship's captain to perform a burial at sea?

If the body cannot be safely preserved and transported to shore, the captain has the legal right to conduct a burial at sea. In most situations, however, the crew will deliver it to a port, where relatives can claim it.

Are there time limits within which a body must be buried?

State laws usually require that the body be buried "within a reasonable time after death." In Utah, for example, burial or cremation must occur within 24 hours of death if the body is not embalmed or refrigerated. The burial of an embalmed or refrigerated body may usually be delayed longer, if necessary, until the family can make the necessary arrangements.

Someone told us that all bodies have to be embalmed. Is this true?

No. Each state has its own laws about embalming, but in general it is not required unless (1) the burial is delayed, (2) the person died from a communicable disease, or (3) the body is being transported out of state. Federal Trade Commission regulations forbid a mortician to tell the family of a deceased person that state or local laws require embalming when they do not require it.

My father asked that his remains be cremated. Are we required by law to provide a casket for the cremation?

No, you are not. State law governs the requirements for cremation, and none of the states require that a casket be provided for a body that is to be cremated. In Maryland and Nevada, it is illegal for a funeral home to require a casket for cremation, and Massachusetts law says only that a "suitable container" must be used.

Katrina requested that she be cremated after her death and her ashes scattered in the mountains in another state. Would Katrina's family be within the law if they followed her wishes?

It depends on the laws of the state where the ashes are to be scattered. Many states—and cities—have laws governing the scattering of ashes from human remains in certain areas. In Indiana, there is no restriction if the ashes are scattered on a waterway, uninhabited public land, or with the consent of a private landowner.

Funerals and Burials

When is an autopsy mandatory?

A coroner will order an autopsy whenever the cause of death is unknown. Autopsies are usually required to establish the cause of death in violent, unexplained, or suspicious circumstances.

Although Jennifer seemed to be in excellent health, she died quietly in her sleep the other night. The coroner has ordered that an autopsy be performed on her remains. Do her relatives have to give their consent before an autopsy can be performed?

A coroner may proceed with an autopsy without the consent of Jennifer's relatives if he believes that her death was unusual or suspicious in any way. Autopsies are often ordered when someone who appeared to be in good health dies suddenly.

Conrad and his family recently purchased a 100-acre tract of land. The family would like to establish a family cemetery on part of the property. Will they be able to do so?

It is very possible that they will not be able to do so. At one time, landowners were free to establish private family cemeteries on their land,

What to Do When a Loved One Dies

One of the most difficult circumstances a person may ever have to face is the death of a relative or close friend. In addition to the emotional impact of the death, there are many hard decisions that must be made, some of them right away. The following list may be helpful if you are responsible for making these decisions:

- If someone dies at home, contact the family doctor or the police or an ambulance service for assistance. If the person who died had recently been under a doctor's care or had a history of illness (such as cancer or heart disease), the family doctor will generally sign the death certificate.
- If the death was sudden or occurred under suspicious circumstances, call the police. If an investigation is needed, they will arrange to have the coroner or medical examiner determine the cause of death.
- If death occurs in a hospital, the attending physician will sign the death certificate. An autopsy may be needed if the cause of death is unknown.
- After the immediate formalities have been completed, call a funeral director to arrange for transportation of the body to a funeral home.

but this is no longer the case. State and local laws increasingly restrict the establishment of private burial plots. Conrad should contact his local government to find out about any regulations covering family cemeteries. Zoning and other local or county ordinances usually set strict qualifications for both where a private cemetery can be established and who can establish and maintain one.

If I buy a cemetery plot, does the purchase price include maintenance of the gravesite?

Yes, if the plot is in a perpetual care cemetery. In many states—Indiana, South Dakota, and Washington, for example—the law requires that a percentage of the sale price of the burial plot be put into a fund for the maintenance of the gravesite.

Ethan obtained a family plot after his mother had been buried elsewhere. What must he do to have his mother's body moved from one cemetery to another?

He must follow the procedures set by the laws of his state. Ethan will also need to obtain permission from the authorities at both cemeteries, and possibly the consent of other members of his family. If consent cannot be obtained, Ethan can seek court approval to have his mother's body moved to the family plot.

- Find out what funeral and burial arrangements should be made. The person who died may have supplied this information in a letter of last instructions or his will. Otherwise, close relatives or the lawyer who drafted the will may know what arrangements were preferred.
- If the person who died belonged to a memorial or burial society, notify a representative of that society of the death.
- Plan the memorial service and final disposition of the body.
- Notify friends and relatives about the services. The funeral home will help you prepare an obituary for newspaper publication.
- Obtain copies of the death certificate. The executor will need them to administer the estate. The funeral home will usually have copies made for you if you request it.
- Give the will to the person named executor of the estate so that he can begin to assume his duties in settling the legal aspects of the estate.
- If there is burial insurance, notify the insurance company or its agent. Also make a list of any other burial benefits that may be available from Social Security, the Veterans Administration, a labor union, or a fraternal organization. Application for these benefits should be made by the funeral home, executor, or the person responsible for paying these expenses.

Funerals and Burials

My uncle Jonathan served in the army. My aunt says he is entitled to a burial payment. If so, how do we apply for this money?

You should contact the nearest Veterans Administration office for an application for burial benefits. Don't hesitate to ask the funeral home for help, if you need it, in obtaining and filling out the forms. The claim must be made within two years of your uncle's death. The burial allowance ranges from $300 to a maximum of $1,100 if your uncle died from a service-connected disability.

Do all veterans of the armed forces have the right to be buried at Arlington National Cemetery?

No. For ground burial, a veteran must have had 20 years active duty, and been retired and receiving veterans' pay. Individuals who receive military honors—the Silver Star, Purple Heart, Air Force or Navy Cross, Distinguished Service Medal, Distinguished Service Cross, or Medal of Honor—are also eligible for burial at Arlington National Cemetery. A columbarium (a vault where urns containing ashes are placed) is available to any honorably discharged veteran.

There are many other national cemeteries operated by the Veterans Administration. Servicemen who die on active duty are eligible for burial in these cemeteries, as are all veterans except those who received dishonorable discharges. Members of the military reserves who die honorably while serving on active duty, as well as some dependents of veterans, are also eligible for burial in national cemeteries.

CHAPTER
17

Victims and Crimes

If You Are a Victim

For courtroom procedures, see Chapter 18, *Going to Court.*

If I am the victim of a crime, do I have a legal duty to report the crime to the police?

No. The law does not require a victim to report a crime to the police. However, informing the police benefits both the victim and society at large. It makes it possible for a victim to (1) receive court-ordered compensation for his medical expenses or property damage, if the criminal is caught; (2) collect reimbursement from a victim compensation fund, if the victim's state has one; and (3) establish details about the crime that may be required by his insurance company. Notifying the police also helps bring criminals to justice.

Graham's car was vandalized while it was parked at a shopping mall. What will happen once he notifies the police?

The police will ask Graham to provide important information—such as when he last saw the car, when he discovered the damage, where the car was parked when it was damaged, and whether he or anyone else witnessed the crime—and to sign a sworn statement attesting that the information is true. If a suspect is arrested and prosecuted, Graham will be asked to testify at the trial. If the vandal is convicted, the court may order him to reimburse Graham for the damage to his car.

After being robbed, Nicole reported the crime to the police. How will she be expected to cooperate during the investigation?

Nicole will be asked to give a statement describing what happened. She may also be shown mug shots or be taken to a lineup and asked to identify the robber. If a suspect is charged with the crime, Nicole will probably be interviewed again by both the prosecutor and the defense attorney. When the suspect is tried, Nicole will be asked to testify about the robbery.

Some neighborhood kids slashed the screens on Jake's porch while he was away on vacation. Jake's neighbor, Luke, witnessed the incident and told Jake who did it. Can Jake make the police arrest the children who are responsible?

No. A private citizen has no legal right to force the police to make an arrest—even when he is the victim of a crime or can identify the offenders—unless certain kinds of domestic violence are involved, such as abuse of a spouse.

Tara called the police to complain that her husband, Rod, was hitting her. When an officer arrived at their house, Tara asked him to arrest Rod, but he refused and told the couple to sit down and work out their differences. Tara feels that the officer neglected his duty. What can she do?

Tara should seek advice from a lawyer or a citizens' group concerned with preventing family violence. If she decides to sue the police department for not arresting her husband, she may have a good chance of winning the lawsuit. Some courts have ruled that in cases of domestic violence where the police refused to arrest the abusive husband, they violated the wife's constitutional right to equal protection under the law.

Abraham's home has an alarm that is connected to the nearest police station. The alarm sounded during a burglary, but the police didn't respond until long after the thief had fled. Can Abraham sue the police?

Probably not. Although the police have a duty to protect the public, this does not make them liable when an individual suffers as a result of their actions or their failure to act. However, a few states have laws that allow an individual police officer to be held personally liable in certain circumstances. Abraham should find out what the law says in his state.

Leah was mugged six months ago, but the police still haven't found a suspect. How long can Leah expect the police to search?

There is no minimum or maximum amount of time allowed for a criminal investigation. Generally, the police will continue their investigation as long as there are leads to follow. However, since Leah's case may receive less and less priority as time goes by, she should keep in touch with the police to check on the status of their investigation.

I haven't heard a word from the police since the day my home was burglarized. Don't they have a duty to keep me informed about the progress of their investigation?

Some states—for example, Rhode Island—legally require the police to notify victims about the progress of their case, but others do not. However, police departments in all states are willing to share information with a victim because the success of their investigation frequently depends on the victim's cooperation. If you call the police officers who are working on your case and ask them, they will probably tell you how your case is progressing.

If You Are a Victim

Hazel's purse was stolen by her nephew, who is a drug addict. Hazel's father said she should press charges. What does this mean?

When a person presses charges, he agrees to cooperate with the authorities in all phases of their prosecution of an accused person. This includes being available for pretrial interviews and testifying at the trial. If Hazel does not wish to press charges against her nephew, she may be asked to sign a written statement to that effect.

My neighbor refuses to return the lawn mower he borrowed from me. I'd like to press charges against him, but the prosecuting attorney has denied my request. Can I force him to take action?

No. There is no way to force a prosecutor to bring criminal charges against someone. However, if you think the prosecuting attorney is abusing the power of his office by refusing to bring charges, you may report him to your state attorney general's office. The attorney general has the authority to overrule the prosecuting attorney's decision not to press charges. In any case, you can still sue your neighbor in civil court.

Rights of Victims

Most states have a Victim's Bill of Rights, which gives the victim of a crime various rights and privileges. To find out if your state has such a bill, contact the office of your local prosecuting attorney or state attorney general. Although the exact provisions of these bills vary, in most states a victim has the right to:

- Be treated with respect and courtesy.
- Be provided with appropriate medical treatment.
- Have his personal property returned as soon as possible.
- Have his case handled as promptly as possible.
- Be informed of the progress of the investigation.
- Be notified of the date and time of any important hearings.
- Be told when the defendant will be released from custody.
- Be protected against threats or harassment by the defendant.
- Be notified of any delay or postponement of the trial.
- Be present at the trial.
- Be provided with a safe waiting area—away from the defendant, his family, and associates—during the trial.
- Tell the court about the crime's effect on his life (except in cases involving the death penalty).

I'd like to see the man who robbed me get put away, but I'm a little nervous about identifying him in a lineup. What will it be like?

To protect your identity, the lineup will be arranged so that its members cannot see you, even though you can see them. The lineup will include the suspect and several other people whose physical appearance is similar to the suspect's. As each individual steps forward, he may be instructed to speak, walk, or turn. You will be asked if you can identify your assailant and, if so, to single him out. To make sure that no one influences your decision, the suspect's lawyer may be present. If he feels that the lineup is unfair in any way, he may later move to prevent your identification of the suspect from being submitted as evidence at the trial.

The police asked Janelle to attend a lineup to identify the man who raped her, but Janelle can't bear to look at the man again. Does she have to cooperate?

No. The victim of a crime cannot be forced to attend a lineup. However, if Janelle refuses to participate—or if she attends the lineup and is unable to positively identify her assailant—the police may have to drop all charges against the suspect.

Can the victim of a crime be required to testify at a suspect's trial?

Yes. If the prosecuting attorney considers it necessary, a victim can be subpoenaed to testify. A victim's testimony is often needed to establish that a crime occurred or to identify the suspect. But even if the victim was not present at the scene of the crime, his testimony may still be necessary. In the case of a burglary, for example, the homeowner may be asked to testify that the defendant did not have permission to be in his home or to take his property.

Estelle's knitting shop was broken into, and a suspect has been arrested. Will Estelle have to be present at the bail hearing?

No, but since bail hearings are open to the public, Estelle is certainly free to attend if she chooses.

The police recovered Tim's stolen television set, but when he went to pick it up they would not return it to him. Why?

The television is probably needed as evidence at the suspect's trial. At that time, Tim may be asked if he can identify the television as his property, and other witnesses may be called to testify that they saw the television in the suspect's possession after it was taken from Tim's home.

Some states, such as Wisconsin, Oklahoma, and Washington, require that personal property be returned to its owner promptly. In Wisconsin, for example, property must be returned within 10 days of its recovery, if possible. However, this does not apply to property that must be tested—such as weapons, currency, and contraband—or property whose ownership is in dispute. Florida encourages the prompt return of stolen property by allowing photographs of the property to be submitted as evidence at trials in place of the actual property. If Tim lives in a state that keeps stolen property until the trial, he will be able to take his television home when the trial is over.

Darren was injured during a fight he had with his neighbor, Morris, over the use of their common driveway. Darren wants to press charges against Morris, but the prosecuting attorney suggested that Darren and Morris participate in a dispute resolution program. What is that?

It is a way to avoid the bitterness and conflict that often follow a court trial, and is especially helpful when the people in a dispute are neighbors, coworkers, or others who must continue to see each other. If Darren and Morris agree to participate in such a program, they will be asked to meet with a mediator, work out their differences, and refrain from violent confrontations in the future.

My sister keeps a can of Mace and a knife in her pocketbook for self-defense. Is this legal?

Most states and localities prohibit citizens from carrying concealed weapons, such as revolvers, daggers, blackjacks, brass knuckles, and other dangerous or deadly devices. Mace is not usually considered a weapon, since it causes temporary discomfort rather than physical harm. However, in some states, such as Montana, it would be illegal for your sister to carry a knife with a blade longer than four inches.

To defend myself from a mugger, I poked him in the eye with my keys. The mugger lost his sight in the injured eye and is now charging me with assault. Can I argue that I acted in self-defense?

It depends on the circumstances. You have the right to use force, even deadly force, to defend yourself against someone who is trying to injure you. However, once you are no longer in danger, you may not use force against an assailant. If you poked the mugger in the eye while he was trying to strangle you, you could claim self-defense. But if you tried to blind him after he had let go of you, and you were no longer in mortal danger, you could be charged with assault.

While Monty was walking down a dark alley, a man came up behind him and pressed what felt like a gun barrel against his back. Monty took out his revolver, turned around quickly, and shot the man; he then realized that the man was holding a piece of pipe, not a revolver. Can Monty plead self-defense?

Yes. When threatened with physical harm, an individual has the right to use enough force to prevent an attack or defend himself from one. Even though Monty's assailant was not actually armed with a deadly weapon, he gave Monty reason to think he was by using an object that simulated a gun barrel. Therefore, Monty was justified in using force to defend himself against his assailant.

After Cecil's sports car was stolen from his garage, he rigged the garage door with a booby trap gun. When an intruder tried to open the door, he was killed by the device. Can Cecil be held responsible for causing the intruder's death?

Yes. Cecil can be charged with manslaughter. Booby trap guns and similar devices are capable of deadly force; and deadly force may be used only to defend someone's life or protect a person from serious bodily injury. The law does not permit a person to use such dangerous devices to protect personal property.

Although Cecil may not have intended to kill the intruder, the prosecuting attorney may argue that if Cecil only wanted to scare away an intruder, he could have loaded the gun with blanks. The prosecution may also try to show that Cecil acted carelessly by installing a deadly device that could not possibly differentiate between an intruder and someone who might need to open the garage door in an emergency, such as a fire fighter or police officer.

Kelly was assaulted by Howard after he got drunk at a party where they were both guests. If Kelly presses charges, can Howard use his intoxication as a defense?

No. In cases of simple assault, such as this one, drunkenness cannot be used as a defense. The fact that Howard was drunk will not excuse him from responsibility for his actions.

If You Are a Victim

Noreen was held up at gunpoint after cashing her paycheck. A suspect was arrested and charged with armed robbery, but now he's trying to plea-bargain to get the charge reduced to assault. Can Noreen prevent this from happening?

No. Only the prosecuting attorney can stop a plea bargain from being negotiated. Noreen's only course of action is to try to persuade the prosecuting attorney to deny the defendant's request to plea-bargain.

Does a victim have the right to know when his assailant will be released on parole?

Usually. In federal cases, the law requires that a victim be notified of when his attacker becomes eligible for parole and when he is actually released from custody. Some states, including Florida, Rhode Island, Washington, and Wisconsin, have similar laws. States that are not legally required to notify victims about such dates usually allow the police department to provide this information upon request.

The man convicted of killing Angela's daughter is coming up for parole. Will Angela be allowed to address the parole board to protest his release?

It depends on where Angela lives. Although no state forbids a victim or family member to address a parole board, some states do not allow such appeals to be made in person. If Angela lives in Texas or New York, for example, she may only be able to address the parole board in writing. Angela should contact her state's parole board to find out if her state has such a restriction.

My cousin suggested that I take advantage of a victim assistance program offered in my state. How will this program help me, and where can I find out about it?

Most police departments and prosecutor's offices sponsor or work closely with assistance programs that help people who are the victims of crimes. In addition, there are programs that provide help for witnesses whose testimony puts them in danger of reprisal. Many of these programs have 24-hour hotlines to handle emergencies. Victim assistance programs provide a number of services, including food, shelter, and medical care; psychological counseling; and advocates who accompany victims to court hearings and help them in their dealings with the police.

A man snatched Marlene's purse and then shoved her in front of a moving car. Her injuries required $20,000 worth of medical treatment. Can she get any financial help from the state?

Perhaps. In 39 states—including Alabama, California, Florida, Illinois, Kansas, New Jersey, New York, Pennsylvania, Texas, and Wisconsin—there are victim compensation funds to help reimburse victims of violent crime. Most of these funds help cover lost wages, counseling and medical expenses, and funeral costs. Marlene can qualify for this aid even if her assailant is never tried or convicted, but not if she lives in the same household, is related to, or has a continuing relationship with him. The police department, prosecuting attorney's office, or state attorney general's office can help Marlene contact the program in her state.

Can a criminal be forced to pay restitution to his victim while he is in prison?

Possibly. In many cases a victim cannot be reimbursed because the prisoner has no money, property, or job. However, if a convict is enrolled in a work-release program, he may be required by the court to turn over part of his wages to his victim. In addition, if a convict is employed while on parole, he can be required to pay the victim a portion of his salary. For certain federal crimes, such as kidnapping, mail fraud, and bank robbery, courts must order restitution or explain why they have not done so.

What Is a Crime?

Emily's attorney told her that she was lucky to be charged with a misdemeanor rather than a felony. What's the difference?

Misdemeanors are less serious than felonies. Misdemeanors are punishable by a fine or brief term in the county jail, and include such crimes as simple assault (assault without a deadly weapon), resisting arrest, and stealing less than $150. Felonies, on the other hand, are punishable by more than one year's imprisonment in the state penitentiary or, in some cases, by death. Burglary, rape, and murder are all examples of felonies.

Warren was notified that the extension he built on his house violates his town's zoning law. Does this mean Warren has committed a crime?

Yes. Violations of zoning laws are usually classified as petty offenses, or infractions. Such violations are less serious than misdemeanors, and are usually punishable by fines. However, if a court orders Warren to remove the extension and he refuses, he could be charged with contempt of court, which is a more serious offense.

Lynn moved to a new town with her pit bull terrier, not knowing that the town prohibited such animals. The town confiscated the dog and served Lynn with a summons that said that she could be fined or jailed. Lynn didn't realize that she was breaking the law. Is she liable?

Yes. Citizens are responsible for knowing what the law is and obeying it. Since pit bull terriers are banned from many communities because they are dangerous, Lynn should have checked local ordinances or asked her real estate agent to check for her before she moved.

Maggie tapes movies from a cable television station on her VCR. Is she committing a crime?

It depends on what Maggie does with the tapes. If she records movies only for her own viewing at home, she is within the bounds of the law, which permits the "fair use" of copyrighted material. However, if Maggie rents or sells the tapes, she will be guilty of pirating or bootlegging, which is a criminal offense punishable by fines of up to $250,000 and a prison sentence of up to five years.

While Pierce was away, his friend Alexis borrowed his car, intending to return it before Pierce came home. Pierce returned earlier than expected, and accused Alexis of stealing the car. Can Alexis be arrested?

Yes. Although Alexis did not intend to steal Pierce's car, she violated what many states call the "joyriding" law, which makes it illegal for a person to borrow a vehicle without the owner's permission. However, Alexis cannot be arrested unless Pierce files charges against her.

What is a victimless crime?

It is a crime that harms society at large, rather than a particular individual. Drug offenses, gambling, and prostitution are considered to be victimless crimes because their participants are willing—unlike the victims of robbery or murder.

Isn't a crime committed against a person more serious than one committed against property?

Not always. For example, the law considers stealing a car to be more serious than punching someone in a barroom brawl; the auto thief would probably receive a harsher sentence than the person found guilty of assault, even though assault is a crime against a person.

Is the failure to act ever considered a crime?

Yes, as illustrated in these examples: if you don't file a federal income tax return annually; if a parent doesn't provide food or shelter for his children; if an employer doesn't provide safe working conditions for his employees; if a citizen doesn't comply with a police officer's request for assistance; or if a doctor doesn't report a patient with a gunshot wound.

Can a person with AIDS be prosecuted for knowingly infecting another person with the disease?

Yes. Since 1986, 22 states have passed laws making it illegal to knowingly engage in conduct that could transmit the human immunodeficiency virus (HIV), which causes AIDS.

If I accidentally pick up the wrong suitcase at the airport and the customs inspector finds illegal drugs inside, can I be found guilty of drug possession?

No, as long as you can prove that the suitcase does not belong to you, and that you therefore did not knowingly or willingly possess the drugs.

Is it true that a person can't be held responsible for a crime he didn't intend to commit?

Yes. A crime has two elements: the criminal act itself and the intent to commit the act. To be found guilty, a person must not only commit a crime but must do so willingly and knowingly. For example, if you were angry at a friend and fired a gun at him and killed him, you could be found guilty of murder. However, if you were cleaning a gun and it went off accidentally, killing your friend, you would not be guilty of murder, because you did not intend to kill him. (But you might be guilty of manslaughter or criminally negligent homicide.) If you were legally insane or mentally incompetent when you killed the friend, you would not be held responsible for his death.

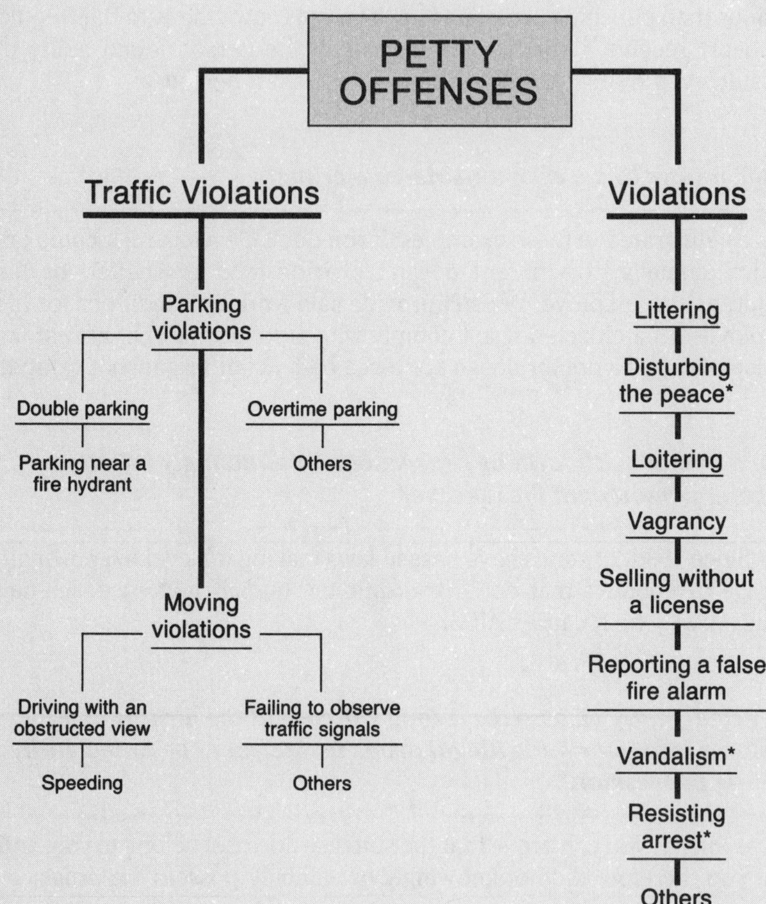

Crimes are divided into two broad categories—petty and criminal offenses—and then subdivided into traffic and other violations, misdemeanors, and felonies. The type of punishment imposed for a crime determines the category: *Violations* are usually punishable by a fine or a short jail term; *misdemeanors* are punishable by larger fines, longer jail terms, or both; *felonies* generally call for more than one year of imprisonment in a penitentiary or for the death penalty. An * means that the offense can be either a violation or a misdemeanor, depending on the seriousness of the offense, and a † means that the offense can be either a misdemeanor or a felony, depending on the value of the property involved and whether the offender used a weapon or had a record of previous convictions.

Are Classified

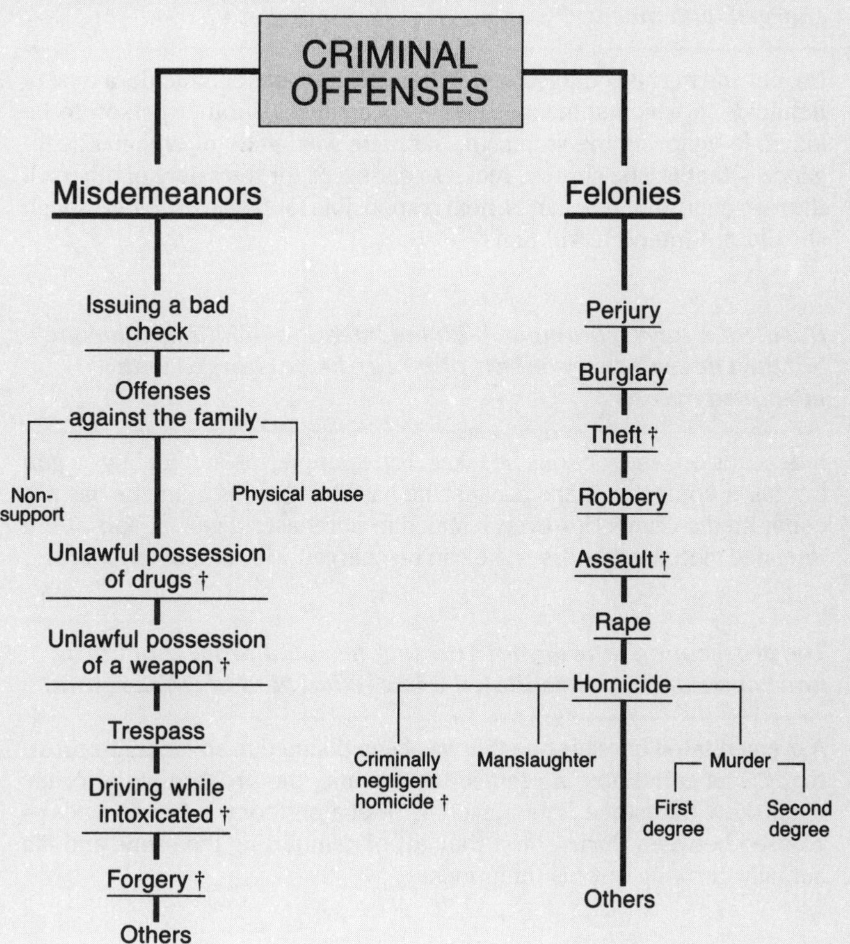

Homicide is divided into four different types: *Criminally negligent homicide* (sometimes called vehicular homicide) is an unintentional killing resulting from indifference or reckless disregard for human life, such as speeding through a school zone. *Manslaughter* is killing someone intentionally in the heat of passion; unintentionally while committing a violation or a misdemeanor; or unintentionally while performing a lawful act in a negligent manner, such as while cleaning a loaded gun. *Second-degree murder* involves malice, which means that the killer must have intended to cause death or to inflict severe bodily harm. *First-degree murder,* the most serious form of homicide, involves both malice and a premeditated decision to kill someone.

What Is a Crime?

Nannette drove her car past a stop sign without slowing down or stopping and hit an elderly man. If the man dies, will Nannette be charged with murder?

No, but she may be charged with criminally negligent homicide, a type of homicide in which someone's negligence causes another person to be killed. By ignoring the stop sign, Nannette was guilty of criminal negligence—that is, she showed reckless disregard for the safety of others. If the man dies, Nannette can be held responsible for his death, even though she did not intend to kill him.

If Malcolm buys a handgun with the intention of killing someone but then doesn't carry out his plan, can he be charged with attempted murder?

It depends on what actions he takes. For example, if Malcolm buys a gun but takes no further steps because he has changed his mind, he has not committed a crime. However, if Malcolm purchases a gun, shoots at the intended victim, and misses, he can be charged with attempted murder.

The prosecuting attorney told the jury he could prove that Curtis had committed a premeditated crime. What kind of crime is that?

A premeditated crime is one that has been planned in advance. To prove that Curtis committed a premeditated crime, the prosecuting attorney must show that some time—even as brief a period as a few seconds—elapsed between Curtis's first thought of committing the crime and his actually carrying out his intentions.

Is an accomplice the same as an accessory?

An accessory is a type of accomplice. An accomplice is a person who helps or encourages someone in a criminal act—for example, the lookout in a burglary. Accomplices can be divided into two categories: the aiders and abettors, who are present when the crime is committed, and the accessories, who are not present.

There are also two types of accessories. An accessory before the fact is anyone who provokes, incites, counsels, or otherwise encourages another person to commit a crime, but who is not present at the scene of the crime and does not take part in committing it. An accessory after the fact is someone who knows that a crime has been committed and helps the criminal to avoid capture or arrest, or to escape from custody.

I've just learned that my son-in-law has been using my daughter as a lookout while he sells illegal firearms. Can she be arrested for doing this?

Yes. If your daughter is serving as a lookout, she is actively participating in committing a crime. This makes her an accomplice in the crime. Even though your son-in-law is the person who is actually selling the firearms, your daughter could be charged with the same offense.

Can a corporation be charged with a crime?

Yes. The law considers a corporation an artificial person, and it can be charged with committing a crime because of the activities of its officers and employees. The penalties for corporate crime usually take the form of a fine. However, officers and employees involved in a corporate crime can also be tried and sentenced to a fine or imprisonment or both.

Rights of the Accused

For more information, see "Dealing With the Police" in Chapter 12, *Your Individual Rights;* also see Chapter 18, *Going to Court.*

My neighbor complained to the police that I was playing my stereo too loudly. Do I have to let the police into the house when they arrive?

No, unless they have a search warrant. The only time the police are allowed to enter your home without your permission or a search warrant is in an emergency, such as if someone inside your home is threatened with injury or a suspect the police are chasing has fled into your house.

If I refuse to allow a police officer into my home even though he has a search warrant, can I be arrested?

Yes. If a police officer has a search warrant, it is illegal for you to hinder his investigation. If you refuse to allow him into your home, the police officer has the right to arrest you on the spot.

What are no-knock laws?

Federal law requires that a police officer—even if he has a search warrant—must knock and announce his presence and the purpose of his visit before forcibly entering a home. Many states—including Alabama,

Florida, Iowa, Kansas, Michigan, Montana, New York, Oregon, Tennessee, and Utah—also have no-knock laws. If a police officer breaks into a home without first giving its resident the opportunity to open the door, no evidence he seizes will be admitted by the court. Officers are not required to knock, however, if they know that no one is home, or if such a warning would give a suspect time to flee or destroy evidence.

Several minutes after a jewelry store was held up, Darrell ran down a nearby street to catch a bus. When the police saw him running, they stopped and frisked him. Was this legal?

Yes. The police have the right to stop and frisk anyone if they have reason to suspect that the person has committed a crime and that he may be armed and dangerous. Since Darrell was running near the scene of a recent crime, the police were justified in thinking that his behavior was suspicious. However, the police would only be allowed to pat Darrell down to find out if he was carrying a concealed weapon. They would not be permitted to conduct a full body search unless Darrell were arrested.

Your Legal Rights If You Are Arrested

If you are accused of committing a crime—whether you are guilty or innocent—our legal system guarantees you certain rights. You have the right to remain silent and not incriminate yourself, the right to be represented by a lawyer, and the right to have a lawyer appointed by the court if you cannot afford one. If you are arrested, before questioning begins you must be advised of these rights, which are summarized in the Miranda Warnings required by the U. S. Supreme Court. You also have the right to:

- Have a hearing before a magistrate or judge, as soon as possible after you are arrested.
- Be notified of the charges against you.
- Have reasonable bail set, if bail is granted.
- Have a fair, impartial trial by jury.
- Be present at all stages of the trial.
- Confront your accusers.
- Have your lawyer cross-examine witnesses.
- Have your lawyer call witnesses on your behalf.
- Be tried for a crime only once.
- Receive neither cruel nor unusual punishment if you are convicted of a crime and sentenced.

Liza was stopped by the police because her car had a broken taillight. The officer offered to check the bulb, and Liza agreed to let him. When he opened the trunk, he found a briefcase full of cocaine. Did the officer have the right to open the briefcase?

No. The police officer had the right to stop Liza's car because the broken taillight was a traffic violation, and to open the trunk because Liza gave her consent. However, to search the trunk or open the briefcase, the officer would have needed (1) Liza's permission, (2) a search warrant, or (3) reason to suspect that Liza was hiding something illegal.

Can a police officer make an arrest without an arrest warrant?

Yes. If a police officer has probable cause to believe that someone has committed a serious crime, then he does not need an arrest warrant—even if the crime was not committed in his presence. To make an arrest for a less serious crime, such as disturbing the peace, an officer must either witness the crime or obtain an arrest warrant.

If Nicholas feels that the police are totally unjustified in arresting him, should he resist the arrest?

No. Resisting arrest is a crime. Even if Nicholas is found innocent of the charges for which he was arrested, he could be convicted of resisting arrest.

The police told me that they've issued an arrest warrant for the man who stole my car. What information does a warrant contain?

An arrest warrant identifies the person to be arrested, either by name or physical description, and lists the charges against him. A warrant usually directs police officers, sheriffs, and other law enforcement officials to make an arrest, but it may also grant that authority to private citizens. An arrest warrant can be issued by a judge, justice of the peace, magistrate, or someone else designated by law, such as a coroner, but it cannot be issued by a prosecuting attorney or police officer. If a warrant is not issued and signed by an authorized person, it is not valid.

Is it true that a person who is arrested is allowed to make only one phone call?

No. If you are arrested, you are entitled to make as many phone calls as necessary to arrange for a lawyer to represent you and to arrange for someone to post bail for you.

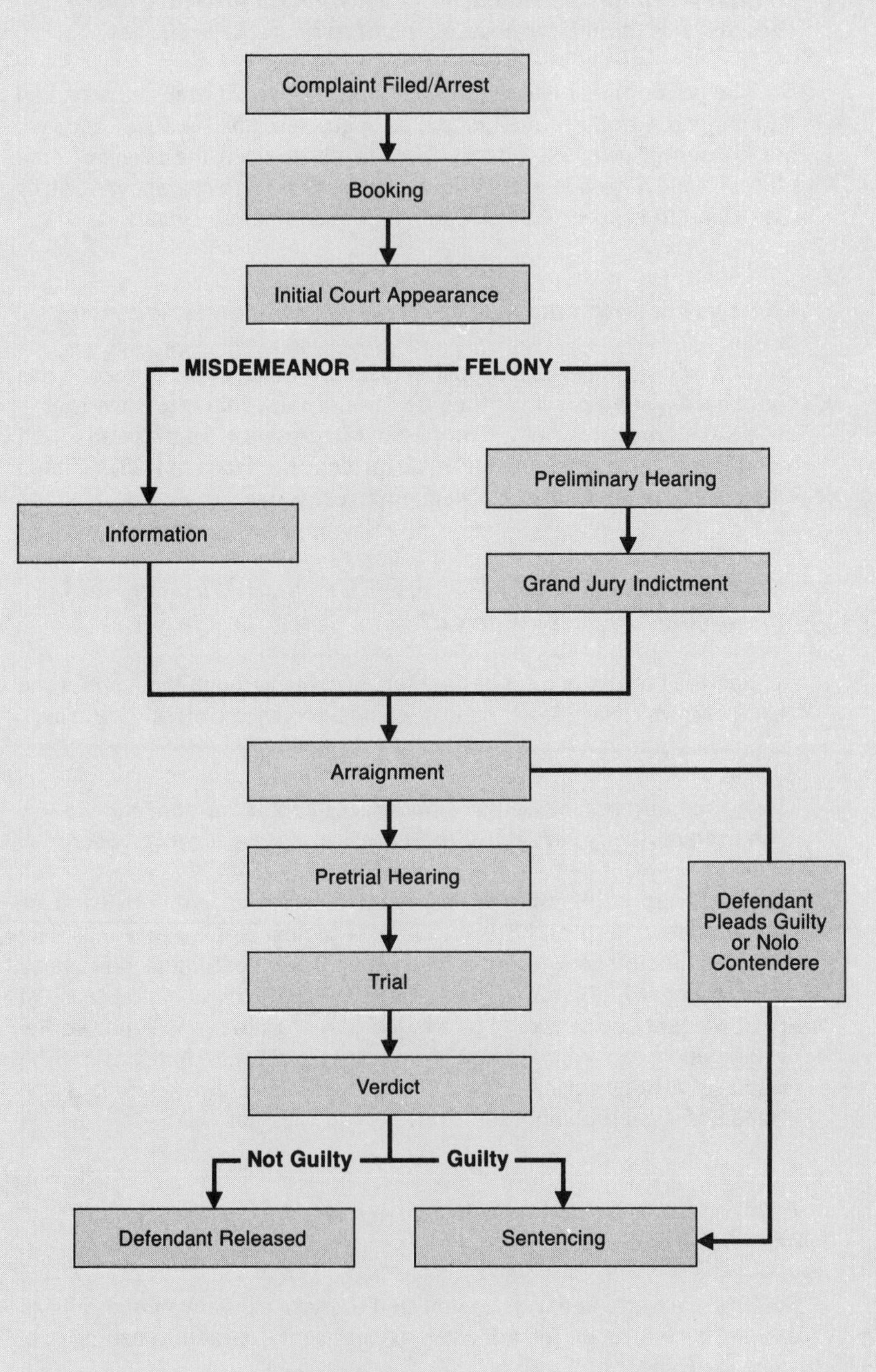
Steps of a Criminal Case
Complaint Filed/Arrest
Booking
Initial Court Appearance
MISDEMEANOR
FELONY
Preliminary Hearing
Information
Grand Jury Indictment
Arraignment
Pretrial Hearing
Defendant Pleads Guilty or Nolo Contendere
Trial
Verdict
Not Guilty
Guilty
Defendant Released
Sentencing

Before a person accused of a crime can be brought to trial, certain steps must be taken to establish that a crime has been committed and that there is reason to believe the accused person committed it. Although the sequence of steps may vary from state to state, most follow this outline:

Complaint and Arrest—After the police investigate a crime, the prosecuting attorney files a written statement (called a *complaint)* with the court, describing the crime and naming the suspect; if a judge decides there is sufficient evidence, he issues an arrest warrant. Upon arrest, the suspect is informed of his rights. (If a suspect is arrested at the scene of a crime, the complaint is filed afterwards.)

Booking—At the police station, the suspect is searched, photographed, fingerprinted, allowed to contact a lawyer, and given a receipt for any personal property that is impounded. For a misdemeanor, the suspect is usually released and assigned a date to appear in court. For a felony, he is usually jailed.

Initial Court Appearance—At this hearing, the judge informs the suspect of the charges and his rights as a defendant. He also decides if the suspect should be released on bail or kept in custody. If charged with a misdemeanor, the suspect can enter a plea at this time; if accused of a felony, he cannot. The suspect's next court date is set.

Information—In this document, filed by the prosecuting attorney, the suspect is formally charged with committing a misdemeanor.

Preliminary Hearing—Some states use this hearing when a suspect is accused of a felony or arrested without a warrant for a misdemeanor. If the judge decides there is sufficient evidence to proceed, he forwards the case to a grand jury; if not, he releases the suspect.

Grand Jury—At these proceedings, the grand jury decides if there is sufficient evidence for the accused to stand trial. If it votes yes, an indictment (a court order) is issued requiring the suspect to stand trial; if not, the suspect is released.

Arraignment—At this hearing, the judge reads the charges to the accused, who is again advised of his rights. The accused then enters his plea. If he pleads not guilty, a date is set for the trial. If he pleads guilty or is allowed to plead nolo contendere (no contest), he waives his right to a trial, and a date is set for sentencing.

Pretrial Hearing—The judge meets with the prosecuting and defense attorneys and reviews the issues of the case.

Trial—The defendant stands trial before a jury or, if he waives that right, before a judge.

Verdict—The judge or jury decides whether the defendant is guilty or not guilty. If the verdict is not guilty, the defendant is released.

Sentencing—The judge tells the defendant what his punishment will be. He may order him to pay a fine or serve a jail term, or he may have him released under the supervision of a probation officer.

Rights of the Accused

Celeste received a phone call from her husband, saying that he had been arrested. What should she do?

If her husband hasn't already contacted a lawyer, Celeste should do so as soon as possible. The lawyer can represent and advise her husband during police questioning and at the bail hearing. If the bail hearing has already been held, Celeste should find out where she can post bail to have her husband released.

Can someone who is not a police officer make an arrest?

In most states, a private citizen can arrest someone without a warrant, but only if he is ordered to do so by the police or if someone has committed a serious crime in his presence. (Some states, such as Connecticut and Oregon, permit citizens' arrests for minor theft, such as shoplifting.) Unlike a police officer, however, a citizen does not have the right to arrest someone simply because he suspects the person has committed a crime. In fact, if a citizen arrests someone who, it turns out, did not commit a crime, the citizen can be sued for false arrest.

When a suspect is told he has the right to remain silent, does this mean he also has the right to refuse to sign any statements?

Yes. A suspect cannot be required to sign a statement or confession after he has claimed his right to remain silent. A statement signed under these circumstances is inadmissible as evidence in court.

Trisha was arrested and held overnight in jail because the police mistook her for someone else. Can she sue for the emotional trauma and embarrassment this caused her?

Probably not. The police cannot be held responsible for a false arrest based on mistaken identity. As long as the police released Trisha once they realized that they had made an error, she has no grounds to sue them. However, if Trisha could prove that the police arrested her even though they knew she was not the person they were looking for, she could sue for both emotional trauma and damage to her reputation. In any case, the false arrest will not give Trisha a criminal record.

Ralph wanted a ticket to the World Series so desperately that he paid a scalper $200 for one. When Ralph handed over the money,

the man identified himself as a police officer and told Ralph he was under arrest. Was Ralph the victim of police entrapment?

No. Since Ralph had decided to buy a ticket from a scalper before he approached the police officer, his intent to commit a crime makes him a perpetrator rather than a victim. Ralph would have been the victim of entrapment only if the police officer had tricked Ralph into buying a ticket that he had no intention of buying otherwise.

Willie committed a crime in one state and then fled to another state. Can the police still arrest him?

Possibly. Although a police officer cannot make an arrest outside the geographical area of his authority, he is still able to make a citizen's arrest. If a police officer saw Willie commit a serious crime, he is within his rights as a private citizen to pursue Willie and arrest him.

My lawyer says he is going to ask the judge for a writ of* habeas corpus *because I am being held in jail without bail. What is he talking about?

Habeas corpus literally means "you have the body." The writ is a court order directing the officials holding you in custody to bring you to court and justify your being held. The court then determines whether you are being held legally or whether you should be released.

A *habeas corpus* writ is often used in criminal cases when the prisoner claims that his constitutional rights have been violated. But it can also be used in civil cases.

Posting Bail

Is bail the same as bond?

Yes. Both terms refer to the sum of money given to a court to release a person who has been arrested and to help ensure that he appears at his trial. When the accused shows up for the trial, the bail money is returned; if the accused does not, the bond is forfeited.

Can I use my credit card to post bail?

It depends on where you live. In most states, bail must be posted by giving the court the full amount of the bond in cash or by having a bail bondsman pay the amount required. However, courts in some states, such as New York and Oregon, permit an accused person to use a credit card to post bail in some cases.

Nelson wants to post bail, but he doesn't have enough money. What can he do?

He can ask a bail bondsman to post bail for him. For a nonrefundable fee—about 10 percent of the bail—the bondsman will pay the amount required by the court to secure Nelson's release. Nelson will probably have to provide collateral, or written guarantees by relatives or friends that they will pay the bondsman if Nelson fails to appear for his trial. If the bondsman thinks Nelson is likely to flee, he may refuse to post the bail. If Nelson skips bail, the bondsman may track him down and bring him back to court. If the bondsman brings him to the proper authorities in a reasonable amount of time, the court may refund his money.

What factors does a judge consider when setting bail?

Since the law does not specify a fixed amount of bail for any particular crime, a judge must use his own discretion in each individual case. He must set an amount that is high enough to deter the suspect from fleeing to avoid trial, but not so high that it violates the U.S. Constitution's prohibition against excessive bail. In making his decision, the judge considers several factors, such as the evidence against the suspect, his financial resources, his reputation within the community, his employment record, and his health.

The judge told Nat that he would be released on his own recognizance. What does that mean?

Nat will be allowed to go free, without posting bail, if he agrees in writing to appear in court on the date of his trial.

Marshall, who has a long criminal record, was denied bail after his last arrest. Can the judge do that?

Yes. In deciding whether to allow bail, a judge has the right to consider a person's past record as well as the strength of the evidence against him in the case that is currently before the court. The judge can deny Marshall bail if (1) he decides that Marshall is more likely to flee than face trial,

(2) Marshall's record indicates that his release might threaten the safety of the members of the community, or (3) Marshall is charged with a crime punishable by death or—if his state has no death penalty—with first-degree murder or any other crime punishable by life imprisonment.

Juvenile Offenders

For responsibility of parents, see "Children in Trouble" in Chapter 2, *Marriage and Family*.

My 15-year-old daughter has been arrested and charged with shoplifting. What will happen to her?

Since your daughter is too young to be treated as an adult by the legal system, her case will be referred to juvenile court. (For most states, 18 is the age at which the law considers a child to be an adult; in other states the age of adulthood is 21.) Officials at the juvenile court will review the charges and your daughter's record to determine whether she should be brought before a juvenile court judge.

If a hearing is ordered, your daughter will probably be released in your custody until the case goes to court. If, at the hearing, the judge finds your daughter guilty of shoplifting, he may put her on probation and allow her to stay at home, assign her to a foster home, or place her in a reform school. The judge will choose whichever option he considers is in your daughter's best interest.

Andy, a 16-year-old boy, stole a car and then wrecked it while he was fleeing from the police. What will happen to him?

If Andy is prosecuted and found guilty of car theft, the juvenile court judge may put him on probation and allow him to stay at home; assign him to a foster home; or place him in a reform school. In addition, Andy may be charged with reckless driving and be prosecuted in traffic court. If so, he will not be entitled to any special treatment because of his age. He may be fined and ordered to participate in a driver safety course. Andy may also find himself in civil court if the owner of the stolen car or anyone injured during the accident sues for damages.

Some of Annabel's older friends were arrested for buying drugs. Even though Annabel wasn't with her friends when they were picked up, she has been charged with "associations contrary to a child's welfare." What does that mean?

It means that by associating with people who were a bad influence on her, Annabel committed a status offense—an act of noncriminal misbehavior.

If the charges are upheld in juvenile court, the judge may allow Annabel to remain at home as long as she does not socialize with these particular friends. The judge could also temporarily assign Annabel to a group home or another setting that he thinks appropriate.

Some neighborhood boys smashed Melinda's mailbox. Can Melinda get them to pay for the damage?

Yes. Melinda should complain to the police so that the matter can be referred to juvenile court. If the boys are found guilty, the court may order them to pay for repairing or replacing the mailbox. The court may also require the boys to do some form of community service.

Ginger's 14-year-old son is too difficult for her to handle. Can the juvenile court provide Ginger with any assistance?

Yes. Ginger can file a complaint against her son, stating that he is a troublemaker and beyond parental control. If the juvenile court agrees, it can provide counseling for Ginger's son or assign a social worker or probation officer to work with the family. If necessary, the court could place Ginger's son in a group home, a foster home, or a reform school until his behavior improves.

Carolyn was picked up for truancy. She is 13 years old. Can she be sentenced for not attending school?

Yes. Most states require children to attend school from age 7 through 15. In Maine children must attend school until they are 16 years old. If Carolyn is prosecuted, the judge has a wide variety of options available to him, ranging from placing the child under her parents' supervision to sending her to reform school. The judge will take whatever steps he considers necessary to make sure Carolyn attends school.

Seymour's parents were notified by the principal of his school that Seymour was being referred to juvenile court. Is this legal?

Yes. Although most juvenile court referrals are made by the police, referrals for status offenses—acts of noncriminal misbehavior, such as truancy and running away from home—are usually made by others. Teachers, principals, and the board of education itself all have the authority to refer a child to juvenile court.

Does a child need a lawyer when he appears in juvenile court?

Yes. Whenever a child is charged with an offense that would be a crime if it were committed by an adult, the child has the right to be represented by a lawyer. If the child's parents cannot afford a lawyer, the court must appoint one for the child. Children charged with status offenses—acts of noncriminal misbehavior, such as truancy or running away from home—also have the right to legal representation. In cases involving a status offense, however, the child may be represented by a guardian *ad litem*—a guardian appointed solely for the purpose of the hearing—who does not have to be a lawyer. Parents may serve as guardians *ad litem* unless they themselves are bringing the complaint against the child, as might be the case with a child who is an uncontrollable troublemaker.

Jackson, who is 17, has been accused of robbery. The police are talking about charging him in adult court. Can they do this?

Yes. Every state has the right to try juvenile offenders in adult court, but this action is usually not taken unless the young person has committed so many offenses that the juvenile court feels it can no longer deal with him effectively. If this is the case with Jackson, juvenile officials will file a court petition to allow him to be prosecuted as an adult and request a hearing to determine if this step is appropriate. In making his decision, the judge will consider Jackson's record of offenses. He will also consider whether the juvenile court has any facilities or programs that could help Jackson. If Jackson is tried as an adult, he will be entitled to the full range of adult rights and subject to adult penalties.

Mary Ann's social worker wants to treat her case as unofficial and put her on probation. What does this mean?

When a child is arrested for a relatively minor offense, such as disturbing the peace, and has had no previous arrests, court officials may recommend that the child be placed under unofficial supervision instead of having a formal court hearing. Under this arrangement, a social worker will work with the child to try to prevent him from committing any offenses in the future. However, unofficial supervision is voluntary, and the child can refuse to participate.

Brent is scheduled to attend an adjudication hearing next month. Is that the same as a trial?

Yes. The purpose of an adjudication hearing is to determine whether the charges made against a juvenile are true. At the hearing, Brent's lawyer will present evidence and witnesses on Brent's behalf and cross-examine witnesses who testify against Brent. If the judge rules that the allegations are true, he may order that a social worker or probation officer complete a predisposition investigation before he determines Brent's appropriate punishment and rehabilitation.

What is a predisposition investigation?

An investigation ordered by a juvenile court judge of a child's background and the situation that caused the child to be brought to court. The investigation is usually conducted by a social worker or probation officer to try to understand the causes of the child's delinquent behavior.

The investigator will generally interview not only the juvenile offender himself, but his family and teachers and any other concerned adults, as well as the victim of the juvenile's offense. The investigator will look still further into the child's background by examining his school and medical records and any previous court records. The investigator will then report his findings to the juvenile court and make recommendations for the child's placement and treatment.

Chester was arrested for stealing hubcaps from a car. The lawyer his father hired to defend him wants the young man to deny the charge, but the father thinks Chester ought to admit his guilt. Doesn't Chester's father get to decide what's best for his son, since he's paying the lawyer?

No. A lawyer has an ethical duty to serve the best interests of his client regardless of who is paying his fee. If the lawyer does otherwise, he is guilty of malpractice. If Chester's lawyer thinks it is in the boy's best interests to deny his guilt, he cannot allow himself to be swayed by the boy's father. The father's best alternative would be to try to persuade his son to confess his crime.

Molly has been charged with stealing money from the church poor box. Her mother and stepfather are afraid that the press will try to sensationalize the case. Will reporters be allowed in the courtroom during Molly's hearing?

No. To protect children from harmful publicity, juvenile court proceedings are held in private, and all facts relating to such cases are confidential. Molly's hearing will be closed to the public, and only those directly involved with the case will be allowed to attend.

After ruling that my brother was guilty of disturbing the peace, the judge ordered him to stay within a two-mile radius of home and be in the house by 8:00 P.M. every night. Does the judge have the authority to do this?

Yes. Once a judge finds a juvenile offender guilty, he has the authority to establish whatever punishment he deems most appropriate. This includes placing curfews and other limitations on the child's activities. If your brother disobeys the judge's ruling, the judge could order that your brother be removed from your parents' custody and placed in a more restrictive setting, such as a group home or reform school.

The judge ordered my husband and me to attend counseling sessions with our son. Will we have to pay for these sessions?

Short-term counseling with court personnel, such as social workers, probation officers, and court psychologists, is usually provided free of charge. If your son receives private counseling, however, you will probably have to bear that expense yourself. If you cannot afford the full fee, your son's probation officer can direct you to counseling agencies with adjustable rates.

Do juvenile court judges always punish children by sending them to reform school?

No. A judge has many options available to him when dealing with a juvenile offender. He could (1) place the child under the supervision of his parents, (2) place the child with a relative, another family, or a foster home, (3) order the child to devote a certain number of hours to community service, (4) order the child to reimburse his victim for any harm he has done, (5) send the child to a hospital or a group home, or (6) place the child in a reform school or other correctional facility.

Stacy ran away from home for the third time, and was found by the police a week later. The juvenile authorities plan to send Stacy to reform school over her parents' objections. Can they do that?

Yes. By running away from home, Stacy was guilty of a status offense—misbehavior that is not a crime but is unacceptable to society nonetheless. When a child commits a status offense, such as repeatedly refusing to obey his parents or teachers, the authorities have the right to intervene and, if necessary, assume custody of the child. Since Stacy has repeatedly run away from home, the court will be even more likely to remove her from the custody of her parents and send her to a foster home or reform school.

Juvenile Offenders

After playing hooky on several occasions, Thornton was picked up for truancy and sent to a reform school with young people who had committed much more serious crimes. Can his parents do anything about this?

Probably not. If Thornton has been placed under the control of the juvenile court, only a judge has the authority to decide where Thornton will live. Although some juvenile courts have separate facilities for different types of offenders, most do not. Consequently, children with behavior problems are often placed with those who have committed serious crimes. If Thornton's parents feel they can control him, they may be able to persuade the judge to release him to their custody. The judge might also allow Thornton to move to a private group home for troubled children.

What is the essential difference between a reform school and a detention center?

A reform school is a correctional facility—staffed by teachers, medical personnel, and guidance counselors—where juvenile offenders live and attend school. Reform schools are usually located in rural areas. Some are secure facilities with locked doors and gates, while others permit their residents more freedom. A detention center is similar to an adult jail. If a juvenile is uncontrollable or if he tries to escape from a reform school, he might be transferred to a detention center. A juvenile might also be sent to a detention center if he commits an offense after being released from reform school.

My son confessed to the judge that he stole a camera. Does this mean that now he'll have a criminal record?

No. Since juvenile court proceedings are considered civil, not criminal, children do not plead guilty to offenses. Instead, they admit that the charges made against them are true. In addition, juvenile records are sealed and confidential, and cannot be released to the public without a court order. These regulations are intended to prevent children like your son from being stigmatized by a criminal record for the rest of their lives.

Rachel was arrested for drug possession when she was 14. If she's arrested again, can her juvenile record be used against her?

It depends on how old she is when she's arrested for the second time. If Rachel is still a juvenile, the judge will be allowed to take her past offense

How the Law Protects Juvenile Offenders

Juveniles accused of breaking the law are granted some special rights intended to protect them because of their age. If a juvenile is charged with a crime punishable by a term in a reform school or juvenile detention facility, he is assured the right to:

- Remain silent, and not incriminate himself.
- Be placed in quarters separate from adult offenders while being held in custody.
- Be notified before a hearing of the charges against him.
- Be released to his parents or guardians after signing a written promise to appear at his trial (unless the child is likely to run away and not come back to court or unless he is dangerous or may himself be in danger if sent back home).
- Be tried at proceedings that are closed to the public.
- Have a record of the proceedings made, in case one is needed for a future appeal.
- Be represented by a lawyer.
- Have a lawyer appointed by the court if he cannot afford one.
- Confront his accusers.
- Have his lawyer cross-examine witnesses.

into account when determining her sentence. Once Rachel reaches adult age (18 or 21 years old), her juvenile offenses cannot be used against her.

Manny is such a troublemaker at school that the principal wants to expel him. Can the principal check the juvenile court's records for previous offenses that will help support his case?

No. If Manny's case was tried in juvenile court, the only people who have access to his record are Manny's parents, the police, the judge, the prosecuting attorney, Manny's attorney, and his social worker. Once Manny's case was closed, his record was sealed and no one can have access to it without an order from a judge.

When Burt was a kid he got into trouble with the law and spent some time in reform school. Does he have to report this when he applies for a job?

No. Burt's juvenile record is confidential. He is not required to report his juvenile offenses to prospective employers, and they will not be allowed access to his records.

Witnessing a Crime

For information on testifying, see "Being a Witness" in Chapter 18, *Going to Court.*

Am I required by law to come to the aid of a crime victim?

It depends on where you live. In Wisconsin, the law specifically requires anyone who witnesses a crime to assist the victim if it is safe to do so. Generally, however, you would not have to help anyone unless (1) you yourself had caused his predicament, for example, if you injured another driver in a car accident, or (2) you had a special relationship with the victim, for example, if the victim were your spouse or child.

A friend of mine gets paid "off the books." Am I obligated to report him to the Internal Revenue Service?

No. You have no legal duty to report someone else's tax evasion to the IRS. However, if you deliberately help your friend conceal such a crime, you will be committing a felony.

Mortie told Alfred that he was going to hold up Anderson's liquor store on Friday night. Will Alfred be breaking the law if he doesn't report Mortie's plan?

No. Alfred is not legally required to report this information to the police. However, if he does, he may be able to help prevent the crime.

If Wilson reports a crime, will it be necessary for him to give his name to the police?

No. Wilson can make an anonymous call to the police. However, if Wilson does identify himself, he will make it much easier for the police to apprehend and prosecute the criminal, particularly if Wilson is the only person who witnessed the crime.

Bonnie saw a man breaking into her neighbor's house and reported the crime to the police. Will Bonnie have to get involved any further?

Possibly. The police may visit Bonnie at home to question her about what she saw, and may ask her to go to the police station to look through mug shots of known criminals. If the police arrest a suspect, Bonnie may be asked to identify the criminal in a lineup. If the suspect is tried, Bonnie may be subpoenaed to testify in court.

While Marcia was walking home one night, she saw a knife fight between two neighborhood gangs. After the police broke up the fight, they asked Marcia for her name and address. Can Marcia be required to testify as a witness?

Yes. Either a defense lawyer or a prosecuting attorney can have Marcia served with a subpoena, a court order requiring her to testify. If Marcia ignores the subpoena or refuses to testify, she could be charged with contempt of court.

My neighbor's six-year-old son, Toby, is the only person who saw an intruder leave Pauline's house after it was burglarized. My neighbor is worried that her son may be called as a witness. Can young children like Toby be forced to testify?

Sometimes. Under a certain age—10 years old in many states—children are assumed by the law to be incompetent to testify. However, a lawyer may use a young child as a witness if he can show beforehand that the child is mature enough to testify.

In order to determine whether a child is competent to testify, the lawyer or judge must question the child in court to demonstrate (1) that the child knows the difference between the truth and a lie; (2) that he understands that he must tell the truth after taking an oath; (3) that his vision and hearing are reliable; and (4) that he knows how to describe what he sees and hears. If Toby passes these tests, he can be a witness even though he is only six years old.

If I sign a sworn statement about a crime I witnessed and some of the information I provided turns out to be incorrect, will I be prosecuted?

No. If you mistakenly give the police inaccurate information, you will not be charged with a crime. However, if you intentionally give false information in a sworn statement, you can be charged with false swearing, a form of perjury punishable by a fine or a short term in jail.

When Ryan saw an elderly woman being beaten by a man, he ran over and tackled her assailant. The man's head hit the sidewalk. Can Ryan be held responsible for the man's injuries?

Probably not. The law permits a person to use force to protect himself or someone else from death or serious injury. Since the woman Ryan assisted was in danger of being seriously injured, Ryan was justified in using force against her attacker.

Witnessing a Crime

Hilary witnessed an assault and reported it. The police arrested a suspect, but he was released on bail. Will the police provide Hilary with protection?

If the police suspect that the person accused of the assault may try to harm Hilary to keep her from testifying at his trial, they will probably offer her protection. But Hilary should not expect to be assigned a personal bodyguard or put under 24-hour surveillance. More likely, the police will warn the assailant to stay away from Hilary and will patrol her home more frequently. If the assailant harasses Hilary while he is free on bail, the judge may revoke bail and order him held in custody until the trial.

A man who identified himself as an FBI agent called Lizzie and asked her several questions about her nephew. Was Lizzie required to answer?

No. In fact, Lizzie should have refused to answer any questions over the telephone. When FBI agents question someone about a suspect, they are generally required to appear in person and show proper identification. The man who called Lizzie may not have been an FBI agent.

CHAPTER
18

Going to Court

Is there a difference between the kinds of cases heard in a federal court and those heard in a state court?

Yes. Federal courts hear cases where any of the following apply: (1) the U. S. government is a defendant or plaintiff; (2) a constitutional law is involved; (3) there is a dispute of more than $10,000 between two states, between a state and citizens of another state, or between citizens of different states; (4) a person is accused of a federal crime, such as tampering with the U. S. mail; (5) maritime affairs (laws of the sea) are involved; or (6) the dispute involves foreign affairs. The U. S. Constitution established the Supreme Court and gave Congress the power to establish other federal courts.

State courts are established by each individual state and deal with disputes between residents of that state or cases that involve state or local law. Examples of the types of cases heard in state courts are divorces and landlord-tenant problems.

I just lost my case in the state supreme court. Can I appeal the decision to the U.S. Supreme Court?

It depends on the nature of your case. The U. S. Supreme Court does not have the authority to hear cases that involve state law unless a federal or constitutional law is also involved or the dispute is between citizens of different states or between a state and a citizen of another state.

How is it decided which court has jurisdiction over my case?

The decision on where your case is heard is based on a number of factors, including whether it involves a criminal or a civil matter, the amount of money or property in dispute, and the county and state you live in. State courts have jurisdiction over the majority of cases involving individuals.

Can a person be put on trial for the same crime in both federal and state courts?

Yes. If a person is accused of something that is a crime under both state and federal law, he can be tried in both a state and a federal court. The state and federal governments are separate entities, and a conviction or acquittal in one court does not prevent a subsequent prosecution in the other. The same holds true for the punishment imposed. However, the sentence in one court might be taken into consideration in fixing the punishment in the other court—for example, one sentence might be suspended. Being prosecuted for violating the laws of two different governments (federal and state) does not result in double jeopardy (being tried twice for the same crime), which is forbidden by the Fifth Amendment to the U. S. Constitution. The prohibition of double jeopardy is aimed solely at preventing prosecutors from bringing someone to trial again in the same court system for the same offense.

Roger was tried and found guilty of knocking Jaclyn down from behind and stealing her purse and watch. Can Jaclyn also sue him for her injuries and stolen property?

Yes. Two distinct legal matters are involved. First, pushing Jaclyn down and robbing her are criminal offenses, and the state has the duty to prosecute Roger in a criminal trial. Second, Jaclyn has the right to bring a civil lawsuit against Roger for her stolen property, for the medical bills she had to pay to take care of the injuries he caused, and for any pain she suffered. Although the two cases arise from the same incident, they are different under the law and do not put Roger in the position of being tried twice for the same crime, which is forbidden by the U. S. Constitution.

Can I be sued for something I did in another state?

Yes. If a person or business in another state wishes to sue you, the court in the other state will determine where the lawsuit should be heard. Generally, the state where the dispute first arose is the proper place for the lawsuit to be filed. Sometimes the court chooses the state in which the greatest number of people involved in the case live. In other cases, the place where a lawsuit is heard may have been agreed upon in advance. For example, a contract may declare which court will hear a lawsuit in the event that the contract is broken.

Doesn't everyone have the right to a trial by jury in all cases?

No. It depends on whether the case comes under federal or state jurisdiction and whether the case is criminal or civil. In all federal criminal cases, the Sixth Amendment to the U. S. Constitution states: "the accused shall enjoy the right to a speedy and public trial, by an impartial jury." In federal civil cases, the Seventh Amendment states: "Where the value in controversy shall exceed twenty dollars, the right of trial by jury shall be preserved."

As a practical matter, however, the majority of federal cases involving lesser crimes and small amounts of money are resolved before they reach a jury trial. Settling a case before it comes to trial can be attractive to both sides, as well as to the court, because crowded court calendars can mean

Our Court Systems

The United States has two court systems, federal and state. They are similarly structured, with one supreme court at the top and a number of courts on the levels below. For example, beneath the U. S. Supreme Court there are a dozen appeals courts, and beneath them about 90 district courts. The arrows in the charts show how cases are appealed from lower to higher courts.

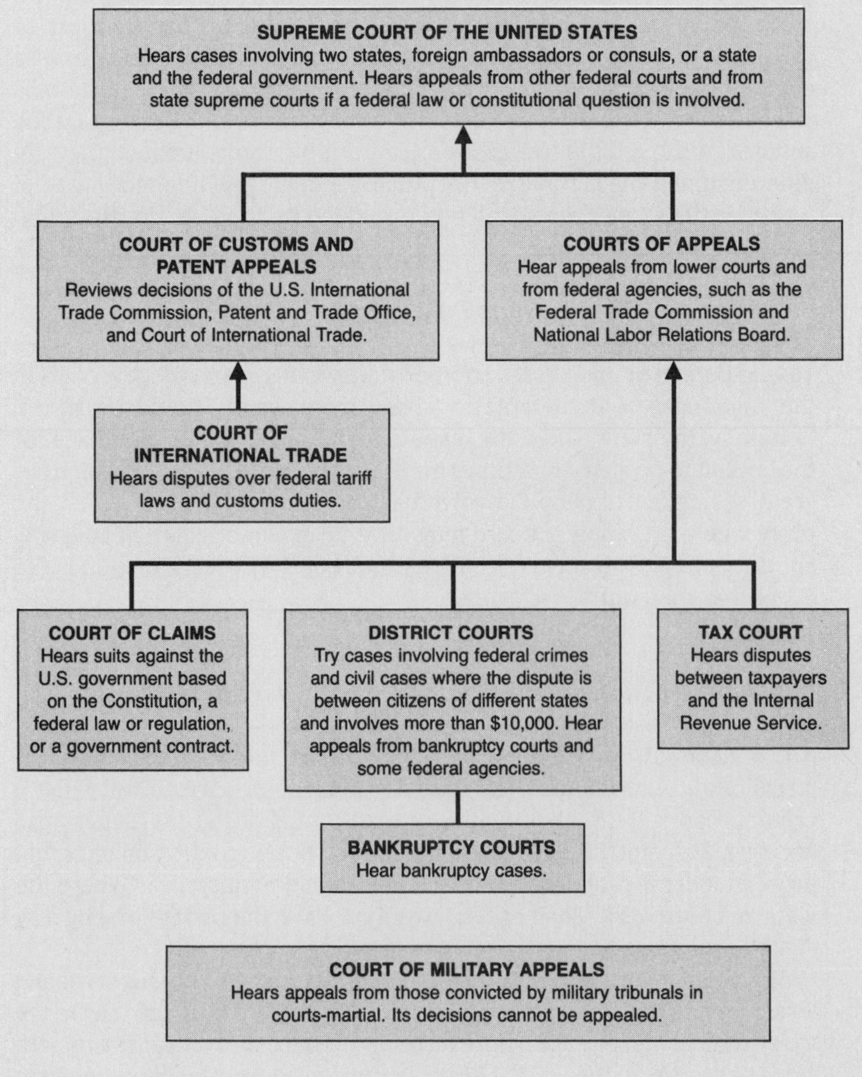

FEDERAL COURTS
SUPREME COURT OF THE UNITED STATES
Hears cases involving two states, foreign ambassadors or consuls, or a state and the federal government. Hears appeals from other federal courts and from state supreme courts if a federal law or constitutional question is involved.
COURT OF CUSTOMS AND PATENT APPEALS
Reviews decisions of the U.S. International Trade Commission, Patent and Trade Office, and Court of International Trade.
COURTS OF APPEALS
Hear appeals from lower courts and from federal agencies, such as the Federal Trade Commission and National Labor Relations Board.
COURT OF INTERNATIONAL TRADE
Hears disputes over federal tariff laws and customs duties.
COURT OF CLAIMS
Hears suits against the U.S. government based on the Constitution, a federal law or regulation, or a government contract.
DISTRICT COURTS
Try cases involving federal crimes and civil cases where the dispute is between citizens of different states and involves more than $10,000. Hear appeals from bankruptcy courts and some federal agencies.
TAX COURT
Hears disputes between taxpayers and the Internal Revenue Service.
BANKRUPTCY COURTS
Hear bankruptcy cases.
COURT OF MILITARY APPEALS
Hears appeals from those convicted by military tribunals in courts-martial. Its decisions cannot be appealed.

GOING TO COURT

STATE COURTS

SUPREME COURT
Hears appeals from lower courts. Cases involving a federal statute or constitutional law can be appealed to the U.S. Supreme Court.

↑

APPELLATE COURTS
(Some states)
Review appeals from lower courts.

↑

TRIAL COURTS
Hear criminal and civil cases and may hear appeals from special courts. (Also called court of common pleas, or circuit, county, district, or superior court.)

↑

LOCAL COURTS
Hear cases involving lesser criminal charges, such as creating a nuisance or violating a housing code, and claims for small sums of money. Names and functions of these courts vary from state to state.

TRAFFIC COURTS
Hear cases involving minor traffic violations.

POLICE COURTS
Hear cases involving violations of local ordinances.

MAGISTRATE'S COURTS
Hear cases involving traffic violations and other minor offenses.

JUSTICE (JUSTICE OF THE PEACE) COURTS
Similar to magistrate's courts.

MUNICIPAL (CITY) COURTS
Hear minor criminal cases and lawsuits for small amounts.

SPECIAL COURTS
Hear particular types of cases.

PROBATE (SURROGATE) COURTS
Hear cases involving wills, estates, guardians, conservators, incompetency, and adoption.

JUVENILE (FAMILY) COURTS
Hear cases involving paternity, child support, and delinquent, neglected, or abused children.

SMALL CLAIMS COURTS
Hear demands for money up to a set dollar limit. (May be a separate court or part of another state or local court.)

CRIMINAL COURTS
(Some states)
Hear minor criminal cases.

COURTS OF CLAIMS
(Some states)
Hear claims against the state.

delays of months or years before a case is heard, and to this is added the time and expense needed to conduct the jury trial itself.

As for state cases, both criminal and civil, state constitutions and laws outline which cases must be heard before a jury. The general rule for criminal cases is that a jury trial is required for any offense for which the punishment is six months' imprisonment or more.

Is a trial by jury generally better than a trial by a judge?

It depends on many factors: whether the case is civil or criminal, whether you are the plaintiff or defendant, how much money is at stake, and how complex the issues are. Many lawyers believe that juries award higher verdicts in injury cases. The defendant in a criminal case usually wants a jury because more people have to agree on guilt.

However, if you are paying your lawyer on an hourly basis, a jury trial will cost you more because it will take more time and create more work for your lawyer. Finally, because of crowded court schedules, it can take longer for a case to come before a jury than before a judge.

Why will it take so long for my case to come to trial?

Several factors could account for the delay, including the time needed by lawyers for both sides to prepare their cases, interview witnesses, and assemble the evidence they need. A crowded court calendar can also delay the start of your trial.

Does my right to have a lawyer at a trial apply to all situations?

Yes, except for small claims court, where lawyers are not permitted in some states. However, you do not have the right to a free court-appointed lawyer unless you cannot afford to hire a lawyer and you face the possibility of imprisonment if you are convicted.

The case against Frank was dismissed because the prosecuting attorney waited too long to bring it to trial. Is there a time limit for bringing a criminal case to court?

The Sixth Amendment guarantees criminal defendants the right to a speedy trial. Although laws limit the amount of time a prosecutor has to bring a case to trial, a defendant will not necessarily be released if the deadline is not met. In Virginia, the prosecutor has either five or nine months to go to trial, depending on whether the defendant is being held in custody, but this deadline may be extended if there are adequate reasons for a delay. For example, a key witness may have been too ill to testify; the defendant may have asked for a continuance; or the defendant's mental condition may have required a delay until he was able to stand trial. Usually, judges decide on a case-by-case basis whether the right to a speedy trial has been violated.

Pretrial Procedures

Sydney received a summons, and his wife was served with a subpoena. What is the difference?

A *summons* is a legal notice given to a person that legal action has been started against him. It states that the person is now a defendant and directs him to file an answer with the court by a specified date. Attached to the summons is a complaint, which details the charges against the defendant. A summons may be prepared by the plaintiff's attorney or an officer of the court. A person receiving a summons would not be breaking the law if he did not appear in court, but his absence would most likely result in the plaintiff's winning the lawsuit against him.

A *subpoena* is a court order directing a person either to appear in court to testify or to produce a document that is relevant to a case. A person receiving a subpoena must appear in court or face charges of contempt of court for ignoring the subpoena.

I received a summons that said I had to file my answer to the lawsuit by a date that was a week before I received the summons. Does this mean I've lost the case already?

No. You must be given adequate notice of the lawsuit and an opportunity to be heard. If the sheriff or other court official has not delivered the summons to you in time for you to meet the court deadline, the court cannot rule that you've lost the case by default. In fact, your lawyer can ask the court to dismiss the lawsuit, since the summons was served on you after the date you were meant to respond.

Darren is suing Blaine. Will Darren automatically lose his case if Blaine never receives a summons?

No. It is possible that a summons was legally served upon Blaine without her having personally received it. For example, the summons might have been left with a family member or at Blaine's place of business. If no one knew where Blaine was, a copy of the summons might have been mailed to her last known address or published in a newspaper. As long as a summons is delivered according to one of the methods described in the state's laws, a plaintiff can pursue his case—even if the defendant never receives the actual piece of paper the official summons is written on.

Is a plaintiff the same as a petitioner?

Almost. The terms *plaintiff* and *petitioner* both refer to a person who initiates some type of legal action or proceeding. *Plaintiff* usually refers to the person who sues in a civil lawsuit or the prosecutor in a criminal case. A *petitioner* is someone who is asking the court, an administrative agency, or a legislative body for a certain action, such as approval to sell property in a deceased person's estate or to have a guardian appointed.

Is a respondent the same as a defendant?

Not necessarily, although both terms are used to describe the person against whom a legal action is brought. If a plaintiff starts a lawsuit or a

Steps in a Civil Case

If you are involved in a legal dispute that cannot be settled out of court, you will probably end up in a lawsuit. A typical civil case usually follows the steps set out below (for the steps in a criminal case, see "Rights of the Accused" in Chapter 17, *Victims and Crimes*):

1. *A complaint* is filed with the clerk of the court. In this document, the plaintiff (the one doing the suing) states his version of the situation and demands *damages*—the amount of money he seeks from the defendant (the one being sued) for his loss or injury.
2. *A summons* is issued by the clerk of the court and is delivered with a copy of the complaint to the defendant, directing him to respond to the charges. If the defendant doesn't respond by the date shown on the summons, the plaintiff may win his case by default.
3. *An answer* to the summons is filed by the defendant, and a copy of it is sent to the plaintiff. The answer is a document in which the defendant presents his version of the case, admitting or denying the charges made in the complaint.
4. *A trial date* is set by the court.
5. *Discovery procedures* may be used to uncover evidence that will

criminal trial, the accused person is called the defendant. If a petitioner initiates some other legal action, his opponent is called the respondent.

Maria has no money for a defense lawyer. How does she ask for a court-appointed attorney?

If her case is a civil lawsuit, the court will not provide Maria with a lawyer; she will have to find and pay for her own. If Maria is a defendant in a criminal case, she should ask for a court-appointed attorney after being arrested or at her initial court hearing. She will have to fill out a financial statement that proves her inability to pay for an attorney.

Timothy was charged with trespassing, but there was no grand jury proceeding before the charges were filed. Doesn't he have the right to have a grand jury hear his case first?

No. Although charges for serious crimes in federal court must be made through grand jury indictments, state courts are not required to follow this procedure. Many states provide for grand juries only in cases involving serious crimes, such as murder, rape, and robbery, but not for such lesser offenses as trespassing.

strengthen the case when it comes to court. Discovery includes depositions (questioning of witnesses and others under oath) and interrogatories (written questions that the defendant or plaintiff must answer in writing under oath).

6. *Pretrial motions,* or requests, may be filed. For example, the defendant may ask that the lawsuit be dismissed, or the plaintiff may amend his complaint, or either side may request a change of venue (ask that the trial be held in a different place).

7. *A pretrial conference* may be called by the judge to discuss the issues in the case with the opposing lawyers. This helps avoid surprises and delays once the trial starts, and sometimes leads to an out-of-court settlement.

8. *The jury is selected* (if one is being used), and the trial begins.

9. *Opening statements* are made by the lawyers for the plaintiff and the defendant, summarizing what each will establish during the trial.

10. *Witnesses* are called by the plaintiff and then by the defendant. The witnesses can be cross-examined by the opposing lawyers.

11. *Closing statements* are made by both sides.

12. *The jury deliberates* (if there is a jury) and reaches a verdict.

13. *The final judgment* is handed down by the court in the form of the jury's verdict or the judge's decision.

Pretrial Procedures

I have been called to testify before a grand jury. May I bring my lawyer with me and consult with him during the proceedings?

You do not have a constitutional right to have a lawyer present in the courtroom when you appear before a grand jury, even if you are the subject of the investigation. However, your lawyer can wait for you outside the courtroom, and you may be allowed to leave the courtroom to speak with your lawyer if you are concerned that answering certain questions may incriminate you.

If a grand jury indicts me, do I face a greater threat of being found guilty at my trial?

No. Your guilt or innocence is decided solely on the evidence presented at your trial. The vote of the grand jury and the opinions voiced by its members are secret and will not be disclosed at the trial.

Cathy's lawyer told her that her case is now in discovery. What is he talking about?

In its broadest legal sense, the term *discovery* means obtaining information about the case. A case is said to be "in discovery" from the time the case is filed until the trial begins. The purpose of discovery is to learn more precisely which issues are in dispute and to obtain evidence. Methods used in discovery include depositions, interrogatories, requests to produce documents, and requests to submit to physical or mental examinations.

What is a deposition?

It is sworn testimony that is given and recorded outside the courtroom (in a lawyer's office, for example), usually during the pretrial phase of a case. It is the main method that lawyers use to gather evidence about a case before it goes to trial. Any witness—including one who is also a plaintiff or a defendant in the case—may be asked to give a deposition.

If a lawyer wants you to make a deposition, you should arrange to have your own lawyer present, since testimony you give that supports one side of the case may be challenged by the lawyer for the other side. Lawyers for both sides will be present. You will be placed under oath by a qualified officer of the court, usually a court reporter or stenographer, who attends the deposition to record your testimony, which may be used as evidence in the trial. Giving a deposition does not excuse you from testifying at the trial: you may have to do both.

Is an interrogatory the same as a deposition?

No. An interrogatory is a written set of questions requiring written answers from a plaintiff or defendant under oath. A deposition involves asking oral questions of any person who may have information relevant to a legal case. The person answers orally under oath, and an official transcript is made of the questions and answers.

I gave a deposition over a year ago. The case is finally coming to trial next week. May I review this deposition before testifying?

Yes. This is an excellent way to refresh your memory about details you may have forgotten in the course of the year. Since the lawyers from both sides in the case will have a copy of your deposition, any discrepancy between the deposition and your testimony will cause them to challenge your memory and truthfulness.

What if I'm ordered to give a deposition and I ignore the notice?

You could be held in contempt of court, an offense that is punishable by a fine or imprisonment or both. If you are either the plaintiff or defendant in a civil lawsuit, the court could find that your failure to respond left it no choice but to rule in favor of your opponent on the issues that the deposition dealt with.

Lewis has been asked by a friend to testify at a hearing. Is a hearing the same as a trial?

No. A hearing is less formal than a trial. Hearings are used by courts to obtain evidence needed to decide legal and factual questions concerning a dispute. Legislative committees, such as those of the U. S. Congress, or public administrative agencies, such as federal or state housing authorities, also make use of hearings to investigate issues or to resolve disputes. If Lewis is subpoenaed to appear as a witness at the hearing his friend is involved in, he will be required to appear or face charges of contempt.

Under what conditions can Pamela's lawyer ask the court to postpone her trial?

A postponement, or continuance, may be requested if it is needed to assure a fair trial. Pamela's lawyer might cite the lack of time to prepare her case or the absence of a witness, defendant, or plaintiff. If important evidence were lost or destroyed or if her lawyer became incapacitated, a continuance could be requested. Another valid reason to ask for a postponement is surprise—for example, if new evidence is presented that is damaging to Pamela's case and her lawyer needs time to analyze it and determine how best to minimize its effect.

My case is scheduled to be tried before a judge with a reputation for being tough in cases like mine. Am I entitled to a different judge if I request one?

No. You cannot expect to be assigned a new judge just because you think the one you have may be too hard on you. However, a judge can be replaced for other reasons, such as if he has a personal interest in the case, a close relationship to either the plaintiff or the defendant, or a personal bias or prejudice against someone involved in the case, or if he might be called as a witness.

Dean is going to be his own lawyer in a civil court case. How can he make sure his witnesses show up to testify?

Dean should subpoena the witnesses. He can obtain subpoenas from the clerk of the court. The subpoena requires the witness to appear on a certain date or be charged with contempt of court.

Will the judge reschedule my case if the witnesses can't appear on the court date?

Possibly. A judge can reschedule, or in legal terms *grant a continuance,* if you can prove that the witnesses' testimonies are important to your case and that no other witnesses can provide the same information. Your chances of obtaining a continuance are much greater if you had had the missing witnesses subpoenaed, rather than simply relying on their willingness to appear.

My attorney tried and failed to reach a settlement with the person whose cats killed my prize parrot. We then took all the steps necessary to prepare for a trial. Now the defendant wants to settle out of court. Is it too late to do so?

No. Because of the crowded court calendars and time needed to complete a trial, the legal system encourages people to resolve their differences outside the courtroom.

I read in the newspaper that a person charged with a notorious crime got a change of venue. What does that mean?

Venue is the county or district in which a trial is held. For example, in a criminal case, the trial is usually held in the county where the crime occurred. Often a change of venue is requested when a plaintiff or defendant believes he cannot receive a fair trial in the county or district where the trial is scheduled. Other reasons to request a change of venue include convenience—for example, if witnesses or evidence are located a great distance from the courthouse—or if the judge turns out to be biased or prejudiced in a particular case.

Courtroom Protocol

Does the general public have the right to sit in the courtroom during a trial?

The right to a public trial is guaranteed by the U.S. Constitution to defendants in criminal cases, but not to those involved in civil cases. Even in criminal trials, however, the judge may bar the public from the courtroom for various reasons: to prevent disorderly conduct by spectators, to protect the identity of witnesses (such as undercover agents), or to prevent overcrowding. The court is not required to provide enough seating to accommodate everyone.

May I bring a friend to court with me if I'm testifying as a witness or if I'm on trial?

Yes, if the judge says the trial is open to the public, you may ask anyone you want to sit in the courtroom. However, if your friend is going to be a witness, he may be barred as an observer until after he has testified. Witnesses may be excluded by the judge when he or one of the attorneys involved is concerned that the witnesses will be influenced by the testimony of others.

Georgia has to appear in traffic court, but doesn't want to hire a babysitter. Can she take her children with her?

Yes, but Georgia will be responsible for their behavior. As a practical matter, Georgia may find it difficult to respond to questions and mind the children at the same time. If she still wants to bring the children to court, Georgia should consider asking a friend to accompany her to the courthouse to help take care of them.

Courtroom Protocol

What will happen to me if I can't go to court on the day I am called to appear?

If you are the plaintiff or the defendant in a civil case and do not show up in court on the day stated in the summons, the court may declare you in default, and you may lose the case. If you know in advance that you will not be able to appear in court, ask for a continuance, or postponement, of the trial to a later date—a delay the court will grant only for a good reason, such as an illness confining you to bed.

If you were subpoenaed as a witness in either a civil or a criminal case and cannot appear as scheduled, you should contact the court officer who issued the subpoena to make other arrangements. Simply failing to appear may result in your being held in contempt of court, a crime that is punishable by a fine or imprisonment or both.

If I plead guilty to an offense for which a fine is levied, do I have to pay my total fine on the day I go to court to make my plea?

It's up to the judge. He may require payment by the end of the day or by some later date. If it is a large fine, the judge may allow you to pay it in affordable installments.

My sister Ursula, who is head of a landmark-preservation group, has offered to be an amicus curiae in a rezoning lawsuit. What does this mean?

Amicus curiae is Latin for "friend of the court" and means a person or organization that has a strong interest in a particular case, but is not involved directly as a defendant, plaintiff, or witness. Ursula will ask the court's permission to file a brief (written statement) on the issues as she sees them from a preservationist's viewpoint.

While Suzanne was testifying, she made a nasty remark about the plaintiff, whose attorney objected. The judge sustained the objection and ordered what Suzanne said stricken from the record. What does this mean?

Strike from the record means to delete a statement made during a trial from the official transcript. The lawyer for either side may request such a deletion when he thinks a witness has given an unthinking or improper answer that may prejudice or mislead the jury. Since the court reporter had already taken down Suzanne's statement, it will be followed by the

Courtroom Dos and Don'ts

Most of us will never have to be a plaintiff or a defendant in a trial. But if you must go to court, take a few moments to review the following guidelines. They will help you put your best foot forward.

- ☑ Attend court proceedings as required. If you have been subpoenaed, you could be jailed for not showing up. If you are a plaintiff or defendant, you could lose your case by being absent.
- ☑ Arrive on time for all scheduled hearings.
- ☑ Dress in clean, neat, conservative clothes, like those you would wear to religious services.
- ☑ Don't try to speak to your lawyer while he is questioning witnesses, listening to testimony, or addressing the court.
- ☑ Never argue with your lawyer in front of the judge or jury.
- ☑ If you have concerns about your lawyer's performance, discuss them with him during breaks, in private.
- ☑ Bring pen and paper to write down comments and insights that occur to you during the court proceedings so you can discuss them later with your lawyer.
- ☑ Be respectful to all the participants in the proceedings: judge, jury, plaintiff and defendant, witnesses, court officials.
- ☑ Speak in a strong voice so the judge and jury can hear you.
- ☑ Don't argue with the lawyers questioning you. If they act improperly, the judge will reprimand them.
- ☑ Answer all questions truthfully; if your lawyer objects to a question, don't answer it until instructed to do so by the court.

attorney's objection and the judge's order to sustain the objection and strike the statement in question from the record. Suzanne's remark will not appear in the official transcript of the trial and the jury will be told not to consider it when deliberating on a verdict.

Trial Procedures

Can I plead guilty or innocent against my lawyer's advice?

Yes, but your lawyer may refuse to continue to represent you. In one curious case in California, an accused murderer blurted out his guilt in court and asked for the death penalty. He was later freed when it was learned that he had not had his lawyer's advice on pleading guilty. Because the defendant had not consulted his lawyer, the court reasoned, he had acted without proper legal advice and was not aware of the consequences of his action; therefore he could not be convicted.

Trial Procedures

Ethan's lawyer has suggested that he plead nolo contendere to the charge of drunk driving. How is this different from pleading guilty or innocent?

Nolo contendere means "I do not wish to contend." It is not a plea of guilt or innocence. However, it is similar to a guilty plea in that the court may impose the same penalty it would have if the person had pleaded guilty. The advantage of a nolo contendere plea is that it cannot be used as an admission of guilt in related civil or criminal proceedings. For example, if a pedestrian is suing Ethan for running him down with his car and severely injuring him, the pedestrian cannot mention the criminal case or use Ethan's plea to prove that Ethan was drunk when he hit him.

Pleading nolo contendere instead of innocent may also be an attractive choice to someone who would rather pay the penalty than face the time, expense, and publicity of a trial. The plea of nolo contendere cannot be used in very serious crimes, such as kidnapping and murder; and in all cases it can be used only with the court's permission.

Can a defendant be excluded from his own trial?

In certain extreme cases he can. Although the Sixth Amendment gives criminal defendants the right to confront witnesses and thus to be present in court, the defendant may lose this right if he repeatedly behaves in a disrespectful manner. On the judge's order, the bailiff will remove the unruly defendant, who will be allowed to return only when he promises the court that he will behave properly.

Can a defendant choose not to attend his own trial?

It depends on the nature of the crime. If the defendant is being held behind bars or if he is charged with a crime that is punishable by death, he must be present at all stages of his trial. Defendants who are charged with lesser crimes may be allowed to waive their Sixth Amendment right to attend their own trials.

If I am on trial, must I testify?

It depends on whether the case is in criminal or civil court. If you are a defendant in a criminal case, you need never take the stand, because of the Fifth Amendment protection against self-incrimination. However, if you are being sued in a civil case, you have no such protection: if you are called to testify, you must take the stand.

Can a defendant who testifies refuse to be cross-examined?

Not as a rule. A defendant cannot take the stand, present his side of the case, and then sit down. The opposing lawyer has the right to cross-examine. However, there may be times when the defendant can "take the Fifth" and refuse to answer when cross-examined. For example, in a civil trial, the opposing lawyer might ask a question that, if answered, could link the defendant to a crime. If the defendant refuses to answer that question, the judge will then decide whether or not the defendant can claim the Fifth Amendment privilege against self-incrimination.

Jared is accused of larceny. Does he have the right to make people testify as part of his defense?

Yes. The defendant can compel witnesses to testify in court by asking the court to subpoena them.

A defendant was held in contempt of court for making derogatory remarks about the judge. What will happen to him?

If the defendant's offensive behavior occurs right in court, it is called *direct contempt*, and the judge usually has the power to impose a penalty immediately, such as a fine or imprisonment. *Indirect contempt* takes place outside or away from the courtroom. An example would be refusing to comply with a subpoena. A hearing (sometimes called a contempt proceeding) would generally be scheduled, at which the accused could defend his actions. The hearing would determine whether or not the individual should be cited and sentenced for contempt of court.

Carla is the victim of a crime, but the prosecutor won't let her testify. Is he allowed to do this?

Yes. A prosecuting attorney has the power to decide how to prepare his case and present the evidence. This includes deciding whom he wants to testify at the trial. Although the victim of a crime generally appears as a witness for the prosecution, it is not required.

Does a witness's testimony become part of the public record so that anyone can read or obtain a copy of it?

Not always. During the course of a trial, a court reporter, or stenographer, writes down everything that is said. Although this transcript may be typed up at the end of each day for reference by the judge and attorneys during the rest of the trial, an official typed copy of the transcript is generally not made unless the case is being appealed. At the time of an appeal, the transcript becomes one of the documents filed with the appeals court. Access to the transcript may be limited by the court; otherwise, anyone may ask to see a particular file.

If I win my case, can the judge require the other person to pay my court costs?

It's possible, but not automatic. Each state has its own laws about when the judge may order a person to pay his opponent's court costs, such as expenses for filing legal papers, having subpoenas served on witnesses, obtaining expert opinions, photocopying, and telephone calls.

Craig won a court judgment against the Zero Company, but before he could collect, the Zero Company went out of business, and the owners started a business under a new name. What can Craig do?

If the Zero Company was a sole proprietorship or a partnership, Craig can seek payment from the owner's or partners' personal assets. The court would issue a writ of execution, which authorizes the sheriff or other official to seize property and sell it to pay the judgment. If Zero was a corporation, business assets may have to be sold to pay the obligation.

How many times can I appeal my case?

Generally speaking, you can appeal no more than twice in the same court system. For example, if you started in a state court and lost, you might be able to take your case to the state court of appeals, and if you lost there, you might be able to go on to the state supreme court. The appeal process in federal courts is similar.

However, there is nothing in the U. S. Constitution about your right to appeal if you lose your case. Federal, state, and local laws outline which cases may be appealed to a higher court; and the appellate courts (courts that hear appeals) have the authority to turn down your request.

When I lost my lawsuit, my lawyer advised me to appeal the decision. Does this mean that I will have to testify again?

No, it does not. When a higher court reviews the decision of a lower court, there is no trial, no jury, and no new testimony. A judge in the appellate court reviews the case, weighs the arguments of the opposing attorneys, and pronounces a decision either to affirm the ruling of the lower court or to overturn it.

Wesley was being tried for attempted murder. The jury returned a verdict of not guilty. Can the prosecutor appeal this acquittal?

No. Allowing the prosecutor to appeal would mean that Wesley would be subject to double jeopardy (he would be tried twice for the same crime)—an action that is forbidden by the U. S. Constitution. In some states, a prosecutor may be able to appeal the acquittal of a person accused of a crime that is punishable only by a fine, but never of one that carries a prison sentence, as in this case.

How the Court Determines Damages

When the plaintiff in a lawsuit wins his case, the judge or jury decides the amount of money the defendant must pay the plaintiff to compensate him for his loss or injury or for any pain or suffering he has to endure, or to punish the defendant for his actions. In legal terminology, the money a court awards in a lawsuit is called *damages.* Damages are divided into two categories: actual and punitive.

Actual damages are awarded to restore, as nearly as possible, a person or his property to the condition existing before the problem arose. In setting the amount of actual damages, the judge or jury considers:

- Lost job income
- Loss of future income (projected on the basis of the person's age, education, job history)
- Hospital, medical, and pharmacy bills (including such expenses as prosthetic devices, wheelchairs, and nursing care)
- Pain and suffering, including that caused by fright, grief, shock, humiliation, or indignity
- Loss of memory or intellectual capacity (temporary or permanent)
- Physical impairment or disfigurement (temporary or permanent)
- Increased living costs (for custodial care or remodeling to accommodate a physical handicap, for example)
- Repair or replacement costs for property

Punitive damages are based on how seriously the judge or jury disapproves of the defendant's conduct, and are linked to how much the defendant can afford to pay as atonement for his misconduct. In some types of cases, the law specifies how much is to be paid. For example, if an employer is found guilty of violating federal equal pay laws, he must pay twice the amount of past wages due to the plaintiff.

Small Claims Court

For consumer problems, see "When You Have a Complaint" in Chapter 9, *Consumer Rights*.

What kind of cases do small claims courts handle?

Simple civil cases that involve small amounts of money—anywhere from a few dollars to $10,000, depending on the limit set by each state. If the dollar amount of a case exceeds the limit, it must be heard in a different court. Common cases that are brought to small claims courts include those of tenants who want their security deposits back from their landlords, and consumers seeking refunds for defective merchandise.

I'm going to small claims court to get my money back for a defective dishwasher. Will I need to question my witnesses?

It depends on how the small claims court operates in your area. Talk with someone who has been through it. Or, if you have time, go to the court and

Taking Your Case to Small Claims Court

If you are involved in a dispute over a fairly small amount of money, you may be able to settle it quickly and easily in small claims court without ever consulting a lawyer. Small claims courts only hear cases where the money in question is under a certain amount—from $750 to $10,000, depending on the state you live in. If there is no small claims court in your area, your case may be heard by a trial court (possibly called circuit, common pleas, county, district, superior, or some other name) or a local court, such as city or municipal, justice, or magistrate's court. You will have a better chance of winning your case if you prepare beforehand, following these steps:

1. Fill out a formal complaint and make a copy for yourself. Many courts have standard forms for complaints. If your court does not, ask the clerk of the court what you should write.

2. Give the complaint to the clerk of the court. He will ask you to pay a filing fee—ranging from $5 to $50, depending on the state. If you win your case, the defendant (your opponent) may be ordered to reimburse you for this fee.

3. Ask the clerk for your court date and the number assigned to your complaint. This number will identify your case; use it in any communication with the court.

4. Make sure that your complaint is delivered to the defendant. Usually the clerk will mail it with a *summons* (an order to file an answer to the complaint by a certain day) or have the sheriff's office deliver it. But if the watch what goes on. There is no better way to prepare for your case. In some courts, you might be expected to "examine" your witnesses, just as a lawyer does. In other places, you might be expected only to introduce your witnesses (ask them to state their names), and then ask them to tell in their own way what they saw. A third possibility is that the judge may ask most of the questions, allowing you to ask about anything important you feel he overlooked. You may also have the opportunity to question any witnesses the store owner brings to court.

Lester received a summons from a small claims court directing him to file an answer to the complaint attached to the summons. What should he do?

Lester should call the clerk of the small claims court to find out if there's an official form for his answer. If there is one, he should obtain this form, fill it out carefully, file it with the court, and send a copy to the person who filed the complaint. If there is no official form, Lester should type or neatly

summons cannot be delivered, you may have to help locate the defendant. The court will not proceed until the defendant receives the summons.

5. If the defendant offers to settle out of court, you may choose to accept the settlement and drop the case. If he files a written answer to your complaint, request a copy so that you will be prepared for the counterclaims he will make in court.

6. If you cannot appear in court on the appointed day, ask the clerk of the court for a continuance (postponement). The defendant can do the same.

7. Appear in court promptly (or you risk losing your case by default). Bring any witnesses with you and whatever documents you think will help prove your claim, such as canceled checks, receipts, letters, and contracts. Have this material organized and neatly arranged in a folder. If damaged property or defective merchandise is involved, and it is portable, bring it with you; otherwise, bring photographs of it.

8. When the judge (or arbitrator) asks you to present your case, explain the facts simply and clearly, without exaggerating or becoming excited. Be brief but thorough. Try to show that your demands are reasonable and that you have tried other means to persuade the defendant to settle with you. Let the judge know if you have brought witnesses, documents, or other evidence.

9. Answer the judge's questions as best you can and allow the defendant to tell his side of the story. If you are allowed, question your own witnesses and cross-examine the defendant's witnesses. After hearing both sides of the case, the judge will announce his decision. If you win, the court will order the defendant to pay you a specified amount of money.

print his own answer. He should use the name of the case as it appears on the complaint, such as *John Doe* v. *Lester Smith*; use the case number listed on the summons; respond to each point in the complaint; sign his name; and return it by the date specified.

Whom and what should I take to small claims court to help me win?

Anyone or anything, within reason, that relates to your case. Witnesses to the disputed transactions and events are especially important. Bring all documents that will back up your position, such as warranties, receipts, contracts, leases, correspondence, and canceled checks. If your dispute is over something you can easily carry, such as a defective radio, bring it with you. If not, take photographs of the item and bring them to court.

Reginald arrived in small claims court expecting to have his dispute settled by a judge. Instead, a court officer suggested that the case be submitted to arbitration. What's going on?

In some small claims courts, where there is only a single judge presiding, people would have to wait months or even years to have their disputes resolved. Therefore, many courts offer the alternative of having the controversy submitted to arbitration. Reginald and his opponent would present their arguments to an objective third person, such as an attorney. The arbitrator would act as the judge and make a decision for the court.

Gisela lost her case in small claims court. Can she appeal?

It depends on where she lives. In some places, the decisions of a small claims court may be appealed to a higher court; in others, only a defendant may appeal; and in still others, no appeal is allowed. Gisela should check with the clerk of her court about the law in her area.

What happens if Mathilda wins her case in small claims court, but can't collect the judgment she won?

Mathilda should ask the clerk of the court to prepare a writ of execution, which the clerk will then issue to the sheriff. The writ authorizes the sheriff to seize and sell enough of the defendant's property to pay Mathilda what she is owed. (Certain types of property, such as a percentage of the value of the family home, tools of a trade, livestock, or other assets may be exempt from seizure under state law.)

Selecting Jurors

Why do some juries have 12 people and some only 6?

Although the U. S. Constitution calls for trial by jury for anyone accused of a crime, it does not specify the number of jurors to be used. In criminal trials where the defendant is accused of breaking a federal law, the jury usually consists of 12 members; but the defense and prosecution may agree to have as few as 6. In state criminal trials, the jury may have as few as 6 members if that is mandated by state law. In all civil cases, federal and state, the jury has at least 6 and no more than 12 members.

Maggie received a legal notice requiring her to appear for jury duty. How did her name get on the list?

Every court system must select its jurors, by a fair and impartial method, from among the citizens in its area, or jurisdiction. This means drawing up a list from a wide cross section of people in the community—using names from tax rolls, city telephone directories, utility records, or car registrations, for example—and then having a public official randomly select names taken from these sources. The individuals whose names are selected, like Maggie, are then notified to appear for jury duty.

Collette, a single mother, received a notice to report for jury duty, but she doesn't have anyone who can take care of the children in her absence. Will the court excuse her?

Perhaps. Collette should call the number given on the notice and ask what she must do to be excused. If she ignores the notice and does not appear on the date requested, she may be arrested and jailed.

Recent service on a jury, illness or disability, lack of child care for small children, and the demands of running a small business are all reasons that might result in a person's being excused from jury duty. Some judges may also excuse members of certain professions, such as police officers, doctors, and schoolteachers.

Will I be paid for the time I spend on jury duty?

Yes, but probably not very much. A juror may be paid no more than a few dollars a day, plus the cost of traveling to and from the courthouse. Generally, jurors are not reimbursed for other expenses, such as child care and meals. However, if the jury must deliberate during mealtimes, the court will provide food, and if the jury is sequestered, the court will provide for lodging.

Selecting Jurors

Hope has received a notice to appear for jury duty for two weeks. Will she be deliberating on a jury during that whole time?

Probably not. In fact, Hope may never sit on a jury. When she reports to the courthouse, she becomes one of a pool of prospective jurors waiting to be chosen to sit on an actual jury. Those in the pool are selected at random for questioning by the prosecuting and defense attorneys, who must then agree on the final composition of the jury for the trial. (This process is called *voir dire.*) After being questioned, Hope will either be asked to stay as a member of the jury or be excused from that jury. If excused, she returns to the jury pool to await another call.

The last time I was on jury duty, a defense lawyer sent me back to the jury pool without asking me a single question. Why would he do this?

Both prosecuting and defense attorneys have a certain number of what are called *peremptory challenges*, which they can use to dismiss jurors for no reason whatsoever. This allows a lawyer to remove a juror if he has a feeling that the person may have a prejudice about the case.

What kind of questions will the lawyers ask me when they're selecting the jury?

They may ask questions about your occupation and education; whether you have any connection or relationship to the plaintiff or defendant; and how much you know about the case, either from personal experience or from the news media. In addition, the lawyers will try to find out if there is anything in your background that will make it difficult for you to be impartial in deciding on a verdict. If, for example, you had once been robbed, the lawyer for an accused burglar might suspect that it would be difficult for you to be impartial about his client. In some courts, prospective jurors are asked to fill out written questionnaires. Lawyers use this information to reject jurors who may be biased.

When being questioned as a prospective juror, Nelson suddenly realized that the defendant was a former business partner of his father's. Should Nelson tell the lawyers?

Yes. If Nelson is selected to serve on the jury and this connection is revealed after the trial begins, the judge could halt the proceedings and order a new trial before a new jury.

Am I likely to be disqualified from a jury if I admit I've read a newspaper account of the case?

No. That alone would not disqualify you, since in highly publicized cases it may be difficult to find jurors who have not heard something about the case. But if you feel you cannot be impartial, and no evidence can change your mind, you should say so during the selection process.

Thomas was selected as an alternate juror. What does this mean?

As an alternate juror, Thomas will sit with the jury in the courtroom and hear all the evidence that the jury hears at the trial. If a juror becomes ill during the trial or is unable to continue for some other reason, Thomas will take his place. Many courts choose alternate jurors to make sure that the case will not have to be retried if a juror is dismissed in mid-trial.

Are jurors ever selected by judges?

No. But once the jury has been selected, a judge may excuse jurors who appear to be unfit to serve. If a juror is ill, disorderly, intoxicated, under the influence of drugs, or is otherwise incapable of fulfilling his duties, the judge may remove that person from the jury.

Bernice will be a juror in a trial that is expected to last several weeks. Must her employer pay her for the days she misses work?

Some states do require employers to pay employees for time spent on jury duty. Even in states where these payments are not required, many employers still pay in recognition of the fact that jurors are fulfilling an important civic duty.

I was selected as a juror for a murder trial. If I say that I doubt that I could vote for the death penalty, will I be removed from the jury?

Not necessarily. You can be removed if you say you would automatically vote against the death penalty regardless of the evidence in the case, or that your opposition to the death penalty would prevent you from making an impartial decision about the defendant's guilt.

In the past, the prosecutor could have jurors who opposed the death penalty removed from the case on the grounds that they could not be impartial. Then, in 1968, the Supreme Court held that a death sentence could not be carried out if it had been imposed by a jury from which all those with general objections to the death penalty had been excluded.

Serving on a Jury

How is the foreman of a jury chosen, and what are his duties?

The manner of choosing a jury foreman varies from court to court. The foreman may be simply the first juror chosen for the trial. Or he can be elected by the jury members or named by the judge. As foreman, he presides over the jury's deliberations and makes sure all the jurors have a chance to express their views. The foreman also acts as the spokesman for the jury in communications with the court; in some courtrooms, he announces the jury's verdict.

Rory fears that he may forget some of the facts being brought out during the trial. What should he do?

Rory may find that when the jury's deliberations begin and he can discuss the case with the other jurors, he will remember more than he thinks he will. But if he absolutely cannot recall important testimony, he or any other juror can ask the judge to allow portions of the record of the trial to be read aloud by the court reporter. In most situations, the judge will permit this rehearing of testimony.

When Doug was on a jury that was hearing a complicated case, he started to take notes, but the judge told him to stop. What is wrong with taking notes at a public trial?

Most courts do not allow note taking, on the grounds that a juror may put too much emphasis on notes that may be incomplete or perhaps inaccurate. Not all courts take this view, however. Doug should check with the judge or a court officer for permission if he feels that taking notes will help him keep the facts of the case straight.

While serving as a juror, Natalie inadvertently heard something on the news that could influence her decision. Should she report this to the court?

Yes. The judge or a court officer and perhaps the prosecution and defense lawyers may wish to question her further about what she heard and its influence on her. If Natalie was shocked, moved to sympathy, outraged, or otherwise strongly affected by what she heard, she might be disqualified from sitting as a juror on this case. If, on the other hand, the news item was not closely related to the major issues in the case, Natalie might be allowed to continue as a juror. The final decision rests with the judge, who must weigh the news item's effect on Natalie.

If a news reporter wants to talk to Bud while he's serving as a juror on a trial, should Bud automatically refuse to discuss the case, or is it OK to answer some questions?

Bud should refuse. A judge usually instructs jury members not to discuss the trial with anyone until it is over—and not even with fellow jurors until all the evidence has been heard and the jury's deliberations begin.

Discussing the trial before all the evidence is presented may lead a juror to form an opinion before hearing both sides of the case. Even if the reporter was not trying to influence Bud, just answering his questions may lead Bud to form an opinion before learning all the facts. If Bud does talk with a reporter, he could be removed from the jury or charged with contempt of court—an offense punishable by a fine or jail or both.

While serving on a jury, Dora saw a fellow juror talking to the plaintiff during a court recess. Should Dora report this to someone?

Yes. Dora should tell a court officer, such as the bailiff or judge, who can discharge the juror from service. All jurors should avoid speaking with anyone involved in the case during the trial—even about topics unrelated to the case, such as the weather or the Superbowl.

If a juror wants to know more about the people, places, and events involved in the trial, can he investigate on his own?

No. Jurors are not allowed to visit places connected with the case without court approval and supervision. Nor are they permitted to question any of the witnesses or read articles about the case. If a juror is caught pursuing his own investigation, he will be dismissed from the jury, and he could also be charged with contempt of court, an offense that is punishable by a fine or jail or both.

Does a jury have to reach a unanimous decision?

In criminal cases, only in some states or if a federal crime is involved. In certain states the jury must reach a unanimous decision only if the defendant faces the death penalty or long-term imprisonment. For less serious offenses, only 10 of the jurors may have to agree—unless the jury is made up of only 6 members, in which case the verdict must be unanimous.

In civil cases, many states, including Massachusetts, Washington, and Wisconsin, allow a jury to return a verdict when five-sixths of the jurors agree on it. In Rhode Island and in federal courts, the plaintiff and defendant may agree before the trial begins that they will accept the verdict of a majority of the jurors.

Serving on a Jury

The judge said that the jury I am serving on may be sequestered. What does that mean?

It means that you and the other jurors will be kept isolated until the trial is over to keep people from influencing your thinking about the case and to prevent you from being exposed to improper information. You and the other jurors will be lodged in a hotel or motel at the court's expense, and any contact or communication with other people will be severely restricted. (Exceptions may be made for family members, so long as they do not discuss the case.) In addition, your reading material may be screened to make sure you don't read news accounts of the trial; and the judge may forbid you to listen to radio or watch television news broadcasts. You will be permitted to leave your rooms only in the company of bailiffs and to travel only to and from the jury room.

The jury Thea is on is going to be sequestered. Thea doesn't want to leave her family during the trial. Can she be excused?

Probably not. Separation from your family is not reason enough to be excused from jury duty unless there are some special circumstances, such as the serious illness of a child. If the trial is a long one, the judge may permit Thea's family to visit her even though the jury is sequestered.

Naomi is on a jury that has been deliberating for almost a week, and the jurors are still not close to the unanimous vote required in the case. What happens if they can't reach a verdict?

If the judge feels that all the jurors have done their best to reach a verdict but remain hopelessly at odds, he will declare a hung jury (meaning the jurors are unable to reach a verdict) and dismiss the jurors. The person who brought the case to court (the plaintiff in a civil case, the prosecutor in a criminal case) must then decide whether or not to retry the matter before a new jury. Because of the time and expense involved, judges hesitate to declare hung juries and will do so only when they are convinced that further deliberations are useless.

After a jury returned a verdict in favor of the plaintiff, the defense lawyer went up to the jurors and asked them why they decided against his client. Is he allowed to do this?

Yes. Although neither the defense nor the prosecuting attorney may discuss the case with members of the jury during the trial, once the case is

Deliberating as a Juror

There is no set procedure that jurors must follow when deliberating. Each jury decides its own way of conducting discussions, settling differences of opinion, and polling its members for a vote. It is important to know, however, that if a juror cannot remember exactly what a witness said while testifying or if there is a dispute among the jurors about certain facts, the jurors may ask that the testimony be read to them or that exhibits be shown to them again.

Before the jurors leave the courtroom to begin their deliberations, the judge will tell them how the law applies to the case and ask them to follow his instructions to the best of their ability. Many judges stress the following points in their instructions:

- Jurors must discuss the evidence presented on all important issues before taking a vote on the verdict.
- Each juror should be allowed and encouraged to express his opinion during the deliberations.
- No juror should be pressured into changing his vote simply to arrive at a verdict more quickly.
- Each juror should weigh opposing views carefully and examine his own viewpoint in the light of those other opinions.
- No juror should hesitate to change his vote if the discussion has changed his point of view.

decided, the jurors are free to discuss it with anyone they choose. Many lawyers, whether they win or lose, like to discuss the trial with jurors after it is over. Some even ask for comments about their courtroom performance in order to improve their skills.

However, no attorney should badger or berate the jurors about the verdict they have given, even though his client lost. Conduct of this sort should be reported to both the judge who presided over the trial and the state bar association.

Serving on a Grand Jury

I have been called for regular jury duty several times, but I have never once been called to serve on a grand jury. How are people chosen for grand jury duty?

The selection process is the same as that for trial juries. A list of local residents is compiled from sources that ensure a representative cross section of the community. Names of people who will serve on a grand jury are drawn from this list.

Serving on a Grand Jury

How many people are there on a grand jury?

Federal grand juries have 16 to 23 members, and state grand juries have 12 to 23 members.

Susan has been chosen as a member of a grand jury. Will she be deciding the guilt or innocence of someone?

No. A grand jury hears evidence to determine whether or not to bring formal criminal charges against a person. After the prosecutor presents the evidence gathered by the police or other investigators, the grand jury decides if there is enough evidence to bring the person to trial. If there is enough evidence, the grand jury will then bring formal charges, called an indictment, against the accused person. If the grand jury does not find enough evidence, all charges against the accused will be dropped.

Are the members of a grand jury paid the same as other jurors?

Generally, yes. State law specifies the amount to be paid to those serving on state grand juries.

Several members of Edwin's federal grand jury left before the deliberations were over. The remaining members continued to deliberate and voted for an indictment. Is the indictment valid?

Yes, as long as 12 jurors voted for it.

If I'm on a grand jury, will I get a chance to hear testimony from the person who is suspected of committing the crime?

Not necessarily. The person under suspicion does not have to be present or play an active part in the grand jury proceeding.

Are grand juries ever sequestered while they are hearing evidence?

No. Other methods are used to preserve confidentiality. A grand jury conducts its inquiry in private, behind closed doors. No one is allowed in except the jurors, prosecuting attorneys, witnesses who are testifying, and the judge and other necessary court officials. Grand jurors are sworn to secrecy, as are witnesses and others in a grand jury proceeding.

Being a Witness

For more information, see "Witnessing a Crime" in Chapter 17, *Victims and Crimes.*

Lori will be a witness for the first time. Is it proper for the lawyer who subpoenaed her to help phrase her answers before the trial?

Yes. The lawyer can discuss her testimony with her, rehearse with her, and advise her on courtroom procedure. But it is improper for him to supply answers for her. When Lori testifies, she must tell the truth on the basis of her own knowledge and observations, not an attorney's.

I am going to be a witness in a child custody case. Who will be questioning me, and how long can I expect the process to go on?

When you take the witness stand, you will take an oath to tell the truth. Then the lawyer who called you will begin the questioning with what is called the *direct examination.* After that, the lawyer for the other side will question, or *cross-examine,* you. If the cross-examination brings up new issues, the first lawyer has another chance to ask questions, or *redirect*; then the other lawyer, too, can ask additional questions, or *recross.*

Redirect and recross-examination can go on for more turns if necessary. Once the lawyers have completed their examinations, the judge may ask you some questions as well, especially if he did not understand your answers or felt important issues were overlooked by the lawyers.

Kendall is nervous about testifying under cross-examination tomorrow. Should he steel himself for a real ordeal on the witness stand?

Cross-examination can have its tough moments, because it is how lawyers challenge the accuracy and relevance of a witness's previous testimony. The cross-examining lawyer will try to show that his client is less damaged by Kendall's testimony than it might first appear. Kendall might be asked to give more details about an event or observation; he might be confronted with earlier statements he made that seem to be inconsistent with his present testimony. The cross-examining lawyer also might ask Kendall about his relationship with the accused person, in order to try to show that Kendall's testimony is biased.

What should I do if I am a witness and the opposing lawyer tricks me into a misstatement during cross-examination?

Tell the lawyer or judge that you made a mistake in your testimony when you answered the question and that you would like to correct or clarify your answer. The judge will allow you to do so. You have the right to explain any of your answers. If you realize your misstatement after you've left the witness stand, let the lawyer who called you know, and he may ask you to take the stand again to correct your mistake.

What happens if I'm on the witness stand and I simply don't know the answer to a question?

If you don't know the answer, say so. If you don't understand the question, ask the judge or lawyer to repeat or rephrase it. Your duty on the witness stand is to answer all questions as completely and truthfully as you can, and that includes admitting you don't know the answer.

Maureen is not sure she saw the defendant hit the shopkeeper, but that is the only possibility that makes sense to her. Should she testify that she witnessed the attack?

No. A witness should never present a logical deduction or a guess as a fact. Maureen should restrict her testimony to her own observations and knowledge. In some situations, a lawyer might ask a witness to make an educated guess based on his knowledge. If Maureen is asked to do this, she should make it clear that her answer is only a guess or estimate.

Does a witness have the right to refuse to answer questions?

Sometimes. If a witness feels his answer might link him to a crime, he may refuse to answer on the basis of the Fifth Amendment right against self-incrimination. Some judges will also allow a witness to refuse to answer if he thinks answering would disgrace him. But if an answer is needed to prove or disprove a key issue in the case, a witness may be ordered to respond. Finally, a witness may refuse to answer questions that probe knowledge gained from privileged communications, such as facts that spouses know about each other, or a lawyer learns in confidential discussions with his client, or a doctor with his patient. What a priest hears during confession is also regarded as a privileged communication.

If I am called as a witness, can I use notes while I'm testifying?

It is in the court's discretion to forbid you to use notes on the witness stand. However, some judges allow you to consult notes to refresh your memory of the facts of the case.

Martin, who is an avowed atheist, is scheduled to be a witness, but he does not want to take the oath by placing his hand on the Bible. Can he be a witness?

Yes. At one time, his objection would have disqualified Martin from being a witness. Now, those who object to taking an oath may say, "I affirm that I will tell the truth," or words to that effect, without placing a hand on the Bible or referring to God.

What is a material witness?

A material witness is one who has knowledge about the case that no one else has. The only eyewitness to a shooting would be a material witness because he can give firsthand evidence about a criminal act.

A material witness may, in some criminal cases, be held in prison against his will to make sure he testifies. But in some states there are limits to how long such a witness can be held. In North Carolina, it is 20 days with possible 5-day extensions. In Wisconsin, a material witness must post bail to ensure his appearance in court. If he cannot put up the money, he can be arrested and held for up to 15 days, during which time he is required to give a deposition (give testimony as he would at the trial).

Harold was a witness to an accident in which a motorcycle hit a pedestrian. The lawyers for both sides have sent him a list of questions to which they want his written answers. Are they allowed to do this?

Yes, but Harold does not have to respond. Written questions that are to be answered in writing and under oath are called interrogatories, and only the defendant and the plaintiff in a lawsuit are required to answer them.

However, the lawyers may compel Harold to give a deposition, in which he orally answers questions that are usually oral, but may be written (and read aloud to him). To do this, the lawyers would serve Harold with a subpoena to appear at a certain place, such as at one of their offices, and they would have a court reporter record his testimony while he answered the questions under oath.

Nicole is a witness in an accident case. Can she send in a written statement instead of going to court in person?

No. Witnesses are required to give their testimony in person, so that lawyers for both sides can question them. However, in exceptional circumstances, such as if Nicole were seriously ill or lived far away, her deposition could be used instead of live testimony.

Being a Witness

Rick was told to wait outside the courtroom until he was called to the witness stand to testify. Why?

Lawyers want to make certain that each witness testifies from his own memory, based on his personal observation and knowledge. Lawyers fear that if a witness hears the testimony of others, he could be influenced, consciously or unconsciously, to reshape his testimony. If Rick is asked to wait outside the courtroom, he must comply.

Teresa is going to be a witness in a criminal trial. She will have an hour's drive to the courthouse and will have to sit there every day until she is called. Can she get paid for doing this?

Yes, if her state has a law providing for witness fees. Such laws usually cover mileage and set a dollar amount for each day the witness must attend court. But the fees can be quite small. For example, in Wisconsin, witnesses are paid $16 per day and 20 cents per mile; in Massachusetts, they receive $6 per day and 10 cents per mile. Michigan makes a distinction between civil and criminal cases; in civil trials, the witness receives $12 a day and 10 cents per mile; in criminal matters, a witness for the prosecution who has come from another state or a foreign country may be reimbursed for his reasonable expenses. Teresa should ask the attorney who called her as a witness if the state has witness fees and what she must do to get paid.

Daisy did not tell the truth while under oath as a witness. What could happen to her?

Lying under oath in court is a crime known as perjury, and is punishable by a fine, imprisonment, or both.

Under what circumstances is "taking the Fifth" a good idea? Is it the same as conceding guilt?

The Fifth Amendment right against self-incrimination allows you to refuse to respond to questions that would force you to implicate yourself in a crime. But if you take the witness stand of your own free will to testify about an event that could incriminate you, you then lose the protection of the Fifth Amendment. You also cannot claim your Fifth Amendment privilege to remain silent if you have been granted immunity from prosecution in order to persuade you to testify. You should always seek legal advice before giving up your right to Fifth Amendment protection.

"Taking the Fifth" is not the same as admitting guilt. A judge or a jury cannot assume that a defendant is guilty merely because he chooses to invoke his Fifth Amendment right not to testify.

Someone Bill is scheduled to testify against keeps phoning him at home. What can he do to stop this?

Bill should inform the police or the prosecuting attorney. Harassing or trying to intimidate a witness is a crime. The person calling Bill could be both fined and jailed.

What types of protection are available to witnesses who may be in danger because of their testimony in criminal cases?

Generally, a witness who is in danger will be kept under police surveillance or even given a personal bodyguard for the duration of the trial. If a witness in a federal case is threatened with violence or if he will be in real danger even after the trial as a result of his testimony, the U. S. attorney general's office will establish a completely new identity for him. It will arrange for documents reflecting the witness's new identity, help with relocating and finding a new job, and provide any other assistance that may be needed. States may administer their own witness-protection programs. To find out about them, contact your local prosecuting attorney's office or the police department.

Glossary

abandonment The voluntary surrender of property or rights with no intention of reclaiming them. Putting your old bicycle out to be picked up with the trash is abandonment; if a neighbor takes the bike and repairs it, you have no right to take it back.

abet To encourage someone to commit a crime.

abrogate To repeal or abolish; for example, to cancel a law by repealing it or declaring it unconstitutional.

abstract Summary or recap; a short history of who has owned a particular piece of real estate.

abuttals Boundary lines around a plot of land.

accessory Person who helps another to commit a crime, but who is not personally at the scene when the crime is committed. An accessory before the fact helps someone plan or prepare to commit a crime. An accessory after the fact helps the criminal hide or get away.

accomplice Person who helps or encourages another to commit a crime.

accord and satisfaction Agreement by a creditor to accept something different from what is called for under the contract he entered. For example, if a mason agrees to pave your driveway and does it badly, he may be willing to accept a lower fee for the job than the one you originally agreed to pay him.

acquit To find a defendant in a criminal trial not guilty; to release someone from an obligation.

action Legal proceeding, such as a criminal trial or a civil lawsuit, undertaken to (1) determine whether or not someone has committed a crime, (2) obtain monetary compensation for a wrong or injury, (3) enforce someone's right, or (4) prevent a wrong from being done.

ademption Selling, giving away, or using up of property that a person has left to someone in his will, so that when he dies the property is no longer part of his estate and cannot be given to the heir as the will provides.

ad hoc Latin phrase meaning "for this," or "for a specific purpose." For example, an ad hoc committee is a group that is formed to study or address a particular problem.

adjournment Temporary or indefinite postponement.

adjudication Act or process by which a court reaches a decision; judgment handed down by the court.

ad litem Latin phrase meaning "for the lawsuit." A guardian *ad litem* is a guardian appointed by the court during a lawsuit, hearing, or other legal proceeding, to represent someone who is considered incompetent because of age or mental condition.

admissible Acceptable for use in a court hearing; relevant to the case.

adultery Voluntary sexual relations by a married person with someone other than his or her spouse; adultery is usually grounds for divorce.

advocate To plead someone else's position or case. A person, such as a lawyer, who argues for a specific position or proposal.

affidavit Written statement made under oath and witnessed by a notary public or other authorized person.

agent Person authorized to act on behalf of another, as in transacting business or managing property.

age of majority Age of adulthood; age at which a person can legally act on his own behalf—typically, age 18 or 21, depending on the state.

aggravated Severe or intensified; for example, aggravated assault involves attacking someone with a dangerous weapon; simple assault does not involve the use of a weapon.

alien Someone from a foreign country who has not been naturalized according to the laws of the country in which he is living.

alimony Money paid by one spouse to an ex-spouse by order of a judge. The term *alimony* is gradually being replaced by the terms *maintenance* and *support.*

allegation Accusation made by someone in a lawsuit; it indicates what he hopes to prove.

amicus curiae Latin phrase meaning "friend of the court." A person or organization who is not involved in a lawsuit, but who may be affected by the court's decision, may with the court's permission prepare arguments or point out information that the court ought to take into consideration when making a decision.

amnesty General pardon granted by a government for a crime, often before a trial or conviction.

amortization Payment of a debt, such as a mortgage, in installments over a specified time period.

annulment Declaration that something is, always was, and will continue to be, void. A court or church order stating that a marriage never existed.

answer Written response prepared by the defendant in a lawsuit, which admits or denies accusations made against him.

appeal Act of asking a higher court to review a case when one disagrees with the judgment of the lower court.

appellate Pertaining to appeals. For example, the federal and state supreme courts are appellate courts because they hear appeals from lower courts.

appropriate To designate money or property for a particular use.

arbitrate To try to help disputants to reach a settlement. Arbitration can be used to settle disputes that might otherwise end in a lawsuit.

arraignment Court hearing in which a judge reads the charges against someone accused of a crime in order to allow him to make a plea of guilty, not guilty, or no contest.

arrears Overdue payments, debts.

arson Crime of maliciously setting fire to a house or other property.

artificial persons Persons created by law, as opposed to natural persons. Corporations are artificial persons.

assault and battery Acts of violence toward another person. The unlawful, intentional touching of someone else. Assault involves a threat or attempt to do physical harm; battery involves the actual touching or striking of the other person. An assault is more serious if it results in serious bodily injury or if it is committed with a deadly weapon (aggravated assault).

assignment Transfer of property rights from one person to another.

attachment Court order, or writ, authorizing the sheriff or other official to seize something a person owns (other than real estate) as security for payment of a court judgment; often the property is sold to get money to satisfy the debt.

attest To affirm that something, such as a signature, is genuine or true.

attorney-in-fact Person who is authorized to act on behalf of someone else in business dealings or for other purposes. The authority to function in this way is given by a letter of attorney, or power of attorney.

attractive nuisance Something on a person's property that attracts children and that is potentially dangerous to them, such as a swimming pool without a fence around it.

bail Release of a person under arrest in exchange for a promise to appear in court to answer the charge that has been made against him. In order to obtain bail, it is usually necessary to post money (also referred to as bail) or a bail bond.

bail bond Surety bond, or written guarantee by one person, called the surety, to pay a certain amount of money to the court if an accused person fails to appear for trial. Generally, an accused person pays a bail bondsman a certain percentage of the bail amount (generally a little more than 10 percent) to act as surety.

bailiff Official who maintains order in a courtroom.

bailment Entrusting of property to another for a special purpose, such as repair or safekeeping. Bringing clothes to a laundry or putting a car in a garage for repairs are examples of bailment.

balloon loan Loan requiring the borrower to make a number of small regular payments and one very large final payment. Often the borrower must refinance the loan in order to make the final balloon payment.

bargain and sale deed Deed that lists the amount paid for the property and states that the property is being transferred to the new owner.

beneficiary Person named to receive property or money, as in a will or insurance policy.

bequest Gift, given through a will, of money or other property that is not real estate.

beyond a reasonable doubt Level of proof required in criminal trials; a jury must be convinced that the defendant committed the crime, not that he probably committed the crime.

bigamy Crime of having two spouses at the same time.

bill of lading Receipt issued by a railroad, trucker, or other transport company, showing which goods have been received for shipment; terms of the contract may also be included.

bill of particulars Document that gives the details of the charges being brought against the defendant in a lawsuit or criminal trial.

bill of sale Documented proof that ownership of property has been transferred from seller to buyer.

binder In insurance, a document providing temporary protection to an insured person. In real estate, an agreement indicating that a person has paid a small sum for the right to buy a particular piece of property.

binding Enforceable; imposing a duty. A binding contract is one in which the people involved are required to carry out its terms.

blackmail Crime of forcing someone to give something of value to keep from having something revealed that would incriminate him or ruin his reputation; extortion.

bona fide Latin phrase meaning "in good faith." Sincere, with good intentions, without fraud or deceit.

bond Written promise to pay a fixed sum of money at a future date and at a specific interest rate—for example, a U. S. savings bond; a type of insurance in which a company or individual will reimburse another person for any loss suffered because of the actions of a third person.

boycott Refusal to conduct business with a person or company until certain practices cease.

breach Failure to uphold one's part of a contract; violation of the law.

breach of the peace Crime of disturbing the peace and quiet of a community with disorderly behavior.

bribery Crime of giving or offering a public official something of value in order to influence his actions.

brief Attorney's written summary of a law case.

broker Dealer or agent who is paid to buy or sell property, such as real estate or stocks.

burden of proof Responsibility of establishing that a disputed fact is true; presenting evidence in court to prove that the facts are as you allege them to be. In a criminal case, the burden of proof is always on the prosecutor, who must prove that the defendant is guilty; the defendant need not prove that he is innocent.

burglary Breaking into and entering a house or other building with the intention of committing a crime.

bylaws Set of regulations adopted by a corporation or other organization that governs the way the company will do business.

canon Principle, standard, or rule; a law of a religious denomination.

capital offense Any crime that is punishable by death.

carrying a concealed weapon Illegal possession of a hidden weapon—such as a gun, knife, or explosive device—on a person's body or within easy reach inside his car.

case law Legal principles established by judges in individual cases and used in deciding similar cases; part of the common law.

casualty Disaster or accident; a person who has been injured or property that has been lost or damaged.

causa mortis Latin phrase meaning "on account of death"; in expectation of death. Gifts *causa mortis* are given because the donor expects to die soon.

caveat emptor Latin phrase meaning "let the buyer beware"; in the past, this phrase was used to warn consumers that they had no legal remedy if they bought defective merchandise that was not covered by a written warranty. Today consumer protection laws reduce the risks of buying defective goods.

cease and desist Order issued by a government agency requiring an individual or a business to stop a particular practice; similar to an injunction, which is issued by a court.

certiorari Order from a higher court to a lower one to prepare a certified copy of a case for review.

champerty Illegal agreement in which a person agrees to pay someone else's lawsuit expenses in exchange for part of the settlement.

change of venue Moving of a trial from one district to another, or from one court to another, in order to assure a fair and impartial trial.

chattel Item of property other than real estate.

chattel mortgage Loan obtained by putting up property other than real estate as collateral.

circuit court Local court, also called county, superior, or district court, which has jurisdiction (legal authority) over a particular area.

circumstantial evidence Indirect evidence; testimony or facts from which other facts, which are important to the case, can be inferred.

citation Written order to appear in court; legal reference to a statute, court case, or other legal authority.

civil action Lawsuit between individuals or companies to get money, stop a particular activity, or enforce a civil right (as opposed to criminal action, in which the state prosecutes someone for violating a law).

clerk of the court Employee who files court documents (pleadings, motions, or judgments), has access to court records, and issues summonses and subpoenas.

closing Final step in buying a house, in which the deed is given to the owner, money is given to the seller, and the mortgage is secured.

codicil Amendment to a will that changes or explains a part of it.

collateral Property or money pledged as security to ensure repayment of a loan.

collective bargaining Process by which an employer and a representative of his employees (generally a labor union leader) make agreements about the workers' hours, wages, rights, and benefits.

collusion Secret agreement made by two or more people to cheat someone or to defraud him of a legal right or possession.

comaker Cosigner; someone who signs a contract or promissory note and guarantees payment in the event that the borrower defaults.

common carrier Person or business that transports people or property for a fee, such as a bus company.

common law System of law based on traditions and customs and on decisions rendered in previous cases (case law) rather than on legislation.

common-law marriage Marriage that is not solemnized by a wedding ceremony. It is created when a couple agree to marry, present themselves as married, and live together as man and wife. Not all states recognize common-law marriages.

community property Property acquired by a husband and wife during their marriage, with each spouse holding a half-interest. Generally excludes property acquired through inheritance or as a gift.

commutation Change; reduction in a convicted criminal's sentence.

competent Possessing all the legal requirements to do something. For example, the law requires a person to have reached a certain age (usually 18 or 21) in order to make a contract, and so children are not considered competent to do so, and if a child tries to enter a contract it can be declared void.

complainant Plaintiff; one who initiates a lawsuit.

complaint Document initiating a civil lawsuit, typically containing a brief description of the facts and what the plaintiff believes he is entitled to; a charge seeking prosecution for a criminal offense.

conciliation Meeting to resolve a dispute in a friendly manner; pretrial technique used to settle differences and avoid a trial.

condemnation Procedure for taking private property for public use. The Fifth Amendment to the Constitution requires that the owner receive "just compensation" for his property.

condominium Complex of apartments or buildings in which different persons own the individual units but all owners have an interest in the common areas, such as stairways, hallways, elevators, and lawns.

condonation Forgiving or pardoning of an offense by acting as if it had not been committed.

confiscate To legally seize property without payment, usually because the owner was using it illegally or did not legally own it. For example, the police may confiscate stolen property from a suspected thief.

consanguinity Blood relationship; kinship. The connection between persons with the same ancestor.

consequential damages Losses, damage, or injuries that are not directly caused by an act, but are a result of that act. For example, in a lawsuit for breach of contract, the profits lost because goods were not delivered on time are considered consequential damages.

conservator Person appointed to handle someone's financial affairs—generally because the person is unable to handle them himself.

consideration Something of value offered in a contract in exchange for something else of value. It is an inducement, such as a money payment, to get a person to perform his part of the agreement. For example, in a contract to buy a car, the consideration given the dealer is the price of the car, and the consideration given the buyer is the car itself. For a contract to be valid, each side must offer consideration to the other.

consignment Delivery of property to someone for resale.

conspiracy Illegal or harmful plot between two or more people.

constitutional law Principles of law established in the U. S. Constitution or in a state constitution.

contempt of court Intentional disregard for the authority or dignity of the court, such as by disobeying its orders or disrupting its proceedings.

contested divorce Case in which only one spouse wants a divorce or in which there is no agreement regarding division of property or child custody.

contingent Dependent on an event, the outcome of which is unknown.

contingent fee Attorney's fee that is dependent upon the outcome of the case or upon factors other than the attorney's time. Often used in personal injury cases, where the attorney receives a percentage of the money awarded to his client if he wins.

continuance Delay or postponement of a court proceeding.

contract Binding agreement between persons or businesses to do or not to do something.

contribution Right to collect from others who are equally responsible for an amount one has paid in excess of one's fair share. For example, if Bob and Jane jointly owe Dan $200 and Bob pays the entire amount, he has a right of contribution from Jane for $100.

conversion Unlawful taking or use of someone else's property.

convey To transfer ownership.

conviction Final judgment in a criminal trial, finding the defendant guilty as charged.

cooling-off period Period of inaction; a time to reconsider. In door-to-door sales transactions, the time given to cancel an order or purchase.

cooperative Multidwelling complex where the tenants lease their apartments, but own shares in the entire complex, forming a corporation.

copyright Legal protection given to the author or artist for the exclusive right to reprint, publish, or sell additional copies of his work for a specified period of time.

corporation Business or organization formed by a group of people, with rights and liabilities separate from those of the individuals involved.

corpus delicti Latin phrase meaning "body of the crime"; something that shows a crime has been committed, such as a dead body with a stab wound or a safe that has been broken into.

cosign To sign a contract as a backup in case the primary signer does not fulfill his part of the contract. Cosigners are often used to back up persons making loan agreements.

counselor-at-law Attorney, lawyer.

counterclaim Claim brought by the defendant against the plaintiff in a lawsuit. If the defendant is successful, the counterclaim may reduce the plaintiff's claim or result in the plaintiff's paying the defendant.

counterfeiting Crime of making a false copy or imitation of something—especially currency—with the intention of passing it off as genuine.

court-martial Court that tries members of the armed forces for violations of military law; civilians and members of the armed forces who commit nonmilitary crimes cannot be brought before this court.

covenant Any written agreement, or contract; clause or specific stipulation within a contract.

creditor Person or company to whom someone owes money.

crime of passion Crime committed impulsively under the influence of a sudden outburst of rage, terror, hatred, or some other overpowering emotion. For example, if a man discovers his wife in the act of adultery and kills her in a fit of rage, he has committed a crime of passion. Passion can be used as a defense against a charge of premeditated murder and may reduce the charge to manslaughter, which carries a less severe penalty.

cross-examination Questioning of a witness by the opposing attorney in a legal case.

curtesy In the past, the property to which a husband was entitled when his wife died. The concept of curtesy has been eliminated or drastically changed by state laws.

custody Responsibility for keeping and caring for a person or property. Also, the legal confinement of a person, as in protective custody or arrest and imprisonment.

damages Amount of money that a court may order the defendant in a lawsuit to pay the person who brought the suit to compensate him for any loss or harm the defendant caused.

debenture Document indicating that a debt is owed and will be paid, usually without putting up any collateral.

debt consolidation loan Arrangement for combining and repaying several debts; the debtor makes installment payments to a single creditor who, in turn, pays the original debts.

decedent Person who has died.

decree Judgment of a court.

de facto Latin phrase meaning "in fact"; actually. Used to describe a government, corporation, officer, or state of affairs that has to be accepted, but is illegal or illegitimate.

defamation Attack on someone's reputation; slander, libel.

default To fail to fulfill a legal or contractual duty.

default decree Court judgment entered against a defendant who failed to appear in court and defend himself; also called a default judgment.

default docket Group of uncontested cases on a court's calendar.

defendant Person who is being sued or prosecuted.

de jure Latin phrase meaning "by right"; legal or legitimate.

delinquent Late in fulfilling an obligation, such as repaying a loan.

demurrer Response by the defendant alleging that, even if the plaintiff's accusations were true, there would be no need to go further with the claim; there is nothing for which the defendant should be made to answer.

deport To send someone back to the country from which he came.

deposition Sworn testimony taken out of court to gather information before trial; a part of the legal procedure called discovery.

descent and distribution State laws governing the distribution of a person's property to his heirs when he dies without leaving a will.

detainer Keeping someone against his will; holding property unlawfully, such as borrowing tools and failing to return them.

devise To transfer ownership of real estate by means of a will.

disbar To revoke an attorney's license to practice law.

disclaimer Rejection of a claim, property, or right; document that rejects such a claim.

discovery Pretrial procedure in which investigations are made to uncover evidence about a case.

dismissal Court order ending a trial before it begins, or while it is in progress but before a verdict is reached.

disorderly house House or building where something illegal is going on that creates a nuisance or threatens the public welfare. Drug houses, gambling houses, and houses of prostitution are examples.

dissolution Termination of a marriage by divorce; cancellation of a contract; termination of a corporation.

dividend Payment of a share of the profits, given to stockholders in a corporation; payment by an insurance company to policyholders with participatory policies.

docket Calendar, or record, of the cases scheduled to be heard in a court.

dower Formerly, what a widow was entitled to receive from her deceased husband's estate. Today, the concept of dower has been either completely abolished or drastically changed by state inheritance laws.

due process Legal requirements that must be met, under the Constitution, before a person can be deprived of life, liberty, or property.

durable power of attorney Authority of one person (the attorney-in-fact) to act on behalf of another (the principal) in business or personal matters even after the principal is determined to be legally incompetent to manage his affairs. Also the document bestowing this authority.

duress Undue pressure or force to persuade someone to do something, such as to include someone in a will or get married.

earnest money Money paid to a seller to show the buyer's intention to carry out his part of the contract.

easement Right to use another's property for a particular purpose, such as the right of the city to run a sewer line across your land.

emancipation Freeing of someone from another's authority or control. A child is emancipated from his parents when he reaches the age of adulthood (usually 18 or 21, depending on state law) or gets married.

embezzlement Crime of misappropriating money or goods by a person to whom they have been entrusted.

eminent domain Authority of the government to take private property for public use for a fair price.

en banc Full bench; a court session for which the number of judges hearing a case is at its greatest. For example, three of the five judges may hear a routine case, but for important cases, all five may be present.

encroach To trespass; to illegally intrude on someone else's land.

encumbrance Anything that lessens the value of real estate or hinders its sale; any claim that someone other than the owner has on real estate. For example, a mortgage is an encumbrance on a piece of land.

entrapment Deception by an official to trick a person into committing a crime he would not otherwise commit.

equal protection of the law Treating a person the same as others and not denying him the protection afforded by the law. The Constitution guarantees this, to prevent the government from favoring one group of people over another.

equitable distribution Fair division of property, as in a divorce, even if only one spouse's name appears on the title or deed as the owner.

equity Decision based on fairness; value of property after deducting the mortgage and other liabilities.

ERISA Acronym for the *Employee Retirement Income Security Act,* the federal law that regulates employee pension plans.

escheat Right of the government to take property when there is no owner, as when a property owner dies without a will or any natural heirs.

escrow Deed, title, or money held by a third person until all conditions of a contract have been met.

estate Everything a person owns or has a financial interest in; the property of a deceased person.

estoppel Condition by which a person cannot change an earlier statement or action if it will cause loss or injury to another person.

evict To force a tenant to move out.

evidentiary Having the quality of evidence or proof.

exclusive occupancy Right of only one person to use real estate.

exculpatory agreement Agreement releasing someone from liability for the consequences of his acts, except for harm or damage resulting from wilful misconduct or gross negligence.

execute To complete; a document is executed when it is signed or when its terms have been carried out. In criminal law, to carry out the death penalty.

executor Person designated to carry out the terms of a will.

exemplary damages Award in a lawsuit in excess of the actual loss; punitive damages; an amount assessed against the defendant to punish him for his actions.

expert witness Someone with special knowledge of a trade, science, or activity, who testifies in court to interpret or explain a fact or other evidence.

ex post facto Latin phrase meaning "after the fact"; routinely applied to a law that makes an act a crime after it has already been committed. The Constitution prohibits such laws.

express Specifically stated or written; a printed warranty with its terms spelled out is an express warranty.

expunge To totally erase or destroy something, such as a charge from a criminal record.

extortion Crime of taking money by force, threat, or misuse of authority.

extradition Surrender by one state or government of a person accused of a crime to another state or government.

fee simple Full rights of ownership in a piece of real estate.

felony Serious crime, such as murder, rape, or arson, generally punishable by imprisonment for more than a year or by death.

fiduciary Person, such as an executor, or institution, such as a bank, that has a duty to act for the benefit of another person because he or it is in a position of trust or confidence.

filing Giving a legal document to the clerk of the court so that it can be placed in the appropriate court records or stamped "received" and routed to other court personnel for further action or review.

fixture Anything that has been attached to a house or other type of real estate and is considered part of the property. A built-in closet is a fixture.

foreclose To terminate rights, as in a mortgage, by taking and selling the property to pay the debt.

forfeit To give up or lose something as a penalty for a crime, for neglect of a duty, or for breach of contract.

forgery Crime of making a false document or altering a genuine one with the intention of defrauding someone.

franchise License to sell a specific brand of product or own and operate a branch of a particular business, such as a fast-food restaurant chain.

fraud Crime of intentionally misrepresenting something for personal gain or to harm someone.

fraudulent Misleading or false.

full covenant and warranty Type of deed that transfers ownership of real estate with a guarantee that no one else has a claim to the property.

garnishment Court order allowing a creditor who has won a lawsuit to have access to the defendant's money or property to collect the debt. For example, if the court allows a loan company to garnishee your wages, your employer must deduct money from your wages to pay the loan company the amount ordered.

grand jury Group of citizens who hear evidence presented by the prosecution in criminal cases and decide whether there is sufficient evidence to establish that a crime has been committed and that the named individual should be tried for that crime. The grand jury does not determine guilt or innocence.

guardian Someone charged with legal custody of a person who has been declared unable to take care of himself.

habeas corpus Latin phrase meaning "you have the body"; a court order directing a person who is detaining someone to bring that person to court and explain why he is being held. Used to obtain the release of a person who is being unlawfully imprisoned.

hearing Proceeding in which evidence is presented or witnesses are heard. Usually less formal than a trial. Hearings may be held before legislative committees or government agencies.

hearsay Testimony by a witness about matters he heard of from someone else, but about which the witness has no personal knowledge.

holographic will Last will and testament that is entirely handwritten by the person making it.

homicide Killing of one human being by another, whether justified (as in war or self-defense) or not (as in manslaughter or murder).

hung jury Jury that cannot come to an agreement and reach a verdict.

illegitimate Contrary to the law; in reference to children, those born out of wedlock.

immunity Exemption from duties or penalties normally required.

impanel To list possible jurors.

incest Sexual relations between two people who are related too closely to be legally married. Incest is a crime.

incriminate To accuse someone of a crime or otherwise imply that he is guilty of wrongdoing.

indemnity Security against injury, loss, or damages. An insurance policy is an indemnity contract under which the insurance company will reimburse you for losses you incur because of injury, loss, or damage.

indict To charge a person with committing a crime.

in forma pauperis Latin phrase meaning "in the character or manner of a pauper"; being unable to afford court costs or other legal fees; being allowed to file a lawsuit without paying costs.

informed consent Agreement to submit to something, such as surgery, made with full knowledge of all the risks and alternatives involved.

infraction Violation of an ordinance, statute, or law.

infringement Violation of a right. For example, the unauthorized copying of a book protected by copyright is an infringement of the copyright.

injunction Court order to do or stop doing something specific.

in loco parentis Latin phrase meaning "in place of the parent"; having parental rights over a child without being the child's actual parent.

inquest Legal investigation by a jury or coroner into the cause of a death.

insolvency Inability to pay debts.

instrument Written legal document, such as a deed, contract, or check.

interlocutory decree Temporary court decision during the course of a lawsuit. Often used during a divorce before the final decree is issued.

interrogatories Series of written questions, given to the plaintiff and defendant in a lawsuit before a trial, which must be answered in writing under oath; a form of the legal procedure called discovery.

inter vivos Latin phrase meaning "between living persons." An *inter vivos* trust is set up during the lifetime of the person creating the trust to provide income to someone.

intestate Having died without leaving a valid will.

joint property Property owned by two or more persons.

joint tenancy Ownership of the same property by two or more persons at the same time, generally with the right of survivorship. Under the right of survivorship, when one owner dies, the property goes to the other owner or owners, and the deceased owner's heirs have no claim to it.

judgment Court decision that resolves a dispute and determines each person's rights and responsibilities.

jurisdiction Power of the court to rule upon certain issues.

jurisprudence Science or philosophy of law; a system of laws.

kidnapping Crime of seizing a person, usually to obtain ransom.

laches Defense raised when the plaintiff has delayed bringing a lawsuit for so long that the defendant has lost the opportunity to defend himself.

larceny Crime of theft; taking someone else's personal goods for one's own personal use.

lease Formal agreement between a landlord and his tenant about the rental of property.

legacy Something other than real estate that is left to someone in a will.

legislation Act of passing laws; laws made by a legislative body.

legitimize To make lawful; to make legitimate the status of a child who was illegitimate—that is, his parents were not married at the time of his birth.

letter of credit Document issued by a bank, promising to back up or pay a businessman's or company's financial obligations in another place, usually a foreign country.

liability Duty or responsibility, such as a duty to pay a debt or responsibility for injuries suffered in an accident.

libel Form of defamation involving a written statement that damages a person's or a company's reputation.

lien Legal claim against property to ensure payment of a debt; it allows the property to be taken and sold if the debt is not paid.

life estate Right to use real estate during the lifetime of an individual who is not necessarily the person who will occupy the land. For example, you might grant the use of your house to your brother until his death, at which time your daughter will be given the house to live in. A person with a life estate cannot pass the property on to his heirs.

limited divorce Divorce without any allowance for support; a decree of legal separation.

liquidate To pay and settle a debt.

liquidated damages Set amount of money a person agrees to pay if he breaks a contract.

litigate To sue.

loitering Crime of lingering idly or prowling about in a public place, especially for the purpose of begging, dealing drugs, or soliciting for prostitution.

magistrate Judge who has limited authority, such as a justice of the peace or a judge in a police court.

maintenance Means of spousal support; synonym for *alimony*.

malice Intent to cause injury, death, or severe harm.

malpractice Professional misconduct; failure to follow the accepted standards set by a profession in providing service to one's clients.

mandate Court order issued from a higher court to a lower one or from a court to an individual.

manslaughter Killing of a human being without malice. It is *voluntary* if it is committed intentionally, as in a fit of sudden passion; it is *involuntary* if it is committed unintentionally—for example, as a result of carelessness.

marital misconduct Behavior that would provide grounds for divorce, such as adultery or desertion.

marital property Things acquired by a couple while they are married.

mayhem Crime of maiming, disabling, or disfiguring someone.

mechanic's lien Claim on property for work done or materials furnished. Failure to pay for goods or services could result in the sale of the property.

mediate To act as a go-between to help settle a dispute.

misdemeanor Category of crime that is not as serious as a felony; generally punishable by a fine or short-term imprisonment.

misfeasance Doing something legal, but in an improper way. For example, cleaning a gun is legal and proper, but cleaning it while it is still loaded is misfeasance.

misrepresentation Incorrect or false statement, whether made deliberately in order to mislead someone or made innocently in ignorance of its falsity.

mistrial Trial that is terminated because of legal errors or the failure of the jury to reach a verdict.

mitigating circumstances Facts or events that, although they do not excuse a person's conduct, reduce the blame for it.

mortgage Document that puts up property as collateral to pay a loan—often a loan made to finance the purchase of the property.

mortgagee The lender in a mortgage agreement, generally a bank or other financial institution.

mortgagor The borrower in a mortgage agreement; the person buying a home who puts it up as collateral for the loan.

murder The crime of intentionally and maliciously killing someone.

naturalization Process a foreigner goes through to become a citizen.

naturalized citizen A foreigner who has met the requirements for becoming a citizen and has taken an oath of allegiance to his new country.

negligence Failure to use the standard of care a reasonable person would use in a given situation.

negotiable Transferable from one person to another. A negotiable instrument is any signed, written agreement to transfer money to another person. Checks, bank drafts, and promissory notes are all examples of negotiable instruments.

negotiate To bargain with someone over something, such as a purchase or terms of a contract; to transfer funds to another person by endorsing a check or negotiable stock or bond.

no-fault divorce Divorce in which it need not be shown that either spouse is at fault, but only that there are irreconcilable differences between husband and wife.

nolo contendere Latin phrase meaning "I do not wish to contest"; a plea of no contest entered by a criminal defendant, which means he does not admit guilt but agrees to be sentenced or punished by the court.

nominal damages Small sum of money awarded by a court to compensate the plaintiff for a violation of his rights or a breach of duty by the defendant, even though the plaintiff has suffered no substantial loss or injury.

non compos mentis Latin phrase meaning "not having mastery of one's mind"; insane; not of sound mind.

nonfeasance Failure to perform a required duty.

notary Public officer who administers oaths and witnesses signatures on documents.

note Written promise to pay.

nuisance Anything that interferes with a person's quiet enjoyment of his property or that disturbs, inconveniences, or harms the public at large. Noisy neighbors and the storage of explosives in a residential neighborhood are examples of nuisances.

oath Formal declaration or promise to do something.

obscenity Offensive material designed to stimulate an obsessive interest in nudity or sex, and lacking any redeeming social value.

obstruction of justice Interference with the operation of a court.

ordinance Law enacted by a city government or other municipal body.

palimony Financial settlement made between two people who are separating after a period of cohabiting without being married to each other.

parens patriae Latin phrase meaning "parent of the country"; the role of the government to protect and be guardian of those people who are legally unable to act for themselves, usually children.

parole Release of a prisoner from part of his sentence provided he meets certain conditions, including reporting to a parole officer at regular intervals. If he does not abide by these conditions, he must return to prison to serve out the rest of his term.

partnership Agreement of two or more people to operate a business with the expectation of sharing the profits and dividing the losses.

party Person, group, or business involved in a contract or lawsuit. For example, the buyer and seller who sign a sales agreement are parties to a contract; the plaintiff and defendant are parties to a lawsuit.

patent Legal protection given to an inventor against the unauthorized use of his invention.

paternity Fatherhood.

penal Relating to punishment.

peremptory challenge Right of the plaintiff's and defendant's lawyers in a jury trial to object to a specified number of prospective jurors without having to give a reason.

perjury Crime of knowingly making a false statement while under oath.

permit License, or written permission, to take specific action. For example, a builder may need a permit to remodel a home.

personal property Anything that can be owned, except real estate.

petition Written request to the court for a particular remedy, stating the facts on which the request is based.

petit jury Trial jury; called petit (French for "little") because it is usually smaller than a grand jury. It weighs evidence presented by both sides in a criminal or civil case to determine the facts on which to base a verdict.

plaintiff Person who initiates a court proceeding, such as a lawsuit.

plea Criminal defendant's answer to the charges brought against him. The plea may be guilty, not guilty, or nolo contendere (no contest).

plea bargaining Negotiation, between the prosecutor and the defense attorney in a criminal case, to reduce the number or type of charges brought against the defendant in exchange for a guilty plea.

pleadings Formal written statements made by the plaintiff and the defendant (the complaint and the answer) in which they state their versions of the facts of the dispute.

power of attorney Authority to represent someone else (act as his agent) and do business in his name. It generally expires when the business in question has been completed or when the person being represented is declared incompetent—unless it is a durable power of attorney.

precedent Court decision or legal case that is used as a guide to help decide a similar case.

preliminary hearing Hearing held to decide if a crime has been committed and whether the accused should stand trial for that crime.

prenuptial agreement Document prepared by a couple, prior to their marriage, which outlines how property is to be divided in the event of separation, divorce, or death of a spouse.

preponderance of evidence In a civil lawsuit, the need to produce evidence that is more convincing than that presented by the other side in order to win the case.

prima facie Latin phrase meaning "at first sight"; something assumed to be true or factual in the absence of evidence to the contrary. Prima facie evidence is evidence presented by one side that is so strong that a judge or jury would decide in favor of that side unless the opposing side presented contradictory evidence.

principal Amount of a debt, not including interest; person primarily liable for a debt; person who authorizes someone to act on his behalf.

probable cause Strong reason to suspect something—for example, that a law has been or is being violated.

probate Court procedure that determines the validity of a will.

probation Permission for a person convicted of a crime to remain free from imprisonment as long as he stays out of trouble and periodically reports to a probation officer.

promissory note Signed document promising to pay a specified amount of money either on demand or on or after a designated date.

pro se Latin phrase meaning "for oneself"; representing oneself without the help of a lawyer.

prosecuting attorney The attorney for the government in criminal cases, who files charges against a person suspected of committing a crime and presents the case in court.

protective order Court mandate preventing the normal operation of the legal system when that might constitute an injustice. For example, if an elderly widow defaults on her mortgage and it is discovered that she intended to make the payments but was too ill to do so, the court may issue a protective order to keep the bank from foreclosing and give her the chance to pay. Also, a court order forbidding one person to continue to annoy or threaten to harm another.

proxy Someone authorized to act or decide for another person; also, the authorizing paper.

publication Public notification of an impending court action—generally by announcing it in a newspaper. Also, making a defamatory statement about someone to one or more others.

public nuisance Activity that is offensive, dangerous, or obstructive to a number of people.

public policy Legal principle saying that no one may violate the public good; the conscience of the people.

punitive damages Money awarded to the plaintiff in a lawsuit in order to punish the defendant for his malicious, negligent, or reckless conduct. It is in addition to any actual losses suffered by the plaintiff and can be used as a warning to others that such conduct will not be tolerated.

purchase agreement Contract for the sale of real estate, goods, or services.

quitclaim deed Document that transfers ownership of real estate, but contains no guarantees that the seller has a valid right to do so, or that others do not have rights to the land.

rape Crime of forcing a person to have sexual intercourse against his or her will.

real property Real estate; land and anything growing on it or attached to it, such as trees, fences, and buildings.

rebut To disprove or counter arguments or evidence presented by the opposing side in a trial.

receiving stolen goods Crime of accepting property that one knows has been illegally obtained.

reciprocity Mutual exchange of privileges between states or countries for their respective citizens. For example, states have reciprocal laws governing drivers' licenses, which allow someone with a license from one state to drive in another.

reckless endangerment Action that is taken without regard for the safety and welfare of others.

recognizance Promise to a court to do something, such as pay an overdue debt. Before a trial, a court may choose to release a person suspected of a crime from custody on his own recognizance: instead of posting bail, the suspect gives the court a written statement that he will appear for trial.

recourse Rights and remedies under the law. In banking, right of someone who holds a check—or other paper containing a promise to pay—to receive payment from anyone who endorses it, even when the person who wrote the check cannot pay.

remainder Ownership rights in real estate that take effect only after the rights of another end. For example, if Paul is given the family house to use during his lifetime, and upon his death the property goes to his brother Nathan, Nathan has a remainder.

remand To send back. An appellate, or higher, court may remand a case to a lower court for further action.

remedy Relief available to the person bringing the lawsuit after it has been proved that his rights were violated. Damages (money) are one type of remedy. A court order compelling a defendant to do something, such as honor a contract, is another type.

replevin Type of lawsuit to recover property that was taken illegally or borrowed and not returned.

representative payee Person or institution designated to receive money on behalf of another person who is unable to handle his personal affairs.

residuary estate In a will, all the property in the estate that is not specifically mentioned elsewhere in the will. A residuary clause in the will names the person or entity that is to receive this remaining property—for example, "I leave all the rest of my property to my beloved wife, Helen."

respondeat superior Latin phrase meaning "let the master answer"; the legal principle making an employer liable for what his employee does in the course of performing his job.

restraining order Court mandate stopping someone from doing something, but valid only until a hearing can be held to determine whether or not the mandate should continue in force.

restitution Restoration of something to its rightful owner; restoration of a person to the position he would have been in if a contract had not been broken.

retainer Money a client pays an attorney; the hiring of an attorney.

reversion Legal interest in property that a person keeps after transferring ownership to someone else. For example, if Carl transferred ownership of his property to Ned for life, with no one specified to receive the land at Ned's death, the property would revert to Carl or his heirs upon Ned's death.

riot Disturbance of the peace by three or more people who act together to terrorize others.

robbery Crime of taking goods or money by force or intimidation.

scienter Prior knowledge that something was going to happen and the deliberate failure to prevent it.

secured transaction Type of loan that gives the lender power to seize the property offered by the borrower as collateral if the borrower defaults on the loan. Car loans and installment purchases are secured transactions.

security deposit Money a tenant pays a landlord to cover any damages the tenant causes or to cover unpaid rent if the tenant breaks the lease.

sentence Penalty handed down to a defendant at the end of a criminal trial.

slander Talking maliciously about a person, or making false statements that injure the person's reputation.

solicit In criminal law, to encourage or ask someone to commit a crime.

specific performance Carrying out a contract exactly as the terms are written—a remedy sometimes ordered by a court when a contract has been broken, especially when monetary damages would be inadequate, as in the case of agreements to sell one-of-a-kind antiques.

status offender Someone whose behavior is unacceptable to society but who has not committed a crime, such as a child who will not obey his parents or teachers.

statute Law passed by Congress or a state legislature that declares, commands, or prohibits something.

statute of frauds Law that requires certain contracts to be in writing to be enforceable, such as contracts for the sale of real estate or of goods valued at over $500.

statute of limitations Law requiring a lawsuit or a criminal prosecution to be filed within a certain period of time for it to be heard in court.

statutory Pertaining to a statute, or law. Required by a law.

statutory rape Crime of having sexual intercourse with a girl (or in some states, a boy) who is under a certain age (generally 16 or 18) and therefore legally incapable of consenting to the act, even though she (or he) did not resist and perhaps even initiated it.

struck jury Jury that is chosen by having each attorney strike, or delete, names from a list of prospective jurors.

sublease Agreement by a tenant to rent premises to a third person during a part of the time the original tenant's lease is in effect.

subpoena Court order to appear and testify at a given time and place.

subrogate To transfer rights to another person.

sue To begin legal proceedings against a person or company or against the government because of an alleged wrongdoing.

summons Court order, or writ, notifying a person that a lawsuit has been started against him and giving the date by which he must go to court to file an answer to the charges against him or risk having a court judgment made against him by default.

surety bond Written guarantee (for a fee) to pay a second person a debt that the bonded person did not meet or to pay for a job he failed to do. For example, a builder might buy a surety bond to cover his work on a house; if something happened to prevent him from completing the job, the surety company would pay to have the work completed by someone else.

surrogate Substitute, such as a surrogate parent; in some states, the title of a probate judge.

sustain To uphold or support. A judge may sustain an attorney's objection during a trial, which means the judge agrees with the objection.

tenancy by the entirety Type of joint tenancy; an arrangement in which a husband and wife co-own property. Neither spouse can sell his or her share of the property without the other's consent, and when one spouse dies, the other automatically takes over full ownership of the entire property without having it go through probate.

tenancy in common Arrangement in which two or more people co-own the same property, but with no right of survivorship—that is, when one of the owners dies, his share of the property goes to his heirs, and not to his co-owners, as it would in a joint tenancy with the right of survivorship.

term life insurance Type of protection that will pay the beneficiary only if the insured person dies within the time specified in the policy.

testamentary Relating to a will; based on, derived from, or established in someone's will, such as a testamentary trust.

testator Person making a will.

title Rights of ownership of property; paper that indicates ownership.

title search Examination of deeds registered locally to make sure that a piece of real estate can be sold without anyone else's claiming rights to it.

tort Any wrong for which a person can be sued, except breach of contract.

treason Crime of attempting to overthrow the government to which one owes allegiance or of actively helping those who are seeking to do so.

trespass Illegal entry onto or interference with another person's land.

trial Hearing in a court of law, before a judge or jury, to determine facts and decide the outcome of a case.

trover Lawsuit to seek compensation from someone who has taken property without permission and converted it to his own use.

truant Child who deliberately and consistently misses school.

trust Arrangement by which one person (the trustee) holds property for the benefit of someone else (the beneficiary). The person setting up the trust is called the grantor, settlor, or trustor.

umbrella policy Type of insurance that increases the amount of protection in return for a relatively small increase in the premium.

uncontested divorce Divorce proceeding in which a couple agrees on such basic issues as child custody, support, and division of property.

usury Crime of charging an illegally high interest rate on a loan.

vandalism Crime of damaging or destroying someone else's property.

venue Geographical area in which a court may hear a case; place where a crime was committed or the events leading to a lawsuit occurred.

verdict Final decision made by a judge or jury.

vest To take effect; to confer ownership or the right to future enjoyment. For example, when your rights in your employer's retirement fund are vested, you are entitled to this money if you leave your job, even if you aren't yet eligible for retirement.

voir dire Old French phrase meaning "to speak the truth"; preliminary questioning of prospective jurors to determine if they are qualified and competent to serve on the jury.

waiver Written statement voluntarily relinquishing a right or claim.

ward Someone who has been legally declared unable to take care of himself and has had a guardian appointed; also, a division within a city.

warrant Written authorization or order to do a specific act—for example, an arrest warrant.

warranty Written or implied statement that a product is of a certain quality or has certain characteristics.

warranty of merchantability Statement or promise that a product will function for the purpose for which it was designed and will conform to industry standards.

whole life insurance Type of protection that is in force as long as premiums are paid, rather than for a predetermined period of time (term insurance). The policy premiums remain the same, with a cash value and dividends accumulating while the policy is in effect.

will Document stating how a person wishes his property to be distributed after his death.

writ Court order requiring a person to do or not to do a specified act.

wrongful death Death caused by the willful act or negligence of another person. Dependent heirs of the victim may be able to sue the person responsible for the death for loss of the support they had expected to receive from the deceased person.

Z Mark used to fill in blank spaces in a legal document, such as a contract, in order to prevent them from being filled in at a later time.

zoning laws Legislation dividing a municipality into districts for the purpose of limiting certain types of building or activity. For example, industry may be banned in some zones.

Index

Abortion, 92–93
Absentee voting, 459
Abuse
  of children, 94–96
    reporting, 89, 95–96
    sexual, 94
  of elderly parents, 96
  of wives, 93
Acceleration clauses, 282, 283, 365
Accessories to crimes, 602
Accidents and injuries, 476–492
  in amusement parks, 488
  in apartment buildings, 163, 478
  to assailants, 594–595, 619
  automobile, 252–262. *See also* Automobile accidents.
  in bars, 485–486
  at baseball games, 489–490
  boating, 491–492
  with borrowed property, 215, 480
  to burglars, 476
  on buses, 484
  to children
    babysitter's neglect and, 77–78
    in camps, agreeing not to sue for, 489
    in day-care centers, 78
    in Little League games, 490
    on others' property, 480–481
    in school football games, 89
    in school playgrounds, 490
    at skating rinks, 490
    in swimming pools, 481, 489
    toy safety and, 374
    while working, 483
    in zoos, 488–489
  to contractors, 181
  defective merchandise and, 374–375, 382
  dogs and, 204–207
  to door-to-door salesmen, 478–479, 482
  exculpatory agreements and, 489
  faulty repairs and, 480
  on golf courses, 488
  helping victims of, 486, 492
  in hospitals, 506–507
  household, 476–483. *See also* Household accidents.
  on ladder, 483
  lawsuits filed for
    criminal charges and, 623
    against government, 485
    lawyers' handling of, 33
    time limit on, 488
    winning, 476–477
Accidents and injuries *(continued)*
  to letter carriers, 482
  liability insurance for, 333–335
  on others' property, 482–483
  in public places, 485–491
  on public transportation, 483–485
  in railway stations, 484–485
  on sidewalks, 333, 485
  in stores
    merchandise displays and, 487–488, 490–491
    wet floors and, 486–487
  in taxicabs, 483–484
  time limit on filing claims for, 488
  warnings and, 483, 488
  workers' compensation for, 401–404. *See also* Workers' compensation.
  in zoos, 488–489
Accomplices to crimes, 602–603
Accountants
  errors made on income taxes by, 299
  tax lawyers vs., 16
Adjudication hearings, 613–614
Adoption, 64–70
  adoptive parents' age and, 68
  agencies in, 66–67
  buying children in, 66
  of foreign children, 65
    citizenship of, 66–67
  grandparents and, 70, 99
  inheritance and, 80
  lawyer needed for, 64
  legal rights of children after, 80
  natural parents' attempts to regain children, 69
  private, bonuses for natural mothers in, 64–65
  putting children up for, 68–69
  returning children after, 67
  by single persons, 65
  Social Security benefits and, 534
  of stepchildren, 69–70, 145
    divorce and, 145
    factors considered in, 68
    noncustodial parent's consent for, 67–68
  by unmarried couples, 65
  unwed father's prevention of, 69
Advertisements
  deceptive, 348–350
    false claims in, 348–349
    refunds and, 350
    sale items and, 350
  misprints in, 350
  photographs used without consent in, 470

Age discrimination, 384, 392, 410, 417, 418, 441, 516
AIDS, knowingly infecting others with, 599
Aid to Families With Dependent Children (AFDC), 291
Airlines, 377–379
  delays of, passenger accommodations during, 377
  fares raised by, 378
  height and weight requirements for jobs with, 384
  luggage lost by, 378–379
  overbooking
    compensation for delays in, 378
    hotel reservations lost because of, 378
Alarms, police's late response to, 591
Alcohol
  barroom injuries and, 485–486
  drunk driving and, 247–252, 342. *See also* Drunk driving.
  guests injured at parties and, 477–478
  minors furnished with, 82
    drunk driving and, 250
    false identification and, 83
Alcoholism
  as grounds for divorce, 131–132
  health insurance for, 323
  losing job because of, 419
Aliens
  Bill of Rights and, 452
  citizenship obtained by, 455, 456–457
  green cards for, 455–456
  professional licenses and, 467
  teaching jobs and, 467
Alimony, 138–140
  amount and duration, determining, 139
  conditions for, 138
  credit card applications and, 274–275
  while divorce is pending, 116
  ex-spouse's death and, 140
  ex-spouse's raises and, 139
  for husbands, 139
  income taxes and, 140
  increase in, 139
  late payment of, 139
  time limit for requesting, 139
  See also Child support; Divorce.
Americans With Disabilities Act, 447, 468
Amicus curiae, 634
Amusement parks, accidents in, 488
Animals
  deer killed on highway, 253
  farm animals, 192
  as pets, 203–207. *See also* Pets.
Annuities, 523
Annulment, 123–124
Antiques, reproductions sold as, 355
Apartments, cooperative, 170
  See also Condominiums; Landlords; Leases; Rented homes.
Appeals of court decisions, 638–639
  small claims court and, 642
Arbitration, 34–35
  for cars that are lemons, 227, 229
  small claims court vs., 642
Arlington National Cemetery, 588
Arrests, 605–609
  of abusive husbands, 591
  without arrest warrants, 605
  bail and, 593, 609–611
Arrests *(continued)*
  false, 608
  forcing police to make, 590
  legal rights after, 604, 608
  in other states, 609
  phone calls after, 605
  by private citizens, 608
  resisting, 605
  what to do for someone after, 608
  See also Crime; Police.
Arrest warrants, 605
Artificial insemination, legitimacy and, 72–73
Assault
  drunkeness as defense in, 595
  self-defense and, 594–595
Attorneys. *See* Lawyers.
Attractive nuisance, 481
At-will employment agreements, 387
Audits of income tax, 302–303
Automobile accidents, 252–262
  blind spots and, 257
  brake problems and, 255, 446
  of children, parents' liability for, 81
  city or state vehicles in, 257
  deaths resulting from, 602
  deer killed in, 253
  dogs and, 206
  drunk drivers, 251–252
  employees in, 445
  expired driver's licenses and, 241
  fault, admitting, 258
  fault of both drivers, 256
  faulty repairs and, 446
  Good Samaritan laws, 261
  helping victims, 253
  hit-and-run drivers, 19, 260–261, 342–343, 344
  insurance rates and, 341–342
  lawsuits after
    insurance, 261, 337
    partnership assets and, 433
    against spouse, 261
  liability, 254–262
    negligence and, 254–255
    of parents for children, 81
    personal vs. business, 437, 445
    releases from, 259–260
  loaned cars, 255
  medical examination after, 260
  money offered after, 259–260
  moving automobile after, 254
  multiple car, 258
  passengers, 255, 261
    releases signed by, 262
  potholes, 257, 338
  pregnant women, 345
  recalls of automobiles and, 262
  rented vehicles, 231
  reporting to police, 252, 260
  seat belt use and, 258–259
  stolen automobiles, 256
  taillight malfunctions and, 257
  taxicabs, 483–484
  traffic tickets and, 258
  undamaged cars in, 253–254
  uninsured or underinsured drivers, 343
  unoccupied parked cars, 253
  what to do after, 259
  witnesses to, 252, 255

Automobile insurance, 335–346
  adjusters for, 344–346
    body shops recommended by, 346
    discussing accidents with, 345
    legal advice, efforts to prevent seeking, 346
  amount of coverage needed, 336–337
  automobile loans and, 339
  cancellation, 340
  car thefts and, 338
  collision vs. comprehensive, 338
  foreign country, coverage for driving in, 338
  hit-and-run drivers, 260–261, 342–343, 344
  lawsuits for more than coverage, 337
  no-fault, 335–336
    lawsuits and, 337
    maximum payments allowed under, 338
  potholes, 338
  rate increases
    accidents and, 341–342
    for drunk drivers, 342
    factors considered, 341
  relatives living in home covered by, 339
  rented automobiles, 339
  reporting requirements, 340–341
  seat belts and, 337
  settlements, 344–346
    body shops recommended in, 346
    disagreements over, 346
    estimates on repairs, 346
    investigations in, 345
    pregnancy and, 345
    releases, 345
  state requirements, 335, 336
  surcharges, 342
  time limit for making claims, 340
  totaled cars and, 339–340
  types, 335
  uninsured or underinsured drivers, 343
Automobile repairs, 236–239
  avoiding rip-offs, 238–239
  blank orders for, 236
  damage to vehicles during, 237–238
  estimates on
    for insurance companies, 346
    lowballing, 237
  faulty, 237, 446
    reimbursement for, 238, 239
    time elapsed since, 238–239
  property in trunk stolen during, 239
  renting automobile during, 339
  storage charges, 236–237
  unauthorized, 236–237
Automobiles
  abandoned, 217–218
  buying, 226–230
    deposits, 226
    lawyers in, 17
    price discrepancies, 226
  children, special seats for, 243
  damaged in car washes, 256
  divorce and, 136
  dogs killed by, 206
  drunk driving, 247–252, 342. *See also* Drunk driving.
  engine replacements, 242
  firearms in trunks of, 464
  homeowners insurance and, 329
  joint ownership, 230, 576–577
Automobiles *(continued)*
  leasing, 231–232
  lemons, 227–229
  licenses, 240
  loans for, 226
    defaulting on, 290
    defective vehicles, 228
    insurance and, 339
    outstanding, selling cars with, 232
  police searches of, 472, 605
  recalls of, 228, 262
  registration
    expired, grace periods for, 242
    out-of-state driving, 240
  renting, 230–232
    accident insurance and, 339
    accidents and, 231
    collision damage waivers and, 230–231
    during repair of defective vehicles, 227
  repairs, 236–239. *See also* Automobile repairs.
  repossession, 229
  sales tax, 226
  seat belts, 243, 258–259, 337
  selling, 232–234
    to children, 232–233
    to friends, 234
    with outstanding loans, 232
    precautions, 233
    during probate of spouse's will, 576–577
    records needed, 232
  service plans, 235–236
  tampering with odometers, 227
  thefts, 598, 611
    damages resulting from, 256
    insurance and, 338
  trading in, before loan approval for new car, 226
  used
    dealers' misrepresentations of, 230
    defective, 230
    with invalid titles, 230
    warranties, 234, 235
  vandalized
    informing police, 590
    in parking garages, 256
  warranties, 234–236
    additional charges, 235
    defects arising during, 234
    extended, 235
    full vs. limited, 234–235
    repairs vs. replacements, 235
    for used automobiles, 234, 235
  See also Traffic tickets and violations.
Autopsies, 586

B

Babysitters
  children injured while in care of, 77–78
  consent for emergency medical treatment, 78
  income tax returns, 300
Bail (bond), 609–611
  credit cards, posting by, 609–610
  denial of, 610–611
  insufficient funds to pay, 610
  setting, factors considered, 610
  victims attend hearings on, 593

Bail bondsmen, 610
Bailments, law of, 211
Balloon mortgages, 179
Bank accounts, 264–272
direct deposits or withdrawals, 102, 531
disputes over balances, 266
joint, 60, 548
death of one owner and, 270
divorce and, 137
money mistakenly credited to, 266
Swiss, 265
See also Banks; Checks.
Bankruptcy, 303–306, 444–445
cosigned loans and, 180
credit and, 306
declaring
alternatives to consider before, 303–304
more than once, 306
employees' pensions and, 519–520
employees' wages and, 397–398
exempt vs. nonexempt property, 304, 305
incorporating and, 438, 444–445
of repair shops, reclaiming property after, 210–211
stockholders' claims, 295
types, 304–305, 444–445
Banks, 264–272
automatic bill payment by, 102, 266
automobiles repossessed by, 229
closed by government, 264
commercial vs. savings, 264
counterfeit money deposited in, 272
direct deposits in, 102, 531
errors made by
in automatic bill payment, 266
automatic teller machines, 266–267
crediting to accounts, 266
time limit for objecting to, 258
foreclosures by, 194–195
paperless banking, 267
safe-deposit boxes, 270–271
safety of money in, 264
service charges, 265–266
illegal, 266
on small accounts, 265
withdrawal transaction fees, 265
as stockbrokers, 298
See also Bank accounts; Checks; Loans.
Bars, intoxicated customers in
drunk driving, 250–251
fighting, 485–486
Baseball games, injuries at, 489–490
Better Business Bureau, 382
Bill of Rights, 452
Bills
automatically paid by banks, 102, 266
computer problems, 280
of deceased relatives, 580
errors, 280
household
divorce and, 137
responsibility for, 56
medical, 509–510
of children, 61
of elderly parents, 100, 107
hit-and-run drivers and, 260–261, 342–343
inability or refusal to pay, 509–510
Bills *(continued)*
nonpayment of
medical, 509–510
property seized for, 291–292
by valuable customers, 443
payment problems, 290–294
spousal responsibilities, 56, 57–58
in two-income families, 56
telephone, late payment of, 291
veterinarians', 206–207
See also Debts.
Bills of lading, 212–213
Binders, purchase agreements vs., 164
Birth certificates
in adoption, 67
for illegitimate children, 71–72
Birth control pills, for adolescents, 494
Blood tests
before marriage, 45
in paternity suits, 72
Boating accidents, 491–492
insurance for, 335, 492
Bond. *See* Bail.
Booby trap devices, 595
Borrowed property, 214–215
damages to, 214–215
secondhand replacements, 215
injuries resulting from, 215, 480
lost or stolen, 214
refusal to return, 215
Breath tests, 247, 248
Brokers and brokerages, 295–296
insurance, 308
real estate, 195–199. *See also* Real estate brokers.
stock, 295–298. *See also* Stockbrokers.
Burglars
injuries to, 476
shooting of, 192, 595
Burials. *See* Funerals and burials.
Buses, injuries on, 484–485
Businesses, 424–450
bankruptcy
employees' pensions and, 519–520
employees' wages and, 397–398
incorporating and, 438, 444–445
reclaiming property from, 210–211
stock in, 295
bulk rate postage discounts for, 425–426
buying, judging price of, 426
changing form of, 436
to protect personal assets, 437–438
closed, collecting court awards from, 638
customers' unpaid bills, 443
in divorce settlements, 136
failures, 444–445
forms of, 424
franchises, 424, 438–440
guarantees required of, 441
home, 188, 425
insurance for, 444–445
licenses or permits for, 425
magazine ads for, 426–427
successful, incorporating, 434
incorporating, 424, 429–430, 433–438. *See also* Corporations.
late delivery, liability for, 446
liability insurance for, 443–445
mail-order, 425
buying from, 356–358

INDEX

Businesses *(continued)*
naming, 435, 442
partnerships, 33, 424, 430–433, 448. *See also* Partnerships.
post office boxes as addresses of, 357, 426
public nuisances created by, 446–447
retail. *See* Stores.
running, 441–448
selling or ending, 448–450
sole proprietorships, 424, 427, 450
starting, 424–430
advertisements for, 426–427
bad credit history and, 430
employer identification numbers for, 429
former employers' lawsuits and, 428
franchises, 424, 438–440
incorporating and, 424, 429–430, 433
licenses and permits, 424–425, 438
loans from relatives, 427–428
mail-order, 425
partnerships, 430–432
sole proprietorships, 427
unincorporated business tax, 429–430
See also Employees; Employers.

C

Cable television, in rented homes, 162
Camps for children, exculpatory agreements and, 489
Cars. *See* Automobiles.
Cashier's checks, 268–269
Catastrophic illness insurance, 320, 322
Cats, accidental deaths of, 207. *See also* Pets.
Cemeteries
Arlington National, 588
gravesite maintenance, 587
moving bodies, 587
private family, 586–587
Certified checks, 268–269
stopping payment on, 269
Chain letters, 356
Chapter S corporations, 437
Charities, pledges to, 291
Checkrooms, 209
Checks, 267–270
amount changed on, 272
certified, 268
cashier's or bank checks vs., 268–269
stopping payment on, 269
direct deposit of, 102, 531
endorsing, 269–270
to other parties, 270
with rubber stamps, 269
government, direct deposit of, 102, 531
signatures forged on, 272
stopping payment on, 269
canceling orders by, 359–360
certified, 269
time limits on cashing, 267
time limits for drawing against, 268
Child abuse, 94–96
reporting, 95–96
by doctors, 95–96
by teachers, 89
sexual, 94
Child custody, 140–146
adoption and, 145–146
children's wishes, 141
consent for medical treatment and, 502
custodial parent's authority, 143
custodial parent's death and, 146
factors considered in, 140
foster home placements and, 62–63
joint, 142–143
judges as decision makers in, 140
lost by both parents, 141–142
mothers given preference, 141
moving out of state and, 141
name changes and, 143
parental kidnapping and, 144–145
parent dating before divorce is final and, 132
parent living with lover and, 141
parent remarriage and, 143, 144
unwed father's desire for, 69
visitation rights, 146–148
Children
abortions, 92
abuse, 89, 94–96
accidents and injuries to
babysitters and, 77–78
in camps, agreeing not to sue for, 489
in day-care centers, 78
in Little League games, 490
on others' property, 480–481
in school activities, 89, 490
at skating rinks, 490
in swimming pools, 481, 489
toy safety and, 374
while working, 483
in zoos, 488–489
accidents caused by, 81–82
adopted. *See* Adoption.
age of majority of, 84
alcohol furnished to, 82
drunk driving and, 250
false identification, 83
birth control used by, 494
boating accidents caused by, 491
born of adulterous affairs, 72
born after unsuccessful vasectomies, 504
brought to court, 632
car seats for, 243
college loans, 283
contracts not enforceable, 166, 220–221, 232, 364
crimes committed by, 611–617. *See also* Juvenile offenders.
custody of, 140–146. *See also* Child custody.
driving violations, 81–82, 245
drugs used or sold by
doctors' informing parents about, 494
parents' liability, 84
employment of, 75–77
income tax on earnings, 300
liability, 77–78
limited work hours and, 76–77
by parents, 76
parents' right to earnings from, 61
expelled from school, 86
foster homes for, 62–63
guardians for, 90–91, 107, 561
home teaching vs. school attendance, 86
housing and, 154, 193

Children *(continued)*
illegitimate, 71–75
birth certificates, 71–72
inheritance, 75, 573–574
naming of child conceived out of wedlock, 71–72
parents' eventual marriage, 71
support, 73–74, 149
visitation, 74–75
inheritance, 77
legitimacy and, 75, 573–574
rights of vs. surviving parents, 579
wills and 558, 559, 571
injured in fight by other children, 82
kidnapped by noncustodial parent, 144–145
last name of, 97–98, 143
legal rights of, 75
legitimacy of, 48
annulment of marriage and, 124
artificial insemination and, 72–73
inheritance and, 75, 573–574
losing job for staying home with, 418
marriage of, parents' right to prevent, 44
medical expenses, 61
medical records, 508
medical treatment, 502
divorced parents' consent for, 502
emergency, babysitters' consent for, 78
emergency, grandparents consent for, 99
in hospitals, 497
parents' religion and, 460
misbehavior by, 81–85, 86–87, 203, 612
missing, 84–85
name changes of, 97, 143
organs donated by, 513
parents' responsibility to support, 62–63
parents sued by, 62
parents supported by, 100–101
police questioning of parents about, 83
product safety and, 374
property sold by, 220–221
religious education, 52, 87
rentals refused because of, 154
runaway, 85
school attendance, 85, 86, 612
school prayer, 87
school records, 88
sex education classes for, 87
stepchildren, 60–61, 98, 534
struck by teachers, 89
support for. *See* Child support.
surrogate parenting and, 70–71
testifying as witnesses, 619
thefts by, 203
truancy, 86, 612
of unwed parents, 71–75, 149
vaccinations, 87–88
visitation rights, 146–148
wills, protected in, 557
windows broken by, 81
as witnesses in court, 619
work permits for, 76
Child support, 148–152
age of adulthood as end of, 149
for adopted children, 146
college tuition, 151
cost-of-living increases, 150
while divorce is pending, 148
ending payments, 149
enforcing payment of, 149, 150
Child support *(continued)*
errors in court records on, 152
garnisheeing wages for, 149
going into debt to pay, 148–149
grandparents' responsibility for, 74
health insurance and, 151
for illegitimate children, 73–74, 149
inability to pay, 151
informal agreements for, 151
late payment, 149
life insurance and, 152
noncustodial parent responsible for, 148
reducing, 150, 152
remarriage and, 152
during separation, 117
time limit on suing for, 74
verbal commitments for, 151
visitation rights and, 148
Citizenship, U.S., 455–457
dual citizenship, 455
of foreign children adopted by U.S. citizens, 66–67
losing, 457
obtaining, 455, 456–457
City ordinances, 454–455
Civil cases
criminal cases vs., 252, 623
steps in, 628–629
Civil rights. *See* Discrimination; Rights, individual.
Civil service jobs, 389
Closings, real estate, 168–169
costs, 168–169
lawyers in, 17–18
prepaid interest, 169
property not turned over, 169
Clothing
checked, 209
defective, 372
dry cleaners or laundries and, 207–209
inappropriate, employees fired for, 415
property lost while trying on, 210
restaurant dress codes, 376
school dress codes, 88–89
stained in restaurants, 376
Collection agencies, 294
College loans, 283
Colleges
parental rights assumed by, 89–90
tuition, child support agreements and, 151
College students, credit cards for, 275
Collision automobile insurance, 338
Common-law marriages, 54–55
legality of, 54–55
living together vs., 55
state laws on, 55
terminating, 55, 132
Community property laws, 59–60
Companies. *See* Businesses; Corporations.
Condominiums, 169–171
assessment fees for, 170
buying, 171
cooperative apartments vs., 170
defaulting on payments for, 195
houses vs., 169–170
mortgages, 180
planting trees outside, 184
rental apartments converted to, 162
right of first refusal on sale of, 200
unfinished work in, 173

Consent forms, 501–502
Conservators, 105, 106–107, 299
  See also Guardians.
Consumer complaints, 379–382
  airlines, 377–379
  Better Business Bureau and, 382
  dry cleaners, 207–209
  faulty repairs, 379–380
  government agencies for, 381–382
  hairdressers' negligence, 380–381
  to manufacturers, 372, 382
  merchandise never delivered, 379
  restaurants, 376–377
  steps for, 380–381
  to stores vs. manufacturers, 372
  travel agents, 379
  See also Automobiles; Insurance.
Consumer contracts, 364–367
  acceleration clauses in, 365
  canceling, 365–366
    by minors, 364
    orally, 366
  deleting objectionable clauses in, 364, 365
  health club memberships, 367
  oral, 366
  price reductions in, for naming potential customers, 365
  printed-form, 364
  repair shop estimates, 366
  right to assign, 364
  sold to finance companies, 364
  time-share vacation agreements and, 367
Contempt of court, 36–37, 637
Contingent legal fees, 29
Continuing care facilities 107–109. *See also* Nursing homes.
Contractors
  bonded, 181
  building codes violated by, 175
  completion of work by, 176, 181
  hiring, 183
  inferior materials used by, 176
  injuries to, 181
  instructions not followed, 174
  liens on property made by, 165, 172
  subcontractors hired by, 181
  supervising of, 175
  warranties provided by, 176
  work redone by, 182
  written agreements with, 182–183
Contracts
  annuity, 523
  binders, 164
  for buying and selling personal property, 218–221
  by children, 166, 220–221, 232
  consumer, 364–367
  for continuing care facilities, 107–109
  of employees, forbidding work for competitors, 391
  loan, language in 286–287
  marriage as, 46
  purchase agreements, 164, 167, 173
  separation agreements as, 122
  service, 370–371
Cooperative apartments, 170
Copying machines, copyrighted material and, 224
Copyrighting, 223–224
  of books sent to publishers, 223
  copying machines and, 224
  patenting vs., 223
  permission to use material under, 223
  public domain and, 223
  of television shows, 598
  of video cassettes, 224
Corporations, 424, 433–438
  automobile accidents while on business for, 437
  businesses called, without legal corporate status, 435
  Chapter S, 437
  criminal charges against, 603
  directors' duties, 448
  forming, 434–435
    attorneys in, 434
    criminal records and, 438
  nonprofit, 436–437
    tax returns, 437
  owners' loans to, 436
  partnerships vs., 430
  personal assets vs. assets of, 441–442
  personal guarantees and, 435–436
  shareholders
    annual meetings required, 447
    liability, 447–448
    minimum number, 433
    restrictions on stock sales by, 449
  unincorporated business taxes and, 429–430
  See also Businesses.
Cosmetics, skin conditions caused by, 374–375
Counterfeit money, 272
Courts. *See* Judicial system; Juries and jurors; Trials; Witnesses in trials.
Courts-martial, 454
Covenants, 190
Credit, 273–277
  alimony and child support income considered in, 274–275
  bankruptcy and, 306
  business start-up and, 430
  divorce and, 274, 275
  establishing, 273
  factors affecting, 273
  marriage and, 273–274, 275
  moving to new city and, 275
  reports, 273, 277
  temporary financial problems and, 276–277
  See also Consumer contracts; Debts; Loans.
Credit bureaus, 276
Credit cards and charges, 278–281
  age discrimination, 275
  applications for
    estimating balances due on, 279
    permissible questions, 278–279
    time limit on response to, 279
  bail posted with, 609–610
  billing errors, 280
  for college students, 275
  debit cards vs., 278
  disclosure requirements, 279
  divorce, effect on liability for, 137
  lost, 280–281

Credit cards and charges *(continued)*
protecting, 281
reducing monthly payments on, 290
revolving accounts, 278
security agreements on purchase slips, 280
separation, effect on liability for, 122
shopping for, 278
spouse's use of, 57–58
telephone orders paid with, 360–361
travel cards vs., 278
Credit life insurance, 314–315
Credit reports, 273, 277
Credit unions, 265
Cremation, 585
Crime, 590–620
accomplices or accessories, 602–603
accused's rights, 472–474, 603–609
in arrests, 605–609
entrapment, 609
frisking, 604
habeus corpus, 609
illegal searches, 605
no-knock laws, 603–604
AIDS, knowingly infecting others with, 599
automobile theft, 256, 338, 598, 611
bail, 609–611
booby trap devices, 595
burglaries, 192, 476
corporate, 603
felonies, 597, 600–601, 606
home recording of videotapes, 598
ignorance of laws and, 598
intent to commit, 599, 602
job-related, 392, 393–394
juvenile, 611–617. *See also* Juvenile offenders.
misdemeanors, 597, 600–601, 606
parole, 596
against person vs. property, 599
pit bull terriers and, 598
plea bargaining, 596
police response time, 591
premeditated, 602
reporting
follow-up to, 590
victims' legal duty and, 590
witnesses' legal duty and, 618
self-defense against, 595, 619
thefts. *See* Thefts.
time allowed for investigation of, 591
vandalism, 256, 331, 590
victimless, 598
victims, 590–597. *See also* Victims of crime.
witnesses, 618–620. *See also* Witnesses to crimes.
zoning law violations, 597–598
See also Judicial system; Trials.
Criminal cases
civil cases vs., 252, 623
steps, 606–607
time limit for bringing to trial, 626–627
Criminal records
false arrest and, 608
incorporating and, 438
of juvenile offenders, 616–617
privacy and, 470
voting and, 459
Crops, as personal property, 202
Cross-examination of witnesses, 36, 637
what to expect in, 651
Custody of children. *See* Child custody.
Customs inspectors, drugs found by, 599

D

Damages, 639
consequential, 369
Day-care centers, 78, 79
injuries in, 78
Death, 586–587
autopsies after, 586
what to do when a loved one dies, 586–587
See also Estates; Funerals and burials; Wills.
Debit cards, 278
Debts, 290–294
Aid to Families With Dependent Children (AFDC) checks and, 291
child support and, 148–149
collection agencies, 294
consolidation of, 290
credit life insurance and, 314–315
of deceased, collecting, 579, 580–581
time limit for, 581
estate settlements, 519
garnisheeing of wages, 294
life insurance and, 292, 317–318, 319
newspaper notices of limited liability for, 58
property seized for nonpayment of, 221, 292
recognizing trouble with, 293
refusal to pay, 292
spousal responsibilities, 57–58
to utilities, 290–291
wills, canceled in, 561
See also Bankruptcy; Consumer contracts; Credit; Credit cards and charges; Loans.
Deeds
divorce and, 137
purchase agreements superseded by, 173
quitclaim, 168
types of, 167–168
where to keep, 172
Defective and unsafe merchandise, 372–375
charges for return of, 373
clothing, 372–373
complaining about, 372, 379–382. *See also* Consumer complaints.
injuries caused by, 374–375, 382
no refunds or return policy and, 372–373
property ruined by, 373–374
replacements vs. refunds for, 373
returning, 372–373
spoiled food, 372
Defendants, 628–629. *See also* Trials.
Delaware, advantages of incorporating in, 436
Deliveries, delays in, 379
Dentists, malpractice by, 506
Depositions, 630–631
interrogatories vs., 631
reviewing before testifying, 631

Deposits
  on automobiles, 226
  to hold merchandise, 219
  real estate binders, 164
  security, for rentals, 158–159
  for telephone service, 291
Deposits and withdrawals, direct, 102, 531
Detention centers, 616
Developers, 189–190
Disability insurance, 325
  Social Security, 545–546
  workers' compensation and, 404
Discrimination
  age, 384, 392, 410, 417, 418, 441, 516
  insurance, 330–331
  racial, 376, 418, 467
  See also Equality under the law; Job discrimination; Sexual discrimination.
Dispute resolution programs, 594
Divorce, 114–119, 124–152
  alimony, 138–140. *See also* Alimony.
  annulment vs., 123, 124
  bank accounts and, 117, 137
  child custody, 140–146. *See also* Child custody.
  and children adopted from previous marriage, 145
  child support, 148–152. *See also* Child support.
  common-law marriages, 55, 132
  costs, 118
  court appearances, 127–128
  court decrees required for, 114
  credit cards canceled in, 117
  desertion or abandonment and, 132
  do-it-yourself kits for, 126
  emergency, 126
  filing, 119, 130
    without spouse's knowledge, 119
  foreign, 126
  grounds for, 130–132
    alcoholism, 131–132
    infidelity, 125, 130
    wife not moving with husband, 130–131
  home, expelling spouse from, 117–118
  jury trials for, 126
  lawyers' role
    first consultation with, 115–116
    hiring, 127
    one used by both spouses, 118
  legal fees, 118–119
    contingent, 29
  length of proceedings, 125, 128–130
  life insurance and, 316, 318
  marital relations resumed during, 121–122
  marriage counseling requirements, 116
  mediators for, 127
  Mexican mail-order, 125
  moving out first and, 116–117
  by mutual consent, 114
  no-fault, 114, 124–125, 132
    property settlement in, 125
    speed of, 125
  non-self-supporting spouse's preparations for, 114–115
  pets and, 136
  prenuptial agreements and, 50
  preventing, 128
  process of, 127–133
Divorce *(continued)*
  property division, 133–138
    accusations of wrongdoing and, 125
    automobiles, 136
    business run by both spouses, 136
    changing, 135–136
    credit card debts, 137
    deeds, 137
    hidden assets, 134–135
    home ownership, 134, 137
    household bills, 137
    inheritances, 136
    judge's approval needed, 134
    methods, 133–134
    pensions, 138
    pets, 136
    prenuptial agreements and, 50–52, 134
    putting spouse through school and, 137–138
    Social Security benefits and, 138, 533
  property taken by spouse before, 116–117
  pro se, 127
  remarriage and, 48, 119
  retrials of, 132–133
  separation before, 114
  serving of papers, 127
  setting aside decrees, 133
  spouse moving back into home, 121–122
  steps in, 128, 129
  types, 124–127
  wills and, 133
  See also Annulment; Separation.
Doctors, 494–496
  consulting after automobile accidents, 260
  experimental treatments prescribed by, 495
  forced treatment, 495–496
  malpractice history, 503–504
  Medicare, 539–540
  information withheld by, 494–496
  patients unable to pay refused by, 510
  prescriptions, 469, 503–504
  privacy rights, 469
    children's drug problems, 494
  refusing treatment, patients' rights in, 494
  See also Malpractice: medical; Medical treatments.
Dogs
  accidents caused by, 206, 207
  gardens destroyed by, 204
  hit by automobiles, 206–207
  injuries caused by, 204–206
    "Beware of Dog" signs, 204–205
    "one bite" rule, 205
    in own yard, 206
  leash laws, 206
  licensing of, 203
  neglect of, 204
  pit bull terriers, bans on, 598
  purebred, impregnated by mutts, 204
  See also Pets.
Do-it-yourself
  divorce kits, 126
  incorporating, 434
  lawyer, acting as own, 19–20
  separation agreements, 121
  small claims court, 640–642
  wills, 553

Door-to-door sales, 358–360
canceling orders made in, 358–360
guarding against schemes in, 359
injuries to salesmen, 482
licenses, 358
misrepresentation of goods, 360
Double jeopardy, 623, 639
Driver's licenses, 240–242
for delivery trucks, 240
expired, driving with, 240–241
accidents and, 241
organ donor's consent on, 513–514
out-of-state driving, 240
practicing driving without, 240
state requirements for, 240
suspension of, 241
for drunk driving, 250, 251
tickets allowed before, 241–242
work-related driving and, 242
Drug abuse
by children
doctors informing parents about, 494
parents' liability for, 84
losing jobs for, 419
Drugs, illegal, found by customs inspectors, 599
Drug testing
of employees, 394
random, 474
Drunk drivers, 247–252
in accidents caused by others, 251–252
alcohol furnished to children and, 250
allowing driving by, 249
arrested while not driving, 249
attorneys for, 250
automobile insurance rates for, 342
driver's licenses suspended, 250, 251
lawsuits against, 78, 252
legal definition of, 248
penalties for, 251
roadblock searches for, 246
tavern owners' liability for damage caused by, 250–251
tests for, 247
Breathalyzer, 248
refusing to submit to, 248–249
sober persons who fail, 247
Dry cleaners and laundries, 207–209
articles lost by, 208
clothes damaged by, 207–209
clothes not cleaned on time by, 209
clothes sold by, 209
Durable power of attorney, 101, 102

E

EIN's (employer identification numbers), 429
Elderly, 100–104
abuse of, 96
children's liability for, 100
credit cards for, 275
direct deposit and withdrawal arrangements for, 102, 531
discrimination, 384, 392, 410, 417, 418, 441, 516
driving safety of, 100
Elderly *(continued)*
government benefits, 101. *See also* Medicare; Social Security.
guardians and conservators, 102, 103, 104–107
health insurance for, 322
incompetence, 101–102, 103
nursing homes, 107–112
power of attorney given by, 101–102
Social Security taxes paid by, 531
state agencies for, 103
unretired, IRA's of, 524
unusual behavior of, 103–104
welfare department investigations, 103
See also Grandparents.
Emergency rooms, uninsured patients refused by, 496
Eminent domain, 189, 193
Employee Retirement Income Security Act (ERISA), 516, 520–521
Employees
in automobile accidents, 445
automobiles of, vandalized on job, 394
of bankrupt companies
pensions, 519–520
wages, 397–398
benefits, 399–401, 428
insurance, 323–324, 420, 538. *See also* Health insurance; Life insurance.
legal plans, 24
maternity leave, 400–401
pensions, 516–523. *See also* Pension plans.
vacation and sick time, unused, 400
children as, 75–77
damages caused by, 398
drug testing of, 394
firing, 414–420. *See also* Jobs: losing.
forbidden to work for competitors, 391
handicapped, 447
hazardous work conditions and, 412–414
absence from work due to, 413
fire hazards, 412–413
lawsuits filed for, 413
reporting, 412–414
hiring, 442–443. *See also* Jobs: applying for.
illegal tasks asked of, 392
insurance, 323–324, 420, 538–539. *See also* Health insurance; Life insurance.
job descriptions of, changing, 390
job discrimination and, 408–411. *See also* Jobs: discrimination.
job-related crime, 392, 393–394
job seeking, 384–390. *See also* Jobs: applying for.
lie detector tests, 394
maternity leave, 400–401
medical records, 508
moonlighting, 391
notice given by, 395
overtime, 442
compensation, 396–397
forced, 396
ownership of materials prepared by, 391
part-time, 399
paycheck deductions, 429
pension plans, 516–523. *See also* IRA's; Keoghs; Pension plans; Social Security.
personnel file access, 390–391
political activities, 392

Employees *(continued)*
raises, 398
searching desks of, 393
searching packages and purses of, 393–394
sexual harassment, 411–412
smoking, 392–393
Social Security, 526–534. *See also* Social Security.
strikes, 406–407, 408
testifying against employers, 392
unemployment compensation, 420–422
unions, 404–408
vacations, 400
wages, 294, 395–399. *See also* Wages.
workers' compensation, 401–404. *See also* Workers' compensation.
Employer identification numbers (EIN's), 429
Employers
bankrupt
employee pensions, 519–520
employee wages, 397–398
benefits provided by, 399–401, 428
former employees, right to sue for starting own businesses, 428
illegal tasks requested by, 392
overtime, 396–397
paycheck deductions, 429
pension plans, 516–523. *See also* Pension plans.
Social Security taxes, 429
wages, docking of, 398–399
See also Businesses.
Employment agencies, fees, 389–390
Engagements, broken, 45–47
engagement rings, 46–47
gifts, 47
third person implicated in, 46
wedding cancellation and, 45–46
Entrapment, 609
Equality under the law, 465–468
age discrimination, 384, 392, 410, 417, 418, 441
equal protection clause and, 465
fraternal organizations, 467
handicapped people, 468
homosexual teachers, 467
professional licenses, 467
rock concert prohibitions, 465–466
smoking, 466
See also Jobs: discrimination; Racial discrimination; Sexual discrimination.
Equal Opportunity Commission, 409
ERISA (Employee Retirement Income Security Act), 516, 520–521
Estates, 548–577
planning, 548–551
estate taxes, 550–551
home ownership, 549
immediate access to cash, 548
inheritance taxes, 549–550
IRA's, 549
joint bank accounts, 548
life insurance, 551
methods, 550–551
reasons, 548
types of property included in, 548
Estates *(continued)*
settling, 574–581
assets discovered after, 581
bills and other debts, 579–581
deadline, 578
executors. *See* Executors of wills.
missing heirs, 581
probate of will, 574–577. *See also* Probate of wills.
property in more than one state, 577
simultaneous death of both spouses, 578
See also Inheritances; Wills.
Estate taxes
estates subject to, 550
inheritance taxes vs., 549
joint ownership of home and, 577
spouse's exemption, 551
Eviction, 160
Executors of wills
buying assets from estate, 579
deadline for settling estate, 578
debts and taxes settled by, 579
declining to serve, 578
duties, 575
lawyers as, 38
from other states, 554
payment of, 578
property sales, 580

F

Family responsibilities, 55–64
foster home placements and, 62–63
spousal, 55–60
community property laws, 59–60
for debts and purchases, 57–59
disabilities, 56–57
household bills, 56
husband's relocation and, 64
to provide support, 55–57
sexual relations and, 64
signature use and, 63–64
of stepfathers, 60–61
support
of children, 60–62, 148–152. *See also* Child support.
of spouse, 55–57
FBI, questioning by, 620
Federal courts, 622–623
Felonies, misdemeanors vs., 597, 600–601, 606
Fences
children's injuries and, 481
neighbors' view blocked by, 185
Financial institutions, 264–272. *See also* Bank accounts; Banks; Checks; Credit; Credit cards and charges; Loans.
Financial planners, 299
Financial records, 271, 303
Fines, paid in court, 634
Firearms, 464–465
Fire hazards at work, reporting, 412–413
Fires
homeowners insurance and, 328
temporary lodgings and, 328–329
in house after signing of purchase agreement, 164–165
in rented homes, 163

Firings. *See* Jobs: losing.
Floater insurance, 330
Floods, homeowners insurance and, 329
Food
  hairs in, 377
  spoiled, 372
  See also Restaurants.
Foreclosures on homes, 194–195
Forgery
  of checks, 272
  of spouse's signature, 63–64
Foster homes, 62–63
Franchises, 424, 438–440
Fraud
  deceptive advertisements, 348–350
  by mail, 357
  in wills, 572
Freedom
  of press, 462–463
  of religion, 459–460
  of speech, 460–462
  See also Rights, individual.
Frisking, by police, 472, 604
Funeral directors, licensing of, 584
Funerals and burials, 581–588
  at Arlington National Cemetery, 588
  cremations, 583, 585
  embalming, 585
  gravesite maintenance, 587
  insurance for, 582–583
  legal authority to arrange for, 583–584
  letters of last instructions, 582–583
  military service and payment for, 588
  package prices, 584
  planning before death, 581
  prepaid, 582
  private family cemeteries, 586–587
  scattering of ashes, 585
  at sea, 585
  telephone inquiries about, 584
  time limit for, 585
  transporting bodies, 584, 587
Furniture
  delayed delivery of, 379
  damaged in moving, 211–212

G

Garage sales
  income tax on earnings from, 300
  warranties, 351
Garnisheeing of wages, 294, 302
Gifts
  from dying people, 216, 549
  promised but not delivered, 216
  taxes on, 300
    inheritance, 549
  valuable, getting back, 216
  to wives
    from husbands, 216
    husbands' right to, 59
Gossiping by neighbors, 187
Government
  insurance offered by, 311. *See also* Medicare; Social Security.
  lawsuits against, 485
  private property taken by, 189, 193
Grandchildren
  adopted by grandparents, 99
  grandparents' authority over, 99
  grandparents' loans to, 99–100
  Social Security benefits for, 534
Grand juries
  confidentiality, 650
  functions, 650
  selecting members, 649
  seriousness of crime, 629
  serving on, 649–650
  size, 650
  testifying before, 629–630
    right to have lawyer in, 630
Grandparents
  adopting grandchildren, 99
  authority over grandchildren, 99
  lending money to grandchildren, 99–100
  rights, 98–100
  support of minor's child, 74
  visitation rights, 98–99, 147
Green cards, 455–456
Guarantees
  implied, 441
  money back, 361
  warranties vs., 367–368
Guardians, 299
  for children, 90–91, 107, 561
  for elderly, 104–106
Guns, 464–465

Habeas corpus, writ of, 609
Hairdressers, unsatisfactory work by, 375, 380–381
Halfway houses, preventing opening of, 190
Handicapped, rights of, 447, 468
Hazardous working conditions, 412–414
Health club memberships
  canceling, 367
  free, as prizes, 363
Health insurance, 320–325
  for alcoholism, 323
  cancellation, 320
  cancer, effect on eligibility, 324
  catastrophic illness insurance vs., 320, 322
  child support and, 151
  emergency room admittance and, 496
  as employee benefit
    leaving job and, 323–324
    losing job and, 420
    working past age 65 and, 538–539
  lying on applications for, 323
  Medicaid, 543–545
  medical procedures excluded, 325
  medical records provided for, 508
  Medicare, 535–543. *See also* Medicare.
  noncancelable, 320
  nonpayment of benefits, 324
  physical exams for people over 65, 322
  preexisting conditions, 323
  questions to ask about, 321
  refused because of serious disease, 322
  riders, 311
  for specific diseases, 322
  to supplement Medicare, 542

Hearing impairments, applying for jobs and, 384–385
Hearings, trials vs., 631
Hit-and-run drivers, 19, 260–261, 342–344
  medical bills of people injured by, 260–261, 342–343
Hitchhiking, 244
Home improvements and repairs, 180–184
  contractors, 181–183
  decorators, 182
  escalating bills, 182–183
  landscapers' liability, 184
  neighbors' objections to color of house paint, 185–186
  painters, 184
  permits, 180
  poor workmanship, 182
  in rented homes, made by tenants, 158
  on rented land, 202
  restrictions on, 180–181
  selling home and, 197
Homeowners insurance, 326–335
  amount to buy, 326
  automobiles and, 329
  double coverage, 327
  fires, 328–329
  floater policies, 329–330
  floods, 329
  liability coverage, 333–335
    for occasional workers' injuries, 334
    for pedestrians' injuries, 333
    reporting requirements, 334
    for swimming pool injuries, 334
    for watercraft injuries, 335
  overdue premium payments, 329
  personal property covered, 329–333
    away from home, 331
    documentation for, 333
    of guests, 330
    jewelry, 329–330
    stamp collections, 330
  refusals to compensate, 332
  for rented homes, 327–328, 332
  replacement cost
    for damage to home, 327
    for theft, 331–332
  temporary living expenses, 328–329
  theft, 330–333
    from automobiles, 331
    damages during, 331
    in high-crime areas, 330–331
    and negligence, 331
    recovery of stolen property, 333
    valuation of property, 331–332
  types, 326–327
  vandalism, 331
Homes
  accidents in, 476–483. *See also* Household accidents.
  alarms in, police's late response to, 591
  building, 174–176
    building codes, 175
    monitoring contractors, 175
    substitute materials, 176
    trees on lot, 174
    undeveloped lots, 174–175
    warranties, 176
    work done after closings, 176
    zoning restrictions, 174
Homes *(continued)*
  burglars, homeowners' right to thwart, 192
  businesses in, 188, 425, 426–427, 434, 444–445
  buying, 163–173
    binders vs. purchase agreements, 164
    closings, 17–18, 168–169
    condominiums, 169–171, 173
    contractors' liens and, 165, 172
    cooperative apartments, 170
    deeds, 167–168
    extensions of purchase agreements, 164
    fires, 164–165
    furnishings included, 172
    government seizures, 166
    inspections before, 173
    lawyers' role, 163
    leaking roofs, 173
    by married couples, 166
    mobile homes and, 171–172
    terms of sales contracts or purchase agreements, 167
    title insurance, 165–166
    title searches, 165
    warranties, 173
  contaminants in, 191–192
  divorce and ownership of, 134, 137
  financing, 176–180. *See also* Mortgages.
  household workers, 188
  insurance, 326–335. *See also* Homeowners insurance.
  joint ownership, 166, 549
    estate taxes and, 577
  lakefront, lake use and, 187
  legal responsibilities of owners, 479
  losing
    babies in adults-only communities and, 193
    bank foreclosures, 194–195
    defaulting on condominium payments, 195
    government seizures, 189, 193
    nonpayment of real estate taxes, 195
    partnership defaults, 432–433
  moving, 212–213
  neighbors, 185–187. *See also* Neighbors.
  noise near, 190, 192
  offices in, 188
  police entry into, 473, 603
  property taxes, 58–59, 190, 191, 195
  rented. *See* Rented homes.
  renting spare rooms, 187
  selling, 195–200
    children's inheritances and, 579
    commissions for nonbrokers, 196
    condominiums, 200
    real estate agents, brokers, and realtors, 195–196. *See also* Real estate brokers.
    remaining in homes after, 200
    repairs, 197
    tax breaks, 300
  sidewalks in front of
    city-ordered paving of, 189
    pedestrians injured on, 333
    shoveling snow from, 188
  trees in yards cut by power companies, 188–189
  widening of streets in front of, 189

Homosexuality
losing job for, 419
teaching and, 467
Hospices, 500
Hospitals, 496–500
anesthesiologists vs. anesthetists, 497
awakening of sleeping patients, 498
choice of physician, patients' right to, 497
consent for medical treatment, 496–497, 500–502
discharge from, 500
emergency rooms, treatment refused in, 496
fathers in operating rooms during cesarean delivery, 497
inability of patients to pay, 509
interns and residents at examinations, 498
involuntary confinement in, 500
malpractice, 506–507
medical charts, 499
parents remaining with children, 497
patients' rights, 498–499
transfers, 499
Hotels and motels
luggage lost in, 210
overbooking, 379
reservations, lost because of airline overbooking, 378
swimming pool injuries, 489
Household accidents, 476–483
admitting knowledge of danger after, 477
to burglars, 476
to guests, 476
intoxication and, 477–478
homeowners' legal responsibilities, 479
inside home, 476–478
outside home, 478–483
to children hired to mow lawn, 483
garden hoses and, 482
hazards to children, 480–481
ice on roof, 482
on porches, 478–479
on sidewalks, 333
in swimming pools, 481
in rented homes, 163, 478
Household workers, workers' compensation for, 188
Husbands
abusive, 93, 591
alimony granted to, 139
consent of, to wives' abortions, 92, 93
gifts to wives from, 216
IRA's for, 524
legally dead, collecting life insurance benefits of, 319
noncustodial, children kidnapped by, 144–145
in operating rooms during births, 497
visitation rights of, 146–148
wives' legal protection from, 94
wives raped by, 94
wives' self-defense against, 93
wives sued by, 261
wives testifying against, 93
See also Divorce; Family responsibilities; Marriage; Wives.

I

Immigrants. *See* Aliens.
Income tax
alimony and, 140
audits, 302–303
constitutionality of, 299
errors made by accountants on, 299
keeping records for, 303
late filing, 301
legal fees and, 301
life insurance proceeds and, 319
minimum income to file for, 300
payment problems and, 301
on profits from garage sales, 300
reporting someone's evasion of, 618
selling home and, 300
on Social Security benefits, 531
spousal responsibility for, 58–59
Swiss bank accounts and, 265
wages garnisheed for nonpayment of, 302
Incorporating. *See* Corporations.
Individual retirement accounts. *See* IRA's.
Inheritances
adoption and, 80
during divorce proceedings, 136
legitimacy and, 75, 573–574
marriage and, 56, 59–60, 558
selling property acquired through, 220
separation and, 122
See also Estates; Trusts; Wills.
Inheritance taxes, 549–550
Injuries. *See* Accidents and injuries.
Insurance, 308–346
agents, 308, 310, 312, 323
automobile, 335–346. *See also* Automobile insurance.
binders, 308
for boating, 335, 492
buying, 309
canceling, 310, 312–313,
claims denied, 344
complaining about, 313
credit card protection plans, 281
disability, 325, 404
for funeral costs, 582–583
government, 311
for hard-to-insure people, 310–311
health, 320–325; *See also* Health insurance.
for home businesses, 444–445
homeowners, 326–335. *See also* Homeowners insurance.
incorrect information on applications, 308–309
items not covered, 312
liability
for businesses, 443–445
for homeowners, 333–335
life, 313–320. *See also* Life insurance.
Medicare, 535–543. *See also* Medicare.
MGIC, 176–177
partial premium payments, 310
plain English in policies, 308
retirement, 523
sexual differences in rates, 311–312
time limit for settling claims, 312

Insurance *(continued)*
title, 165–166
workers' compensation, 401–404. *See also* Workers' compensation.
Interior decorators, dissatisfaction with, 182
Interrogatories, depositions vs., 631
Investments, 295–299
in bankrupt companies, 295
financial planners, 299
IRA's, 523–526, 549
Keoghs, 523–526
lost stock certificates, 295
of married couples, 295
savings bonds, 298
swindles, avoiding, 296–297
U.S. Treasury Bills, 298
See also Stockbrokers.
IOU's, 285
IRA's (individual retirement accounts), 523–526
age limit for contributing to, 524
beneficiaries of, 549
contributing to, 524
Keoghs vs., 523–524
for married couples, 524
penalties for early withdrawals, 524
restrictions, 526
SEP's, 525
setting up, 526
wills and, 526

J

Jewelry, 214, 218, 220, 329–330
Jobs, 383–422
accidents, 401–404, 437
applying for 384–390
arrest and conviction information, 388–389
at-will agreements, 387
civil service, 389
employment agencies, 389–390
false information given, 386, 415
fingerprinting and photographing, 387–388
height or weight requirements, 384
illegal interview questions, 385
impairments and, 384–385, 386
lie detector tests, 388
medical history, 387
physical examinations, 386–387
psychological tests, 388
references, 386
unfulfilled job promises, 387
union shops, 405
discrimination, 408–411
age, 384, 410, 441
aliens as teachers, 467
bankruptcy and, 306
Equal Opportunity Commission, 409
forced retirement, 410
physically impaired, 384–385
promotions, 410
racial, 418
religious holidays and, 411
sexual, 408–410, 518
Jobs *(continued)*
losing, 414–420
back wages and, 416
for destroying company property, 416
for drug or alcohol abuse, 419
for false information on job applications, 415
group medical insurance and, 420
for habitual lateness, 415–416
for homosexuality, 419
improper firing procedures, 415
for inappropriate clothing, 415
for jury duty, 416
for no reason, 415
for not reporting theft by other employees, 419
pensions and, 418
for prolonged illness, 416
for refusing to do illegal tasks, 419
for refusing transfers, 418
right to know reason for, 414
for staying home with children, 418
for union organizing, 405
See also Employees; Employers.
Judges
cases rescheduled by, 632
jury selection, 645
as lawyers, 14
requesting change of, 632
trial by jury vs., 626
Judicial system, 622–655
courtroom protocol, 633–635
courts, 622–625
criminal vs. civil offenses, 623
delays, 626
federal courts, 622–623
juries, 643–650
grand, 629–630, 649–650
See also Juries and jurors.
jurisdiction decisions, 622, 623
juvenile court, 612, 613, 614
pretrial procedures, 627–633
right to lawyer, 626
small claims court, 19, 379–380, 640–642
trial procedures, 636–639
witnesses, 651–655. *See also* Witnesses in trials.
See also Trials.
Juries and jurors, 643–650
alternate, 645
deliberations, 649
discussing case after trial, 649–650
foremen, 646
grand, 629–630, 649–650
hung, 648
investigating cases on their own, 647
news reports on case and, 645, 646
note taking by, 646
number of, 643, 650
reporters speaking to, 647
right to trial by, 623–626
selecting, 643–645, 649
sequestering, 648
serving on, 646–650
speaking with plaintiff during trial, 647
testimony reheard by, 646
trial by judge vs., 626
unanimous decisions, 647

Jury duty, 643–644
excused from, 644
on grand juries, 649–650
losing job because of, 416
name list for, 643
payment for, 644, 650
by employers, 645
Justices of the peace, 14
Juvenile court
children referred to, by schools, 612
lawyers for children in, 613
press barred from, 614
Juvenile offenders, 611–617
adjudication hearings, 613–614
"associations contrary to child's welfare," 611–612
auto theft, 611
counseling, 615
criminal records, 616–617
curfews and limitations, 615
drug offenses, 611–612, 616–617
lawyers for, 613, 614
legal protection of, 617
beyond parental control, 83, 612
predisposition investigations, 614
punishments, 615, 616
reform schools, 615, 616
restitution for damages by, 612
running away from home, 84–85, 615
shoplifting, 611
tried in adult court, 613
truancy, 612, 616

K

Keoghs, 523–526
IRA's vs., 523–524
restrictions on investments in, 526
setting up, 526
wills and, 526
Kidnapping, by noncustodial parents, 144–145
Knives, carrying, 544

L

Lake, right to use, 187
Landlords, 159–163
homes entered without notification by, 161–162
repairs not made by, 159–160
tenants' property seized by, 161
See also Leases; Rented homes.
Laundries. *See* Dry cleaners and laundries.
Laws
city ordinances, 454–455
state differences in, 454
types of, 453
Lawsuit, steps in, 628–629
Lawyers, 14–42
accident lawsuits and, 33
acting as your own, 19–20
for adoptions, 64
age of, 21
ambulance chasing, 39
Lawyers *(continued)*
appeals not filed on time by, 42
associates, 38–39
automobile purchases and, 17
big firms vs. individuals, 22–23
for buying homes, 17–18, 164
cases refused by, 22
choosing, 21–25, 127
clients coached, before testifying, 36
clients testifying despite disapproval of, 36
confidentiality, 34, 41
conflict of interest, 40–41
contempt of court charges against, 36–37
court-appointed, 629
details of case revealed to, 35
dissatisfaction with, 32
divorce, 29, 115–116
choosing, 127
for financially needy, 119
shared by both spouses, 118
what to bring to, 115
drunk driving charges and, 29, 250
"Esq." title used by, 14
ethics, 38–42
as executors of wills, 38
family, 15, 19
fees, 26–31
contingent, 29
court costs and, 28
disputes over, 30
estimates, 27
firing lawyers and, 37
hourly vs. flat, 26
inability to pay, 24–25
incidental expenses in, 28
income tax and, 301
itemized bills, 28
legal assistants' work and, 28
negotiating, 26
paid by opposing party, 30–31
referral, 31
refunding, 29–30
retainers, 27–28
saving on, 27
setting, 26
splitting, 31
withdrawal from case and, 30
firing, 37
first consultation with, 21
grand jury testimony and, 630
for guardianship hearings, 104–105
hit-and-run drivers found by, 19
inappropriate advice given by, 42
for incorporating, 434
judges as, 14
for juvenile offenders, 613, 614
from law firms vs. legal clinics, 24
legal language used by, 14
malpractice, 38
monitoring performance of, 31
opinion letters, 32
paralegals and, 16
personal feelings toward, 21–22
power of attorney agreements and, 20
practicing in other states, 20
privacy rights and, 469
probating wills without, 574, 576
pro bono work of, 16–17
referral services, 22
retirement of, 37

Lawyers *(continued)*
right to, 17, 626, 629
rural vs. big city, 23
second opinions, 31
for separation agreements, 121
settlement offers refused by, without clients' approval, 41–42
for small claims court, 19
soliciting business, 39
as specialists, 15, 16
for tax problems, 16
timetables provided by, 32
for traffic tickets and violations, 19, 246
trial facts published by, 41
type of clients accepted by, 17
when to consult, 17–21
wills drawn up by, 552–553, 555
withdrawing from cases, 30
witnesses coached by, 651
witnesses cross-examined by, 36
working with, 31–37
Leases
breaking, 158
business, sidewalk displays and, 443
changing before signing, 154
expired, 155
rent increases and, 156
for mobile home parks, 156
no-sublet clauses in, 156
precautions before signing, 154
tenants without, 155
unwritten, 155
See also Landlords; Rented homes.
Legal clinics, law firms vs., 24
Legal plans, as fringe benefits, 24
Legislators, slanderous statements of, 461
Legitimacy
annulment and, 124
artificial insemination and, 72–73
divorce during pregnancy and, 71
inheritance and, 75, 573–574
parents' eventual marriage and, 71, 573–574
support responsibilities and, 73–74, 149
See also Unwed parents.
Letters of last instructions, 582–583
Liability insurance, 333–335
for businesses, 443–445
for occasional workers' injuries, 334
for pedestrians' injuries, 333
reporting requirements of, 334
for swimming pool injuries, 334
for watercraft injuries, 335
Libel, 463
Licenses
boating, 491
for businesses, 424–425, 438
dog, 203
for door-to-door salesmen, 358
driver's, 240–242, 250, 251, 513–514
marriage, 44–45
for undertakers and funeral directors, 584
Lie detector tests, 388, 394, 442
Liens on property, 165, 172, 221
Life insurance, 313–320
accidental death policies vs., 316
automatic premium loan, 316
Life insurance *(continued)*
beneficiaries, 316–320
collecting by, 317
dead before death of insured, 318–319
inquiries made by, 318
naming, 316, 318
policies owned by, 317–318
bought by mentally ill persons, 315
child support and, 152
credit, 314–315
debts and, 292, 317–318, 319
divorce and, 316, 318
double coverage, 313
endowment insurance, 315
estate planning and, 551
income tax and, 319
legally dead spouse and, 319
payments after death of insured, 580
as retirement insurance, 315, 523
shopping for, 314–315
smoker vs. nonsmoker rates for, 314
suicide and, 320
wills and, 319
Lineups, 593
Living together. *See* Unmarried couples; Unwed parents.
Living wills, 510–512
benefits, 511
euthanasia and, 512
medical records and, 512
moving to new state and, 511
periodic renewal of, 512
states without laws for, 510–511
Loans, 282–290
acceleration clauses, 283
applying for
false statements in, 282
after first refusal, 284
for automobiles, 226, 228, 290, 339
college, 283
to corporations from owners, 436
cosigning, 289
bankruptcy and, 180
default and, 289
debt consolidation, 290
defaulting on
cosigning and, 289
life insurance and, 292
finance charges, 284–285
forgiving, 284
between friends, 288–289
late payments on, 285, 288
legalese vs. plain English, 286–287
loan-sharking, 284
misunderstanding terms of, 282
payable on demand, 282
personal finance companies and, 285
precautions, 282
promissory notes vs. IOU's, 285
refused
reapplying after, 284
right to explanation for, 283
to relatives, 99–100, 289
repaying ahead of time, 285
terminating (accelerating), 282–283
two people sharing, 289
See also Credit; Credit cards and charges; Debts; Mortgages.
Loan-sharking, 284
Lost and found property, 217–218

Lots
for mobile homes, 171
undeveloped, buying, 174–175
Lowballing, 237
Luggage, lost, 210, 378–379

M

Mace, 594
Mail
chain letters, 356
consumer complaints sent by, 382
fraud, 357
postage discounts for businesses, 425–426
post office boxes and, 357, 426
sexually oriented, stopping delivery of, 471
tampering with, 470
Mail-order businesses, 356–358
Major medical insurance, 320–322
Makeup, skin conditions caused by, 374–375
Malpractice
accidents in hospitals, 506, 507
dental, 506
legal, 38
medical, 503–507
addiction to prescription drugs and, 503
checking doctor's record of, 503–504
consent forms, 501
foreign objects left inside patients, 505
illegible prescriptions, 503
infections caught in hospitals, 506
injections, 506
prescriptions by phone, 503
unauthorized amputations, 505
unsuccessful surgery, 504
vasectomies, 504
Manslaughter, 599, 601
Marriage, 44–52
abroad, 49
of adopted and natural children, 48
annulment, 123–124
automobiles and, 230
blood tests for, 45
broken engagements, 45–47
breach of promise, 45–46
children's guardians and, 91
child support and, 152
common-law, 54–55, 132
credit history and, 273–274
debt and, 58
of first cousins, 48
home ownership and, 166
inheritance and, 56, 59–60, 558
investments and, 295
IRA's and, 524
as legal contract, 46–47
legal requirements, 44
licenses, 45
of minors, preventing, 44
persons authorized to perform, 48, 49
prenuptial agreements and, 49–52, 61, 134
property and, 58–60
restrictions, 47–48
safe deposit boxes and, 270
separation and, 119–122
Marriage *(continued)*
sexual consummation, 49
Social Security and, 528
of unwed parents, legitimacy of children and, 71
waiting period before, 44–45
wife's name change, 96
See also Divorce; Family responsibilities; Husbands; Unmarried couples; Unwed parents; Wives.
Marriage counseling, 116
Material witnesses, 652
Maternity leave, 400–401
Medicaid, 543–545
appealing decisions of, 544–545
applying for, 543
limits, 544
losing benefits, 544
Medicare vs., 535
personal needs allowance, 544
Medical insurance. *See* Health insurance; Medicare.
Medical records, 507–509
of children, 508
doctor's death and, 509
of employees, 508
living wills as part of, 512
medical insurance and, 508
privacy rights, 507
right to see, 499, 507–508
Medical treatment
bills for, 509–510
for children, 61
for elderly parents, children's liability for, 100, 107
hit-and-run drivers and, 260–261, 342–343
of children
babysitters' consent for, 78
grandparents' consent for, 99
parents' consent for, 502
parents staying in hospital during, 497
consent for, 500–502
emergency
babysitters and, 78
inability to pay and, 496
malpractice. *See* Malpractice: medical.
unauthorized surgery, 502, 505
See also Doctors; Hospitals.
Medicare, 535–543
appealing decisions of, 536–537, 541–542
automatic enrollment in, 537, 538
for children, 539
deductible, 541
for disabled, 535–536
doctors' fee increases and, 540
enrollment in, 537, 538
for home care, 542
insurance to supplement, 542
job-related benefit plans and, 538–539
limits to coverage, 543
Medicaid vs., 535
medical care in foreign countries and, 543
nursing home patients, 541
participating doctors, 539–540
Parts A and B, 536–538
retirement and, 535
Social Security and, 537
time limit for submitting claims, 540
working past age 65 and, 539

MGIC (Mortgage Guaranty Insurance Corporation), 176–177
Military service
burial at Arlington National Cemetery and, 588
civil service jobs and, 389
courts-martial, 454
funeral payments for, 588
Minimum wage, 395
Miscarriages, prescribed medications and, 504
Misdemeanors, felonies vs., 597, 600–601
Missing children, 84–85
Mobile homes, 156, 171, 172
Money, 264–306
counterfeit, 272
lost, finding, 217
Money market accounts, errors in, 268
Moonlighting, 391
Mortgage Guaranty Insurance Corporation (MGIC), 176–177
Mortgages, 176–180
balloon, 179
for condominiums, 180
due-on-sale clauses, 177
on inherited property, 561
insurance, 176–177
interest, prepaid at real estate closings, 196
payment problems and, 194
renting homes with, 180
seller-financed, 177
spousal responsibilities and, 58
transferring
original owner's responsibility and, 178–179
rates raised in, 177
types, 178–179
Motels. *See* Hotels and motels.
Motorcycles, riding without helmet, 243
Movies, review boards for, 463
Moving
bills of lading, 212–213
estimates, 212
liability for damages during, 212
Murder, 601, 602

Name changes, 96–97
of children, 97, 143
National Guard, U.S., 454
Naturalization, 455, 456–457.
Negligence, 476–477
in automobile accidents, 254–255
consumer safety, 374–375
by hairdressers, 380–381
homeowners insurance and, 331
Neighbors, 185–187
color of house disliked by, 185–186
dispute resolution programs for conflicts with, 594
dogs owned by, 204, 206
driving across property, 186–187
fences erected by, 185
fires caused by, 328
gossiping by, 187
in lakefront homes, sailing rights and, 187
Neighbors *(continued)*
noisy, 185, 190
peering into windows, 471
property damaged by, 186–187
thefts by children of, 203
trees of, 185
No-fault automobile insurance, 336
maximum payments under, 338
No-fault divorce, 114, 124–125, 132
property settlement, 125
speed of, 125
No-knock laws, 603
Nolo contendere pleas, 636
Nonprofit corporations, 436–437
tax returns filed for, 437
Nonsmokers, rights of, 466
Notaries public, 16, 21
Nude sunbathing, 471
Nuisances, 186, 192, 446–447
attractive, 481
Nursing homes, 107–112
abuses in, 109, 112
beds reserved for hospitalized patients in, 111
bribes for admission to, 109
choosing, 108
continuing care facilities, 107–109
involuntary confinement in, 107
liability for bills from, 107
Medicare, 540–541
privacy, 111
release from, 110
rights of patients in, 110
room transfers, 111
thefts in, 111–112

Obscene materials in mail, stopping, 471
Obscene phone calls, 471
Odometers, tampering with, 227
Offices in homes, 188
Older people. *See* Elderly.
Opinion letters, 32
Option contracts, 219
Ordinances, city, 453, 454–455
Organ donations, 513–514
Overtime, 396–397, 442

Painters
damages caused by, 184
extra money demanded by, 184
Paralegals, 16
Parents
adoptive. *See* Adoption.
alcohol served to children by, 82
child abuse, 94–96
child custody and, 140–146. *See also* Child custody.
children employed by, 76
children remembered in wills, 556–559
children's abortions and, 92

Parents *(continued)*
children's medical treatment
confidentiality between child and doctor, 494
consent for, 502
religion and, 460
children's name changes and, 97, 143
children's religion, 52, 459
children's school attendance, 85, 89
children supported by, 62–63
children's use of contraceptives and, 494
elderly, abuse of, 96
foster, 62–63
guardianships and rights of, 91
home classes by, vs. school, 86
liability of, for acts of children, 81–82
preventing child's marriage, 44
questioned by police, 83
remaining with children in hospitals, 497
sex education and, 87
sued by children, 62
supported by children, 100–101
surrogate, 70–71
unwed, 71–75. *See also* Unwed parents.
visitation rights of, 146–148
See also Child custody; Children; Child support; Juvenile offenders.
Parking garages, vandalism in, 256
Parking tickets, 242–243
Parole, crime victims and, 596
Partnerships, 430–433
agreements for, 430–432
information in, 430–431
oral vs. written, 431–432
approving new partners, 432
automobile accidents of partners and, 433
corporations vs., 430
decision making in, 432
jointly owned property and debts of, 432–433
limited, 432
retiring from, 433
setting up, 431
stealing from, 33
to transfer businesses to children, 448
trial periods for, 432
Part-time workers, benefits for, 399
Patents, 221–223
Paternity suits, 72, 73
blood tests in, 72
Pawnbrokers, 213–214
Pedestrians, right of way and, 244
Pension Benefit Guaranty Corporation (PBGC), 519–521
Pension plans, 516–523
bankrupt companies and, 519–520
benefits for workers over 65, 517
changing jobs, 518–519
disabled employees and, 519
divorce and, 138
of employees who worked for more than one company, 520–521
employers required to set up, 516
ERISA and, 418, 516, 520–521
firings or layoffs to avoid paying on, 418, 519
mergers and, 521
for older employees, 516–517
Pension plans *(continued)*
part-time employment and benefits from, 521
reductions of companies' contributions to, 519
sexual discrimination, 518
Social Security and, 531
spouse's death and, 522
taxes withheld, 522
terminated employees and, 518
types, 516–517
for union members only, 517–518
vesting rights in, 518, 519, 520
ways of receiving benefits, 522
See also IRA's; Keoghs; Social Security.
Permits
for businesses, 424–425, 438
for renting spare rooms, 187
Personal finance companies, 285
Personal property, 202–224
crops as, 202
found by others in trash, 203
insuring, 329–333. *See also* Homeowners insurance.
real property vs., 202
on rented property, 202
selling, 218–221
by children, 220–221
joint ownership and, 219, 220
with liens, 221
option contracts in, 219
papers needed, 220
by pawnbrokers, 213
reneging on agreements in, 219–220
by repair shops, 366
written agreements, 218–219
tangible, 202
Personal property taxes, 58–59
Personnel files, right to see, 390–391
Petitioners, plaintiffs vs., 628
Pets, 203–207
accidents caused by, 206, 207
dangerous, 207, 598
divorce and, 136
found on public property, 203
gardens destroyed by, 204
hit by automobiles, 206–207
injuries caused by, 204–206
leash laws, 206
licensing of, 203
neglect of, 204
purebred dogs impregnated by mutts, 204
in rented homes, 162
trusts for, 565
veterinarians and, 205
in wills, 560
See also Dogs.
Picketing, 406–407, 461
Piece-rate workers, overtime for, 396–397
Plaintiffs, petitioners vs., 628
Plea bargaining, 596
Police
abuse reported to, 89, 93, 94, 95, 96
arrests by, 605–609
false, 608
in other states, 609
for refusing to help them, 474
victims' inability to compel, 590
automobile accident reports, 252, 260

Police *(continued)*
crimes reported to, 590
crime victims' cooperation with, 590
drunk drivers and, 247, 248, 249
entrapment by, 608–609
frisking by, 472, 604
late responses of, to alarms, 591
no-knock laws, 603
parents questioned about children by, 83
random drug testing by, 474
refusing to help, 474
and rights of citizens, 472–474
roadblocks, 245–246
runaway children and, 85
searches by, 472–474
search warrants and, 603
time allowed for investigations, 591
victims informed about progress of cases by, 591
Polygamy, religion and, 460
Possession as nine-tenths of law, 202
Postal Service. *See* Mail.
Post office boxes
as business addresses, 426
mail-order firms with, 357
Potholes, automobile accidents caused by, 257, 318
Power of attorney, 20–21, 101–102
Prayer in schools, 87, 459
Predisposition investigations, 614
Pregnancy
automobile insurance settlements and, 345
divorce during, 71
father's identity questioned, 72
marriage to man who is not father of child during, 71–72
maternity leave, 400–401
paternity suits and, 72
school attendance during, 86–87
vasectomy, unsuccessful, 504
See also Abortion.
Prenuptial agreements, 49–52
canceling, 50–51
contesting of divorce prohibited in, 50
forced by spouse's parents, 52
hidden assets, 134
oral, 51–52
property rights in event of death, 50
religious upbringing of children, 52
stepchildren protected by, 61
what to include in, 51
Prescriptions
drug addiction, 503
illegible, 503
miscarriages due to, 504
by phone, 503
privacy rights and, 469
wrong dosages, 503
Press, freedom of, 462–463
edited interviews, 462–463
government suppression of information, 463
libel, 463
motion picture review boards, 463
privacy rights, 470
trials, 462
Price tags
"as is" on, 355
inaccurate, 351
unauthorized discounts, 355
Priests, confidentiality of, 469
Primary care givers, 500
Privacy, right to, 468–471
access to government files, 469
commercial use of photos, 470
conversations with lawyers, doctors, or priests, 34, 41, 469, 508
juveniles' criminal records, 470
mail and, 470, 471
medical records and, 507
neighbors peering into windows, 471
newspaper photos, 470
nude sunbathing, 471
in nursing homes, 111
prescriptions, 469
recording telephone conversations, 468
Prizes
free health club memberships, 363
for listening to sales presentations, 362–363
sweepstakes, 362
Probate of wills, 574–581
assets discovered after, 581
changes in will provisions, 580
deadline for, 578
debts of deceased, 579, 580–581
dying without will and, 577
executors. *See* Executors of wills.
insufficient cash in estate, 579
without lawyers, 574, 576
lost wills, 567
missing heirs, 581
photostatic copies of wills, 576
process, 574
property in more than one state, 577
requirements, 576
selling property during, 576–577
simultaneous deaths of both spouses, 578
taxes, 579
See also Estates; Wills.
Pro bono work by lawyers, 16–17
Product safety, information on, 374
Promissory notes, 285
payment demanded on, 293
Property
acquired during separation, 122
bailments, law of, 211
bankruptcy, 304, 305
borrowed, 214–215
damage to, 214–215
injuries resulting from, 215, 480
lost or stolen, 214
refusal to return, 215
checking
in checkrooms, 209
with hotel bell captains, 209–210
community, 59–60
damages to
borrowed, 214–215
by dry cleaners or laundries, 207–209
by neighbors, 186–187
by pets, 204
in restaurants, 376
divided in divorce, 133–138. *See also* Divorce: property division
gifts, 216

INDEX

Property *(continued)*
held as evidence in trials, 593–594
jointly or communally owned, 220
selling share of, 219
lost and found, 217–218
marriage and, 58–60
pawnbrokers and, 213–214
personal, *See* Personal property.
pets as, 203–207. *See also* Pets.
possession of, 202
prenuptial agreements and, 49–52, 134
real estate
personal property vs., 202
See also Condominiums; Homes; Rented homes.
reclaiming from bankrupt businesses, 210–211
seizures of
by creditors, 221, 291–292
by government, 189, 193
by landlords, 161
selling, 218–221
by children, 220–221
joint or communal ownership, 219, 220
with liens, 221
option contracts in, 219
papers needed, 220
by pawnbrokers, 213–214
reneging on agreements in, 219–220
by repair shops, 366
written agreements, 218–219
separation agreements and, 122
shipping, 211–213
stolen
automobiles, 256, 598, 611
while borrowed, 214
buying, 213
in stores, 210
at work, 210
valuable, unknowingly buying, 218
Property taxes, 58–59. *See also* Real estate taxes.
Prosecuting attorneys, forcing action by, 592
Pro se divorces, 127
Psychiatrists, confidentiality of, 495
Public domain, 223
Public nuisances, 446–447
Public transportation, accidents on, 484–485
Purchase agreements
binders vs., 164
deeds supersede, 173
extensions on, 164
terms of, 167
Purses, stolen at work, 210

QR

Quitclaim deeds, 168
Racial discrimination, 376, 418, 467
Railroad stations, injuries in, 484–485
Railroad workers, Social Security and, 529
Raises, 398
Rape, by husbands, 94
Real estate. *See* Condominiums; Homes; Rented homes.
Real estate agents, 195–196
Real estate brokers, 195–199
allegiance of, 196
commissions
negotiating, 197
when house is not sold, 197–198
when house is sold for less than asking price, 198–199
houses undervalued by, 199
realtors or agents vs., 195–196
services provided, 196
types of listings used, 198–199
working with, 197
Real estate taxes
challenging assessments, 190, 191
homes lost by nonpayment, 195
spousal responsibility for, 58–59
Realtors, 195–196
Rebates, 363
Recognizance, suspects released on own, 610
Record clubs, 356
Records,
birth certificates, 67, 72
court, 634–635, 637–638
important papers, 271, 303
medical, 499, 507–509
Redlining, 330–331
Reform schools, 615–616
Refunds
from continuing care facilities, 109–110
from fired lawyers, 29–30
replacements vs., for defective merchandise, 373
Registrations, automobile
driving in other states and, 240
expired, grace periods for, 242
Religion, freedom of, 459–460
medical treatment of children, 460
polygamy, 460
school prayer, 459
state facilities used by church groups, 459
store closing laws, 460
working on the Sabbath, 411, 460
Rent
increases
expired leases and, 156
notice periods for, 157
overdue, seizure of tenants' property and, 161
roommates and, 53, 157
Rented homes, 154–163
cable television in, 162
children not accepted in, 154
converting to condominiums, 162
eviction from, 160
fires, 163
heat not furnished, 159
homeowners insurance, 327–328, 332
improvements, 202
made by tenants, 158
injuries, 163, 478
landlords' entry into, 161–162
landlords' refusal to make repairs, 160
landlords' refusal to rent, 154
with mortgages, 180
moving out of
breaking leases, 158
giving notice, 157

INDEX

Rented homes *(continued)*
neighborhood noises and, 158
overdue rent, 161
pets, 162
rent increases, 156, 157
rent strikes, 159
roommates, 157
security, inadequate, 159
security deposits, 155, 158–159
spare rooms, 187
subletting, 156
tenants' rights, 160–161
See also Leases.
Rent strikes, 159
Repairs, faulty
automobile accidents caused by, 446
injuries due to, 480
refusing to pay for, 379–380
Repair shops
bankrupt, reclaiming property from, 210–211
property sold by, to pay for repairs, 366
See also Automobile repairs.
Repossession, 283, 364, 365
of automobiles, 229
Resisting arrest, 605
Respondents, defendants vs., 628–629
Restaurants, 375–377
"All you can eat" ads, 375
clothing stained in, 376
dissatisfaction with service, 376
illness caused by food, 377
jacket and tie rules, 376
seating, 376
superlative claims for food, 375–376
Retainers, for lawyers, 27–28
Retirement
early, 530
forced, 410
of lawyers, 37
Medicare and, 535
from partnerships, 433
raising legal age for, 527
Social Security and, 530
Retirement insurance, 523
Retirement plans. *See* IRA's; Keoghs; Pension plans; Social Security.
Rights, individual, 452–474
Bill of Rights, 452
equality under the law, 465–468
freedom of press, 462–463
freedom of religion, 459–460
freedom of speech, 460–462
of handicapped, 384–385, 447, 468
to have firearms, 464–465
police and, 472–474, 604
to privacy, 468–471
taking away, 452, 454
to trial by jury, 623–626
in U.S. armed services, 454
U.S. citizenship and, 455–457
to vote, 458–459
Roadblocks, searches for drunk drivers at, 245–246
Rock concerts, bans on, 465–466
Roller coasters, injuries on, 488
Roommates, 157
Runaway children, 85

S

Safe-deposit boxes, 270
Sailing on lakes, neighbors and, 187
Sales tactics, 351–355
"as is," 355
discounts, 349
false advertising, 348–350
garage sales, 351
inspection of goods, 351–355
prizes, 362–363
salesperson's claims, 351, 355
scams, shams, and swindles, 352–354
sellers' misrepresentations, 355
unauthorized discounts, 355
wrong price tags, 351
Savings bonds, 298
Scams, 352–354
School, 85–90
attendance at
parents' liability for, 85
truancy and, 86, 612
children referred to juvenile court by, 612
children struck in, 89
dress codes, 88–89
expulsion from, 86
flag saluted in, 462
home classes vs., 86
injuries in, 89, 490
prayer in, 87, 459
pregnant students in, 86–87
reform, 615–616
religious education, 87
sex education, 87
truancy, 86, 612
vaccinations, 87–88
School records, 88
Scofflaws, 242
S corporations, 437
Searches, 393–394, 472–474, 603–605
Search warrants, 472, 473, 603, 605
Seat belts, 243, 258–259, 337
Security deposits, for rented homes, 155, 158–159
Selective Service registration, sexual discrimination and, 466
Self-defense, 594–595
of wives against husbands, 93
Self-employed persons
income taxes, 300
Keoghs, 523–526
Social Security taxes, 528
Separation, 119–122
agreements, 114, 116, 119–120
consulting lawyers for, 121
mutual, vs. judicial separation, 120–121
property division, 122
what to include, 120
child support during, 117
dating after, 121
inheritance from spouse and, 122, 571
liability for credit card purchases during, 122
property acquired during, 122
See also Annulment; Divorce.

INDEX

SEP-IRA's, 525
Sermons, slanderous statements in, 461–462
Service contracts, 370–371
Service plans, for automobiles, 235–236
Sex education, 87
Sexual abuse of children, 94
Sexual discrimination
club membership, 467–468
drinking age, 465
insurance rates, 311–312
at job, 408–410
in employment tests, 408
equal pay, 408
pension plans, 518
promotions, 409–410
reporting, 408–409
separate facilities and, 410
Selective Service registration, 466
Sexual harassment 411–412
Sexually oriented mail, stopping, 471
Shams, 352–354
Shipping, damage during, 211–212
Sidewalks
accidents on, 485
paving, 189
Signatures
forged on checks, 272
of spouse, use of, 63–64
Simplified employee pension—individual retirement accounts (SEP-IRA's), 525
Skating rinks, injuries at, 490
Slander, 461–462
Small claims court, 379–380, 640–642
appealing decisions of, 642
arbitration vs., 642
cases handled by, 640
collecting judgments awarded in, 642
lawyers in, 19
questioning witnesses, 640–641
summonses from, 641–642
taking cases to, 640–641
whom and what to bring, 642
Smoking
nonsmokers' rights, 466
in workplace, 392–393
Social Security, 526–534
appealing decisions, 536–537
applying for, 529
benefits for stepchildren and adopted children, 534
calculating benefits from, 529–530
collecting, 529–531
deaths not reported, 534
dependents' benefits, 532–534
based on spouse's work record, 532–533
from both former and current spouses, 533
for children, 534
divorce and, 138, 533
for grandchildren, 534
lump-sum death benefits, 534
direct deposit program for, 102, 531
disability benefits, 545
early retirement, 530
earnings limit, 530
earnings records
errors, 529
obtaining, 527
income tax on benefits, 531
Medicare Part B and, 537
pensions and, 531
Social Security *(continued)*
qualifying for, 526–529
for railroad workers, 529
remarriage and, 528
survivor's benefits, 534
remarriage and, 533
working past age 65, 530–531
Social Security taxes, 300–301, 429, 528, 531
Sole proprietorships, 424, 427, 430, 450
Speech, freedom of, 460–462
flag salute in schools, 462
nonverbal expression, 460–461
picketing, 461
slander, 461–462
Speeding tickets, 244–245
SSI (Supplemental Security Income), 546
Stamp collections, insuring, 330
State courts, 622–623
States
Bill of Rights and, 452
different laws in, 454
States of emergency, 454
Status offenders, 612
Stepchildren, 60–61
adoption of, 69–70, 145
prenuptial agreements for protection of, 61
providing for in wills, 557
Social Security benefits, 534
stepfather's last name taken by, 98
stepparents' responsibilities, 60–61
Stock
in bankrupt companies, 295
replacing certificates for, 295
Stockbrokers, 295–298
banks as, 298
churning, 297
discount, 296
going out of business, 295–296
insider trading, 297–298
suing, for giving bad advice, 296–297
Store detectives, 472
Stores
accidents in
breaking merchandise in, 487–488
icy sidewalks, 485
while looking at displays, 490–491
wet floors, 487
property lost while trying on clothes in, 210
sales tactics, 351–355
Strikes, 406–407
judges' orders to end, 408
rent, 159
Subchapter S corporations, 437
Subletting apartments, 156
Subpoenas, 632
summonses vs., 627
Suicide
life insurance and, 320
terminally ill patients, 512
Suits, 628–629
Summonses
late arrival of, 627
not received by defendants, 627–628
from small claims court, 641–642
subpoenas vs., 627
Supermarkets, spoiled food in, 372
Supplemental Security Income (SSI), 546

INDEX

Supreme Court, U.S., 622, 624
Supreme courts, state, 622, 625
Surgery
  consent forms, 501
  malpractice suits, 505
  unauthorized, 502, 505
  unsuccessful, 504
Surrogate parenting, 70–71
Sweepstakes, 362
Swimming pools, injuries in, 481
  homeowners insurance and, 334
  at motels, 489
Swindles, 296–297, 352–354
Swiss bank accounts, 265

T

Taxes
  estate. *See* Estate taxes.
  gift, 300
  income, 299–303. *See also* Income taxes.
  inheritance, 549–550
  personal property, 59
  real estate, 59, 190, 191, 195
  reporting evasion of, 618
  sales, 226
  Social Security, 300–301, 429, 528, 531
  unincorporated business, 429–430
  voting and, 458
  withholding of
    on employees' paychecks, 429
    on pension checks, 522
Taxicabs, accidents in, 483–484
Teachers
  child abuse reported by, 89
  children referred to juvenile court by, 612
  homosexuality, 467
  students struck by, 89
Telephones and telephone calls
  after arrests, 605
  consumer complaints made by, 382
  deposits for, 291
  funeral cost inquiries made by, 584
  obscene, 471
  prescriptions given over, 503
  recording conversations, 468
  sales made by, 360–361
Television
  advertisements, 361
  cable, in rented homes, 162
Tenants, 159–161. *See also* Landlords; Leases; Rented homes.
Thefts
  of automobiles, 256, 598, 611
  homeowners insurance and, 330–333
  by minors, 203, 611
  in nursing homes, 111–112
  on-the-job, 393–394
    losing job for not reporting, 419
    of purses, 210
  of personal property in automobiles, 330, 331
  from rented homes, 332
Tickets. *See* Traffic tickets and violations.
Tips, deducted from wages, 395
Title insurance, 165–166
Toys, children injured by, 374
Trademarks, 224
Traffic tickets and violations, 242–247
  alcoholic beverages in car, 249
  automobile accidents, 258
  for children not in car seats, 243
  classification as crimes, 600–601
  drunk driving, 247–252. *See also* Drunk driving.
  fines, inability to pay, 247
  fines, unpaid
    boots on automobile tires and, 242
    jail as penalty for, 243
    in other states, arrests for, 246
  hitchhiking, 244
  jury trials for, 246
  lawyers in court appearances for, 246
  for motorcyclists without helmets, 243
  parking, 242–243
  pedestrians' right of way, 244
  reckless driving, 246
  seat belt use and, 243
  for speeding 244–245
  stop signs, not yielding right of way at, 244
  for taillight malfunctions, 243
  yellow lights, driving through, 244
Travel agencies, 379
Treasury Bills, U.S., 298
Trees
  cut down by contractors, 174
  growing over property line, 185
  planted in front of condominiums, 184
  tangled in power lines, 188–189
Trespassing, 185, 192, 476, 479, 480
Trials, 627–640
  amicus curiae in, 634
  appealing verdicts, 638–639, 642
  civil, steps in, 628–629
  collecting judgments, 638
  courtroom protocol, 633–636
  defendants, 636–637
  delays, 626
  determining damages, 639
  for divorces, 126
  hearings vs., 631
  judges, changing, 632
  by judge vs. jury, 626
  juries, 643–650. *See also* Juries and jurors.
  lawyers fired during, 37
  out-of-court settlements vs., 632
  pleas in
    guilty or not guilty, 635
    nolo contendere, 636
  postponing, 631–632
  press barred from, 462
  pretrial procedures, 627–633
    depositions, 630, 631
    discovery, 630
    interrogatories, 631
    plaintiffs vs. petitioners, 628
    subpoenas, 627, 632
    summonses, 627–628
  procedures, 636–639
  property held as evidence, 593–594
  public attendance, 633
  public record of testimony, 637–638
  remarks stricken from record, 634–635
  respondents vs. defendants, 628
  for traffic violations, 246

Trials *(continued)*
  venue, change of, 633
  victims forced to testify at, 593
  witnesses, 651–655. *See also* Witnesses in trials.
  See also Judicial system.
Truancy, 86, 612
Trustees, 566–567
  challenging appointment, 567
  death of, 566
  duties, 566
  firing, 567
  guidelines for, 564
  mismanagement by, 566, 567
  in other states, 566
  parents as, 566
Trusts, 562–565
  age specifications in, 565
  amending, 565
  creditors and, 564
  current vs. future assets in, 564
  decisions on amount paid from, 564
  established in wills, 562–563
  for friends, 564–565
  living, 562–563
  money received before termination of, 565
  for pets, 565
  spendthrift, 564
  support, 563–564
  terminating, 565
  testamentary, 562–563

U

Undertakers, licensing of, 584
Unemployment compensation, 420–422
  firings for misconduct, 420
  job training programs, 422
  quitting, 420–421
  refusing transfers and, 421
  for self-employed, 449–450
  state differences, 421–422
  union lockouts and, 421
Unincorporated business tax, 429–430
Unions, 404–408
  automation and, 405
  employees' right to petition for, 405
  fines imposed by, 406
  firings and, 406–407
  joining, 404, 405
  lockouts, 421
  nonmembers helped by, 405
  pension plans only for members of, 517–518
  picket lines, 406
  retirees' benefits and, 407
  slowdowns, 407
  strikes, 406–407, 408
Union shops, applying for jobs at, 405
Unmarried couples
  abortion, 92
  adoption, 65
  breakup of, 53
  child custody, 141
  common-law marriage vs., 55
  living-together agreements for, 52
  wills, 53–54
Unwed parents, 71–75

Vacations
  as employee benefits, 400
  for religious holidays, 411
Vaccinations, of school children, 87–88
Vandalism, 600
  of automobiles, 256, 590
  by children, 590, 612
  homeowners insurance and, 331
Vasectomies, unsuccessful, 504
Veterinarians
  bills, 206–207
  legal responsibilites, 205
Victims of crimes, 590–597
  aiding, 618
  assistance programs for, 596–597
  bail hearings, 593
  charges pressed by, 592
  convicts' restitution payments to, 597
  cooperation of, in investigations, 590
  crimes reported by, 590
  dispute resolution programs, 594
  informed of progress of cases, 591
  lineup identification by, 593
  police asked to make arrests by, 590–591
  property held as evidence, 593–594
  prosecutors asked to press charges by, 592
  rights of, 592
  self-defense, 594–595
  testimony required of, 593
Videocassettes
  copying of, 224
  home recording on, 598
Visitation rights, 146–148
  of grandparents, 98, 99, 147
  of parents
    changing, 146
    children's refusal to see parent and, 147–148
    child support, 148
    while divorce is pending, 146
    living with lover and, 147
  of unwed parents, 74–75
Voting, 458–459
  absentee, 459
  choosing state for, 458
  criminal records and, 459
  eligibility, 458
  taxes and, 458

Wages, 395–399
  bankrupt employers and, 397–398
  deductions from, 429
  docking, 398–399
  equal, for persons with same job, 398
  garnisheeing of, 294, 302
  method of compensation and, 395
  minimum, 395
  overtime, 396–397, 442
  raises, 398
  tips deducted from, 395–396
  unpaid, 397

Warranties, 367–370
on automobiles, 234–236
buying on credit and, 292
express vs. implied, 367–368
full vs. limited, 234–235, 368–369
guarantees vs., 367–368
for home improvements or repairs, 182
late mailing of cards for, 369–370
multiple, on one product, 369
neglect, abuse, or mishandling and, 370
in purchase agreements for homes, 173, 176
"repair or replace" in, 370
seller out of business, 370
terms, 368–369
Warrants
arrest, 605, 606–607
search, 472, 603
Weapons
carrying concealed, 594
right to have firearms, 464–465
Wills, 552–581
adopted children and, 80
challenging, 572
changing, 567–569, 580
by codicils, 568
after death of one spouse, 570–571
when necessary, 569
child custody provisions, 561
children born after writing of, 559
children cut out of, 558, 570, 571
children protected in, 557
children's marriage prohibited in, 558
codicils, 568
contesting, 570–573
incompetence as grounds for, 572
oral promises and, 570
payment of inheritance delayed by, 573
steps in, 572–573
copies
photostatic, 576
signed, 555
debts canceled in, 561
divorce and, 133
do-it-yourself forms for, 553
dying without, 573–574, 577
executors. *See* Executors of wills.
fraudulent, 572
guardianship of children and, 561
handwritten, 553
heirs named in, 556–561
beneficiary's death, 568
children, 556–557, 558–559
friends, 559–560
people living abroad, 559–560
pets, 560
prohibitions against marriage, 558
remarriage and, 556, 557
stepchildren, 557
houses left, 560
mortgages on, 561
IRA's and Keoghs in, 526
joint, 552
death of one spouse and, 570–571
lawyers in writing of, 552–553, 555
life estates established in, 560–561
life insurance, 319
living, 510–512
losing, 556, 576
Wills *(continued)*
making, 552–555
minimum age for, 552
moving to different state and, 556
need for, 552
oral, 553–554
organ donations indicated in, 513
points to consider when making, 559
probate of, 574–581. *See also* Probate of wills.
proceeds from property bequeathed in, 572, 580
property in more than one state, 577
revoking, 568–569
separation and, 571
specific items listed in, 560, 571–572
stepchildren, 557
storing, 556
tearing up, 569
trustees named in, 566–567. *See also* Trustees.
trusts established in, 562–566. *See also* Trusts.
unmarried couples and, 53–54
on videotape, 553
witnesses to, 554–555
beneficiaries as, 554
court testimony required of, 554–555
number, 555
See also Estates.
Withholding
on paychecks, 429
on pension checks, 522
Witnesses to crimes, 618–620
children as, 619
crimes reported by, 618
forced to testify, 619
incorrect statements made by, 619
protection of, 620
telephone inquiries to, 620
victims aided by, 618, 619
Witnesses in trials, 651–655
atheists exempt from swearing, 653
children brought to court by, 632
compelled to testify by defendants, 637
cross-examination, 36, 637, 651
Fifth Amendment, invoking, 654–655
friends brought to court by, 632
harassment and intimidation of, 655
lawyers' coaching of, 651
logical deductions of, 652
lying by, 654
material, 652
mistatements made by, 651–652
notes used by, 652
payment for, 654
protection of, 655
questions asked of, 652
required to give testimony in person, 653
in small claims court, 640–641
subpoenaing, 627, 632
testimony of, in public record, 637–638
unable to appear on date called, 634
waiting outside courtroom, 654
Witnesses to wills, 554–555
beneficiaries as, 554
court testimony required of, 554–555
number, 555

Wives
abortions, 92, 93
abused, 93, 591
alimony, 116, 138–140, 274–275
child support paid by, 148
credit histories, 274
divorce. *See* Divorce.
husband moving and, 64, 130–131
husbands' gifts to, 216
husbands testifying against, 93
husbands' unemployment checks and, 422
IRA's for, 524
legal protection from husbands for, 94
life insurance proceeds on legally dead husbands collected by, 319
married name, 96
police asked to arrest husbands by, 591
raped by husbands, 94
retirement benefits of deceased husbands, 522
self-defense of, against husbands, 93
spousal responsibilities of
community property laws, 59–60
for debts and purchases, 57–59
sexual relations, 64
support, 55–57
sued by husbands, 261
See also Marriage.
Women
discrimination against, 408–410, 467–469. *See also* Sexual discrimination; Sexual harassment.
searched by male police officers, 474
sexual harassment of, 411–412
Workers' compensation, 400, 401–404
benefits, 401
disability insurance and, 404
Workers' compensation *(continued)*
duration, 404
firings for filing claims, 403
for house cleaners, 188
for injured employees unable to do heavy work, 404
for injuries caused by fights with other employees, 403
for injuries due to coworkers' pranks, 403
for injuries in company softball games, 402–403
lawsuits and, 401–402
for nervous breakdowns, 402
for new workers, 401
previous injuries and, 402

X-rated materials in mail, stopping, 471
Zoning laws, violation of, 597–598
Zoos, injuries by animals in, 488–489